The Esoteric Secrets of Surrealism

"This book is a necessary resource for those readers interested in, or rather compelled by, the implicit and explicit relationships between surrealism and the initiatory forms that comprise the great traditions of the esoteric and occult arts. The author, whose enthusiasm for his subject is equaled by his erudition, provides for the first time in English translation numerous excerpts from noted surrealists commenting directly on the subject at hand, whether it be divination, astrology, dark romanticism, the Celtic world, or alchemy, magic, Voudoun, Gnosticism, and mythopoesis. His exegesis and conclusions are ripe and should provoke the reader not only in terms of encountering the texts and works discussed throughout the various ages and contexts they were created in but also in recollecting, or revisiting, quite personal moments that have acted as levers or axial junctures from which much else evolved. A much-needed looking-glass into a still evolving gyre in which science, as a capacity for astute observation, and poetry, where our internal and external theaters merge, have ever the potential of reaching new syntheses."

ALLAN GRAUBARD, COAUTHOR OF *INVISIBLE HEADS: SURREALISTS IN NORTH AMERICA—AN UNTOLD STORY* AND AUTHOR OF *AND TELL TULIP THE SUMMER*

The Esoteric Secrets of Surrealism

Origins, Magic, and Secret Societies

Patrick Lepetit

Translated by Jon E. Graham

Inner Traditions
Rochester, Vermont • Toronto, Canada

Inner Traditions
One Park Street
Rochester, Vermont 05767
www.InnerTraditions.com

Copyright © 2012 by Éditions Dervy
English translation copyright © 2014 by Inner Traditions International

Originally published in French under the title *Le Surréalisme: Parcours souterrain*
First U.S. edition published in 2014 by Inner Traditions

All rights reserved. No part of this book may be reproduced or utilized in any form or by any means, electronic or mechanical, including photocopying, recording, or by any information storage and retrieval system, without permission in writing from the publisher.

Reproduction of the plates, including downloading of ARS member works, is prohibited by copyright laws and international conventions without the express written permission of Artists Rights Society (ARS), New York.

Library of Congress Cataloging-in-Publication Data
Lepetit, Patrick, author.
 [Surréalisme. English]
 The esoteric secrets of surrealism : origins, magic, and secret societies / Patrick Lepetit ; translated by Jon E. Graham.
   pages cm
 Includes bibliographical references and index.
 ISBN 978-1-62055-175-2 (pbk.) — ISBN 978-1-62055-176-9 (e-book)
 1. Surrealism. 2. Symbolism in art. 3. Occultism in art. 4. Freemasonry and the arts. I. Graham, Jon E., translator. II. Title.
 NX600.S9L4613 2014
 700'.41163—dc23

2013022217

Printed and bound in the United States by P. A. Hutchison

10 9 8 7 6 5 4 3 2 1

Text design by Brian Boynton and layout by Virginia Scott Bowman
This book was typeset in Garamond Premier Pro with Garamond Premier Pro and Gill Sans used as display typefaces

Inner Traditions wishes to express its appreciation for assistance given by the government of France through the National Book Office of the Ministère de la Culture in the preparation of this translation.

Nous tenons à exprimer nos plus vifs remerciements au gouvernment de la France et au ministère de la Culture, Centre National du Livre, pour leur concours dans la préparation de la traduction de cet ouvrage.

In memory of

Sarane Alexandrian and Alain-Pierre Pillet

⸺●⸺

I would like to thank the following individuals for their information, advice, help, and/or encouragement: Christophe Boulanger, Alain Buyse, Roger Dachez, Christophe Dauphin, Pierre Dhainaut, Marie-Christine Dubois, Pierre Drachline, Guy Ducornet, Elie-Charles Flamand, Paul-Armand Gette, Charles Jameux, Jean-Pierre Lassalle, Philippe Lemaire, Bernard Roger, Paul Sanda, Jean-Claude Silbermann, Tara Solti, Jacqueline Storme, Jehan Van Langhenhoven, and Jean Van Win.

Contents

Foreword by Bernard Roger — xi

Introduction: Tolerance and Acceptance of Difference — 1

1 Under the Sign of the Goose: Surrealism and Liberation of the Mind — 7

2 Surrealism and the Sacred — 35

3 Surrealism and the Labyrinth of the Mind — 84

4 Surrealism and Divination — 116

5 Surrealism and Astrology — 142

6 Surrealism and Dark Romanticism: "In the Closed Palace" — 156

7 The Unappeasable Shadow of Arthur's Companions: Surrealism and Celticism — 175

8	Surrealism and Alchemy: "You with Lead in the Head, Melt It Down to Make Surrealist Gold"	216
9	Surrealism and Magic	257
10	Surrealism, Freemasonry, and Voodoo: *Ogun Ferraille,* the Elect Cohen, and the Great Tradition	300
11	Surrealism and Gnosticism	348
12	Surrealism and Tradition: Occult Sources, Histories of Orders and Churches	371
13	Surrealism and Myth	397
14	Keeping a Level Head?	428

Notes	444
Bibliography	473
Index	499

The science that I undertake is distinct from poetry. I do not sing about the latter. I force myself to discover its source.
　　　　　　　　COMTE DE LAUTRÉAMONT, *POÉSIES II*

For the time being my intention has been to see that justice was done to that hatred of the marvelous which rages in certain men, that ridicule under which they would like to crush it.
　　　　　　　　ANDRÉ BRETON, *MANIFESTOES OF SURREALISM*

I systematically refuse to look for anything in a painter but a poet. So am I using literature as my judge? No, I am looking as a cretin, a medium, a savage, a prophet.
　　　　　　　　ROGER GILBERT-LECOMTE,
　　　　"*CE QUE DEVRAIT ÊTRE LA PEINTURE, CE QUE SERA SIMA*"

Exegetes, in order to see clearly, erase the word surrealism.
　　　　　　　　PAUL NOUGÉ, *HISTOIRE DE NE PAS RIRE*

In the crush of guests, visitors are rare.
　　　　　　　　PHILIPPE AUDOIN,
　　　　　　　　COMMENT ACCUEILLIR DES VISITEURS

The Surrealists, 1933
Front row, left to right: Tristan Tzara, Salvador Dali,
Paul Éluard, Max Ernst, René Crevel
Back row, left to right: Man Ray, Hans Arp, Yves Tanguy, Andre Breton
(photo by Anna Riwkin-Brick)

Foreword

The last café where André Breton and his friends met was La Promenade de Venus in the neighborhood once home to Les Halles. Breton was often the first one there, arriving every day around six o'clock. He would take a seat in the middle of a banquette in the room whose windows looked out on rue du Louvre. One evening, although the place was almost empty, he found someone sitting in the "seat perilous," as Philippe Audoin called it. This individual was none other than Eugène Canseliet, who had casually dropped in to relax over a drink, entirely unaware of the daily meetings that took place there.

Both men were equally surprised and delighted. That evening, Fulcanelli's disciple took part in the group discussion, surrounded by the congenial interest that had dispelled many of the misgivings of some members.

This completely improbable encounter, an exemplary manifestation of objective chance, provides a good illustration of the problem implicitly posed by Patrick Lepetit's book, concerning the apparent oxymoron created by the simultaneous presence of a demand for the most total liberation ever expressed and a powerful attraction to so-called "traditional" thought inside a revolutionary movement.

The author's investigation rests entirely on statements collected from the texts by a large majority of the people—lifelong militants or fellow travelers for a few months, close companions or distant sympathizers—who took part in the development of the surrealist movement until its dissolution in 1969, and in its extensions whose activity can still be seen today in Paris and elsewhere around the world.

The author's unorthodox method casts a bright light on the relations that Breton and his friends maintained at various times with the many different approaches to the invisible, which are far too often lost in the confused gray blend of "the occult." One of the qualities of this light is to remind us that the adjective *surrealist* is totally foreign to the notion of the "supernatural." The surrealists know that the surreal is in the real, just as the mage knows that the invisible is in the visible and the alchemist knows that the infinite is to be found in the finite—and the Great Work consists of its extraction.

It is impossible to overstate the significance of the fact that René Alleau, who knew Antonin Artaud and was with him during his final moments, could tell Breton that it was his earlier involvement with surrealism that led Artaud to take the road of adventure to "the open entrance of the closed palace of the king."

Like a reflection in the mirror of this magic conjunction, Alleau's lectures at the Hall of Geography in Paris toward the end of 1952 inspired a tempest of interest for alchemy among the members of the group, raising many questions about its nature and purpose, but primarily on the nature of its mysterious "primal matter."

This period of the movement, which saw the opening of the gallery whose name, L'Étoile scellée (the Sealed Star), was chosen by Breton from among several names suggested for this "matter" in a list compiled by Alleau, would long bear the imprint of one of this star's luminous points in which surrealism and alchemy, those two paths of high poetry that, in the words of Jean-Louis Bédouin, "never merge although they intersect," overlap in broad daylight. Some of the companions in this adventure were moved by an impetuous desire to learn how to set off on the quest for the "Golden Fleece," attracted by the dark underground paths toward which the study of the books dealing with this work would take them.

This was an attempt to gain access to the depths of a domain stripped of all orientation and landmark, "a labyrinth in whose center," writes René Alleau, "the secrets of the high science are hidden in a column like the books of the Temple." How could a trajectory of this nature fail to recall to them the direction—vertically parallel although at a palpable distance—that André Breton defined as the one necessary to take with an eye to "the total recuperation of our psychic strength," a "vertiginous descent within us, the systematic illumination of hidden places and the gradual darkening of others?"

At this stage, the path suggested by the surrealist project is similar to that of alchemy, as it is to that of Freemasonry, whose initial trial was discreetly described by two members of the current Paris group, quoted by Patrick Lepetit, as like a "descent to the bottom of the volcano or only to the cave, vitriol."

Here is where the secret common to surrealism and these two traditional disciplines is to be found, and it is black in color. It is the foundation of the marvelous, the cellar of the doorless tower from where the prisoner of the high chamber can be heard singing, the beautiful longhaired Rapunzel.

Where could such a labyrinth wind its way, if not to the heart of the "old ocean" hailed by Comte de Lautréamont? Surfacing at the dawn of time with the birth of humanity were magic, astrology, alchemy, and sacred rituals, which were then followed by tarot cards and crystal balls, as if from the hands of a magician.

Diffused within these mother waters, a "new myth" seems to be dreaming itself into being by fits and starts since surrealism's genesis. It is precisely this dream's eyewitnesses whom Patrick Lepetit has convoked to achieve his meticulous work, which is remarkable and unprecedented, especially with regard to the method followed for making visible certain paths on which "it is possible," as Pierre Mabille wrote, "to feel a new system of liaison between man and the universe."

We can only marvel at the feat of chance that ensured that the untraceable Fulcanelli's two books appeared in the same decade that Breton's *Manifestoes of Surrealism* were published, recalling the perennial nature of the extremely ancient "art of Hermes." In this temporal meeting between alchemy, whose treatises and practice urge "the student of science" to "follow nature," and the birth of the surrealist project, which stipulates the individual must gain access to his or her deepest nature to remake human understanding, within these two fortuitously contemporary manifestations, we must perforce recognize the traces of parallel paths toward the fulfillment of the primordial and constituent desire of man: the free and boundless expansion of awareness.

This man represents precisely that quality in all humans that "remains forever motionless in the center" of the whirlwind mentioned by André Breton, but he is also the "Son of science," the twin brother of "philosophical Mercury." The Freemasons called him Hiram. It is his task, under one or another of these names, to achieve the revolution described by Patrick Lepetit in his splendid book.

Throughout this penetrating study, which truthfully extends over surrealism's relations with everything found on "the other side of the bridge," Patrick Lepetit, without ever scattering "cursed bread to the birds," discreetly indicates the curtain of mist from which the silhouette of the disturbing yet marvelous closed castle emerges.

BERNARD ROGER

Bernard Roger joined the surrealists in 1950 and was close to André Breton. He contributed the essay "Plan for a Cinema at the Bottom of a Lake" in Paul Hammond's *The Shadow and Its Shadow: Surrealist Writings on the Cinema*. An expert on alchemy, Roger's best-known book is *Paris et l'alchimie*.

Bernard Roger was a close friend of the painter Jorge Camacho. They both remained members of the group formed around Vincent Bounoure after the official dissolution of the movement in 1969.

INTRODUCTON

TOLERANCE AND ACCEPTANCE OF DIFFERENCE

What is the topicality of our dreams?
ANNIE LE BRUN

This book, born from meeting Paul Sanda in his House of the Surrealists in Cordes-sur-Ciel in August 2007, is a valid instance of objective chance: "the whole of those phenomena that display the invasion of daily life by the marvelous" (to borrow Michel Carrouges's definition). The long discussions we shared took us from surrealism to esotericism through a variety of specific figures, particularly Philippe Audoin and Gérard de Sède, as well as Maurice Baskine, who was in Paul's debt for finding a choice refuge in the Cordes-sur-Ciel Museum of Modern and Contemporary Art. Several months later, I received a letter from Paul Sanda addressed to members and friends of the House of the Surrealists (an art and alchemy center whose utmost purpose is to provide a place for the avant-gardes and the traditions to meet). The letter informed me of the turmoil roiling the association and the surrealist spectrum following the participation of its leader as a bishop in the Rosicrucian Gnostic Apostolic Church, of which I had known absolutely nothing until then. A personal note added to the letter invited me to briefly respond on this matter, in the name of "tolerance and acceptance of difference." I have been long convinced that, as Jean Schuster wrote in *La Brèche* in May 1962, "surrealism is, from a certain angle, an intellectual effort to dissipate the fog released by confused minds claiming to open, with a single key, a world whose complexity they dread above all else," and I have been aware of the quest, in the words of Jean-Louis Bédouin, "of a total freedom, whose guarantor would be, or rather could only be, total awareness."

I began writing a response that over the years became this book bearing the mark of one of the last of Breton's texts, his foreword to Jean-Claude Silbermann's first exhibition in 1964, titled in a way that could be described as premonitory and very much in the tone of this study: "Poetry Is at This Price."* It would probably be helpful to quote a few lines from the original here.

> From the philosophy of "enlightenment" one should not only retain but consider as established beyond doubt the premise that in terms of man's aspirations there is not the slightest reason to infer any design in nature, whether intelligent or moral, from which any kind of principle of methodology might conceivably flow. No permissible speculation can possibly conclude in the necessity of a God, even one abstracted from the insane and despotic images imposed by the established religions. Nevertheless, even if that supreme aberration of anthropomorphism, which parades the label "God," represents the ultimate rock on which the analogical principle has foundered; the fact remains that for mankind this process answers an organic demand and can only escape becoming fixed in the rigid likeness of a disastrous entity if—while also making use of the resources of Hegelian dialectic—it ensures that it is neither held in suspicion nor subjected to limitations but, on the contrary, offered every possible stimulation. Poetry is at this price.

---

*The title is taken from one of André Breton's last texts, his foreword for the exhibition of works by Jean-Claude Silbermann in 1964.

This book was also inspired by my long-held desire to restore to their proper context the elements used against the surrealists by Jean Clair in his vicious little pamphlet *Du Surréalisme considéré dans ses rapports avec le totalitarianisme et les tables tournantes* (Considerations on Surrealism's Relations with Totalitarianism and Table Turning). I should make it clear that I am well aware that Michel Carrouges already tackled this matter in his book *André Breton et les données fondamentales du surréalisme* (André Breton and the Basic Fundamentals of Surrealism) at the beginning of the 1950s, but his approach can be viewed as partial because it is now dated and primarily focuses on Breton. Its reliability is also made suspect by the hints of religiosity that clearly appear in this passage from his *La Mystique du surhomme* (The Mysticism of the Superman):

> The fundamental purpose of all great modern literature can be summed up as the complete conquest of Heaven and Earth against God: it is the new titanesque and Luciferian Apocalypse![1]

A similar criticism was stated by Eddy Batache, who, in his *Surréalisme et tradition* (Surrealism and Tradition),[2] studied Breton's thought from a Guénonian perspective, which is fairly narrow, as René Guénon believed that surrealism was an agent of "counter-initiation."

And, as Alain-Pierre Pillet suggested, it is singularly difficult to identify what Jean Decottignies calls "the untraceable identity of this far-reaching movement." I think it is necessary to state explicitly that what I mean by "surrealists" is first and foremost the personalities listed in *Dictionnaire général du surréalisme et de ses environs* (General Dictionary of Surrealism and Its Surroundings)[3] by René Passeron and Adam Biro, by Alain-Valéry Aelberts and Jean-Jacques Auquier in *Poètes singuliers du surréalisme et autres lieux*,[4] and by Gérard Durozoi in his monumental *History of the Surrealist Movement*,[5] as well as in the various reviews both past and present, in France and abroad, that claim the surrealist label (*BLS, Surréalisme, Supérieur Inconnu, S.U.R.R., Analogon, Phosphor,* and so forth). Those reviews are close in spirit and are collaborative efforts (also including *Infosurr, Cahiers de l'Umbo, L'Or aux 13 Îles* . . .) even if they only involve the persistence of a *spirit,* as the history of the movement was "officially" terminated on February 15, 1969, essentially taking collective activity with it, that "communism of the spirit," which cannot be separated from it.

However, we should also recall what José Pierre said in his Naples lecture (published as a supplement to number 177 of *La Quinzaine littéraire*): "If someone asked me what the surrealist movement was today . . . I would answer that it is *the sum total of individual, even contradictory surrealist activities that are manifesting in one way or another throughout the world*. It should be understood that these activities encompass both singular individual behavior and a specific use of creative faculties. . . ."* In other words, according to Pierre Daix, it involves "surrealism in its restrained configuration of successive groups in liaison with Breton or under his authority, as well as in its broader acceptance of all those who took part in it, even furtively."[6]

An article written by the Czech theoretician Karel Teige in the Prague review *ReD* in 1930—and translated long afterward by Petr Kral for Alain and Odette Virmaux's book *Roger Gilbert-Lecomte et le Grand Jeu*—also casts light on the matter (an insider's perspective, to boot). Le Grand Jeu is a group of young poets and painters, led by René Daumal and Roger Gilbert-Lecomte, based in Reims and active at the end of the twenties and at the beginning of the thirties. When it split at the beginning of the thirties, some of its members joined the surrealist group itself and the others, although remaining "independent," kept close to the ideas of the movement.

> The scattering of the surrealist movement, the conflicts between its various original or more recent factions, is simply one essential aspect of any movement that is romantic by nature and inspiration. Despite the gap between groups and factions, despite their reciprocal, strong hostility, something yet remains that could be defined as "surrealist atmosphere: a night of ghosts and some confused, nagging, fantastic dream, a night that seems to witness the resurrection of a long lost,

---

*[Pierre's italics. Unless indicated otherwise all italicized, all-capitalized, and otherwise highlighted phrases in quoted passages are those of their authors. —*Trans.*]

barbaric, infantile, and animal world where no border lies between reality and unreality or action and dream. This is the atmosphere of surrealist works, whether poems, novels, films, essays, or accounts of dreams, paintings, or sculptures: whether it is Breton, Aragon, or Eluard, Chirico, or Desnos, Ribemont-Dessaignes, Soupault, or the members of the Grand Jeu. A Maldororian night![7]

Teige then listed the reviews around which the various factions gathered at the beginning of the 1930s, citing *Le Grand Jeu, Bifur, Variétés, Documents,* and *La Révolution surréaliste.* While still an associate of Breton, Henri Pastoureau (a bit of a provocateur) made the following observation in an April 1946 letter to Michel Fardoulis-Lagrange, declining the latter's invitation to collaborate on his parasurrealist review, *Troisième Convoi:*

> There has never been a surrealist group *per se,* only a certain number of people at any given time predisposed to advocating a set of ideas. They have been sustained over the last twenty-five years, but a little like Lichtenberg's knife—sometimes their handle is changed and sometimes their blade. One idea can vanish; a new idea appears, and so on. Only a few have endured from surrealism's beginnings (and that is not an iron-clad certainty). The same goes for the people—they were never the same. This does not upset me; I don't presently want surrealism to be unified, and I don't see why there couldn't be several groups gathered around specific affinities.[8]

Charles Jameux, a member of the last organized surrealist group, objected to this idea and echoed the image of the far-reaching movement suggested by Decottignies, saying that the various groups—including the international ones, which puts the notion of their autonomy of action in context—function like a star around that of Paris. André Breton, by virtue of his uncommon personality, was the "cement" assuring the cohesion of the whole. Alain Jouffroy, in issues 123 and 124 of *Opus* (April–May 1991)—despite his regrettable confusion that made him lend to Arthur Rimbaud what by rights belongs to Lautréamont—rightfully adds, based on his personal experience:

> In reality, for the truly independent spirits, all those who took part at one moment or another in the surrealist movement, the group took the place of their own family. They saw in it their long lost brothers and continuously rediscovered its history, which became commingled for them with a saga starring adventurers and explorers of all kinds, all emerging from the challenge hurled by Rimbaud against the society of his time. What is extremely liberating about this family, in comparison to real families, is that each of us could return without having to play the role of prodigal children or the reconverted.

In his book *Les Fruits de la passion* Jean Schuster noted, "The group embodied surrealism's insertion in history. . . . But the group is not *the whole of* surrealism."[9] Jules Monnerot reminds us of all those who only passed through, but without whom surrealism would not have been what it was: "something essential to surrealism lies in these temporary surrealists."

1
Under the Sign of the Goose

Surrealism and Liberation of the Mind

The spiritual aspirations of the surrealists, displayed in their faith in a supernatural reality—a surreality—must be understood in the context of modern religious awareness. Everything in this movement suggests a camouflaged religion: its sect-like structure, its use of manifestos and codes of belief, its origin in underground Bohemian culture, its attraction to the occult and the heterodox. Even the blasphemy and iconoclasm surrealists used against the hegemony of reason and bourgeois morality ironically bring to mind the double-edged power of the taboo that confirms its source—however greatly it has been reversed—in Catholic tradition, in what has been called "the Catholic crisis of consciousness." My purpose is to show that the religious origins of surrealism illuminate the entire movement.[1]

The above phrases by Celia Rabinowitz were quoted by Guy Ducornet in his book *Le Punching Ball et la vache à lait* (The Punching Bag and the

Milk Cow), which is about the lack of comprehension that has always been an integral element of American university criticism of surrealism. However, the United States is not alone in this. In fact, these extracts from the article "Surrealism and Modern Religious Consciousness" by Professor Celia Rabinowitz, published in 1987 by the American Theosophical Society, are of no value, in my opinion, because they incontrovertibly show just how greatly one can be mistaken—unless this is an attempt at recuperation—about a movement that never stopped proclaiming its refusal of religion, particularly Catholic, Apostolic, and Roman varieties. I do not doubt for a moment that a Breton or a Péret would have expanded his field of secular anathemas today to others, like Jean Schuster did in his *Lettre à André Liberati contre les acolytes de Dieu et les judas de l'athéisme* (Letter to André Liberati against the Acolytes of God and the Judases of Atheism):

> Didn't a Jewish psychoanalyst recently declare in the columns of *Le Monde* that the greatest tragedy of the Jewish people after the holocaust was mixed marriages? The state of Israel—notwithstanding the good reasons for its existence—follows a theocratic plan connected both to the fable of the chosen people and to the anti-Arab racism that is constantly simmering there. It is pointless to single out the dreadful old man in Tehran and the torture and murder he orders. Far worse is the darkness that has fallen on the minds reduced to the Qur'an, the exclusion of the concept of freedom, and the conditions imposed on women, worse than in any past or present society![2]

Marcel Jean sensibly observed in his text "Un banquet de têtes" (Talking Heads Banquet) in 1996, "People will say all this anticlericalism 'is outdated. . . .' What should really be outdated are all current forms of patriotism, clericalism, and fundamentalism."[3]

It is, however, just as inappropriate to claim, as Montague Summers did in his 1938 article "Surrealism and the Gothic Novel" (also cited by Guy Ducornet), that "the fundamental weakness of the surrealists—what am I saying!—the rot that eats away the entire movement is their crass materialism. . . . They deny the supernatural." Again, we need to agree on what this notion means!

Such equally unacceptable misinterpretations could be usefully countered by this quote, taken from Sarane Alexandrian's autobiography, *L'Aventure en soi: Autobiographie:*

> Those who have believed (or pretended to believe) that Breton was lapsing into theosophy or parapsychology are taking people for fools; furthermore even the great occultists dismissed theosophy, starting with René Guénon who attacked it in two books as a "pseudo-religion."[4]

The following quote from Alain Jouffroy's "Lettre Rouge" (Red Letter) is also helpful: "Surrealism, as has been said, is not a school. It cannot be reduced to a style and does not even offer a unique way to feel: it opens a door onto all the unknown qualities of the mind!"[5]

But this extract from the collective tract of the May 24, 1951, issue of *High Frequency* really sets the record straight:

> Neither a school nor a sect, surrealism is much more than an attitude. In the most aggressive and total sense of the word, it is an adventure: an adventure of humanity and reality casting each other into the same movement. With all due respect to the spiritualists who are at their tables lowering the lights in order to conjure a shadow, surrealism continues to define itself in relation to the life whose forces it has never ceased exalting while attacking secular alienation.

It is these factors of alienation that surrealism has always attacked with the greatest virulence. We must note the permanence of its refusal, in man's name, not of belief but definitely of all transcendence, especially that embodied in a revealed god, particularly the god of Christians. "Find a heaven at ground level," Michel Leiris declares in *Le ruban autour du cou d'Olympia*.[6] Against religious thought, surrealists gave priority to a certain kind of magic thought, the source of what Sarane

Alexandrian called (citing Cornelius Agrippa) "occult philosophy."

Everything in the discourse of the group's principal figures exhibits the strength of this refusal, especially those close to it in France and especially Belgium. It took the malevolence of Roger Vaillant, a fallen member of the Grand Jeu turned Stalinist henchman, who used false citations in his 1948 book *Surrealism against the Revolution* to accuse the primary organizer of the group of claiming it was necessary "to reinvest the artist in his religious duties!" Citations on this topic, over the years and from various pens, are not lacking, such as Breton's "God, who no one describes, is a swine." This statement accompanies his observation that "lucidity is the greatest enemy of revelation," which echoes René Daumal's opinion of God, whom he describes as the "Désir Imbécile d'Éclairage Universel,"* as well as his more abstract "that limited state of any consciousness, which is Consciousness grasping itself without the help of any individuality or, if you wish, without the support of any particular object." Louis Scutenaire stated, "Believing in God is the equivalent of killing yourself. Faith is only a form of suicide." We also have Ghérasim Luca's extremely radical observation from 1941:

> When the bourgeoisie sends armies blessed by priests onto the battlefields . . . I furiously scream the same obscurantist and prophetic howls addressed to the Creator: "Monster, whose inconceivable ferocity engendered the life inflicted on innocents you dare condemn in the name of some kind of original sin, who you dare punish by virtue of who knows what clauses, we would really like to force you to confess your shameless lies, your inexpiable crimes! We would like to hammer on your nails, push on your thorns, and cause your blood to painfully reopen your dried wounds! This is something we can and will do, by desecrating the quietude of your Body, Profaner of ample vices, Abstractor of stupid purities, Cursed Nazarene, lazybones King, cowardly God."

---

*[*Dieu* is the French word for God; the phrase is also an acronym, and it can be translated as "imbecilic desire for universal enlightenment." —*Trans.*]

We should not overlook Robert Desnos, who in his 1924 book *Liberty or Love!* (La Liberté ou l'amour!) skillfully wielded anachronism and derision when alluding to

> Christ, accompanied by his twelve sirens, wending his way to his destiny; an ebony sky against which a blood-red cross stands out, to his left and right are Egyptian papyri, the debris of a Greek column with its capital at its foot, and telegraph lines on the horizon.[7]

Georges Ribemont-Dessaignes, in his novel *Ariane,* wrote what seems to be a parody of the Gospel of John: "Finally, I see a large throne with a minimal paint job on which the man with the flasks and the colorless face was seated. He was still dressed in casual garb although he had kept his bowler hat on. His gaze met mine. I asked: so who is that? Someone told me: But that is God!"[8]

Continuing in this vein, Julien Gracq provides this description of a Christ descended from his Calvary into the Segréen farmland in his contribution, "A Nightmare," in the catalog for the exhibit Le Surréalisme en 1947 (Surrealism in 1947):

> Now standing next to me, his gaze burning into mine with the impudence of a depraved Adonis, was a gnome with a dirty little yellow beard who came up to my belt. He had the unspeakably wretched air of an old wrinkled urchin, a cheeky and bewitching beggar demanding alms while offending you with his wounds like a bait and switch.

And it is not at all necessary to be a scholar, except one with a certain slight bias, like Jean Clair, who sees in the description by the author of *Paris Peasant* of gas pumps as so many "great yellow gods, great red gods, great green gods," as "profane *signa*, illuminations of a higher reality of which they are the lower inscription, to hear Louis Aragon snickering sarcastically."

René Crevel, never one to be left behind in these matters, denounces in *Les Pieds dans le plat** the "men in black . . . paid by the rich to talk about eternity" and with no beating about the bush puts on trial "the obscurantist 'good lorder,' his morality of enslavement, his mysticism of torture."

Benjamin Péret, one of the most ardent denigrators of all forms of the opium of the people, expanded the debate in these terms: "God must be killed. . . . The Christian religion represents the greatest obstacle to the liberation of Western man. . . . Its destruction is a matter of life and death," all the more so because, as Ghérasim Luca points out, "the pyres of the Middle Ages are still burning!"

In his book *Égregores ou la vie des civilisations* (Egregores or the Life of Civilizations), Pierre Mabille predicted Christianity's imminent end, and he provided a magisterial analysis of its perverse effects in his unsparing case study of the saint in *Thérèse de Lisieux*:

> Confronted by the total misery caused by the last centuries of Christianity with its divorce from human and social reality, humanity can only strive to live by rejecting this woeful teaching, or perish by remaining hooked to their cherished destructive pessimism.[9]

Charles Jameux also saw it as a "woeful teaching," one without any foundation. He aired his deepest feelings on the subject in 1980, bringing the discussion back to its correct existential dimension: "I believe man created God out of whole cloth using the debris torn from him by time." This message is relayed perfectly and amplified by surrealist collages by various artists. In "Un banquet de têtes" Marcel Jean eloquently reminds us, "Saint Augustine believed in monsters and thereby came to the logical conclusion that dragons, chimera, guivres, griffons, Panotti, and other Sciapods were 'God's creatures.'" This is a perilous assertion if we compare it to Jacques Prévert's teratology, with its popes

> whose fruit heads are greedily eaten away by a caterpillar, its lion-headed hermits and goat-headed angels, its intestine-headed

---

*[*Les Pieds dans le plat* means "putting my foot in it." —*Trans.*]

officiating priest holding out the Eucharist to a flayed-head baby Jesus; its Virgin Mary topped by a cephaloidal clitoris, its painter whose bestial face gapes with hilarity as he paints a Saint Veronica, and its ladies of Port Royal, Augustine's disciples, who display ape heads, or faces made hideous by grimaces and insane laughter.[10]

Nor does Marcel Jean overlook *A Little Girl Dreams of Taking the Veil,* Max Ernst's collage album, which exhibits the artist's "free thought"—as does much of his other work—just as sardonically as Jacques Prévert's example.

Filmmakers also refused to be left behind. Louis Buñuel's film *L'Âge d'or,* which portrays the Duke de Blangis as a Sulpician Christ figure straight out of *120 Days of Sodom,* almost earned the film's producer, Le Vicomte Charles de Noailles, excommunication (!) from the church. Meanwhile, Buñuel's *Un Chien Andalou* (An Andalusian Dog) repulsed the right-minded, despite their skill at wielding loaded sticks (a sign of those times), by establishing a parallel between the Marist Christian schools and the "grand pianos filled with donkey carcasses" that the star of the film dragged behind him with a rope.

Buñuel made three important surrealist-related films: *The Exterminating Angel,* with its backdrop of the Exodus and the Apocalypse; *The Milky Way,* which featured the Spanish heretic Priscillian of Avila,* Jesuit and Jansenist duelists, and the Marquis de Sade as a torturer; and *Simon of the Desert,* a major part of the work of Buñuel, the friend of Federico García Lorca and the early Salvador Dali, which he called "an appeal to the irrational, the obscure, and all the impulses that come from my deepest self."[11] Together, they illustrate this remark by Buñuel, confided to Tomas Pérez Turrent and José de la Colina: "Surrealism† is not an aesthetic for me, not just another avant-garde movement, but something that engages my life in a spiritual and moral direction."[12]

---

*Priscillian of Avila was a neo-Gnostic who was executed by the church in 385.
†Octavio Paz wrote, "Surrealism is not a poetry but a poetics and even more, in the most decisive fashion, a vision of the world."

In 1960, the Belgian Marcel Mariën* caused a scandal with his film *The Imitation of Cinema* (with Tom Gutt and Jane Graverol), an "erotic Freudian farce against the Church."[13] The film faced prosecution, and the Belgian Catholic Office of Cinematographic Censor labeled it as a "film unworthy of a civilized country," blasting it as "a sacrilegious parody of Christianity combined with an obscenity that exceeds the wildest imagination. This film, totally devoid of any artistic value, is undoubtedly the work of a psychopath."[14] But as noted by Bernard Schmitt and Marie-Dominique Massoni, "Sacrilege is not profanation because it partakes in the sacred."[15]

For good measure, Mariën's friend Roger Van de Wrouwer echoed his playful provocation by exhibiting his painting *The Elevation,* which showed Pope John XXIII drinking a Coca-Cola. This was an acerbic, humorous critique of both the church and the emerging consumer society.

Jean Schuster, in his 1990 article "The Discreet Charm of God," after stating he does not belong to "any religion," attacks God in all his guises, both as a burdensome material presence ("The specificity of the Christian God, perverse and subtle where the Jewish and Islamic Gods are crude, is *to be* as overwhelmingly massive as possible in the terrestrial spaces men have built in his glory") and as a spiritual void ("The alleged discretion of God clearly illustrates the theological impoverishment of the Christians, devoid since the Reformation, with a few sublime exceptions of any spiritual authenticity").

True, it is possible to read these same attacks on God in Schuster's earlier arguments: "Religion is a bond between man and God. Love is a bond between a man and a woman. It is a fine thing that a woman can transform and divert toward her flesh these oblations that would otherwise have gone to this unpleasant phantom."[16]

Jean-Claude Silbermann, in a lecture given to the students of the Cergy School of Art in 1999, denounced both God and his servants.

---

*This is the same Mariën who was unfortunately a Stalinist and who snickered discreetly in 1955 in his magazine *Les Lèvres Nues,* "You one-legged people, Lourdes will make you a fine leg but it won't get you very far."

It is definitely impossible for me to believe in the existence of this frightful creature, this gutted, eyeless doll named Jehovah, Allah, Christ, and a lot of other names, which the vital sentiment of world unity can well do without, causing no harm—and his servants: I need only list the shady and absurd practices of priests, rabbis, imams, and other bureaucrats of the divine. Kneelers and squatters alike who show heaven their assholes, at best, only kneel or squat before their own image. . . .[17]

Closer to the present, in his 2005 text "On the Necessity of Being an Atheist to Feel the Sacred," Guy Girard confirms the permanent—or rather "classic"—nature of this rejection in the surrealist circle of influence. Citing its intellectual basis, he explains:

I am an atheist. This is a poetic certainty. I feel the idea of the deity is undoubtedly the most criminal the human mind was ever able to formulate against its own freedom, and I admire the philosophical atheism of Sade or Bakounin!

The world is there, I take part in it, living like this with billions of individuals knowing everything is filled to the brim, so full there is really no room for any hypothetical divine presence.[18]

But the most iconoclastic charge is undoubtedly the one dated April 30, 1975, and published in 1988 in *Lettres à la cantonade* (Letters to No One in Particular), signed Pierre Schumann Audricourt. This was the collective pseudonym used by José *Pierre*, Jean *Schu*ster, Jean-Claude Silber*mann*, Philippe *Aud*oin, Jean-François Bo*ry*, and Claude *Court*ot to publish the letters they wrote and distributed selectively in 1974 and 1975 in an attempt to maintain intellectual contact following the end of collective activity. Philippe Audoin writes:

All the same, there is something equally repulsive as God—man. Not in and of himself but insofar as by manufacturing God, man chose to enslave himself to what inside was most cowardly, senile, and fundamentally repugnant. God is fabricated in the image of what man bears and feels the need to evacuate for want of being able to accept it without disgust. God is, therefore, excremental by birthright, and expelled from the body and spirit.

For good measure, Audricourt/Audoin adds, reversing the signs and wonderfully confirming Ferdinand Alquié's observation, "Surrealist blasphemy does not insult God but believers," those who Prévert says with his inimitable humor in the poem *Talking Heads Dinner in Paris, France*, "believe, those who believe to believe, those who bleat-bleat."

If God is the excrement of the nonreligious man (believer) he is also his food. The religious man, on the other hand, does not stoop to this. It is hardly as if he feels the need to spit on God, unless in the event of a friendly orgy. He is quietly satisfied to be divine (which is the least of things) and to transform everything that comes not from him but to him into so many helpful little Gods. This is how he can have all the gods he wants or deserves at his disposal. . . . So many birds he wants to charm and who select him for their perch. Sometimes they overburden his left shoulder as if trying to ensure he walks properly. The religious man limps. He has a goose foot . . .[19]

It is not surprising that Audricourt/Audoin puts us on the trail of several important clues. The goose, in extremely ancient Greek myths, is the guise in which the goddess Nemesis would have suffered Zeus's amorous assaults, which led to the conception of the beautiful Helen. But the goose is also, as shown by Louis Charpentier in his book on the two Jameses and the mystery of Compostella, an avatar of the sun freshly emerged from the primordial egg, the messenger between the Earth and the other world.[20] Ancient Egyptians believed that Amun, "the Hidden One," the god ruling over both the earthly and divine worlds, associated with the vital breath, the pneuma of the Greeks, was the guarantor of an eternally restarting creation. He was also believed responsible for hatching the cosmic egg holding the sun; among other things he was represented as a goose of the Nile whose honk gave birth to the world. In this context, it is interesting to note that the goose game* is a typical Egyptian game going back to the first dynasty, whose purpose is to free the sun from the darkness. According to Pierre Mabille, its path "is reminiscent of labyrinths," in which, as Jameux says, "When the adept reaches certain points, [he is] obliged to retrace his steps and undergo ordeals" in the hope of "penetrating to the heart of the secret."

A surrealist equivalent of this game was created by the combined talents of Yves and Jeanette Tanguy, Suzanne Muzard, André Breton, Georges Sadoul, and Pierre Unik during a stay in July 1929 on the isle of Sein, the Gallic Sena renowned for its Druid college. "In Celtic tales . . . supernatural beings take the form of birds during their life,"[21] Jean Markale reminds us, and the goose foot, which was a Druid symbol, has always been perceived as a *sign* of the goose, that is, the initiate. More on this to come . . .

Extremely virulent—and eternally vigilant—anticlericalism is therefore a salient characteristic of surrealist thought. It can be verified on countless occasions in the history of a group that would often be divided by "the religious question," such as the Carrouges affair† in 1951 that prompted a number of departures.

Additional evidence can be seen in the 1957 tract "Coup de semonce" [Warning Shot], which condemned Breton's former friend Simon Hantaï, who had organized, with Georges Mathieu and Stéphane Lupasco, "Templars of Bad Painting," an event José Pierre called "manifestations of a fundamentalist and fascistic spirit." This included the Commemorative Ceremonies of the Second Condemnation of Siger de Brabant, who was a thirteenth-century heretic condemned by the Inquisition but redeemed by Dante. Pierre went on to describe it as that "vile tyranny whose head, whatever mask it wears, is in Rome." In a more profound and less polemical way, Victor Crastre claimed, "Night fell upon the world the day when Christianity insisted upon 'consolidating' Aristotle's theories with its own." (It should be noted, though,

---

*[This game is better known in the English-speaking world as snakes and ladders. —*Trans.*]
†The Carrouges affair is detailed later in the book.

that thanks to the return of neo-Platonic idealism, a certain period of the Middle Ages was opposed to Aristotle's rationalism.) So it should come as no surprise that Breton spoke of a knowledge that "would simply be a re-knowing and a kind of return to sources." We should remember that this could not "stand as a security deposit for a narrow-minded conservatism" or permission for "the restoration of political forms from a bygone age."[22]

In fact, it is an extremely virulent and unsparing condemnation, which was still being echoed in 1991 by Annie Le Brun in her *Qui vive: Considérations actuelles sur l'inactualité du surréalisme* (Who Goes There, subtitled Topical Considerations on the Nontopicality of Surrealism), with her remarks on "the vile sweat of the being connected to a divine principle."[23] Breton never compromised on this *avowed* atheism (which led Michel Carrouges in his book *La Mystique du surhomme* (The Mysticism of the Superman) to inscribe him in "the purely Promethean tendency"[24] of modern literature next to Sade, Nietzsche, and Mallarmé), no more than did the majority of Breton's friends: "Everything that is doddering, squint-eyed, infamous, sullying, and grotesque is contained for me in this single word: God."[25]

This opprobrium was clearly extended, of course, to his apostles. "An apostle, on the whole," Philippe Soupault writes in *En joue!*[*] "is a maniac." It also included his saints. André Pieyre de Mandiargues, in his poem "Somewhere in the World," clearly depicts how much they were exploited by the right-thinkers, against a backdrop of Francoist tyranny:

> *The sacred heart of the murderers is on vacation,*
> *The faces of Saints Ignatius and Dominic*
> *Look like the jaws of the guardia civile.*[26]

But Christianity's vicar is not spared either! Breton, whose material situation was hardly flourishing, took a job[†] with Pierre Lazareff on the Voice of America radio during World War II, only on condition

---
*[*En joue!* means "take aim!" —*Trans.*]
†Breton said that he accepted the job at Patrick Waldberg's urging.

he never had to talk about the pope. According to Jean Schuster in his *Lettre à André Liberati*:

> In New York, Breton would not hear of being involved in any way whatsoever promoting a personality he regarded as a usurper of spiritual values, to whom he denied all moral authority, and whose complacency toward Hitlerism only added a timely justification for his refusal. Later he stated: "The political event is only the good conscience of those who gather around the mystic table to ceaselessly invent this repugnant, faceless God."[27]

The reader cannot help but note in passing that while Peter's successors are considered to be "usurpers" of spiritual values, said values are thereby not entirely devoid of interest. Whoever said vicar may be—either Gérard Legrand's "clown Pious XII," or one of "those popes with bird names,"* according to Prévert, or John XXIII—changes nothing. Pope John XXIII's encyclical, *Pacem in Terris*, was similarly condemned and deconstructed by Claude Dumont, who labeled it a "shady text" in the October 1963 issue of *La Brèche*.

> What we are looking at is the openly declared rebirth of a kind of Christian fascism, justified by "the divine origin of the authority," to the extent its author feels the need to conclude his analysis of "the necessity of authority" with one of his familiar pirouettes: "This is why the DOCTRINE we have just presented is suitable for every kind of truly democratic regime." Theocratic would sound more appropriate.

This opprobrium is extended not only to the vicar but also to all his representatives! Beyond his sarcasm, Paul Nougé peremptorily concludes his 1934 *Letter to an Aesthete Dominican*, cited in issue 912 of the review *Europe*, devoted to the Belgian surrealists, with this hard-hitting phrase: "The sole grace we can still wish for you is to find within yourself

---

*[The French word for "pious," *pie*, also means "magpie." —*Trans*.]

the honesty and courage to simply regard us as mortal enemies of what you represent and defend with such delightful clumsiness." Ernest de Gengenbach (who also sometimes signs his texts Jean Genbach), in an ideal position for voicing his opinion, describes the suffering he felt "living perpetually with males and with men whose sinister garb always made [him] think of flights of crows over deserted fields in November." In his *La Conscience démonique* (The Demonic Consciousness), Charles Duits cites "the obstinate violence with which all true poets attack the Church."

> In their eyes, the priest is first and foremost a *falsifier*, who makes the oracle say something other than what it said. . . . He is also an *impostor*, who uses a speech without virtue, meaning one without magic, and believes—or pretends to believe—that the echo has the same power as the voice. He is finally a *usurper* and a *persecutor* who, not satisfied with taking the place of the authentic representative of the sacred, condemns it to silence or the flames.[28]

"American surrealists" of the latter part of the twentieth century, quoted by Guy Ducornet in his introduction to the book *Ça va chauffer! Situation du Surréalisme aux U.S.A. (1966–2001)* (*The Forecast Is Hot!*),* noted, "The fundamental experience of poetry enabled us to recognize religionists as the colonizers of the Marvelous: brutal exploiters whose means and ends are explicitly anti-poetic," which obviously disqualifies them yet again—once and for all.[29]

The opprobrium is also sometimes extended to the very symbols of religions, for example, when the Grand Jeu group mocked Judaism by asserting "true circumcision is that of the heart." Christian symbols are also targeted, notably the cross. In his 1948 text titled "Tutuguri," about a Tarahumara rite, Artaud wrote in what may well be anger mixed with terror, "It is not sufficiently known, and not at all in Europe, how dark a symbol the cross is . . . the cross is an abject sign and . . . its material needs to burn. . . ." In this context, it is interesting to turn our attention

---

*The Forecast Is Hot! is a collection of the statements issued by the surrealist group of Chicago led by Franklin and Penelope Rosemont. Guy Ducornet has translated this book into French and written an introduction.

to—but without exaggerating its importance for it is all anecdotal—the case of Ernest de Gengenbach, a student of the Jesuits and a "former seminarian turned surrealist anarchist" and self-proclaimed "mystical pirate." He was born in Gruey-lès-Surance in the Vosges region in 1903 and died in 1979 in Châteauneuf-en-Thymerais, in the Eure and Loir. Leiris called him "half mythomaniac, half adventurer" in his book *L'Age d'homme.** Maurice Nadeau, in his *History of Surrealism,* called him "the most colorful and disturbing figure of the movement."[30] Julien Gracq, in his study "André Breton ou l'âme d'un movement" (André Breton or the Soul of a Movement), made him "[the] most provocative, [the] most profane and [the] most sacrilegious of surrealism's adepts," or more specifically "of the surrealist Luciferian sect, which concerned itself with occultism, sorcery, spiritism, and mediumship." Gengenbach recalls this, in a tone combining horrified hindsight and guilty conscience, in *Judas or the Surrealist Vampire,* his "ghost story/biography!"

In 1925, after *La Révolution surréaliste* published a letter with a photo of its author in his cassock (in the fifth issue), Breton met in Troyes this young, slightly deranged cleric, who was flirting with suicide as a way to "escape this world." Ernest Gengenbach, alias Father Judas, his double, or even the Abbey priest who was forbidden to wear clerical dress because of his profane love affairs, claimed to have a split personality (a complaint he shared with some other members of the movement), which was expressed in a perpetual "small shuttle between Satan and Christ," a constant, completely schizophrenic back and forth between worldly life in gay company and religious retreat among the monks, "where he had the habit of going several times a year to rest and get back on his feet," but which he also saw as a prison or a sanctuary. In his article "La vie poétique d'Ernest de Gengenbach" (The Poetic Life of Ernest de Gengenbach), Jean Decottignies described this "shuttle" as the expression of that individual's *"cantilevered"* life, a life whose true formula is osmosis, the "entanglement of two existences." He then went on to say, "Moving from one to the other, it was not change he tasted but their reciprocal contamination—fundamentally perverse and profaning." Decottignies stressed that "the Church and its sanctuaries

---

*[*L'Age d'homme* means "manhood." —*Trans.*]

of all orders were the choice site for his mental chimeras; moving from the world to the cloister is like traveling from reality to unreality. This way, he did not have an impression he was traveling from surrealism to Christianity, but was fully assuming the former's requirements," thereby illustrating in some way the dilemma encountered by those "within whom the sacred asks to exist" but "in whom the loss of a universal God is consummated."[31] Jules Monnerot would later express it in these terms: "Either 'we are not in the world' or 'we are there to ensure he is no longer there.'"

But the real choice was expressed in these terms in the preface to Gengenbach's *Satan à Paris* (Satan in Paris).

> So, if everything is poisoned and corrupted, we are obliged to choose either pure and simple suicide, or the re-creation of the world with the marvelous power of the imagination, the mystical rebirth through prayer and faith, knowing that "supernaturalism is the point where poetic experience and mystical experience coincide."

"A ghost caught between life and death," said Ernest de Gengenbach, who was convinced that he was the satanic reincarnation of Dom Robert Jolivet, an abbot of Mont-Saint-Michel who went to England during the Hundred Years War. Gengenbach would be a traveling companion of surrealism for several years, although he confessed in his correspondence that he remained "attached to the pure and indulgent, gentle figure of Christ." After his first meeting with Péret "at the café," Gengenbach was punctuated by a magisterial slap in the face, as the "priest" had made the mistake of introducing himself while wearing the clerical garb of cassock and "ecclesiastic Roman cape," although he had had it lined with white satin.

In July 1926, responding to a request by Breton for his thoughts about the question of religion, Gengenbach responded in a letter—two letters, in fact—as well as "notes from retreat" at the Benedictine Abbey of Solesmes, which can be found almost word for word in *Satan à Paris*. These would be published in the eighth issue (December 1, 1926) of *La Révolution surréaliste*, where he writes:

> The West causes me atrocious suffering, my entire personal and distant being yearns for the East, and if there is no other means to get there than through the fire and blood of this entirely rotten West, then long live the Revolution.

After repeating "there is no such thing as a religious question," he goes on to say:

> Religion, like God, is a word devoid of meaning for me. It is dogmas, rites, theater, intellectualism, and so on. The cloisters allow the neurotic and hypersensitive to live in a place where they will be left alone . . . Cloister dwellers don't give a damn about the world.

He then concludes that he has found *"no solution"* to his existential malaise, "nor any detour or acceptable pragmatism." All he has left is "faith in Christ, cigarettes, and the jazz records [he] loves," and, paradoxically, *"surrealism* especially." It may well have been, despite all, the tone of these letters that convinced Breton to make an introductory speech at an April 3, 1927, lecture—reprinted in its entirety in *Judas or the Surrealist Vampire*—given by Jean Genbach (another transparent pseudonym of the defrocked priest). This lecture was conceived, as described by the anonymous author of the preface to the reprinted edition of *Satan à Paris,* as "a desperate attempt to 're-enchant' through transgression, a world that has lost its sense of the sacred." The man, giving this lecture at Adyar Hall,* introduced himself as a man "consciously possessed by demons," vacillating between Catholicism—insofar as it was heir to "the Orphic mysteries and the initiatory rites of Ancient Egypt and even India"—and Satanism, a Satanism in the style of a Clovis Trouille rather than a true transgression (see plate 1).

Breton, in his introductory remarks at that April 3 lecture, cited Jorris-Karl Huysmans, a description of Gengenbach that will also be

---

*Adyar Hall was the appropriately decorated premises of Helena Blavatsky's Theosophical Society; Breton noted its "décor."

used by Jean Decottignies talking of a "surrealist avatar of Durtal," the hero of Joris-Karl Huysman's book *La-Bas*.

Gengenbach also published a Sapphic novel, *La Papesse du diable*, under the pseudonym Jehan Sylvius, said to be cowritten with Robert Desnos, but this is doubtful. He also wrote several largely autobiographical works, which revealed true internal torment, such as *Satan à Paris*. In it he makes this confession:

> I already admitted with no false shame that I was a former monastery priest and with all the insolence characteristic of surrealism's adepts, I cut pyjamas out of a bishop's cassock. Certainly, I needed a great deal of courage to say all this, without concern for the skeptical, cynical smiles of those who have been duped by literature, and without worrying about all those psychiatrists in search of their next madman.[32]

The monastery used as the "black" theater of black masses and sabbaths, of which, of course, he was never in charge, was Mont-Saint-Michel, which is specifically consecrated to the vanquisher of the Evil One. Gengenbach, nonetheless, had been brought there on vacations while still a student by a Dominican who had provided "lengthy explanations on how millions of invisible demons roved in our world since time began, since the serpent of Genesis seduced Adam and Eve by promising them they would become gods." This is a Mont-Saint-Michel that oddly echoes the tone of the English gothic novel:

> Beneath the abbey crypts . . . Satan lives in an underground castle in the rock where he has rendezvous at night with all the drowned souls from lakes and oceans, suicides, those who have been driven mad by anguish, all those stuck in a rut, and all those mestizos and exotics soliciting here and there in the Montmartre night clubs!

This Mont-Saint-Michel that recurs continuously in Gengenbach's writings also figures in the backdrop of a snapshot found in Breton's papers, in which Gengenbach, clad in clerical dress, is proudly "enthroned" in the company of a very beautiful woman. (Is this Mary, that "Divine, Loving, Protective, Consoling Maternity"? Or else she could be the Temptress, with "her body of Diana the Huntress and the head of a stained-glass Virgin," with eyes "like two small Morning Stars smiling from the other side of death.") There is little doubt that this snapshot may have inspired Breton's response to one of Gengenbach's particularly unforthcoming answers during the fourth session of their sexuality investigations on February 15, 1928.

> Your Mont-Saint-Michels, your lovesick Virgins only interest me in connection with your sexuality![33]

Since we are speaking about a priest's sexuality, one who was always surrounded by pretty women, "priestesses or . . . magicians," I should mention the many descriptions of black masses that liven up Gengenbach's books. He uses what Jean Decottignies calls a "sacrilegious speech that combines the lexicons of religions and eroticism in a baroque symbolism." What is more, it was more or less inspired by the theories of the father of red (sexual) magic, the American occultist Pascal Beverly Randolph (1825–1875), which were translated into French by Maria de Naglowska in 1931 under the title *Magia Sexualis*. This work irresistibly brings to mind the Georges Bataille of *The Story of the Eye*—without the incandescence.

Founder of the Brotherhood of the Golden Arrow, Maria de Naglowska also passes as a continuer of Eugene Vintras's work of Mercy ("Saint Séverin, which Vintras's heresy had already made the site of a strange rite," *Astyanax*, by Mandiargues).* Maria de Naglowska is cited in *L'Expérience démoniaque* (The Demonic Experience), and Sarane Alexandrian devoted a text with the evocative title "Maria de Naglowska and Feminine Satanism" in *Les Libérateurs de l'amour* (The Liberators of Love).[34]

Gengenbach, who would be ordained a Vintrassian priest (a priest of the para-christian sect founded by Vintras) at the end of his life, had

---

*Maria de Naglowska is considered as the continuer of Vintras. "Astyanax" is the title of a poem by Mandiargues. The work of Mercy is the name of Vintras's "sect."

long been fully apprised of "feminine Satanism," insofar as he had the good fortune to number among his conquests a young woman baptized by Pierre Péan as the She Devil of Caluire.[35] This Lydie Bastien, responsible for the arrest of Jean Moulin,* was a young woman who also had a passion for spiritualism and occultism. Gengenbach said in his autobiography, *L'Expérience démoniaque*†—a perfect title in this instance—that she had the "undulating, glacial soul of a reptile." The subscription bulletin for what was undoubtedly the first edition of the book *Judas or the Surrealist Vampire* in 1930, "The Sign of the Black Eagle," also includes a fine sample of Gengenbach's prose, which merits reading because of its confused nature.

> Then the earth grew cold again, vainly watered by the blood of Christ, to suddenly gape open to swallow the Cross in Golgatha's sides, but from the earth reheated and fertilized by the sperm of the hanged man, Judas, the marvelous mandrake will emerge.[36]

The author then says, "This is how a Satanic and Prussian hussar should think of death," although we are told in the same book's preface by its alleged editor that "[Father Judas] was initiated by the surrealists into occultism and magic, and he underwent many fairly dangerous paranormal experiments . . . that [put] his mental equilibrium to a rude test."

Laurent Beaufils in his book on Malcolm de Chazal[37] cites an extremely interesting extract from the cleric's memoirs, in which Gengenbach states:

> Man can be restored to his original vocation of sorcerer, mage, medium, and seer, a vocation that has been obscured and smothered by all the religious obscurantisms and all the darkness producing mystification of the Church that seeks to dominate humanity, not enlighten it.[38]

---

*[Moulin was the leader of the French resistance during World War II. —*Trans.*]
†[*L'Expérience démoniaque* was written under the name of Brother Columban de Jumièges. —*Trans.*]

This sentiment shares some aspects of the quest of Breton's friends. It even seems that "in the higher spheres, in the secret councils of the Eminences and Excellencies of the ecclesiastical hierarchy, they were terrified by this example of sacrilegious and profane apostasy exhibited publicly," by this odd figure who said, "It is precisely because I was a churchman that I want people to know what the men of the Church have made me: a desperate man, a rebel, and a nihilist!" This prompted the famous Thomist philosopher and Leon Bloy disciple, Jacques Maritain, deftly assisted by a charming young woman, Mercedes de Gournay, to encourage him to repent. Maritain was mocked by the surrealists as "a member of the Société d'Entreprise de Néo-Conversion Cocteau, Maritain, Reverdy et Frères," with which Gengenbach swore he had no involvement. Among the "brothers" in question, we also find a certain Maurice Sachs, author of *The Sabbat,* who enjoyed an even more fiendish notoriety under his nickname "Gestapette" during the Occupation!

At a later date, the seminarian—it seems he never moved past this stage—who had officially broken with the movement in 1935 following the suicide of Crevel, would even venture the opinion in a brochure bearing the improbable title *Surréalisme et christianisme* (Surrealism and Christianity),[39] in which he mistook his desires for realities and spread rumors, usually linked, at the time, with the Freemasons of the so-called wisdom grades, that "he was certain the surrealists are joining Lucifer."

This impossible synthesis is by an author who views, among other singular perspectives, "this reverse mystic" Breton as both his "Luciferian mentor" and a reincarnation of Pietro di Luna, who ruled in Avignon under the name of Benedict XIII, the "excommunicated pope who was always excommunicating." This earns us the highly comic description in *Judas or the Surrealist Vampire* of a "mysterious figure" accompanying the devil, if you please, "also in clerical dress but the silk lining of his habit was Roman purple. The unknown individual wears a magnificent satin cape the same color as the cassock worn by the pope in the Vatican." This individual, who is none other than "His Excellency Peter of the Moon, the reincarnated phantom of the former Antipope of Avignon ... is the same individual the abbey priest recognizes, despite his mask, as André Breton, founder in Paris of the surrealist Luciferian sect!"

I would like to rectify this papal portrait, which was echoed in the 1930 tract *Cadavre,* which attached that same label to Breton—and stuck. I can put forth the notion in company with Marcel Jean and Arpad Mezei (see chapter 5, note 13) that "pope" in the hermetic sense of the word is the fifth arcana of the tarot, the representative of the spiritual man—spiritual but not divine—and, therefore, say with Charles Duits:

> Breton was a pope, yes. But he was a true pope, meaning a spiritual sovereign, a pontiff, who held his crown from the Individual. Men can neither elect nor depose him....

A more judicious label might be "fratriarch," to use the term coined by Régis Debray, as any detailed examination of Breton's work will reveal his great sensitivity and receptiveness to his comrades' contributions.

Gracq sharply criticized *Surréalisme et christianisme* and announced that he was going to write a clarification of Breton's relationship with esotericism, which earned him a letter from Gengenbach, dated June 3, 1947—now in the Nantes Library archives—in which he tried to explain himself without managing to emerge from his characteristic wooly thinking.

> It is quite possible that the formidable ecclesiastical imprint I was given surrendered me like a choice prey to the hallucinatory illusions of illuminism and the mythomania based on chimaera and evangelical legends!

Yet, at the same time, this same Gengenbach wrote the following in his *Adieu à Satan* (Goodbye Satan), while hailing the "sublime approach of the seeker of the Absolute," that is, Breton:

> Surrealism is a mysticism without theology ... but the mysticism of a regressive spiritual evolution using poetic and magical knowledge to attain an esoteric human Golden Age ... to attain a legendary past, illuminated by the dazzling lightning flashes of the Light-bearer Angel. If you prefer, surrealism is a kind of mystical

poaching in the forbidden gardens of the Earthly Paradise to steal the fruits of the Tree of Science. It involves rediscovering the secret of the Great Work, of proceeding to the alchemical re-creation of Man and the Universe . . . after having rediscovered and learned anew what has always remained the hermetic property of a few rare initiates!

May I dare conclude that Gengenbach, the embodiment of some of the movement's ambiguities, may have been perfectly aware of the antinomy: "Surrealist in Christ"? But this was a Christ, who, as Gengenbach himself pointed out, "died in rather dubious company, surrounded by two bandits and a high-class hooker from Galilee at his feet"—a demystified Christ. Unless we consider the matter more soberly and realistically, as did Charles Jameux, saying that the encounter with the unstable, possibly insane Gengenbach, who was nonetheless a man of learning and most importantly defrocked,[40] was perceived by the surrealists as a "godsend" by virtue of the symbology which this meeting hid while remaining basically superficial and of little importance, if not to say—and this settles the matter—derisory. "This is how the pollutions, which psychoanalysis is unable to drain, rise like a religious gesture in the soul, at the heart of the lives of the saints, the exalted, and the lunatics of the church," Malcolm de Chazal noted (as someone who would know).[41]

Getting back to the pope as well as to bring this digression to a close, Artaud declared in his first address* to this individual:

We don't have anything to do with your canons, index, sin, confessional, and clergy; we are thinking of a new war, a war on you, Pope, dog. Here the spirit confesses to the spirit. From top to bottom of your Roman masquerade, the part that triumphs is the hatred of the soul's immediate truths, against these very flames, which burn even inside the spirit.

---

*There is a series of texts, not books, written by Artaud in the mid-twenties called "Addresses" (to the Pope, to the Dalai Lama, etc.).

Visible Catholicism will be razed for reason of idolatry and the current pope condemned to death as a traitor and a Simoniac.

In 1990, Michel Leiris described the Dalai Lama, relatively spared criticism during Artaud's time, as being "as creepy as any other high cardinal" in *Entre augures* (Between Omens).[42] He even appears as an arch manipulator to the Czech* group's Eva Svankmajerova, who wrote an article on him in the form of an open letter similar to Artaud's, which appeared in the second issue of *Analogon* in 1990[†]: "So you suggest we all could put our legs behind our neck for a laugh, in order to radiate an innocent or even single-minded innocence. You charlatan!"

While René Crevel attacked science-worshipping idolatry in *L'Esprit contre la raison* (The Spirit against Reason) in 1927, saying it gave the masses an illusion of spiritual progress through the most hypocritical kinds of wordplay without ever losing sight of its useful ends or the personal profits to be made from its new discoveries, it was not until the 1930s, if we can believe André Malraux's text in *La Tête d'obsidienne* (The Obsidian Head), that Breton's distrust of science began to manifest. Here is the dialogue between Breton, who was looking over some Hopi kachinas, and the author of *Man's Hope:*

> "Do you know where the religious center of the Hopi Indians was?" "In Nevada, I think?" "No, in Los Alamos." And since it was in Los Alamos that the Americans were then working on the atomic bomb, they chased out the Indians. "That doesn't surprise me," he [Breton] replied with his look of a discouraged medicine man. "I don't believe in coincidences: magic takes over from magic."[43]

To write, as Carrouges did in his 1950 book on Breton that "the pure and simple negation of the value of science only smacks of that childhood malady of surrealism, which at a certain period was respon-

---

*The Czech (and Slovakian) group was created in the thirties and is still working.
†[The first issue of *Analogon* was published in the years of the Prague Spring back in 1967; issue 2 could not be published until after the Velvet Revolution removed the totalitarian government in 1989. —*Trans.*]

sible for their tendency toward a kind of magic idealism" seems more like an attempt to convince himself of this since the risk of nuclear catastrophe was so great at that time to the members of the group and their friends. For example René Alleau described how "shadows are printed on the asphalt of the streets of Hiroshima and Nagasaki of the first human beings to be disintegrated thanks to the progress of contemporary science and industry."[44] You be the judge! After the Second World War the science "of the scientism proponents" (Jean-Louis Bédouin) and the technicians, seen as a vector of a religiosity of reason and "descriptive knowledge of phenomena" rejecting "tangible emotion" (Pierre Mabille) and the scientists themselves, "knackers with diplomas," were condemned to face the same opprobrium as religion. Consider Yves Bonnefoy's advocacy of "an aggressive physics of the irrational" or the intransigent attitude of Gérard Legrand in "Rationalisme et raisons de vivre" (Rationalism and Reasons to Live), the seventh "Surrealist Bulletin" published in *Le Libertaire* of November 30, 1951, which stated:

> In this regard, we cannot forewarn revolutionary thought too strongly against a narrow-minded rationalism that is still common today in certain "scientific" milieus, a rationalism that is quite mistakenly assumed capable of carving a path toward atheistic emancipation. . . . Beyond the contrived opposition, conjointly maintained by the religions and positivism, between the "body" and the "soul," or between the various mental functions, this study (a dispassionate and attentive one of occultism, which will separate the true from the false) is of a nature to prepare the advent of REAL LIFE.[45]

This is a fairly moderate position, it is true, when compared with the radical one presented by Roger Gilbert-Lecomte in the autumn of 1930 in his text "L'Horrible Révélation . . . la seule" (The Horrible Revelation . . . the Only One), in *Le Grand Jeu*, n° 3.

> We can oppose to the universality of scientific reason—based on mathematics—a universality of immediate intuition in other

domains of the spirit. However, this new aspect of the universal cannot be grasped by all human consciousness; it can only be attained at the price of long training and a full evolution that determines the suitable state for this revelation.

Science, all things considered, whose *face* Duits thought, "[Breton] sought, among other things, to *transform,*" once it denied the principle of analogy and set itself up as an "unsurpassable truth," was thereby placed in the same sack as religion, which undoubtedly reinforced the common postwar accusations against the movement of an irrational, occultist deviation. Consider the following, from *Unmask the Physicists, Empty the Laboratories,* a tract* from February 1958:

> If religion was long the opium of the people, science is well placed to take up the baton. Protests against the arms race that some physicists today put on a show of signing, only clarify for us all the more their guilt complex, which is really in every case one of the most heinous vices of mankind. We know the refrain: the breast that is beaten too late, the pledge made to the bleatings of the herd by the same hand that arms the butcher. Christianity and the police states that are its distorting mirrors have accustomed us to it.... From Jesus on the cross to the laboratory assistant who is "anguished" but incapable of abandoning the manufacture of death, hypocrisy, and masochism equal each other.

Ten years later, in *André Breton a-t-il dit passe* Charles Duits pronounced his own definitive judgment: "The amazing blindness of the scientists is a direct consequence of the inhuman idolatry that characterizes the scientific attitude." This antiscientist position called for some greater nuance, but, as we shall see, it would find an echo: "The edifice of science remains, for the most part, a castle of ghosts" appeared in the text *Prague aux couleurs du temps,* which was signed in 1967 by several

---

*This tract was probably written by Breton himself and signed by twenty-nine members of the group. It is quoted in *Tracts surréalistes et déclarations collectives,* vol. 2 (Paris, Eric Losfeld, 1982).

members of the Czechoslovakian group, which, at that time, was enjoying a brief resurgence. The following passage, though, taken from the first issue of *La Brèche* in 1961, shows that a dialectical process aimed at surmounting the contradictions was then being sketched out.

> As poetry, within its own symbolism, is incapable of explaining the paradoxical aspect of the image, and scientific logic is incapable of grasping the paradoxical aspect of atomism, a new language must be used, which, drawing rigor from science and analogy from poetry, would become a poetic science alone with the capability of penetrating both the domain of the image and that of phenomena, and thereby explain creation.

The philosopher Ferdinand Alquié (who was close to Breton) agreed with this idea in a lecture at the Cerisy-La-Salle symposium in July 1966.

> Science reveals relationships between objects that are physical laws, with whose help we construct a rational system of the object called physics. It truly seems to me that the essential surrealist requirement is to proclaim that this way of understanding and grasping the world is insufficient. It stresses there are many other relationships between objects that are not seen, that are not grasped by scientific reason: meaning that there is more *being* in the world than what scientific knowledge reveals to us. Consequently magic, spiritualism, and objective chance remain to be ways of revealing relationships overlooked by science.

This opens up incontestable perspectives. Down with dogmas, all dogmas, Duits proclaims nonetheless, because "the current orthodoxy is a prison whose windows look out over a void and whose door opens on to death!" Yet I have spoken only of Breton's mistrust of science. As the imaginary is only one aspect of reality, the author of *Les Vases Communicants* (Communicating Vessels)—in a direct line of descent from his German Romantic "precursors" like Novalis, who were all more or less heavily influenced by the scientific spirit—was not hostile a priori to science. Breton believed it was possible to reconcile it with the nonrational. But mirroring Guénon's position in *The Crisis of the Modern World*, he condemned its consequences (Charles Jameux notes) due to technical and technological inflation, both on the plane of thought and that of daily life. It was not a question of tossing everything out; it was a question of perspective. As evidence, we have, in the third issue of *Médium* (May 1954) the amazing "Surrealism and Probability" by the doctor, philosopher, and statistician Pierre Vendryès (1908–1989) on the construction of a probability theory of human autonomy, perfectly illustrated, in the author's opinion, by notions dear to the members of the group, like objective chance. Introduced in 1942 in his book on life and probability and founded on the first "mathematic modeling of biological regulation," this theory established that "the true nature of chance is relational" (Pierre Vendryès quoting scientist Jacques Lorigny).[46]

This theory was sharply criticized by a certain Guy Debord in *Les Lèvres Nues* because, and this is why it is interesting, "it results in freeing humanity from the constraints of universal determinism," in the very words of the theory's inventor.[47]

This is how surrealism became defined as a "search for a path of knowledge and salvation . . . attention to everything that lifts man above himself or seems, at least, to draw him out of himself," as Ferdinand Alquié suggests in his *Philosophy of Surrealism*. This movement, essentially devoted to the total liberation of the spirit and the transformation of the "severe and inert world in which it is stipulated we live," has been viewed as obscurantist, anticlerical, and even atheistic—anticlerical and atheistic by its own intent—and as such has been rejected by the bourgeoisie, with the notable exception of a few "eccentrics" like Edward James, Nancy Cunard, Peggy Guggenheim, and the Noailles;* rejected, that is, by the church and all the thurifers of the established order. But the truth, as Jules Monnerot notes, is that "the surrealists' aggressive attitude was directed against the *official* fallen replacement of the *sacred* and the caricatured symbol of the *serious;* it is what sacrilege is to the sacred."

---

*The Noailles, Viscount Charles and Marie-Laure, were rich patrons who subsidized and helped the surrealists Dali, Buñuel, Man Ray, etc., by financing films and buying paintings.

2

SURREALISM AND THE SACRED

The incessant human sedition . . .
GÉRARD LEGRAND

Things are much more complex than they appear at first glance, even if "the beyond, all the beyond is present in this life"[1] and deserves closer attention. We should clearly acknowledge that surrealism has, as Michel Carrouges stated, a complete "metaphysical progression," and as Marcel Mourier put it, "Of all the surrealists, Breton is the preeminent (and only?) metaphysician, in the etymological sense of the word: someone whose chief concerns continuously carry him beyond nature, toward the 'true life,' which always 'absent,' as Rimbaud puts it, may be primarily elsewhere."[2] Hence, a "singular philosophy of immanence, according to which surreality would be contained in reality itself and not superior to or outside it," assuming "that there is nothing invisible that tends to manifest through the framework of the visible world,"[3] as Breton writes in *Signe Ascendant* (Rising Sign). This is a philosophy that perhaps closely resembles that *monotonous* metaphysics mentioned by Breton in 1926 in *Self-Defense* when quoting Count Hermann Keyserling, with whom he stands wholeheartedly.

They only ever speak of the One in which God, soul, and the world merge together, the One which is the most profound essence of all multiplicity. It is also only pure intensity, which targets life itself, that nonobjective reality from which objects flow like sudden incidents.

Alquié (in his *Philosophie du Surréalisme*) offers this idea:

And if, in order to realize man, he rises against all dualisms, his fidelity to human experience, his sincerity, his lucidity lead him in many cases to recover truths that the dualistic philosophies brought to light. Finally, calling himself the enemy of metaphysics, Breton arrives often—by his own ways—at truths taught by metaphysics by following the other path that leads closest to truth, poetry, provided its language remains scrupulously faithful to the truth of man, which makes him appear, in spite himself, a messenger of transcendence.

And he adds, "Surrealism, refusing any hereafter apart from this world and professing a doctrine of immanence, is, nevertheless, inasmuch as it disqualifies the objective World, the messenger of some transcendence." The Quebec writer Fernande Saint-Martin made a similar observation in 1959 when she said that the movement's "fundamental tendency" was that of "a philosophy reacting against the nominalist idealism of classical philosophy, a return to the concrete, toward the understanding and adequate evaluation of the object ... an object [that] continues to define itself however in extreme subjectivist, if not to say magical terms."[4]

From the very start, like a "squirrel in the cage of its condition," to use Georges Ribemont-Dessaignes's expression, Breton,

absolutely incapable of consenting to the fate allotted [to him], refused to adapt his existence to the derisory conditions of all existence, for though it harps on social alienation and hopes for salvation *in the future* surrealism sees also that the unhappiness of consciousness is not linked only to its history but to its eternal condition. It is commonly accepted that every metaphysic originates in the disappointment engendered by reality (italics added).[5]

In 1955, Jean Schuster and Simon Hantaï, cosigners of the article "Une demolition au platane" (Demolition by Plane Tree), which appeared in the fourth issue of *Médium,* expressed the wish that surrealism's horizon could be a "meta-human condition." It is this "Promethean revolt colored by the refusal to be born of the flesh as much as to find a place in the natural order"[6] about which José Pierre speaks, echoing Michel Carrouges, who dubbed it "mystic atheism" (a term not devoid of ulterior motives). This is a revolt that has become exacerbated only since romanticism, as well as in symbolism, and finds its extension in surrealism—albeit in a highly different way. We find in *Le Grand Jeu* this remark from Roger Gilbert-Lecomte: "Man in his current state is inevitably condemned to the abject state of limitless misery."[7]

Breton thought it necessary to distrust the vision of the world provided by our senses, as it is naturally limited by their imperfect and unreliable nature, which means we should be constantly seeking to recover the unity between perception and representation, between signifier and signified, and between true and beautiful. Even if, as Alquié says, "Breton recovers the truths [of the] dualistic philosophies," it clearly seems that, at least in the movement's initial phase, we see a monism postulating that "God" and humans are of the same essence, a monism found also in the thought of Angelus Silesius (the adopted name of Johannes Scheffler, 1624–1677). This German Jesuit, a doctor and mystic poet, wrote the phrase, "Where are you running, don't you know heaven is within you?" He also shares the position of Georg Wilhelm Friedrich Hegel, who said, "Pure Reason completely free of any limit or restriction whatsoever is the deity." Artaud, in his *Héliogabale ou l'anarchiste couronné* (Heliogabalus or the Crowned Anarchist), explained "monotheism [as] that unity of all things that hinders the whim and multiplicity of things," which he calls "anarchy," and writes, "To have a sense of the profound unity of things is to have a sense of anarchy—and of the effort made to reduce things by bringing them into unity."[8] But here is Alquié again:

Unlike Hegel's disciples, Breton, refusing to let a state or a party judge in his place, maintains the solitary rights of a thought discovering itself in its first certitude. The truth that he announces is, by that, metaphysical, and it is no accident that the words sur-realism and meta-physical have the same structure.

Like it or not, there is in the surrealist quest, and has been since the start, next to its violent rejection of the world as forged by society—social man bogged down in his egotisms of class, caste, or others, whatever our deceptive senses allow us to see—there is a search for the absolute that aims at restoring the lost unity, especially when it involves "the unity of the soul whereas we harbor several consciousnesses."[9] At the same time, Aragon proclaimed in 1924 that "surreality, the relation in which the mind brings notions together, is the shared horizon of religions, magic, poetry, dream, madness, intoxications, and of stunted life, that trembling honeysuckle you think is enough to populate reality for us."[10] Presumably coming from a milieu (or family) "remaining . . . faithful . . . to the occult tradition of the Marranos," as suggested by Sylvère Lotringer,[11] Antonin Artaud made fairly similar observations in his 1936 lecture "Surrealism and Revolution," given in Mexico, when he reminded his audience:

> Surrealism opened a way to get back to the secret of things. Like the Unknown God of the Cabiric Mysteries, like the Aïn Souph [sic], the living hole of the abysses in the kabbalah, like the Nothing, the Void, the Non-Being devourer of nothingness of the ancient Brahmas at Vedas, we can say what surrealism is not, but to say what it is we must employ approximations and images. By a kind of incantation in the void, it resuscitates the spirit of the ancient allegories.

We should note Artaud's reference to the *En Sof* of Issac the Blind (1165–1235), meaning the "Endless." This is the kabbalistic expression for absolute transcendence, which is infinite and, more importantly, hidden. Its male part is the Kaddosh Barouch Hou and its female part the Shechina (also the immanent divine presence), which brings to mind the couple formed by the Gnostics' Sige and Propator. Artaud may also have confused the *En Sof,* "God thought by God," and the *Aïn,* nonbeing or the potential to be nonmanifested. As indicated by Guy Casaril in his book *Rabbi Siméon Bar Yochaï et la Cabbale,* the Shechina "is a typically Jewish concept, yet if you can compare any kabbalistic idea with a certain popular Christian perspective, it is clearly the idea of Shechina. Couldn't this personification of femininity, gentleness, humility, love, and charity correspond to the idea of the Virgin Mary in Christian tradition?"[12] Gengenbach, who remained close to Artaud, speaks in *Adieu à Satan* about "this Holy Spirit that is none other than the Eternal Feminine of God."

At this same time, Artaud, whose voice still held authority even though his remarks could not claim to represent the entire surrealist movement, wrote (in a text on the work of sculptor Ortiz Monasterio):

> Surrealism seeks a higher reality and, to attain it, destroys temporary forms in quest of what in the language of the ancient Vedas is called the *Non-Manifested.* . . . Imbeciles have called the surrealist movement destructive. It is undoubtedly destructive of transitory and imperfect forms, but this is because it is looking beyond forms for the occult and magical presence of a fascinating unreality.

These institutions come from afar: Jean-Louis Barrault, in an homage titled "L'Homme-théâtre" (The Man-Theatre) that appeared in 1957, revealed that "*Tantric Yoga,* the Egyptian Book of the Dead, the Upanishads, the *Golden Verses of Pythagoras* were the books that Artaud soaked through by magical desires gave [him] to read before his internment."[13] In his article "Rationalism et raisons de vivre," Gérard Legrand, who would play an important role in the writing of *L'Art magique* (The Magic Art),* ably summarized the matter in a few lines.

> In its effort to give man a means of knowledge and action finally in his size, surrealism cannot fail to overturn the prevailing notions

---

*I talk extensively about *L'Art magique* later in the book. As for Legrand's contribution to *L'Art magique,* he is the cowriter of the book in a way, but he has never been credited. He has never claimed to have been more than a "collaborator."

on the role of LANGUAGE and poetry, an activity that it wrests from the context of literature and from all conformism—even conflicting—of moral or political origin. Consequently, the surrealists' attention was held by the phenomena of occultism to which their desires to restore to dream and imagination their rights naturally drew them.

Further on, he added, "The necessities of the antireligious struggle cannot let us forget how certain aspects of magic and myths continue to correspond to the most audacious movements of what we have been able to name 'THE INCESSANT HUMAN SEDITION.'"[14] In fact, granting occult symbolism the interest it deserves does not necessarily expose one to the religious transgression it may carry. It only gives full range to Charles Baudelaire's observation, "The imagination is the most scientific of faculties for it alone gives us the key of universal analogy."[15] The explanation for the surrealists' interest in esotericism in all its forms is undoubtedly basically there, especially if we consider this suggestion of Daniel Beresniak, who, contemplating the message of the humanist John Amos Comenius in his book *La Rose et le compas: Rose-Croix et franc-maçonnerie* (The Rose and the Compass: Rosicrucianism and French Masonry), states:

> The so-called esoteric tradition (Rosicrucian, alchemical) teaches neither submission nor indifference to the established order. To the contrary, this tradition is revolutionary. But contrary to what naive ideologues may think, this tradition teaches that in order for the revolution to succeed, it must first take place inside the individual. The ideologues' mistake consists of expecting improvement of the quality of life, the end of injustices, and the advent of a fair and enlightened society from a simple reformation of the political and social structures of the city . . . it is absurd to imagine that the social "body" can experience a metamorphosis that has not been experienced by each individual that makes up that society—and this metamorphosis is the fruit of perseverant, methodical labor. On the other hand, this essential work on the self does not prevent propos-

ing reforms that would give a greater number of people the means to carry them out.[16]

This had been a recurring debate—although formulated differently—inside the movement. Max Ernst, according to Marc Alyn in the article "Birth of a Galaxy," which appeared in *Aujourd'hui Poème* in May 2007, "was in quest of a grail that he called 'beyond painting': a parallel universe in which the imagination becomes one with space as well as time." Octavio Paz, meanwhile, went so far as to write in *Alternating Current,* "The so-called human condition is a point of intersection with other forces. Perhaps our condition is not merely human."[17] Finally, it is fair to recall that Breton was convinced, as he writes in *Entretiens* (Interviews), "that man, originally in possession of certain keys, which held him in close communion with nature, lost them and since then more and more feverishly persists in trying others that do not work." Breton, according to Jean Schuster, "spent his life forcing the locks of reasoning and reasonable reason with all the keys that an 'attraction proportional to his destiny' put into his hands,"[18] even if he never went as far as the Grand Jeu's "technicians of despair," direct heirs of the preceding decades' occultism and revolt (which included political revolt). René Daumal defined the Grand Jeu as a "somewhat initiatory community." It was so initiatory that its early members called themselves "brothers," recalls Léon-Paul Quint, quoting Pierre Minet. "An essential aspect of [these brothers'] thought" crystalized around the notion "that a man could, by following a certain, allegedly mystical method, attain the immediate perception of another world, which was incommensurable to his sense and irreducible to his understanding."*

It was again Daumal who, on the matter of initiation and the initiatory course, would later write, in *Mont Analogue* (Mount Analogue), in allegorical and luminous fashion:

> Keep your eyes fixed on the way to the top, but don't forget to look at your feet. The last step depends on the first. Don't think you have

---

*I should note in passing that the major figure of reference for the Grand Jeu was Rimbaud.

arrived just because you see the peak. Watch your feet, be certain of your next step, but don't let this distract you from the *highest* goal. The first step depends on the last.

Breton did not travel as far in this domain as Georges Bataille, whom André Masson depicted as an "unpledged adjunct" to surrealism with his group Acéphale (which means "headless man"). This group stood apart from the magazine of the same name, which was somewhat exoteric and was published between 1936 and 1939. Bataille, whom Annie Le Brun called a reverse mystic, placed this magazine under an ambiguous sign, as shown by this phrase on which this "sacred conspiracy" was founded: "WE ARE FEROCIOUSLY RELIGIOUS and because our life is the condemnation of everything recognized today, an inner requirement compels us to also be imperious." In "The Threat of War," a text written for the fifth issue of *Acéphale,* Bataille goes so far as to say:

> If we propose to follow human destiny to its very end, it is impossible to remain alone, we must form a veritable Church, we must claim "spiritual power" and form a force capable of development and influence [capable of creating the] conditions for the "fulfillment" of human possibilities.

This statement clearly offers justification for Marcel Lecomte's judgment in "The Theme of the Last Moment," an article published before his death in the issue of *L'Arc* dedicated to Georges Bataille in May 1990: "The demystification in Bataille certainly moved him to act upon religion: nonetheless, he kept its secret dimension just as it is also quite palpable, from reading Bataille, that he did not wish to retain the tradition although he took it into account." It is quite logical, therefore, for longtime agnostic André Masson to say (in "Acéphale or the Initiatory Illusion," his 1980 interview with Paule Thévenin in the first issue of *Cahiers obliques*), "We are not for a religious world but we are for a world in which the sacred exists." He then says that "the sacred is not necessarily divine" and that "in this sense there is something better, even in surrealism," although conceding, "basically, there is still a slight slip into the mystical in all this!" He did acknowledge his own part in all this. In his text about Bataille, *Le Soc de la charrue* (The Plowshare), whose title was inspired by William Blake, he recalled the emblem that illustrated the cover of the review, saying, "It was my job to draw the Idol!" This is a "slight" slip! No doubt we should see it as a stylistic device.

Pierre Prevost, who, as Charles Jameux reminds us, participated with Bataille and Maurice Girodias "in the adventure of the creation of the review *Critique*," mentions in his article "New Mystics: From Georges Bataille to Maurice Blanchot" the gist of their initial conversations from the time Bataille was preparing to write *L'Expérience Intérieure* (The Inner Experience):

> The subjects discussed were most often related to what he told me one day: "I had an experience of the divine that was so strong that it is hard for me to talk about it." In fact, he talked quite a bit and enthusiastically urged me to read Angela de Foligno, Catherine of Sienna, John of the Cross, Teresa of Avila. All these authors are great Christian mystics.

They were all also old acquaintances for him according to Prevost, who stressed how "in *Le Coupable* (The Guilty One), which appeared in 1944 (from Gallimard), Bataille informs us: 'I began to read Angela de Foligno's *Book of Visions* while standing up in a packed train.' It was also during September 1939, he went on to say, that he also read the great Spanish mystics: Saint John of the Cross, Teresa of Avila, and others."

Less well known than the Grand Jeu, but following its example in 1936, the Acéphale group adopted an "initiatory approach" and a "ferociously religious" exterior. Among its members at that time were Colette Peignot (who also used the name Laure) and Isabelle and Patrick Waldberg, who later wondered how they all could have fallen for Bataille's mystic schtick for so long. Other members included Robert Lebel, Georges Ambrosino, René Chenon, Georges Duthuit, and possibly Jacques Lacan, Pierre Klossowski, and Roger Caillois. Acéphale* was defined as a "more or less mystical" secret society that was "more or less Gnostic (but stripped of any confessional infection in its gnosis of nonknowing) by Michel Camus (in his preface to the reprint edition of this review by Jean-Michel Place in 1995). Maurice Blanchot deemed it an "unavowed fellowship (rather than 'society,' as in *The Fellowship of the Ring*!)," while Bédouin depicted it as practicing "a kind of Dionysian worship, contradictorily inspired by Christian mysticism and Nietzschean will power."

Philippe Macaire tells us:

> A community was therefore formed [Macaire was NOT a member of the group] in order to bring man to the impossible. An internal journal was created and rules decreed. Time was divided between sacred and profane. Rites† took place based on the lunar cycle at night in a forest near Paris. We had initiations, established taboos, and worshipped earth and fire. We dreamt of a headless man. We imagined a sacrifice. We laughed. And Silence was the operative word.[19]

It is plausible that this forest was the spot where their nightly meetings were held and the following event, recorded by Pierre Prevost, occurred.

> One day, at the beginning of 1940, he [Bataille] shared this confidence with me: "Alone, one summer evening in the silence of the forest, I saw the sky gape open and experienced something analogous to what the great mystics describe."

This group, which Masson refused to join, honoring his proclaimed, stubborn refusal of secret societies, took as its purpose (a purpose that

---

Acéphale was also a magazine. It was reprinted in 1995 by Jean-Michel Place (editions) in book form with an introduction by Michel Camus.
†Concerning the existence of ceremonies in the Saint-Germain Forest, André Masson told Paule Thévenin: "That's the secret. I believe that, yes [meaning they did take place]. No human sacrifice but ceremonies certainly. All the same there was an embryonic secret society."

was never totally achieved, it seems, for the participants never spoke of it) the practice of rituals that remain a mystery in the Saint-Nom-la-Bretèche Forest,* "the celebration of joy in the face of death."[20]

These rituals were supposed to culminate in a double human sacrifice, perhaps closely modeled on the one Artaud describes in a September 13, 1932, letter to Jean Paulhan (and inserted in the article "Le Théâtre de la cruauté" [The Theater of Cruelty]).

> In the practice of cruelty there is a kind of higher determinism, to which the executioner-tormenter himself is subjected and which he must be determined to endure when the time comes. Cruelty is above all lucid, it is a kind of rigid control and submission to necessity. There is no cruelty† without consciousness and without the application of consciousness.[21]

But doesn't the word *sacred* basically come from the Latin *sacer,* "sacrifice"? "This mad scheme," Michel Camus says:

> to found a religion on a ritual murder or its simulation would later be seen as an aberration by Bataille. With some hindsight, he would see its "comic" side and admit its origin in his overly exalted reading of the history of religions and in *the quasi religious or even magical atmosphere of surrealism* (italics added).

All the same, Masson points out that "Breton found this idea of a secret society quite appealing and that the culmination of all this was the surrealist exhibition following his return to Europe in which Breton accepted the idea of an initiatory exhibition. A rapprochement occurred there‡ between Bataille and the surrealists," and Masson admitted

---

*Saint-Germain-en-Laye is on the northern side of the forest and Saint-Nom-la-Bretèche on the southern side.
†It is important to grasp what Artaud truly means by cruelty. As observed by Jean-Michel Royer, "The cruelty he proclaims is that of all creation, it is the suffering of the man torn from his rest and stretched into Being."
‡The rapprochement was on the level of ideas because there had been misunderstandings between Bataille and the surrealists before the war.

to sharing the opinion aired by Paule Thévenin, according to which "Bataille [would have] tried to form an initiatory school with the College of Sociology"—with his personal research on the forms taken by the sacred. There would also be the abortive attempt to create a Socratic college after the Second World War. An extreme approach was certainly at work with the Acéphale group, although when we think of Jean Benoît and his *Execution of the Will of the Marquis de Sade*...

Furthermore, doesn't Breton, in the *First Surrealist Manifesto*, say, "Surrealism will introduce you into death, which is a secret society," then in the *Second Surrealist Manifesto* say, "It is important to reiterate and maintain here the 'Marantha' of the alchemists, placed at the threshold of the work to stop the profane.... The public must be absolutely prevented from entering if confusion is to be avoided. I add that it should be held exasperated at the door by a system of challenges and provocations. I demand the profound, veritable occultation of surrealism." Finally, in the *Prolegomena to a Third Surrealist Manifesto or Not*, "There are new secret societies seeking to define themselves during multiple conciliabules at evening in the ports." Meanwhile, in 1948, Julien Gracq noted in his *André Breton, quelques aspects de l'écrivain*:

> The group never portrays itself as an open community, swollen with a boundless contagion; rather the idea of a closed and separate *order*, an exclusive companionship, a phalanstery that tends to be enclosed in some undefined kind of magical walls (the meaningful notion of a "castle" is lurking in the vicinity) appears to have asserted itself on Breton from the start.... From the idea of this closed society, that Breton had already conjured around himself, to the idea of *secret society*, it is only a step. This step, Breton took expressly in the *Second Manifesto*.

This thought was shared around this same time by Gengenbach when he declared in 1952, "You have tried, BRETON, to create a kind of initiatory brotherhood, an idealist secret society, of the type propagated by Orphism and then Manicheism." Raymond Queneau, in his roman à clef, *Odile*, alluded to this iconoclastic temptation Breton was fond of, writing, "Anglarès joked about certain overzealous disciples* who 'would have liked us to form a secret society with statutes, initiation stunts, and secret signs, just like an American fraternity,'" a phenomenon he ungraciously explained as due to "the theosophist background of some of them [who] haven't yet managed to treat these old tall tales with the scorn they deserve."[22]

On a more serious level, Hester Albach, in her tragic and unclassifiable investigation and study on Nadja, *Léona: héroine du surréalisme* (Léona: Heroine of Surrealism), says, quoting one of her contacts, "The surrealists formed a veritable, finely-structured order."[23] This confirms Gracq's initial suggestion, while that of Alain Jouffroy in issue 123–124 of *Opus international* (April–May 1991), a special issue titled "André Breton et le surréalisme international," goes one step further than Breton when he expresses his wish for "a complete rereading of the surrealist movement" that would allow "the necessity for new secret societies that will be all the more effective as they will be undetectable."

In July 1971, in the third issue of the *Bulletin de liaison surréaliste*, Jean-Louis Bédouin, who had earlier observed in his book on André Breton that "it was sometimes not disloyal to criticize surrealism for striving toward the secret society," speaks of "a *fraternity* that remains the distinctive feature of the surrealist movement when compared to all other artistic or political groups." He may provide an explanation here for the violent and highly emotional nature of the various internal crises when evoking with a tad of nostalgia "the fairly unique *egregore* that we formed around Breton and with him" (italics added)! We should also note that this word *egregore,* dear to Freemasons as members of a discreet if not secret society, was also used by Philippe Audoin and Pierre Mabille, with the latter offering his own completely enlightening definition: "I call the human group that is endowed with a personality that is different from that of the individuals who form it an *egregore* (a word formerly used by hermeticists)."

Charles Imbert elaborates on this notion, saying, "Although inspired, nurtured, and animated by a group, the egregore is in fact profoundly archetypal and trans-personal in nature." He follows this

---

*"Anglarès" is the name Queneau gives Breton in his novel.

remark with a very interesting observation: "This calls upon a major presupposition that consciousness can exist independently of the body, a question far from being resolved that resides at the base of positions between materialism and spiritualism."[24] It is not entirely absurd to connect this to the desire expressed by Roger Gilbert-Lecomte in *Le Grand Jeu* to work on "the creation of the group's collective soul."

The third issue of *La Brèche* (1962) also cited Mabille's suggestion in his *Notes on Symbolism* (1938) that "certain human groups of common persuasion [could] constitute a dynamic aggregation capable of subduing outside forces." Later in Quebec, Claude Gavreau, in a lecture on the work of Roland Giguère, spoke of the "surrealist egregore, meaning the collective gathering in a synthesis that was foreign to all that was scattered or random," even though he adds "the only egregore that now exists is the romantic egregore." Jean-Jacques Lebel, when examining the exquisite corpses made from the fragments of engravings by Yves and Jeannette Tanguy, Jacqueline Lamba, and André Breton in the Oise region during the summer of 1938, notes how Breton

> mentioned the *egregore,* the collective psychic being that permits each active participant to surpass his own subjectivity by intensifying it to the maximum possible extent, in order to attain a radical state of intersubjectivity.[25]

Philippe Audoin, meanwhile, in his book on the surrealists, borrowed the expression "aristocracy (not of blood but) of miracles" from Jules Monnerot, who described the group this way when he likened it to being more akin to a Germanic *Bund* (an association of the chosen), yet conceded there were "in surrealism modest substitutes for rites of initiation."[26]

Charles Jameux, who spoke of a "form of elitism," confirmed for me that it was necessary to have presenters to meet Breton, who never hesitated to kick out unwelcome guests, and to attend the daily reunions *"au café."* He noted that this referral process smacked in "a certain way of how a secret society" operated, leading the "members and their spouses [into] a life that was not entirely profane." Audoin drives the point home in this respect when he names "one of the principal temptations that continuously obsessed the group and which it never quite accepted or abandoned: that of transforming into a secret society."

> What the surrealists had primarily and almost secretly in common, was the equivalent of a spiritual experience, of a plunge deep into the unexplored pits of *inspiration;* its results—texts or paintings—were made public but the effect of change and revelation it had on its participants were purely inexpressible. These people, together, *had seen something.* One could talk about it, write about it, discursively, but essentially the message barely reached its outside recipients—except to *tempt* them. How not then contemplate turning one's back on the profane so as to only ponder on this unearthed treasure whose inventory had just begun to be taken. And how to stand up for taking one's bearings in the real or alleged operations—it hardly matters—of the so-called occult sciences.

Whatever the case may be, it is striking to note, outside of any esoteric reference, that the journalist Claire Lefebvre, reporting in the daily paper *La Voix du Nord* on January 10, 2010, on the awarding of the Jean Arp Prize to Pierre Dhainaut, thought it just dandy to headline the story "Pierre Dhainaut Was Initiated by André Breton."

Let's be clear, though, the "materialist" Breton, who in an internal document in 1925 called for the "creation of a new kind of mysticism" and who already then possessed a vast knowledge of esotericism, was dangerously fraternizing, through the work of "the playing hooky teacher," Lewis Carroll, who was also an Anglican pastor, with immaterialist idealism, particularly the "philosophy of de-realization" of Bishop Berkeley, a figure mentioned outright in *Nadja* particularly. The thought of Hegel, on the other hand, whom Breton claimed to follow, is not exempt, if we believe Jean Wahl, of influences from Jacob Böhme,* who, perhaps inspired by the kabbalah, was not exactly an advocate of

---

*There are two possible spellings for the first name: Jacob or Jakob (used in particular by Louis-Claude de Saint-Martin or Sédir) and, for the last name: Böhme or Boehme.

materialism, an opinion that was corroborated and reinforced by these lines of Vincent Bounoure, speaking about German philosophy in the sixth issue of *La Brèche* (June 1964):

> All the materialist currents have collected if not their lights, their enlightenment in Hegelian thought, which is heir to much more shadow than generally admitted. But this was the shadow favorable for inspiration, the shadow of enduring nights that obliges the human gaze to manufacture its own light and break out of its prison with the power of thought. This is still in our opinion the virtue of this audacity that it brings us close, despite the chains of their faith, to the will that animated Rabbi Simeon bar Yochaï,* Jacob Boehme, and Saint Martin. Whether Hegel read Louis-Claude de Saint-Martin's *L'Homme de désir* (The Man of Desire)[27] or not, it is the same emblem he raised in the middle of his philosophy, making it the most effective methodological instrument" ("Le Paradoxe de la communication").[28]

Charles Duits, meanwhile, casually slips in a digression in *André Breton a-t-il dit passe:* "The *spiritual* revolution is not seen completely. Breton was much closer (for example) to Gurdjieff than to the even great writers with whom he's been compared," adding, still in that book, "Gurdjieff was like this, according to those who knew him. He was *heavy*. Breton was also *heavy*. It is interesting to note that *heavy*, according to Philippe Lavastine, was the original, true meaning of *guru*." Duits, who had heard about G. I. Gurdjieff in New York from the new companion of Jacqueline Lamba and the first cousin of Kay Sage, his friend David Hare, whose mother was a disciple of this teacher, also granted the highest importance to the teachings of Gurdjieff, "one of the faces of [his] inner Deity." In his novel *Ptah Hotep,* Duits depicted Gurdjieff, although he had not met him personally, under the features of Mullah Nasroddîn, "a completely bald man with a huge mustache

---

*Simeon Bar Yochaï, who lived in the eleventh century, has been mistakenly attributed with authorship of the Zohar.[29]

whose ends curl up and who seems more like a warlord than a hermit." He is "a Dervish, for this is the name given to us, and this name means Madman, and we are called the Madmen of Laha"—much in the same way, I would say, as the disciples of Mevlana. It is worth pointing out here that Gurdjieff gladly attributed his original maxims to a certain Mullah Nassr Eddin, undoubtedly the Nasr Eddin Hodja, the Mullah Nasroddin, the legendary ulema of Eastern folk tales from the Sufi tradition.

Duits was also quite close to Georges Saint-Bonnet, a former member of the Gurdjieffian "phalanstery" of the Avon Priory near Fontaineblue, whose teaching profoundly influenced him. The shadow of Gurdjieff, "a thundering mage with a gigantic, stratified ego" (according to Nora Mitrani), a "monumental figure" and even a "black angel" (in his own words as recorded by Duits), in truth an amazing figure of twentieth-century esotericism, who would soon soar over surrealism and its close vicinity, particularly over Daumal and his Grand Jeu friends, especially after their meeting with "a man for whom the search for truth took precedence over everything."[30] This man was Alexander Salzmann, faithful follower of the future author of *Beelzebub's Tales to His Grandson*, whom they met in November 1930 at Joseph Sima's home and then later at the home of his wife, Jeanne, in February 1931. It was undoubtedly sooner than this for Joseph Sima, unless it was Sima's father,* as he had written with Salzmann a book on the baroque architecture of Prague in 1926. The Yugoslavian surrealist Oskar Davico (1909–1989), who had been involved with the work of the group and therefore had heard Salzmann's fabulous stories, later confided that they were "the greatest influence of his life."

Gurdjieff's teaching sometimes mirrors Pierre Janet's theories in *L'Automatisme psychologique* (Psychological Automatism),[31] which also influenced Breton. More proof of the attention he aroused can be found in the form of a quote from Gurdjieff at the end of the "Almanach surréaliste du demi-siècle" (Surrealist Almanac of the Half Century).

---

*Sima's father met Salzmann before his son, but it's not possible to say exactly which of the Simas, the father or the son, wrote the book with Salzmann.

A case file of six pages assembled by Jean-Louis Bédouin appeared in the third issue of *Médium* (1954), following the publication of Louis Pauwels's book on *Monsieur Gurdjieff* (with whom the author had frequently spent time), which clearly exposed the questions raised about this figure. Bédouin raised in particular questions surrounding the heavy-handed methods Gurdjieff employed.

> This program is not to everyone's taste—not to ours in any case. Would I say though that the lesson it imparts does not seem so detestable in itself? Given by a man who comes from the East, at a time when the assizes of Western consciousness are tottering, it cannot help but be intensely displeasing to licensed spiritual advisors, first and foremost Christians.

We can easily see where a common platform could take shape: "Doesn't [this doctrine] teach man that he should be his own God or not exist? Under these conditions, why would this man-God have need of the *other*?" It nevertheless remains true that beneath the undeniable interest displayed by the surrealists, they remained quite wary, as shown by the fact that they alternated giving space in their columns for the writings of Jacques Bergier, who considered Gurdjieff to be an agent of Hitler, and Louis Pauwels, who viewed him much more favorably, although he was not a follower. We can lastly find a trace of the author of *Meetings with Remarkable Men* in the works of Charles Jameux, who, exhibiting the high esteem in which he held Gurdjieff, was not loath to write in his book *Le Vaisseau de feu* (The Vessel of Fire), "I would like history to remember the names of Breton, Bataille, and Gurdjieff from my lifetime, and those names alone perhaps to the exclusion of others."[32] He then revisited this topic in his book *Souvenirs de la maison des vivants* (Memories from the House of the Living), concerning the hard road he had to travel through suffering in order to reeducate his battered body:

> I would of course then think back to Gurdjieff, and the teaching attributed to him, minus (or except) its mechanics. We are not so

far from those blinding sparks perceived by the author of *Beelzebub* in Central Asia at the beginning of last century![33]

Guy Dupré,* meanwhile, mentions a "Breton whose third eye is open to the black light of Eliphas Levi, the white light of Fabre d'Olivet, and the violet light of Saint-Yves d'Alveydre. Not to mention Fulcanelli."[34]

From the *Littérature* era[35] and even from the time that a list was drawn up of works that had contributed to "the formation of the poetic mentality of [their] generation," as proposed to Jacques Doucet in 1922, the names of Hermes Trismegistus, Lulle, Flamel, Cornelius Agrippa, Saint-Martin, Swedenborg, and Péladan appear (as noted by Marguerite Bonnet in the notes on the *First Surrealist Manifesto* in the first volume of Breton's *Oeuvres complètes*). These are names we shall continue to encounter throughout this book, and they are practically the same, moreover, as those that appeared under the pen of Marko Ristic, "one of the Belgrade Thirteen," in his response to the inquiry *Celjust Dialektike* (The Jaw of the Dialectic) in the *Nemoguce Almanach* (The Impossible Almanac). Spomenka Delibasic took note of this in the thirtieth issue of *Mélusine,* the journal of the Center of Surrealist Research, which was specifically dedicated to Nadrealizam, which is the Serbo-Croatian name for surrealism.[36]

The names of Cornelius Agrippa, Raimon Lulle† and his *Ars Magna,* Abraham the Jew, Basil Valentinus, Pythagoras, Jacob Böhme, Cagliostro, the kabbalah, "the alchemical fortress of Khunrath," symbol of the *scientia occulta* of Hermes Trismegistus, which opens a breech toward the achievement of the Great Work and

---

*Dupré, who isn't credible in other domains, previously used these remarks in his article "Unique Annie," published in 1982. The "Unique Annie" is none other than Annie Le Brun, presented by the author as follows: "*Pasionaria* of heroic surrealism, in her, André Breton has found a heir in whom he can both be satisfied and take pride: eldest daughter of his underground Church, and whose surrogate mother would be 'Michelet's young witch with the gaze of the moor,' or one of the mysterious dedicatees of Rimbaud's Illuminations: Louise Vanaen de Voringhem or Léonie Aubois d'Ashby. Baou! In twenty years, Annie Le Brun has won her place in the black sun."
†Raymond Lulle in French and Ramon Llull in Catalan.

the philosopher's stone all study the work of Marko Ristic, which clearly shows that Breton's approach was not an isolated phenomenon. As it can also be clearly seen in *L'Art magique,* in 1957:

> The development of civilization and the incessant progress of technology has not totally eradicated the hope in the human soul of resolving the enigma of the world and diverting to its benefit the forces governing it. Every time the old Faustian dream has taken possession of humanity, it has revealed trails—off of the road said to be safe and, what's more, prescribed as mandatory—which at first glance seemed quite snarled but which proved possible to gradually untangle. They are the paths offered us by the various hermetic disciplines called traditional because they presume a chain of transmission that comes down to us from the depths of time.

The allusion to the "Faustian dream" appears again at the end of this same book (*L'Art magique*), in this luminous passage in which the authors assert that surrealism sets in motion at "the disposal of the activity *of the imagination*":

> a veritable pact with the unknown and the *unmeasured,* a pact whose modalities can vary from one mind to the next but which remains no less comparable to the oath of the Samothracian initiates to never reveal the Kabirian mysteries, and better yet, to the famous "pact with the devil" of the medieval sorcerers—save that here it insists one refuses to sell their soul to God or men.[37]

We then find in Breton's writings this phrase, among others, which gives food for thought.

> Everything tends to make us believe that there exists a certain point of the mind at which life and death, the real and the imagined, the communicable and the incommunicable, high and low, cease to be perceived as contradictions.[38]

Although he explicitly states in his 1952 interviews that said point "can never be located on a mystic plane," Breton nonetheless assured the students of Yale, "This is not *only* a view inherited from the occultists, it reveals an aspiration so profound that it is essentially this aspiration that surrealism will have undoubtedly appear to have embodied" (italics added). It would be easy for Jules Monnerot to write the following in his harsh review of Maurice Nadeau's *History of Surrealism* (published in the September 1945 issue of *Confluences*):

> The antinomies in surrealism's deepest intent do not reconcile on the verbal plane of justifictory reason. They are experienced in the alternating cycle of hope and despair, night and day, inhalation and exhalation. And transcendence haunts surrealism!

"Did this notion of a supreme point occur spontaneously in his mind," Victor Crastre rightly wonders, "or did kabbalistic texts inspire Breton? It hardly matters! It fits in so well with the very notion of surrealism that it cannot fail to develop in it like a seed in favorable soil."[39] Jean-Louis Bédouin, while reminding us that the "fundamental fact, from which the surrealist demand takes shape, the revelation of the true functioning of thought," does not hesitate to acknowledge that "it is probable, as Michel Carrouges attempted to establish at this same time that the site of this reconciliation of the opposites could be identified as the 'originating point of creation,' which, for the tradition, also symbolizes 'the totality of reality.'"[40] However, the 1957 tract "Coup de semonce" (Warning Shot) clearly indicates, "And in fact, if surrealism intended to *profane* the values of Christian society, this has never led to the profanation of the very ideas of the 'sacred' and of 'revelation,' or with greater reason still, of morality: very much to the contrary, it has always accused Christianity . . . of having vulgarized and transformed the 'sacred' and 'morality' into a pure, indefinitely extensible, *positivism.*"[41] This sentiment was reformulated by Guy Girard in 2005:

> I think this is how surrealism should redeploy, at the risk otherwise of losing all utopian impetus, these approaches to the sacred (once

they have been adopted) that are so decisive in the poetic dimension," a poetry that is "subversion," a "sacred that vanishes once the dogma is convened."

How would it, in fact, be possible to separate poetry from the sacred? This "Great Sacred" was mentioned by Breton himself at the beginning of the 1950s in a letter to Judit Reigl about her painting *They Have an Insatiable Thirst for Infinity,* which was inspired by Lautréamont (see plate 2). This does not involve the writings of Paul Claudel, of La Tour du Pin, and those of their consorts (Patrice de La Tour du Pin is another Christian poet), but something much deeper and essential, evoked in a particularly elegant fashion by Gabriel Bounoure (discoverer of surrealist Georges Schéhadé). This critic for the journal *NRF,* who could hardly be suspected of excessive sympathy for automatic writing, which he labeled "surrealist coprolalia,"[42] writes:

> So varied, so insanely sensitive, so black, so desperate, so full of rumors of the world, so carried away by a time that is unknown or immobilized inside a moment of bliss, all today's great poems testify to man's aptitude to speak to the man above the abyss—as if the poet deemed it possible to make himself the creator of man with his breath, for the space of a second—as if he deemed it possible to make of his complicated and miserable singularity the manifestation of this absolute simplicity—that undoubtedly none could refuse to call Being.[43]

It may also be helpful to recall, as noted by renowned ethnomusicologist Jean During, that the sacred and esoteric travel through symbolism is "the tangible form of all initiatory teaching."[44]

Although the word rarely appears in his writings, some such idea of the sacred (as Georges Henein says, "There is no ersatz sacred") was accepted by Breton, who wrote his daughter Aube on September 13, 1956, "You know I have a sense of the sacred, and I am not moderate in my aspirations,"[45] on condition that it was considered self-evident that the spiritual element only takes form in the individual's mind, that is, with the following reservations:

The surrealist concepts of love, of liberty, of a certain extra-religious sacred have moved and for a large part served as a model for modern sensibility. These ideals, these ways of feeling do not fundamentally differ from the first formulation they were given.[46]

This is implied but in a much more radical way by Roger Gilbert-Lecomte, upholder of an experimental metaphysics "absolutely divorced from all religion,"[47] when he states in the foreword to the first issue of *Le Grand Jeu,* "All the great mystics of all religions would be ours if they have broken the shackles of their religions that can't subjugate us," before stating more explicitly in "L'Horrible Révélation . . . la seule," "No one can be a seer and adept of a religion or any kind of system of thought without betraying his vision." He then concludes with this phrase, which holds a double meaning: "Our prophets are in our midst."

The same thing, with due consideration to the reservations called for in his case, can be found in the work of Ernest de Gengenbach, who, with his distinctive rhetoric in *Judas ou le vampire surréaliste,* observed in words whose meaning we will see later again:

> There are individuals who have wished and been able to dream their lives and live their dreams. These ambitious, audacious beings sought to possess the Keys, to force the doors of the Ivory Tower of Mystery, to steal the Fire of Heaven. They are the great adventurers of the Unknown.

In *La Poésie moderne et le sacré* (Modern Poetry and the Sacred), Jules Monnerot, a man who would be close to the surrealists for a time despite the deplorable way he strayed toward the end of his life, emphasized, "The men within whom the sacred asks to exist, turn their backs on everything preserved, represented, and signified by religions that are no longer anything but ritualism—ritualism that is nothing but the rampart of what the profane reckon the most vulgar—and refuse to take any part in it."[48] Again in *L'Archibras,* in April 1967, in his article "A l'ordre de la nuit: Au désordre du jour," Jean Schuster makes clear:

It is not the least of Breton's merits that he disputed religion's ownership of words like *soul* or *sacred,* spurning both the critique of a restricted positivism and the spiritualists' attempts of annexation,[49] to charge these words with an immanent meaning. That they still have more presence at the present time in the shadow of the Churches than elsewhere is no reason to fear a congealing of language with the force to overburden us. Getting a foothold on this terrain, even if it may be a minefield, is part of the surrealist project and forms one means among others for attaining the true functioning of thought.

Péret is equally free of doubt about this struggle, and in *The Heart of the Comet* (1955) he explains:

If human love is sacred, it is because in reality the very notion of the sacred follows so directly from love that without it, no sacred is conceivable (divine love being only a misappropriation of human love for ends that in sum are primitive). In vain will one seek any other origin for the sacred—even in its most irritating accepted meanings (sacred love of country) or its most vulgar (the sacred bonds of the family)—than human love, through all the distortions which have been inflicted upon it.

We seem to have strayed quite far from sacred and/or sacrifice! But the Artaud of *Heliogabalus or the Crowned Anarchist* had earlier observed:

The sacred spirit is the one that remains pasted upon the principles with a force of dark identification, which resembles sexuality—the sexuality on the plane the closest to our organic spirits, to our spirits blocked by the thickness of their fall. This fall about which I asked myself if it represented sin. For on the plane where things rise, this identification calls itself Love, one form of which is universal charity, and the other more terrible form becomes the sacrifice of the soul, in other words the death of individuality.

In this quest for the sacred and meaning, we make "a breach by pulling out all the stops," as Gérard Legrand says in the eighth issue of *La Brèche* (The Breach). Breton, in fact, as shown by his article on Marcelle Loubchansky in *Le Surréalisme et la peinture* (Surrealism and Painting), is marked by the philosophers of the dawn of reason—Empedocles, Parmenides, and Heraclitus—as are Char, Calas, and Legrand himself.[50] Many others were similarly influenced, such as Ithell Colquhoun, who calls up Empedocles several times in her writings and paintings, Scrutenaire and his "Ephesian," or Caillois, who confirms devoting himself to them with a true "fervor" ("in particular Parmenides, many of whose passages from fragment 8 he still knows by heart"[51]). They were primarily rediscovered through Nietzsche and the Acéphale team, a group that numbered among its members Masson, about whom Bataille would write in "The Star Eaters":

There where a wind blows that breaks the weak voice of the aesthetic, André Masson does not find himself in the company of Matisse or Miro; the place where he speaks with all his strength would echo with the aggressive voices of Heraclitus and Blake, with the voice of night and the sun of Nietzsche.[52]

Yves Battistini, a close friend of René Char, writes the following with regard to the little that has survived of the work of the first of these Greek philosophers in his book *Trois Présocratiques* (Three Pre-Socratic Philosophers):

The enthusiastic fervor of these Orphic and Pythagorean pages makes it a truly *mystic book*—a hierophany even, experience and revelation sung and lived by a man who was the mirror of concentration in which glowing iridescently—coming together before manifesting—were the *presences* of unsuspected worlds.

In his presentation of the philosopher of Agrigento, Battistini next notes:

Identifying the subject and the object, Empedocles poetically moves into a universe where all enchantment was possible, where the abolished opposites ceased to limit the time and space of the body and thought. He speaks of the wheel of Orphic births, how he was once "bush, bird, mute fish in the sea," and these words sound familiar to those who know the aphorisms of Novalis. [53]

Or of a Taliesin, I would be tempted to add. What we also find here is a portrait of the philosopher quite close to the one Peter Kingsley paints in his book.[54] Using his great erudition, Kingsley's chief concern is to also connect Empedocles to a much earlier Orphic and Pythagorean current, and even to a certain "shamanic tradition of Central Asia," which, according to him, would have wended its way through Egypt, then the Middle East, before finally reaching medieval Europe by way of Spain. By putting Empedocles back in his historical context, this British scholar shows the fundamentally mystical nature of this Greek philosopher, whom he does not hesitate to make, not a precursor of Aristotle, as is the orthodox view, but truly a thaumaturge, if not an outright sorcerer.

While Odysseus Elytis, a key figure of Greek surrealism, with Andreas Embirikos, says in his great poem *Axion Esti* (1951), "the voice of Heraclitus causes devastation," and while he makes numerous allusions to the pre-Socratic philosophers, he is primarily influenced by a symbology of numbers that apparently owes much to Pythagorean tradition. "The number of each verse, referring mainly to Pythagoras, corroborates its exoteric meaning," notes Xavier Bordes. This is clearly the context in which we need to understand the reference to the "Tetractys" at the end of the first part of the text, "Genesis." Xavier Bordes also notes that "the word 'Orient' needs to be read in its proper meaning: Orient as that which orients, whence rises the sun of thought, of Sophia, the mystic, polar Orient, a kind of North, which would explain the prevalence of the Boreal wind, the wind out of the north in all this poet's writing." As Breton says, "There is too much North in me!" And in the deceptively more playful style that distinguishes his work, author Raymond Queneau even parodies Heraclitus in his book *Pierrot mon ami* (My Friend Pierrot). In it he has one of his characters—Posidon [*sic*] the innkeeper—say, to great effect, "A person never washes his feet twice in the same water."[55]

True, Georges Henein observed in a 1963 letter to Charles Duits (and thereby slammed a few doors shut), "Greece offered a possible dimension for man but our 'enlightenment philosophy' posits a non-scalable man as a starting principle. The matter is thus a dead end." However, this "extra-religious sacred" that all the great nineteenth-century seers sought in the fallow territories of reason, "those fairly sleazy domains" (said Audoin) from which sprout the flowers of evil and weeds of all kinds, was something that Breton and many of his friends expressed great interest in because they stalked this area persistently after noting its poetic dimension. Like it or not, their desire for reunification of opposites and the recovery of lost powers makes them authentic seekers. Bédouin's book on Breton clearly reveals the movement leader's thinking in this domain.

> Through the work of his direct predecessors—Baudelaire, Nerval, Rimbaud, Lautréamont—he tends, in fact, to precise its filiation with an infinitely vast spiritual current: the esoteric tradition. It should be understood that we consider the phenomena of this esotericism from the perspective of the *knowledge* they may bring us or permit us to attain. We do not stop at the hypothesis of a single truth, henceforth lost for most people, which this tradition preserves, the key to which only a few rare initiates hold. We see in esotericism, under often quite disparate forms, the manifestation of a spirit of constant *opposition* to the traditional norms of reason, knowledge, religion, and so forth. This spirit of opposition cannot lack ties to ours and its past manifestations are capable of enlightening and helping us imagine our human world on completely different bases.[56]

The same author formulated this with even greater clarity and precision in *Vingt Ans de surréalisme: 1939–1959* (Twenty Years of Surrealism: 1939–1959).

Alchemy of the verb, these words demand to be taken literally. In other words, I think it is no longer a matter of writing "subjective" poetry, of exalting—in the way one deems most propitious at satisfying emotional needs—the "course of things," but that, by departing from horizons in which "the other is sunk," we are committing to a path that, though different from that of alchemy, is no less perilous, and leads straight to a distant domain in which man, after his battle with the Dragon, should emerge as the glorious son of the luminaries, [whose goal is a real transformation of] "the opaqueness that is within us into philosophical gold!"[57]

Even the extreme rationalist Roger Caillois (although he did initially pass through the Grand Jeu group) confessed in *Le Fleuve Alphée* that he had read Emanuel Swedenborg, Hoene Wronski, William Blake, Saint-Yves d'Alveydre, the *Pimander,* and even the accounts of the table turning in Guernsey,* and so on. This tendency can be seen starting with the *Manifestoes of Surrealism,* in which Breton writes, "We cross through with a shudder what the occultists call *dangerous country*." This remains perfectly obvious even if Breton categorically refuted it in an interview with *Le Monde* journalist Jacqueline Piatier in 1962 when she asked him, "Should we conclude then that surrealism has become an esotericism?" He abruptly responded, "No. Those words are employed without rhyme or reason!" And yet, in his March 1948 interview with Aimé Patri, Breton said the following, and for good reason since it was evident from the time of the journals *La Révolution surréaliste* and even *Littérature,* after having mentioned a number of books dealing with the relationship between poetry and tradition.

> Be that as it may, for the past twenty-five years† this way of seeing has always been implicit in surrealism. Those who claim the contrary are lying, and shout themselves hoarse trying to maintain an untenable position.

---

*["Table turning" refers to Victor Hugo's experiments with mediums. —*Trans.*]
†"The past twenty-five years" in the extract refers to the time since 1923.

Duly noted. Perhaps we should be talking of "occultation" again! This taste for hermeticism even influences the highly elaborate image of woman that the author of *Mad Love* created, a woman naturally in tune with the marvelous. Ondine, Melusine, Esclarmonde, the woman-child or femme fatale, the reversed double in any case, were all evidence of a continuous attempt to reconstitute the primordial androgyne, specifically on the part of the occultists, a reconstruction whose "necessity" Breton proclaimed in the fourth issue of *Médium* in January 1955.

André Pieyre de Mandiargues, playing on his last name, called himself "arrogant lover of the word, mocking beggar" and would even go so far in his interviews with Francine Mallet (published in 1975 as Le désordre de la memoire) to advance an iconoclastic theory.

> If André Breton recognized a goddess of love, it was much less Venus than Diana, the cold queen of the night, the woman's reflection in the mirror's silver, the lunar and feminine principle according to the alchemists and masters of an esoteric tradition that lingers in the pages of *Arcanum 17* as it does in the sculptures of numerous cathedrals.

Diana is the one who, jealous of her own image, doomed the hunter Acteon—in whom Giordano Bruno showed an interest in his book *The Heroic Frenzies*—to such a cruel death. The Greek equivalent of Diana is Artemis, from the Greek *artemes,* meaning "safe and sound." An apparent enigma,* Diana's key may have already been provided in Jean-Louis Bédouin's article "Eros and the Death Instinct," in issue 4 of *Médium*.

> A certain female figure is thereby the magic mirror in which this or that phase of the mind's progress is reflected. This mirror can be an instrument of white magic as well as one of black magic. It is sometimes both and the type of woman inside of whom darkness and light face off is not the least illuminating of those whose image we retain. In her the fires of passion are refracted, the

---

*Diana is a killer and her name means safe and sound. At least a paradox!

flames of forbidden knowledge. Essentially nocturnal, the woman then reveals the treasure of a daylight the profane cannot even imagine.

This is why it is permissible for this curiosity of the occult as an undeniable and profound characteristic of the thought of the spokesman of surrealism—taking into consideration the very nature of Breton's writing—to be identified with this *Me,* who, in 1924 in *Introduction to the Discourse on the Paucity of Reality,* explained, "The fearless soul plunges into a land with no exits, where eyes open without tears." A land or a past! Marcel Lecomte, in Michel Fardoulis-Lagrange's magazine *Troisième Convoi,* in 1947, delivered, thus, these rather disconcerting considerations:

> Some of André Breton's most recent notes and allusions . . . cast light on a series of approaches whose final stage can be detected in Breton: a stage that could consist of an absolute poetic and magical knowledge of the world. I believe the moment has come to examine what could be called the Golden Age complex, which has left a deep imprint on surrealist consciousness, several particularly rich elements of which can be found in Breton. Breton hears the voices of the esoteric human past. Sometimes they only speak to him in a kind of murmur. . . . These voices orient his thought. They propel his desire for the knowledge of certain traditional assumptions, and I am using this term in the sense of its most secret density, to reach man so that he might free and transform himself and recreate himself through them.

After, Paul-Émile Bourdas, the leader of the Quebec automatists, confided to poet Claude Gauvreau in a 1954 letter:

> Concerning the Breton of *Arcanum 17,* like you I find great beauty in the "revelation" of the "redeeming" role of the "woman-child." Add to that the idea of "resurrection" which you find there as well and tell me if we are not dealing with Christian poetry of the pur-

est sort? Revelation, Redemption, Woman-Virgin, Resurrection, and Eternal into the bargain![58]

Octavio Paz is even more explicit when he writes:

On the other hand, the word *revelation* shines in many of [Breton's] texts. Speaking is the noblest activity of all: revealing what is hidden, bringing the buried word back to life, calling forth our double, that Other which is us but which we never allow to resist—our suppressed half. Then quite clearly, revelation is resurrection, exposure, initiation. It is a word that calls for rites and ceremonies.[59]

As additional evidence there is also this passage from "La Montagne des signes" (The Mountain of Signs), written in 1936 in Mexico by Artaud, for whom "all dreams are reality":

I remember suddenly that there were in History, Sects which inlaid these same signs upon rocks, carved out of jade, beaten into iron, or chiseled. And I begin to think that symbolism conceals a Science. And I find it strange that the primitive people of the Tarahumara tribe, whose rites and culture are older than the Flood, actually possessed this science well before the appearance of the Legend of the Grail, or the founding of the Sect of the Rosicrucians.[60]

A possible response to Artaud appeared fifteen years later in Malcolm de Chazal's book *Le Rocher de Sisyphe* (The Rock of Sisyphus) about Mauritius.

It so happens that in my prospecting in the mountains and my subsequent researches in the starry vault, I discovered as if by a miracle, repetition of hybrid myths with identical principles here as above, myths with animals' heads on human bodies like those the Hindus conceived with their Ganesh and Hanuman, and the Egyptians with their Thoth, Anubis, and Amon.[61]

This is easily explainable when we know that *"the Original Religion was a religion of signs and nomination:* Eden, where the stone condensed the universal verb and symbolized the Setting of Truth" (capital letters and italics are by Chazal) and, as Chazal makes it clear, that "Stonehenge, the menhirs, the carved mountain are all so many proto-ancient remnants of this Religion of Stone, fallen from its high peak of the Symbol toppled from its summit of quintessence."[62]

Chazal then went on to say, in 1973:

> Everything concerning prophecies and life is inscribed in the mountains. Whoever can lucidly read the mountains* shall know the future. . . . I who have lived among them and who sees them with the impressionist eye of the visionary; this is what I have seen: everywhere slopes and crests are scattered, recumbent effigies, the outlines of sphinxes, initials clearly chiseled, *like* hieroglyphs, signs, human gestures.[63] (Italics are mine because Chazal would have tended to see the hand of God here instead.)

More evidence can be found in this significant text, "From What Distance!" published by Michel Leiris at the end of the 1950s in his book *Haut Mal*.

> *Equal to the hadj*
> *as to other makers of trouble and pilgrimages*
> *when one has plunged where I have dived*
> *and returned from where I have been*
> *removed from the oily ink of sensational news items*
> *one has a clear right*
> *whether wearing his hat or not*
> *the polyhedron or the most beautiful pink one*
> *to a small piece of black sun.*

---

*Jules Monnerot rightly observed in *La Poésie moderne et le sacré*, "More than one ethnographer or theoretician has noted in parts of the world quite far from one another, the suggestive value of unusual rocks—because of their position, shape, color—that the 'primitive' imagination easily invested with powers!"

This is Gérard de Nerval's black sun, of course, as well as that of William Blake and Odilon Redon, about whom Stéphane Mallarmé wrote:

> But all my admiration goes straight to the grand inconsolable Mage and stubborn seeker of a mystery he knows does not exist but which he pursues forever for that very reason, out of mourning for his lucid despair, because it was once the truth!

A dead-end region! Even Atlantis is mobilized, and echoing Roger Gilbert-Lecomte's question, "Is death the lost secret of Atlantis?" (Gilbert-Lecomte was "seeking the ancestral soul of the Atlanteans"[64]), Artaud's text "The Rite of the Kings of Atlantis" (in which its author alludes to the end of *Critias*) maintains:

> However mythical the existence of Atlantis may be, Plato describes the Atlanteans as a race of magical origin. The Tarahumara, who I regard as the direct descendants of Atlantis, continue to devote themselves to the worship of magical rites![65]

Malcolm de Chazal also mentions the Atlanteans in *Le Rocher de Sisyph*, stating that they "base their architecture on star-shaped construction," but he also says, "Everything seems to indicate that black magic was at its peak among the Atlanteans and would have been the very cause of their downfall." Later, in this passage from his lengthy poem "The Return of Spring,"* Gérard Legrand tried to put things back in their proper place:

> *What Atlanteans?*
> *Those ancestors who drag themselves through their final*
> >   *oyster beds*
> *In a cloud of steam from a furrow these frail, red men*
> *Who have never existed outside the imperfect delusion*

---

*Legrand began writing "The Return of Spring" in 1951, and it was published in 1974 by Le Soleil Noir.

Of a prophet (I restore the poetic effect to them
Like that philosopher who clasped the copper of statues
Mute and covered with snow).

Then, in 2001, after the attacks of September 11 which so much inspired Jean Clair, Guy Girard, and Marie-Dominique Massoni of the Paris group of the surrealist movement developed a "reverie on the imaginary geography of Agarttha" in their text "37° North, 73° East and Several Hundred Leagues Below Ground." This pure myth of Agarttha was only created at the end of the nineteenth century from the texts of Louis Jacolliot and Saint-Yves d'Alveydre, for whom, Jean Van Win reminds us, it was an "initiatory center . . . keeper of our planet's secret archives: a kind of ultra-Masonic lodge."

René Guénon, basing his view on Swedenborg, saw it as the refuge of the "true Rosicrucians," twelve in number (!) who had "withdrawn to Asia from Europe" bringing with them "the true initiatory knowledge." This is undoubtedly why Guénon took an interest in the Fraternity of the Polaires, which was founded by Cesare Accomani and allegedly connected to an esoteric Himalayan Rosicrucian center. Guénon even went so far as to reread and correct Accomani's manuscript of *Asia Mysteriosa,* which the author published under the name of Zam Bhotiva in 1930. Girard and Massoni's text ends as follows:

> Agarttha enthuses us not only because one of its openings is located beneath Afghanistan, but also because others can be found in all places charged with a poetic or symbolic significance. Descent to the bottom of the volcano or only to the cave, vitriol.[66*]

Agarttha is also "the underground kingdom of universal tradition," to which Daumal—citing not only the authors of *The Mission*

---

*The word *vitriol* is the acronym of a phrase dear to occultists, *Visit interiora terrae, rectificandoque, invenies occultam lapidem* (Visit the interior of the earth and, by rectifying, you shall find the occult, or hidden, stone). The hidden stone in fact designates the philosopher's stone. For the Freemasons, it was rather, as Oswald Wirth says, "the corner stone (the core of crystallization) of the intellectual and moral construction constituted by the great work" (cited by Daniel Ligou in *Dictionary of Freemasonry*).

of India (1910) and *The King of the World*[67] but also Ferdinand Ossendowsky and his *Beasts, Men, and Gods*—refers in the third issue of *Le Grand Jeu* with respect to Nerval! It is true that he places this world, "if it exists, exactly in the slopes of Mount Analogue,"[68] which has remained unknown to men until the present for complex physical reasons and by virtue of its *inaccessibility by ordinary human means*. This is perhaps the same kind of peak as that "Mount Universal" that Chazal describes as a

> spiritual gauge of the heavens [that] sends us dancing with the light of its gestures gloved in invisibility [and] provides the music of elevation, the only perpetual and divine music.

It is true that Daumal's unfinished text dedicated to Alexander Salzmann and titled *Mount Analogue* is presented as a "novel of non-Euclidian and *symbolically authentic* alpine adventures" (italics added). In any case these various, fleeting allusions to Asia are all the more surprising inasmuch as the surrealists in general seemed to take scant interest in the thought of the Far East. However, this observation taken from Charles Duits's *André Breton a-t-il dit passe* brings it irresistibly to mind while opening certain perspectives on it:

> A person creates a false image of initiation when he confuses it with the acquisition of knowledge and powers. An initiate is the man who is fully alive and the teacher is the man who reveals the true meaning of life. Breton watching a butterfly revealed . . .

We perhaps could find the reasons for what could be perceived as a form of mistrust, one revealed at a fairly late date though, in the 1954 article "Orient to Disorient," written by Adrien Dax in the second issue of *Médium*, with these observations that resound like a critical echo of those of Guénon.

> In the disarray of a time when the traditional frameworks have been shaken to say the least, the regret for the lost harmonies between

man and the world cannot fail to be once again kindled. By preference, for it seems far too certain that the light cannot emerge from anywhere else, their gaze remains turned to the East and the expectation—more or less acknowledged—for some new spiritual dawn still supports, on this side, an illusory hope.

With the exception—but they were playing the Grand Jeu—of René Daumal, who had learned Sanskrit and translated excerpts from the Upanishads, Rig Veda, and Bhagavad Gita; André Rolland de Renéville, who seems to have been sufficiently acquainted with "the ancient Bardo Thôdol or Tibetan Book of the Dead" to advance the notion that it "curiously anticipated the procedures of psychoanalysis," and Roger Gilbert-Lecomte, for whom "Asia was long the refuge of the sole true life of the spirit,"[69] that is the mystic life, the members of the surrealist circles (of influence) seem to have only given cursory attention to Asia and its traditions—except the I Ching—in spite of the famous map of the world published in *Variétés* in 1929. Two exceptions, who were but somewhat marginal figures to surrealism as well, were Georges Bataille and André Masson, who, as the latter indicated in his interview with Paule Thévenin, had been acquainted with "the Zen doctrine" since the Acéphale era. Artaud was also an exception, as shown by the third issue of *La Révolution surréaliste*. Artaud advised Anne Manson in an August 1937 letter, as he had already done with Jean-Louis Barrault, to read "the Bardo Thôdol, the Egyptian Book of the Dead, the Tao-Te-Ching, and the VEDAS, *and drop all the rest!*" (Capital letters and italics are his!) Another peyote fan, Charles Duits, although attracted by Henri Corbin, "despite his gratuitously circumspect and heavy academic language" on the thought of the masters of the "Iranian Inner world," discovered Zen through Daisetz Teitaro Suzuki's *Essays on Zen Buddhism*[70] around 1956. Someone—since the note wasn't signed—had already reported on Zen in the second issue of *Médium* in February 1954. An ad for these essays, which had been translated by Daumal (and later graced with a preface by Carl Jung), could still be found in the January 1955 issue. Duits says that he considers this discovery as "one of the great turning points in my life."[71] In the second issue of the bulletin *Médium, Information surréaliste** in December 1952, a short, unsigned review that focused attention on Suzuki and his book *The Zen Doctrine of No Mind* was undeniable evidence of the surrealists' interest, which "showed how Zen Buddhism reconciled the opposites and abolished all dualism at the price of emotional suppression."

The anonymous reviewer continues:

Atheistic and repudiating any idea of soul, Zen thought undoubtedly represents the highest point attained by philosophical speculation inasmuch as it aims at a transposition onto the plane of the spirit the notion of "continuum" championed by modern physics!

This moreover is precisely what held the surrealists' attention, insofar as Adrien Dax, in February 1954, recalling the prejudices of Breton's friends toward Tagore† and the "dubious effusions of the Bengali mystic," again stressed in very clear terms:

Conversely, what we know of Zen Buddhism—less stained, it is true, of such a fairly overflowing affectivity—seems far from having inspired as warm a welcome today. This thought in fact remains devoid of all referential criteria, and the behavioral freedom it implies, toward both morality and religion, fortunately does not correspond with what a certain West expects of the East.

Conjuring up the initiatory "old man" of Zen, Duits notes in his book on Breton:

The essence of the teaching is passed silently from the teacher to the disciple. How? I don't know. Nobody does. We see a man eating, laughing, ranting, lighting his pipe, walking. We "watch the old

---

*There were first the eight issues of *Médium, Information surréaliste* and then the four issues of *Médium, Communication surréaliste*.
†Rabindranath Tagore (1861–1941) was an Indian (Bengali) poet, writer, playwright, painter, and philosopher. His work was very popular in Europe at the beginning of the twentieth century. He was awarded the Nobel Prize (Literature) in 1913.

man," we live at his side. Nothing is transmitted. But little by little, how to put it, we become "denser." Breton transmitted this way; he transmitted himself. His good and bad times alike . . .

Breton necessarily had his own opinions about Suzuki's work, as he cites a Zen saying in the article he wrote on Yahne Le Toumelin in *Surrealism and Painting*. Suzuki, whose teaching, according to Sandra Lisci,[72] left traces in the work of Remedios Varo, also drew the attention of Roger van Hecke, a member of the Tokyo group for a time[73] and above all of Guy Cabanel, whose interest in this matter is irrefutable: He discussed it in the first issue of *Bief* (November 1958) and still recently considered these texts fundamental. He did so with good reason perhaps: Adrien Dax, in the same review, compared the poems in Cabanel's collection *À l'animal noir* to "Zen dialogues." Later, as he confided to me personally, Jean-Claude Silbermann took a very close interest in it, as did Alain Jouffroy, who in *Manifeste de la Poésie Vécue* cites the "true Far East" in which he "finally approached the point where the world ceases not only to be perceived contradictorily, but begins to be seen as the sole possible world." In the same book the author would even venture to describe *"poetry as satori."*[74]

But the Japanese surrealist Fukuzawa Ichirô himself outlined the limitations of such a comparison, in a way that is extremely interesting with respect to his perspective, in *Surrealism and Japanese Forms*.

> A surrealist spirit can be found, to a certain extent, in Zen. However there are elements where they do not commingle and, therefore, it is best to deal with them separately with no further ado. But with respect to what is in the mind, in the sudden burst of enthusiasm that carries them off in quest of the divine, they are identical.[75]

Roger Caillois also reported how he found "Lao Tsu's axioms so obviously true and how some unknown kind of intoxication made me repeat the litanies of the Bhagavad Gita over and over to myself." This Bhagavad Gita troubled René Daumal in the same fashion.

In an article of *La Revue des ressources*, on the other hand, Régis Poulet notes René Char's interest in Lao Tsu and an even greater interest in the poet Jetsun Milarepa (1040–1123) who was one of the great teachers of Tibetan Buddhism, the founder of the Lineage of the Gold Rosary, and a poet cited by André Rolland de Renéville in *L'Expérience Poétique* in 1938. Char hailed Marie-José Lamothe's French translations of the Tibetan's works, writing, "Milarepa's work enchanted me. My thanks to Marie-José Lamothe for her ardent, passionate gift embroidered with grace from the auspicious Land of the Snows." Marie-Claude Char told Régis Poulet in a letter dated February 21, 1992, that the "major book he admired was Milarepa's *One Hundred Thousand Songs*," and while it is true that the poem "The Convalescent," published in 1983 in *Loin de mes cendres* (Far from My Ashes), is framed by two anecdotal citations of the yogi, it seems more prudent to describe these as convergences rather than influences. We should remember that the interest of Breton's friends was drawn more to Oceania, Africa, or America than Asia!

Benjamin Péret translated and provided extracts from the *Book of Chilam Balam of Chumayal*, which was discovered in the Yucatan in the nineteenth century. They were presented in the "Almanach surréaliste du demi-siècle" as a collection of texts of a mystical nature, truly "symbolic formulas of religious initiation written at different eras by the Indians, probably priests" and in which the reproduced figure of the "Querant" cannot help but bring certain Tarot cards to mind. Clearly, then, very few occult or hermetic* domains escaped the surrealists' curiosity, even if, as Ferdinand Alquié notes, we have to admit that with the exception of Breton "the knowledge of this domain held by the young people of the time of the hypnotic sleeps was quite scant" and even though "the German Romantics, the initiated, and the illuminati are not mentioned in the *First Surrealist Manifesto*." He is still quick to state, "while the sources of surrealism are not to be found in esotericism," when we take into consideration the depth of the German romantic influence, the approach and study of this kind of thought had to have made itself felt fairly quickly—and to long-lasting effect. We cannot overlook some ambivalent areas such as

---

*"Hermeticism. N. Occult tradition that takes its name from Hermes Trismegistus. Cultivated during the Middle Ages, hermeticism presumes mysterious relationships between all the portions of the visible and the invisible universe. This alleged science is confused with occultism, magic, alchemy, etc." (*Nouveau Larousse universel*, vol. 1).

when Philippe Audoin mentions—at a much later date—Paul Le Cour's extremely traditionalist review *Atlantis* in the seventh issue of *La Brèche*. Le Cour was Guénon's bugbear, but Robert Amadou described him as "one of the most reliable instructors, one of the truest mystagogues of our time." He was also, as Jean-Pierre Laurant tells us, the spiritual heir of the *hieron* of Paray-le-Monial, this "Catholic anti-masonry" in the expansion "of the movements of reparation by the Sacred Heart," led by the Jesuit Victor Drevon. Lecour's review is thus one we could call reactionary: a review of which the traditional Martinist Order under the leadership of Victor-Émile Michelet will be quite close.

These explorations were never made to the detriment of a direct political involvement centered on various political connections depending on the times, something that was true of the surrealist movement since its beginnings, even if violent criticisms about these explorations were laid against a person, which could even lead to exclusion from the group. These reproaches could come from either outside or from within the different circles at this or that time. Ithell Colquhoun, for example, was one of the most interesting representatives of British surrealism, which she had discovered in 1931. She was also one of the major figures of twentieth-century occultism.* She refused to abandon her research in this domain, which she had been engaged in since 1927, and was forced to

---

*"Occultism. N. Science of occult things. Occultism is a survival of humanity's primitive notions at a time when ignorance assumed a cause and mysterious agents for all phenomena. Its domain, which falls between that of religion and that of science, embraces facts that seem to display intervention by forces that escape all rational explanation. Occultism, which formerly included magic, astrology, alchemy, and various forms of divination, is reduced today to spiritualism, which tends to establish relationships between the world of the living (physical or earthly plane) and the dead (astral plane)" (*Nouveau Larousse universel*, vol. 2). Robert Amadou, specifying that "the word is of nineteenth-century provenance, from a time shortly before Eliphas Levi, who ensured its success," proposed his own definition: "Occultism is all the theories and practices founded on the theory of correspondences, which is to say the theory according to which every object belongs to a single group and maintains with every other element in that group a necessary and intentional relationship, which is nontemporal and nonspatial. Its theories deal with kingdoms and correspondences, which are the analogical type, and the tradition that transports the doctrine into its various expressions. Its practices ranges from mantics—or divination—to magic and alchemy. Occultism culminates in theosophy" (*Occident, Orient: parcours d'une tradition*).

distance herself from the English group following an April 1940 meeting at the Soho restaurant Barcelona, where the participants had been summoned to reassert their allegiance to the main principles of surrealism as defined by the group's leader, E. L. T. Mesens, who was the former disciple of E(sote)rik Satie. This was also the basis for the group's rupture with Toni del Renzio, who would write in his 1944 manifesto "Incendiary Innocence," "To ensure no misunderstanding of what is being said here, let it be repeated that the occultists, Christian Rosenkreuz not the least among them, have supplied surrealism with the form as well as the *content* of some of its boldest and totally recalcitrant assertions."[76]*

About this meeting, in 1976 Ithell Colquhoun would say, "I said that I wanted to be free to pursue my studies in the domain of esotericism† as I

---

*Toni (Romanov) del Renzio (dei Rossi di Castellone e Venosa) (1915–2007) is one of the major hidden figures of the British surrealist group. He was excluded for challenging "the authority" of Mesens and trying to restore a little vitality to a group that had become anemic since the beginning of the 1940s and was condemned to disappear in 1951 with the closing of the London Gallery.

†Concerning esotericism, I would like to cite Frédéric Lenoir, who is definitely highly versed in these matters, from "L'Homme ne peut se passer de mythes ni de symboles," his contribution to the popularized "20 Clés pour comprendre le ésotérisme" (special issue, Le Monde des religions, n° 10, 2009). "The adjective esoteric comes from the Greek esotirokos, 'to go within.' An Alsatian Lutheran scholar, Jacques Matter, created the word esotericism in 1823. This 'portmanteau' word only exists in the different meanings its speakers attribute to it and overlays a group of thought trends connected to each other through history and located outside any specific religion. Esotericism moreover exhibits certain characteristics: it tends to reunite the varied knowledge present in all philosophical and religious traditions with the idea that a primordial religion of humanity is concealed behind them. This is why it almost always refers to a Golden Age when the human being possessed knowledge that was subsequently scattered in various religious currents. Another component is the existence of a continuum between all parts of the universe, in the plurality of the levels of visible and invisible reality from the infinitely small to the infinitely large. This doctrine of 'correspondences'—on which the practice of alchemy, among others, is based—regards nature as a huge living organism through which a spiritual flow travels that gives it its beauty and unity. It so happens that only magic and esoteric philosophy can elucidate the mysteries of this enchanted nature. Finally, its final element is the central place of the imagination as mediation between the human being and the world." According to Amadou again, "Esotericism refers to the internal, and to the entrance into the internal; of man, the world, God in their depths, which is Wisdom. Esotericism is that philosophy in which

deemed best (the opposition to this aspect of surrealist activity comes from a whim of Mesens, insofar as Breton, Dominguez, Dr. Mabille, Masson, and Seligmann, and other continental surrealists pursued research like this without it raising questions),"[77] which clearly shows so many years later the depths of the feeling of incomprehension and injustice she must have felt then. It is true that the lady, whom Michel Rémy defined in the *Dictionaire général du surréalisme et de ses environs* as "surrealism in a perpetual state of 'fantasmagic' on the convulsive paths of occultism," did not pull any punches, being a member of the Ordo Templi Orientis, an organization already suspect for allegations of practicing sex magic. The Ordo Templi Orientis was founded at the end of the nineteenth century by two Masons, Karl Kellner and Theodor Reuss. Reuss was a thirty-third-degree Mason of the Scottish Rite, which did not prevent him from having incriminating sympathies for National Socialism, and it was connected to the Rite of Memphis-Misraïm (of which Reuss was the world grand master) and the (Swedish) Swedenborgian Rite, which would ultimately be led astray by the devilish Alastair Crowley, as was his religious arm, the Gnostic Catholic Church. The name of this occult poetess is also associated with the founder of the Hermetic Order of the Golden Dawn—although she was not a member—the Scot, Samuel Liddell "MacGregor" Mathers (1854–1918), to whom she dedicated a book in 1975, *The Sword of Wisdom*.

Elie-Charles Flamand, who collaborated on *Médium,* where he wrote reviews like "La Ville mystère" (n° 4), on Jacques Yonnet's *Les Enchantements de Paris*[78] and its description of the "second life" of the occult city, and participated in the preparatory questionnaire for *L'Art magique,* was similarly excluded from the Parisian group in 1960 for "ruiniform esotericism." Though Breton signed the letter of rupture, he maintained their personal friendship. Born Charles Flamand, a trained geologist and paleontologist as well as an ardent fan of jazz, this

---

(continued from p. 75) occultism culminates—there is nothing of one without the other, but are they even separate?" For Sarane Alexandrian, in his *Histoire de la philosophie occulte,* "Occultism is the overall theory of the occult virtue of things; esotericism is a mysterious means for approaching the primordial tradition of humanity, from which all religions arise."

undeservedly obscure poet chose early on to combine his name with that of the prophet Eli, who represented "divine fire and the illumination it confers," as he explains in his book *Les Méandres du sens* (The Meandering of Meanings).[79] This prompted Marc Kober to suggest, "Elie-Charles Flamand would be the metaphysical quest made tangible through the mediation of poetic work."[80] Flamand met André Breton, René Alleau, Eugène Canseliet, and Robert Amadou in the same movement, evidence of a selective eclecticism, and he placed the first stone of his work with the collection, *À un oiseau de houille perché sur la plus haute branche du feu*,* whose primarily initiatory nature leaps off the pages. In the 1960s he was the author, Canseliet tells us in his introduction to the republished edition of the *Mutus Liber*,† of

> the illuminating text for the magnificently illustrated three volume set of the pictorial schools of the Renaissance, which have recently been published by the Lausanne publisher, Rencontre editions. This lavish trilogy brings together in this order, the Quattrocento, the Cinquecento and the powerful birth parented by these two ages in France, Flanders, Holland, and Germany . . . it is, in short, a veritable goldmine that offers vast resources to the untiring efforts of the hermeticist!

Other books that followed include *La Lune feuillée* (The Wavy Moon), with a preface by André Pieyre de Mandiargues, the same Mandiargues who, Robert Sabatier recalls in volume three of his summa on French twentieth-century poetry, "Compared his poems to those engravings that illustrate the wonderful treatises of the ancient alchemists, which display a surrealist phantasmagoria ahead of its time."[81] *Attiser la rose cruciale* (Arouse the Crucial Rose) appeared in 1982, about which Marc Kober said it "resounds like a Rosicrucian collection." It contains this verse with a Nervalian tone: "Sometimes I have

---

*Flamand's book was published in 1957 by Henneuse, with illustrations by Toyen (Marie Cermínová).
†For the new edition of the *Mutus Liber*, Flamand rediscovered "two graceful copperplate engravings" at the Saint-Ouen flea market.

seen my inner darkness adorned with a radiant rift." This impression is confirmed by Kober, who concludes that the poet "tirelessly extracts the fervid heat of a black sun from one book to the next," combining the highest standards with the greatest openness with respect to his choice of themes, displaying the widest sense of esotericism in the vicinity of René Guénon, as in the poem "À contre-mort."

> *Friends of the keeper of survivals*
> *Keep watch further ahead*
> *And flay your corrective confessions.*

Sabatier sums up Elie-Charles Flamand as "the metamorphosis of initial surrealism into spirituality, into sacredness!"

Éleonore Antzenberger, in an article about Whitney Chadwick's book *Women Artists and the Surrealist Movement,* expresses the following criticism, which at least goes to show that even reviewers find themselves under pressure to remain in reason's crosswalk.

> The author's insistence on the "esoteric content of the works"* is also this book's weak point. The enrollment of the feminine imaginal realm into a telluric/chthonic tradition occupies almost a third of the book while other aspects are held at arm's length. Although its presence is incontestable, esotericism undoubtedly does not justify the systematization of its appeal![82]

Undoubtedly this divergence is too absolute.

As early as 1930, Robert Desnos, bitter about his expulsion from the movement, stigmatized its occultist penchant. In his pamphlet *Third Manifesto of Surrealism,* he declared, with undeniable polemical intent:

> Believing in the surreal is to repave the path of God. Surrealism, such as it has been formulated by Breton, is one of the gravest dan-

---

*The works of the women surrealists.

gers to which we expose our freedom of thought, the most devious trap into which we let our atheism fall, the finest auxiliary to a renaissance of Catholicism and clericalism.

The attacks against this path taken by surrealism, simply reasserted after the Second World War, triggered misunderstandings that often had detrimental consequences for the group as a whole. One such misunderstanding about the nature of "hermeticism" appears to have helped cause the rift with *Le Libertaire* at the beginning of the 1950s. Evidence for this appears in the following extract from "Double Star," a letter written by Schuster to a "Group of militants" and signed by the majority of surrealists who had published letters in this anarchist newspaper.

> It is worth dissipating an ambiguity concerning the word hermeticism. You are surely aware that it designates a philosophical, scientific, and poetic tradition going back to Antiquity that has come down to us thanks to its occultation as it is a *revolutionary opposition* to the modes of thought defined in the West by the merger of Christianity and rationalism. Again on this point, we feel we have explained ourselves with sufficient clarity.* But it seems that you are using the word "hermeticism" in its most common and broadest meaning, encompassing everything that escapes rational comprehension.[83]

This approach was fruitless, and the collaboration did not resume. Sometimes the rejection was the work of close colleagues, such as Paul Nougé,† the brains of the Belgium surrealist group. Faithful to the specific options of the Brussels group at this time (and to his own scientific training as a biochemist), Nougé wrote the following in his preface

---

*In the *Bulletin Surréaliste* in *Le Libertaire;* José Pierre, *Surréalisme et anarchie*.
†The same Paul Nougé wrote in his book *Propositions* in 1927, "We have the intuition of an order of deeds, of powers . . . that we label as *spiritual*," and later, speaking of "mysticism," "We place the accent on the occult *powers* of the mind: we *believe* in these still unknown occult powers of the mind" (Nougé's italics). Then, in 1933, in "Les images défendues," a text published in the fifth issue of *Le Surréalisme au service de la révolution*: "Our open eye passes over many things that in the physical sense of the word remain invisible!"

("Les Points sur les signes") to René Magritte's 1948 Brussels exhibition, about the international exhibition in Paris Le Surréalisme en 1947, an exhibition whose character was strongly—and intentionally—initiatory.

> And they pretend to recognize the theoretical expression of a purely experimental thought in pretentious and incoherent ravings in which sordid superstitions and milky mysticisms are tangled together. Appearing here are tarots, horoscopes, premonitions, hysteria, objective chance, black masses, kabbalah, voodoo rites, ossified folklore, ceremonial magic. There is no longer any question of citing André Breton, who deserves to be outcast.[84]

This will not prevent Nougé from participating again in 1964 in reviews—such as *La Brèche*—directed by the "autocrat" Breton! Yet Breton's companion in exile, René Étiemble, who has been entirely—and rightfully, as we shall see—forgotten today, was not to be left behind in this regard. In his contribution to the special issue of *NRF*, "André Breton et le movement surréaliste," published in 1967, Etiemble bemoans the "line of weakness" that appeared after World War II on the "leonine mask" of the author of *Arcanum 17* in these words:

> How sad, indeed, to see him going astray far too often on the paths of unreason, the sinks of "magic!" This, alas, is the fate of those who refusing organized worship also refuse experience and reason. A man of faith, a sectarian, if only Breton was satisfied to merely bless or curse his own, Father Divine of the white man [sic]. But the tarot! But Saint-Yves d'Alveydre! But Martinez [sic] de Pasqually! When I saw Breton prefer Fulcanelli to Renan, who one century before the discovery of the Dead Sea scrolls foresaw and grasped the Essene doctrine, or the *Dictionary of Occult Sciences* to the dictionary of atomic energy, I better grasped why, despite his courage, rectitude, and need for justice, he had wandered from one political sect to the next. I can clearly understand that Fourier's socialism would be preferred to Marxism; but rather than placing his hope on some oddballs why didn't he become a Taoist?

Let's ignore the "Father Divine," undoubtedly spotted when leafing through *On the Survival of Certain Myths and Several Other Myths in Growth or Formation,* "staged" in 1942. But so much confusion, conformism, and incomprehension is alarming, especially as Étiemble had already attacked Breton by more or less accusing him of obscurantism in an article in *Les Temps modernes* titled "Le Requin et la mouette" (The shark and the gull) in 1947.

Yves Bonnefoy acted in similar fashion. While reasserting his admiration for the author of *Pleine Marge,* he could not refrain from noting:

> And it is true that to really understand Breton, we have to ask ourselves if he was always as faithful to this great possible that opened his poetic intuition for him in his life as he lived it . . . if he did not, in other words, dream of substituting for "ardent reason" a gnosis, out of attachment to the increasingly attractive idea of other laws of the world than those to which we are subject: a hidden reality as postulated by esotericism, that religion without reason.[85]

But this is nothing compared to the bad faith—unless it is ideological blindness and/or intellectual dishonesty—displayed by Jean Clair,* like a modern Bernard Dorival of wretched memory, in his

---

*My words may appear excessive when speaking of Clair's intellectual dishonesty. Yet it is impossible that this renowned art historian is unaware of what he is doing when he separates the rest of the movement's activity from what he calls "the surrealist aesthetics," a distinction the surrealists always refused to make, when he goes in the most radical direction by sanctimoniously merging the adjectives *surrealist* and *extravagant,* or when, starting on page 16 of his book *Du Surréalisme considéré dans ses rapports avec le totalitarisme et les tables tournantes* he offers no less than eight perspectives for approaching Breton, each more negative than the last. These are in the style of "Was Breton . . . a Beast of the Apocalypse eating heretics? A Trinity of Evil? An *Emblema diabolico,* tracing his opinions and gestures in the political monsters of his time?" In other words, Satan or some other diabolical figure or else one of their scarcely presentable avatars of the Hitler or Stalin variety! Fortunately we have been warned straight off that the author is not putting surrealism on trial (page 9). But who cares! The bilious Jean Clair, as a worthy henchmen and authentic reactionary in the cultural domain, received his just reward for a zeal and ideological doggedness quite in keeping with the times—a seat in the *Academie française!* (Jean Clair was elected at the Académie Française in May 2008.)

pamphlet *Du Surréalisme consideré dans ses rapports avec le totalitarisme et les tables tournantes* (Surrealism Considered in its Relationships with Totalitarianism and Table Turning)[86] or in his article "Surrealism and Demoralization of the West," published in *Le Monde,* on November 22, 2001. Both of these are exacerbated expressions of "the small-minded resentful mediocrity of a certain French cultural bureaucracy,"[87] for the same could be said about Victor Hugo and his table turning or Nerval and his legend of Hiram in *Le Voyage en Orient* (Journey to the East).

I should say that the presumptions of the "darkly bilious," which is the title of Clair's autobiography, are fairly weighty: "Art," Clair barks, "was a knowledge and a pleasure, at least until the seventeenth century. It was the unified field of a body of knowledge . . . essentially a science of observation and description, in the service of precise sensory perception." This is undoubtedly one of Clair's subtle allusions to the countless religious representations of hells, paradises, Pantocrator figures, ascensions, and other more or less mystical lambs, unless he is referring to the paintings adorned with unicorns or other varied fabled animals and planispheres haunted by Cyclops, dog-headed men, Blemmyes, Skiapodes . . .

We can see how significant his opinion is when measured by the yardstick of sensory perception! Jean Clair, the sworn opponent of all the avant-garde movements of the twentieth century—except maybe futurism, who knows why—accuses all the creators who took part in these movements of having, by pen or paintbrush, paved the way for totalitarianism and attempted to usurp (the crime of *lèse-majesté*) the legitimate power of politicians, who alone are capable of making their people happy. Politicians who we have seen—and are able to see—never make any mistakes and, if they do, apologize and retire from office!

His utter lack of empathy makes him equally incapable of understanding how the tragic death of millions of young men on the battlefields of a Europe in full moral and human collapse is enough to explain the emergence of a morbid attitude propitious for the development of spiritualism and a widespread disgust for the values that presided over the disaster. These sentiments blooming amid the ruins led to the frenzied headlong rush into the pleasures that characterized the Roaring Twenties, and Lotte Eisner expresses them with great sensitivity in *The Haunted Screen,* when discussing the emergence of expressionist theater in Germany: "The ghosts that had already haunted German Romanticism revived like the shades of Hades when they drank blood."[88] Such intellectual impoverishment suffices to stress the essential role played by such conservatories of the marvelous like the House of the Surrealists in Cordes-sur-Ciel!

These critical if not dubious epiphenomena notwithstanding, it is quite clear, as noted by Alain Jouffroy, that at least in the field of the plastic arts, "It is common knowledge today that *fantastic art* is the exoteric term representing the esoteric and occult reality of surrealism."[89] Therefore it is well worth returning to this hermeticism, used as one arm among others for subverting reality and seeing through it "without rallying," as Philippe Audoin stresses, "to the mystical or religious presuppositions it inspires" to this esotericism that to the great displeasure of argumentative priests of all stripes runs through its works, in all its forms in almost all languages, and on almost every continent.

3

SURREALISM AND THE LABYRINTH OF THE MIND

The ghosts ate at the windows.
                               JEAN-PIERRE DUPREY

"The ghosts trigger rites," said my voice, harmonizing with the shadow's echoes.
          JEAN-PIERRE DUPREY, *LA FIN ET LA MANIÈRE*

"Here the land of phantoms begins." These are the *different* beings (perhaps) that René Crevel's old friend Pavel Tchelitchew depicted in his painting *Hide and Seek** (see plate 3), the very same ghosts about whom Duprey would write shortly before killing himself in 1959:

> They are coming, they are coming! Their colors stabbed into the water, their image hiding mirrors, only an absence embodies them for us, a presence disembodies us![1]

---

*Tchelitchew's painting was exhibited at the Museum of Modern Art in New York City in 1942.

I, of course, intend to discuss the "period of hypnotic sleeps" (1922) mentioned in Breton's text "The Mediums Enter." This was the experiment "of a mystic path about which it would be vain, until further notice, to try to discuss in terms of reason" and "resumption of a *quest* that the nineteenth century had spread beyond all other so-called poetic concerns," as Breton will sum it up in his interviews with André Parinaud, a period characterized by behaviors comparable to those of the "convulsionaries of Saint Medard." Jouffroy describes it as close to "a veritable metaphysics of vertigo," in which, as Robert Desnos states, one "collides with thick darkness in which hazy shadows make vague sweeping gestures." Aragon adds, "With all the devices of terror, we hold our hands out to ghosts."[2] This is a far cry from Maurice Henry's sympathetic shroud wearers! René Crevel, who had received the "start of a spiritualist initiation"[3] during an encounter in Normandy with a Madame Dante [*sic*] and her theosophy adept friends,[4] is a perfect illustration of how surrealism was transforming then into what Michel Carrouges describes as "a vast system of wiretaps and spectral projections in the dark." It also shows how its adepts were venturing onto the terrain of spiritualism, despite the distance Breton—like Guénon—exhibited. Guénon made his views clear in his book *L'Erreur spirite* (The Spiritualist Error) about "depressing spiritualist literature" and the sectarian theories of Allan Kardec (the pen name of Léon-Hippolyte Rivail, 1803–1869), which, based on "the exogeneity of the dictating principle, in other words the existence of spirits," were more or less presented as a divine revelation, one based on science in denial of the marvelous.

We should not forget that standing behind spiritualism, as Charles Jameux showed me, is everything that falls into the jurisdiction of psychoanalysis, perceived as a plunge into the components of the human mind. Thus it would be more accurate to say that they were venturing onto the terrain of a certain kind of mediumship stripped of its spiritualist clutter. This is not so far from the automatic writing that Breton, simply seeking to explore possible supranormal "second states," would more or less compare to "the automatism inherited from mediums" in *Artistic Genesis and Perspectives of Surrealism*, as it appears in the paintings of the miner Augustin Lesage, the well digger Fleury-Joseph Crépin, and the American slipper manufacturer Morris Hirshfield. In *Point du jour* (Daybreak), Breton also mentions Fernand Desmoulins, the Count of Tromelin, Madame Fibur, Machner, and Petitjean, also "the mediumistic [texts] like those (admirable incidentally) cited by Denis Saurat in his book *Victor Hugo et les dieux du peuple*"[5] and even the narrative *From India to the Planet Mars,* published by the linguist Victor Henry. This book recorded the words of the "surrealist in language" Helene Smith (born Élise-Catherine Müller, 1861–1929), the future siren of the keyhole (personification of knowledge) in the *Jeu de Marseille,* the surrealist playing card deck, was dictated to Théodore Flournoy, "the fascinated fascinator"* (i.e., hypnotist), between 1895 and 1900. Helene Smith was the woman to whom Nadja was referring when she cried out, "Helene is me," and whom Annie Le Brun also discusses in her 1984 article "L'Inconscient de la seduction," reprinted in her book *A Distance.*

In any case, the reproductions of "Martian" or "Ultra-Martian" texts and landscapes, and "Uranian" symbols produced by Helene Smith were given pride of place in issue 3–4 of *Minotaure,* despite the clearly mystical turn taken by the work of this medium. In the latter part of her life she heard celestial voices! Other seekers, and most serious, had already taken this route, for example, Emanuel Swedenborg published a treatise titled *Concerning the earths in our solar system, which are called planets: and concerning the earths in the starry heavens together with an account of their inhabitants, and also of the spirits and angels there: from what hath been seen and heard.*[6]

Carrouges, however, in his paper on objective chance delivered at the Cerisy symposium on surrealism in July 1968, recalled "the importance attached by Breton in a text from *Point du jour* to the major explorations of Myers and Flournoy," and in particular, he added in his book *André Breton et les donnés fondamentales du surréalisme* (André Breton and the Basic Concepts of Surrealism). Myers was famous for his "Gothic psychology" on "the subliminal world and the automatism of the mediums." Carrouges went on to say, "The surrealists accept the

---

*This nickname was given to him by Annie Le Brun.

arguments of spiritualism no more than did Flournoy. Nor are they prepared to place their blind trust in mediumnistic revelations."[7]

This proximity, nevertheless, between the experiences of mediums like Victorien Sardou or Helene Smith and Breton's friends is clearly underscored by Jean-Louis Bédouin in the monograph he wrote on Benjamin Péret (published by Seghers), in which he recalls an episode during a hypnotic sleep session on October 2, 1922, during which the author of *Trois Cerises et une sardine* (Three Cherries and a Sardine) describes "what he [sees] on another planet, extremely far from earth." In fact, isn't it somewhat logical to see the young surrealists, completely permeated as they were with a "fin de siècle" spirit whose echo reverberated through the 1920s, to display signs of huge interest in the "occult" and to seek in parapsychological manifestations and spiritualism a third way between the rationalism of a triumphalist science promising yet brighter tomorrows, on the one hand, and a religion that is losing speed but still powerful and that persistently claims, despite its compromises, to offer moral comfort to a rather disoriented humanity, on the other? Charles Duits sums up the matter quite well in his book on Breton when he writes:

> A substratum then showed itself—one of his substrata as he had several. One that the majority of his "admirers" refuse to see, forgetting that automatic writing was discovered by mediums, and pretending to be unaware of the *subjects* of [his] principal works.

Something along the same line was detailed in the review *Médium,* which was published between 1952 and 1955, another period of "wild years" preceding the outbreak of the colonial war in Algeria and the mobilization of conscripts, an era that was, according to Philippe Audoin, one of "the mass raising of insatiable and sometimes charming ghosts." But there was also what Charles Duits wrote after May 1968— the time of a crisis of another nature—in the preface to *Ptah Hotep:*

> Not a single line in this book is mine; I have only transcribed the words dictated to me by the luminous voice and described the scenes revealed to me by the invisible hand!

In his *Journal,* as in his unpublished text *La Seule Femme vraiment noire* (The Only Truly Black Woman), also named the *Treatise,* Duits also said he was in communication and dialoguing with entities he respectively named B(etty) and Sophie or the "goddess." In fact, contrary to the players of the Grand Jeu, especially Gilbert-Lecomte and Daumal, who would sacrifice their health following their paths to the bitter end, Breton's friends only abandoned their explorations of trance states, at least as a systematic activity, because of the risks they posed to some individuals. As Breton notes:

> For years Robert Desnos abandoned himself bag and baggage to surrealist automatism. For my part, I tried to hold him back from the time I began to fear his personality structure would not bear the strain. Yes, I continue to believe there is the danger of disintegration once you go beyond a certain limit on this path. This would be too long a story. He was upset with me but you needed to be there to know how close he came to the edge of the abyss several times. It was at this price as well that inspiration (in the romantic sense of the word) was not only restored to all its rights among us, but also no longer had to accept any limit to its empire.[8]

"Watch out," Caillois wrote as an epigraph to a chapter in *Le Mythe et l'homme* (Myth and Man), "by playing a ghost, you become one!" Single-mindedly focused on his outbursts, Carrouges, who saw in the abandonment of these kinds of experiments "one more proof that beyond all disintegration [surrealism] is looking for a reintegration," was seemingly unaware that both Breton and Aragon had psychiatric medical training. Aragon, in his 1924 text "Une vague de rêves" (A Wave of Dreams), indicates, in a fairly premonitory fashion, another aspect of the problem on which the vicissitudes and tragic end of Desnos—the author of *Liberty or Love!*—would cast a singular light.

> In other circumstances, were Desnos to cling to this delirium, he would become the leader of a religion, the founder of a city, the tribune of a people in revolt. . . . We soon witnessed the

birth of an age of collective illusions—but were they illusions after all?

Others would really get into this delirium, and Desnos would be their victim! But who would dare cast the first stone at him when, at almost this same time, Roger Gilbert-Lecomte wrote, "We are a handful of ten. Give me only one hundred students and I will destroy the Sorbonne, the Institute, the College of France, and introduce the New Knowledge."

Jean-Pierre Duprey* explains in highly inspired language:

> It is clearly the hour where I SEE† my corpse! And like every night, the castle opens its invisible doors to Esteva's two eyes, to the Carmilla's double fire, this shadow-enchantment, this specter and woman shadow, which haunts me night after night, between the dog‡—which is a wolf—and the large wild cat. And henceforth, SHE no longer leaves me, laying upon me the common weight of a two-voiced silence. . . . And like each night, thus, she stares at me this way with her gaze of black fire in whose depths I lose my eyes; and her contact then, which penetrates me beyond even myself, causing me to shout outside my life . . . whose projection is being announced on OTHER PLANES.[9]

We cannot help but see Victor Brauner's *Strigoï the Sleepwalker* (1946) wandering nearby, a Romanian *strigoï* that is none other than

---

*The fact that Duprey baptized one of his characters Carmilla cannot help but bring to mind Joseph Sheridan Le Fanu's novel *Carmilla*, published in 1871 (Arles, France: Actes Sud [coll. "Babel"], 1996), which was also illustrated in 1983 by Leonor Fini. This Irish fantasy writer, born in 1814 and died in 1873, was heir to the English gothic novelists whose work was heavily inspired by the thought of Emmanuel Swedenborg. Duprey wrote of his Carmilla, "She lifts the soul-black Veil of the closed hair, so that a face appears! And if the face is not, She lifts the void—the Voice of On High is a point of the Down Below. . . !"

†There's a pun, here: VIS in French can be understood as SEE (past tense) or LIVE (verb: vivre, tense: present).

‡["The dog" is a play on a French expression for twilight: *entre chien et loup*, "between dog and wolf." —*Trans.*]

a phantom momentarily associated with the artist's recurring memory of the somnambulist of Fălticeni, a memorable figure from his childhood.

Marc Alyn writes in "Birth of a Galaxy," his article about Robert Desnos, that he "sleeps at will, and the beyond, 'all the beyond,' speaks through his mouth." In his studio on the rue Blomet, Desnos, in 1922, had begun "a series of mediumistic drawings in which the automatism of the gesture corresponded to the dreamlike nature of the representation." Breton alluded to them briefly in the *First Surrealist Manifesto*, speaking of two images by Desnos—*Romeo and Juliet* and *A Man Died This Morning*—which had been published in issue 36 of the review *Feuilles Libres* as the drawings of madmen.

Sarane Alexandrian reminds us in his book *Création, Récréation*[10] that the author of *Arbitrary Destiny* created these works with "eyes closed, his head propped against the table in a state of hypnotic trance": before transposing them "into paintings that were merely colored copies of what he had drawn" and to which he (Desnos) granted high value. Desnos thought, and he wrote it about Max Ernst, that "for the poet hallucinations do not exist, only the real exists"—even if Breton makes an odd allusion to the "powers of darkness" in the *First Surrealist Manifesto*.

This cannot help but bring to mind the passage in *L'Erreur spiritiste* in which Guénon observes:

> Some of these forces (which manifest during spiritualist séances) could be said to be truly *demonic* or *satanic;* these are the forces that sorcery notably brings into play, and spiritualist practices can also often attract them, although unintentionally. The medium is an individual whose unfortunate constitution puts him or her in contact with everything that is least advisable in this world, and even in the lower worlds.

Concerning those deep states of altered consciousness that lead to trance, which the members of the Grand Jeu group would also explore a little later by different means, Aragon states in "Une vague de rêves":

These repeated experiments kept the men who underwent them in a state of growing and terrible irritation, of crazy nervousness. They lost weight. Their trances grew longer and longer. They no longer wanted to wake up. They went to sleep watching someone else sleep, and then conversed like people from a blind and faraway world; they quarreled, and sometimes we had to wrench the knives from their hands. Real physical ravages, and the difficulty, after repeated attempts, of pulling them out of a cataleptic state that seemed to pass over them like a whisper of death would soon force the subjects of these extraordinary experiments, at the pleading of those who watched them leaning out from the parapet of wakefulness, to break off the exercises that neither laughter nor doubts had been able to disturb.

It should be noted that during one séance Crevel seems to have persuaded a few of the participants to hang themselves, while at another an entranced Desnos pursued Paul Eluard with kitchen knife in hand. This is a perfect example of the *split* personality[11]* that Artaud talks about in *On the Balinese Theater* as the "double who is terrified by the apparitions from beyond," "this double who at a given moment hides behind his own reality." Other examples include Unica Zürn's *L'Homme-Jasmin* (The Man of Jasmine), which describes "impressions of a mental illness"† in which soars the shadow of "the Other inside

---

*In one of the notes of his article on Nerval, "Comme une suite à un ajour d'Arcane 17," published in issue n° 6 of *La Brèche*, Robert Guyon notes about the "parasite *double*": "Egyptian doctrine mentions the existence of a *double* that still plays a dubious role when the dead individual was not worthy to be proclaimed 'like the gods.'" And Philippe Audoin, in *Maurice Fourré, rêveur definitif,* clearly states, "Obsession with the double can be found in various forms in all civilizations: it is the *Ka* of the Egyptians, the inviolable *Shadow* of the Indians, the Christian *Soul*, etc. In our day the double has adopted a new name: the Unconscious, which quickly divided itself up into different authorities: the *Id,* the *Ego,* the *Superego*. This can be refined yet further by measuring the degree of awareness accompanying the occasional emergence of one of the hypostases of the new Trinity."

†Unica Zürn also provides her own singular account of mediumship: "The hypnotism at a distance has begun again. The mutual work proves to be extremely beautiful. She has become a medium, the sole state of which she is worthy. She can rest (continued on p. 92)

her,"[12] and Stanislas Rodanski,* *Lancelot in the Vale of No Return,* who depicts himself as "prey to voices . . . clad in [his] phantom,"[13] victim "of the powerful influence of a Masque that seeks to make [him] its creature."[14]

We then come to the prince in this kingdom of the split: Jean-Pierre Duprey[†] who "doubles and splits in two" in *Derrière son Double* (Behind His Double), "each of them like a glorious, dark angel, the ghost of both his double and its opposite."[15] All of these authors, with their individually distinctive features, are splendid examples, similar to Guy de Maupassant's Horla, whose muzzle pokes through in the pages of *On the Survival of Certain Myths and Several Other Myths in Growth or Formation* . . .

(continued from p. 91) assured that a new signal will be knocked-out to help her whenever she hesitates before drawing the next line. This collaboration is filled with harmony. The result is of great quality—but is suddenly ruined because he does not stop knocking, and in the end she tears up this document in a fit of sad rage. What did their joint drawing depict? One can see a clear division between a seemingly dead couple on the ground and a very white paradise above." Is it absurd to imagine this as a tragic rendition of the primordial androgyne of the alchemists? And could the Celt's Tir-na-Nog be the backdrop here? As René Daumal wrote in *Mugle,* only published in 1978 by Fata Morgana, "Each of us carried the other entirely inside."

*"'Who am I?' Always the same revenant, which amounts to saying still another," wrote Stanislas Rodanski in "La Nuit verticale," included in Alain-Valéry Aelberts and Jean-Jacques Auquier's *Poètes singuliers du surréalisme et autre lieux.* This cannot help but bring to mind Breton's metaphysical interrogation at the opening of *Nadja,* "Who am I . . . indeed why would it not all come down to knowing who I haunt? I must admit that this last word is misleading . . . it makes me while still alive play the role of a ghost, it obviously implies what I must have ceased to be in order to be *who* I am," as well as Nerval's, "I am another—and perhaps even hostile." It is again Rodanski to whom we owe the following passage: "At the head of a body formed by aspects of the personality, the author is separate from what manifests him. Decapitated, the head witnesses the life of his body's ghosts" (in *Artère,* n° 20, Winter 1985). The passage on the totem, with an incontestably magic dimension formed by a bloody seagull's wing and an old rudder on the beach of Penmarch is mentioned several times in what I know of his work and therefore seems particularly important to Rodanski.

†Duprey, born in 1930, committed suicide in 1959, a suicide evoked by Yves Elléouët in *Falc'hun* when he talks of "the avenue du Maine where someone hung himself." Duprey had written earlier, in 1946, "Because of you, my dear hanged man, my half-brother, my companion in anguish, I have denied the already seen, the already false, the already known."

How true Duprey's claim that "death is a double sign" and Gilbert-Lecomte's assertion that "everyone carries their own corpse on their back. Fulcanelli confided to Canseliet, "Our star is alone yet it is double." It so happens, writes Maurice Fourré in *Tête de Nègre,* that this double is "an omen of our death perhaps."[16] Fourré's phrase, Françoise Leclercq-Bolle De Bal suggests, after Edgar Morin, is "undoubtedly the sole great universal myth because it corresponds to a life experience: it is seen in the reflection, in the shadow, it is felt and sensed in nature; it is present in dreams."[17] And, still after Morin, a friend of Marguerite Duras and Dionys Mascolo and a fellow member of what was known as the group of rue Saint-Benoît she calls "ego alter" [which means "me otherwise"] this double "that possesses . . . within itself all the malefic powers of the self and all the major powers of the superego."

Who could say, for example, just what Loplop, this "personal ghost," specifically meant to Max Ernst, the "superior of the birds?" In Victor Brauner's works as well, a man born under the sign of Gemini, we note the "constant and disturbing presence" of the theme of the often malevolent double that arises from the depths of the fairy tales and legends that had fed the painter's childhood, as established by Margaret Montagne in "The Myth of the Double," her contribution to the catalog *Victor Brauner: Surrealist Hieroglyphs.*

Confides another Romanian, Ghérasim Luca in *Le Vampire passif,* clearly laying out the problem of the nature of this double:

> I always had the impression of being thought like Rimbaud and Lautréamont, but it never occurred to me that this other that thinks like me could step out of myself and appear before me in as tangible and concrete a way as any other external object. This time Déline Fetish* is thinking me.

Ferdinand Alquié cites a letter from Joë Bousquet, who wrote him, "What would you say if I told you that sometimes I feel to the point of delirium that I am thought?"

---

*Déline Fetish is an object Luca created for a woman he loved.

Perhaps it is Carrouges, tying together the themes of the ghost, the double, and objective chance, who can provide an acceptable answer to these questions by replacing the expression "dark powers" with a much more neutral reference to "manifestations of the unconscious" when he explains:

> Feeling like you are a ghost is a mental phenomenon that possesses an extremely concrete meaning. It indicates the extent to which one can feel like a stranger to oneself, to become disoriented in his normal ego awareness and be dragged down into subterranean layers of the mind, threatened by remote grumblings that rise from the underground lava of the mental labyrinth. The outside world begins to be shaken by the early symptoms of a seism of unknown nature. The individual then detects a vast framework within words, images, and thoughts he does not know, and in the interference of his ego and the world, he sees a subtle network of premonitions and magic coincidences. His own mind becomes the field of projections from dark powers.

Should we conclude from this, in the words of William Blake, that "everyman is in his Spectre's power?" And whoever says "double" is suggesting, in the absence of twinship, something disturbing, as in some of Brauner's paintings, or even monstrous, as in the novellas "Napoleon"[18] or "Jules César,"[19] both by the "surrealist mantis with the satin jaws,"* Joyce Mansour, or something androgynous, "all the magic of the mirror residing in that of the double."[20] The existence of a reflection is by nature perturbing, as underscored by Gilbert-Lecomte, who commented, "Whoever comes face to face with his double shall die." Mabille makes it all the more unsettling by saying, "Reflections and echoes lead to the center of the unconscious, to the origin of dream, to the place where desire confusedly expresses itself." Unless the mirror detours us via its reflection from the essential, inspiring disgust, as it does Jameux:

---

*Mansour was called this by Alain Joubert.

> This is why I hate mirrors, the degrading mirrors in which the man I am speaking of likes to arrogantly contemplate the reassuring and revolting face of his own little self that should make him vomit. Why not cover all the mirrors with a veil like the Student of Prague, and *dare direct your gaze inward* (italics added)?[21]

So it is a reflection and therefore a mirror that is an artifact, that allows passage to the other side of appearances if not travel between worlds. The mirror, "the most banal and most extraordinary of magical instruments," as Pierre Mabille says, is the one essential object to cover in the house of a dead man, in order to prevent his double from lingering. Rodanski, for example, spoke of it quite often in his texts, notably *Lancelot and the Chimera* or *La Victoire à l'ombre des ailes,* clearly establishing the link between dream and reality that object presumes.

> Uncovered mirrors create a translucent path. I indiscriminately aspired to transfiguration, penetrating this world that is only the sequel to the other, if it is no longer the same by virtue of what happened there, I spy a sign of life, contingent on all that foreshadows an individual's life, deliberate where once it was only a suspicion.

In his text "Ouverture Italienne," Claude Courtot explores his relationship to time, in a slightly desperate variant of Rimbaud's suggestion that real life is elsewhere.

> I walk on the edge of time that fascinates me like a mirror. At that very hour, I see you in this mirror and I see someone talking to you and who resembles me so closely that I would happily think it is me—all of me—if I did not simultaneously feel the sensation that I was still existing outside the mirror in a kind of temporary lower realm.[22]

Unica Zürn in *The Man of Jasmine,* another gripping description of the loss of self, obliquely exploits, as Mandiargues says in his preface, "the kinship of the narrative with a mirror and the aspect of mirage presented by the confession there. Furthermore it seems to me that the narrator continuously pursues her double through writing and questions it about what life has yet in store for her, she who is in the world reflected but not contained by the mirror. A split the reader cannot witness without anguish, if he knows the esoteric interpretations of the phenomenon." He then adds, "Unica Zürn's double in the silvering of the mirror where she remembers herself takes us farther, lower, higher, than any heroine in a novel."

Another possible destination is that place where premonitions take shape for the chosen few, as in Mandiargues's *Des cobras à Paris*.

> The vapor of breath or cigarette smoke in the narrow café, the air becomes murky, a halo appears on the glass of the mirror in which reflections sickly express themselves [and] appear as if they had climbed from the table.... Galet could take pride in being the only person in the world who knew how to look into mirrors.

This has a potentially tragic denouement thrown in: "The mirror died in a spiral of flame," as Rodanski wrote. Roger Gilbert-Lecomte, in the text for Sima's 1930 exhibition The Mystery of the Face, had noted earlier, "Under the sign of the HUMAN FACE there are worried eyes contemplating worrying mirrors where their faces of the depths live." Fourré, meanwhile, in *La Marraine du sel* (The Godmother of Salt), indicates, "Dead is the glass in the paradise of mirrors, which casts light on the hell of the face." This is because mirrors as interfaces or points of passage are assuredly objects smacking of a disturbing strangeness. "Nothing is better demonstrated today then the sur-normal vision in mirrors," writes René Sudre.

In any case, Breton noted in his 1962 text, "Pont Levis" (Drawbridge) that Mabille had already underscored their importance in the spring of 1938, in a text specifically titled "Mirrors" in the eleventh issue of *Minotaure*: "As to mirrors he lets us know that, if it is possible to find a comparison for our minds there, we must admit that 'its silvering consists of the red flow of desire.'" The doctor's understanding of the matter went much deeper in *Le Miroir du merveilleux* (The Mirror of the Marvelous), underscoring that "the mirror engenders the first metaphysical interrogations . . . causes us to doubt the evidence of our senses . . . poses the problem of illusions."

To a certain extent, perhaps because it, too, possesses a "magnetizing property" that "charges" the spectator, the cinema, although through a mediation of a more directly artistic nature, exists "in a blessed darkness conducive to illusions."* Precisely, the cinema raises the problem and takes the relay of mediumistic-like explorations in an approach that aims to give body to the beings of the night whose legitimacy Desnos had underscored in a 1927 article in *Le Soir* titled "Les rêves de la nuit transportés sur l'écran."

> And how not identify the darkness of the cinema with the darkness of the night, and films with dream! Blessed are those who enter the theaters with their heads still full of the tumult of their imaginations and ride double with their black and white heroes. . . . Isn't it consequently natural that the cinema would try to project dream on the screen? But if the attempts that have not failed utterly are rare, wouldn't this be because they misread the essential characters of dream, their sensuality, their absolute even baroque freedom, and a certain atmosphere that specifically conjures up infinity and eternity? It is for want of crossing through these uncleared domains, for want of developing in this surreal light, that so many films are inadequate or ridiculous.

Even better are Breton's remarks in the article "Comme dans un bois," which he contributed to *L'Âge du cinéma,* the review founded by Robert Benayoun, Georges Goldfayn, and Ado Kyrou: "It is a way of going to the movies the way others go to church." He then explains, "I think that from a certain angle, regardless of what is playing, it is here that the only absolutely *modern mystery* is celebrated." There might be good reason to recall here what the cinema—especially in the '20s— owed to Paul Philidor's "phantasmagoria," which was made famous

---

*These quotes are from André Breton and Robert Desnos.

at the end of the eighteenth century by Étienne-Gaspard Robert (1763–1837, known by the stage name Robertson, sometimes Étienne Robertson) chiefly due to a memorable séance held at the Capuchin monastery in Paris, which seems to have featured a skillful use of mobile retro-projection to recreate the world of the gothic novel.

Nor does Carrouges, recalling that "the works of the mind are also carried out on the inner dark room where mental images reveal themselves by being projected on the screen of consciousness," fail to emphasize that "films can open disturbing perspectives to us ... on the worlds that possibly surround us." Sometimes this phenomenon occurs in an oblique way, as in the case of Charles Duits. In his "Les Fantômes"—a phenomenon he analyzes as "concentrations of the mental substance that survives the individuals who produced it"—he describes his "completely inexplicable vision" in the ruins of the Château de Lacoste on September 27, 1966.

> You could have said I was watching the projection of a film. What was singular about this film was that the ruins played the role of the screen. They remained perfectly visible. But I saw them through the image of what the castle must have been like in the fourteenth century.

And he goes on to say, "I knew perfectly well I was looking at an *image:* I was not dreaming at all."[23]

There is also the case of Roger Caillois, who, when recounting his memories in *Le Fleuve Alphée,* explains with regard to reading the books of Jules Verne, "I preferred the *Castle of the Carpathians,* the forerunner of a kind of television or cinema in relief. The projection of recorded images replaces the ghostly apparitions of the gothic novel in it."[24] This perfectly underscores the nature of the connection between the poetic, dream image as it springs from writing, and its cinematographic transposition. Sometimes this idea is expressed in a more clear-cut fashion, and not necessarily innocently. For example, Yves Elléouët, in *Falc'hun,* speaks this way about what goes on in the dark halls:

Music announces the appearance of the ectoplasms. . . . He dreamt the film as much as saw it. . . . The dialogs of the film become dreamlike. The figures on the screen become distorted and transform into nothing but the play between light and shadow leading an incomprehensible Sabbath in slow motion.[25]

True, Artaud wrote in his 1927 article "Witchcraft and the Cinema":

Essentially the cinema reveals a whole occult life with which it puts us directly into contact. But we must know how to divine this occult life. . . . Raw cinema, taken as it is, in the abstract, exudes a little of this trance-like atmosphere eminently favorable for certain revelations.

It is also undoubtedly favorable to that "knowledge of the human abysses" of which Roger Gilbert-Lecomte spoke in *L'Alchimie de l'oeil: Le cinéma, forme de l'esprit* (Alchemy of the Eye: Cinema, Form of the Mind) in 1932. For Elléouët, the atmosphere is of the same nature, only "the disturbing strangeness" does not show up on the spot. But it can be found in the same work, by means of this image: "The earth was like a medium in a trance slowly expectorating an ectoplasm (this phenomenon is visible on several photos of Eusapia Paladino, for example, 'materializing' a ghost)." This also brings to mind some of Louis Darget's photos from the end of the nineteenth century. It is hard not to think of Darget when looking at some of Raoul Ubac's photos (*La Nébuleuse*, 1939), the "photo-graphics" from Jindrich Heisler's *De la même farine cycle* (1943), or even the work of the American surrealist Clarence John Laughlin, who was close to the Arsenal group, such as his evocatively titled photograph, *The Lamia Returns* (1973).

In the steps of Caillois, who convoked lamiae, empusae, and succubi pell-mell in his book *Le Mythe et l'homme*, Breton noted a woman's "forehead painted with the word Lamia" by Paollo Ucello (the first painter cited as a precursor of surrealism) "in the renowned frescoes of Santa Maria Novella" in his *L'Art magique*. Concerning the vampiric lamia he said:

She was the Lilith of the rabbis, the female faun who attempted to seduce Adam and engendered the phantomatic creatures of the desert; she is the vampiric nymph of curiosity (Plutarch) who can put in or remove her eyes at will and gives the children of men the venomous milk of dreams.

"After all," Duits tells us in "Science et magie" (part of *La Conscience démonique*):

> If we cannot perceive the "fluids," "waves," "effluvia," "vibrations," "auras," etc., that does not necessarily mean that these phenomena are illusory. It can also mean that for one reason or another we have lost the ability to perceive them or, what amounts to the same thing, not all of us have developed this faculty.

In "Les Fantômes," another part of *La Conscience démonique,* he shows that this ability has not been lost by recounting the episode of the "Scandicci Villa," near Florence, and the "*black woman*" who haunts it. "She was truly a *shadow* with the appearance of what photographers call a negative. She was like smoke with a fixed outline. During the day—for she was visible during the day—when she passed in front of a window, she became vaguely translucent." This clairvoyance, if I dare use that expression, is sometimes more scattered. Additional evidence is offered in Philippe Audoin's text on the Lallemand Hotel in Bourges, which he files under "the imprecise and disconcerting category of *discreetly* haunted houses." "Nothing here like the ghost castle" he adds, "but a place where the feeling of a presence, in no way malevolent, is felt from the start and grows until it arouses a slight uneasiness. We are welcomed—but by whom?"[26]

It is true, as Alquié observes in *The Philosophy of Surrealism*, that

> ghosts, whose return surrealism hopes for, cannot be seen by us, and can only appear as forces of the night when illuminated by some kind of light. In fact, the ghost that was seen one evening on the

Place Pigalle by Chirico, Aragon, and Breton, looked like a child selling flowers.

At least if we can believe Chirico's diagnosis! Members of the group gathered around Vincent Bounoure in France at the beginning of the 1970s performed experiments similar to the ones of the 1920s. Robert Guyon's article "Surrealists Seek Medium for Automatist Experiment," in the first issue of the *Bulletin de liaison surréaliste,* throws new light on the activity of their predecessors using the research of René Sudre (1880–1968). Sudre was the more or less legitimate heir of Pierre Janet and Frederic Myers* and played a lead role in the International Psychic Institute (in French, the Institut métaphysique international). Guyon's article relies most heavily on the third chapter of Sudre's book *Introduction à la métapsychique humaine* (Introduction to Human Metapsychics).

> René Sudre observes that in certain abnormal circumstances, some subjects abruptly abandon their customary personality to adopt a completely different one. He calls this phenomenon *prosopopeia* (from the Greek meaning theater mask, character). The study of prosopopeia will confirm an important notion: the kinship of somnambulistic, hypnotic, hysterical, and meta-psychological states. These states are all more or less characterized by the same tendency of personality modification. It could be said they reveal a personality breakdown.[27]

As early as what they would call a simple experiment in automatic writing, *The Magnetic Fields,* Breton and Soupault acknowledged they had experienced hallucinations, which the former suggested in a letter were potentially fatal. Francis Gérard, in the first issue of *La Révolution*

---

*Frederic Myers (1843–1901) is considered an important early depth psychologist who influenced, in particular, Pierre Janet, Théodore Flournoy, and Carl G. Jung. Pierre Janet (1859–1947) is one of the founding fathers of psychology and a major psychotherapist in the field of traumatic memory and dissociation. Janet also influenced André Breton who had received a training in psychotherapy during World War I.

surréaliste, confessed that "it seemed that the person who practiced this exercise could no longer disconnect from it totally!" By the same token they were always given broad consideration, Charles Jameux claims, as "there is a hallucinatory world inside us that we are not equipped to explain."

Jameux is in a good position to speak about this. Following a very serious car accident in November 1994 that left him in a coma for some time, he felt on several occasions "a very acute and pronounced feeling of (his) own death," which reminded him "of the Near Death Experiences (NDE) you read about in popular magazines." He related these experiences in *Souvenirs de la maison des vivants* in a style that fails to conceal the incredulity he felt in hindsight.

> The eyes of the motionless, prostrated body see the weightless spirit rise and, I could say, soar while the eyes of the spirit in glory—surrounded by luminous rays—overlooking everything from the top of the dream, see the body in its decline, stretched out and motionless. This sense of dissociation irresistibly brought to mind the gift of double sight mentioned by seventeenth-century Scotch writers attuned to the myths of our origins.

And this:

> Another time, I experienced a kind of vision. I was dying. My being was wending its way through what could be described as a wide corridor that had a dazzling light at its exit. When I reached the end of the corridor, I was swallowed up by this light.

Not being particularly drawn to mysticism, Jameux could not explain in an intellectually acceptable manner the decidedly strange visions that assailed him at this time other than by the high doses of morphine he received. There is no doubt that the mouths of shadows—unless it is Lautréamont's "immense vagina of darkness"—can prove voracious, as was earlier mentioned regarding Victor Hugo's entourage in Guernsey (see page 62), particularly for the unique Jules Allix!

Under the impetus of Alena Nadvornikova and Jan and Eva Svankmajer at the onset of the twenty-first century, the Czech surrealists launched into the production of mediumistic drawings, thereby reliving the very old spiritualist tradition of Bohemia and Moravia. This illustrates perfectly the ongoing nature of surrealist investigations.

They may also be the kinds of studies that confer full meaning on the complete title* of F. W. Murnau's film *Nosferatu*—the "most beautiful film in the world," according to Desnos.† The idea for this film was inspired by the Irishman Bram Stoker's *Dracula* and was suggested to the German filmmaker by the producer Albin Grau, a close associate of Aleister Crowley, whom Breton, who had dreamed of the monster, cites in *Les Vases communicants*. This book includes a photograph of this creature: "When he was on the other side of the bridge, the ghosts came to meet him."[28]

"If we do not know the ghosts that will come to meet us when we reach the other side of the bridge, how distressing to think we could remain among them the little man we are on this side. We shall stop being that man when they stop being ghosts," Schuster says in *Les Fruits de la passion*, before going on to say, "Concerning Breton, I invite this to be read in a silent interrogation still waiting for a response, not like someone who built the bridge, but as someone who gave himself to the ghosts."

If the idea of a bridge, therefore, of a crossing, suggests Michel Carrouges (with all the ulterior motives we have a right to surmise from him) interests the surrealists, wouldn't it be because it provides them with a solution to the problem of the "cyclical, and consequently irremediable, misfortune of human destiny"? This cannot help but bring

---

*[The subtitle of *Nosferatu* is *A Symphony of Horrors*. —*Trans*.]
†Lotte Eisner, in her book *L'Écran démoniaque* (The Haunted Screen), writes, "In fact, seeing this film again today, one cannot fail to be struck by what Bela Balazs called 'the glacial currents of air from the beyond.'" The subtitle of *Nosferatu* seems to have left a lasting effect on the members of the surrealist group, insofar as in 1938, in *Le Mythe et L'homme*, we find from Caillois's pen this phrase of the highest interest: "Hardly has the traveler set foot in Greece than, as in the country of the vampires, the ghosts come to meet him."

Markale's observation to mind (whose echo we shall hear further on) in his article "Rome et l'épopée celtique," that this is a "frequent epic theme in Celtic literature. The bridge or its equivalent, the ford, is a frontier that cannot be touched. It is the contact point between two worlds, that of the living and that of the beyond," of the Sidh and the mounds.[29]

The author of the first French book on this "exceptional 'shadow tamer,'" Charles Jameux similarly points out in his *Murnau* (one of the rare books devoted to the seventh art by a member of the movement) how in *Nosferatu,* a film that paradoxically marks "the eruption of open air and nature into the German cinema," after crossing the bridge, "the hero enters an imaginary world . . . where the values of the countryside are suddenly reversed: it seems to him that he is traversing a world of anti-matter bathed in the strange light of dream."[30] This helps clarify Alquié's suggestion that "the prestige of Desnos, mentioned in *Nadja,* stems from the facility with which he makes this transition and crosses the bridge."

Contradicting Michel Carrouges, who had put forth the notion in *André Breton and the Basic Concepts of Surrealism* that "the bridge that led to the domain of the phantoms had been destroyed" and that from this point of view, "free circulation no longer existed," and instead endorsed his idea that "the point of projection for revenants and their strange domains is the living man himself, in flesh and blood," Wolgang Paalen, "who showed us time and space more as a shaman than a physicist,"[31] spun this metaphor to its conclusion with equal facility but much more tragically:

> On the other side of the bridge it will no longer be phantoms coming to meet me—the glass mountain whose glaring reflection sometimes blinds me and which far too often has only reflected my own face will open for me and restore intact the treasure of my childhood.[32]

A Totemic Landscape then. Unless it is the *Paradise of Phantoms* (dedicated though to automatons) mentioned by Benjamin Péret in the December 1933 *Minotaure,* in a phrase that curiously echoes Carrouges:

"Because every man is a revenant that lurks in the ruins of paradise!" Charles Jameux mentions again, in his book *Murnau, Nosferatu* and the "great wind of freedom that blows from it," and quite rightly observes that this film "on love and death, magic and fear," a "voyage into pure interiority," overlays a certain number of the surrealist themes of first importance, which may explain the enthusiasm this film aroused in Breton, and that I have already examined or will examine in the course of this book.

Jameux decodes the film as follows:

> Hutter, in quest of the *secret*, has to go down into the castle crypt thereby symbolically retracing the psychological itinerary that travels from the consciousness to the unconscious state. Having entered by transgression (the bridge) the land of memory and the past (the country of the ghosts), and done so at a critical time (Saint George's Night), he is led to descend to the heart of his thought's architecture (the castle) and to confidently enter, impelled by his intuition, its central point (the castle crypt). It is on this condition alone, uncovering his own fear, that Nosferatu is revealed to him.

This proximity is one also recognized by Julien Gracq in his 1981 preface to Michel Bouvier and Jean-Louis Leutrat's *Nosferatu*. In this text he weaves together a network of familiar correspondences.

> Prepared far in advance and remotely foreshadowed in my childhood years by reading the *Castle of the Carpathians,* clustering around those enthralling images imported entirely from gothic novels and Wagnerian opera, from *The Old English Baron*[33] and *The Flying Dutchman* alike, a definitive derealization of the Transylvanian landscapes by creating a more perilously haunted Scotland, promoted to the status of the land of ghostly activity, *Nosferatu* represented to me both a summa and a limit, a treasure—thanks to the infallible accuracy of the poetic instinct, like a glance from a plastic eye.[34]

Jameux also strongly suspects, moreover, that Murnau, if not "an 'adept' of the alchemical concept or even the disciple of a teacher of the science of Hermes" (which is not supported by any documented proof), was at the very least a "hypersensitive and superstitious individual" whose aesthetic bears the stamp of an "attraction for the noumenal realms, anxious to reveal life's hidden face (I should say occulted)." And he emphasizes that "certain details . . . certain signs, are implicit in his work, which should hasten the genesis of 'the alchemical hypothesis' of that work," compelling us to "consider his artwork from beginning to end in accordance with an alchemical correspondence and symbology." This may even better explain the surrealist infatuation for his work.

As I have already mentioned Péret, this seems like a good time to note that Marcel Jean, who, like Kurt Seligmann, took a strong interest in heraldry, represented Péret "with Gules in an annulet of vair enclosing a gold fusil" in the "Almanach surréaliste du demi-siècle"! The "Almanach," published under the direction of Breton, is a collective work, a collection of drawings, paintings, and various texts. And while we are on the subject of heraldry, Elléouët also touched on it with the sketches published in the final pages of *Tête cruelle*, in which he speaks of "violent death on moors quartered by gules" and "birds perched on oaks/–Sinople," just a word to indicate, with the Gracq of *Les Eaux étroites* (The Narrow Waters), that "the emblematic bonds woven at the beginnings of ancient families between the name, the arms, the colors, and the device cannot help but shed light on their origin" and especially that the art of the blazon, which originated in the twelfth century out of the necessity for combatants to recognize each other in medieval melees, takes its name from the Old German *blasen*, "to blow," which belongs to the same semantic field as the Latin *spiritus* and the Greek *pneuma*. "To blazon," Joseph Péladan said as early as 1910, is "to incarnate an idea in its form!"

Taking an opposite approach to the Gothic image with which the ghosts are usually identified, Giorgio de Chirico, a man who Breton says "is only touched by mystery," in his book *Hebdomeros* (first published in 1929) combines ghosts—and this may be a reminiscence of his youth in Greece—with the blazing sun of noon, that is to say "the hour of phantoms that are much more interesting and unique than those that ordinarily appear to us on the stroke of midnight in abandoned cemeteries or the wan light of a moon breaking through storm clouds, in the middle of the lonely ruins of a cursed castle, ghosts that all of you as well as I know quite well from having known them since our earliest childhood." Although the air in Chirico's work has, as Georges Ribemont-Dessaignes said in 1928, "the strange aridity of the Latin twilight"!

Nevertheless, it is also this characteristic of disturbing singularity that will prompt Desnos to observe about Erckmann-Chatrian's *Fantastic Tales* in 1940, "Yet a ghost in the hot sun of high noon would be even more terrible."[35] But there are some who go even further, like Aragon, who in *Une vague de rêves* dares to write about the hypnotic sleep sessions.

> The great shock of such a performance necessarily called for delirious explanations: the beyond, the transmigration of souls, the marvelous. The price of such interpretations was incredulity and sneers. *In truth, such interpretations were less false than was supposed* (italics added).

Like Elie-Charles Flamand who recalled a bizarre event, in "Souvenirs sur Stanislas Rodanski," which he contributed for a special issue of *Supérieur Inconnu,* in autumn 2007:

> It was during the very mild winter of the year 1955 that I took a photograph of you that once developed, was revealed to be a paranormal document. You were concentrating with your eyes closed and a release of spiritual forces materialized in a powerful fluid was coming out of you. Bushes of lightning emerging from your feet enveloped your body and your forehead was crowned by a white flame. Such effluvia are naturally so subtle that the eye cannot perceive them, but the emulsion on the photographic film can sometimes record them. So, you possessed parapsychological abilities (as is often the case with artists).

This cannot help but bring to mind Victor Brauner's painting *Heron of Alexandria* (see plate 4) as well as the works of Adrien Dax, of whom José Pierre (*Le Surréalisme Aujourd'hui*) extols the "particularly inspired graphism in which the graces of 'Modern Style'* and the disturbing fluidic emanations of mediumistic artists combine," comparing them quite poetically to "the dance of Ariel in the clearing of the sky through which comets travel." Once again we should acknowledge that we are not so far from Louis Darget.

Like Marko Ristic, again, expanding on an idea expressed by Breton in *Surrealism and Painting* during an interview with Feliks Pasic that was published in 1971 by the Yugoslavian newspaper *Borba*, titled "For the Eighty Years of Max Ernst."

> I want to stress the mediumistic, more exactly metempsychotic, nature of his appearance among us. Inexplicably reincarnated in this magician, besides several extraordinary phantoms, were Hieronymous Bosch, Leonard da Vinci, and Cornelius Agrippa. It is not by chance that the archmage Agrippa was born so close to Max Ernst's birthplace. He was one of the greatest occultists of all time as well as a philosopher, doctor, alchemist, and author of the treatises *De Occulta Philosophica* and *De Nobilitate Praecellentia Foeminei Sexus*. Is it possible to find a painting that corresponds better to the fantastic theories of Agrippa on the three worlds, on the spirit in germination in the universe, on the divine kabbalistic radiation, on the magical forces of things and elements, and so forth, than that of Max Ernst?[36]

Cornelius Agrippa de Nettesheim (1486–1535) was the first thinker to classify the practices inherited "from the gnostics, alchemists, and astrologers of the Middle Ages" under the label of "occult philosophy." (Breton owned several copies of his *De Occulta Philosophica* as early as 1924.) Seligmann tells us this man's religion was "a blend of

---

*"Modern Style" refers to the artistic movement of the final years of the nineteenth century and the first years of the twentieth, called in France "Art Nouveau."

Christianity, Neo-Platonism, and kabbalah," and he also notes that "his study of Plotinus, Iamblichus, and Porphyry plunged [him] into the supernatural and the occult" so deeply that "his enthusiasm for these philosophers of the marvelous prevailed over his critical sense."

In a similar vein, Ghérasim Luca, in *Le Vampire passif* (The Passive Vampire; written in Bucharest in 1941), when speaking of the world of "tomorrow," predicts:

> Ghosts will be common and accessible, and there will no longer be any need for that pretentious ritual of trance séances for mediumistic phenomena to occur: in a world where mediumship will be a common quality, the projections of our unconscious occur naturally like a slip of the tongue.[37]

This echoes Antonin Artaud in the text "To Have Done With Masterpieces," included in *Le Théâtre et son double* in which he wishes for "a theatre that induces trance, like the dances of the Dervishes and the Aissawa," or in the different essays that make up the collection *Les Tarahumaras*. Pierre Mabille, citing William Seabrook, examines in his book *The Mirror of the Marvelous* the type of radical trances of Haitian zombies, specifying that they are the result of the manipulation of "diabolical imaginations . . . haunted by the desire to bring a part of humanity down to the state of automatons, devoid of independence, personal needs, psychological anxiety." This is the "possession phenomena" that Breton observed in a 1953 interview (published in *Entretiens*) has "always been one of surrealism's poles of interest."

During his first stay in Brazil (between 1929 and 1931), Benjamin Péret took an interest in that country's African religions, which he claimed to study from a poetic viewpoint. This resulted in a collection of thirteen heavily documented articles around the theme "of an initiatory journey in the mystical labyrinth of African thought," which were published from November 25, 1930, to January 30, 1931, in the *Diario da Noite* under the generic heading "Candomblé e Makumba [*sic*]." The article "When the Poet Meets the Ethnologist: The African Religions of Brazil" by Leonor L. de Abreu, in the exhibition catalog *Benjamin*

Péret et les Amériques, shows how "as a veritable pioneer, Benjamin Péret lends himself to psychological, social, geographical, and exotic states of openness," and how, "first among his peers, he performs the task of a true 'ethnographical surrealism.'" He studied the *candomblé,* "the purest expression of the African religion," whose "organized worship goes back to the first decades of the nineteenth century," and especially the *macumba,* "the illegitimate daughter of candomblé, indigenous beliefs, and the gradual simplification of the rite in the white milieu where it still survives,"* which is also "more permeable to expressions of popular Catholicism" and "synonymous with black magic." Péret familiarized himself with these "two rites [which] are centered on the phenomenon of trance possession . . . employing ritual sacrifices" against a backdrop of dancing and beating drums, "both having recourse to divinatory practices and implementing magical-religious activities" during ceremonies that reach their height when "the deities begin to come down, in an order of precedence and 'possess' their 'horse,' through the ritual phenomenon of trance, i.e., when the dancers are seized by convulsions and "fall from the saint." This is the same vocabulary we find in voodoo.

"Péret," Abreu adds, "is one of the first authors to report on a ceremony of 'counter-witchcraft, of white magic,' the umbanda, which comes out of the macumba and integrates, by re-crafting them into a new synthesis, African, indigenous, and Catholic elements with the white spiritualism of Allan Kardec!" Everything is connected . . . In any case, she adds:

> In the Afro-Brazilian religions and their mythology, the poet discovers what constitutes the very motor of poetic creation: magical, mythical thought that harms logical certitudes and the obvious principles of causality. The marvelous in the raw state is in tune there with daily life, myth is still fecund there as is magic—the common denominator uniting the wizard and the poet—still operates there at an unconscious level.

---

*This quote and the last one in this paragraph are by Péret; the others in this paragraph are by Abreu.

This is a lesson Péret will never forget.

Around this same time, Michel Leiris, who defined himself with his customary lucidity and ruthlessness in *Images de marque* as "an atheist worshiper of the moon; a positivist starved for miracles; a miscreant inconsolable over the death of the fairies, and a skeptic armed with his icons, talismans, and personal ex-votos. Someone who has been disenchanted talking of trying to bewitch himself again. A fan of myths who demands they not be myths,"[38] shared an interest equaling Péret's in these matters, particularly after his sojourn in Africa with Marcel Griaule. Even in his most strictly scientific works, like *La Possession aux Génies 'Zar' en Éthiopia du Nord* and *La Possession et ses aspects théâtraux chez les Éthiopiens de Gondar* (Possession and Its Theatrical Aspects Among the Ethiopians of Gondar),[39] on the Zar ceremonies and their priestess Malkam Ayyadou, he was openly and professionally fascinated (as he would also show in the case of voodoo worship) by the phenomena of possession and trances connected to this "institution, a survival of religions that preceded Christianity in these lands."* Annie Le Brun, in *De l'éperdu*,[40] even ventures the hypothesis (after working on an unpublished notebook by Leiris and discovering that he "had entirely developed under the sign of Roussel") that "Raymond Roussel would have been the *zar* of Michel Leiris," exercising over him "a veritable grip and influence that seems to have registered far more deeply than something literary and in a semiconscious/semiunconscious way for close to fifty years."

> *Proud Flame*
> *and stiff blade*
> *the friend of sylphs and fairies*
> *WIFREDO LAM*
> *true elf or sprite*
> *with frail but rapid fingers.*

Like his friend Michel Leiris, who wrote the above poem in 1986,

---

*"These lands" refers to Ethiopia and even the entire horn of Africa.

the Cuban painter Wifredo Lam was also marked by the cases of possession he witnessed both in Haiti and Cuba. The half-human, half-horse figures in a number of his paintings cannot fail to remind us that in Caribbean worship, the individual possessed by the "saint," the *loa* of voodoo or the *orisha* of Santeria, is called the "horse," which is depicted in a fairly obvious way in a painting like Lam's *Clairvoyance* (1950) (see plate 5).

This mediumistic-possession relationship naturally brings us to shamanism, that vision of a cosmic balance in which man is one with the cosmos, defined by Roger Caillois in *Le Mythe et l'homme* as a manifestation of the "power of the individual struggling against the natural order of reality," an approach that leads to magic, in other words something coming from the "primitive need of the ego to disengage from an ungraspable reality and acquire power with the aid of magic."[41] This phenomenon is also considered among other forms of "primitive" thought in its relationship with surrealism and dream by Jules Monnerot in *Modern Poetry and the Sacred,* which undoubtedly explains why Breton valued Monnerot's book so highly (if we can believe the short note added by Gérard Legrand in the *Dictionnaire général du surréalisme et de ses environs*). Breton and Legrand also explained in *L'Art magique* how "shamanism is based on the possession of the sorcerer by his spirit, a possession conceived in the form of a sexual dominance obtained during an epilepsy fit." They go on to say, "The extreme personality dilution of the shaman, simultaneously a neurotic, medicine man, and (sometimes) official wizard of his tribe, probably cast its shadow over the pre-Hellenic oracles by way of Thrace over Babylon, and more certainly over Tibet. . . . But shamanic influence was also exercised over the old artisanal folklore of Lithuania, the Slavic countries, and perhaps even further west."

Shamans are a distinct kind of intercessor; because they are most often tied to so-called primitive cultures, they also make a regular appearance in the surrealist universe—implicitly or explicitly—such as in the works of Ithell Colquhoun or Jacques Hérold. There is also Roger Gilbert-Lecomte's magnificent text "Horrible Révélation . . . la seule," which recalls that man ought to remember that "his

Being is the home of countless Spirits: the ancient Soul of the Clan, the Manes of the ancestors and his Animal Father, and his Plant Elder, and the Father of Stone, and finally the Father Spirit of the Universe in miniature." Starting in 1927, Masson began giving "the painter's gesture the value of a rite," according to Sarane Alexandrian, and started producing "sand paintings" to which he would later add feathers and seashells, which earned him the nickname of Feather Man from his friends. Roberto Matta proceded similarly in the 1960s with his series *Cuba Frutto Bomba* by adding Cuban dirt to the paint, which allegedly conferred to the works "a sacred, and so to speak telluric, character" in order to "make [it] a mirror of the earth."[42]

This brings to mind Max Ernst wearing the feather hat of a Hopi wizard when welcoming his friends to his property of Huisnes in Touraine, so close to the alleged location of the Abbey of Thélème, or using the reproduction of a ritual Indian mask in his sculpture *The Capricorn* (1948). Breton's taste for American Indian and Eskimo masks is well known, less so is Matta's *Automatic Portrait of Federico Garcia Lorca*.[43] This portrait, with its Cyclopean eye, inevitably conjures up these masks, just as it recalls the automatic and poetic nature of all shamanic speech. Stephen Schwartz also analyzes the shaman, stating, "The 'false death' of the shaman, the 'real life' of the surrealists: these emblems are our surest guides in the boundless quest in which we are engaged. Our need for light is insatiable."[44]

The somewhat more marginal work of artist Jackson Pollock (who was influenced by Picasso, Miro, Matta, Ernst, and Masson), a seminal figure of abstract expressionism (which Robert Motherwell said would have been better called "abstract surrealism"), was undeniably influenced by automatism, shamanism, and its totems, and more broadly by American Indian cultures, not to mention Jung's depth psychology—which he knew by way of his first analyst, Dr. Joseph L. Henderson. This was shown in Pollock's paintings, such as *Birth* (1938–1941) (see plate 6), in which an Eskimo mask has been identified, *Guardians of the Secret* (see plate 7), or *Gothic* (painted during the time he was close to Peggy Guggenheim). With respect to *Guardians of the Secret* (1944), Leonhard Emmerling went so far as to suggest an influence from the theosophical teachings of Krishnamurti and Rudolf Steiner, both linked at one time or another to Helena Blavatsky or to her school, before adding:

> There is nothing surprising then if certain signs inscribed in the center rectangle, which should represent or contain the mystery, are probably inspired by the fourth book of *De Occulta Philosophia* by that great connoisseur of kabbalistic literature cited earlier, Agrippa von Nettesheim. Pollock knew this work from having seen two illustrated pages from it in the February–March 1942 issue of *View*.[45]

Cornelius Agrippa and *View*—again!

Inasmuch as we find ourselves among more or less malevolent powers, let's add that the path of the surrealists during their American exile even crossed that of the Great Old Ones, Cthulhu, Dagon—the monstrous half-man, half-fish hybrid that makes a brief appearance in the Bible—Nyarlathotep, or Yog Sothoh, who had been awakened by the son of an Egyptian Rite Mason, Howard Phillips (H. P.) Lovecraft. Lovecraft, who was highly versed in the field of fantasy literature, as shown by his book *Supernatural Horror in Literature,* was the author of texts he called "Gothic horrors," which possess elements reminiscent of Lautréamont, namely through their "horrifying reversal of the Christian thematic."[46] Robert Allerton Parker was the first to devote a text to the author of "The Dunwich Horror," with "Such Pulp as Dreams Are Made On" (which also examined the work of Lovecraft's friend Clark Ashton Smith, whose name had already appeared in "First Papers of Surrealism" in issue 2–3 of *VVV* in March 1943). Franklin Rosemont of the Chicago group and even Gérard Legrand in France were quick to follow suit; an article by Legrand, "H. P. L. and the Black Moon," appeared in the first issue of *Médium*. In it Legrand writes, "Lovecraft's grandeur resides in nothing less than the creation of a personal mythology that makes modern history look ridiculous. Scattered in pulp magazines until his death, this mythology is evidence of authentic occult knowledge treated with total freedom." He then concludes this article, "Rarely has so much rigor been used to evoke abysses." Robert Benayoun, in a brief item titled "Babel Revisited," appearing in the fourth issue of *Médium,* sharply attacks the translator of an unnamed work by the "hermit of Providence," but which could easily be *The Color Out of Space,* an ad for which appeared at the back of this same issue. Benayoun described the American's "book . . . as spun from shadow" and saw in it "the greatest endeavor of collective panic of the half-century, the sure progression through the awareness of an anxiety drawn from the source of the ages." He also took the trouble to praise the author's "imperturbable, anachronistic, and solemn style."

Legrand returned to this subject in *La Brèche,* n° 8 (November 1965), adding, "Religious historians generally contain theosophists who don't know it—those who Lovecraft criticized (not without naïveté) for their 'blissful optimism.'" Remedios Varo, Jean-Pierre Duprey, and the future leader of the Phases group, Edouard Jaguer—contrary to Breton—also greatly esteemed the American, according to the testimony left by Jaguer personally in his book *Le Surréalisme face à la littérature* (Surrealism at the Hands of Literature),[47] as did Yves Elléouët. While deploring Lovecraft's rudimentary style, Julien Gracq, who seems to have particularly liked "Dagon," also felt Lovecraft was participating in the renewal of the novel by the efforts of imagination his books presume,[48] whereas Mandiargues reports in *Le Cadran lunaire** on "the success of Lovecraft's once scorned writings and of the audience granted to the people of his school." Finally, Sarane Alexandrian, in his *Histoire de la philosophie occulte* (History of Occult Philosophy), makes this observation, whose full importance we shall see later: "A book on twentieth-century gnosis should also include the fantasy novelist H. P. Lovecraft, who was inspired by the Syriac text by Teodor bar Konaï on manicheism." Konaï was the eighth-century author of a *Liber Scholiorum,* which "stands out," Jean Doresse tells us, "by the strange nature of certain heresies it helped save from oblivion."

---

*[A *cadran lunaire* is a moon dial as opposed to a sun dial. —*Trans.*]

4

SURREALISM AND DIVINATION

An anonymous will to clairvoyance...
ALAIN JOUFFROY

What the Seers see is always identical.
ROGER GILBERT-LECOMTE,
"L'HORRIBLE RÉVÉLATION... LA SEULE"

A catchphrase from an early 1920s surrealist flier read, "You who do not see, think of those who see," which perfectly, though obliquely, explains the group's position on clairvoyance, including both the poets' experiments and the fortune-tellers' daily experiences, although Pierre Mabille would write twenty-five years later, "Unfortunately, we know almost nothing about clairvoyance" (when discussing William Blake, whom his contemporaries called "mad Blake," but whom Mabille considered "one of the most important prophets of modern times... expounding on what our truth is and will be for centuries"). Mabille notes:

> Psychiatrists regard it as a mental derangement, a pathological symptom, a hallucinatory modality. But who gave them the authority to

take the extremely deplorable average man as term of comparison and as symbol of the normal?

... Clairvoyance is generally a temporary state that is triggered by a powerful psychic upheaval, an exacerbation of sensibility connected most often to a crisis of passion.

... While the nature of the visionary phenomenon remains obscure, the conditions favoring its formation are better known to us and we *retrospectively* analyze with greater acuity the psychological and social mechanisms that created the convulsionaries of Saint-Médard, the illuminated prophets of the Cévennes, the Cathar martyrs, and which, more generally, are at the origin of various artistic and religious sects.

This observation lucidly takes us straight to the heart of the matter. Additional reinforcement to the idea is provided by a notion we will see reemerge in another context: "In the vision as in the dream, the unconscious, dissatisfied with reality, builds a world *commensurate with its desire.*"

"The phenomenon of poetic clairvoyance," Marc Eigeldinger writes in his "Notes on the Poetics of Clairvoyance," "arose out of German Romanticism,"[1] and it was so widespread that Hegel felt comfortable stating in his *Philosophical Propaedeutic,* "The poet is a seer." Victor Hugo next installed "poetry in the 'fullness of the great dream' thanks to its imagination's visionary and prophetic power." However, it was Rimbaud who made it an "instrument and mode of consciousness with which the poet explores the space of his being and his soul," the product of a "promethean and satanic experiment performed in the movement of revolt, in the confrontation with the threats of madness or death," an experiment during which "the poet's ego becomes *an action* through an expansion commensurate to humanity and the world," inhabited as he is by an *impersonal process,* by the awareness of being, to use Jung's terminology, "a collective man that bears and expresses the unconscious and active soul of humanity," and who "participates in the sphere of archetypes and projects itself in the universal where it discovers the sources of poetic substance." (This is Jung's terminology, as reported by Marc Eigeldinger.)

Charles Duits, in *Vision et hallucination: L'experience du Peyotl en littérature* (Vision and Hallucination: The Experience of Peyote in Literature), in 1960, proposed a similar though more lyrical and mystical approach to the poet as "not a man who puts words together, but as a man who sees and believes" and of vision as a "more acute perception":

> What is vision? The perception of unity. I call a visionary anyone who has this perception, even if no figure accompanies it. He is the man in whom the existence of the multiple and the other does not destroy certainty, the man who foresees the irradiation of the One through variegation and diversity. He is actually a visionary because appearance is a laceration.

In the same vein, Vera Linhartova in *Joseph Sima* observes:

> The original meaning of the word vision is "perception of a supernatural reality," synonym of "apparition," "revelation," or "illumination," and Sima is therefore a visionary as he is fundamentally incapable of imagining plastic forms outside a total vision of the world. Before being a painter, he is a thinker and a visionary, a Seer in the sense of the word as understood by Breton and the poets of the Grand Jeu . . .

In other words, Sima was a man seeking to synchronize the real and the imaginary.

Breton, in *Daybreak,* explains in a way that is a bit staggered but finally quite logical if we recall the importance he grants to automatic writing, that the visionary is first and foremost a listener who feverishly notes "this unforeseen and unforeseeable confidence of the subconscious to the conscious that he above all seeks to capture for purposes of clairvoyance,"* without completely understanding it before being gripped, in a second phase, by illumination. He revisited this in "Silence

---

*Carrouges in *André Breton et les données fondamentales du surréalisme.*

Is Golden"[2] in which he wrote, "The great poets have been 'auditories' not visionaries. At any rate, in their case vision, 'illumination' is not the 'cause' but the 'effect.'"

It is therefore quite natural that, at their level, the seeresses, these "pythonesses born of the coitus of gas and stream," according to Michel Leiris, priestesses of divination and the "sole tributaries and guardians of the secret," would be honored in a 1925 letter in which "the poet who never wears a mask"*[3] declares, "Everything the future surrenders to me falls into a marvelous field. . . ." So it is all the more natural that Breton in the *First Surrealist Manifesto* also pointed out, "The surrealist voice that shook Cumae, Dodona, and Delphi is nothing other than the voice that dictates my less wrathful discourses." It is the voice that Schuster (in *Les Fruits de la passion*), citing Yves Battistini, invites us to "listen to like the sibyl of Heraclitus 'whose delirious voice proclaims words without light, finery, or perfume, crossing through the voices of millennia by virtue of the god that gives them life.'" This "same voice," a critical Caillois tells us, "arose from the entrails of dazed virgins, murmured in the foliage of divine oaks, fell from the lips of an angel for a kneeling prophet, and is what we hope today will draw into the light the eddies of the totally animal stream of blood and desires that rolls in the depths of each individual a dark, fiery lava."[4]

By all evidence Breton granted the highest importance to the oracular dimension: "Yes, I cannot be mistaken here, yours is clearly this tone that is rarely attained and maintains itself without difficulty, the oracle," he wrote to the young Charles Duits in 1943. Unica Zürn published in 1967 a set of anagram poems and etchings, *Oracles et spectacles,* on which she had been working for at least four years. It is interesting in this regard to note that René Char, in *Seuls demeurent* (Alone Remain), written between 1938 and 1944, takes his distance from the movement with the phrase, "The oracle does not make me its vassal" (which can be interpreted in a number of ways).

In the text of "L'Horrible Révélation . . . la seule," Roger Gilbert-Lecomte, acting as a spokesperson for the entire Grand Jeu, inasmuch as

---

*"The poet who never wears a mask" is the name the Czech surrealist Viteslav Nezval gave Breton in his book *Rue Git-le-Coeur.*

André Rolland de Renéville, who regarded clairvoyance as "a new mode of consciousness," had expressed a similar opinion in the second issue of their review, confided five years later, "Clairvoyance is experimental metaphysics." In a footnote, Gilbert-Lecomte makes what, I believe, is a major point about this "experimental metaphysics."

> Hasn't this metaphysic been sensed by the philosophical tradition of Pythagoras, Heraclitus, Plato, Plotinus, the Gnostics, Apollonius of Tyana, Denis the Aeropagite, Giordano Bruno, Spinoza, and even Hegel for which the culmination of the dialectic is the concrete notion?

These are the names of a lineage we should keep in mind. Truthfully, there should be no surprise about this predilection for divination in people who adopted Rimbaud's motto, "The poet should make himself seer." The same is true of people like Max Ernst, who declared, "I have created a seer out of the blind man I once was," or Breton, who quoted the famous phrase of Novalis in his second Haitian lecture: "The totally conscious man is called a seer." Breton also noted that "the expression 'All has been written' should be taken literally." It is true that the distinction made here between visionary and seer is fairly vague.

In her book *Surréalisme et sexualité,* Xavière Gauthier mentions—between anathemas—a drawing of Brauner's, on the margins of which the painter noted:

> This woman whose hair has transformed into a bird of prey, and whose eyes are haloed by luminous rays while retaining the opaque light of those who do not see, is a seer who wears the symbols of great abundance on her luxurious, magic robe. In her right hand is the flower of fire that opens the secrets of the imagination, in the left hand the void that counterbalances it.

These attributes confer the nature of a "both benevolent and dreadful magician [on her]." She is benevolent and dreadful because, as Pierre Mabille says, "Every sermon casts a kind of enchantment."

And what about the colorful Madame Rosa depicted by Clovis Trouille in 1944 or of the implausible portrait of Madame Sacco, who was also frequented by Max Ernst and was the very same who inspired Artaud's August 1926 *Lettre du Voyant* (dedicated to André Breton) and whose photo and address can be found in *Nadja*? Nadja, herself, was provided, it seems, with solid abilities in this domain—"always, naturally in what the spiritualists call a clairvoyant state, in a constant, perfect state of availability," as Nadeau sums it up. She knew it, too, as shown by the self-portrait she did of herself as a seer, one of her rare surviving drawings.

There is also the disturbing, wild-eyed marquise Luisa Casati, Gabriele D'Annuzio's muse, who dreamed "of being a living work of art" and never went anywhere without her crystal ball, whom Man Ray photographed in 1922 for *The Portrait of My Soul* (see plate 8).

In *Le Bridge de Madame Lyane* (The Bridge of Madame Lyane), Georges Limbour describes the "extra-lucid Madame Raffa, who reads in a glass ball, surely the world in there is miniature like the one seen when looking through opera glasses the wrong way." This ball, the preeminent tool of visual automatism, is one she opens "like the fruit of hope." Limbour allows this "merchant of illusions," Madame Raffa, who first used her gift charitably before making it the mainstay of her profession, to speak for herself, and here are her remarks, which have the merit of reflecting all the ambiguity of the surrealist position on seers:

> Chiromancer? No . . . the hand: a pretext for meditation, the weight of the hand soft and inert like that of a corpse, fat or bony, their heat rose inside me, these hands inspired me, the intoxication of knowing exalted my pride, I talked, I invented, I thought I knew everything. . . . My friends talked of my gift, and I was consulted as if I were an all-powerful and dreadful priestess. There were those whose skin and gestures were charged with meaning and confessions, those whose faces were stamped with signs and whose secret rose to the surface of their eyes, rich with prophecy material. . . . How I loved the fate of men! I often cheated, despite my gifts, when my sight

grew weak, when I was groping in the dark, and perhaps then, so close to lying, I brushed against the truth. I used ruse and deceit, and even information taken in advance. A charlatan's gimmicks? No, no, I looked for help to walk the labyrinth and the night.[5]

This good lady is absolved, moreover, by Michel Carrouges, who states in his book on Breton, "Aren't the seers using tarot cards, tea-leaves, and crystal balls looking for devices to project beneath their eyes of flesh the sights they have a hard time discovering in the zone of their subconscious where they enter into contact with that of their clients and even with others?" And then, as René Sudre says in his book *Introduction à la métapsychique humaine,* which Carrouges also cites:

> The faces of cards, tea leaves, the flocculations of egg whites, etc., are means of stimulating the unconscious vision. In these last two cases and in analogous forms of divination, a grouping of particles or a tangle of variously colored lights offer points of concentration to the subject and induce hallucinations.[6]

It is also one of Sarane Alexandrian's fictional heroines, Hermine de Charménil, who boasts of having "cast [the horoscope] of all her friends." He explains in his book *L'Homme des lointains* (The Man of Far Places) that she is skilled in the art of casting horoscopes and a good fortune-teller, although not professional. The remarks this upper middle-class woman at loose ends lets fall under Alexandrian's pen are highly significant and testify to the author's interest in this matter beyond his fictional character: "There are all sorts of elements in the palm to interpret," she says to another character, Simon.

> In any case your fate line is extraordinary. You will always land on your feet, no matter how far you fall. Your head line, which curves around your Mount of Luna shows that you are ruled by fantasy, and this cross tells me that it will cause you lots of trouble. Your heart line, which vanishes in your Mount of Saturn, reveals there will always be misfortune and tragedy in your love affairs. Finally,

> I see in your life line that you will die a violent death, but that you will live to a ripe old age.[7]

In a tone closer, and for good reasons, to Artaud and the Leonora Carrington of Down Below, we have Unica Zürn's text "MistAKE" (in *MistAKE et autres écrits français*), which she wrote probably in Paris in 1964, as indicated by Rike Felka, in her foreword to the French writings, "Feuille volante franco-allemande" (Franco-German loose sheet). According to Felka, Zürn, Hans Bellmer's companion in suffering, who yearned "to feel guided, to follow a sign, to be connected to her surroundings by the messages she received,"[8] displays, in a hesitant language, her interest in divination: "Watch out for the letter *M*." These were the words of the gypsy in Palavas, who looked inside her hand. This can easily be interpreted as the echo of concerns shared by many other members of the group and its circle of influence. Queneau gently makes fun of cartomancers and clairvoyance in general in *Odile,* and Crevel, in *Are You Crazy?* draws an unflattering portrait of his Madame de Rosalba, a character inspired by a real fortune-teller, Madame Diris, whom he frequented at this time. He calls his character a "chamber witch, Batignolles oracle," someone who knows how to read in "the book of hands and fate" and goes into a trance to eventually provide her visitor advice worthy of any country bonesetter. However, it is Leiris, in his extremely odd book *Aurora,* who provides the most negative image, albeit in a context charged with mystery.*

> Many years ago the entire city of Aigues-Mortes had been plunged into perpetual darkness, a night as thick as black coffee, and beside

---

*How can I avoid pointing out, if only as coincidence, the existence of a book by Jacob Böhme titled *Aurora oder die Morgenröte im Aufgang* (1682)? Moreover, Leiris also recorded, in *L'Âge d'homme,* a dream he had in July 1925, in which some very beautiful female seers, especially beautiful when seen in their "astral" aspect, had set up shop in a brothel and finally appeared, "after diverse incantations, accompanied by the burning of certain materials, dances, cries, etc.," for what they truly were: vampires. In addition to the psychological approach that can be taken of this dream account, the way in which it combines several themes dear to the surrealists—sexuality, clairvoyance, and vampirism—is noteworthy.

its walls a hideous fortune-teller shuffled her cards, she who always confuses ALWAYS with NEVER, never NEVER with ALWAYS, and can only pronounce "baby's cry" as the "end is nigh," so rotten are her teeth.[9]

Rodanski would later share this scarcely flattering opinion: "To tell the future is to make a calculation that calls on one to perish." Duprey reacts even more bitterly: "The knowledge of Love begins in the lines of the hands to finish in a wallflower of two different fleshes!" It is true, as Sophie Bastien observes in her article "Photography and André Breton: An Illustration of Objective Chance," that

> by a metonymic relationship, the seer returns to the esoteric world of which the surrealists were fond and to the intuitive intelligence they cultivated. Breton consulted the seer for this reason, which makes her a catalyst of objective chance. She also harks back, by a synecdoche this time, to her tool of the trade, the crystal ball, which Breton considered to be a paranoiac screen, thereby referring to this major concept developed by Salvador Dali. *Nadja* offers some examples of its implementation and *Mad Love* will make it a theme by connecting it to chance. The seer therefore combines in her person with unfailing consistency the operating ideas of surrealism.
>
> The majority of the predictions we know proffered in 1927 by Pierre Piobb in his lectures on Nostradamus at "the hall of the Theosophical Society in Paris" [and] "published that same year by ADYAR Editions," but prepared in 1924, were obtained by means of clairvoyance, and smack of parapsychology. Such a large number like this have been noted—the vast majority—that many researchers have developed the habit of thinking there is no other means for explaining a prophecy besides clairvoyance.[10]

The "prophet" of this movement, whose "essays . . . on surrealist painting, like his poems, were teeming with premonitions and predictions,"[11] was Robert Desnos. This author of *Trois Livres de prophéties* (Three Books of Prophecies), which were fairly much in the same spirit as the above-named Nostradamus and sometimes quite singular, especially in the first book, writes in the sixth issue of *La Révolution surréaliste* (March 1926):

> Prophecy is within the grasp of everyone, just like memory and, for my part, I see no difference between the past and the future. The sole tense of the Verb is the indicative present.
>
> *Prophet without obeying my reason in any way*
> *But prophet by my passions,*
> *Prophet of the Heart*
> *Passion of the heart*
> *Passions of dream*
> *And by the Breath.*

The man saying this then adds, "German city, what is your name? Nuremberg! Famine and plague will exempt your excise duties at no expense in 1929!" before talking of "Nagasaki visited by the fusion of iron and fire" (but in 1991). And perhaps the Dutch should be worried as he also announced in a way that was equally veiled and menacing:

> *And schism will torment your final days pope number*
>   *XVI*
> *with regard to Australian and Gaelic defections*
> *And the sea shall cover Holland up to its quasi*
>   *republican*
> *Council*
> *And reborn from the shadows the ancient race of the*
>   *tempted and the creators of heavens.*[12]

Still on the subject of prophets and prophecies, Breton, whose great interest in Jean-Pierre Brisset, the author of *Prophéties accomplies* (Fulfilled Prophecies),[13] is well known, mentions in "Pont Levis," the very beautiful text devoted to his friend Pierre Mabille, through their discussions in Salon-de-Provence, the city of Nostradamus, regarding "the enigma of the *Centuries*,"* a work on which Pierre Piobb, Mabille's mentor, had worked greatly despite (or because of) the puzzling nature of "this blend of dazzling light and thick shadows, of formal allusions and impenetrable enigmas."

With *Le Secret de Nostradamus* (The Secret of Nostradamus),[14] Piobb reminds us that it was only in 1862, thanks to the priest Toiné, that the "alleged Michel de Nostradamus," whose book was printed in 1668 by "Jean son of Jean . . . and the Widow, a renowned widow whose progeny is well-known," finally "become popular again," and, letting enthusiasm carry him away a bit, he added these lines:

> Did Nostradamus invent all this? I can immediately tell you no. The prophet clearly says he had documents that came down from his ancestors. These were Hebrew documents of Egyptian provenance, as well as Persian documents.

The former represented all or part of the "documents of the initiatory crypts of the Egyptian temples" and the "geometrical, cosmographical, and algebraic formulas" with which "the biblical texts, the psalms, the Torah, and the Temple of Solomon were made." The others "originated from ancient Persia, that of the Magi," to be exact. We can clearly see here the kind of environment—one propitious to the marvelous—in which Pierre Mabille evolved under the tutelage of the highly esteemed author Pierre Piobb.

But it was Caillois, that "enemy of the interior" as Sarane Alexandrian puts it, who confessed in *Le Fleuve Alphée* (The Alph River) of his attraction to the Camisard women, those "prophetesses, terrible dark angels, violent, somnambulistic warriors," notably "Isabeau Vincent, whose ugliness transformed into beauty during her mediumistic crises." He provided in *Pontius Pilate,* his remarkable alternate history published by Gallimard in 1961, his most beautiful visionary figure with the purely fictional character Marduk, although the book

---

*The full title is *Les Prophéties de Michel de Nostredame*. The book is divided in parts called "centuries."

is primarily a formidable contemplation of "the evasive, evanescent, history of the world, at least one of the infinite virtualities of this history." At the Roman prosecutor's request, the prophet explains that "if this religion* triumphs, the years will no longer be counted from the time of the founding of Rome but from the birth of the Teacher of Justice." Carried away by his vision, Caillois tells us:

> Marduk had the impression of conjecturing and inventing plausible hypotheses. . . . He was convinced that he was imagining everything, to which his knowledge and intelligence contributed. But in reality . . . he merely was perceiving a vast invisible spectacle, offered to him unawares.

Thus unconsciously!

We can even ask ourselves what is the nature of the interest that some members of the group and its immediate circle, namely Breton himself, displayed for numbers. Breton could see the number 1713 in the initials of his name, and underscored that it is the date of the publication of George Berkeley's *Dialogues between Hylas and Philonous*, which includes the water fountain mentioned in *Nadja*. And he concludes *Arcanum 17* with these lines:

> Eternal youth. "1808 = 17:" birth of Nerval. Publication of the Theory of Four Movements and the General Destinies.

Man Ray signed some of his drawings with a 11112, which is the stylized representation of his own initials. André Rolland de Renéville, who according to Cyril Loriot is "the greatest of the forgotten men of *Le Grand Jeu*" and "the writer who, in the opinion of . . . René Daumal and Roger Gilbert-Lecomte was the closest to them both humanly and on the plane of theoretical power and performance," explains in detail in *L'Expérience Poétique* (The Poetic Experience) how "the symbology of Nerval's sonnet Artémis only takes on its full meaning when compared to the first teachings of the kabbalah on numbers." It is significant that

---

*"This religion" refers to Christianity.

in support of his position he quotes an extract from René Allendy's book *Le symbolisme des nombres, essai d'arithmosophie*. Queneau, a trained mathematician, also granted a particularly noteworthy importance to the symbology of numbers, as Marie-Noëlle Campana-Rochefort clearly demonstrated in her paper titled "The Numbers in *The Blue Flowers*." After pointing out that "*The Blue Flowers,* through a precise numerical architecture, expresses an entire traditional or Eastern cosmogony metaphorically," and to be exact makes reference to Plato and the "I Ching," she lists names, the majority of which are memorable.

> This permanence of number takes part in a literary tradition that was revived by Queneau and defended by Dante or Butor, with the help of Victor Hugo, Baudelaire, Balzac, and others: the number is a much more powerful sign than the linguistic sign. While words succeed at explaining the world, the number is their secret root.[15]

This is all the more so, according to Marie-Louise von Franz who said, relying on Jung's preliminary work, that "the number also represents the archetypes of the collective unconscious and would therefore be connected to everything produced by human imagination!" Unica Zürn, meanwhile, writes in her "Notes Concerning the Final (?) Crisis," published in *The Man of Jasmine*, about June 6, 1966, "the 6–6–66, a date she finds worthy and meaningful": "she *knows* that these apparitions can only be visible on that day, for that day's date in which the number 6 is repeated so many times is dedicated to death." But Artaud's approach, which, in *New Revelations of Being* (1937), combines horoscope, arithmology, and tarot, and Marianne Lams of the Grand Jeu's approach, which adds geomancy to the list, are the ones that raise the most questions.

In the same spirit, Breton, also notoriously interested by the tarot and the *Book of Thoth*,* did not disdain to tell fortunes, as Charles Duits reveals

---

*"*The Book of Thoth*, the alphabet Moses made the great secret of his kabbalah," Eliphas Levi states in his *History of Magic*. Levi believed the tarot had been born in Palestine. Several decades earlier, Jean-François Alliette, alias Eteilla, a disciple of Court de Gébelin, wrote that the tarot-Ta-Rosh, the doctrine of Mercury, had been created in 2170 BCE from the *Book of Thoth*. The Greeks incorporated Hermes Trismegistus into Thoth.

in his book on Breton, nor even curl up with them in reverie. Regarding the tarot, Antoine Court de Gébelin, a pastor and a Mason of the Lodge the Nine Sisters, who was the spiritual father of the Rites of Memphis and Misraïm,* had no fear about declaring the cards' Egyptian origin and divinatory vocation at the end of the eighteenth century in his encyclopedia *Monde primitif, analysé et comparé avec le monde moderne.*

In his text "D'un Poème-Objet," published as a foreword to the 2008 edition of the original manuscript of *Arcanum 17,* Henri Béhar recalls that Breton "long took an interest in tarots, mainly since his sojourn in Marseille, where he undertook an investigation on the origin of card decks in the municipal library, inviting his friends to redraw the major arcana of a deck in the spirit of the surrealist movement," before adding that "in New York, he asked the eminent historian of magic, Kurt Seligmann, to procure notes for him on this subject on which he planned to devote a study." This study would eventually center on the seventeenth arcanum, symbolizing, Béhar says, "the Star, Eternal Youth, Isis, the myth of resurrection, etc.; hope, and the eternal renewal that cannot become fossilized." In *L'Art magique,* Breton writes, "One lone divinatory and apodictic system had the fortune to inspire numerous representations, which are well preserved and of high aesthetic values: the tarot." It is perhaps significant here to note that one of Duit's first published texts, in n° 2–3 of *VVV* in March 1943, "The Day Is an Attack," is on a new conception of the tarot proposed by Matta and Leonora Carrington.

This is the same Matta whose four arcana—the Lovers, the Chariot, the Stars, and the Moon—illustrated the original Brentano's edition of *Arcanum 17* in 1945. Several years earlier, the cover of n° 3–4 of *Minotaure,* composed by André Derain, who was never a surrealist, was adorned by representations of four figures from the major arcana of the Tarot of Marseille—the Juggler, Strength, the Hanged Man, and the Fool—under the eponymous face of the Minotaur. An adept of the divinatory arts, like Apollinaire or Masson, Derain† offered in the same December 1933 issue

---

*At the end of the eighteenth century the Rites of Memphis and the Rites of Misraïm were two different Masonic rites. They merged later and became "Memphis-Misraïm."
†Breton (who was then close to Derain) had written in a 1924 letter to Jacques Doucet that he considered Derain to be "the greatest modern portrait painter." (This quotation is taken from Daix's *Les Surréalistes.*)

a "Criterion of Aces." This was a poetic text with highly esoteric connotations on the Aces of Wands, Swords, Pentacles, and Cups—the respective symbols of fire, air, earth, and water—beginning with the remark, "A word to the wise!" This was followed by this incontestably esoteric passage:

> Place of the unrepentant Juggler, orator painter whose mouth will be sewn shut with strong leather laces like a shoe, shoe of the Hanged Man "twelfth card." Here neither Good nor Evil nor Time nor Space, nothing but the Eternal Present, privilege of the Image/Image that gives life to the one who desires it. Troubled souls anxious about the Future, the Aces give you reassurance. There is no Future, we predict it!! And we defy the demon that deals us the cards.[16]

While it is true that Tériade* was still at the helm of the magazine at this time, Breton already had the authority to review the material he selected.

By all evidence, the tarot as a "divinatory and apodictic system" could not help but arouse the interest of Breton and his friends by virtue of the fact, as shown by the Freemason and Catholic Emile Grillot de Givry[†] in his book *Picture Museum of Sorcery, Magic, and Alchemy* (which they knew quite well), that the tarot had

> no origin, of any kind. It remains a mystery, an enigma, a problem. At best, it is in harmony with the symbolism of alchemy, another intangible doctrine that has traveled an underground road through

---

*Tériade's real name was Stratis Eleftheriades or Eleftheriadis, but he is always called "Tériade."

†Robert Amadou writes about Grillot de Givry (1874–1929) in his postface to the French edition of Kurt Seligmann's *Le Miroir de la magie* (The Mirror of Magic), "He was a student of the occult, to use the language of Papus ["Papus" is an alias] and his friends at the beginning of the twentieth century, he was a scholar, almost a believer in occultism, he was a "specialist." J. K. Huysmans . . . confessed his surprise that he could both be a 'Freemason of the Order of Misraïm and good Catholic.' But this dual affiliation characterized this individual."

the centuries, avoiding both religion and science yet establishing a foothold in both of their domains.[17]

Arthur Edward Waite (1857–1940), an eminent member of the Golden Dawn, even maintained, with a very "ecumenical" intent, that "tarot reflects a sacred doctrine, mysteriously transmitted and vouched for by philosophies like alchemy, kabbalah, the Rosicrucian mysteries, up to Masonic rites, for which it constitutes a living synthesis." Pierre Mabille, investigating the origin of the decks in a more general way, notes in *The Mirror of the Marvelous* that tarots, "like dice, like small bones, are used by the hierophant when he questions fate." Then, independent of its intrinsically poetic nature, the tarot functions on the principle of analogy to which the surrealists were so attached.

Simone Perks, in her article "Fatum and Fortuna: André Masson, Surrealism, and the Divinatory Arts," which appears in the third issue of *Papers of Surrealism*,[18] argues that "the fact that these motifs are consistently repeated suggests that they are unlikely to be without meaning for the surrealists," mentioning specifically the image of "a mysterious door opening on a gaping and unfathomable future of illusions and hopes," to use the words of Grillot de Givry, which Perks cites. Perks views the figure in some of Masson's presurrealist works from the early 1920s, particularly *L'Homme à l'orange* or also *Homme dans un intérieur*, as modeled on the Juggler; "the Mage in the highest sense of the word," as stated by Gérard Van Rijnberk, and underscores it has the "omnipotence of a god" according to Wirth and is "the Aleph" for Seligmann, who adds:

> He is pointing at the above and the below, confirming the teaching of Hermes Trismegistus that here below all is like that which is in heaven, that the little world, man, contains all the elements of the universe, and that the study of man will make us understand the wonders of the whole creation.[19]

The Juggler, who is traditionally partially clad in blue (the color of the spiritual) and partially in red (the color of matter) also symbolizes the balance between opposites. In his article "Alchemical, Kabbalistic, and Occult Symbolism in the Work of Pablo Picasso and His Contemporaries,"[20] Marijo Ariëns-Volker postulates that Picasso in 1907, as a forerunner, had depicted the devil's hand (androgynous and winged) as seen in the fifteenth arcanum above the head of the leftmost figure in his painting *Les Demoiselles d'Avignon*. We next have Giorgio de Chirico, the painter about whose work Breton writes in *Entretiens*: "Painting like this, which only retains those outside aspects that stir up mystery or allow the omen to be freed, tends to form one with divinatory art and the Art, strictly speaking."[21] He added, in the same interview with André Parinaud, that this work "tends to rehabilitate the divinatory arts of Antiquity." Chirico was not spared by these more or less conscious influences, as this passage from *Hebdomeros* gives us good reason to believe:

> He finally found himself in the presence of this man, this apostle, whom he had more than once imagined in his childhood reveries as going through the world with a pack on his back and a pilgrim's staff in his hand, his head high and his eyes shining, like all those who walk over deserted plains toward white-walled towns—for they know that brothers are awaiting them there and feverishly waiting beneath the arcades at the gates.[22]

How is it possible to not see this as the Fool in person—although without his dog—to not see him as the Fool, "who contains all the negative and positive Arcana of the deck,"* entering the painter's dream world with its "divinatory and transfigurative"† nature on an equal level through the magic of writing? He is going there, and this is worth emphasizing, to meet mysterious "brothers," about whom everything gives the impression that they are initiates, promethean members like him of some secret society devoted to humanity's happiness. He is introduced as an apostle. "Devoted to the cleft / to the clientele of the cleft / at your command of cleft and cutting the current: / THE FOOL

---

*This quote is by Marcel Jean and Arpad Mezei.
†This quote is by Michel Carrouges.

/ almost alone / in his bad company," seeking to "organize / desire, to upgrade the night," and "to give the indeterminate, loss, absence, and incompleteness, especially incompleteness its due," as Jean-Clarence Lambert wrote in 1980 in his collection *Le Noir de l'azur*.* In this book, "where the play of tropes and structures is deployed around the figure of the Fool, who emerged from the tradition and alchemical imagination," the poet deemed it wise to liven up the table of contents with a "note on the Mat or the Fool" borrowed from the preface written by Roger Caillois for Oswald Wirth's *Tarot*, which I will quote:

> Final arcanum of the tarot. . . . It could undoubtedly be added to any combination one wished to develop: a kind of joker before the fact, the ultimate concession or excess of triumph, the chance within chance itself and subsidiary Unknown that corrects the detected unknown element.

In his book *Bourges, cité première* (Bourges, Initial City), Philippe Audoin stresses that the fool is "a madman . . . posing as a pilgrim" who "carries no number. He possesses no rank as if he is above all rank, as if he encompassed the totality of meanings, desires, and fates." He adds, on another plane, and here again I am slightly jumping the gun, that it is "permissible to recall that for the adepts, the substances involved "from the beginning to the end of the Work" for creating the philosopher's stone are called mercury "because of the natural volatility and instability of these substances, which the ancient authors customarily called the Fool—or the Traveler."[23]

Breton's curiosity about this deck, whose first card depicts a magician and whose last card (is?) a fool, would never wane. In *L'Art magique*, with the complicity of Gérard Legrand, he analyzes the highly potent sixteenth arcanum, the House of God, which features a crenellated tower in which he saw a depiction of the "mythical Tower of Babel, whose name means 'God's Gate.' This is the transcription of the Semitic term 'Beth-el,' which the Greeks transformed into *betyl*, the

---

*Lambert's book was published by Galilée with numerous illustrations by Karel Appel, "painter of our joyful apocalypse."

word used to designate the aeroliths that have been the subject of worship since the dawn of time (the black stone of Mecca is a good example)." Compare the information above with what Canseliet wrote in his commentaries on the *Mutus Liber:*

> The betyl, for Altus,* can be equated with Jacob's *bethel,* which in Hebrew means the *house of God.* . . . The betyl is identified as identical to the black stone that fell from the sky and was swallowed by Saturn, and possessed the dual virtues of oracle and divination. It can be seen, first in its natural state, then cut and carved over the emblems XXII and XXXVI among the fifty luxurious engravings by Jean-Theodore de Bry for Michaelis Maierus's *Atalanta Fugiens* (1618).

In *Heliogabalus or the Crowned Anarchist,* Artaud also mentions the "Betyls, the black Betyls or Stones of Bel," which "emerged from the fire" and "are like the carbonized sparks of the celestial fire."

Getting back to Breton's description of the sixteenth arcanum, he then adds, speaking specifically of the Italian tarot known as the Charles Sixth Tarot:

> The tower, covered with cracks as if from an interior explosion, remains intact. In fact it is a giant energy container, the skeletal structure for the sanctuary intended to polarize the magic power contained in "thunder stones."

At a later date, even after former members of the group or those once close to it returned to reason (Caillois, for example), they continued to interrogate the cards, if not the stars! Other names that should be added to the list of surrealist adepts of tarot divination include the "benevolent magician" Valentine Penrose and Gala Dali. Also in this list are Seligmann, Ernst, Brauner, and even Leonor Fini, whose book *Rogomelec*[24] features the brother Taro who uses the Marco Polo Tarot for divination.

---

*Altus is the pseudonym used by the author of the *Mutus Liber.*

As did Freemason and Martinist Oswald Wirth in his book *Tarot des imagiers du Moyen Âge* (1923) and many others before him, André Breton interpreted the Star card in his book *Arcanum 17*. This card portrays a naked young woman, kneeling by a pond, as a symbol of truth. (She is entirely nude as she has just emerged from the well.) She holds a vessel in each hand and is spilling the contents from the golden urn in her right hand into the stagnant water. At the same time she is spilling the contents of the silver vessel in her left hand on the arid wasteland behind her. She is thereby circulating the energies she holds, by virtue of which she embodies the cosmic heartbeat. The two containers appear to be inexhaustible. The liquid flowing from the left vessel seems to keep the possibly paradisiacal vegetation of the site alive, particularly the acacia branch in the background to the right of the woman. This would be the "desert mimosa that adorned Eastern tombs," according to Wirth, and "a tree that imprisons the debris of dead wisdom," according to Breton. To her left is a rose on which a butterfly is resting. The Greeks regarded the butterfly as a symbol for the soul, and Charles Duits said it is "the messenger of another world in this world, a world men call death and they fear it."

Wirth presents the rose in bloom (a duplicate of this card appears on page 32 of the *Arcanum 17* manuscript) as a flower of love and beauty representing everything that enriches life on Earth. Breton states:

> Barely glimpsed a little while ago, the rose expresses in whiffs all of sacred Egypt in the trembling night. The rose is, vertiginously turned in on itself, the collar of the ibis, the sacred bird, and from it rise all the riggings that human dreams might need in order to recover on a tightrope and to make their white soles, split like the veins of leaves, glide again along the wire stretched between the stars.

Above the beautiful young woman, who is also given the very pretty name Pourer of the Morning, eight stars with eight points of varying size are shining. Five of these stars are yellow and three are blue. The largest of these stars, which is yellow, is directly above the woman at the upper edge of the card. Some believe this is Maia, one of Zeus's lovers, with whom Hermes was conceived. Breton calls it the "Morning Star" and the "Dog Star or Sirius." For others, such as Wirth, it is Lucifer, the light bearer, in other words Venus or the Ishtar/Astarte of the Sumerians, who deified stars to such an extent that the ideogram for *star* in their writing means "god." Ishtar, who inspires souls with the desire to take body, demands of human beings the courage to face life's struggle with joy. The kneeling figure could thereby be an incarnation of this deity, a worthy heir of the ancestral mother goddess (whom we shall revisit later in chapters 7, 9, and 11), who reveals the most exalting aspects of the beauty of the world and nature. She could also be a personification of Eve, the mother of humanity. With the seven others, the large star signifies the clarity of night that guides the spiritual aspirations of human beings, without whose help they would strive in vain. The seven smaller stars, often identified as the Pleiades, Atlas's daughters transformed into a constellation by Zeus, who was seeking to spare them from the unwelcome advance of the blind hunter Orion, can be divided into two groups: three yellow and four blue and red, but this depends on the deck, forming a septenary related to to Ishtar or Venus. The smallest yellow star is placed directly above the kneeling woman's head, evoking the star that watches over each of us and filters cosmic influences. The other, slightly larger two, located on either side, symbolize the lunar influence on the right and the solar influence on the left. The lunar side works on the imagination and feelings, whereas the solar influence affects consciousness and reason. Their placement in the card cannot help but bring to mind the positions of the sun, the moon, and the master of the lodge in Masonic temples. The four blue-red stars form a square, relaying the influences of Mercury, Mars, Jupiter, and Saturn, which all represent astrological and alchemical principles. Papus, who believed the tarot was "the original book of initiation in antiquity," created his own version around 1910, a version in which, like Eliphas Levi and Oswald Wirth before him, he compared the arcana with the letters of the Hebrew alphabet. He noted in his book *Le tarot des bohémiens: La clef absolue de la science occulte* that the original Hebrew letter corresponding with the seventeenth arcana depicted a stylized tongue and mouth, in other words, speech.

"Spare the spirits of the star!" Unica Zürn wrote in one of her anagram poems, which relied on no automatism whatsoever.

A star, as Bernard Roger recalls, "has served forever as a guide to nocturnal navigators whether over the oceans of the globe or over the philosophical sea of the Argonauts."[25] Echoing him, Jorge Camacho notes the star "has shown the solitary sailor his route over the high seas. By faithfully following it throughout his long voyage, he is sure to reach port safely." The star burns with such an intense gleam in the surrealist imaginal realm that in 2004, the Czech painter Martin Stejskal organized a large exhibition near White Mountain in which it "was declined in all its natural, cultural, as well as mythical aspects, in the union of traditions (astrology, kabbalah, alchemy, Freemasonry) as in the poetic union of the male and female in each individual, borne by the work of surrealist friends, and by the uncarved stone placed at the castle entrance that bore this phrase that sings in our hearts like a magical couplet: constructed on the side of abyss, on philosopher's stone..." as Marie-Dominique Massoni points out in issue 5 of *S.U.R.R.* However, "You can never see this star like I saw it. You don't understand: it is like the heart of a heartless flower," as Nadja, the "magician," says.[26]

A harmony founded on the spiritual in all its forms, love of humanity in all its beauty, we can thus clearly see the richness of the esoteric domain approached this way by the surrealists, who incidentally made the Star, in the Deck of Marseille, the symbol for the suit of Dreams, whose face cards are Lautréamont, Alice in Wonderland, and Freud. This deck was conceived (these things are never invented) between the Villa Air Bel and the café Au Brûleur de Loups.

As noted earlier, tarot symbology never completely left Victor Brauner, as shown by his 1947 painting *The Surrealist* (see plate 9), which is clearly modeled on—and includes many of its symbols—the Juggler, also called the Magician, of the first arcanum. This painting depicts the destiny of the man battling against the underground currents of the occult. That same year he created *The Lovers, Messengers of the Number* (see plate 10), which depicts the same magician in the company of a secretary bird-headed female pope of his own invention, inspired by the second arcanum. This painting is a "*conjunctio oppositorum,* which is one of the basic principles of the hermetic vision of the world," as Verena Kuni notes in the catalog devoted to the work of this Romanian painter by the Pompidou Center in 1996. The lemniscate-shaped hat of the Magician, like an elongated figure eight, may explain the infinity symbols that accompany the artist's signature on so many of his paintings.

True to himself—to his egocentricity and personal symbology—Dali depicted himself as the Magician of the tarot he designed to please his wife Gala, who also appears in it as the Empress. Each of the seventy-eight cards of this superb "universal tarot" is a collage, with that of the Magician depicted in front of the ribbed vault of a Gothic cathedral.

The signature of Jacques Abeille appeared in *La Brèche* and then again later with that of Vincent Bounoure's friends in the *Bulletin de liaison surréaliste* and the magazine *Surréalisme,* in which he figures on the contents page of the second and last issue with the *Blason Fugace-Fugace Blason* diptych that already holds the embryonic form of the fabulous world of *The Statuary Gardens,*[27] and the image is placed beneath the sign of divinatory tarot. The opening lines of the book *Le Veilleur du jour* (The Day Watchman)—Abeille's extraordinary novel written during 1976 and 1977—introduce a "mountebank," depicted in a way by illustrator Michel Guérard that leaves no doubt he is identical to the one in the traditional tarot deck we have been discussing, save for the fact he is masked. The author describes this figure as "a character in a multicolored costume preparing to fold up a small stall," who offers his customer the opportunity to hear "the voices of [their] fate" by means of cards "adorned with great noble figures, cards whose length made them appear narrower than those of ordinary decks." After shuffling them briefly, his interlocutor, the "traveler, turned over the first card." Jacques Abeille tells us:

> Seen on it is a high tower whose top, with its gilded crenellations and stone settings, had been knocked over by a bundle of flames from on high. A colored rain from the heavens was also falling over the building. Two figures appear to be falling headlong so slowly

toward the foot of the building they seem to be soaring, and are touching, perhaps feeling the ground with their hands, as if in acknowledgment. Hills extend into the distance under a blue sky. The top of the tower is a destroyed crown.[28]

Here again Arcanum 16, the House of God, is easily recognizable, incorporated in this instance into the abolished tower of Gérard de Nerval, whom the author calls "my most intimate friend" in his dedication.

This is simply one of many examples from this book, as other familiar figures such as the Fool or the Hanged Man fleetingly appear in its pages.

Jean Markale in his article "Mystères et enchantement des littératures celtiques," which appeared in *Médium* in January 1955, proposes an original reading of Arcanum 9, the Hermit, which carries us under new skies.

> If we compare the ninth card of the Tarot to Merlin, an identification becomes evident. The Hermit could possibly be Diogenes, but he is also Merlin, Merlin the Madman, Myrddyn, the Welsh bard, who after the battle of Arderyd, *went mad* and became a hermit in Kelyddon Forest and wrote poems with a prophetic tinge, of which some traces remain.

Also in the Celtic mists and descended in a direct line from her abortive attempt in the 1930s to join the Golden Dawn, where the tarot played an important role, we have the Wheel of Fortune (Arcanum 10, symbolizing the alternations of life and the law of the cycles), which Ithell Colquhoun took on in the 1940s before presenting a complete tarot in 1977. That was the Taro Pack, which used her distinctive spelling and whose suits were the same as those of the most traditional decks: wands, cups, swords, and coins, and were the subject of a series of paintings she created also in the 1940s.

In *Perfect Balance* (1932), the Romanian painter Jules Perahim painted (although in the background) a figure in the exact posture of the Hanged Man of Arcanum 12, the symbol of self-renunciation.

Marina Vanci-Perahim tells us he was "reading the occultist Papus and his Tarot of the Bohemians at that time, which showed him the analogy between the twenty-two letters of the Hebrew alphabet and the twenty-two Major Arcana of the tarot."[29] I think I am within my rights to compare the young heroine of Toyen's painting *No Performance* to this figure, if only because she is in the same position, except the rope holding her up cannot be seen and the legs of Toyen's young woman are not crossed in a "tau" shape, as is the case with the traditional figure. Conversely, the female figure of Brauner's *Murmur of the Wall* (1945), while not hanging, is standing upright in a vaulted doorframe, and her enormous head fits its rounded contours perfectly. Her arms are crossed over her chest, and her legs form the "tau" shape.

In his book *A New Model of the Universe*, Gurdjieff's disciple P. D. Ouspensky wrote a short poem for each of the Major Arcana. This is what he wrote about the Hanged Man:

> *Behold! This is the man who has seen the Truth.*
> *New suffering, such as no earthly misfortune can*
>   *ever cause . . .*

Near the figure in Toyen's painting, whose face is concealed, contrary to that of the traditional hanged man, which can be seen glowing with a kind of bliss that seems incompatible with the situation in which he finds himself, there is an object (in addition to a Ku Klux Klan–type hood) that resembles a whip or some other object capable of being used in a *Story of O* type of sadomasochistic ceremony, an impression that reinforces the symbolic meaning of the card, with its image of the "free and sacrificed adept," according to Eliphas Levi.

Next, we cannot help but look at Marcel Duchamp's *The Bride Stripped Bare by Her Bachelors, Even (The Large Glass)* differently when we know he also called it *The Hanged Woman*. Mandiargues, talking of Arcanum 18, the Moon (Imagination), deemed it revealing to admit in his response to the questionnaire accompanying *L'Art magique*, "This tarot card dictated a long fragment of the poem *Hédéra* to me in 1943 (from 'In the midst of blood-covered reeds' to 'I see you through this red gaze—In the chill instant of your nakedness—Surrounded by rushes, orioles, and trout')," amounting to twenty-two verses out of a total of 251.

It is impossible to miss the singular nature of the following verse from "Hédéra," a poem which was dedicated to Meret Oppenheim.

> *Specter of the Sabbath the large cerambyx*
> *Cast a goat shadow over the forehead that reflects*
> *The white of a beech over the dampened grass*
> *A horned eye flouts the tranquil flesh*
> *The beautiful palaces where dwells my pleasure*
> *Bristling with tails curling into stingers*
> *Round elytrons of fire-bearing antenna*
> *Long banded feet in blind flight*
> *For a crushing of ass heads*
> *Seeping already in horrible sepia spurts.*

How could we fail to see in the reference to the "beautiful palaces" an allusion to the famous alchemical work by Eirenaeus Philalethes (whose real name might have been George Starkey), *An Open Entrance to the Closed Palace of the King,* the same book that inspired Colquhoun and Carrington? Most importantly, how could we fail to see flourishing there those same poisonous plants that haunt the etchings and drawings—compared by Mandiargues to some of Alfred Jarry's graphic work—of the "satanic and perverse" Aubrey Beardsley (as described by Jehan Mayoux), the heir to the pre-Raphaelites, who was esteemed so highly by Hans Bellmer, who considered him one of his teachers? Couldn't tarot and other arts of divination, as Simone Perks suggests, have been "another potential method for achieving a more direct relationship with nature and the self" for the surrealists?

5

SURREALISM AND ASTROLOGY

A very great lady, who is quite beautiful and comes from ... far ...

ANDRÉ BRETON

In their search for a supreme model of order and harmony, the priests lifted their eyes to the heavens. A meticulous, ceaseless observation of the heavenly bodies led them to that wisdom we call astrology.

KURT SELIGMANN, *THE MIRROR OF MAGIC*

Consider Leiris, who in *Aurora* paints a landscape over which "the moon curves its transparent horn, similar to the glass bend of the alchemist's retort, while the stars stack up their surprising grimoires." Then there is Toyen, the secretive, dazzling Marie Cermínová, on whom Marcel Jean bestowed a coat of arms emblazoned with "a silvered blue window, with four vert wings placed at the corners" (Marc Kober's "Marie-Vieil-Or" [Mary Old Gold].* According to Radovan Ivsic, Toyen was "silent and

---

*Marie-Vieil-Or is only the name Marc Kober gives to Toyen with a reference to her origin (Prag) and her interest in alchemy.

attentive like an Indian whose attractive blue gaze seems made to see what others do not," and Breton called her "that Superintendent of hookey school." We are in her debt for such soaring works of art as *At the Golden Wheel, At the Black Sun,* which brings to mind Eliphas Levi and François di Dio at the same time, and *At the Gold Tree* (1951), inspired by the signs that are "luminous from the inside not the outside." Her paintings carry the color names (black and gold) of the workshops of old Prague—"the magical capital of Europe"—and its Alchemist Street.

Toyen is, therefore, emblematic of those many surrealists whose work has proven to be shored up by the three columns of occultism that are magic, alchemy, and astrology, or "higher astronomy." The Arab alchemist Muhammed ibn Zakariyya Razi (also known as Rhazes) called alchemy "lower astronomy," and to Breton and Gaston Bachelard it "smacked primarily of magical psychology."[1] Philippe Audoin believed alchemy migrated into Europe from "Saracen Spain with Neo-Platonism, [becoming] for a long while the principal and perhaps sole Western esoteric science." These final two "minor mysteries" (alchemy and astrology) were dear to Guénon, and all three had varying degrees of affiliation to the sacred.

From the point of view of traditional occultists, we can latch on to Robert Amadou's approach that appeared in the *L'Art magique* questionnaire. This could clearly define the context in which the surrealist interest in astrology was centered, despite Amadou's allusions to "metaphysics" and "superhuman beings."

> Astrology encourages a metaphysical self-knowledge, thanks to its contact with symbols and the superhuman spirits that govern the universe associated with it. This knowledge finds fulfillment in a liberating experience. Astrology commits a human being to rise above the stars. We can find this idea in Plotinus. The stars have two faces. One looks down, toward men, the other looks up, toward the One. To the extent that astrology helps us know ourselves psychologically and procures a metaphysical experience for us through the contemplation of symbols, to the extent it helps us better understand the structure of the cosmos—this is fundamental—and to the

> extent it allows us to have better commerce with the intermediary powers, it allows us to pass over to the other side, the side where the stars themselves are looking toward their upper faces.

While the "intermediary powers" may leave us cold, the reference to Plotinus is far from being devoid of interest, as is the less direct inference to hermeticism and the system of correspondences between above and below! André Barbault also refers to this system of correspondences in his response to the questionnaire "The World Upside Down?" on the potential consequences of space exploration, published in the third issue of *La Brèche* in September 1962.

> The field of astral determination, which astrological observation endeavors to explain, is that of the personal structure of the human soul in all its subjectivity: the psychological microcosm responds to the geocentric macrocosm in a system of anthropocentric references.

Astrology, "a very great lady, who is quite beautiful and comes from so far that she cannot fail to keep [one] under her charm,"[2] was never excluded a priori by Breton, who had been initiated into its mysteries by Valentine Penrose. But he did have some reservations. "There are many kinds of knowledge, and astrology could certainly be one of them, and one of the least negligible, provided the premises are monitored and that what is a postulate be taken as a postulate."[3] These reservations are partially clarified somewhat vehemently by Gérard Legrand in *Le Libertaire* when he condemns "with disgust the clowning of horoscope merchants." He also mentions in his book *André Breton en son temps* Breton's "practical attitude" (he sometimes cast his friends' horoscopes), "which was both deferential and somewhat detached" toward this "science"* and adds that in this instance what fascinated Breton was "the astrologist's practice, his more or less evolved sense of analogy, his psychological dexterity, and not at all a 'belief' in the 'truth'

---

*It is quite interesting to note that Legrand's opinion matches that of Marcel Boll, founder of the Rationalist Union, who in his book *L'Occultisme devant la science* notes that "the value of the various kinds of occultism is essentially psychological in nature."

of his 'readings.'"4 In any case the science Jung claimed rises "from the depths of the human soul," and which had its actual origins in Chaldea and Egypt, Breton regarded as "holding one of the world's highest secrets."5 This was a conviction that Raymond Queneau, with his customary humor, satirized in *Odile,* with the following tirade uttered by Anglarès/Breton:

> I have always despised mathematics . . . but I have to admit that it has its use, for example, calculating probabilities, as it therefore provides a scientific basis for astrology.

In any event, the poet was "an excellent horoscope caster," as noted by Sarane Alexandrian in his *André Breton par lui-même.* He follows this with an observation worth quoting.

> In fact, Choisnard in his *Astral Influences* (1893) noted that the Saturn Uranus conjunction, which only occurs every forty-five years, signifies a "profound love of science, search of the mysterious, and a heightened need to educate oneself." Choisnard then wondered: "Who knows, perhaps the conjunction of Saturn with Uranus will bring about the birth of a new school of science?" It so happens that this conjunction took place between 1896 and 1898 and characterized the birth chart of Breton, Aragon, and Éluard.

With respect to this phenomenon, Marc Le Gros, in his *André Breton et la Bretagne* (André Breton and Brittany), states:

> André Breton was born in Tinchebray in the Orne on February 19, 1896. Forty years later he drew his birth chart with his own hand in green ink, his fetish color. Among other zodiacal considerations the key to which escapes us, he says, "Saturn and Uranus are conjunct." It is also interesting to notice that this sign in "conjunction," which is also, in the phosphorescent Vert escutcheon, the major sign of the alchemists, can be seen on the cover of the six issues of *Le Surréalisme au service de la révolution.* It is never a question of coincidence or

wasted steps for him. But among this forest of symbols, it is a simple small note that shines for us and gives us food for thought.[6]

Then, among the disturbing elements that are hard to interpret but are definitely significant, how can we overlook the fact, noted by Georges Sebbag, that Breton made the decision at the beginning of the 1930s to alter the day of his birth, saying he was born on February 18, not 19, thereby changing his astrological sign by choosing Aquarius over Pisces.[7] Gilbert-Lecomte, in "L'Horrible Révélation . . . la seule," expresses in particularly poetic fashion the relationship to astrology that the surrealists and their friends felt.

> The Sky is the cosmic Giant whose head has three eyes. Go as far as you can from yourself, rediscover the ancient hope that slumbers in the entrails of the last sorcerer of the last clan of savages. And you shall remember that the fortuneteller, who is several times normal human size, when he stands erect at the top of some high place, knows he is the Node-of-the-Worlds. According to the fascination of Influences, he knows that the Sun is his right eye, the Moon his left. He knows that the caverns of the Vast Space are also in his body, Aries in his head, Taurus in his throat, Gemini in his arms, Cancer in his chest, Leo in his heart, Virgo in his kidneys, Libra in his entrails, Scorpion in his penis, Sagittarius in his thighs, Capricorn in his knees, Aquarius in his hamstrings, and Pisces in his feet. He knows that each of the Planets lives in the organs of his body and in the lines of his hands to the line of Mars and the lunar mound, that his fingers have dedicated the thumb to Venus, the index to Jupiter, the middle finger to Saturn, the ring finger to the Sun, and the pinky to Mercury.

This cannot help but bring to mind this observation by Seligmann in *The Mirror of Magic*:

> In the astrologer's language, symbols and allegories were adopted, which were as many enigmas to the profane. The sun sheds tears;

Jupiter was surrounded by courtiers; the moon traveled in a carriage and accepted various crowns from the stars she approached, the crowns of bad weather, of wrath, of joy . . .

Artaud in *Heliogabalus or the Crowned Anarchist* reveals the great importance he granted astrology by borrowing some of his elements from one of the major works by Antoine Fabre d'Olivet (1768–1825), *Philosophical Views on the History of the Human Race* (1822). An orientalist, poet, theosophist, and more or less spiritualist healer, Fabre d'Olivet (who was also mentioned by Rolland de Renéville in *The Poetic Experience*) adhered to the ideas of the French Revolution (experiencing both ups and downs) and was even suspected of being a Jacobin by the Consulate, which earned him vindictive persecution at the hands of Bonaparte.* *The Golden Verses of Pythagoras* (1813) and *The Hebrew Language Restored* (1816), which will be mentioned by Gérard de Nerval in his discussion of this immensely erudite and somewhat mystical individual in his book *Les Illuminés* (The Illuminati), reveal Fabre d'Olivet to be a possible missing link between the illuminism of the eighteenth century and early romanticism. Antonin Artaud was undeniably inspired by this original thinker when he spoke of the "schism of Irshu," born of the realization that "the world far from descending from a single principle is the product of a combined dualty [*sic*]" leading to a war between the sexes. This is especially evident when he lingers over "the Zodiac of Ram inspired by God," its "races of stars arranged by groups," and its "twelve divisions" that "are equivalent to the number 12, which is the number of nature in the Pythagorean tradition," to which "respond like organic echoes" "the four major human races."

Completely in the spirit of the times that saw the creation (in 1935) of an Astrological College of France by a former engineering student from Saint-Etienne, Maurice Rougié, astrological themes frequently appeared in the movement's various magazines and publications, such as, for example, the extremely detailed horoscope of Arthur Rimbaud drawn up by Paul-Chardon in issue 3–4 of *Minotaure* in 1933. Similarly, the reputable

---

*During the Consulate, Bonaparte is not called "Napoleon."

doctor Pierre Mabille published "The Birth Chart of Lautréamont" in issue 12–13 of the same review and drew up Aube Breton's astral chart the same day he delivered her into the world. This activity seems to have been fairly commonplace, given the fact that Benjamin Péret's chart is housed in the Nantes Municipal Library, and that we also have that of Yves Elléouët, which Breton drew up shortly after they met.

In 1937, Artaud proposed to *NRF* that he write an "article of *clarification* concerning astrology at the present time," which was not preserved and was rejected by Paulhan, who argued he was not sure "Astrology-Science had ever existed."

It is true that interest in astrology could be confined to pure and simple superstition, such as when Vitezslav Nezval, for example, the future pillar of scientific materialism in Czechoslovakia, mentions "the unlucky signs" surrounding his visit to Paris for the International Congress of Writers in Defense of Culture in 1935. "Literally unlucky," he writes in the book titled *Rue Git-le-Coeur*:

> A month before leaving for Paris, I received, to my great joy, an astrological calendar on which the predominant astral influences for each day were displayed. I had seen in Prague that it was dangerous to keep a calendar like this in the home because, if our imagination is the slightest bit demanding, we will succumb to the predictions of our horoscope so thoroughly that when an allegedly unfavorable day arrives, we find ourselves incapable of undertaking any activity. Unfortunately, this year was placed under very evil constellations, and some of them coincided with my trip to Paris. To avoid, under the effect of a subjective interpretation influenced by these astrological anticipations, covering in advance some of these days full of menacing signs with the black veil of mourning, I decided not to bring this ephemeris to Paris.[8]

This soothsayer's talk, filled with the idea that man is the plaything of higher powers, seems to be shared by Rodanski, who, in *Requiem for Me*, conjures up "those intelligent masks depicting the powers of [his] fate!"[9] In notes only published after his death, Charles Duits, repeating and expanding on what he had said earlier in *André Breton a-t-il dit passe* (whose "occult part" was clearly seen by Jacques Abeille), drew up this amazing self-portrait in the stars:

> I was born in Paris on October 30, 1925. I am therefore a Scorpio: I should immediately add that I attach a certain value to this sign. It is my portrait that makes of the natives of this sign, astrologers. My reason tells me that it is the work of chance. But I do not believe in chance, and I doubt reason could provide a true image of this extravagant world. This does not mean that I believe in astrology like I believe the earth is round. However, by my complicated nature, my critical mind, my taste for a corrosive lucidity that easily turns into self-hatred, I am clearly a Scorpio. It takes me years to do what others do in several months, and this is not surprising because I am under Saturn's influence. But my rising sign also connects me to Sagittarius, to which I owe my love of the remote, the spiritual, the inaccessible, and the divine, this movement I easily recognize in that of the Centaur who soars upward without being able to tear himself away from the ground to which he is joined by the animal part of his being. Venus in Sagittarius explains my passionate love of the beautiful and my vision of the divine through woman. Feminine beauty epiphanizes the divine for me.[10]

In his book on Breton, Duits even provides astrological causes for the tensions between him and his "mentor" over the years. "As a Scorpio, I could not tolerate Breton's solar, Jovian side. He threw my nocturnal powers into ferment. These powers escaped the Leo's domination. But they were exasperated by the serenity of this domination. They pressed darkly against the frontiers of the kingdom of light. . . ."

Mandiargues also displayed enough interest in this topic to say in his 1982 interviews with Yvonne Caroutch:

> When I was around seventeen or eighteen, shortly after 1925, at the very time I was discovering Rimbaud, Lautréamont, modern poetry,

and surrealism, I also discovered esotericism and was avidly reading Eliphas Levi and Rudolph Steiner. Later, around 1933, I met Max Jacob and of everything he was able to tell me, I especially remember his astrological experience.[11]

Mandiargues granted such importance to the astrological signs of the artists he discussed in *Quatrième Belvedère* (Fourth Belvedere), for example, that he mentioned them systematically, even emphasizing in a 1981 article about Isamu Noguchi that "astrology should not be a joking matter." More significantly, in his *Pour saluer la naissance de Sibylle*, he noted that when his daughter Sibylle was born, "The Sun was in Leo, and the Moon was sixteen days old."

At the end of 1950, Jean-Pierre Duprey and Jacques Hérold produced "Le Temps en blanc" (Time on Spec), "a prediction poster," like a horoscope, that they plastered on the walls of Paris on April 30 to May 1, 1968. It was published by Le Soleil Noir in 1970 in *La Forêt sacrilège et autres textes* and shows on the date of "7/5."

> AND THE MIRROR WILL BE FORCE
> The gaze plunged
> The night sea will congeal the air and water the full water, its polished pale hair of eternity that the tide will toss and reject, like nets, in cold wave, in frosted glass. . . .

It also shows on the date of "12/6."

> And you fall asleep facing the vampire and your slumber will have black wings . . .
> (Several rediscovered signs will contain forever, in all shapes thereby fixed, the alphabet of ancient passageways.)

In a somewhat more theoretical approach Marcel Jean and the Hungarian surrealist Arpad Mezei stated in the chapter "The Master of Time" in their book *Genèse de la pensée moderne dans la littérature française* (Genesis of Modern Thought in French Literature):

Medicine and astrology are perhaps the oldest of all the sciences. It was also clear that originally the two sciences—that of men and that of the world—were closely linked. In hermetic tradition, the universality of the human personality possesses a cosmic meaning: the microcosm of the personality reflects the exterior macrocosm. . . . Astrology is a synthesis of two freshly roughed-out perspectives; the earth revolves around the sun and each month, each new phase, corresponds to the causal order—which is dual inasmuch as each phase of the day is also measured by the zodiacal hour. Every manifestation of reality (for example birth of the human individual) is therefore dominated by the sign of the birth month as well as by the ascendant; but moreover, it is under the influence of the planetary constellation, the arrangement of the planets in the heavens at the time the event took place. The horoscope thereby produces the synthesis of the causal movement of the generating cycle with the specific determinants of each elementary element.

The two writers, alluding to the precession of the equinoxes, then add at the bottom of the page, "We can note, in this regard, that the precessional shift would appear to remove all value from the stellar constellations as 'influences' in astrological calculations." In another 1970 article, Arpad Mezei,* an expert in psychology of the personality and a founding member with Endre Rozda of the European School in Hungary ("the third essential manifestation of surrealism"),[12] provided this particularly enlightening view of the relationship between "astrological thought, which seeks to determine the concrete individual according to a combinatory process, mapped out in correspondence with phases of development—symbolized by the signs of the Zodiac—and the sectors of human activity: the Houses" and the movement that interests us:

---

*Between 1947 and 1949, Arpad Mezei also cowrote an essay with Marcel Jean, "Genèse de la pensée moderne dans la littérature française" (Genesis of Modern Thought in French Literature; republished in 2001 by Henri Béhar in the *Bibliothèque Mélusine, Éditions de l'Âge d'Homme*) in which both men displayed their extensive knowledge of kabbalah. The cover copy presented Mezei as a "psychoanalyst, psychologist, graphologist, and alchemist in his spare time."

All the phases and sectors that serve as foundations, then determine the Adam Kadmon, the primordial man, of which every individual is only a derivation through combinations. According to this ancient doctrine, the concrete individual appears as the whole of the determinations of ideal outside entities. I was inclined to consider this play of symbols as a myth artistically crafted from broad empirical observations. But from personally working with the help of modern personality tests, I discovered that all that had been developed from a series of more or less undefined blots (interpretation of chance images, the completion of unfinished drawings, and so on) have an inevitable correspondence among them and simultaneously with the apparently aleatory construction of astrology. Rorschach blots can be classified similarly in a parallel way and the corresponding elements always have the same meaning. In the case of Rorschach, the "climate" of the ten test tables was determined by Minkowska, Dr. Booth, and with greater precision, F. Mérei. Their tests have an exact correspondence with the meanings of the Houses, which were determined by adepts long ago.[13]

It clearly seems that here the human sciences are joining the tradition. Or we could leave the last word to Malcolm de Chazal, who stated in *Le Mauricien* in 1960, "On Earth itself there are analogies and correspondences, and astrology in the poetic order."

In a neighboring category, but on a much vaster scale, we should mention Guy René Doumayrou and his sacred *Géographie sidérale* (Sidereal Geography). This is the game of snakes and ladders in space and time, a celebration of the "continuous wedding of Earth and Sky in the bed of human settlements, cities, temples, castles, laid out like a vast mind snare for daily use." His sidereal geography draws on heraldry and astrology to reveal the "concealed promises of a possible harmony" whose "future and actual materialization . . . can only occur through the *concerting* power set in motion through the rediscovery of the paths of the Star." The word *sidereal* is from the Latin *sidus,* which is also the root of the words *desire* and *regret.*

A Hyperborean ray captured at *Stonehenge* ("hanged stone," the hanging stone that is the emerald fallen from Lucifer's forehead), following a geodesic line, illuminates the southern sea at *Lluchmayor* (the greatest light). At the crossing of the Path of the Star that "His eminence Saint James of Galicia" fixed at *Compostella* (*compos stellae:* "master of the star"), the Zodiacal rose was made to flower, the heraldic emblem of *Toulouse* (*tholos:* "the dome") imprinting upon the Occitan lands the methodical signature of the twelve signs of the astrological heavens.[14]

In this book, Doumayrou looks over a number of certain castles in southwest France because, as Breton wrote, "Once and for all poetry must reemerge from the ruins / In the finery and glory of Esclarmonde."[15] He looks at castles from Montsegur to Bruniquel or even from Queribus to Penne of Albigeois (dear to Noël Arnaud and especially Jean Malrieu) in search of the manifestation of cosmic harmony in their geographical location. A word is due here to Jean Malrieu, who, like Noël Arnaud (and Joë Bousquet, René Nelli, Adrien Dax, and Henri and No Seigle, as well as the Cordes resident Francis Meunier and also Gaston Puel), reinforced the Cathar-Occitan touch Breton had already given surrealism, very much like Joseph Delteil ("Cathar in My Soul"), who confided in *La Deltheillerie:*

> It pleases me to imagine I had a Cathar grand-grandmother and a Perfecti: Rixende du Teilh. . . . She was an archdeaconess and on top of that mistress of the Count de Foix. Hail Rixende du Teilh, burned alive at Montsegur on the Field of the Cremated in 1244![16]

Pierre Dhainaut wrote the following about the founder of the magazine *Sud:*

> How could Jean Malrieu avoid mingling his steps with those of the Faithful and the Perfecti? The archives of his country and the remnants spoke of them ceaselessly and more importantly his poems summoned them. . . . What attracted Jean Malrieu was

not Catharism but the persecuted and tortured Cathars, it was Montsegur. He did not turn this into an allegory.

And further on:

> Despite his frequent use of Cathar and Christian vocabulary, Jean Malrieu's religion remains, in fact, a solitary one. Do poets have any other religion? Would they still be poets if they conformed to rites and dogmas? Jean Malrieu repeated enough times, "I am a heretic of every faith." And this God that was finally given a name as the final word of *The Cathar Castle,* what does it matter what the theologians think about it, what was it for Jean Malrieu? "The desire for the name of God is only one of the names for the God of desire," one of his Perfecti says.[17]

In the steps of Tristan Tzara, who had taken part in the creation of the Institute of Occitan Studies in Toulouse at the end of the Second World War, and who, Henri Béhar recalls, "erected a bridge between the Pythagorean and kabbalistic traditions and the renaissance by the intermediary of the Troubadours" through his later study of anagrams, Georges Goldfayn, in the seventh issue of *Médium* (May 1953), contributed an article titled "Rebis," which says:

> We know that the Gnostic current shaped the inspiration of the Cathar troubadours who were the first in the West to sing of passionate love. But the occult meaning of their concerns vanished at the time their legacy was incorporated by the Church.

Taking into account the nature of that incorporation, this is understandable although not quite true. The Belgian painter Jacques Lacomblez also visited Montsegur in 1958 on the recommendation of Marcel Lecomte and André Breton, and he later explained to Claude Arlan the reasons for this visit: "What really interested me about the Cathars was specifically this Gnostic aspect," and I will also have to speak about it again, that had earned him the defamatory label of "mystic" from "several small procurers of a fundamentalist surrealism."

On a decidedly more anecdotal but still significant plane, I am enticed to mention a ring "crafted by [Jean] Filhos, that [Mandiargues] never went anywhere without, in which a gold setting held a small stone from Montsegur."[18] Mandiargues who, in *The Moondial,* spoke about Lueg Castle near Trieste and "the *spulgas* of the Sarbathes that were the last redoubts of the Cathars who barred some caves in Rousillon with high, sometimes crenellated walls." It seems Nora Mitrani was mistaken when she said in *La Flamme et son ombre,* "All that remains of the Albigensian heresy is Esclarmonde's luminous smile...."

6

SURREALISM AND DARK ROMANTICISM

"In the Closed Palace"

The marvelous envelops and bathes us like the air but we do not see it....
CHARLES BAUDELAIRE, *SALON DE 1846*

Surrealists in general have always shown a great interest in castles and buildings of all kinds, which are often haunted by more or less material and/or malevolent entities, whose origins lie in what Michel Carrouges claims "appears to primarily be that strange series of stories that made up the gothic novels and, before them, the chivalrous romances," "those books in which terror is the main character."[1] These books sometimes include the theme of ghosts and other night tales such as Clara Reeves's *Old English Baron or The Ghosts Revenged* and *The Sleepwalking Lovers*. These ruined buildings are the architectural manifestation (at least in the so-called gothic novel) of "that English soul, whose presence can be obscurely perceived among the ruins of the abbeys and monasteries broken up by Henry VIII or those castles destroyed by Cromwell's troops."[2]

After speaking enthusiastically in the *First Surrealist Manifesto* about the gothic novel in general—that excessive genre with its 138 authors—a pan-European literary phenomenon* that spanned the last half of the eighteenth century and the first third of the nineteenth, Breton returned to it in *Les Vases communicants,* where he wrote:

> There is nothing more exciting than this wildly romantic, ultra-sophisticated literature. All these castles of Otranto, Udolpho, the Pyrenees, Lovel, Athlin, and Dunbayne, rent with huge cracks, honeycombed with tunnels, persist in leading their fictitious life and offering their strange phosphorescence in the darkest corner of my mind.

Not without irony, Julien Gracq stated the following in his "Note to the Reader" for *Au Château d'Argol* (The Castle of Argol), a work described by Annie Le Brun as a "crystal of darkness, skillfully reconstructed to recover "the lightning-like efficacy of certain apparitions, here and now."

> It does not seem possible to cast aside the always gripping repertory of instable castles, sounds, lights, and ghosts in the night and in dreams, which enchant us primarily by their utter familiarity, and give our feelings of unease their essential virulence by forewarning us in advance we are *going* to shiver, without committing the most vulgar kind of transgression.

It is true that the shadows of Edgar Allen Poe and the Honoré de Balzac of *Beatrix* are also hovering over this novel. In *La Forme d'une Ville,* he will later slip in a very direct allusion to "the passive malice typical of closed off places, the *black castle.*"

Perhaps validating Carrouges's observation on the "castle's silhouette" in his texts as "the geometric point of the interlacings of his

---

*The Marquis de Sade, with his specificity and his excesses, would be one of the most splendid representatives, as well as Matthew Lewis's *The Monk* (1796), about which Breton went so far as to say that "the breath of the marvelous animates it entirely."

myths," Breton in *L'Art magique* returns to this theme with respect to the romantic vision in its relationship to the inner world. "It is helpful to recall that Goya's time was almost the same as that when the Pyrenees were being filled—in Europe's 'frenetic' literature—with castles and monasteries populated by brigands performing the most shameful practices." He adds that an "underground current connects these 'gothic novels' to the works of Sade."

Here are a few observations that in their convergence also illustrate the importance of the castle, defined by Breton as the "predestined . . . site . . . for carrying out a particular kind of mediumistic activity that manifests" when a person has abandoned himself to dream. Annie Le Brun describes the castle as "the clandestine meeting place for the European imagination" in that "night tradition" which, according to Nora Mitrani, "forms the royal lineage from Romanticism to Surrealism." It may be possible to attach lineage to "a remote initiatory tradition" by virtue of "the succession of ordeals that occur with increasing frequency, with each more difficult than the previous, to overcome" a "prophetic tradition of Western poetry."* This theme even passes over into certain aspects of the popular novel, inasmuch as Caillois detects a gothic novel influence in some of these novels: like *The Mohicans of Paris* by Alexandre Dumas, "*The Mysteries of Paris*† is sometimes strongly reminiscent of *The Mystery of the Castle of Udolpho*." And especially, Caillois adds in a footnote, because of "the preponderant importance of caves and underground passages." Gengenbach in *Judas ou le vampire surréaliste* provides a splendid example of this kind of place and climate when he describes the "subterranean manor" on the deserted isle of Tombelaine off of Mont Saint Michel. "Here Satan has a young nun raped [by] former priests and defrocked monks every night, clerics who have escaped or been driven away from their presbyteries and monasteries," clerics who, moreover, "play billiards with skulls carved in ivory."

Antonin Artaud, whom Breton would describe in his *Entretiens* (Interviews) as "very handsome . . . [and] when he moved [he] dragged

---

*Quotes by Annie Le Brun, followed by Octavio Paz.
†[*The Mysteries of Paris* was written by Eugene Sue. —*Trans.*]

behind him a Gothic landscape pierced throughout by lightning," prepared a photomontage at the beginning of 1930 intended to interest a film producer in his "adaptation" of Matthew Gregory Lewis's *The Monk,* in which Buñuel and then Ado Kyrou also took an interest.* But Artaud's would be a *Monk* "stripped bare, down to the quick,"† as Jérome Prieur put it in the issue of *Obliques* dedicated to Artaud.

Jacques Bernard Brunius offered unpublished fragments of William Beckford's *Vathek,* with an introduction. Paul Eluard wrote a preface—in which he alluded directly to Lautréamont—for *The Castle of Otranto,* the practically automatic novel by Horace Walpole. Breton also wrote a preface to *Melmoth the Wanderer,* "the great Satanic creation" (noted Baudelaire) by Irishman Charles Robert Maturin, the "surrealist in despair." As if by contamination, Julien Gracq published the already cited *The Castle of Argol* in 1938, whose *Environs* Kurt Seligmann explored in 1941.

André Pieyre de Mandiargues, meanwhile, under the pseudonym of Pierre Morion, wrote, in 1953, *L'Anglais décrit dans le château fermé,*‡ with its "marine dungeon of Gamehuche," comparable to "the Sadian athanor of the Château of Silling in a high valley of the Black Forest," "A sacrilegious castle in which crimes too pure for the light of day are born and achieved," as Duprey says in *The Sacrilegious Forest*!

Out of conformism, no doubt, William Beckford never went, at least *in writing,* to the ultimate end of an undertaking that cannot help but bring to mind that of the Divine Marquis. "Emmured we were 'au pied de la lettre.' Outside it is winter grey and cold, but for

---

*In 1972, Ado Kyrou (1923–1985) created a feature-length film, *Le Moine,* inspired by Lewis, from a screenplay by Luis Buñuel and Jean-Claude Carrière. Carrière, describing the screenplay, said, "Ultimately, very little of the book remained. We eliminated everything concerning the bloody nun and introduced a new character, the Duke of Talamur, who is not in the book." As for the film, he added, "Years later, Buñuel gave the screenplay rights to a friend, Ado Kyrou. He made a film, but it did not really succeed, to put it mildly." Kyrou also made a movie on Freemasonry for French television.
†Breton called Matthew Gregory Lewis "a surrealist in the beauty of evil."
‡Mandiargues's story brings to mind what Beckford, in his *closed castle* of Fonthill during the orgiastic celebrations of Christmas 1781, which were more or less organized by the Comte de Loutherburg, a friend of Cagliostro, lived in real life.

three days following doors and windows were so strictly closed that neither common daylight nor commonplace visitors could get in," the author of *Vathek* wrote in 1838, as cited by Jean-Jacques Mayoux in "La Damnation de William Beckford" in *Sous de vastes portiques*, whose author does not fail to emphasize (like André Parreaux) the comparisons that can be made between Beckford, on the one hand, and Sade and Blake, as well as Nerval, on the other. Mayoux also speaks of the "surreal character" of this work, adding, "For its time, *Vathek* is clearly the first major hallucinatory evocation of our literature." It can also be noted that the narrator in Edgar Allen Poe's novella *The Domain of Arnheim* explains that the death of the owner of these gardens "has given to Arnheim a sort of secret and subdued if not solemn celebrity, similar in kind, although infinitely superior in degree, to that which so long distinguished Fonthill."

The Château of Silling appears again in a 1969 painting by Toyen, with clearly tragic connotations, whereas Magritte had given us, in 1959, his vision of *Le Château des Pyrénées*, which illustrates in a gripping manner a much earlier verse by Daumal: "The cloud suddenly falls, it is a block of stone." Then there is the reference by Octavio Paz in *Eagle or Sun?* (1949–1950): "The castle crowning the rock is made of a single lightning flash." Not to mention that "small Celtic castle" that is the Rose Hotel in its night, a refuge, flanked by the Sun and Moon bar, for the "dreamers of the Setting Sun." Or in *Tête-de-Nègre* (Chocolate Brown),* Deodat XIV, "opposite the 'Sun King,' a sun shadow, a black sun on whose surface the excesses of sex and blood are glistening," as Philippe Audoin puts it. Maurice Fourré describes this Deodat XIV as "a nonagenarian baron with an ebony mask" in his Languidic castle. By the way, according to Philippe Audouin, all of Fourré's work can be placed in the wake of the gothic novel, most particularly of *Melmoth the Wanderer*, whose *Return* was celebrated by Jean Terrossian in a pastel drawing with that name in 1960.[3]

Slightly expanding on this castle theme in his article "Le noir des sources" (The Dark of the Springs), Philippe Audoin notes, "Still

---

*[In addition to "Chocolate Brown," the title *Tête-de-Nègre* can also mean "Turk's Head" or "Negro Brown." (And it is a chocolate-covered meringue.) —*Ed.*]

passable underground tunnels link the Castle of Otranto with that of Argol: travelers here cannot fail to stumble upon Mallarmé's stairs of Igitur while en route, and Huysmans's cellars of Tiffauges."[4]

Couldn't these underground passages, whose "entanglement . . . leads us astray like entangled plants,"* in which "the appearance of the smallest torch rends the darkness and causes alarm with the same dazzling brilliance as the storms without," be those "of the being," to which we are drawn, as Annie Le Brun says, by the "incomparable energy" of Sade's work, unless they are, as Jung maintains, the site of the alchemical katabasis, the descent into hell to which the beginning of the process leading to the Great Work is compared.

Around this same time (in 1962), Valentine Penrose, practically identifying with her character, lyrically analyzed *Erzébet Bathory: la Comtesse sanglante* (Erzebet Bathory, the Bloody Countess), who, according to Bataille in *Les Larmes d'Éros* (The Tears of Eros), "allegedly drew from [Sade] the howl of a wild beast."[5] Bathory's story had already partially inspired Bram Stoker's *Dracula* as well as Leopold von Sacher Masoch's *Fountain of Youth,* which Walerian Borowczyk brought to the screen in 1974—starring Paloma Picasso. It could be said that a Sadian atmosphere† reigned in Barthory's austere Hungarian fortress of Csejthe Castle during the time Rudolph II ruled over Prague and the Holy Roman Empire.[6] This Hapsburg emperor (1552–1612), who figures prominently in the subject matter of this book, had a pronounced interest in the esoteric arts, especially alchemy and magic. He exercised a decisive influence on the art and thought of the central European Renaissance. "King of fortune tellers and horoscope casters, emperor of alchemists, chiromancers, and necromancers,"[7] protector of mages and astronomers who had hastened there from all over the continent to take advantage of his largess, Rudolph II was also the powerful patron of Giuseppe Arcimboldo (1526–1593) at a time when analogies were believed to exist between creative nature and a man's artistic work.

---

*These could be the metaphorical plants of the "Gothic forest." (There are also many disturbing, unsettling forests in gothic novels.)
†As Caillois points out in *Le Mythe et l'homme,* a female automaton also appears in Sacher Masoch's novella, programmed to kill her partner during their amorous embrace.

Emblematic of this period when attempts were made to push back the frontiers between the mineral, plant, and human, Arcimboldo, a key figure of the imperial court (who was the subject of a study by Mandiargues) was the creator of odd "composed heads" whose renown was so prominent they became the origin of an entire art genre: the Arcimboldesques. The persistence of the Arcimboldian "imaginal realm," which gradually evolved into a kind of "fantastic naturalism," would not fail to leave its mark on the much later work of Magritte, Toyen, Jindrich Styrsky, Roland Penrose, and Richard Oelze, not to mention Ernst, Paalen, and Matta.[8] Of course this list should include Jan Svankmajer, whose short 1989 film with the Arcimboldian title *Flora* stars a character composed of plants in full decomposition.

It is easy to imagine Blodeuwedd, who was "flower-born," in Svankmajer's character (as we are in the old Celtic lands of Bohemia). She was, according to Jean Markale, the female figure entirely created out of plants and flowers in the Welsh story of Arianrhod and Gwyddion, with the complicity of the "shaman-Druid" Math.

In the middle of the 1950s, Leonora Carrington, who "remains in the tradition of Walpole and Ann Radcliffe,"[9] wrote *The Hearing Trumpet*, after her fantastic tale *The Starry Castle*. Her story also includes an abbey and a castle, but with a smidgeon of her humor, whose disturbing strangeness had already been highlighted in Breton's *Anthology of Black Humor*, unless it was an outcropping of the "*Uralptraum*, the 'fundamental nightmare,' that forms the primordial element of the magical-religious experience," as cited by Gérard Legrand in his rich contribution to the questionnaire accompanying *L'Art magique*.

A short time later, Yves Elléouët, with the help of two friends, Pierre Jaouën and his sister Anne-Yvonne, wrote a still-unpublished novel, *Portrait of a Castle*, that tells the story in the form of a poetic narrative of the return of a young man to the castle of his youth.[10] Trying again in the middle of the '60s, Elléouët coauthored an "epistolary gothic novel" with his friend Charles Estienne, an art critic who was also a friend of Breton and the surrealists but more importantly a huge fan of *Melmoth the Wanderer*, and the latter's wife, Marie-Hélène. It also remained unpublished. In this book, *Morimont*, "an alarming vampire . . . brought about the undoing of his sister-in-law, the poor Mathilde de Leuses."

In the same spirit, Leonor Fini, another person who was close to the surrealist group but jealously independent, published a book titled *Rogomolec* in 1979. The title of this book is "a Hebrew word, which in a very old and singular dictionary," Jocelyne Godard tells us, defines as "he who stones the king." It recounts the story of a feast in a monastery (Léonor Fini owned or rented a monastery in Nonza, in Corsica) and a palace haunted by monks, about whom it is impossible "to tell what gods [they] claim to be," and a hanged man, the whole story within a strange, "magical and nightmarish" ambiance close to that of dream and equally ambiguous.[11] The novel is not without kinship to *The Castle of Argol* by her friend Julien Gracq, with its Chapel of the Abysses.

Jacques Lacomblez, discussing architecture in an interview, said:

> I have very bad taste in architecture; in my opinion not much has been created since the castles of Louis II of Bavaria! I truly love ruins, on the other hand, especially the monastery ruins of Caspar David Friedrich, but the rest leaves me quite cold![12]

Farther east, a major figure—since 1970—of the Czech group whom we briefly mentioned earlier is Jan Svankmajer. Bernard Schmitt said of him:

> Surrealist, in other words, an alchemist, Svankmajer is a resident of Prague to boot, which is to say a citizen of one of the world's focal points whose magic no visitor, even one coming directly from Disneyland, could fail to feel . . . this same magic is at work in all his creative efforts.[13]

Svankmajer's short film *Otrantsky Zamek* (Castle of Otranto, 1979) is a fairly free and ironic, documentary-like adaptation of Walpole's book. Marie-Dominique Massoni and Bertrand Schmitt call Svankmajer "both theoretician and experimenter, craftsman and researcher, explorer and seeker." His films include a *Faust, Jabberwocky,* and *Alice,* which are evidence of his fondness for Lewis Carroll, as well as *Fall of the House of Usher* and *The Pit, the Pendulum, and Hope,* which bring Poe to mind. We should also note with Massoni and Schmitt that we can find in his work

> traces of the pansophism and multidisciplinarity that governed the court of Rudolph II. Hence, undoubtedly, Svankmajer's fascination with mannerism and everything connected to the golden age of the imperial court of Prague such as alchemy, astrology, Arcimboldo's paintings.

From 1981 until her death in 2005, he had worked with his wife, Eva, on the restoration of Stankov "Castle," a "former Celtic temple and old sixteenth-century dwelling," which he is seeking, according to Pascal Vimenet, to transform "into something similar to the Facteur Cheval's Ideal Palace crossbred with a surrealist dream," or, according to Guy Girard, "into the ideal castle of the surrealist adventure."

The great Italian specialist of dark romanticism Mario Praz, in his substantive work *La Chair, la mort et le diable* (Flesh, Death, and the Devil), mentions in these terms—and by indicating paths others have not failed to follow—the surrealists' taste for this kind of literature.

> If we next turn toward the surrealists, we find a Sadist theme holds a large place in their works: in the collages of Max Ernst (*The Hundred Headless Woman, A Week of Kindness*) corpses, chained women, and so on abound, the entire arsenal of gothic novels blended with elements of an entirely different nature, based on the poetics of Lautréamont, which is centered on the formulation: the fortuitous encounter of an umbrella and a sewing machine on a dissection table. The Sadist theme is quite prominent in books like Gracq's *Au château d'Argol,* Mandiargues's *Dans les années sordides* and so forth.[14]

Carrouges stresses that "Breton made ... an admirable social psychoanalysis of the myth of the castle in gothic novels: 'Ruins only appear abruptly and so charged with meaning that they are visually expressing the collapse of the feudal system.'" But according to Péret, who notes in his article on the gothic novel that "we need to place man's revolt against the outside world as the origin of the gothic novel, and revolt against the human condition itself, this phoenix born again from its own satisfaction,"[15] Annie Le Brun has no trouble showing, in her book *Les Châteaux de la subversion* (The Castles of Subversion), that while we can actually read "the death agony of and nostalgia for feudalism there," this fairly terse Marxist explanation cannot explain the fact that the "taste for castles seems to have gathered together those for whom poetry—in contrast to people primarily focused on social revolution—was the ultimate yardstick of human revolt," those who had chosen "the radical lack of topicality of poetry advancing always masked over the crest of time." Furthermore, notes Yves Vadé, "one of the characteristics of these novels is their reconciliation of the marvelous with historical time."[16]

"Social psychoanalysis," "Sadist theme" (to which I prefer the term *Sadean*), and, citing Breton again, "perfect adequacy to a given historical situation," the novel "of terror" thereby illuminated proves to be an "observatory of the inner sky," in some way a "veritable theater of *inner operations*."[17] It is, if not only, in the words of Anne Ubersfeld, "Un balcon sur la terreur," at least a kind of "pathognomonic" foreshadowing "of the great social disorder that would possess Europe at the end of the eighteenth century" ("Limites non-frontières du surréalisme").* Then it appears next as the "essential fruit," according to Sade, of these upheavals, the curious literary expression, "occult foundation of the Romantic interrogation," according to Le Brun, emerging from a more or less collective unconscious, of what had been first implicit in the political landscape of the era before becoming the groundswell that overturned the ancient order. In his second Haitian conference in 1946, Breton, summarizing his remarks, explained:

---

*"Limites non-frontières du surréalisme" is the title of a lecture delivered by Breton in London in 1937.

Ruins, as the preferred décor of the gothic novel, stealthily appear full of meaning insofar as they reveal the collapse of the feudal period, the inevitable ghost that haunts ruins is an expression of the intense fear of the return of the powers of the past, the underground corridors in which the actors venture every now and then represent the difficulties and perils encountered by the individual seeking to carve a path to the light. . . . As for the devil, who is never far away throughout these novels and who without having lost any of his dreadful power chooses to present himself under the aspect of a dazzling angel, I believe it possible to announce that he personifies the Revolution itself.

Annie Le Brun, again in *Les Châteaux de la Subversion,* develops this theme, which finds its culmination in *Sade: A Sudden Abyss,*[18] realizing around what Swinburne described as the "immense, explosive, inexpressible phantom" of this atypical but perfectly authentic Freemason who conspired "against the order from which reason takes its haughtiness"[19] the junction between the liberation of desire and political emancipation. If all this literature, indeed, finds its only appeal as an "absurd wall of shadow barring the landscape of the Enlightenment," it proves to be primarily "a space of uncertainty and obscurity, haunting as a piece of darkness torn from the night of which we are made," that it brings back to the surface! A balcony over nothingness to a certain extent! Carrouges asks, "May not the immense prestige Sade enjoys from the surrealists partially stem from the fact that he has taken up anew, in a new form perfectly acceptable to atheism, the theme of terrifying castles?" This provides an ironic echo of Doumayrou's assertion, "There is no life except for the castle!"*[20]

Man Ray's portrait of Sade—the future Genius of (the) Wheel—has the Bastille in the background, while Jacques Hérold's contribution to the surrealist card deck called *Le Jeu de Marseilles* includes Lamiel as an

---

*There's a pun, here. In French, *mener une vie de château* means "live a life of luxury." The meaning of Doumayrou's sentence would be something like: Isn't there another life than a life of luxury, une "vie de château."

extraordinary Siren of (the) Wheel (revolution) with "a burning brand at her fingers," who is holding a castle on her knees with its three towers thrusting up from a conflagration. Traces of this same Lamiel, a fiendish character of Stendhal's, can also be found in the work of Brauner and Max Walter Svanberg.

In the screenplay of a film on surrealism that Robert Benayoun wrote at the request of Breton to counter the premature attempts to bury the movement in May 1964 by Raymond Nacenta of the Charpentier Gallery with the complicity of Patrick Waldberg (a film that never advanced past the stage of rushes), a section can be found subtitled "The Surrealists at the Désert de Retz." This site was emblematic of their taste for masks and the more or less perilous castle serving as a meeting place for the members of a (if not secret) discreet society, placed under the aegis of high ancestors and the sign of mystery.

> In the Marly Forest, dark figures masked in white cardboard are gathering together in the bushes. They enter through the sinister, dilapidated gate of a PRIVATE PROPERTY. The identical masks give the scene the atmosphere of a Louis Feuillade film with lighting by Magritte. They head through the woods toward a ("fluted and diagonally truncated") circular tower formed from ten concave facets: a scabrous *folly* built in 1785 by R. de Monville for the sole purpose of fêtes galantes. The approach of the silhouettes is viewed from various angles, showing a pyramid, Doric columns, and a ruined pagoda, which surround the building. The visitors crowd the entrance to the tower.... Perhaps recognizable are André Breton, Mandiargues, Soupault, Joyce Mansour (selection to be determined).... Strange hosts are waiting on the half-crumbling spiral staircase. There is a young man in romantic dress and an eighteenth-century Marquis, both are *faceless* (a stocking conceals the faces beneath their wigs). Collages created from photos taken in various nooks of the tower, and through our editing, will permit us to include many other guests: Swift, Lichtenberg, Fourier, Rimbaud, Baudelaire, Forneret, Jarry, Roussel, Vaché,

Cravan, Péret.* At the foot of the staircase, a terrifying phantom: Jean Benoît in his necrophile costume. The guests vanish one after the other into the tower. A distant shot of the tower: desolate impression. Who knows what is taking place there now?[21]

The Freemason Swift's arms are as follows: "gold with a vert tree, struck by a bolt of lightning in gules moving from the sinistral canton on the top"; that of Lichtenberg: "sable with a gold gallows and a rope in gules topped by a lightning rod, placed on the dexter"; that of Fourier: "a gold field sowed with sable stars and purple lodestones with azure poles"; that of Rimbaud: "ermine with sable escutcheon in the center charged with a gold fess surcharged by five natural bezants: black, white, red, green, and blue, laid out along the fess"; that of Jarry ("surrealist in absinthe"): "the first half based on the Arms of Poland (silver field with eagle in gules), with the second vairy in three traits of sable and gold with a silver unicorn salient, both topped by a vert chief charged with two gold wheels, bisected by a gold saber with a purple dragon placed in one pallet overlying the partitions"; that of Roussel: "silver field with a gold patience placed in two pallets (*armes à enquerre*)"; and finally that of Vaché: "Vairy and counter-vairy in three tiers of gold and purple, with a silver chief charged by two facing sable sphinxes, placed over the partition."

I should say a word here about the Désert de Retz, the most beautiful of the "Anglo-Chinese gardens" from the eighteenth century (of which there were many). Built between 1774 and 1789—and thus a balcony over the Terror, if there ever was one—near Chambourcy by François Nicolas Racine de Monville, these abandoned gardens of Retz consist of around twenty "follies" (forty-seven were planned) on nineteen acres. Israël Bidermanas, also known as Izis (1911–1980), Prévert's pal, has left

---

*Almost all these figures have been given coats of arms in Marcel Jean's "Quinzaines héraldiques" in "Almanach surréaliste du demi-siècle." "Almanach surréaliste du demi-siècle" is a collection of articles, poems and drawings published by the surrealists in 1950 under the supervision of André Breton, as a special issue of *La Net*. "Les quinzaines héraldiques" is a series of coats of arms devoted to people the surrealists admired or who themselves were surrealists.

us some superb photos of these gardens. Gustau Gili Galfetti, who discusses them in his book *Maisons excentriques* (Eccentric Houses), says:

> It is wondered if the construction of these follies was dictated by the Masonic ritual of a lodge about which we are not even sure he was a member.[22]

In any event, the premises have an initiatory character, and we know that their owner received the grand master of the Grand Orient of France, Philippe of Orleans—the future Philippe Égalité—there as well as the author of *Dangerous Liaisons*, Choderlos de Laclos, who was also a Mason. About eighty feet high with a diameter of seventy-five feet, the tower (the Column), broken as in Masonic temples, was Racine de Monville's dwelling and was built around a central staircase. Symbolizing "Reason competing with the Supreme Being," it represents, Vincent Nocé says, "the tower of Babel, in which all the world's cultures crossed paths and which God destroyed for its excessiveness," hence the marks carved on it, as though left by lightning bolts. Babel is Breton's "cracked tower," which is to say the House of God, Arcanum 16 of the Marseille Tarot, which, as we have seen, is a symbol of the fragility of human constructions built on the sand of desire and destroyed by the very force of this desire. Nocé goes on to say:

> The Boulder at the entrance, a Platonic figure, organizes the passage of chaos into the world of knowledge. The Universal Mind wends its way through the civilizations (the Greek column, the Roman temple, the nomad's tent, the Chinese pagoda) culminating in the perfect form of the pyramid on the top of the hill, giving shelter to the purity of ice [the pyramid was used to keep ice]. In counterpoint, it is perhaps no accident that the chapel, baptized anew as a Gothic church, has been left [deliberately] in ruins at the bottom of the valley.[23]

So it is hardly surprising that the Désert de Retz, like the Sacred Grove of Bomarzo (as described by Mandiargues), the Tatin house, and the Facteur Cheval's Ideal Palace inspired the surrealists. It is impossible for any doubt to be nurtured with respect to this emblematic site. Breton had conjured it up earlier in the *First Surrealist Manifesto*.

> I am thinking of a castle half of which is not necessarily in ruins; this castle belongs to me, I can see it in a rustic spot not far from Paris. . . . Several of my friends have moved in. . . . The spirit of demoralization has taken up residence in the castle.

Among the friends in question was Jacques Baron, whose *Pick-me-up et les Femmes-Poètes,* which was written around 1927 and 1928 but only published recently, begins, "It is not chance that led me to this ancient castle perched on a rock in the middle of the sea," a castle beneath which, moreover, extends a vast network of rooms and underground passageways. Breton, in fact, alluded to it again from another angle in "Limits not Frontiers of Surrealism."

> My own search trying to find the most favorable place for receiving the great annunciatory waves held me spellbound, theoretically at least, in a castle only beating one wing.

Nor should we forget that the athanor of the alchemist sometimes takes the shape of a crenellated tower.

We owe the definitive words to the ever-tactful Audoin, writing in *La Brèche* in 1964:

> Irreducible to being simply picturesque, the Castle is still for many a place of fear and mad hope, and the armor, the impossible to conjure specter of the Other: the *first* person. It hardly matters that this Middle-Ages panic matches the worst clichés on more than one point and may even be complete fiction; if it is charged with that dark part lacking any admissible application of contemporary sensibility to help reveal, as if its negative, the temptation of the Unique—and its freedom.

But the message is sometimes more sibylline, like that found in the famous phrase from *Mad Love,* "The star castle built of philosopher's stone opens on the side of the abyss," or in this ethnopoetic observation by Péret:

> I think of the dolls of the Hopi Indians of New Mexico, whose heads sometimes schematically depict a medieval castle. It is this castle I am going to try to enter. There is no door and the walls have the thickness of a thousand years.

There is also this statement about Wassily Kandinsky from the *Diamant des apparitions* by José Pierre: "In the agate castle standing above the black lake of slumber, there are hermetically sealed doors to each domain, which require new keys for every step forward." It could be said that these last two are as sealed as Silling in *The 120 Days of Sodom*. The message can be even simply disturbing, like the recurring image in this passage from Elléouët's *Falc'hun:*

> All this was crowned by the ruins of the immense castle of Morvan-les-Briez with all the solitude of its stones. It advanced with its ageless prow in the clouds. You could say it was a heavy stone boat suspended at the heart of the village and similar to an anxious bird. This gigantic echo chamber rose up beyond the sea and the green and blond lands. It was clearly a large, sad bird made of stone, falling to pieces alongside the streets. An old dead barbarian, it was gradually crumbling over an ascending road that resembled a pig's spine. It could be heard falling apart. Sometimes at night, a block, from which time had erased all signs of stereotomy, would tumble down its crusty sides and bounce off the road, wounding it with a scratch.

We also have these lines of Jean-Pierre Duprey dedicated "To the castle of all metamorphoses and enchantments whose towers are the envelop of shadows of which each crenellation drips midnight at the invisible hour."[24]* Mandiargues also portrays several castles, particularly in *The Moon Dial,* that for want of being closed offer interesting characteristics and whose mysteries he attempts to pierce. There is the castle of Lueg, for example, in Slovenia, "which brings to mind a building toy for colossal children" because of its location "inside this cave whose mouth can be seen gaping in the rocky wall" and whose "rooms . . . only have true walls on three sides as the fourth . . . serving as the back wall is the rock surface itself, raw, rough, cold, and menacing as if, by means of revolt or cataclysm, the mountain had burst into the home," nature seeming this way to create a disruption to human order. There was also, "shaken out of reveries," the "Spy of Pulia, whose nasty name designates a castle still known as Castel del Monte, built for Friedrich II of Hohenstaufen and the favorite residence of this emperor." It "was the meeting place of the Germanic spirit with the Italian (Latin), Norman, Greek, and Arab," designed as "this starry prism and perfect polyhedron, a philosopher's diamond cast on arid earth between the East and the West," a place marked by the symbology of numbers "conceived as a projection or objective representation of that ideal and semiutopian empire described by the *Liber Augustalis,* ten years before the castle was built." Not to mention what "both owe to the treatises of Aristotle (and to those of his Arab commentators, who formed a large part of Friedrich's entourage) as well as the more secret teachings from the Pythagorian tradition."

But this message, as I mentioned earlier, could also be perceived as merely objective chance grasped as a manifestation "in real life" of a "vast network of stupefying reminiscences, premonitions, and coincidences," like that suggested by the photograph in *Nadja* of the Saint-Germain-en-Laye château that served as a refuge for the pretenders to the English throne—the Stuarts—under the reign of Louis XIV. According to Brother Bertin du Rocheret, this is where the first Masonic lodges on French soil were military lodges, from a Masonry that was sometimes described as "Jacobite"†—formed by Scots and Irishmen‡—were born.[25]

---

*The poet adds, in *La Forêt sacrilege et autres textes,* "If you see loopholes, know there is a black hand clenched there."
†The supporters of the Stuarts.
‡The Lodge of the Walsh-Dorrington Regiment recorded on the table of the lodges of the

To close the loop on castles and related notions that could have a close relationship with the "art of memory" (a subject we shall revisit), we can read in this same magazine (*Points de Vue Initiatiques*) an article by Charles B. Jameux, who was a member of the circle close to Breton in the three years preceding his death. In it he says:

> It was fourteen years ago, I believe in 1980, that I took part in a dialogue during which the philosopher Henri Tort-Nougès* compared the Scottish rite to a huge mansion, more specifically a castle. He said this castle contained thirty-three rooms (or chambers) and that each of them contained a treasure.

Thirty-three rooms, thirty-three degrees in the Old Scottish Rite, and thirty-three treasures! Even if we do not overlook the fact, noted by Paul Bancourt, "that the impregnable fortress designates the boundaries that the human form uses, in its hardening, to oppose all attempts by the individual to enter his own inner world," it is perhaps Mabille who ultimately gives us one of the keys to the enigma in his book *The Mirror of the Marvelous*. In his introduction, he likens his book to a collection of "admittedly enigmatic" plans that permit "the discovery of a mysterious castle, not far from the well-traveled paths, hidden by undergrowth and thickets." This castle, in which "nobody lives today," but where "though the perception of compact presences indicates it is the center of life," he identifies it several lines later as . . . the marvelous.[26] Mabille, an initiate who had crossed some thresholds (like Jameux, who said "one must cross through a door that opens 'on the interio'"), adds toward the end of this book these sibylline phrases that subsequently take on their full meaning:

> The Temple is located at the very heart of the castle, now grown to the size of a holy city. What building is it? There is only one,

---

(continued from p. 172) GODF (Grand Orient De France) at the Orient of Saint-Germain-en-Laye on the date of March 25, 1688. Not to mention the alleged existence of a lodge "consisting of Scots and Irishmen who were supporters of the Stuarts," in the same Orient starting in 1649.

*Tort-Nougès was later the grand master of the Grand Lodge of France.

Solomon once lived there. We are still on the square [the place in front of a church], close to the door. . . .

This is a marvel, colored, of course, by mystery.

Closing the loop, Kurt Seligmann indicates in *The Mirror of Magic:*

In every human being there is a child who only wants to play, and the most attractive game is mystery. The mysterious content of the human soul wanders through the meandering corridors of a mythical labyrinth, with underground congregations with candles (or illuminated by candles), secret passages in the double walls of castles, and treasures hidden in the halls!

The marvelous, hemmed with sedition, is the "original milieu," as Jean-Louis Bédouin puts it, of the group, and according to José Pierre it "engages the individual's deepest desires and leads him to freeing himself from the constraints of logic and the social order." This is marvelous, which, as Breton writes in "Pont Levis," "gleams at the farthest point of the vital movement and engages the entire emotional realm," but which is sometimes, as for Duprey in *Prospectreuses,* the ultimate rampart against madness.

At the edge of madness . . . between the two eyes of nothingness . . . at the ultimate border of the lightning bolts, stands self-erected in a single threadlike tip plunged into the HEART OF THE BOTTOM: the LAST tower of the castle of Estern.

This was not the case for Artaud, who speaks of Ville-Evrard as a "kind of castle of slow death."

7
THE UNAPPEASABLE SHADOW OF ARTHUR'S COMPANIONS

Surrealism and Celticism

We are all from Quimper.
LOUIS SCUTENAIRE

The poet is the one that advances toward others like advancing toward his own ghosts. The quest of the Knights of the Round Table has no end.
RADOVAN IVSIC,
CASCADES

The surrealists were impassioned by Gallic art, seen as the "telluric key . . . [that] elucidates the meaning of an ancestral message,"[1] and more broadly, by the Celticism, a product of that "North" from which a large number of initiatory traditions claim to originate, with its "natural fortification of granite and . . . fog." In this they followed the lead of Guillaume Apollinaire,* with his *Enchanteur Pourrissant* (Rotting Enchanter), which was decorated with André Derain woodcuts. Armorica interested them in particular, "that barbaric peninsula / where the bones of the earth pierce through its skin of herbs and thorns,"[2] and "this secret domain [where proliferate] mosses, lichens hanging from the low branches of old oak trees stooped with age, the slopes planted high with pollard trees, gorse bushes, and broom, the crumbling granite scree in which open the lairs of the heraldic ermine, the solitary menhirs on a hill in the moors from which at twilight can be seen the ringing steeples in four or five sleepy villages, the large wayside crosses studded with deities possessing the power to do anything (love, healing, and a good death), the old haunted marshes, the Troménies,† and the elf circles."[3]

We find many Bretons among the surrealists, such as Yves Elléouët, Aube's husband, to whom Breton wrote in 1956, "You are also Lancelot of the Lake in the game of analogies when I play it by myself." Elléouët was the Merlin of the imaginary portraits in *La Brèche* and one of the most splendid embodiments of this figure according to the catalog

---

*Apollinaire's coat of arms, according to Marcel Jean, is "azure and sable in bend sinister with three silver hillocks, the tallest of which is topped by a fountain, and two gold flames on the chief, all overlying the partition." Marcel Jean also observed (with his friend Arpad Mezei, in their *Genèse de la pensée moderne dans la littérature française*) that the poet's writings "incorporated orthodoxy with European and Asian heresies, Gnosticism, Celtic myth, and so forth concurrently, all essentially connected to the notion of modernism." He then ventured the following hypothesis: "Of the trinity of the soul, body, and spirit crucified on Mount Calvary, it is the body alone that is mortal. At least this is what Apollinaire claims in his very curious *Enchanteur Pourrissant*, funerary Christmas, reversed Nativity, which stages the central figure of medieval myths, Merlin the Enchanter, and in which not only the three Magi who are only the shadows of the true Magi, but many other mythological figures come, melancholically, to pay homage to the body of the Enchanter rotting in the grave. This is the overly close connection with love that kills the body; the Enchanter dies by will of the woman he loved."

†The Troménies are processions that take place in Locronan every summer. A "Grand Troménie" takes the place of the "Small Troménies" every seven years, and it includes twelve major stops on the second and third Sundays in July. It is much longer (12–13 kilometers) and much more deeply rooted in what is undoubtedly a pre-Christian tradition. Saint Ronan could be, as Jean Markale says in his book *Les Saints Fondateurs*

for the New York exhibition of 1961, and the author of the "bardish" *Falc'hun*—which Elléouët thought of calling *Horus*—and *Le Livre des rois de Bretagne*. The surrealists, hungry for the marvelous in all its forms, explored—especially starting in the 1950s—this Western path of the tradition, whose proximity they acknowledged: "The fellowship of the Round Table, the passionate quest for an ideal treasure that no matter how stubbornly it conceals itself is always portrayed as within hand's reach, rather easily symbolizes a warranty in the background—with vague repercussions—for some of the most typical contemporary phenomena, among which is surrealism,"[4] notes Julien Gracq, whose play *Le Roi Pêcheur* (1948), with an implicit reference to the Celtic god Nuada, was regarded as "fully surrealist."

And when I speak of the Western path of the tradition, I am thinking of the phenomenon of transmission which accompanied the arrival of Christianity in Armorica and other Celtic lands: from the last Druids to the first Breton "saints," that Audoin describes as "this minor people of gods baptized on the sly," "born on the wrong side of the blanket," which "the church is trying to dust off today," to its own detriment, for "they held the thread that still connects it to the Sacred," there has

---

(continued from p. 176) *de Bretagne et des pays celtes,* considered "the phantasmatic image of the Celtic Druid turned Christian priest" and "the crystallization of all the Druidic beliefs that remained alive in the populace beneath the veneer of Christianity." Breton spoke of these pardons (a religious procession in Brittany, unique of their kind) in the text he wrote for Yves Tanguy during his stay in New York in 1942: "The Procession of the Grand Troménie, all lace caps and velvet sleeves, circles the 'block' three times (as they would say in the States where Breton and Tanguy were then in exile), and then the faithful wheel off to follow in Saint Ronan's footsteps, looking straight ahead, paying no attention to the rustling of the hedges and ignoring the ditches, thickets, and bogs." Gwenc'hlan Le Scouëzec, in the *Guide de la Bretagne mystérieuse,* a source of inspiration, incidentally, for Elléouët, notes about them: "Surprising celebrations in this modern world, these festivals remain very much alive. It can be clearly seen that through its ancestral systems and beliefs, which are hundreds sometimes thousands of years old, Locronan, inextricably blending paganism with Christianity, has remained the center of the sacred land of Porzay, and the rites that occur there touch the deepest chords of the Breton soul. There is a local curse that threatens, "He who has not done the Troménie in his lifetime will do it in death by moving forward a coffin's length each day." This clearly shows how heavily the notion of the sacred weighs in the Breton imagination.

been a slippage of knowledge, a merger rather than eradication. The first Druids who accepted Christianity seem to have converted spontaneously, because of both the proximity of the esoteric essence of the two religions and the Celts's desire to save whatever could still be saved. Their means included a Celtic Church endowed with extremely singular characteristics, as illustrated first by the Pelagian heresy (which is noteworthy by its assertion of absolute free will), then following that church's absorption by the Roman Church in accordance with Charlemagne's political wishes, by means of legends and other folktales that were starting to be codified then (i.e., around the eighth century CE). These legends and tales now make up the Matter of Britain, that is to say of Armorica as well as of Ireland and Wales, in short those "regions," Pierre Mabille says, "in which Christianity merely blended the pomp of its rites to earlier religions, which remained at ground level." When he uses the expression "at ground level," it would probably be helpful to cast the light shed by these words of Adrien Dax to reveal the following nuance:

> We are told [the Gauls] worshipped a great god of night, and lunar myths, whose connections with the powers of biological renewal are well known, held primordial importance for them. We can feel that Night clearly remains here the mother of all wonders, and it is perhaps for an otherwise more profound reason than that of assigning the vanquished god the position of the eternal adversary that we can find in the Gallic Cernunnos a foreshadowing of the medieval Satan.

This may be why Adrien Dax, who saw in this culture "the first signs of an expressive tendency whose Cause has always remained that of Freedom itself," wrote in the fourth issue of *Médium*:

> It seems . . . that dualism, the constant reference of Celtic thought, often remained the indication of a true spiritual liberty and undoubtedly this is why the keepers of all the absolutisms have always risen up against them in their repression of the Manichean heresies and

other domains. I should say straight off that several extremely interesting contributions, like these references to the apocryphal gospels and, notably in Robert Boron's *Roman de l'histoire du Graal*, that of Nicodemus, which grants a particularly important place to Joseph of Arimathea, are closely tied to the Cistercian abbey of Glastonbury in Somerset. It may be helpful here to recall what Canseliet's good friend, the poet Philéas Le Besgue, revealed in his article "L'Essai de Rénovation Philosophique du XVIIIe siècle et le Celtisme," published in 1933 in the magazine *Atlantis,* n° 46. Relying on recently published books by Henri Hubert and Eugène Anitchkoff,[5] Le Besgue first recalls that among the "major currents traveling through the centuries, some openly, some, so to speak, underground," we must include "the Celto-Romantic ideal that gives supremacy to the notion of Beauty and considers Intuition as the preeminent creative faculty, leaving purely logical Reason the sole task of organizing and assembling." This ideal "was developed in its mystic form over the course of the Middle Ages thanks to Eastern religious influences whose effects only persisted in the West because of the presence of forgotten traditional elements and certain legacies buried in people's subconscious."

Reiterating Henri Hubert's theories, Le Besgue then adds:

What survived of Druidic culture in the unconscious of those people of Celtic origin in Germany, Gaul, northern Italy, as well as the British Isles, encouraged the Medieval expansion of Manichean-like doctrines permeated by Gnostic Johannism. These doctrines are embodied in *The Divine Comedy* as well as *The Romance of the Rose,* and in the work of Rabelais. They helped inspire the vocation of a Saint Francis of Assisi, paved the way for Luther and Calvin, instigated the sect of the Rosicrucians . . . and the illuminist philosophies of the eighteenth centuries. Romanticism itself, which took its name from the Breton Romans of the Middle Ages, plunged its roots there.

Next, relying on Anitchkoff's writings, Le Besgue says:

With respect to the episodes of the Arthurian legend, they would be based on Manichean concepts known in the West before the Slavic Bogomilism, and in any case autochthonous and independent. . . . This is how, in the various lands where Celtic atavism slumbered, more or less Gnostic and Manichean concepts began to bloom, in other words concepts that are Pythagorian and Druidic in spirit, although Druidism may have died without leaving direct heirs, something that remains unknown.

Le Besgue then cites Anitchkoff again, explaining, "The celebrated romance of *Lancelot-Grail* was thought out and conceived in England under the direct influence of Joachim de Flore's system. The provenance of Galahad's name confirms this." Bogomilism and Gnostic Johannism give Le Besgue grounds to conclude (and we should keep the paths this opens in mind):

The Gnostics claimed that Man could deliver himself from Evil through Science, meaning by knowledge of the Invisible World. This is salvation through Thought and no longer through Faith and Sacrifice. It opens the door to Pride. We have to accept it was a slippery slope. But the corner stone on which the purest Western tradition rests is nothing other that the Secret Gospel of the Round Table and the Grail.

Getting back to King Arthur, whose mighty figure soars over his work, Gracq implicitly assimilates him with Breton—whose Lancelot in this instance would be Rodanski—in the foreword of *Le Roi Pêcheur*, for example. With respect to the well-known phrases on the resolution of contradiction referred to earlier (chapter 2), did he not write, "A natural slope helps convince us that but for the difference of vocabulary, they could have invariably been uttered by the mouth of King Artus in his castle of Camalot"?

In 2009, in her book on Nadja[6] (Léona Delcourt), Hester Albach mentioned something she heard while conducting her research: "Breton was nicknamed the 'pope' but the surrealists make me think rather of medieval paladins with Breton as their king. They were friends and equals, but in the final analysis, each owed obedience to the king." Yves Elléouët seems to be commenting on this in *Tête cruelle* with his "Ermines over the petrified face of the last / king of Brittany."

Henry Miller, an author who spent time with the group, refers to this same Arthurian corpus to talk about the meteoric Joseph Delteil, about whom he writes (and which the man in question proudly repeated in his book *La Deltheillerie*), "If we could read his heart, we would find in it the ancient and noble spirit of a knight in quest of the Grail." In his book on Breton, Jean-Louis Bédouin, meanwhile, alludes to "the behavior of all those who, like Breton, are resolved to pursue an adventure whose course they may not have the right to alter," adding, "They wished to be wanderers, and it is with good reason they can be thereby compared to the legendary knights of Arthur's court, who never consented to stop or allowed anything, even fatigue or monsters, to stop them."

In 1927, Michel Leiris, with Jacques Baron, a native of Nantes, visited Quibcron, where "there was an old fairy who, as throughout Brittany, presided over the beauty" of the fishermen.[7] Leiris was not left behind in emphasizing the mythical aspect in its purest form of these medieval texts, as shown by this passage from his book *L'Age d'Homme* (Manhood):

> Among the legendary narratives, which I most loved as a child and which have not ceased to amaze me, figure the stories of the Round Table, which I first read not in their complete form, but in little illustrated booklets for children, extreme condensations that were perhaps all the more striking for having been expurgated, because all the accessory details were removed and nothing remained except the very essence of the myths.

This is myth in its purest form, certainly, but necessarily its most ethereal, as Leiris goes on to say, thereby introducing the sexual note that cannot remain out of sight for long when speaking of surrealism.

As a child, I was enthralled by these fabulous adventures filled with wizards, knights, and impossibly chaste damsels at the same time that the confusions of puberty stirred within me.

In 1937, like Roger Gilbert-Lecomte but not with the same goals, Antonin Artaud, shortly after his return from a Mexican trip that had fallen short of his expectation, took the path to Europe's Far East—Ireland. He was perhaps on the trail forty years later of Yeats's friend, the great dramatist John Milington Synge, about whom Soupault had already written a text in the fifth issue of *Littérature* and whom Breton deemed worthy of inclusion in his *Anthology of Black Humor*. Artaud was seeking "a very ancient tradition in its Western form," and despite the fact that he was "worn out by ceaseless suffering," he disclosed its profound reasons in a letter to his family. The letter was posted from Kilronan, the main port of the Aran Islands, in that "primitive Ireland," as Adrien Dax later observed in his article "The Topicality of Celtic Art" in the fourth issue of *Médium,* whose poetic sources remain as limpid as they are unknown. In this letter Artaud revealed:

> I am looking for the last authentic descendant of the Druids, the one who possesses the secrets of Druidic philosophy, who knows that mankind descends from the god of death "Dis Pater" and that humanity must be destroyed by water and fire.[8]

We know that this trip was cut short, but the concerns of the author of "The Nerve Meter" are no less edifying. In this regard, who could say what Breton and his friends in 1948 and again in 1949, after "having at least symbolically embarked in the bark of the dead that crosses back and forth between Raz Point and the Isle of Sein," according to Philippe Audoin, went looking for the ancient Sena on this island? This Sena, as indicated by Pomponius Mela and cited by Pascal Bancourt, was the home of colleges of

> priestesses called Gallicenae, [or Senae] who are thought to be endowed with singular powers, so as to raise by their charms the

winds and seas . . . to turn themselves into what animals they will . . . to know and predict the future and . . . to cure wounds and diseases incurable by others; but this they do only to navigators who go thither purposely to consult them.

This island, where these priestesses held court before the advent of Christianity, was also where their remote descendants still practiced sun worship when, in 1613, Dom Michel Le Nobletz, called *ar belleg foll* (the mad priest), went there to preach the Tridentine Counter Reformation, with its allegorical "cards" of the paths of heaven and hell. The ancestors of those who made these mission pictures, the famous *taolennou*, still used these cards in Lower Brittany until the 1950s.

Returning to Andre Breton,[9] we see him depicted by Claude Roy, who writes, "Yes, we met the Enchanter Merlin on earth at the end of his journey through the century."[10] Breton wrote these words to Robert Tatin* in November 1962:

> The tradition, I know of no other than the one which bears you and which I have always understood intuitively. You and I love it superbly veiled, as it is, but, in our depths, we grasp for ourselves alone its dazzling nudity, just like it arises for Taliesin's *Battle of the Trees*.[11]

This is the Taliesin who appears in Apollinaire's *Rotting Enchanter*, and the one who became a poet by drinking from the Grail's ancestor,

---

*Robert Tatin (1902–1983) was an outsider artist but not at all naïve. He was a kind of "Facteur Cheval" for the Laval area in the Mayenne, and his creation is still "inhabited." He was a friend of Breton and Fini, of whom he left splendid statues, as well as of Jean Dubuffet and Oswald Wirth, the Freemason and author of important books on symbolism. When looking at the dragon that watches over the entrance to his home [now a museum —*Trans*.] how not to think of the ogre or of the Proteus that Pier Paulo "Vicino" Orsini and Pietro Ligorio used to decorate in the sixteenth century the sacred grove or "park of monsters" of Bomarzo in Latium? Mandiargues described this latter location as "a spot that only resembles itself and no other" in his book about it, with photos by Georges Glasberg, *Les Monstres de Bomarzo*, which was published by Grasset in 1957. This site, if we can believe Ragnar von Holten, as cited by Karel Srp, even exerted its influence on Toyen!

Ceridwen's cauldron. Ceridwen, Elléouët tells us, is the "mother of Afang Du, the black beaver." For Jean Markale in "Mystères et enchantements des littératures celtiques" (Mysteries and Enchantments of Celtic Literature), she is the "Isis of the Cymric Celts."[12] Taliesin, who, according to Markale again, "appears as an initiate, truly an adept, the keeper of the strangest mysteries of material or spiritual life," received the cauldron "so that he could take from it the noblest of inspirations, the *Awen*," knowing that this container is "the equivalent of the veil of Isis uplifted, the symbol of higher initiation." Taliesin was the Welsh bard who wrote the poem "Cad Goddeu" (Battle of the Trees), in which, again according to Markale, "Celtic initiation is surely revealed" and "in which each tree holds an esoteric meaning." Taliesin's verse could not have failed to inspire Jean-Claude Charbonnel in his search for the "New Ys." Quoting this poem, Charbonnel says:

> I have been a raindrop in the air, the darkest of stars, the light of lanterns; I have been a huge bridge cast over three score Abers, the provisions of a feast, sponge in the fire, tree in the mysterious grove. . . .

This Taliesin with the "masticated beard," of whom George Cocaign, known as Troadic Cam in Elléouët's *Book of the Kings of Brittany*, is the reincarnation, is the same Taliesin who appears obliquely in the writings of Ithell Colquhoun in her 1972 collection of poems *Grimoire of the Entangled Thicket*—this impenetrable thicket is his property!—and especially in *The Waterstone of the Wise* in 1943, where an allusion to the poem "The Spoils of Annwn" subtly conjures the appearance of an Arthur who is not yet king.

In the foreword to his play *Le Roi Pêcheur*, Julien Gracq suggests an interesting reading track.

> But the two major myths of the Middle Ages, those of Tristan and the Grail, are not Christian; many of their roots reveal they are pre-Christian. The concessions that most often leave their mark on their confabulation cannot blind us to their essential function as an alibi.

The absolute strangeness of "Tristan" cutting through the ideological foundation of an era so resolutely Christian has been shown by Denis de Rougemont. If possible, the Round Table Cycle meets every attempt of delayed baptism or pious fraud with even greater rebellion. The winning of the Grail—it is scarcely possible to be mistaken about this—represents a terrestrial and almost Nietzschean aspiration to a superhuman status so aggressive that it would definitely accommodate this prudish coating poorly, one that is haphazard in a Christian context that could not be any more inconsistent.

But I should note that Marcel Jean and Arpad Mézei allude in their book *Genèse de la pensée moderne dans la littérature française* to the "solar myth of the Round Table, which was Christianized in Medieval chivalrous romances of the Arthurian Cycle by a tradition that was quite certainly Cathar originally." Jean Schuster associates the Grail (in his text "The Discreet Charm of God") with the "Roman arched thought of Bernard de Clairvaux," whereas Markale claims in his *Médium* article "Mystères et enchantements des littératures celtiques" that "the original concept of the Grail was purely and simply alchemical in nature and represented the philosopher's stone, the fruit of the adept's slow, patient efforts." Philippe Audoin may present the most convincing argument in his book on Breton (whom he depicts "as a Grail knight, the most ardent, the most often and best portrayed, the most adventurous, the one who has left and whose return is awaited"*) for this surrealist infatuation with the Matter of Britain, in which, as Markale says, "more than anywhere else, all the texts are coded and all the gestures are sacred." Audoin writes:

> It is emphatically worth noting that while the Arthurian geste became increasingly fascinating to Breton, it was in proportion to what it retained of myths before evangelization or more specifically Romanization, and in which he felt an emancipatory force capable

---

*In the game of imaginary portraits published in *La Brèche* in 1961, André Breton appears as the duke of the Black Mountain, whereas in his book about Breton, Charles Duits describes him as "the Broceliande Forest in a three-piece suit."

of countering the yoke of a humanism he believed responsible for the many chains imposed on imagination and desire.

Charles Jameux clearly confirmed that, although originating from Lancelot Lengyel's book[13] and exhibited in the articles "Triumph of Gallic Art" (1954) and "Present of the Gauls" (1955), the interest of *Arcanum 17*'s author for Celtic numismatics and their authentic rehabilitation rested on the realization that it revealed the strength of this thought far older than Roman imperialism as well as the existence of a fundamental divergence from the Latin spirit as the vision of the world is expressed by means of a reading "grid" that "gives access to transcendence"! Not to mention, as Jean-Louis Bédouin points out in *Vingt Ans de surréalisme: 1939–1959* that "getting ever more free of the Greek vision, commanded by anthropomorphism, and subject to stasis," the "dizziness" born of this particular notion of reality "responds to the profound need to replace man in the course of the stars and constellations" while "translat(ing) the action by which Celtic thought *opens* the petrified form, or at least one closed in upon itself, to put it in communication with cosmic energies." And it was the Druids, endowed—according to the ancient authors—with "superior intelligence, capable of grappling with the most abstruse problems, and disdaining mundane things," who were credited with having seen on the Macedonian coins that had inspired Celtic artists "the secret of man's relationship with the universe as well as indications of what may make him more conscious of his destiny," as Breton wrote it. However, as Lengyel stresses, surprising relationships with certain contemporary discoveries can be established.

> According to modern physics, the world of solid, visible forms is only the expression of energy. It clearly seems that the Gauls were committed to a path of research of these creative rhythms of the cosmos and attempted to depict their effects.

"Couldn't Gallic art, smothered by Rome, be found again in the blossoming of subterranean instincts that have remained mysteriously alive?" This idea borrowed by Breton to Lengyel in "Triumph of the Gallic Art" undoubtedly has some connection with the idea that a Western tradition, the bearer of a "philosophy that we may consider to be that of *true enlightenment*," would have been able, despite Romanization and its replacement Christianity, to hold its own through thick and thin.

In an October 22, 1980, letter to Vincent Bounoure, Charles Duits goes back even farther in time, recalling Breton's judgement on "appalling Greek philosophy," and his opinion about the "origin of evil" for which "Christianity is the most monstrous expression."[14] Confirmation of this view is offered by Jean Markale's books (and Markale was also a contributor to the surrealist magazines *Médium, Le Surréalisme, même* and *La Brèche*), in which he explains the way in which the Celts in general developed "an extremely sophisticated occult metaphysics that resisted Christianization," as Fabrice Flahutez will latter put it.[15] Yes, Christianity was resisted, but beyond it so was that Latin spirit abhorred by Breton who says:

> Latin civilization has had its day, and for my part, I ask that we unanimously give up trying to save it. It now seems no more than the last rampart of bad faith, old age, and cowardice. Compromise, ruse, promises of calm, vacant mirrors, selfishness, military dictatorships, the reappearance of the "Incroyables" (the "Dandies" of the French Revolution), the defense of congregations, the eight-hour workday, more burials than in the plague years, sports—there's nothing left but to give it all up.

Antonin Artaud wholeheartedly shares this opinion on the Romans when he vituperates, in *Heliogabalus or the Crowned Anarchist*, against

> this race of slaves, merchants, pirates, encrusted like crab-lice on the Etruscan earth; race that never had any spiritual viewpoint but sucking the blood of others; that never had any idea save defending its treasures and coffers with the help of moral precepts.

For the sake of completeness, I should mention Yves Elléouët's addition of "the Saxon enemy" in *Falc'hun* to these many denunciations, which echoes the analysis ventured by Ithell Colquhoun in her book on Ireland, *The Crying of the Wind*.

> The Celtic substratum in Britain, and to a lesser extent in France, is the collective equivalent of the unconscious in the individual [which] explains why the Anglo-Saxon strain, which plays the role of superego . . . distrusts and despises the Celtic strain, the incalculable id.

Perhaps we are entitled, again following Markale (whose pedagogical role for the group in this domain should be indicated), to see another reason that can explain the group's predilection for Celtism in the fact that

> for all time, and this is not a criticism but a laudatory observation, the Celts possessed a frenzied imagination; they always preferred imaginary wars and victories to real battles. They thereby conquered the entire world, around Arthur, in a bizarre dream blending the most exuberant kind of fantasy, boundless megalomania, and the obstinate quest for the Beyond.[16]

Exaltation of Celtic culture could thereby be viewed as a tool, making it possible to challenge reason as the heir of Rome, via Christianity, but this reason is not always necessary. The Czech painter Josef Sima, for example, who was highly influenced by the imaginal realm of Greco-Roman antiquity, as shown by the paintings with evocative titles like *The Return of Theseus (Theseus)* (1933), *Souvenir of the Iliad* (1934), and *The Despair of Orpheus* (1943), seems to have borrowed the castle motif (which appears in the 1931 painting *Landscape with Torso*) from the Matter of Britain. In her book on the painter, Vera Linhartova says, "This is the enchanted castle set within the whirlwind of the clouds, the revolving castle of the Grail quest." Further on, establishing a direct link with Daumal's *Mont Analogue*, she shows that "encircled by a wall of rays altering the field of vision and deviating the course of ships, this Mount is only accessible two times a year, on the solstices, by a narrow opening pierced on the tangent of the same sunlight," then suggests with feigned innocence some extremely interesting comparisons: "Couldn't the revolving castle of the Grail legend be accessible in the same way, following the same cosmic rhythm?" Couldn't we also access it in the same way "Merlin in his enchanted circle," whose "stupid history with Vivian" was, according to one of the heroines of Daumal's novel, "invented after the fact by allegorists who no longer understood anything?" Merlin, "by his very nature . . . is concealed from our eyes inside his invisible wall and can be found anywhere."

Merlin's "prison of air," Markale suggests in his *Médium* article "Mystères et enchantements des littératures celtiques," "is not a true prison, but a voluntary disinvolvement from the world resulting from the knowledge of great secrets that allows man to grasp the vanity of earthly agitation." This explanation has the added merit of "rehabilitating" Vivian, the "catalyst" and "the agent who directs the spiritual forces [of the old Druid] in the same way Beatrice served as Dante's initiator . . . with an idea of regeneration through sublime love."

Marc Saporta has clearly emphasized in the group work *André Breton ou le surréalisme même* that "Philippe Audoin and Marguerite Bonnet have highlighted the significance of this site of mystery and enchantment that in the Melusine tradition as in the life and work of the poet, was the magical edge of the *Breton* forest." This forest has always been closely linked to the castle and was a source of fascination long before the writing by Breton of "The Triumph of Gallic Art" in 1954 and "Present of the Gauls" in 1955,[17] and it continued during his lifetime, as in the title of the international exhibition at D'Arcy Galleries in New York in 1961: Surrealist Intrusion in the Enchanter's Domain.

A surrealist "on his best days," the "old Will," meaning Shakespeare, was hailed by Guy Cabanel in *Croisant le verbe* (Crossing the Verb).[18] The Bard, as he is known to the English, is indirectly summoned in Breton's *Alouette du parloir* (Parlor Lark, 1954) through the figure of Titania, the queen of the fairies in *A Midsummer Night's Dream*, who has come "from the other side of the mirror" as a delegate of the "powers of night." She also was the inspiration for three important paintings—particularly *Titania Caressing the Donkey-Headed Bottom*, which was shown at the Zurich Kunsthaus, by the Swiss-Anglo preromantic painter Johan Henrich Füssli (1741–1825), whose later influence on Blake and Beardsley was pointed out by literature historian Jean-Jacques Mayoux. Mayoux goes on to say that Füssli "invited artists to explore a neglected region, that of dream," which he "had never left."[19]

The ass/lover whom Titania tells, "I will slowly drive you out of your body, you will take on the transparency of air and become my spirit familiar," is the same as the title character of *The Golden Ass* of Apulieus (or rather, of his predecessor, Lucius de Patra). This takes us into the neighborhood of the mystery cults, not to mention the god with the donkey head of the gnostics, the demiurge Ialdabaôth! And not to mention the hermetic ass, the Âne-Timon, the "Antimony of the Sages," the primal matter of the alchemists.

As I just mentioned Beardsley (1872–1898), to whom Mandiargues devoted a tombstone collected in his *Musée noir*,[20] it is a good time to recall here the interest in the Arthurian legend he shared with the members of the pre-Raphaelite Brotherhood and their epigones, namely Edward Burne-Jones (1833–1898) and Dante Gabriel Rosetti (1828–1882). They both provided copious illustrations of the Arthurian legend, by means of paintings and engravings as well as by stained glass and tapestries. Burne-Jones depicted Merlin as a Renaissance scholar, and his *King Cophetua* lent its name to a very fine text by Gracq.

We cannot fail to mention Yves Tanguy of Locronan, a small village where a complete solar ritual was still performed in May and June into the twentieth century. His close friend Marcel Jean described him as "azure with a gold sphere." He was also called the "surrealist Druid," and Breton said he was "in permanent contact with terrestrial magnetism."[21]*

---

*Breton's allusion to terrestrial magnetism perhaps deserves comparison to this somewhat melancholic phrase from *L'Amour fou*: "I regret having discovered these ultra sensitive zones of the earth so late." It can also be compared with several observations in *Les Eaux étroites* by Julien Gracq concerning "places [that] enigmatically lift a veil over

The ashes of "this seer in his element," along with those of his second wife, Kay Sage, were scattered, at her request, by Pierre Matisse above the sunken city of Ys in Douarnenez Bay. This gives a specific meaning to the conclusion of the text "What Tanguy Veils and Reveals," published in *View* in 1942 by Breton, whom the painter, after their rupture at the end of the 1940s, nicknamed "the A. B. of the Dead."[†] His evocation here of "Yves behind the grating of his blue eyes," perhaps in the marvelous palace where Dahut is awaiting the propitious moment to reappear, is completed by Patrick Waldberg's observation that "a submerged Brittany is ringing out from the depths of his work." Tanguy, in fact, left his eminently personal mark on surrealism, and this account by his niece, Geneviève Morgane-Tanguy, deserves to be heard:

> He was quite brilliant on the subject of Druidism, having studied since his arrival in America all kinds of "witch stories" from around Salem but which were in fact the remnants of rites once practiced in these regions as they once were in Ireland and Armorica. He consulted books on the Celtic civilizations, on the origins of the Celts and Druidism, on their philosophy, their magic powers, comparing them to Indian magic, their healers, their herbs, their sacred language, their incantations, and their shaman's spirit journeying, comparing all that with India and Egypt.[22]

Tanguy also dreamed, according to Josick Mingam, "of hearing of a connection between the Carnac in Morbihan, Brittany with the Egyptian Karnak."[23] This passion, Chantal Vieuille tells us in her *Kay Sage ou le surréalisme américain* (Kay Sage or American Surrealism), was shared by his companion.

(continued from p. 190) the future [and] carry in advance the colors of our lives," those places connected to "force fields that the Earth guards for each of us singularly under tension," about which he adds, "More than the 'kiss of the planets' dear to Goethe, there is reason to believe that our life-line is confusedly illuminated by this."

†There is a pun, here, on "la Baie des Trépassés," the Bay of the Departed, Bae an Anaon in Breton, at the end of the Finistère, facing the isle of Sein.

The two artists were equally enthused by histories of magic, sorcery, superstitions, and rituals. Occultism occupied a large place in their intellectual research, under the guise of conjuring up the Egypt of the pharaohs, the Brittany of the Druids, the Mayas, the Indians, and to end up again with surrealism.[24]

In the years of 1925 and 1926, in other words directly after his discovery of Chirico* and his decision to devote himself to painting, Tanguy, whose father was interested in pre-Christian Celtic culture and frequented the symbolist and occult milieus of Paris, wrote:

> *O Giantess*
> *Show me your mountains*
> *And your torrents*
> *Show me your forests and clearings*
> *Show me your herbs and flowers*
> *But the features of her face*
> *Remain troubled, and*
> *She goes off, floating into the distance.*
> *A low voice says:*
> *If you wish to know more,*
> *Look deeper, deeper.*[25]

To avoid interpreting Tanguy's "giantess" as a figure of the "Matter-Mother," the primordial great goddess who may be an ancestor of Mélusine—at least in Gaul—and who will haunt his whole work, Gordon Onslow Ford fittingly says:

Planet Yves is a manifestation of the feminine side of the psyche that has been manhandled or repressed by the patriarchal society in which Tanguy was raised.[26]

---

*Chirico's coat of arms, according to Marcel Jean, was "silver companioned by vert under the shadow of an azure setting sun." Among the artists who made a deep impression on Tanguy, we must include Hieronymus Bosch.

This confirms Breton's intuitive insight in "What Tanguy Veils and Reveals":

> The Mothers!—we feel a tremor of Faust's terror, like him we are paralyzed by an electric shock at the mere sound of these syllables, which conceal the all-powerful goddesses who are impervious to time and place, "some seated, others coming and going as it may chance." The Mothers: "They will not see you, for they only see those *beings* who are not yet born" (Goethe). Human thought blazes forth, then soon fizzles away, when it contemplates these divinities, thanks to whom everything possible tends constantly to become manifest.

Restoring to them what may be their true face, Jean-Louis Bédouin, in his article "Eros and the Death Instinct" that was cited earlier, makes a particularly gripping comparison of these deities with the heroine of Pauline Réage's *Story of O*.[27]

> Beneath her night bird mask, O comes from a time long before Christianity. In some way, she is the original night ruled alone by the powers of sex and blood that engender and destroy in the same sacrificial act. These are powers beyond the control of religion now.

Wouldn't this goddess also be shining at the heart of the Wifredo Lam painting *Light of the Forest*?[28] In this work, Lam, "exploring the unconscious through myths, paints a woman based on the goddess, the original mother, echoing the surrealists who were seeking the unconscious through archaic and primitive images." It may well be this same "entity" in the burst of multiple facets of the feminine of whom Max Walter Svanberg was thinking when writing for the 1959 Eros exhibition:

> But She is always a vision in transformation and just when you think you have caught Her She flees, perhaps leaving the hands of her would-be worshipper behind Her, covered in gold dust.

She is the one of whom Sarane Alexandrian was thinking when he put these words into the mouth of his Simon Fontanier, the hero of his 1960 novel *L'Homme des lointaines*.

> I was recently asked if I believed in God. I said no, but I should have added that I believe in the Goddess. In fact, it seems to me that the universe is governed by a maternal, wise Feminine principle, whose symbolic manifestation is the night.

Twenty years later, Duits, in a letter to Vincent Bounoure, went so far as to raise the question of the goddess directly:

> Is it possible in 1980 to replace "the God of absurd and provocative memory" ceaselessly stigmatized by surrealism with a Goddess? This would proclaim that the rising sign about which Breton spoke in one of his most inspired texts represents the formation of the authentic lover of Wisdom who grasps, thanks to his infallible intuition, that the Feminine Principle is the sole object the Masculine Principle can worship in the trialectical sense of the verb—both sexual and spiritual—and that the occultation of this fact is the cause of the Age of Darkness and that the end of this occultation marks the beginning of the Age of the Dawns.

In 1997, Markale echoed Duits in his book *Le Grande Déesse: mythes et sanctuaires* (The Great Goddess: Myths and Sanctuaries)[29] when proclaiming:

> No, the Great Goddess is not dead, and the shadow of the Virgin of the Beginnings extends more than ever over a world in full interrogation about its future.

But Tanguy, "guide from the time of Druids with mistletoe," and Duits, "like a stained-glass saint" (as he was described by Anaïs Nin), are not the only ones to be thus haunted by the anima. Philippe Audoin also notes the following about Maurice Fourré's book *Le Caméléon mys-*

tique (The Mystical Chameleon), with an allusion to sacred geography and its assumed rites (see chapter 5) as a bonus:

> In fact, the "plot" is placed in Bourges, whose central nature Fourré takes pains to note, and it is quite true that this city has, since Celtic times, been regarded as one of those "navels" through which the profane visible world can communicate with the sacred invisible world governed by the great chthonic Mothers. In short an ideal spot for an initiation.

Markale, mentioning a "cosmogonic concept dear to the Celts," speaks about one of these "omphalos in which the rays of the sun converge."[30] It so happens that Audoin was already quite familiar with this location by virtue of having written *Bourges, cité première*, which was published by Julliard in their "Places and Gods" collection, directed by Gérard de Sède. Audoin examined the singular features of this city in this book, particularly the relationship between alchemy and architecture. Then, from the pen of Fourré, an Angevin native, we find in *La Nuit du Rose-Hôtel* (The Night at Rose Hotel), "Neighboring Brittany and its mystic fogs already spreading unease in the hearts.... An empty porch swing, over the leaden surface of Lake Ys, tows King Gradlon's daughter by her necklaces in its phosphorescent wake." Dahut, "the good witch," is the personification of the goddess of waters and a cousin to Melusine and to the Vouivre—the "guivre" and its "guivrets" of Apollinaire—and to the Irish banshee, sometimes depicted as a lady of the Sidhs, a wandering figure from the other world, often depicted as a siren, like Flory, the abbot's diabolical mistress in Gengenbach's *Judas or the Surrealist Vampire*. It is Dahut again who so beautifully embodies "occulted feminine sovereignty . . . submerged beneath the waves, in the dark depths of the unconscious," and who, "when she reappears in the light of day," will make possible "the realization of the harmony of the world" and "the lost paradise to be restored where rules, all-powerful and eternal, the sun-woman, she who bestows life and procures the intoxication of love," as Markale says in "The Triple Face of the Celtic Woman."[31]

Regarding Breton's preface for Fourré's *La Nuit du Rose-Hôtel,* Marc Le Gros indicates quite cleverly:

> So when [Breton] comments in a footnote, "the quest for the Grail is not far away," it is fairly clear that the admission is equally relevant for him and that what is at work in each of them is the same desire to magically appropriate the chosen land again, that Brittany, which is both the primordial land but also the final land where the gold of the thousandth morning will rise. A land for which Broceliande is not only the mythical emblem, but in a more profound way a kind of symbolic navel with a cord of black sap, marvelously concentrated and shining with a blinding light.[32]

This is also why Breton, Elléouët, and Gracq all give an unexpected if belated wink at François-René Chateaubriand, whom Breton deems a "surrealist in exoticism" and who Elléouët says is "crushed under the cross on his islet," in an allusive manner in "Not Wilted on My Lapel," one of the last poems in his last collection in the case of Elléouët, and more emphatically but also more emblematically, in the case of Breton, as a kind of accepted return to the source, as it can be seen in his interviews with André Parinaud:

> As a child of Brittany, I like the moors. Their flower of indigence is the only one that has not wilted on my lapel.

From this perspective, it is fairly amusing and symptomatic to find this in a 1956 letter addressed to Yves Elléouët by Aube's father:

> You are a composite of the ferocious and the exquisite whose seductive virtue I did not feel before meeting you. There is something of Chateaubriand as well, I do not want this to offend you; you know that what I tell you is said with great affection.

As for Gracq, he had written, in 1960, a text on Chateaubriand, "The Great Peacock," which ends with this admission: "We owe him almost everything." And he talks in *La Forme d'un Ville* (The Shape of a City), which was his reminiscence of Nantes, about the "broom and heather [that] continue to orchestrate in [his] memory the phrase from *René* to which their image has been bound since the time he was introduced to the book: 'During the day I would wander the vast heaths, which would end up becoming forests.'"[33] Rodanski makes a similar observation concerning his identification with the Breton countryside in the closing lines of *Lancelo et la Chimère,* an unclassifiable book from the beginning of the 1950s:

> After a long sojourn in the land of shadows . . . I will go back into the house that a famous magician, a divine friend always seals over his loyal supporter. . . . At the end of this account, it, in fact, seemed assured that I should find the house and know the girl of the Vale of No Return. She only takes life (or exists) at midnight, when the doors become ethereal until dawn crumples faces into pale sheets. I am one of those for whom the world is an eye, interminably on the strand.

And it may even be Penmarch Strand, to which he attributes so much importance. "Penmarch is where the dying Tristan had himself carried to watch the sea for Yseut [*sic*] the Fair's return." It is actually this romance of Tristan and Iseult that serves him as a landmark, even though he later chose another emblematic hero.

> This Celtic romance has fascinated me since childhood. In 1947, I remember often telling Vera [Hérold] that I was Tristan, the abbreviation given to my first name—Stan instead of Stanislas—being the last syllable of Tristan. I have often mused on this romance since then. I do not think it is such a good subject for a story. But I trust too much to fate to not recognize that, if it permeates my being, objective chance—beautiful as the encounter of a rudder and a white wing splattered with blood on the edge of the sea—has justified it. To run the risks of this adventure with the minimum chance of imposture, I decided to henceforth attribute myself another figure

who had been much less exploited by art, a figure who under another name would all the same be as often mixed up with intrigue as with an interlacing path and to whom—by the admission of his legend—potions and hypnotic sleeps were not spared: Stanislas Rodanski, 1927–19__. Frequentative individual (claims to be Lancelot), plays at jack of clubs.[34]

Lancelot, the "jack with white weapons," associated with the shamrock, is the emblem of water spirits, and, ironically, of luck. Lancelot is also "the utopian and sympathetic Lancelot" Mac'Horn, the husband of Florine Allespic in Maurice Fourré's *La Marraine du Sel*,[35] the very same author whose pen left these words to be read:

> *I am a man of the West*
> *A small dark Celt*
> *The sun and fog share my heart*
> *My soul under the changing sky*
> *Colors*
> *With a thousand fires*
> *Smiling among the tombs I weep*
> *Among the flowers*
> *Ever a pilgrim of something else*
> *Pilgrim*
> *Of*
> *Always Something Else.*[36]

But, of all these young men who Charles Estienne says "walk on the shore like the first men and who find again the spirit of the Picts, Scots, and Celts of the megaliths in their works,"[37] it is undoubtedly Yves Elléouët who best awakens the myths that are dearest to the Bretons (of all Celtic lands). In an article published in *Surréalisme,* issue 2 (June 1977), Markale takes pains to state, "The Celtic myth is there in all its splendor [and] Elléouët is permeated by it as no poet ever before," then adds, "Falc'hun lurks on the border of two kingdoms, those of the living and the dead, with no clear idea as to which is his." Elléouët, for example, lets us witness the resurrection of a Troadic Cam reminiscent of the Cerne Abbas giant in Dorset or Dagda, the great Irish Druid god with the club, and summons "Ahès, Dahut, Mary Morgane," a pre-Christian figure or even a truly demonized anima who is unique in every sense of the word, "red-headed Mary Morgane" or "Ahès of the vert eyes," "luminous daughter of the King of Cornwall," "the maddest of all the women of Ys with its sea gates." There is yet another example when he describes the equally torrid and phantasmatic loves of a Georges Cocaign imagining himself as "Merlin the Enchanted in the middle of a bubble of air where no part of Broceliande has suffered any change" with "(his) fairy Vivian," who is "the desirable red-haired Lady." But the best example of that revival of the Celtic myths under Elléouët's pen is perhaps to be found when he evokes the names and lives—carefully revised and corrected—of the more or less legendary kings, bards, and saints of Celtia, Graillon [sic] of "the broken heart," and Guénolé, Salaün, and Myrddin, Hoël "with his Broceliande eyes," and Samson, Erispoë, and Llywarc'h-Hen, Judicaël, and the 7,777 saints, Nominoë, Alain Barbe-Torre, and the "Rothéneuf family contorted over the rocks: a clan overwhelmed by the weight of its turpitudes," although placed under the patronage of Saint Budoc, born from the chisel wielded by the naïve artist Father Fouré in his High Folly, and "others, yet others, with no concern for genealogies and precedence, blending History's contestable dates in a tumultuous wine."

Among these, inasmuch as it is impossible to draw a line between the real and the imaginary, is Falc'hun himself, described as follows by Michel Leiris in his preface: "a proud fellow . . . skirt chaser, barroom brawler, and casual dreamer of old stones, ruined castles, and other pieces of incriminating evidence of the romantic ceremonial." All this is contained in a pantheist world in which "the wind . . . is the friend of every solitary moment" and "presses a little harder against the woman's waist" before "[raising] its enormous head" in the "vaginal night," where "the hours flow by into the ears of the dead" who "mop up their wounds at the crossroads," where "the sea licks itself and marks the sands with its singing nails" and "the harsh Atlantic . . . chews the bodies of the dead in its cold furnace."[38]

Michel Dugué also underscores in a few words the nature of the bond spun this way by Elléouët between surrealism and Celtism.

> Cocaign and Falc'hun are individuals who suffer from attempting to change life. This is clearly their challenge and their quest is imbued with this fantastic demand, thereby intersecting with the errantry of the ancient Celts in search of the Blessed Isles. This quest is doomed to be pursued endlessly.[39]

Writing about Elléouët to Aube Breton in a 1983 letter, Per-Jakez Helias said, "If there is a metaphysic for us Celts—which I believe—Yves is certainly the man who felt it most strongly." This is the same Yves Elléouët who in a letter to Gallimard refused to allow the word *bard* to be tacked to his name. He said it would be a parody, bringing him down to the level of "all the Breton imagery for cracker boxes, à la Théodore Botrel." He had chosen "substantial allies" from among the surrealists and from overseas who were Celts like him, "drunken wanderers/chock full of bitterness," such as James Joyce, Samuel Beckett, and Dylan Thomas, whom he had discovered in Jacques B. Brunius's translation.[40]

On the other side of the English Channel we have Ithell Colquhoun, who deserves a place apart. She was directly influenced by Robert Graves's monumental study (himself a writer of Celtic origin) *The White Goddess,* which is about the pre-Christian deity who ruled over the Tuatha de Danaan and governs the inspiration of poets. Graves writes:

> A true poem is necessarily an invocation of the White Goddess, the Muse, the Mother of All Living, with the ancient power of arousing fright and lust—the female spider or queen bee whose embrace is death.[41]

In a word, she is the incarnation of the magical powers with which the surrealists adorned women in their erotica: "Every woman is the Lady of the Lake."[42]

But Colquhoun was also influenced by the work of the Irish occultist, poet, and Nobel Prize winner William Butler Yeats, an influential member of the Golden Dawn and artisan of the Celtic Revival, as shown, for example, by one of her paintings from 1949, *The Battle Fury of Cachullin* [*sic*]. An official Druidess and a member of the Order of the Keltic Cross, this artist, who was a descendent of the great Scottish clan of Colquhoun, whose lands occupy the west bank of Loch Lomond north of Glasgow, attended numerous *gorsedds* (assemblies) in Brittany and Cornwall, where she ended her days in the Valley of Lamorna, between the *finis terrae* of Land's End and Saint Michael's Mount. Taking into account the dual Masonic and Druidic affiliation of this woman, it is not irrelevant to recall that modern Druidry owes its awakening to a curious figure who was a friend of Jean-Théophile Désaguliers, the kingpin of speculative Freemasonry, and to numerous members of the Royal Society like John Toland (1670–1722), for example.

Toland, an attentive reader of Giordano Bruno and the author of *Pantheisticon* (1720), as well as the books *A Summary of Ancient Irish Christianity* (1718) and *A Specimen of the Critical History of the Celtic Religion and Learning* (1726), proclaimed the renaissance of Celtism in 1716. In the autumn of 1717 (!) he created the Druid Order, which, after his death, would be headed by his successor, the Freemason William Stukeley, who was also a member of the Royal Society, an assembly of "scientists" and clergymen that had been more or less founded on the initiative of Isaac Newton and which was a breeding ground for the executives of the newly formed Masonic Order.

Another figure of the Druidic revival of the eighteenth and nineteenth centuries (this time in Wales) was the poet and probably Freemason Iolo Morganwg (born Edward Williams, 1747–1826), who was a friend of William Blake (and the counterpart of the Scotsman James Macpherson). Macpherson is supposed to have collected ancient folktales throughout Scotland. And Iolo Morganwg is supposed to have collected other ancient folktales in Wales. The creation of the gorsedd and the modern image of the Druid by Morganwg was inspired by the myths and structures of Freemasonry, as Andrew Prescott indicated,[43] a process that would culminate a short while later with *The Origins of Freemasonry* by Thomas Paine, another friend of Iolo Morganwg, who openly proclaimed Masonry as the "conservatory of the religion of the Druids!"*

"Tomorrow! Tomorrow, we will go to the grove with the skeletons of Ossian draped in white robes," Jacques Baron wrote in 1922!

In 1951, Ithell Colquhoun published a short hermetic narrative (115 pages), probably finished around 1940, that owes much to the gothic novel and to the Grail cycle, as well as to MacGregor Mathers's *The Book of the Sacred Magic of Abra-Melin the Mage—The Goose of Hermogenes*, one of the rare names of the philosopher's stone. Michel Rémy explains that it is "an alchemical vision of the transmutation of things,"[44] but it is also a plea on behalf of the now deposed Great Goddess, the embodiment of the sacred feminine. Eric Radcliffe writes, "This book was described as the most sustained surrealist text in the English language" and adds that it was "in fact 'surreal' according to Breton's criteria." In 1955 Colquhoun published *The Crying of the Wind: Ireland*, then in 1957, *The Living Stones: Cornwall*, in which she passionately speaks of the attraction the myths and landscapes of these

---

*It may be helpful to recall here what Jean Markale, citing Julius Caesar's *De Bello Gallico*, said in his article on Rome and the Celtic era: "The Druids 'feel their religion does not permit them to entrust the content of their teachings to writing . . . because they do not wish their doctrine to be divulged nor do they wish their students, relying on writing, to neglect their memory.'" It is clearly visible here that there was a "restoration of the tradition." The few fragmentary pieces of knowledge we have on Celtic religion have most often come down to us through Irish or Welsh manuscripts compiled by monks, and therefore are scarcely reliable. In 1812, an author even tried to demonstrate that the secret of the Freemasons resided in the origins of their order, which he traced back to the religion of the Druids and their alleged sun cult. This author, a key figure of the American Revolution who was also active in the French Revolution, was Thomas Paine. He, moreover, was very likely not a Mason, and he ends his posthumously published work, *The Origins of Freemasonry*, as follows: "And from the remains of the religion of the Druids, thus preserved, arose the institution which, to avoid the name of Druid, took that of Mason, and practiced under this new name the rites and ceremonies of the DRUIDS." The Scotsman James Macpherson (1736–1796) "translated" and "arranged" as he pleased the Gaelic poems attributed to Ossian (Usheen),** which would become one of the sources of romanticism. **"Usheen" is the real Celtic name of "Ossian," which is one of Macpherson's "arrangements."

Celtic lands, with their cromlechs and other standing stones, hold for her because of their magical nature. These stones were sometimes the subject of her paintings, as in *The Dance of the Nine Virgins* (1940),* *Sunset's Birth* (1942), or the *Pénil des mennirs* (1943), the title Ithell Colquhoun herself gave to her painting (see Eric Radcliffe's book, in English)—some Celtic landscapes Toyen would also paint on a later date with her superb *Ile Quellern* (1958)†—as were their sacred wells or caves, which she regarded as "energy geysers" at the sacred sources of a pantheism that compelled her to write, "I am identified with every leaf and pebble, and any threatened hurt to the wilderness of the valley seems to me like a rape." Underscoring her fondness for legends about "the little people," Eric Ratcliffe describes Colquhoun as a "natural sensitive" endowed with an "acute sense of life force, psychic power, or ancient meaning of the message stored in some granite masses, in old stone crosses, stone circles, menhirs, dolmens, and so forth in this former territory of the Dumnonii, which stretched to well beyond the eastern boundaries of Devon from the west of Cornwall."

Colquhoun often makes subtle allusions to works by French writers in the titles of her paintings: *Lukewarm Rivers* (1939) is borrowed from Mallarmé's poem "Tristesse d'été" (in which *river* is singular, though). *The Approximate Man* is from Tristan Tzara's collection of the same name, and *Communicating Vessels* (1941) is inspired by Breton's *Les Vases communicants* (1948).

Another Englishwoman, to be exact an Anglo-Irish woman, who describes the apocalyptic appearance of the Grail to the residents of a retirement home in her book *The Hearing Trumpet,* Leonora Carrington

---

The Dance of the Nine Virgins is composed of seven drawings.
†The stone site involved here is undoubtedly Boscaven, but three stone circles near Land's End are called "the nine maidens," and there is a fourth circle near Bodmin, not to mention the "Merry Maidens" of Bunyan, whereas *Sunset's Birth*'s context is the Men an Tol, also called Crick Stone, a hollow circular megalithic monument located in Morvah near Lamorna. The "nine maidens" irresistibly brings to mind the nine girls whose breath warms the cauldron of the Master of the Abyss in Taliesin's poem "The Spoils of Anwyn," which is included in Markale's anthology *Les Grands Bardes Gallois*. The *Pénil des Mennirs* owes its title—in which the word *menhir* is misspelled—from Jarry's poem *Les Jours et les nuits* (1897), possibly via Breton's *Nadja,* which quotes from it.

was also influenced by the work of Robert Graves and inspired by Celtic art and myths, as indicated by Delmari Romero Keith in a recent study of the artist. In this text he writes:

> Salomon (Salomon) Grimberg acquired the notion of "magic art" that will be used later by Breton to grasp the works of Leonora, and has meticulously examined the interpretation of Celtic myths. The impressive legacy left by the Celts can be measured by their high mastery in the drawing of flora and fauna. Plants have religious significance in accordance with their shapes as spirals, undulating brambles, lotus or palm leaves, or concentric circles. The images of the deities, hybrid monsters and mythic animals, were adorned with plant motifs. This calligraphy is reminiscent of the *Book of Kells,* an extremely elaborate manuscript created by eighth-century Irish Christian monks, whose convoluted style is close to Leonora's.[45]

This cultural influence seems to have been large enough to inspire Trieste native Leonor Fini's painting *The Alcove: Interior with Three Women* (circa 1939), a portrait of Carrington as a Celtic warrior queen (see plate 11). This is the same Leonor Fini whose heroines, according to Marcel Brion, come down "from the deepest inner kingdom to the kingdom of the Mothers," again. Her approach can also appear quite close, sometimes, to that of Yves Tanguy, in Constantin Jelenski's opinion, as cited by Jocelyn Godard in his *Léonor Fini ou les métamorphoses d'une oeuvre.*

> The imaginary society created by Leonor Fini is clearly matriarchal and is so seemingly because she recreates the spiritual organization of primitive societies that were also matriarchal. This is not the sign of feminine dominance but of affiliation with a very old form of worship.

Unica Zürn's "Les Jeux à Deux," a very odd text more or less written at Hans Bellmer's instigation and which forms one of the four parts of *L'Homme-Jasmin,* features a seemingly fragile heroine she calls "Norma," as fragile as her in any case, who is "a resuscitated woman among the dead, a dead woman whose aura has not left the house," but also "a Druidess [who] knows she is listening to the forbidden music of the departed Druids, which awakens the desire for death in lovers," and which gives her companion Flavius "her first intimate confidences like a secret she whispers to him in the language of the Druids... that dreadful lineage of the night."

The major importance of the Celtic theme shines through again in the words of Annie Le Brun, who writes:

> The Broceliande Forest was burning during this summer of 1990. Of all the disasters in the news, this one took place within me slowly, the time it took an ash-filled wind to tarnish the monochrome of fawn(-colored), dark, foggy, or acidic transparencies in which I still expected to see the clearings of the marvelous loom up.... But from the very existence of the Vale of No Return or the Lost Rock, the Fountain of Barenton or the Castle of the Lake, each spring restored to the notion of the quest its luxuriant foliage of plant necessity. Brushing past the bark of the trees of Broceliande Forest or rediscovering their black gleaming in the *romances of the Round Table,* I know that I have drawn from this "gold-spattered, green setting" a physical taste for errantry I could never separate from the sense of poetry. I am speaking of a way of trembling while advancing through the silent water of the air, a certain allure acquired with the assurance that the beat of our temples responds to the blind drums of time, and again the salubrious, mad pleasure of no longer being anything but the terrifying trajectory of the possible, confronting reality until rediscovering the stream of blood, of blood spilled, of blood pearled, of blood exchanged, the breathless blood that irrigates the spaces of desire.[46]

These are the very places that were magisterially conjured up with the village of Tréhorenteuc, which is the gate of the forest, between Néant (Nothingness) and Folle Pensée (Mad Thought), some fifteen years earlier by Julien Gracq in *The Narrow Waters.*

This subject continues to obsess creators in the surrealist circles of influence, as traces can still be found in the 2000 catalog for the Phases exhibition in Arras in these lines of Gilles Petitclerc's poem ("Pour Suzel Ania"), a painter of the group working in Saint-Brieuc.

> You who have drunk all the gold of this Vale of No Return, though without soothing the distress of oblivion, I recognized you in the night of the red man. You bathed him in a little milk and a little honey as you once bathed the moor for whose sake we lost the North.[47]

One must also mention *Le Château périlleux* (Castle Perilous) by Jean Yves Bériou,[48] with a reproduction on the cover of a superb lithograph by the combative Portuguese surrealist Mario Césariny de Vasconcelos, which depicts the Tour Saint-Jacques in Paris.

"There is little need to stress," Philippe Audoin points out, "what the tables of the café owe to the Round Table"*: a nonhierarchical bias although there were several seats perilous, including that of Breton in which no one dared or felt legitimate enough to sit after his death."[49]

Moreover, even the "leftist opposition" noted the constant presence, in surrealist thought, of the Matter of Britain, and incidentally of the Grail mythos in its various versions unified by the gleam of the marvelous.

> All the characteristic elements of Celtic literature supplied the base material out of which postwar surrealism dreamed of constructing a new mythic image. These themes and their sacred dimension have been present since the movement's origin.[50]

Yes, they were sacred, like everything that touches on the afterlife, especially in these *Finistères*† of Europe!

---

*Allusion to the habit the surrealists had to meet every day in various cafés in Paris.
†Finistère, or *Finis terrae* in Latin, refers to peninsulas like Cap Finistère in France, or Cabo Finisterre in Galicia, Spain.

And as Fabrice Flahutez notes:

> This other world that runs through the work of Tanguy, Matta, and Breton during the 1940s is an unveiling, rather, of the invisible world surrounding us (which is not empty), a kind of new dimension inhabited by beings that interact with the living, the dead, and nature."[51]

In other words, according to them, Samain is every day and the sidhs, those mounds that serve as communicating doors between the home of the dead and our own, remain permanently open in the black light of the Ankou* from the folktales collected—with retouching—in *The Barzaz Breiz* by the French equivalent of Macpherson, Théodore Hersart de la Villemarqué, in the eighteenth century, or in *The Legend of Death in Lower Brittany* by Anatole Le Braz in the nineteenth century. This Ankou was frequently and magisterially portrayed by Yves Elléouët (who is far from being as well known as he deserves), who installed this myth so deep into the heart of reality, the two became inextricably merged.

> I go back in time to the land of the long-haired men wearing ribboned hats and pleated breeches over their thighs. They speak in harsh voices and live in thatched huts from which straggles the smell of smoke. Shadows wait at the crossroads for those returning from a distant brawl or drinking binge. Sometimes at night the screeching axle of the fatal cart can be heard. It rolls with a loud clatter over the white paths; skulls bang together between its sides. The ghastly coachman stares at the road with his empty eye sockets in a face clenched like a fist.

This coachman, Jos l'Ankaw, perhaps "the Great Purveyor," is "older than memory and voice." He states, "I am the knight of the cart, I know everyone and one day or another, everyone will know

---

*"L'Ankou" is a popular representation of death in folktales or the granite of the churches in Brittany.

me."[52] These are images that echo Philippe Audoin's observations in his article "Baron Zéro," in which he discusses Maurice Fourré and his *Tête-de-Nègre*.

> In this hilarious and gloomy liturgy, Fourré similarly incarnates in the *Ankou*, the complicit double and frightfully affectionate associate of every so-called living thing. And he bluntly signs the hecatomb: "The so-named Maurice / is responsible / for ALL." Mr. Maurice is the enigmatic conductor of an "Angevin panel truck" that travels, like the squeaky-wheeled cart of the Celtic Grim Reaper, the ensorcelled nights of the *Ar-Coat*.[53]

No one has felt as deeply in both mind and body this kind of confusion between myth and reality as Charles Jameux (also of Celtic descent), as he relates in this strange story of a visual and auditory hallucination he experienced during a long hospital stay in 2004. He was lying on his bed when he heard "music, singing, and dancing" coming from above his room. He then tells us:

> At this very moment, turning to look at a window on my right—a window that turned out to be nonexistent—I saw an extraordinary scene. On the front steps of the hospital, solemnly descending in silence the few stairs to the entrance, was a single file procession of all the participants of this imaginary nocturnal celebration. At the front were peasant women in black velvet with lace aprons.... Each was wearing a headdress. Next, saddled horsemen came slowly down the steps of the perron. They were dressed in the old traditional costume I could still see at folk gatherings when I was a child: striped pants or slightly puffy trousers, black shoes and hats with silver buckles, jackets with gold embroidery.

When Jameux tried to find out more about this beautiful folklore group the next day, he was assured it was only a dream—one with a singular power of suggestion, we must admit, but with all the attributes of dreams: silence, gravity, slowness, and majesty in an unreal atmosphere.

No doubt this is the reason why, at the end of his book *Souvenirs de la maison des vivants,* revisiting what he called his "rite of passage of death and resurrection," he gave special thought to all the caregivers who brought him back to life. He compared them to the "fairies" of the "beautiful Celtic myths of [his] Brittany," "gathered in a radiant, sparkling, silent circle dance . . . above his sick bed," here again in that unreal atmosphere characteristic of dream.

An anecdote told by Jehan Van Langhenhoven, who shared the adventure of *La Crécelle Noire* (the black rattle) with Jacques Abeille in particular, lets us grasp once and for all the magical essence of Brittany.

> There was no bed left. I was ten years old. I had to sleep with Louisette, a religious zealot in her opulent forties. A crucifix and pious engravings decorated the walls of her room. Her breasts were heavy and her sex was hairy. Then in this deep Brittany of the '60s, in the land of wayside crosses, fairies, and wizards (a perverse mixture), immanent for the first time, terribly and incurably immanent, I, of course, made up my mind to believe.[54]

There is certainly the detail of immanence, but finally wouldn't the "Caesar" (if I can put it that way!) of the Promenade of Venus have let slip a "disillusioned *Tu quoque*" (you, too)? As for me, I would have been close to saying, if I dared, "The Mass has been said."*

In the same domain, but through the prism of objective chance, the "circumstantial magic" of which Breton, who describes it in *Mad Love,* says he is the "haggard witness," there were many group members who studied the phenomenon of death omens (the *intersignes*) with great interest. These were what Paul Sébillot, in his 1882 book *Traditions and Superstitions of Upper Brittany,* called *avènements* or *avisions,* that is, messages of misfortune. The Celts believed these messages came from the beyond, these "great isolated messages with an entirely new ring to them," to which "can be granted the

---

*[This is an idiomatic expression that means "The die is cast." —*Trans.*]

highest value of a *sign*,"[55] one of the facets of these beyond-the-grave legends being the "Maouès-Noz," "kneeling in [their] wooden half-crates,"[56] "who must absolutely be made to shut up,"[57] those "diabolo-waisted washerwomen of the night who beat on the sides of the rivulets the shrouds of those about to die."[58] And they may also be rising to the surface in the title of the poem "Au Lavoir noir" (At the Black Wash House). Another facet, yet, is the White Ladies, such as Fourré's "transparent Visitor, the final envoy of all powerful sorceries." Philippe Audoin in his book on this author, also indicates, "I noted earlier that Mr. Maurice[59] liked to pass himself off as Baron Zéro, probable counterpart of the dreadful Baron Samedi of Haitian Voodoo"—and consequently a relative of Hervé Télémarque's *Baron Cimetière* (1962). Audoin also adds in his article on Baron Zéro that this "Baron Samedi is the Saturnine Ankou of Antillean rituals": we shall revisit these rituals later in chapter 10.

It so happens that in Fourré's posthumous novel, *Tête-de-Nègre,* the Angevin author writes, "The Baron Zéro! A death omen (*un intersigne*) of our Death perhaps," audaciously marrying in one sentence the Celtic imaginal realm to the more colorful one of the Caribbean. The Breton cook from *La Nuit du Rose-Hôtel* by this same author also lives "in a silent world of death omens, with the familiar procession of their dead." Without his ever pronouncing the word, we can consider this event to be similar to one Michel Leiris alludes to in his book *Manhood,* when he discusses the death of his uncle.

> His death, like my father's (which occurred some years later) coincided with a heavy snowfall. All his life he had never been able to see snow falling without feeling a kind of dizziness.[60]

It is also from this angle of the malefic premonition that I believe we should view Gracq's scene of the "Gaelic cross," on which Albert carved Heide's name beneath "a veil of shadow" that suddenly appeared in the cemetery in *The Castle of Argol*, which Breton regarded as a "surrealist reading of the Grail myth."

This is also how we should understand, despite the risk of overdetermination, Mabille's "The Painter's Eye," published in *Minotaure*, n° 12–13. This is an article about the eye enucleation suffered by Victor Brauner in 1938, which he had so often anticipated in his paintings and drawings. The doctor "rejected the hypothesis of chance and demonstrated, through the painter's work and life, the strange necessity of the accident."*

> Can the facts be explained by a persistent premonition or was the painter the victim of some kind of bewitchment? Don't mutilated shapes set magical forces in motion, creating a psychic environment in which the accident would be the inevitable result? The two theories do not rule each other out.

But Alain Jouffroy is much more circumspect. "No explanation," he states in his 1959 book *Brauner*, "psychoanalytical or otherwise, is enough to totally reduce the shadow this tragedy introduced in us. . . . An 'adventure' like this can only inspire in the mind of the person who experienced it, an absolute mistrust toward all the rational systems that seek 'to explain' its mechanism."

---

*Brauner lost his left eye when intervening in a fight between Esteban Frances and Oscar Dominguez. René Passeron, in his *Histoire de la Peinture surréaliste* (Paris: Le Livre de Poche, 1968), indicates that Mabille saw it as an action that was sought for with strong masochistic overtones, for the purpose of rejoining the initiates of the mysteries of the beyond, who, in antiquity, were considered to be "blind" to the world. In Alain Jouffroy's account of Brauner's mishap, from his book *Victor Brauner* (Paris: Musée de Poche, editions Georges Fall, 1959), the author adds, "A glass was thrown. Victor received a hundred fragments in his left eye. An X-ray revealed that these fragments were arranged in such a geometrical way that it would have required an expert to put them there deliberately."

There have been several works of art related to Brauner's eyes. In 1931, Brauner painted his *Self-Portrait with Enucleated Eye,* and in 1932 he did *Mediterranean Landscape,* where the eye of the main male figure is pierced by a sword held by a capital "D," as in Dominguez. In 1936, during his vacation on the Black Sea, Jules Perahim tried to paint a portrait of Brauner. Unable to reproduce the eyes, he drew them separately in the lower left-hand corner with a lead pencil; the left eye had a disturbing, strange character. And from 1935 to 1938, Brauner produced an impressive number of drawings and paintings featuring an enucleated eye.

As the author of the poem "Nuit du Tournesol" (Night of the Sunflower), with its proclaimed anticipatory dimension, Breton also admired Chirico's *Premonitory Portrait of Guillaume Apollinaire* as man and target, "foreshadowing" the wound the poet took at the temple in 1916, painted at a time "when we know the kind of importance [the painter] granted to divinatory concerns."[61] Breton recalled on occasions—in *The Treasure of the Jesuits* (1927) and in the "Lettres aux voyantes" (1925), in particular—his prediction of a Second World War that would burst out in . . . 1939. This vision was also illustrated by Jules Perahin with his *Before the Storm* and Richard Oelze with *Erwartung* (Waiting), which was analyzed by Wieland Schmied this way: "The time to come reveals itself."[62] Henri Béhar, in his text "On a Poem-Object," which accompanies his transcription of *Arcane 17,* analyzes this phrase from "Prolégomènes à un troisième manifeste du surréalisme ou non," written in 1942 under a very similar angle.

> There is the marvelous young woman who at this very minute, beneath the shadow of her lashes, is walking around the great ruined chalk boxes of South America, one of whose glances would call into question the very meaning of belligerence.

Béhar views this as a prediction of Breton's meeting with Elisa (Breton's third wife).

He wrote, "No one can rid me of the idea that this phrase is just as premonitory for him as the famous 'Night of the Sunflower' that heralded his meeting Jacqueline Lamba. And I cannot prevent myself from seeing the silhouette of Elisa standing out here. Coming from Chile, she would only appear 'for real' one and a half years later." Béhar also explains that if Breton "recognized" Elisa in December 1943, it was because she "embodied the woman he dreamt of meeting" at the age "of the first pictorial emotional confusion" in which he discovered Dante Gabriel Rosetti's *Beata Beatrix*. It is of course obvious that these things are easy to decipher after the fact, but how can you understand the phrase of Artaud, sent to Jean Paulhan at the beginning of June 1937, as anything but a premonition? Shortly before his fateful trip to Ireland, Artaud, whose sensitivity in this domain is easily imagined, wrote, "In a little while I will be dead or in such a situation that I will no longer need a name." Fourteen months later, he was committed to Ville-Evrard Mental Hospital, where he would become number 262 602.

"But there are no causes, are there? There are only *presages*," Claude Tarnaud writes in *De (Le Bout du Monde)* (From [the End of the World]). In *The Passive Vampire*, the Romanian Ghérasim Luca shows evidence of a similar faculty when he writes:

> I finished my work at one in the morning and I placed the objects* on the mantel. Slipping into bed, I was scared to fall asleep because I had the premonition there would be an earthquake during the night. I was awoken at four in the morning by a terrible earthquake, the walls cracked, the wardrobes were tossed to the center of the room, books fell all over, objects and glasses broke noisily. While the earthquake lasted, I kept shouting that I had foreseen it, and this gift of clairvoyance that I discovered for the first time increased my terror.

It is impossible to read these magnificent lines by Desnos in *Poems to the Mysterious Woman*, at the junction of love and premonition, without intense emotion:

> I have so often dreamed of you, walked, spoken, slept with your phantom that perhaps I can be nothing any longer than a phantom among phantoms.

With his text "Before the Curtain," included in *La Clé des champs* (Free Rein), Breton, citing in a footnote several "evidential examples for the benefit of skeptics," goes so far as to venture an amazing suggestion:

---

*Luca here refers to what he called O.O.O., for "objectively offered object," objects he was then making.

Now it may be that surrealism, by opening certain doors that rationalism had boarded up for good, had enabled us to make here and there an incursion into the future, on condition that we should not be aware at the time that it was the future we were entering, that we should become aware of this and be able to make it evident only a posteriori.

Again, in "Le Pont suspendu," which recounts a strange phenomenon of premonition connected to a small painting offered to him by Luis Fernandez,[63] Breton echoes the already dated works of the Irishman John William Dunne (1875–1949), an aeronautical engineer by training and the author of the book *An Experiment with Time*,[64] which had a curious theory of consciousness that claims to supply an original explanation for the phenomena of premonition and makes possible a new kind of dream analysis by means of the notion of serial time, which is based on the fact that variable time can only be conceived as an element of a series. His research also left a mark on Raymond Queneau's novels *The Bark Tree* (1933) and *The Blue Flowers* (1965).

It is true, as Vera Linhartova writes, that "poetry, according to Sima, is a premonition of the world in becoming" (but this observation undoubtedly applies to other creators as well as other forms of creation), once "the poetic imagination, by accepting the rift between the known world and other possible worlds, stands surety for their reintegration into world *one*." Michel Carrouges gives this helpful insight into the works of Frederic Myers and Théodore Flournoy:

In fact, we find in their works very precise indications on the place held by stupefying coincidences, premonitions, and encounters in the lives of mediums and in those of many people who did not believe in the gift of clairvoyance during a period around the year 1900. The bulk of these phenomena—provoked or not—involved relationships between the living and the dead. The large place held in surrealist writings by ghosts, haunted castles, mediums, seers, and the idea of automatic writing reflects a similar climate."[65]

In fact, according to Chirico, as cited in *Surrealism and Painting:*

One of the strangest sensations bequeathed us by prehistory is the sensation of foreboding. It will always exist. It is like an eternal proof of the nonsense of the universe. The first man had to see omens everywhere; he had to shudder at every step.

And did not Breton himself write in 1923, in *Earthlight,* "Veiled premonitions are descending the stairs of the buildings." Unless they are precisely ghosts or more devoted apparitions, as in "The Journal of an Apparition" by Robert Desnos[66] ("We come across supernatural presences in incredible landscapes"), or even "deleterious emanations," "powers that until further notice remain quite obscure," like those at Fort-Bloqué in *Mad Love,* for example. Meanwhile, Roger Gilbert-Lecomte, in "L'Horrible Révélation . . . la seule," proclaims, "Man in the world is a belly of forces exuding their magic powers and receiving the beneficial or malefic inflow of all beings and all things."

8
SURREALISM AND ALCHEMY

"You with Lead in the Head, Melt It Down to Make Surrealist Gold"

But be forewarned, take not vulgar gold and silver, for they are dead; take ours that are living.

THE COSMOPOLITE OR
THE NEW CHEMICAL LIGHT

A surrealist flier from the 1920s proclaimed, "You with lead in the head, melt it down to make surrealist gold."* This advice was repeated in the fourth issue of *Médium* in 1955, and it should be no cause for surprise that "people who undertook the transformation of the world and life based on a concept of the world and life far removed from mercantile rationality recognized the figures and a language they had personally conceived for their specific project in the teachings and communica-

---

*[The French expression *avoir plomb dans la tete*, which literally translates as "lead in the head," means "to have both feet on the ground, to have common sense." —*Trans.*]

tions crafted by the alchemists."[1]* This is especially pertinent if, quoting René Alleau, we recall with "one of alchemy's first historians, Lenglet-Dufresnoy," that the "masters of this traditional science are the most illustrious dreamers humanity has ever known." Bachelard also offers this clarification: "All Alchemy was penetrated by an immense sexual reverie, a reverie of wealth and rejuvenation, by a reverie of power."[2] We cannot avoid saying a word or two about alchemy here, about which Alleau (whom Breton met at the beginning of the 1950s) would state in one of his famous lectures:

> Alchemy offers an order of reference: nature that ceaselessly alters what it produces without changing its laws. Knowledge of nature should permit the removal of the *cherubim* guarding the garden where the tree of life grows: this is the true revolt.[3]

I should like to linger for a moment on the significance of the encounter of the surrealists with René Alleau, which an eyewitness, Jean-Louis Bédouin, despite some reservations, emphasized in his book *Vingt Ans de surréalisme: 1939–1959*:

> That the author of *Aspects of Traditional Alchemy*, Fulcanelli's disciple and Eugène Canseliet's friend, by his own admission, went off to win the "Golden Fleece" after having known surrealism, confirms in noteworthy fashion the analogical purpose Breton discusses of surrealist and alchemical explorations. The fact his path intersected again years later with the path the surrealists had taken shows that the different paths taken by Alleau and his fellow seekers, and by Breton and the poets sharing the same concerns, encircled the same

---

*"The ancient Jewish, Greek, Syrian, and Arab scholars most likely bestowed this name [that of alchemy] on a sacred science, a set of esoteric and initiatory bodies of knowledge, to the ancient 'sacerdotal art' whose teaching was founded on the mysteries of the sun, source of light, heat, and life," Michel Bounan wrote an introduction to René Alleau's (short) book *Alchimie* when he republished it in 2008. Bounan writes in the preface to Rene Alleau's *Alchimie*, a reprinting of the "Alchemy" entry from the *Encyclopedia Universalis*.

axis like the two serpents on a caduceus. From either end of their dual evolution, the two paths never merged, although at certain points they crossed and juxtaposed each other.

On a side note, Alleau, when he took part in group activities, vigorously attacked Jung and his *Psychology and Alchemy* (as in the third issue of *Médium* in 1954), particularly rejecting the idea that "the symbols of the adepts and the teachings of the masters as well as the illuminations of Art and the flames of Nature" can emerge from the collective unconscious, as the Swiss native defined it. Jung's fellow Swiss, Kurt Seligmann, was less doctrinaire here. In any event (and setting aside any kind of transcendence), it is obvious that sixteenth-century alchemy (its golden age) was consistently represented as "a science aiming to recreate and perfect by art what had been created and left imperfect by nature," with a "demiurgic side" aiming at "correcting the work of God"[4] while retaining a "technical [aspect] of spiritual realization" so adroitly demonstrated by Guénon.

In *The Mirror of Magic,* Seligmann supplies details that are particularly revealing about the surrealists' interest in alchemy; incidentally, they bring to mind Rimbaud's verse about the hand with the pen being equal to the hand on the plow.

> His imagination being ceaselessly directed toward the *marvelous,* the hermetic philosopher no doubt took great pleasure in his studies. It is not hard to understand why alchemy is called an art. It is because it is based on the imagination as much as it is on manual dexterity (italics added).

Robert Amadou's view from his book *Occident, Orient: parcours d'une tradition* (West and East: The Journey of a Tradition) is well worth noting: "Alchemy is based on the permanent correlation between the material phenomenon and what takes place on the spiritual level."[5] Eugène Canseliet, for whom hermeticism is a veritable parallel religion and who believes "alchemy assumes ecumenalism, as it is universal and achieves the accord of science and religions," goes even further, stating in his commentaries on the *Mutus Liber* (which we shall revisit) that "mythology, its gods and heroes, like the religion of Christ, apostles, and evangelical pomp, only finds a solid explanation and real value in the many undeniable relations it exhibits with alchemy and its materials and operations." Leaning on the "exegesis" of the Benedictine Dom Antoine-Joseph Pernety, he adds, "Mythological polytheism permitted alchemical authors to conceal the paths leading to the Stone much more effectively than the means authorized by the linear monotheism of the Christian *Revelation* and the mystery of the *Cross*."

Seligmann then shows, "As in the time of Gnosticism and Neo-Platonism, the legend and philosophy of the East and West were syncretized into an amazing image of the universe. The paradise of theology and that of Greek philosophy, the monsters of the East, the mythical figures of Hellas, all come together under the sign of Hermes." The ramifications of what he suggests can only keep raising questions over the course of this book.

This "science" has therefore always deemed itself sacred, and its "language . . . is based on analogies, antimonies, oppositions, or conjunctions of the opposites existing in the natures of the outside or macrocosmic order and the interior or human order; [this science] takes its bearings from the other traditional sciences: astrology and astronomy, mysteries and metaphysics, magic and divination."[6] Most importantly, it "does not fail to fit into the vast current that takes the regeneration of man as its primary purpose. This regeneration appears to be, in the Christian context of Western alchemy, a response to the doctrine of original sin, but is clearly fundamentally different (as is easily verified) as it is nonreligious in its essence."[7]

A slightly more in-depth examination of *Nadja, Mad Love,* and *Arcane 17,* in particular, as found in Richard Danier's book *L'Hermétisme alchimique chez André Breton,* shows that alchemy forms a veritable red thread that runs throughout this entire opus. Hester Albach confirms this, at least for *Nadja,* as indicated by Philippe Noble in the foreword of her book about Léona Delcourt. "Throughout *Nadja,*" Hester Albach tells us, "Breton used coded language to describe the stages of the alchemical 'great work.'" It reflects, in fact, disturbing analogies, if I dare put it that way.

> The secrets of the alchemical process are not transmissible. Never has any alchemy manual communicated anything but clues, a trail through myths, symbols, analogies in the language of the birds, or narrative structures deliberately offering an erroneous chronology. This is true of *Nadja,* where it is explicitly stated that the story has no preordained order. The same holds true for the photos in the book. They tend to make certain descriptions superfluous, just like the enigmatic engravings illustrating alchemical works. It is up to the reader to interpret them, which he will do in accordance with his degree of initiation.

However Albach also shows that Breton was never a "practicing alchemist." In support of her claim she cites an October 11, 1952, letter to René Alleau in which the surrealist states that he "persists in stumbling over the necessity that he is unable to make the 'practical work' of alchemy organically his own and of what makes this work of alchemy be what it is and not something else," adding, "Despite that I do not assume being so easily reduced to a purely poetic grasp of alchemical texts, which I've long found much too 'ethereal' to satisfy me and not leave me out of sorts."[8]

All the same, it is striking to observe that when he undertakes his rehabilitation of the art of the Celts (in the previously mentioned articles that appear in *Surrealism and Painting*), which "springs from a vision of the infinite that dissolves the concrete and leads to the abstraction of the visible," Breton cannot refrain from referring to alchemy.

> One perceives a sparkling, magnetic thread streaking across these medals, which is comparable in its glory to that which the alchemists of other ages attributed to *nostoc* (from the Greek *tokos* and *noös*), that terrestrial alga, which is supposed to evaporate in the rays of the sun and to which they gave a variety of names (as they did to the *Emerald of the Adepts*), for example, cuckoo-spit, star-jelly,

witches' butter, spring-froth. . . . There is nothing surprising about this if one remembers that *nostoc* means literally *giving birth to, generating the spirit,* which is perfectly applicable to the Gallic coinage. Primarily they aim to be radiant coin—the cosmic radiance.

Philippe Sollers, describing his first meeting with Breton in the June 5, 2008, issue of *Le Nouvel Observateur,* says:

> What did he speak of on that day with his impeccable diction? To my great surprise, nothing but alchemy!

This is telling of how much the subject worked on him. Jacques Van Lennep has also stressed this kinship between the thought of the adepts and that of the primary theoretician of surrealism.

> André Breton's writings reveal more than mere allusions to the hermetic art and one concludes from reading them that the approaches of surrealism are not at all foreign to alchemical concerns. . . . In short, Breton appears particularly sensitized to alchemy, and *this is in no way some game of a scholar tempted by occultism but reveals his crucial interest in a gnosis that contains the spirit of surrealism in ferment* (italics added).[9]

Jacques Van Lennep also suggests the poet no doubt remembered that the "Great Work" for Eliphas Levi was nothing other than "the conquest of the central point wherein dwells the balancing force." Moreover, in *Second Manifeste de surrealism,* Breton himself bluntly stated:

> I would appreciate your noting the remarkable analogy, insofar as their goals are concerned, between the surrealist efforts and those of the alchemists. The philosopher's stone is nothing more or less than that which was to enable man's imagination to take a stunning revenge on all things, which brings us once again, after centuries of the mind's domestication and insane resignation, to the attempt

to liberate once and for all the imagination by the "long, immense, reasoned derangement of the senses" and all the rest.[10]

In *Lettres aux voyantes,* he also stated:

> The man of today . . . scarcely believes in the invention of the philosopher's stone by Nicolas Flamel, for the simple reason that the great alchemist seems not to have got rich enough from it. One may well wonder how the obtaining of more than a few bits of gold could have interested him, when it had been, above all, a matter of building up a spiritual fortune. . . . We are searching for, we are on the track of, a moral truth.[11]

On the track! This brings to mind Seligmann, who said, "More than one initiate preferred the path of perfection to perfection itself." We even sometimes see, shyly peeking through, in the course of the *Second Surrealist Manifesto,* for example, an allusion to the transmission of this knowledge by "supernatural means"—and even by an angel!

> Is the admirable fourteenth century any less great as regards human hope (and, of course, human despair) because a man of Flamel's genius received from a *mysterious power* this manuscript, which already existed, of Abraham the Jew's book, or because the secrets of Hermes had not been completely lost? I do not believe so for one minute, and I think that Flamel's efforts, with all their appearance of concrete success, lose nothing by having thus been helped and anticipated (italics added).

Again in *L'Art magique,* Breton deplores "the irreparable loss of the paintings drawn under the guidance of Nicolas Flamel at the Charnel House of the Innocents, paintings of which the *Book of Abraham the Jew* only give us a vulgarly executed souvenir."

This Nicolas Flamel, Eugène Canseliet (who in passing reminds us that he is the proud holder of the title Frère Chevalier d'Héliopolis) tells us in his article "Hermétiques Rudiments d'Héraldiques" (published in the January–February 1975 issue of *Atlantis*), had the blazon of an alchemist rather than a writer, which "bore a fess separating three bouquets of flame on the chief from a crescent moon pointing down with its two horns above." Flamel was a writer, in fact, who, according to MacGregor Mathers in his introduction to his translation of *The Book of the Sacred Magic of Abra-Melin the Mage* (1890) would have left us only twenty-one small "pages of bark and papyrus." Mathers also noted that the transcriber of this manuscript, allegedly dating from 1458, a translation of which he made public, would have been a certain Abraham the Jew of Wurzburg, a contemporary of Flamel—and Faust! Around this same time of Mathers's writing (at the end of the 1920s), Michel Leiris appears to have shared with André Masson "a love . . . of hermeticists and Paracelsus" at 45 rue Blomet. Here "next to works of low magic like the Petit Albert, the great occultists like Paracelsus, as well as Ramon Llull's *Ars Brevis* and Leonardo Da Vinci's *Treatise on Painting,* could be found."[12] Leiris finished his peculiar story *Aurora* (which would not be published until after the war) as follows:

> Further away from me, my vitrified gaze was fixed to the top of the cathedral spire of Notre Dame, quite high up on the right. Neither Semiramis nor the Queen of Sheba built this temple, but, it is said, that carved into its stones are the principal secrets of Nicolas Flamel, more enigmatic than even those of Paracelsus.[13]

Some time later, 1968 to be exact, in the catalog for the Princip Slasti (Pleasure Principle) exhibition, Philippe Audoin, who like Breton claimed to be merely an amateur when it came to alchemy, enlisted Dame Pernelle's husband (Flamel) under the surrealist banner to embody the symbolic link between the banks of the Seine and those of the Vltava. He writes in "La Fontaine de Fortune" (The Fountain of Happiness):

> This is the effect of a certain optical hindsight: the staircase Marcel Duchamp's *Nude* descended becomes that of the Tour Saint-Jacques;

an endlessly spiraling wingnut and armor-piercing vehicle of what the modern spirit can most aggressively offer when it comes to drillings in the dawn of time—and casting, toward an inverted coronation of the one that signs, in the clouds, the tetramorphic chiasmus, the increased form of Nicolas Flamel's *Awaited Bride*. We know that when Flamel was said to have died, the adepts of the Sublime Science had already found a haven beneath the great heretical porch of Notre Dame. Later, all those who appealed to the whim of Emperor Rudolph knew the figures that the Parisian writer had drawn on the Charnel House of the Innocents. Alchemical gold was struck secretly in Prague and Paris, as if at the two stable poles of an intransitive universe, which underlays the official world of tottering courts and religious massacres.[14]

As similar as these poles may be, in Prague the Golden Street of the Alchemists overlooks Stag Moat, where, Gustav Meyrink tells us in *The Angel of the Western Window,* bears fed on the flesh of these same adepts and initiates.

Nicolas Flamel, the "ruril [native] de Pontoise" (the famous name is eventually uttered and repeated), lived in the Châtelet quarter near the church of Saint-Jacques-de-la-Boucherie (which is now destroyed). This was at a time when alchemy, despite its condemnation in the papal bull "Spondent pariter quas non exhibent," issued by the pope of Avignon, Pope Jean XXII (also an alchemist), often shared common ground with the clerics and was casually practiced behind the closed doors of the monasteries. All that survives of the church "at the geometrical center of the labyrinth of the capital" is that "temple dedicated to hermeticism"; according to Elie-Charles Flamand that is known as the Tour Saint-Jacques. This quarter thus gives Paris a bit of an air of an alchemical city, like Prague certainly, but also Bourges. All three are built over an inextricable lacing of caves and underground passages, which is confirmed by these lines by Joris-Karl Huysmans in his *Gilles de Rais: La Magie en Poitou,* which was published confidentially in 1899:

During this era,* the hermetic center in France was Paris, where alchemists gathered beneath the vaults of Notre Dame and studied the hieroglyphs of the Charnel House of the Innocents and the portal of Saint-Jacques-de-la-Boucherie, on which Nicolas Flamel had written in kabbalistic emblems the preparation of the famous stone.

"A magnificent building built between 1508 and 1522 on the site of a building called Hotel de la Rose, on the very spot where pilgrims gathered before setting off on their journey to the song of Ultraeïa [Onwards] following that 'Way of Compostella' [that] every hermeticist [should] therefore . . . travel in their turn with perseverance, at least symbolically," the "brilliant" Tour Saint-Jacques, "tottering" like a sunflower that "remains the traditional departure point toward the Elsewhere," has caused the spilling of a lot of ink, in particular by Breton, who mentions it notably in *The White-Haired Revolver*, *Mad Love*, and especially *Arcane 17*, in which we can read:

> You can imagine how this narrative was able to reawaken the exaltation that the Saint-Jacques Tower has produced in me for quite some time, and that several of my earlier writings or remarks bear witness to. It's especially true that my mind has often prowled around that tower, for me very powerfully charged with occult significance, either because it shares in the doubly-veiled life (one because it disappeared, leaving behind it this great trophy, and again because it embodied, as nothing else, the sagacity of the hermeticists) of the Church Saint-Jacques de la Boucherie, or because it is endowed with legends about Flamel returning to Paris after his death.

These returns were notably detailed in the *Second Surrealist Manifesto*, when Breton admits accepting "that someone named Paul Lucas" was able to encounter

---

*"This era" refers to the fifteenth century, thus "in full flamboyant Middle Ages" to use Bernard Roger's term.

Flamel in Brusa at the beginning of the seventeenth century, that this same Flamel, accompanied by his wife and one son, was seen at the Paris Opera in 1761, and that he made a brief appearance in Paris during the month of May 1819, at which time he was purported to have rented a store at 22 rue de Cléry.

Let me reiterate, these legends were part of the spirit of the time inasmuch as Apollinaire's friend Leo Larguier, cited in *Le Flâneur des deux rives* (The Idler of the Two Banks),[15] also refers to them in 1936 at the end of his novel *Le Faiseur d'or, Nicolas Flamel* (The Gold Maker, Nicolas Flamel).[16]

Describing the affinities between Hérold and Breton and their meeting at the foot of the Saint-Jacques Tower in his article "Jacques Hérold et le surréalisme," Jean-Paul Clébert mentions the following anecdote concerning one of the alleged returns of the alchemist—unless it was Gérard de Nerval.

We know that Breton, in an "aperture" grafted on *Arcane 17*, recounted the strange adventure of the painter Halphern to whom a black man appeared, another phantom of Nicolas Flamel. Condensing his story as much as possible to give it more weight, Breton did not mention that Hérold had climbed to the top of the tower and introduced himself to the head of the weather bureau there. This bureaucrat of the "magnetic fields," a total realist and advocate of scientific method, did not believe in spirits and yet he reported to the painter that one day when he was sitting at his desk filing papers, he suddenly saw a man before him dressed in black with a black hat, silently standing there without moving. In the time it took to call his secretary to ask the reason for the presence of this individual in this private place not open to the public, the man in black had disappeared, with no clue to how he left.[17]

This Châtelet quarter was placed under the sign of Saint James, brother to Saint John, who was the patron saint of doctors and alchemists. Saint James was believed, according to the *Golden Legend,* to have in Spain gotten the best of Trismegistus—the initiated initiating—whose occult knowledge he consequently had to manage. This undoubtedly fascinated Breton. Part of that fascination was due to the fact that this was where Gérard de Nerval had lived and hanged himself with what he claimed to be the Queen of Sheba's garter, as reported by Théophile Gautier. Perhaps, Leiris claims in *Aurora,* because of "two semiphantomatic creatures each bore half of this name: Aurélia and Pandora." In any case, the "late rare G.," a widower of a star left to his own devices in the "night of his destiny," was a great occultist poet and allegedly a masonic initiate who left behind a rough draft for a play titled *Nicolas Flamel.* "Do not wait up for me this evening, because the night will be black and white." These are the colors of the Beauseant and the Mosaic Pavement. And the echo answers with the voice of Jean-Pierre Duprey: "Now the night is a clear door," which he crosses through like Dante or Orpheus. "Your abysses are my stations, Shadow of shadow, I follow you!"[18]

But I spoke earlier of Marcel Duchamp, precursor and close traveling companion; how would it be possible to overlook the alchemical nature of *The Bride Stripped Bare by Her Bachelors, Even,* a work he began in 1915—after he met Rudolph Steiner's friend Kandinsky and read his book *Concerning the Spiritual in Art*—then abandoned in 1923. Nadia Choucha notes:

> The male and female elements in *The Large Glass* attempt to achieve union and thus a sense of "wholeness." This sense of perfection and wholeness was symbolized in alchemy by the androgyne, a divine and unified being that is both male and female. The androgyne is a symbol of the undifferentiated consciousness sought by the alchemists, when all opposites are reconciled. Duchamp was a modern alchemist and *The Large Glass* is his "Great Work."[19]

But the most interesting thing is the way Choucha backed up her claim.

Finally it is worth quoting two alchemical parables from the seventeenth century, which Duchamp must have used as a starting point for his work. These passages are to be found in Albert Poisson's *Théorie et symboles des alchimistes*.[20]

Poisson quotes these two anonymous texts.

> *Diana [the virgin goddess] no longer wears*
> *her garment,*
> *So that marriage becomes more desirable.*
> *From two noble suitors, both fencers,*
> *The Bride receives delicious water*
> *So that she can bathe her own body,*
> *For her groom.*

That which is below, without wings, is the fixed or male.

That which is above, that is the volatile, or to put it another way, the black and obscure female, she who is about to seize control [of the alchemical work] for several months. The first (below) is called sulfur, or instead heat and dryness, and the second (above) is called quicksilver, or frigidity and humidity.[21]

In *Heliogabalus or the Crowned Anarchist,* Artaud associates this "black feminine" with Proserpine, "the woman incarnated in hell and who never gets much out of it." According to Robert Lebel's book on Duchamp,[22] the artist never rejected this possibility, and Alexander Roob reported that he was content to make the sibylline observation, "If I ever performed alchemy, it was in the only way it is permitted today, which is to say unknowingly."[23] Duits, meanwhile, in his book on Breton, noted, "The question could be raised if Duchamp was not seeking to colonize what the occultists called 'the subtle worlds.'" In any case, beyond his rapport with alchemy, Duchamp, acting as if nothing was up, as was his habit, raised—and not only with his hijacked version of the *Mona Lisa*—issues whose scale Paz summed up quite admirably when he stated, "The last image of the Christian Virgin, the Ideal Lady of the Provencals, and the Great Goddess of the Mediterraneans, is *The Bride Stripped Bare by Her Bachelors, Even.*"

Picasso, as we have already seen, was close to Parisian esoteric circles. André Salmon, who dubbed him the prince-alchemist, revealed, says Marijo Ariëns-Volker, that in 1912 the true title of *Les Demoiselles d'Avignon* was *Le B . . . philosophique.**

Anne Tronche's article "Une morphologie totémique de l'invisible" reminds us that Wifredo Lam had a "magnificent knowledge" of "alchemical heraldry" and had "put together a particularly important library in Havana of scholarly books tracing its history and successive interpretations," which was ultimately scattered when his studio was ransacked. She adds, "Finding symbols that stimulated his imagination in the grimoires of the Adepts, he put them to work to the benefit of his pictorial space . . . in accordance with the analogical procedures they inspired."[24] This no doubt is the reason for the proliferation of alchemical symbols and signs in this Cuban painter's work, as shown, for example, in the painting *Nativity (Annunciation)* (1947) by the presence of something that can only be interpreted as an "alchemical egg." Anne Tronche suggests a plausible reason for his infatuation: "His interest for alchemy is probably explained by his wish to give status to the presence of the invisible within the visible, a form to the intensity of thought restored to its true inner light."

Similarly, Magritte—despite the opinion aired by his friend Nougé in 1948—does not reject, a priori, any connection between his work and alchemy, as shown by an interview between Jacques Van Lennep and Françoise Brumagne.[25] The author of a book published in 1966 on art and alchemy, Van Lennep, then a young art historian, gave a lecture in May 1967 on one of Magritte's paintings, which was on display at the Royal Museums of Belgium. In it he established a link between Magritte's 1926 painting *L'Homme du large* (The Man of the Open Sea) (plate 13) and Breton's famous phrase from *Arcane 17:* "Osiris is a black god." He made this claim only after a conversation with the artist as well as with one of Magritte's colleagues and friends, Belgian surrealist

---

*"B . . ." stands here for "bordel," a rude word we use in France. But this "B . . ." can also stand for "bain," which can also be read as the "philosophical bath," a rite that precedes the coniunctio on the path toward the philosopher's stone.

Marcel Lecomte (1900–1966), who had introduced Giorgio de Chirico's work to him. Lecomte was one of the editors of *Correspondence* and the author, "with a keen interest in alchemy and esotericism," of the book *Le Sens des tarots* (The Meanings of the Tarots).[26] He had also published studies on the Cathars and the Bavarian Illuminati. In May 1947, this same Marcel Lecomte also published an article in the fourth issue of *Troisième Convoi* titled "The Lost Secrets," in which he stated:

> It has already been a few years since people began thinking that surrealist painters were concerned with lost secrets. . . . Their conduct in the presence of the invisible and before the infinitely complex expansions of reality could not fail to draw inspiration from those dreams of black magic, those dreams of the demonstrative and enchanting re-creation and isolation of the elements of a "strange reality" already experienced by Cornelius Agrippa and, with him, several seers of that time under the effects of their operations.

Van Lennep's communication, says Brumagne, interested Magritte enough that he took the trouble, shortly before his death, to answer the young lecturer, mentioning in passing his "interest" in alchemy. In fact, *The Man of the Open Sea,* whose title, most likely inspired by that of a film shot by Marcel L'Herbier in 1920, was suggested to Magritte by Lecomte personally, would seem to owe more to Fantômas than to Egypt. I am tempted to conclude "if it does not kill everyone."

Toyen, whose interest in alchemy (as I mentioned earlier) shines through her many paintings inspired by the signs on the old houses of Prague, also did a portrait of Breton in her drawing cycle *Neither Wings nor Stones; Wings and Stones* (1948–1949), which was created shortly after she moved to France to stay (see plate 12). In this portrait, Breton is "in the center of three overlapping triangles" and "surrounded by allusions to the four elements (the flames represent fire, the swallows air, the minerals the earth, and the pool represents water)." It is a portrait of which an alchemical reading could be made, at least according to Phillipe Audoin in "The Fountain of Happiness," cited in Karel Srp's *Toyen, une femme surréaliste*.[27] This cycle of drawings, some of which were drawn on the Isle of Sein, seems to have served as a matrix for a number of her 1951 works, with strong esoteric connotations.

Sailing somewhat off the shores of surrealism, strictly speaking, but clearly in the same spirit, René Daumal, the poet who declared, "Never, no never will any book be as sincerely mine as *Aurélia*," and the author of the very beautiful "Nerval le Nyctalope" (Nerval the Day-Blind) felt an interest at the beginning of the 1930s at least equal to Breton's for the "art of music," as the adepts also put it. His pursuit of studies undertaken during the adventure of the Grand Jeu and even before authorized Jean Biès to write in his regard:

> Alchemy appeared to Daumal in its true guise: a sacrificial, sacramental science of terrestrial substances. If every metal is clearly gold that knows not itself, every word is virtually a vibrational particle of Spirit.... Henceforth, Daumal never claimed to be doing anything but transmuting "the black work"—domain of anguish and illusions, and the viscous darkness of the *materia,* in which the mercurial waters remain congealed—into "the white work"—the kingdom of luminosity; moving his poetry from Solve to Coagula; or if you'd rather, from Chaos to Order, from Earth to Heaven.[28]

A better emphasis of the analogy between the royal art and poetry would be hard to find. This analogy, while definitely varied on several levels, is undoubtedly one of the most reliable footbridges connecting the group led by Breton with the friends of Daumal and Lecomte, even if their main criticism of the group was that it was not radical enough. They even went so far as to call the surrealist approach inspired by their elder "an amusing science."

Artaud was not fooled and established closer ties with the Grand Jeu, then wrote an article for Jules Supervielle's magazine *Sur* in Buenos Aires titled "The Alchemical Theater," which he compared to the "Orphic mysteries." In this text (which Bedouin's *Vingt Ans de surréalisme: 1939–1959,* after René Alleau, would quote later), Artaud notes—in conformance with his main concerns—"a mysteriously identical essence" in "the principle of the theater and that of alchemy," before vigorously demonstrating "the extent to which poetic intuition can sometimes match up with the traditional truths."

> We must believe that the essential drama, the one at the root of all the Great Mysteries, is closely associated with the second phase of Creation, that of difficulty and of the Double, that of matter and the materialization of the idea.
>
> Now these conflicts which the Cosmos in turmoil offers us in a philosophically distorted and impure manner, alchemy offers us in all their rigorous intellectuality, since it permits us to attain once more the sublime, *but with drama,* after a meticulous and unremitting pulverization of every insufficiently refined, insufficiently matured form, since it follows from the very principle of alchemy not to let the spirit take its leap until it has passed through all the filters and foundations of existing matter, and to redouble this labor at the incandescent limbo of the future. For it might be said that in order to merit material gold, the mind must first have proved itself that it was capable of the other kind, and that it would have earned it, would have attained to it, only by assenting to it, seeing it as a secondary symbol of the fall it had to experience in order to rediscover in solid and opaque form the expression of light itself, of rarity, and irreducibility.[29]

Even the poet René Char of the 1930s was not indifferent to these alchemical speculations, and while Georges Mounin in his *Avez-vous lu Char?* claims he does not know where René Char "found these images borrowed from the chemist's vocabulary," and says that *Le Marteau sans maître* testifies to a certain predilection for "volumes of ether," the "block" and the "pinch of sulfur," "the jet of vitriol," "the iron hand," "the platinum wedding band," "the verdigris of the spades, "the leaden grass," "the wild radium," "the red bird of the metals," it is not hard to detect allusions, subtle as they may be, to the Ars Magna (Great Art).

Despite everything, how could I omit Salvador Dali, who in *The Passions According to Dali* (1968) writes, "Having made my entire life a work of alchemy, I gladly consider myself a descendent of the Catalan,

Ramon Llull," the same Llull, "the Archangelical, illuminated Doctor," to whom so many surrealists alluded. As noted by Juliette Murphy in the catalog published in 2009 by the Gala-Salvador Dali Foundation for the exhibition L'Alchimie des Philosophes (The Alchemy of the Philosophers):

> This thirteenth-century mystic philosopher and native of Majorica was a figure of reference in Dali's work. The introduction of the world alchemy (from the Arabic "Al-kimia") into the Catalan language is attributed to him.[30]

This exhibition was based on the magnificent artist's book created in 1976 on the initiative of the Port Lligat painter around classic texts of both Eastern and Western alchemy—among which an extract from *La roman de la Rose* is quite prominent—selected under the guidance of René Alleau, and illustrated, of course, by the "Master" who was also responsible for the presence on the box that contained this entire production, of "Llullian wheels." In his work on the ten prints, Dali, who owned a copy of Serge Hutin's *A History of Alchemy* (Marabout, 1971), multiplied (including by the use of colors) the allusions to the philosopher's stone, Ouroboros, the Emerald Tablet, the labyrinth, and even the androgyne, a recurring theme for him since the '30s.

The famous "Fronton-Virage," the preface written by Breton for Jean Ferry's *Une Étude sur Raymond Roussel,* cites Fulcanelli, "the highest modern authority" in the domain of alchemy and the author of *The Mystery of the Cathedrals* and *The Dwellings of the Philosophers,* a good twenty times. The leader of surrealism seems to consider the influence decisive enough to conclude, "I feel the work of Raymond Roussel needs to be reexamined from top to bottom on that basis." More reserved concerning the method used, Jean Schuster addressed the following criticism to Ferry in the first issue of *Médium:* "I strongly fear that your deliberate hostility toward anything closely or remotely touching on esotericism will considerably shrink the scope of what you are looking at."

This continuous interest in alchemy inspired Breton's friendship with René Alleau, the man who suggested in 1952 naming the new surrealist gallery À l'étoile scellée (subtly alluding to Dom Pernety), even if the language of the birds permits a second reading here. Breton was also a friend of Eugène Canseliet's, a man who was the disciple of the mysterious Fulcanelli, whom he called the "Adept Fulcanelli." Others in the group also shared this interest for alchemy; Elie-Charles Flamand in particular, who, according to Canseliet, was "particularly smitten with the alchemical mystery," recounts in his book *The Meanders of Meaning* his discovery of the Bastie d'Urfe, the alchemical dwelling cited in "Fronton-Virage." There were also Maurice Baskine,* the "tramp philosopher," who introduced Fulcanelli to his friends, Victor Brauner† and Philippe Audoin, whose *Bourges, Premiere City* was inspired by the theories developed in Fulcanelli's *The Dwellings of the Philosophers*. This latter book is an extensive study of the secrets of the royal art that are concealed in the architecture or interior decoration of the principal monuments of Bourges, in which an Alchemy Street also

---

*On Baskine, Sarane Alexandrian writes in his autobiography, "I enjoyed Maurice Baskine, the phantasopher with the large round glasses (he called his concept of life *phantasophy*) looking for the philosopher's stone in an athanor in his house in Fontenay-sous-Bois, and who would leave behind beautiful alchemical painting, a new Tarot deck, a triptych on the Great Work, and a magical object, the Photoron with mirror." This large triptych, accompanied by many other works by this *phantasopher,* are displayed today in Cordes-sur-Ciel Museum of Modern and Contemporary Art, housed in the House of the Great Falconer. Aimé Patri wrote, with regard to this artist, "Baskine is that student of Nature who knows how to extricate from the darkest matter the fire that smolders and gleams when it comes into contact with a mind still in possession of its original gift." Baskine was also discussed in 1947–1949, by Marcel Jean and Arpad Mézei in their book *Genèse de la pensée moderne dans la littérature française,* as a keen astrologer.

†"He [Victor Brauner] baptized his new villa [near Varengeville-sur-Mer, Seine Maritime], 'the Athanor,' the name of the crucible of the philosopher's stone, faithful in this way to alchemy as a source of his inspiration," writes Benoît Decron, in "Mythologie et la fête des mères" (in the Brauner catalog, *Cahiers de l'Abbaye Sainte-Croix,* n° 84, 1997). And Didier Ottinger says, "By baptizing his house and final studio this way, Brauner supplied the key to his artistic undertaking that from then on assumed the appearance of a boundless desire and a permanent quest for unity. Beyond the logical scarifications of the analyst or scholar, the Athanor is the symbol of Brauner's poetic work, which reconnects and welds together what cold reason has put asunder." Coincidence or not, this also served as the title for an anthology his friend Gellu Naum published in 1968. Naum, along with Virgil Teodorescu, was one of the sole members of the pre–World War II Romanian surrealist group to stay in his native land—but that is another story!

existed. Incidentally, Audoin's article "Quand sel y est"* (in *La Brèche,* n° 7, December 1964) took a long look at the heraldic art, which the author of *Two Alchemical Dwellings,* Canseliet himself, claimed was "derived from that same language high initiates maintained was that of the birds and consequently the 'gay science or gay savoir' of the phonetic kabbalah."†[31] Nor should we overlook the man Alleau called "our dear Benjamin Péret"[32] and the Czech Vitezslav Nezval,‡ the Milanese Arturo Schwarz, and even Roger Caillois, who confesses, in *The Alph River,* that he "read Strindberg's alchemical pamphlets," or even Jorge Camacho, "descendant of the Tainos," who was "lurking around a bevy of initiatory texts, Trismegistus, Albert le Grand,§ Paracelsus, Sendivogius."[33] Camacho told Gérard Durozoi in 1998:

> I can place my initial interest in alchemy around the year 1968. . . . It goes without saying that the hermetic science that began interesting me at that time fit neatly in the context of a revolt, in this instance

---

*There is a phonetic pun, here, on the title and the name for Canseliet, which are pronounced the same way.

†In his text "Before the Curtain," Breton also talks about the "phonetic kabbalah," which he associates with the works of Rimbaud, Duchamp, Desnos, Brisset, and Roussel, with another quote: "It is in the tradition of the Cabala, Ambelain reminds us, to assert that in the 'world of sounds' two words or two sounds with related resonances (and not only assonances) are indisputably related in the 'world of images.'" This is, of course, Robert Ambelain, author of *Franc-Maçonnerie d'autrefois: Cérémonies et rituels de Memphis et de Misraïm.* Fulcanelli, in *Les Demeures philosophales,* had in fact written, "The language of the birds is a phonetic idiom solely based on assonance. Therefore, spelling, whose very rigorousness serves as a check for curious minds . . . is not taken into account."

‡"In the street of the Gold Makers in Hradchany / one could almost say that time never passes / If you want to live five hundred years / drop everything and apply yourself to alchemy," Vitezslav Nezval wrote, as quoted by Angelo Ripellino in his book *Praga Magica.* With respect to Nezval (1900–1958), Philippe Soupault notes in his preface to *Prague aux doigts de pluie et autres poèmes,* "He was taken, not without reason, for a dreamer, in other words a man who gives his complete attention to what men overlook most of the time. He smiled at the stars, lent an ear to murmurs and echoes, followed their gleams, spoke with beings who did not wish themselves named. . . ."

§Albertus Magnus was the German theologian, philosopher, and scientist who taught at the Sorbonne in the thirteenth century, which the Place Maubert (Magister Albertus) still serves to remind us of today.

one of a philosophical nature against all dogmatic and academic concepts of Nature. If surrealism plays an essential role in this other notion of reality, as vast and extensive as can be imagined, it is gripping to note a certain parallelism between their respective quests. Since then I have never been able to separate the word "Alchemy" from that of "Liberty," even if it appears paradoxical! Moreover, I had the good fortune to meet, at the beginning of my study of the science of Hermes, Bernard Roger,[34] Eugène Canseliet, and René Alleau. Thanks to them, I was able to enter the way of traditional alchemy directly without any detours, thereby removing from my path all speculations of an occultist nature and other pseudo-mystical doctrines that always graft themselves like parasites on the admirable body of this science and adulterate it.[35] This is the same Camacho who Jean-Claude Silbermann told me "had been at the furnace." The same Camacho (when he was not signing his works with his pseudonym "Ohcamac") who held an exhibition in 1969, Le Ton Haut,[36] "with a clearly esoteric connotation."

This is the same Camacho* whose painting *The Green Candle* (1970) (see plate 14) David Nadeau revealed was directly inspired by an engraving of the Flemish painter Otto Vaenius (or van Veen, 1557–1626), another who had passed through the court of Rudolph II. In 1983 this same Camacho was responsible for organizing the collection *Petite bibliothèque d'alchimie traditionelle* at Fata Morgan Éditions, whose first published title was Eugène Canseliet's *L'Hermétisme dans la vie de Swift et dans ses voyages,* which he personally illustrated. Camacho in 1991 then published, with the Brussels's publisher La Pierre d'Alun, *Le Hibou*

---

*On Jorge Camacho (1934–2011), the great painter born in Havana, François-René Simon notes in *La Quinzaine Littéraire,* n° 1036, "An infinite number of signs haunt his paintings, engravings, and drawings, references to deep and perennial roots that will guide him in both the possession of primitive objects and the representation of shamanic powers as well as in the individual's most deeply buried instincts, personalized by anthropoidal and clawed forms that haunt the very shadows they seem to be made of. Nothing except death will have stopped his dialogue between inner world and outer world, each time linking a series of canvases to one of his personal themes: alchemy, Raymond Roussel, death, flowers, the South, birds, the gods of force and the spirits of life, and so forth." It was Francois-René Simon who described Camacho as a Taino descendant.

philosophe, which contained commentaries of fifteen eighteenth-century alchemical devices placed under the aegis of the master, Canseliet, again and "based on experimentation by fire," according to his accomplice Bernard Roger, who wrote the preface. These devices, says Bernard Roger, were taken from a book found by chance "in a Prague bookstore during the splendid summer of 1968 when flowers of hope were still springing up that were soon crushed beneath heavy boots." Bernard Roger at that time had already provided "The Emblems of Monbel Street" (the area in the Seventeenth Arrondissement) for issue 2 of *L'Archibras,* in October 1967, which was inspired by the works of Fulcanelli and Canseliet. He ended it with these words:

> It would take too long to describe all the emblems with which a noble traveler marked his passage here. . . . These figures found on monuments from eras that are so far from one another are ageless. They do not belong to daily time; they testify to the existence of another "time" in which the notion of duration has been abolished. All that remain are the rhythms marked out, in the sky of both the large and small world, in the complex rhythms of the celestial luminaries. This is the *sacred* time to which belongs the undying chain of the "Children of Science."

This same Bernard Roger provided an alchemical reading ("Melius Spe Livebat," in *L'Archibras,* n° 6, December 1968) of the events of May 1968, comparing the young people in revolt to "the morning star, the mad garbed in foliage, the green vitriol, the mysterious place where vibration becomes a body." He went on to say in this article, "The water of life was in them, death can do nothing against the light being born; death is only a cardboard mask consumed by fire." In the seventh issue of this same magazine (March 1969), in an article titled "Le jour de l'étoile," he stated, "It is permissible to consider the liberation of the 'Artist' under the angle of a foreshadowing of that of the human species in its totality, toward which he is working in silence. Like every authentic revolutionary, like every poet, the Child of the Art should be first and foremost a seer."

Canseliet's name has now cropped up a few more times. This "Philosophus per Ignem," as Patrick Rivière referred to him, was born in 1899 and died in 1982. But is this not the same man who wrote this in his book *L'Alchimie expliquée sur ses textes classiques* (Alchemy as Explained by Its Classic Texts):

> Certainly, André Breton was well acquainted with Alexandre-Toussaint Limojon de Saint Didier's *Hermetic Triumph* from which he took the highly philosophical idea for his [1947] surrealist exhibition, especially that of making its visitors walk through the sand in a narrow passage inside a cavernous labyrinth. I deliberately repeat Limojon's image here: "Our practice in fact is a path in the sands, where we should seek as our guide the North Star rather than the remnants that can be seen imprinted there."[37]

Is he not also the man "who in his preface to René Alleau's book," as shown by Jean-Louis Bédouin, "speaks of that "disturbance of the logical balance of profane consciousness" as the "primal material and consequently the *chaos* of the Great Work on the mental and spiritual plane, which the alchemist cannot abandon without immediately returning to the ordinary manipulations of chemistry manuals?" Bédouin adds, "Coming from who it does, the importance of this clue cannot be emphasized too strongly taking on as it does extended range in the rest of the text: "therein resides the esoteric explanation of certain poetic works, the justification of the *inspired* poets who are labeled as *cursed*." Recall in this regard, with Yves Duplessis, "the gnostic sense of life's whirlwind that devours darkness" (*Le Surréalisme*), and which could explain, for example, Rimbaud's sonnet "Vowels," which itself is not without kabbalistic connection with Raymond Roussel's *Dust of Suns*.

Jean-Claude Silbermann also testified to this alchemical permeation of the movement in a 1993 text titled "Le Saumon, la cerise et le gardien du trait"* (The Salmon, the Cherry, and the Guardian of the Line):

---

*"Le Saumon" is part of a collection of articles published in book form under the title *Le Jour me nuit* in 1999, but it was written in 1993.

I do not have the expertise to detect the reasons and place the circumstances (Christianity? The Renaissance? The Enlightenment?) that led us to sever ourselves from our own original myths. However there is at least one traditional discipline in the West: alchemy. The "Children of Science" have perpetuated into our day "the art of Hermes."[38] In this century, poets—Jean-Pierre Brisset, Raymond Roussel, Ghérasim Luca, Guy Cabanel—were aware enough to slip the bridle off the "horse of speech." Artists, for the most, part from surrealism and in a specific, decisive way, among them Jorge Camacho[39] perhaps managed for a moment "to fix the volatile," and to "volatilize the fixed." But this traditional art is, like all others, transmitted by *initiation,* in study and the reading and re-reading of *inspired* texts. "Its secret is . . . the key—and it is a key whose only lock is its own trail."[40]*

For Brauner, it is even a Dame Pernelle, "a fairy woman with her face and hair haloed in light" [according to Xavière Gauthier] who has the privilege to discover and offer to the world the painting *The Philosopher's Stone* (1940), "that stone bearing the sign of the sun." The palette of Ithell Colquhoun shines no less brightly with all the fires of alchemical symbolism that permeate so many of her canvases, all those *Alchemical Figures* she painted between 1938 and 1967, in combination with the sephirotic tree stemming directly out of the kabbalah. Sometimes, as in the '40s, it was associated with the androgyne—which brings us back to the rebis, the double being—or with the homunculus (*The Homonculus I* and *II,* 1940)—"a wax (or clay or pitch) figure similar to the golem . . . used by the wizards of black magic," G. Scholem tells us. This figure was dear to Paracelsus and to Roger Caillois who talks about it in *Le Mythe et l'homme,* referring for more quotes in "Gustave le Rouge's book *La Mandragore magique (Téraphim, Golem, Androïdes, Homoncules),* Paris, 1912." These two figures can also be found in Colquhoun's novel *The Goose of Hermogenes.*

---

*Jean-Claude Silbermann confirmed to me, though, when we met on March 13, 2009, that his knowledge of alchemy was much less profound that that of Jorge Camacho or Elie-Charles Flamand.

Starting toward the end of the 1970s, Colquhoun's titles became even more explicit, such as *In the Alembic* or *Primal Fire* (both are 1978). As mentioned around 1930 in one of her first texts published, *The Prose of Alchemy*, which in its twelve pages explores the glimmerings of its iconography, the royal art clearly seems to have provided Colquhoun the philosophical and spiritual framework that gave her access to the surreal. She most likely frequented operative alchemists and mentions in this regard, in *The Sword of Wisdom*, a "nuclear reaction triggered by an unknown procedure." It was however the Jewish kabbalah, which postulates that the fall of Adam prompted the separation of the male and female principles and awaits the return of the One of the mystic union of the Kaddosh Barouch Hou and the Shechina, on which she based her spiritual alchemy, as did, perhaps, Breton himself, who owned a silver kabbalist chain, which is housed today in the Nantes Library. It had formerly belonged to Marcel Schwob, a writer highly esteemed by Breton, and it was undoubtedly given to him by Claude Cahun, whose real name was Lucie Schwob. It is perhaps worth mentioning here that the leader of the surrealists speaks in *Arcane 17* of "the allegorical field that maintains every human being was thrown into life to search for a being of the opposite sex and only the one who is paired in all respects, to the point where the one without the other seems like the result of the dissociation, the dismembering of a single block of light,"* and proclaims in "On Surrealism in Its Living Works," "the necessity to rebuild the *primordial Androgyne* of which all traditions tell us." The reunification of these two principles, but also heaven and earth, mind and matter, the *conjunctio oppositorum*, is the true purpose of the Great Work, the necessary condition for the restoration of harmony in nature. The androgyne is equally omnipresent in Brauner's work—and is depicted there sometimes in a powerfully symbolic way, as in *The Birth of Matter* (1940).

In Ithell Colquhoun's text "The Waterstone of the Wise,"[41] a title

---

*It is interesting to note that in this passage, Breton uses the word *thrown*, which can be interpreted as an allusion to the Fall, the word *search*, which evokes the "quest," and finally the expression "block of light," for which, no doubt, a gnostic connotation could easily be found.

probably borrowed from an early seventeenth-century alchemist, Johann Ambrosius Siebmacher, author of *Hydrolithus Sophicus seu Aquarium Sapientium* (The Aqueous Stone of Wisdom or the Aquarium of the Sages), she repeated the arguments Breton developed in *Prolegomena to a Third Surrealist Manifesto or Not* (1942), an extract from which appears in the *New Roads, 1943* anthology. She also proclaims there, like Toni del Renzio, author of the introduction to the part of the book devoted to surrealism, the necessity for a new myth, founded on astrology and alchemy, in particular on that famous union of the opposites that should dialectically permit their resolution. She grants this "science" so much importance that *The Goose of Hermogenes* opens with a more or less explanatory extract from Eirenaeus Philalethes's *The Metamorphosis of Metals* (1668). The novel's structure is modeled on the twelve stages necessary for achieving the Great Work (according to the mythical Basil Valentinus), each represented in a chapter marking out the spiritual progression of the narrator Corolla. According to Canseliet, this same Basil Valentinus (whose "Twelve Keys of Philosophy" he introduced in the fourth issue of *Médium*) was the individual Fulcanelli considered "his primary initiator." Seligmann mentions "Basil Valentinus, the pious monk of the fifteenth century," whose alleged writings in fact date from the seventeenth century and "are probably by J. Thölde von Frankenhausen in Thuringia."

Like his friend Ghérasim Luca, who writes, "For us, the dream of the alchemists, like all dreams, belong to one reality," Hérold, with his *Potable Gold,* also demonstrated a very clear interest in alchemy, described in these terms by Frédérick Tristan in 1987: "Alchemy then, but by air and water and almost never by earth nor fire, the work here opens out without falling into excessive black." Hérold wrote, "This is what I would have wanted my painting to be, the invasion of the body by a substance that is simultaneously both solid and liquid, crystalline, luminous, subtle, potable gold, the elixir of the alchemists."[42]

With his poem "Gypsy Queen" (written when he was in Havana in 1968 and now part of his fifth poetry collection, *Ruisseau des solitudes*), André Pieyre de Mandiargues proposes an "essay of interpretation and *appropriation* of an alchemically emblematic figure" (italics added).

This poem ends with the following lines:

> *The adept has been diverted*
> *The book of wisdom is shut*
> *And the cup of the smoking heart*
> *Is ready to go back to the open sea*
> *In the song of the magnificent wind.*

The word *appropriation* seems a perfect choice, and the author's imagination appears poised to follow tracks that are rather new but will become rapidly familiar to him after his discovery of a "Yugoslavian" painter, Popovic Alekse Ljubomir, known as Ljuba, about whom Mandiargues feels "obliged" in *Un Saturne gai: Entretien avec Yvonne Caroutch* (A Gay Saturn: An Interview with Yvonne Caroutch) to "utter a sacred word, but one that has become sullied today: *alchemy*." He ends with the following sentence: "Couldn't Ljuba's craft, in which a rapid glance distinguishes a purification and crystallization of the image or images, and a sublimation of the work's pictorial elements, be a variety of that of the ancient adepts?" Mandiargues, who in this instance is relayed by José Pierre, alerts us moreover that the work of this mannerist painter (although authentically surrealist) proves to be an "esoteric art oriented by vast readings, as well as a spiritual meditation and an interrogation of the nature of man and that of the universe," which in this instance clearly has to do with a vision of the world marked by alchemical thought.

To drive this point home, Mandiargues dedicated to his friend (in *The Drunken Eye*) an ode worth quoting in its entirety for the way it fits so perfectly within a context with such strong hermetic connotations:

Ode to Ljuba

Emperor Rudolph, if he returned
If he regained the androgynous throne
Transformed from Hadrian's Tivoli to the Hradchin
Beneath the scepter of a lunatic esotericism
I know that he would find the ideal imagemaker
In the person of Ljuba

> *Master in the present*
> *Of Mannerism past and future.*[43]

Jacques Van Lennep does not fail to underscore that "the two dreams were born to dissolve into one another," as alchemical art attained its height when mannerism was triumphing in the courts of Central Europe during the century of Paracelsus and Cornelius Agrippa. It was a time when "science got on well with madness," a time that was perhaps "the most anguished as well as the most nerve racking of our civilization."[44]

Another close associate of surrealism inspired by the royal art was Maurice Fourré, author of *La Nuit du Rose-Hôtel*. In his book *Maurice Fourré, rêveur définitif,* Philippe Audoin said of Fourré that alchemical references were detectable in the work of this Angevin writer and wondered if he had at his disposal "at the end of his life, at the end of all his 'travels', a knowledge of an esoteric nature that he taught covertly to those with the ears to hear him. . . ." Audoin also reminded his readers that Breton himself had not rejected this hypothesis. At the end of a rapid but precise skimming through Fourré's texts, Audoin concludes that while "the alchemical reference throughout is not debatable . . . it does not authorize . . . a more systematic attempt to go much farther down this path." He had suggested somewhat earlier that "the old magician who designates himself as the 'enigmatic alchemist in a carriage' undoubtedly knew much more than he let on about the meaning of the philosophical WORK," noting that "in this regard his Basilic* is revealed as REBIS under the guise of a Traveling Salesman: Clair Harondel, the fickle Mercury, carrier of three suitcases that are respectively black, white, and red. He is also seen in the darkened corridors of the Richelieu Hotel caressing a stuffed cat, the Fool of the tarots!"

Audoin then adds in his previously mentioned "Baron Zéro":

It may not be by chance that shortly after the chapters titled MERCURY and THE MULTICOLORED ALPHABET, Fourré

---

*Basilic was one of the characters in Fourré's *La Marraine du sel*.

placed THE EMERALD SCAFFOLD in which this quasi-acroamatic passage can be found: "a cone of <u>darkness</u> / enshrouds / the <u>sulfured</u> night / overshadowing with <u>black</u> lace / out to the sorcerous <u>waters</u> / the <u>tablet</u> <u>of</u> <u>emeralds</u> / of <u>plant</u> joy / where lurks / the Initiating <u>Metallurge</u>." I have underlined all the words belonging to the most common alchemical vocabulary; you will agree that their profusion makes any coincidence highly unlikely!

Should we then imagine that Fourré, as an astute reader of works devoted to occultism, was only flitting through this neighborhood in quest of an "initiation . . . undoubtedly one of a more personal than traditional nature" like a number of the members or close associates of the group? In any event, it is still Audoin who shows that "the desire to mark out, with deftly arranged standing stones and death omens, the stages of a spiritual path is hardly dubious either."[45]

Meanwhile, Jacques Simonelli, in his text "À la recherche de Fol-Yver" (In Search of Fol-Yver), "with its green pyramids standing like farm worker huts around the dreary prison of Roy . . ." reminds us that the "alchemical Quest" is, "for Fourré, the symbol of every spiritual path."[46] This article, in which Simonelli studies in detail the alchemical symbolism contained in *La Marraine du sel,* as well as in Fourré's other novels, notably *Chocolate Brown*[47] and *Le Caméléon mystique,*[48] follows the same direction taken by Philippe Audoin. Its author emphasizes that "Abraham . . . is linked to a group of the prime matter: 'Grandgousier tossing arsenic into a tankard of Rabelais,' is similar to the 'old arsenical dragon' that without the intervention of the alchemist cannot free itself from the 'vile sulfur' that holds the pure mercury inside."* He then adds, after noting that Clair Harondel's suitcases are the colors of phases of the Great Work, that "Florine† like the Soline of *Chocolate Brown* and the Jocelyne of *Le Caméléon mystique* is a solar heroine, bearer of the values of the alchemists' sulfur."

---

*In *The Godmother of Salt,* Abraham is the first husband of the novel's main character, the witch and magician Mariette Allespic, who is "oddly immutable and magical in her fascinating stiffness."
†In *The Godmother of Salt,* Florine is the daughter of Mariette Allespic.

Couldn't we see the "royal couple," the cherished king and queen of the alchemists, in this "wax couple" who "was once *dissolved* in the sun," after having been enthroned in the display window of the Allespic shop in "the geometrical town of Richelieu," which Michel Butor says is "as sharp as the ax of an Ancien Régime executioner?" In Prague, where the interest of the surrealists in the cursed sciences is as old as it is deep (it goes with the territory), the texts of Fulcanelli and Canseliet were translated on the initiative of Svankmajer, Stejskal, Ivo Purs, and Karol Baron, as was *Aspects de l'alchimie traditionnelle* (Aspects of Traditional Alchemy) by René Alleau, who traveled there on that occasion. In 1989, Martin Stejskal and Stanislas Zadrobilek organized the Opus Magnum exhibition, which echoed Arturo Schwarz's exhibition, held during one of the Venice Biennales, on the relationship between art and the quest for the philosopher's stone. This exhibit, Bertrand Schmitt and Marie-Dominique Massoni tell us in the book *Svankmajer E & J Bouche à Bouche* (E & J Svankmajer Mouth to Mouth), "offered an itinerary that first led underground. An enormous stone skull containing armloads of wheat at the entrance welcomed the visitor who, once over the threshold, would see the reconstruction of an ancient laboratory, *The Black Virgin of Celetna Street*, with film sets designed by Eva Svankmajerova. The rooms of the stages displayed a series of interpretations of plates from the *Mutus Liber*, executed by Eva Svankmajerova, works by Czech and Slovakian surrealists, a documentary by Martin Stejskal, or an alchemical laboratory as seen by Jan Svankmajer, echoing the one in the basement."[49]

It is not irrelevant that Eva Svankmajerova worked on *The Mute Book* (dating from 1677 and attributed to Isaac Baulot the Elder), "a book in which all hermetic philosophy is represented in hieroglyphic figures, which is dedicated to the merciful God, *Thrice good and thrice great,* and dedicated to the sole sons of the art," unless it should read "to the sons of the art and the sun," as Canseliet shows in his introduction to the reprint edition in 1967 (italics added).[50] It is also worth emphasizing here the extent to which all this retrospectively swept aside the prejudices that were formulated by the Parisian members of the movement when they met their Czech and Slovak friends during the brief thaw of the Prague Spring. Confusing legitimate discretion for shameful laxity, they wrote in 1967:

> The reaction that normally followed the weakening of socialist realism's positions resulted in a more or less disorganized, sincere appeal to the forces of the subconscious, thereby bringing about the blooming of fantastic paintings and sculptures—occasionally morbid in nature—instead of a surrealist renewal strictly speaking.[51]

Prague, "sung by Apollinaire," as Breton recalls, is one of the "high holy" places of surrealism, a city whose atmosphere Valentine Penrose (a poet whose work Whitney Chadwick tells us is "full of references to mysticism, alchemy, and occultism") recreates so well in her book *Erzébet Bathory: The Bloody Countess*.

> Vampirism, occultism, alchemy, necromancy, tarot cards, and, above all, ancient black magic, were the fruits of this city of narrow streets that was surrounded by forests. It was here that peddlers came to replenish their stocks of little books with their irregularly printed characters, their pages ornamented with woodcuts portraying devils holding their tails under their arms and looking askance at those who had conjured them up.... The immense cursed science invaded everything.[52]

Despite the "fantastic" nature of the description, it is not surprising that this city where "it seemed wizards, astrologers, seers, necromancers, magicians, the vendors of long life, and miracle workers of the eternal lamented in the black wind whistling through the chimneys,"[53] this city that is "studded with spires, undermined by deep alleys that buried themselves in cellars, led to cemeteries and opened on to the towering walls," this city that "spells out time on astronomical clocks" and "where the paths of charlatans, mystics, spiritualists, sorcerers, rabbis, and angels cross"[54] continues to exercise a powerful enchantment over the imagination.

But all this should not let us forget Theophrastus Bombastus von Hohenheim (1493–1541), also known as Paracelsus (the Mage of Keyholes in the Marseille Tarot deck), who is among surrealism's great ancestors. Chazal would claim that this nonoperative alchemist and wandering pantheistic doctor "healed analogically, like so many others." He was influenced by the thought of the Florentine Marsilio Ficino, as well as that of Johannes von Heidenberg, better known as Johannes Trithemius (1462–1516). Trithemius was the author of books on theurgy, magic, and angelology that sometimes used the gematria of the kabbalists, as well as of the famous *Steganography,* the title of his most famous book, in particular. He was also the founder of the Sodalitas Celtica, a neo-Platonic initiatory society whose members included Cornelius Agrippa and Johannes Reuchlin, the spiritual heir of Pico Della Mirandola, for whom "magic was not the use of dark demonic forces independent of the laws of the universe. It is a natural operation that science can explain or will explain one day but which takes advantage of 'secrets' and 'mysteries,' in other words the insufficiently known properties of natural phenomena."[55] An adept of "the science of talismans" and convinced of the oneness of matter given life by spirit, Paracelsus established correspondences between the different parts of the human body and the outside world. He had a pronounced interest in the "invisible ailments" connected to faith and the imagination. Still he wrote, "He who knows himself implicitly knows God." But this is a God imagined as the eternal source of the universe. He saw the source of all truth in the unity of God and nature (which is the deity's activated thought), a truth which could be decrypted thanks to the existence of the play of correspondences between celestial bodies, plants, metals, and man. In fact, as noted by Alexandre Koyré in an article published in 1933 in *La Revue d'histoire et de philosophie religieuse,* "'nature' as seen by Paracelsus—and as generally seen by the philosophers of the Renaissance—was perceived as life and magic. Magic is natural because nature is magical."[56]

In the system of Paracelsus, man is impure but superior to nature because of thought. He appears as a microcosm, the reflection of a macrocosm of which he has kept only a mere portion—his soul. For as Koyré (who was also published at this time in *Bifur,* Georges

Ribemont-Dessaignes's review in which a number of "dissident" surrealists found themselves) indicates, the world "is first and foremost the product of the fall, Lucifer's fall and that of his angels, and it was created as a prison for spirits."[57] This kind of gnostic thought carries the idea of "reintegration" in embryo, "a very influential doctrine that later flourished. Through Böhme and Weigel and others* it became the basis of the entire modern theosophical movement,"[58] as well as German romanticism.

In her footnotes to the anthology of texts by André Masson, *Le Rebelle du surréalisme: Écrits* (The Rebel of Surrealism: Writings), Francoise Levaillant cites Masson's poem "From the Top of Montserrat" (published in the eighth issue of *Minotaure* in June 1936), which includes the following:

> *And PARACELSUS: his two hands resting*
> *On the sword of wisdom*
> *In intimacy with the stars and stones*
> *In love with the caverns of humanity*
> *With the belly of the universe.*

She also says, "It is curious to see the interest shown by an educated public of the 1920s in the doctrines of the occultist scholar and doctor."[59] And she mentions René Allendy, Antonin Artaud, Jean Epstein, and Michel Leiris as fans of Paracelsus, unaware that Ithell Colquhoun's cat answered to the name of Theophrastus Paracelsus (according to Eric Ratcliffe). Ratcliffe also notes that the title of the work this English author devoted to Mathers, *Sword of Wisdom,* was directly borrowed from Masson's poem.

Kurt Seligmann, pursuing his exploration of the foundational texts of esotericism, would provide an English translation of the "prognostications" of the German thinker (i.e., Paracelsus) with thirty-two engravings in issue 2–3 of *VVV* (March 1943). These prognostications were first published in Strasbourg in 1530 (thus earlier than Nostradamus's *Centuries*) and rediscovered in the nineteenth

---

*The Protestant mystic Valentin Weigel (1533–1588).

century by Eliphas Levi. Allendy felt they gave off an odor of brimstone: "It does not seem doubtful to me that the *Prognostic* had a revolutionary meaning with respect to the Church and to the aristocratic governments."[60]*

It was also Paracelsus whom Alberti Savinio included among his "new friends" in his *Life of Henrik Ibsen*. It was also to Paracelsus that Roger Caillois expressed his gratitude in *Le fleuve Alphée* (The River Alph), citing his name next to those of Ruysbroek the Admirable, Meister Eckhart, and especially Giordano Bruno.

> His theory of signatures helped me greatly, thirty years later, when I was imagining how to present a concept of recurring forms necessarily at work in a countable universe.

It was also a book by Paracelsus that the young vagabond of *Aurora* was reading, a book Leiris—or the narrator of the book provides a lengthy description of ending this way:

> Finally, on the last page, like a sort of diagram summarizing the content of the text, there was a reproduction of the escutcheon of Paracelsus, comprising a red alembic drawn on a star-studded black background inside which burned a white salamander and from which blond hair rose like wisps of smoke. The whole thing was

---

*For more on the Rosicrucians, see Gérard de Sède's book *La Rose-Croix*. His family was related to Clement V, the pope responsible for the destruction of the Templar Order, and he was also a member of the surrealist group La Main à Plume during the War. In March 1943, he published a collection of poems, *L'Incendie habitable,* with the editions of that same group. For the first printing it included a dry-point engraving by Gérard Vuillamy, a Swiss friend of Seligmann and Paul Eluard's son-in-law. After leaving the movement, Sède turned to writing books for the general public devoted to the Templars, the affairs at Rennes-le-Château and Marsal, prophecies, and the Cathars, in which his investigative sense combined with his flair for the mysterious worked wonders, strictly speaking, even if it is likely he was manipulated in some cases by dubious characters (see Michel Fauré, *Histoire du surréalisme sous l'Occupation*). One of his best-known works, *Les Templiers sont parmi nous,* caused a stir in its day. It is probably no coincidence that Marc Saporta's preface to the book *André Breton ou le surréalisme même* was titled "Les Surréalistes sont parmi nous" (The Surrealists Are in Our Midst).

accompanied by this motto, most appropriate for the greatest man ever to seek the philosopher's stone: "Or Aura."*

It is still the language of the birds, but couldn't *Aurora* also be Sophia, the wisdom dear to Jacob Böhme at "'the golden hour' (*aurea hora*), the hour when the night of ignorance and the destructive putrefaction of matter comes to an end," as suggested by Alexander Roob?[61]

As we are discussing Paracelsus, who was—as well as was Heinrich Khunrath (1560–1605)—the Rosicrucians' precursor, I should also mention "a secret fraternity of alchemists, the 'Brothers of the Rose Cross,' who were similar to the Freemasons,"[62†] and who were placed beneath the patronage of a very mysterious "Elias Artista."[63‡] The mythical Christian Rosenkreutz is credited with the founding of this fraternity of the "City of the Sun" (Héliopolis!)[64] in the fifteenth century and the writing of three books published between 1614 and 1616 that formed the body of this society's doctrine. Kurt Seligmann called these three books, the *Fama Fraternitatis,* the *Confessio Fraternitatis,* and the *Chymische Hochzeit* (Chemical Wedding), "a solitary flower in the arid baroque German literature connecting the magic of Paracelsus to the nineteenth-century Romanticism." They

---

*"Or Aura" translates as "Will have gold."

†The high Rosicrucian grades of Freemasonry—such as the Sovereign Prince Rose-Croix—do not have much in common, except symbolically, with the Rosicrucian Order as presented here.

‡In 1784, the Abbot of Brumore swore that the Swedish theologian Emanuel Swedenborg was no Rosicrucian but was a friend to "the extraordinary man who called himself the name of Elias Artista in several books appearing in northern Germany . . . one of the prodigies of our century. A man of the humblest birth, without education or study, guided by a kind of supernatural enthusiasm, he learned almost every language in less than two years. He has written several books, always in the tone of an inspired being, especially his *Treatise on the Great Work* that all those who put their faith in it regard as the key to the art." There is one small problem: there is a good century between the "Elias Artista" who allegedly knew the first Rosicrucians and the alchemists of Rudolph II of Hapsburg's entourage (died 1612), on the one hand, and he who was allegedly the friend of Swedenborg (1688–1772) whose real name was probably J. H. Schmidt! It is true that time for the adepts . . .

were apparently written by Johann Valentin Andreae, among others, based on the *Corpus Hermeticum* and texts by Joachim de Flore (which we will revisit) and the English neo-Platonist John Dee, who was the model for Shakespeare's mage Prospero in *The Tempest*.[65]* Dee was a philosopher, skilled mathematician, *and* alchemist (among other things, as was often the case with Renaissance scholars), who did not establish clear-cut boundaries between the various domains of knowledge.

In his book on the Rosicrucians, *Les Rose-Croix,* Roland Edighoffer indicates that

> Adam, the mysts[†] of Ancient Egypt, of Eleusis, the Brahmans, Gnostic sects, hermetic brotherhoods, and the communities of Sabaeans or Arabs, are clearly the mythical ancestors of the Rosicrucians to the extent they share a certain number of "mythemes," and this isomorphism exists, although one of the principal authors, Johann Valentin Andreae, sometimes undervalued or denied it.

Stressing that the three books are quite different in their content, he adds:

> In the final analysis, the secret of the Rosicrucians, as it emerges in the *Confessio,* is the possession of the gnosis the *Corpus Hermeticum* says "is the achievement of the science, itself a gift from God. For all science is incorporeal and the instrument it uses is intellect itself," that tutelary angel that guides the soul.[66]

---

*Concerning John Dee (1527–1608), Frances A. Yates, in her article "The Hermetic Tradition in Renaissance Science," writes, "The evidence allows us to place John Dee historically as a later variety of the Renaissance mage—Rosicrucian, Paracelsian, and alchemist—with a desire to develop the applied sciences for the benefit of his fellows, overflowing with plans for advancing science, and accused of being a sorcerer in the court of public opinion. Dee felt he was a persecuted innocent."

†"Myst" is the name given to a man who has been initiated in the ancient cults, Eleusis, etc.

The *Fama Fraternitatis,* which takes the form of a nicely constructed story enjoyable to read although rich in symbolism that remains hard to grasp, seems to describe, according to Edighoffer, "God's hierogamy with his creation," opening the way to the study of the functioning of the universe to which the "initiates" at the origin of the scientific revolution of the following century will devote themselves. The harmony restored this way, Edighoffer adds, is announced at the beginning of the book by "the mysterious sign accompanying the letter of invitation addressed to Christian Rose-Cross," "the hieroglyphic Monad borrowed from John Dee (which) symbolizes perfect unity, the Alpha and the Omega, the transition of the Trinity into a Quaternity encompassing creation in the regenerative sacrifice of the cross," a sign that is strangely similar to certain figures depicted in Wifredo Lam's paintings.

It is also interesting to note that the *Fama Fraternitatis,* which clearly seems to have attempted an answer to "the crisis of European consciousness in the seventeenth century," advocated, in order to save humanity from its straying, "the gathering of an elite of impartial scholars free of prejudice who would have powerful material means at their disposal and would be capable of directing those who direct the people."[67] This would ultimately be the goal of the Invisible College, probably founded in 1645 by Robert Boyle, John Locke, Christopher Wren, and Samuel Hartlib, English translator of some of Andreae's works. The goal was continued by the British Royal Society, created in 1660 on the initiative of Isaac Newton, the renowned father of the theory of universal attraction as well as an alchemist, which is not widely known. Newton was very interested in the Rosicrucian Order, and, as Frances A. Yates points out in her 1977 article "Did Newton Connect His Maths and Alchemy?" he also appeared to be "a hermetic philosopher" and "an enthusiastic reader of Jacob Böhme," in the words of Paul Vulliaud. Between 1680 and 1684, he wrote a commentary on the Emerald Tablet and was also determined to discover "the blueprint and exact proportions of the Temple of Solomon," which, "drawn by God himself," then "should reflect (it was believed) the divine plan of the universe." Likewise, Elias Ashmole had also created a society for this purpose in London earlier.

In any case, we should acknowledge, with Serge Hutin, from his book *Les Disciples anglais de Jacob Boehme* (The English Disciples of Jacob Böhme), that "the influence of the Rosicrucians on the founders of the Royal Society, particularly on men like Robert Boyle and Joachim Poleman, is much more than a legend."[68] And we should note that it was Charles Stuart (King Charles I), thanks to the work of John Sparow and his son Charles II, who officially introduced the work of this thinker into England.

Not many specific details are known about the Rosicrucians, but the names most often put forth as assumed members of this probably informal group include the Dominican Thomas Campanella, author of *The City of the Sun;* Robert Fludd, the "seeker" cited by Artaud and the propagator of the ideas of the kabbalists, of Böhme, and of Paracelsus; Francis Bacon and his *Nova Atlantis;* Christopher Wren, the rebuilder of London after 1666; Jan Amos Komenski, also known as Comenius; and the doctor of Rudolph II, Michael Maier, the author of *Atalanta Fugiens,* and Gottfried Leibniz, but also John Locke and René Descartes, who at least looked for them throughout Europe. Others include the astrologer William Lilly and the English "antiquarian" Elias Ashmole, who bore the pseudonym Mercuriophilus Anglicus and was one of the first "accepted Masons" (in 1646), with Robert Moray (in 1641), who was the future kingpin and first president of the Royal Society (known as the Royal Society of London for Improving Natural Knowledge after 1663), which paved the way for the advent of so-called speculative Freemasonry. But perhaps it would be better to follow Frances A. Yate's proposal (while suggesting a possible Dee-Maïer-Ashmole-Newton filiation) and sensibly leave on the sidelines all considerations about the existence of a secret society and only retain the term "Rosicrucian" to "characterize an entire phase of the hermetic tradition in its relationship to science," a "transitional phase between the high Renaissance and the seventeenth century," in order to lift the ambiguities connected with the negative connotations surrounding this current of thought, representing, in her words, "a later form of the magical traditions of the Renaissance."

Like Pierre Mabille, who cited *Chemical Wedding* in *The Mirror of the Marvelous,* or Robert Guyon, who spoke of it in his article "Comme une suite à un ajour d'*Arcane 17*" (Like a Sequel to an Update of *Arcane 17*)[69] André Breton was well aware of the speculations surrounding the existence of this very secret society—if it truly existed—and its alleged founder, as shown by this passage from *Artistic Genesis and Perspectives of Surrealism,* where he writes:

> Paalen's art seeks to realize the synthesis of the myth still in the process of formation and those that are supposed to be fully developed, to embody the new myth in his own flesh. He has undertaken nothing less than to cast a blinding light on the night falling inexorably over humanity, and to this task he brings the rarest encyclopedic intelligence of our time, armed, moreover, with passion's great flashes of lightning. His painting has the wings of that miraculous bird with iridescent plumage, which appears in the *Chymical Marriage* of Simon [*sic*] Rosenkreuz, and has the power to restore life.[70]

Moreover, whether coincidence or objective chance, the Lion (and we should remember here what emphasis was often placed on Breton's "leonine" appearance) is responsible in this same *Wedding* for guarding the entrance to the mysterious royal castle that Christian Rosenkreuz reaches at the end of his journey to the *East* and the ascension that follows . . .

In any event, it should be noted that a trace of Breton's taste for hermeticism and alchemy can even be found on his tomb in the Parisian Batignolles Cemetery. A distinctive ornament distinguishes this grave from its neighbors. This is the Star Castle, the sealed star, a (philosopher's?) stone in the shape of a three-dimensional Seal of Solomon that the poet found shortly before his death in the Dordogne town of Domme, once haunted by François Augiéras.*

Now, as noted by Marguerite Surany in her book *Alchimie du vis-*

---

*[Augiéras was the author of *The Sorcerer's Apprentice*. —*Trans.*]

ible à l'invisible (Alchemy from the Visible to the Invisible), "The seal of Solomon is the initiatory mark of the philosopher who becomes a sage."[71]

Artaud wrote in *Heliogabalus or the Crowned Anarchist,* "The world above and the world below are reunited in the six-pointed star, the magic Seal of Solomon, and both end in a point, the visible like the invisible, the created like the uncreated."

This keen interest for the Star, the Arcanum 17 of the tarot, but also for the Adept, who often describes himself as an "artist," the first manifestation of the Great Work, which "teaches him . . . that he has not found the light of the mad but that of the sages," in the words of Eugène Canseliet, merely reinforces the alchemical "profession of faith" that served Breton, the author of *Fata Morgana,* as an epitaph: "I seek the gold of time." In other words, he seeks "the meaning of eternity," as René Alleau says in *Passage Breton* (a documentary shot in 1975 by Robert Benayoun and Michel Polac). If we take the word of Victor Crastre, a former Marxist from the editorial board of *Clarté* who became a fellow traveler of the movement, history could eventually validate his theory. Crastre writes in *Le Drame du surréalisme* (The Drama of Surrealism):

> I have no desire to raise an inventory of the scientific discoveries of the half-century. My only intention is to show that the aim of the high science was also that of surrealism: the interpretation of the universe was to be accompanied by its transformation. Isn't it puzzling to note, for example, that the dream of the alchemists was realized on the day Rutherford obtained the transmutation of nitrogen into oxygen (1919), thus carving a path for those scientists who obtained gold through the transformation of a mercury isotope in 1949.[72]

At the very least, "whether they were occupied with Flamel in the 1920s or by Fulcanelli in the 1950s, the surrealists have no other objective than to restore to their rightful place those powers of the mind that have been repressed most fiercely, for a radical recasting of understanding," as indicated by Vincent Bounoure* in 1977 in his article "The Surrealist (!!) Turning point," anthologized in *Moments du surréalisme* (Moments of Surrealism), even if out of prudence as a good scientist trained in one of the most prestigious French engineering school, he goes on to say that "the interest in traditional doctrines can only be understood from the perspective of an open anthropology—open mainly on history."[73] This is inevitably the case, for history is not far away, if we believe this friend of Georges Bataille, Doctor René Allendy, as cited by Gérard de Sède, who states:

> The idea of alchemical transformation by itself and the ideal of transmutation automatically lead, on the social plane, to a reformist attitude that assumes a revolutionary nature when confronting institutions with immutable and definitive pretensions.[74†]

Keep in mind as well what Breton tells us, after Guénon in his preface to Maurice Fourré's *La Nuit du Rose-Hôtel*, that "historical facts only have value as symbols of spiritual realities."

---

*It is important though to underscore the considerable importance, comparable to that of Vratislav Effenberger in Czechoslovakia, of Vincent Bounoure in France. Both in fact figure, deservedly so, as theoreticians and leaders of the "second generation" of their respective groups. Bounoure, who was never blinded by "reason," remained ever conscious of his limitations. "It is only with scandal that symbolic thought can oppose positive thought whose tyranny and intolerable pretension become day after day more assured without any valid compensation." For him, the "hermetic work . . . appeared as a specific case of a general poetics."

†René Allendy was the author of a thesis on medicine and alchemy and the organizer at the Sorbonne of the Group of Philosophical and Scientific Studies for the Examination of New Tendencies, which notably hosted a lecture by Roger Gilbert-Lecomte on "The Metamorphoses of Poetry" in 1932, then in 1933 those of André Rolland de Renéville and Antonin Artaud. He was a close friend of Georges Bataille and, most importantly, a strong supporter of Artaud, whom he attempted to psychoanalyze. He died in Montpellier in 1942. His first wife, one of Artaud's "daughters of the heart to be born," Yvonne or Vonia, died in 1935. She helped finance and organize productions at the Alfred Jarry Theater.

9

SURREALISM AND MAGIC

The magical night is not close to dissipating.
BENJAMIN PÉRET

Have you felt the black lace of her magical enchantments slipping through the night, in a circle of hearts pierced by a needle and heads severed with a pair of scissors?
MAURICE FOURRÉ, *La Marraine du sel*

Surrealism has always only been a new sort of magic for me.
ANTOININ ARTAUD, *À la Grande Nuit*

To the extent that "the very essence of magic is naught but a nocturnal belief in the efficacy of desire and feeling," then "poetry is magic for the sake of magic, magic without hope," says Jules Monnerot. "The poet is a magician who devotes himself to rites for their own sake, and expects nothing from them, except the *Erlebnisse* [experience] that becomes one with the very act of performing these rites." He goes on to say, "The hope of slaying an enemy, of seducing a loved one is naively expressed in magic. At a time when belief in magic is no longer a powerful social reality, hope is dissociated from the representations it electively colored." Truly—and Monnerot himself is not fooled! The third discipline of occultism is magic "that seeks, according to Legrand," to reconcile and combine the powers of nature and desire,"[1] and "is nothing but a wish [taking effect] by the appetite of the desire of the being," in the words of Jacob Böhme. Thus related to immanence (as Guénon also thought, although he deemed it "of a lower rank") and made possible according to Novalis (and Breton) by love, it is in no way a minor aspect, and could even be said to play a major role, which mainly through analogy is simply consubstantial to surrealism. This would be "the *universal analogy* that is the same we have seen among the theoreticians of magic," the analogy on which the esoteric approach systematically relies, to the extent in which, to quote Rolland de Renéville's postwar text *L'Experience poetique,* "it continuously connects the human being, understood as a small universe, to the large universe into which he is integrated." Analogy is, in fact, at the heart of surrealist thought, which uses it to set words free, to show the way to the *Signe Ascendant* (Rising Sign), the title of a Breton text that begins with these words:

> I have only ever experienced intellectual pleasure on the level of analogy. For me the sole *obvious fact* in the world is governed by the spontaneous, extra-lucid, insolent conjunction established under certain conditions between two different things whose conjunction would never be allowed by common sense.

From a strictly hermetic point of view, Audoin (as he says in an appendix in his book on Bourges) thinks it "is not only a picturesque means of expressing thought; it accounts for a profound truth and manifests a universal law." Octavio Paz in "Baudelaire as Art Critic: Presence and Present" defines it as follows:

> Analogy is the highest function of the imagination, since it fuses analysis and synthesis, translation and creation. It is knowledge of and at the same time a transmutation of reality. On the one hand it

is an arch that joins different historical periods and civilizations; on the other, it is a bridge between different languages: poetry, music, painting.²

Thereby, this "philosopher's stone of surreality," in the words of Jean Brun in the *Dictionnaire général du surréalisme et de ses environs,*³ naturally has much in common with language, particularly poetry. This is confirmed by the well-known question concerning the relationship between reality and language that casually emerges from *The Introduction to the Discourse on the Paucity of Reality:* "Wouldn't the mediocrity of our universe essentially depend upon our power of enunciation?" It also confirms the related idea, expressed in "On Surrealism in Its Living Works": "Surrealism . . . was born of a far-reaching operation having to do with language," whose purpose was the "rediscovery of the secret of a language whose elements would then cease to float like jetsam on the surface of a dead sea," but also its "'prime matter' (in the alchemical sense)." For good measure, Breton added, "The spirit that makes such an operation possible and even conceivable is none other than that which has always moved occult philosophy."

This question of the relationship between reality and language is one that will always haunt surrealists, as it does Arpad Mézei, who in his article "Liberté du langage" (Liberty of Language), published in the catalogue for the 1947 exhibition, writes:

> The surrealists show that the word is a multidimensional construct. Once a set of signs, language becomes visible as a set of symbols. This way of seeing language is not far removed from what existed in the magical civilizations, because the interchangeability of reality and language, by reason of words' multidimensional nature, is the basic, key principle of all hermetic activity.⁴

It is again Paz who notes:

> There is a strong magical element in Breton's view of language. He not only made no distinction between magic and poetry; he was also

convinced all his life that poetry was a force, a substance or energy truly capable of changing reality.[5]

This is where the science of names comes in, the linguistic magic that comes from the kabbalah (in other words, the tradition), "an impure mixture of religion and magic,"[6] "a belief in language grasped as an absolute,"[7] which presumes the world "is basically constructed on the basis of numbers and letters."[8] In his *L'Experience poetique,* Rolland de Renéville writes concerning the kabbalah:

> We know that, according to this tradition, the successive order of the letters would present a summary of the sidereal system, and would symbolize the signs of the Zodiac in particular, that furthermore, each letter of the alphabet constitutes a power whose number and form would be capable of acting upon the cosmic forces to which they correspond . . . and that each letter is both a starting point and the arrival point for a thousand correspondences.

Seligmann meanwhile defined it sometime later as "a metaphysical or mystical system through which the initiate knows God and the universe," a "knowledge [that] lifts him above common notions and allows him to understand the mysterious meaning of creation." As a method of interpretation of the Bible, involving the practice of the *Tserouf* (letter combinations) among other things, the kabbalah (the *religious* kabbalah) expanded rapidly around the twelfth or thirteenth century, based on "ancient traditions whose original form was lost" and perhaps also on the writings of the Platonic philosopher and Hellenized Jew Philo of Alexandria. It flourished in the third major center of the flowering of medieval Jewish thought—the Languedoc. This was during the time Catharism was developing, which offers two reasons that could partially explain the undeniable gnostic influences as well as the neo-Platonic ones that can be perceived in it.[9] "An oriental source for the theology of the cabalists," Jean Doresse explains in his *Les Livres sacrés des gnostiques d'Egypte* (The Secret Books of the Egyptian Gnostics), "was the *Raza Rabba,* the 'Great Mystery,' a now vanished text that had been nourished by Gnostic speculations on the Aeons." Sarane Alexandrian, who writes on this topic at length in his *History of Occult Philosophy* after making the distinction between the philosophical kabbalah and the religious kabbalah, then, on the methodological plane, between the speculative and the operative kabbalah, summarizes the matter.

> We find in the philosophical kabbalah as in the religious kabbalah, speculators (Agrippa, Reuchlin, Postel), who employ gematria, notaricon, and themoura* in order to extract new information on the Holy Scriptures; operators, who introduce various kabbalistic techniques into medicine (Paracelsus, Robert Fludd, Van Helmont) or into the exploration of the invisible; and finally, in the nineteenth century, conciliators (Fabre d'Olivet, Eliphas Levi, Stanislas de Guaita), who strive to find a definitive accord between theory and practice.

Guy Casaril slightly modifies this list in his book on Rabbi Bar Yochaï (a legendary figure according to Sarane Alexandrian) with his observation:

> If we draw up a list of the principal authors on whom the kabbalah exerted an influence: Pico Della Mirandola, Reuchlin, Agrippa von Nettesheim, Paracelsus, Guillaume Postel, Robert Fludd, we cannot help but see that despite their different origins and philosophies, they all or almost all possessed a common character trait: attraction to the *occult*. All or almost all of them sought a truth beyond the rational and for that reason were suspected of heresy.

But Casaril condemns "the 'mages' of the second half of the nineteenth century: Eliphas Levi, Stanislas de Guaita, Papus in France," whose "books on the kabbalah systematically combined with alchemy and magic reveal practically no understanding of its spiritual message."

In this respect, the Polish scholar Jan Potocki (1761–1815), who,

---

*Gematria, notaricon, and themoura are procedures for reading the sacred texts. These procedures make up the Tserouf.

like Beckford and Blake, was once close to the Jacobins but whose writings are close in spirit to English gothic novels, said in his *Manuscript Found in Saragossa* (of which Roger Caillois published a critical edition in 1958; there was also a deluxe French edition with twenty-one etchings by Leonor Fini in 1961):

> In Hebrew, every letter is a number, every word a learned combination of signs, every sentence a terrible formula, which, when correctly pronounced with all the appropriate aspirations and stresses, could cause mountains to crumble and rivers to dry up. I do not need to tell you that Adonai created the world by the Word and then made himself into a Word. Words strike the air and the mind; they act on the senses and the soul. Although you are not initiates, you can easily grasp that they must be the true intermediaries between matter and every order of intelligence. All that I may tell you about it is that every day we are growing not only in knowledge but also in power.[10]

It is this conception of the connection between language and the power of negation or generation, a poetic power in the etymological sense, that allowed this great—and discreet—purveyor of kabbalistic thought (in whose crown the Zohar is only the most beautiful jewel), the Rabbi Juda Ben Betsalel Löw of Prague, the "Maharal, initials of the Moreinu Ha Rav Loew" ("Our teacher, Rabbi Loew") (see plate 15) as Michel Löwy reminds us,[11] to give life to a creature of clay, the Golem. He did this with—or so it is said—the sacred word *emeth* (truth, and "seal of God" for the kabbalists), more or less borrowed from the *Sefer Yetzirah*,[12] but also with the sacred phrase *shem ham phorash*, which can be found in other traditions.

The Golem, a term that in the Talmud is also used to designate Adam before he was imbued with the breath of God, as indicated by Gershom Scholem in his book on kaballah symbology,[13] is also the mythic figure of the German expressionists, such as Paul Wegener and Henrik Galeen, for example, with *Der Golem* (1914), then Wegener again with Carl Boese with *Der Golem: Wie Er in die Welt Kam* (1920).

Later, the Golem was depicted by numerous surrealists, such as Kurt Seligmann, who featured him on the cover of *View* (December 1940–January 1941). There was also the Gurdjieff disciple David Hare, who titled a work this way in the fourth issue of *VVV* in 1944, not to mention the "Autotaraphis Introspector Golem" that appeared in Victor Brauner's 1948 autobiographical *Biosensitive Ultrapainting;* it was accompanied by a figure baptized Victor, with a "v" with a laurel wreath followed by the infinity sign and a note "to the initiation ceremony." The Golem also made many other appearances in 1944 and 1945 in the works signed by this Romanian painter, who adored Meyrink's book *The Golem.*

It is interesting to note that Brauner combined, in the name of his character, the Golem itself and the *taraph,* as he did in certain writings dating from 1945 (now housed in the archives bequeathed by the artist to the Pompidou Center), writings that Margaret Montagne in *The Myth of the Double* cites:

> The taraph is one of the very first images created by the Hebrew people during their long exile in the desert. While they were headed to an as yet unknown destination in answer to an unconscious need, [it] became the first image to be used for magical purposes and later proved to hold considerable power. The Golem, serving the secret inner man, and endowed with taraphic powers, finds itself facing a world that is both increate and re-created. . . . The taraph is the image of the increate reality headed toward an unknown destination.

The Golem is also "that old man who inspires pity," according to Louis Scutenaire in several comic yet touching verses that reveal that

> *If the Golem is marked by the sign of infinity he says*
> *where the first two phalanges meet*
> *on the middle finger of the right hand*
> *it is because he burned himself on the coffee pot*
> *at dawn when passing the coffee.*

The Golem even made an appearance in good company in Paris at the Gallery Les Yeux Fertiles in 2002 for the exhibition by Enrico Baj, *Ubu Totem Golem*, whose catalog was written by Fernando Arrabal. But just as it is possible to give this creature life by the word, it also is possible—would this word be sacred—to take back this life by simply erasing the first letter, leaving only the word *met* (death), which sounds very similar to LE MAT, the fool of the tarot, who is a symbol of the return to celestial night.

The Golem, which no doubt still sometimes haunts the streets of Prague, unless its ashes remain housed in some walled-up attic of the Old Synagogue, is also the hero of the novel *Golem*, by Gustav Meyrink (who has already been mentioned in chapter 8), and a story by Achim von Arnim who was greatly admired by Breton. In *Artistic Genesis and Perspectives of Surrealism*, Breton also evoked the "golems that include Bellmer's doll," the same doll that Alain Jouffroy wrote in 1959 could "be considered as one of the most effective objects of counter-enchantment ever invented by a man to free himself from the whole oppressive system of surveillance through work and the formation of a family that society perpetuates in all lands and under all political regimes, around each and every one of us."[14]

Upping the ante, José Pierre states:

Of course, Bellmer must have been haunted on more than one occasion by the old legends revolving around the Golem or by the example of Mary Shelly's Frankenstein. Yes, how to give life to creatures produced by desire in its pure state—and at the same time as impure as possible: a woman who is only breasts, or a sexual organ, or spiked heels.[15]

This is an idea that could even bring us back to magical eroticism or the sacred feminine!

"Seligmann,"[16] notes Fabrice Flahutez, "describes how the Golem, literally meaning 'shapeless matter,' was supposed to function according to the sixteenth-century kabbalah by placing the word 'truth' on the front of the still shapeless and lifeless object."[17] Analogically speaking then, out of the word comes life! Or, according to Annie Le Brun, expanding the scope of this subject:

> In other words, it could be that the famous "secret for creating an earthquake" consists of using the analogical impetus, not only to change from one being to another, but to switch from one state to a myriad of others, acting as an intermediary between the real and the imaginary in order to precipitate the imaginary's transition into the real.[18]

And it is so because for the surrealists, language's true function is primarily subversive and aims at (re)enchanting the world: "The path of hermeticism and occultation, that Argol could not avoid taking, is undoubtedly the price to pay in this 'black night' for recovering liberty," writes Dominique Rabourdin.[19] Frances A. Yates, in her article on the hermetic tradition in Renaissance science, shows that Marsilio Ficino (1433–1499), a key figure in the Florence of the Medicis of what in a somewhat reductive sense, perhaps, has been called the "Neo-Platonist of the Renaissance,"[20] cultivated a new audience (in the West) for the texts attributed to Hermes Trismegistus, the *Asclepius,* in particular (Latin version of the *Perfect Discourse*), whose heroes were "the Egyptian priests who were said to know how to harness celestial influences and through this magic knowledge capable of giving life to the statues of their gods." It is not hard to establish a connection—tenuous as it may be—between ancient Egypt and the myth of the Golem. But it should be clearly understood that poetic analogy, which shares with mystical analogy the distinction of transgressing the laws of logic, is "fundamentally different . . . insofar as poetic analogy in no way assumes, within the framework of the visible world, the existence of an invisible one trying to manifest itself," the existence of "any kind of beyond."[21] Breton adds a warning about the dangers of spiritualist parasites, followed by . . . a quote from the Song of Songs and another from Swedenborg! This is the same Swedenborg whom Daumal and his Grand Jeu friends esteemed so highly that they*

---

*[Rolland de Renéville specifically was critical. —*Trans.*]

criticized Breton and the surrealists for, they said, not knowing his works. When Milan Dedinac (1902–1966), cofounder of the Belgrade surrealist group and consequently "one of the Thirteen of Belgrade" had come to Paris in 1925 to study Swedenborg's works at the Sainte-Geneviève Library.[22]

We should not lose sight of the distance that Breton tried to maintain—somewhat ambiguously—with respect to "irrational" manifestations, whatsoever: about magic "common to all peoples," Sarane Alexandrian rightly notes: "We must clearly grasp that what Breton valued here was a primordial sacredness, the root of all authentic poetry: 'I stick to the great poetic mystery,' he said with respect to occultism."[23] This would seem to be corroborated by Breton and Legrand here:

> It is beyond doubt that a certain *imaginary* magic (corresponding to the vehicle of a persistent narcissism, which gives the development of Greek mythology its originality) has permeated Mediterranean culture virulently enough so that later spirits as varied as Desiderio, Gustave Moreau, and Giorgio de Chirico rediscovered the sense of magic there, still confused with poetry by the Platonic tradition.[24]

In the same spirit, Gérard Legrand, closely allied from 1955 on with Breton on the writing of *L'Art magique* and thus in the know, although he seems to tackle the matter with the greatest caution, writes in his book about Breton:

> The old word "magic" often reappears in Breton's earliest texts as the most convenient designation for this "poetic element" that sometimes surrounds us and where things and beings fascinate us. The sovereign emotion that then captures us, life in its most precarious aspects and worse, closest to death . . . seems to reabsorb itself totally in this emotion that transforms it. What could be more normal than for those who made it their task to master these considerable efforts, the magicians of every age, to be invited by surrealism, as the at least legendary bearers of such effects.[25]

It is seen this way no doubt because, according to the great occultist Lotus de Païni (whom Breton cites in "Fronton-Virage"), "Magic is a pervasive knowledge of the soul as well as an essentially positive science of the body which is made of soul." This same Lotus de Païni, whose name appears in *L'Art magique* and Roger Caillois's *La Fleuve Alphée,* is the one "who condemned in the legend of Golgatha the *end* and not the beginning of the sacred, henceforth voided of all magical substance and doomed to vegetate on 'the dry wood of the intellect'" (see the 1957 tract "Coup de Semonce"). Lotus de Païni, or more exactly Elzevia Gazzotti (1862–1953), was a follower of Rudolph Steiner since 1913, to whose memory she dedicated her book *The Magic and The Mystery of Woman* in 1928. She was a friend of the Penroses, and Breton probably discovered her fairly late, maybe in 1954: he dedicated a very symbolic collage to her in 1962. This is probably why the situationist Raoul Vaneigem deemed it wise to say in his *Cavalier History of Surrealism* (written under the name Jules-François Dupuis) that while "she never participated in the movement," she was noted and acknowledged, "like so many others," by the surrealists.

In 1957, after a fairly long and painful gestation, *L'Art magique* came out in a 3,626-copy print run as part of the "Forms of Art" collection in the French Book Club. Its title was borrowed from Novalis, and though it was imposed on the author, by itself it shows the immense interest in this subject held by Breton, who thought, "There may be a cruel lack of magicians in our society." And this interest is even greater than Legrand's earlier citation would allow us to presume, since it appears that in the intellectual spheres as opposed to what takes place in the scientific milieus "every principle for going beyond the level of current consciousness . . . resides and can only reside in magic, in the sense of the traditional science of the secrets of nature." The importance of this essay is ably summarized, moreover, by Nadia Choucha, who indicates:

> Breton was to place surrealism as a twentieth-century manifestation of an ancient magical tradition in art, stretching back into prehistory. In his book, *L'Art magique,* magic is seen as an innate capacity of humanity that always resurfaces, especially after long periods of

rationalism, and which can never be entirely suppressed by religion, science, or politics. It is a symptom of the desire for the autonomy of the imagination and freedom from constraints, a thirst for the unknown, the mysterious, and the unsettling experiences of life that can be valuable in extending human knowledge and power. These goals, in fact, were also surrealist aims from the start of the movement, and by the 1950s Breton openly acknowledged its place in the occult heritage of Europe, perhaps as an attempt to give more prominence to this misunderstood and ignored tradition, which, nevertheless, has never died out and has remained to the present day a valuable source of timeless knowledge.[26]

The authors of *L'Art magique* began this important book by finding a more precise definition for the word *magic:*

No one will contest the fact that it encompasses all those human procedures whose purpose is the imperious domination of the forces of nature through resorting to secret practices of a more or less irrational nature. One of the characteristics of magic is to be "absolutely restrictive," which is what radically distinguishes it from religion. The forces or powers invoked are assumed to be incapable of resisting what is asked of them, they are ordered to comply under pain, in many circumstances, of punishment.

Another difference from religion, which advocates resignation, is that "magic presupposes protest, or more precisely revolt," which makes it preeminently interesting, of course, and explains why it was condemned by the churches. The authors then compare their definition with those of other seekers and scholars, from Hume to Lévi-Strauss to Freud and Frazer. From the latter they borrow the opinion "that a law of sympathy . . . would be capable of governing the relations of nature and man to the benefit of the latter" because "the means man has at his disposal to achieve this aim are none other than those that govern the association of ideas, either through similarity (imitative magic), or by contiguity in space and time (contagious magic)." Here we are back at analogy! But Legrand had already maintained similar opinions in 1951 in *Le Libertaire,* namely stressing, "And the greatest of ethnographers, although a rationalist, James Frazer, was compelled to write: 'If it has been the child of error, it [the Black Art] has yet been the mother of freedom and truth.'" Legrand went on to say:

> But that which in magic and occultism, stripped of its metaphysical backdrop, cannot fail to interest us, seems to me to come down to these two major fields of investigation that complement each other: 1. The elaboration of a DYNAMIC concept of language, based on ANALOGY and appealing to the inexhaustible forces of the unconscious and the imagination. 2. The desire for a universal knowledge.[27]

To complete the picture, Breton and Legrand bring in Eliphas Levi. Levi was one of the first members of the Societas Rosicruciana in Anglia (founded in 1867), which was the "mother" of the Hermetic Order of the Golden Dawn, and he was also "the author of *Dogme et rituel de la haute magie,* the one who, going against the grain like none other in a nineteenth century consumed by the illusion of progress, was to take up the task of reconnecting with such a tradition." According to Eliphas Levi, "There is only one dogma in Magic and it is this: the visible is the manifestation of the invisible in exact proportion to the things that are unappreciable by our senses and unseen by our eyes."

This notion is close to that of the poets and "tends to exalt as much as possible and praise to the skies precisely what the rationalist mode of thought—which claims to be the sole path of progress and has imposed itself as such—can only, it goes without saying, unrestrainedly belittle." In 1957, we see the old mistrust of reason displayed as pure as it was on the first day! Now, according to Breton:

> Individuals [remain] for whom magic is something other than an aberration of the imaginative faculty, which only has a place in the remote past and only merits study for the purpose of understanding what the dawn of human history may have been like. Individuals of

this stripe swear that not only did it exist, there *still exists* an active magic possessing very real powers and boast of being able to judge and speak of it *from the inside*. . . . Called cranks, and even more often imposters, they are denied any say in the matter, which seems the height of the arbitrary. Extremely jealous of its prerogatives, here, as elsewhere, discursive knowledge intends to remain the sole master of the terrain.

This belief is so deeply rooted in him that it borders on superstition. At the time he was writing *L'Art magique*, Breton even believed he was victim of a curse. He wrote to Pierre Molinier:

Nothing appeared more simple to me in the beginning but to my astonishment, mysterious, increasingly large obstacles came into play, the worst of which is an anxiety that never leaves me night or day.

For Breton, "in these domains, disoccultation is perilous."[28] Guy Dupré even claims he feared he would be the victim of a deadly curse like Papus.

Banished by the institutionalized religions and the keepers of rationalism (and of the modernity it engenders) alike, magic could not help but draw the attention of the surrealists, especially if, as Frazer said, quoted by Breton in his preface to the 1947 exhibition, "daughter of Error, it is however the mother of Freedom and Truth." And yet as Sarane Alexandrian emphasized in his *Histoire de la philosophie occulte*, there is "no Western magic without the foundation of Christianity, of which it was sometimes the dissenting voice and sometimes the supererogatory interpretation." Seligmann, moreover, at the conclusion of his *Le Mirroir de la magie*, puts his finger directly on what can be considered the real points of contact between magic and surrealism, although the latter word never appears: "In its purest form, magic—in Christianity—arose from man's desire to take part in the divine *through knowledge*, to attain happiness through his will, not in the afterlife but in the here and now." Again immanence and again magic thought as liberation factor!

Some close associates of the movement go even further. There is the case of Artaud, who noted in *Cahier 391* in January 1948, two months before his death:

> *No one wishes to believe in the fabulous, major*
> *Decisive importance*
> *Of magic*
> *In the dynamic structure of the world . . .*
> *No one would ever have the idea to believe that magic*
>   *could be a science*
> *A mechanically applied process whose effect is therefore*
>   *just as verifiable*
> *As that of a brake of the clapper of a bell or of a lever.*

For Artaud, it was "a link, a power of 'communication' with the awesome efficacy [that] alone could heal the rupture between words and things, ideas and signs, culture and life," but "it was not that Masonry / that symbolic system / that theurgy / that psychurgy" he condemns in *Cahier 398*. This anagram of *image** appears in a number of both his published and projected titles, such as *50 Drawings to Murder Magic* and *Extermination of Magic,* which clearly reveal the somewhat malefic, harmful, dark nature magic held in his eyes despite the great distances he traveled in search of its possibly regenerative qualities. As he said in Mexico, in 1936, "The rationalist culture of Europe has failed, and I came to the land of Mexico in search of the foundations of a magical culture that could still spring forth from Indian soil," wishing "that one would compel the emergence of an occult magic from a land with no resemblance to the egotistical one that stubbornly tramples over it and cannot see the shadow falling upon it." And it is so because, as he adds in "Theater and Culture," his preface to *The Theater and Its Double,* probably written following his return from America, "The Mexicans harness the *Manas,* the forces that sleep in all forms, which

---

*[The word *magie*, which is an anagram of the word *image*, is French for "magic" —*Trans.*]

cannot emerge by simple contemplation of these forms for themselves but stem from a magical identification with these forms." He then concludes, "And the old Totems are there to hasten communication." According to Ado Kyrou, quoting a "project-letter to Maurice Garçon" in *Le Surréalisme au cinéma* (Surrealism at the Cinema), Artaud even wrote a screenplay for a "film on sorcery and the occult sciences," which has unfortunately been lost.[29]

Péret, in a more playful vein, published a short play in issue 3–4 of *Minotaure* titled "In the Paradise of Phantoms." It was illustrated with about thirty reproductions of automatons, including figures such as Heron of Alexandria, Roger Bacon, and Albertus Magnus, in whose mouth he puts the following words: "The magical night is not close to dissipating, and it is not an apple falling on the head of a man that will turn a reasonable moon into a mad sun, an automatic sun. . . ."

Among other faithful members, we should mention Toyen and her work, "in which a timeless night seeps . . . through hieratic ghosts (or 'specters'), in crack-covered bodies, and whose sole substance is that same night."[30] Gérard Legrand, writing about this artist, who was originally a member of the Czech group Devetsil, in the questionnaire accompanying *L'Art magique,* said, "Toyen's painting offers . . . the example of a gradual development of the being that conforms entirely with the pattern of magic." A half-dozen of her paintings are mentioned as signposts marking this progression, which Legrand notes "were pointed out by the artist personally." These include *The Mage Kings* (1925), *The Red Specter* (1934), *The Myth of Light* (1946), in which Legrand detects a "system of references" based on alchemy, and *At the Black Sun*. He then concludes, "Eventually, a completely integrated magical awareness in Toyen's recent works seeks the very *ontology* of apparitions, with an eye to the initiation of others into a 'practical truth' that germinates in the sea and in fire." This conforms to the diagnosis made earlier by Péret in the monograph he devoted to her.

> The entire work of Toyen aims at nothing other than the correction of the outside world in accordance with a desire that feeds and grows on its own satisfaction.[31]

The German writer Unica Zürn, in "The House of Illnesses," written in 1958 and which is the last part of *The Man of Jasmine,* also records some observations on magic that cannot help but recall Artaud and equally merit our attention.

> Having experimented (with black magic, N. de l'A.) on (her) own body, (she) wished at whatever cost to spare others this experience: Goethe—and I have also read this in Strindberg—instantly warns against the danger of projecting ideas of love or hate too strongly toward someone far away. Nevertheless, we cannot get rid of black magic, even if we follow the lessons of these two great poets and refrain from projecting our thoughts, in order to avoid mentally forging powerful and unseemly bonds with just anyone or anything, we cannot be sure that others will act the same way.

"How much it costs," she adds bitterly, "to hold black magic at a distance and not believe in it!"

Duits, in *The Demonic Consciousness,* a later text but one that clearly reflects the concerns of an entire lifetime, also raises questions about the relationships between *science and magic,* and makes this observation:

> If we study humanity's history, we see that mankind have always believed in magic. We can well ask ourselves on what grounds such a durable, stubborn, and universal belief rests. While it is true that science is efficacious, it is surprising all the same that millions of people spent such a long time inventing it, that we had to await the Renaissance for the disheartened magician to abandon the traditional methods of his art.

Duits deduces from this, "It follows that either we are fooling ourselves when we believe magic is ineffective (we only have false, insufficient, fraudulent information at our disposal) or else *the magician has different purposes in mind than those we attribute to him.* We can at least imagine that the magician does not share the same aims as the scientist and therefore may not be as ineffective as we suppose." Unless "magic was once effective, and its efficacy has gradually decreased"!

In Autumn 2009, however, it seems that Jan Svankmajer did not share the pessimism of Duit's judgment insofar as he wrote the following in his article titled "Fetish," which appeared in the second issue of *Phosphor* (the magazine of the Surrealist Group of Leeds):

> We are all convinced of the omnipotence of desire. We describe the imagination as the "queen of human faculties" and we take the side of the "possible" against the "real," but for this to result in anything concrete, it has to be confirmed by a "contract." This is the reason humanity created the fetish, insofar as a contract can only be concluded with an outside entity. A fetish is an independent subject, even if it is the expression of our desire and even if you have invested your entire imagination in its creation, contributing the maximum quantity of "possible" to it. It is perhaps only your product, but by charging it with your most secret desires and sticking the nail in its "flesh," you are establishing a contract with it with an eye to the realization of your desires, thereby transforming your subjective creation into an objective reality, that of a partner endowed with the "higher power" you have bestowed upon it with your faith in its capabilities.

These are the words of a magician!

This echoes the radical opinions voiced by Radovan Ivsic during the "Magic and Writing in the Congo" symposium in Brazzaville on June 2, 1993, a talk reprinted in his book *Cascades:*

> I believe the current world crisis is connected to a crisis of magic, even if this connection is far from obvious. My pessimism in this regard is only equaled by my conviction: if we are able to come up with a remedy for this crisis of magic, the world can only be all the better for it.

Ivsic then states that he is "taking the notion of magic in its broad sense, which for [him], blends into that of poetry." The author of *Airia* feels this somewhat worrying situation is connected with the current state of subservience almost everywhere, and therefore "the impoverishment of language" which is responsible for making us forget "what terrible power words can carry." And he concludes his talk by declaring that "the sole recourse remaining to us is to rediscover, or more exactly try to reinvent from the depths of our solitude," a magic that is as Benjamin Péret said, "the flesh and blood of poetry."

Although she never considered herself as a surrealist, strictly speaking, despite the obvious affinities, we cannot overlook the first phase (pre-1965) of Leonor Fini's work (often akin to mannerism and that I have already compared to that of Yves Tanguy), which also smacks, at least partially, of magic and more broadly the occult. As evidence: the magazine *La Tour Saint-Jacques* devoted a special edition to her in 1955 titled "The Magical Painting of Leonor Fini," with articles by Serge Hutin, Marcel Brion (the patron of *L'Art magique*), and Jacques Audiberti. In a short text, Castor Seibel also observes:

> Refusing any prior transcendence with a prideful gesture, Leonor Fini nonetheless bases her painting on another kind of sacred. This is how she creates, over the vacuity of fêtes, a ritual invested with the power of mythic acts. The theme that haunts her—and indicated in the titles of some of her paintings—is initiation: initiations, you feel, whose hierophanies are beauty and life. Initiation with an immense power of conjuration.[32]

Bacchanals, sabbaths, ceremonies, fêtes more or less galants, or alarming rituals, "sumptuous orgies" to borrow Jean Genet's term, inspired her. These were always bathed in a nocturnal clarity, as in *The Far End of the World* (1949), or at the very best haunted by reddish gleams, as seen in *Friendship* (1958), works that Jacques Audiberti described as "melancholic, finely worked, highly elaborated paintings entirely misted over by another both desired and desiring inner world, yet with plates and reliefs showing on the surface."

Her friend Victor Brauner, after mentioning the "primordial chaos," saw "the history of matter and life, beyond the present and the past" in her work. Springing from this past we see disturbing chthonic deities, sphinxes and other human/animal or human/plant hybrids, victims of the *Equivocal Metamorphoses* (1953)— but aren't they all! Mandiargues writes in a short text titled "The Story of Psyche":

> Metamorphosis is a magic word if ever there was one, insofar as it actually designates an act of magic that brings about a change of shape, a major transformation, and if magic is involved it is through the action of a magician, of a wizard sometimes—or a god.[33]

In her article "Masks and Metamorphoses," Jacqueline Chénieux-Gendron adds that one of the principles of surrealism resides in this direct passage from metaphor to metamorphosis that guarantees the "reality effect."[34] Fini's sphinx, meanwhile, cannot help but bring to mind these lines from the pen of Joseph Péladan:

> The sphinx smiles at his boundless future; he has reconstituted his original unity, being both man and woman, he knows that one day he will reconstitute his original unity, for he is both man and god.

Yves Bonnefoy writes that Fini, "the modern heiress of an old knowledge, that of the fairies," gives us with *La Pensierosa* (1954), *The Guardian of the Red Egg* (1955), and *The Moon Woman* (1955), among other paintings, her vision of what it has become commonplace to call the sacred feminine in the "lapping of the worlds in the retorts of who knows what demiurge," as Claude Louis Combet wrote in *Leda's Mirror*.

And since, with the sacred feminine, we are tackling, albeit indirectly, love relations and magic, so splendidly evoked by Mandiargues in his last novel, *Tout disparaîtra* (Everything Will Vanish),[35] it is worth recalling what Ghérasim Luca guardedly noted in *The Passive Vampire*:

> I sense as if by an echo from a remote distance that the events in which I've been taking part over the last few days exceed what one meant up to this day by the concept of love. I do not know what part

of it is magic and what part of it is love, I know neither the place where these two terrible nuances of black meet nor the place where they separate, but I do know that the lover should be doubled by a magician, in order to be able to approach, without being terrified, these sublime deformations of darkness.

Luca then goes on to say, "I am perhaps thinking of a magic that is not unrelated to the libido, but as long as the forces at work retain their mask of ashes, I will speak about them in an obscurantist manner."

It would clearly seem that what is involved here, being a product of amorous passion, governs the actions of Mariette Allespic, the "witch and magician" who in Fourré's *La Marraine du sel,* "slays [her husband, the unfortunate Abraham] with her potions," a man who appears initially to the narrator as "the ghost of smile—hailing the ceremonious shadows of the Duchesses and the peers casually heading toward the gold fringed stools," the "revenant from another world," showing on the surface of another time or space. Hence, perhaps, this recurring interest, already mentioned, for the figures that emerge from demonology, the succubi and other incubi, like Toyen's *Strange Visitor,* which first appeared, in the early issues of *La Révolution surréaliste* (see, for instance, Aragon's "Entrance of the Succubi" in number 6 in March 1926), and which would be mentioned again thirty-five years later when we are told that the first conversation between Breton and Elléouët centered on succubi—whose ugliness Aragon, admitting his "scant personal experience," had been quick to emphasize.

Succubi also seem to have haunted Ernest de Gengenbach in a singular fashion. Citing Aragon's text, he mentions a "phenomenon that is metaphysical in nature," which he described in his *Adieu à Satan:*

> What happened to me, however, on the psychic level was not at all of the same order . . . because my desire for embrace and amorous communion instead of being satisfied was exasperated in an agonizing way by my ex-lover who, already possessing all the secrets of sexual magic, sadistically did her utmost to make me suffer the veritable tortures of Tantalus. After occultly disrobing by leaving her physical

envelope, she suddenly appeared molded in a vaporous tapering dress that wound around her fluidic body in the voluptuous spirals of a siren-like lasciviousness. I wanted to hurl myself on her, greedy for her embrace, for ecstasy . . . but she vanished like the curls of smoke of a deluxe cigarette smoked by a Venus of pre-Christian mythology. . . . Nothing happened on the level of carnal, sensual realizations and yet I came out of these nocturnal adventures completely dispossessed of my vital fluid. . . . There could be no doubt, I had been vampirized by a succubus!

Later, addressing Breton himself, he confides:

I personally wished to go much farther than you, and not being fulfilled nor getting my fill from mortal, terrestrial, carnal creatures, I experimented with succubi.

Succubi and incubi also put in regular appearances in Brauner's sketchpads, and one of his drawings, reproduced in the catalogue accompanying the exhibition *Victor Brauner: Surrealist Hieroglyphs* at the Menil Collection, Houston, in 2002, bears the following, particularly significant notes in the form of captions: "Incubi, Succubi, Ephialtes, Lycanthropes, Werewolves, Ghosts, Specters rendezvous here my eternal friends. You speak the language of a world of inspiration that is also mine."[36] This last word is underlined twice!

It is also surprising to note that while their companions often perceived them as magicians and the keepers of beneficial powers, the women surrealists tended to depict themselves rather as witches, as shown by a number of works, notably those of Leonor Fini, or the *Hexentexte* (The Witches' Texts) by Unica Zürn, published in 1954.

In his preface to the French edition of *The Man of Jasmine*, Mandiargues notes Unica Zürn's "taste for the kabbalah," which he describes as "quite strong" and tangible "from the very first pages" of the book, especially in this woman's work obsessive with anagrams. Speaking of herself in the third person, "as if contemplating herself," says Mandiargues, she significantly asked herself a little later:

Has she become a witch? The feeble breath from a human mouth that produces a huge whirlwind?

From his initial contact with the group in 1937, Kurt Seligmann, "in search of the marvelous in the book learning of the ancient alchemists and occultists,"[37] despite "his deceptive professorial appearance" and his figure "of a good man of common appearance," displayed great interest in medieval heraldry as well as the art of the North American Indians, more specifically the Indians of the high Skeena region in the Pacific Northwest, which he was the first surrealist to visit (in 1938) in order to collect information and objects on behalf of the Musée de l'Homme, an experience he related in his article "Dialogue with a Tsimshian" published in *Minotaure*.[38] His visit shortly preceded that of Wolfgang Paalen, the future organizer of *DYN,* and Alice Rahon to British Columbia and Alaska in 1939. Pierre Mabille tells us in an article published in the magazine *Derrière le miroir* in 1949:

> Seligmann's character is most singular and mysterious. . . . Nothing in his outer appearance or daily behavior is at all surprising save that he was always here, unchanging, for some twenty-five centuries. He was living in Jerusalem when the Romans invaded it. He knew the secrets of the Temple and kept them. He was in Alexandria and frequented Ptolemy's library; he rued the ransacking frenzy of the Barbarians and took the wise precaution to rescue valuable papyri. He had a house in each of the Hanseatic cities during the Middle Ages and the Renaissance, because that was the true center for the thought then in gestation, his books piled up in semidarkened rooms, and he was smoking a pipe at a window that discreetly looked out over the twisting streets where all the peoples of the West came to exchange their wealth and fabulous tales. Sometimes, on the square, fire rose from the pyres kindled by sectarian passions and human hatred; other times lively bands of people cavorted there during carnivals and fairs, their joyful cries echoing in his garret. From time to time Seligmann disappeared to travel around the world, either for visiting strange peoples or

because he was in Italy for gallant extravaganzas during which, for the space of a night, man loses his footing and goes beyond his sordid condition.

Duits describes Seligmann in no less exalted terms:

But beneath his Swiss exterior, Seligmann hid a love of numbers and mystery, an essential crack, and who knows what kind of corrosive spirit whose triumph his suspicious death may have marked!

There is nothing surprising about the fact that under these conditions the paintings of such an "adventurer" would depict odd, more-than-human characters bearing capes and crested helmets, banners, valances, and other heraldic devices, who meet in violent battles that sometimes smack of the *danse macabre*. His engravings, meanwhile, reveal the influences of sixteenth-century Swiss and German engravers (particularly Urs Graf, to whom he paid tribute with the painting *Homage* in 1934; Niclaus Manuel Deutsch and his *Judgment of Paris,* with a clearly alchemical resonance; Matthias Grünewald; and Albrecht Altdorfer—all artists haunted by war and death), representatives of the late German Gothic or early mannerism, and "German and Swiss painters of the Lansquenets," of whom Jacques Lacomblez also admitted to being quite fond (in his conversation with Claude Arlan).

Jean-Claude Dedieu, in his preface to Leonora Fini's *Fêtes secrétes: Dessins* (Secret Fêtes Drawings), also writes:

The invention and "fantasy" of Leonor Fini's style has a certain affinity with the imaginal realm of the Gothic Renaissance. The svelte, elongated nature of the bodies, their elegant postures, the sharp line that tears them from their torpor and projects them to the surface of themselves is reminiscent of Bellifontain *manner* as well as the inflexion, sinuousness, and active grace of Pontormo's figures. The macabre fêtes transpose memories of Hans Baldung Grien. The Lansquenets of Urs Graf, the knights of Niclaus Manuel

Deutsch reincarnate inside a space with different dimensions: here they are vulnerable and undone.[39]

In this regard it is interesting to point out that Bataille, equally sensitive to the work of "Baldung Grien" as he calls him, claims, "In short, surrealist painting . . . represents the mannerism of today," adding, "Its quest for fever" betrays "the taut violence without which we could not free ourselves from convention." It may also be interesting to note that this aesthetic, which blossomed in Prague in particular during the reign of Rudolph II, inspired (in a perhaps somewhat emblematic but in any case very meaningful way) André Pieyre de Mandiargues to say:

Mannerism, hungry for technical knowledge (architecture, perspective, anatomy), deeply influenced by esoteric traditions (alchemy, astrology, magic), open to the feeling of nature, impassioned by eroticism, appeared with a style we could call revolutionary. Its visibly intense affinities with dream allow us to consider it an art of liberation, capable of both satisfying the secret nostalgias of the human being and uncovering the marvels and monsters his unconscious reveals.[40]

Michel Onfray, in his *Métaphysique des ruines* (Metaphysics of Ruins), discussing the paintings of Monsu Desiderio, even if he did not share the surrealists' analysis of this artist's work, offers from another angle a definition of mannerism that can be equally enlightening.

Mannerism's style is sometimes defined this way: a liking for the strange, rare, and extravagant, a passion for the extraordinary, astonishing, and the horrible, a quest for the allegorical, monstrous, revolting, and bizarre. Others add, complete, or clarify this definition by saying that it is necessary to include the desire for the marvelous, a penchant for seeing excellence in the ambiguous and aberrational, and a talent for the obscure metaphor and allusion, sophistry and the inventive. . . ."[41]

We can top off this portrayal with these clarifications from Jean-Claude Dedieu:

> This awareness in sensibility, this critical hindsight are an essential mark of the mannerist aesthetic which, whatever the era to which it belongs, produces from the world a subjugated, spiritual, and *readable* image of the world.[42]

What more is there to say about this style that, born in Italy around 1520 in reaction against the balanced forms and proportions characteristic of the Renaissance, would prosper into the beginning of the seventeenth century with its compositions that called into question spatial positioning and the equilibrium of forms? What more can we say about its harsh lighting and aggressive colors, its elongated, over-elaborated figures frozen in improbable postures, and its obscure, sophisticated allegories? In *A Gay Saturn: An Interview with Yvonne Caroutch,* Mandiargues, with respect to his former companion, Meret Oppenheim, says, "We can compare her art to Klee just as we can to the ancient master Altdorfer, and the Lansquenet painters Graf or Manual Deutsch"—often mentioned, indeed!

In his book on Toyen, Karel Srp states, "Some of Toyen's paintings created shortly after 1960 may also have been influenced by this curiosity about mannerism" which is, "primarily in its Arcimboldo-like version," an influence that, although visible at the beginning of the 1940s, truly "manifested" in paintings like *The Nightingale and Night Are Here* (1960), *The Lava of Waiting* (1961), and *Stream in the Distance* (1962).

This debate would be resumed in the book on Jan Svankmajer published under Peter Hames's supervision, in which Michael O'Pray considers the mannerist influence on this Czech filmmaker's work, which Svankmajer acknowledges, as well as that of Arcimboldo and curiosity cabinets, and also their impact on his relationship to surrealism.[43]

In 1939, Kurt Seligmann and his wife relocated to the United States (the first of many expatriates), where they settled for good. A collaborator on both *View* and *VVV,* Kurt Seligmann was known within the circle of the European intellectuals in exile, through his erudition and his library, as an expert on esotericism. He was therefore the individual to whom Breton turned to perfect his knowledge of this field, which he had already skirted, but which he would only be fully involved in after the war. In *Genesis and Artistic Perspectives of Surrealism,* in 1941, Breton noted:

> As a very young man Jarry conceived (his poetic drama) *Caesar Antichrist* "with places where everything is figured through armorial bearings and certain characters are double." Kurt Seligmann, who had been instructed in this art of heraldic symbolism, and whose first mission seems to have been to elucidate its mysteries, has gone out to meet all the phosphorescent secrecy the medieval "night can offer." From these expeditions he brought back the pure forms of human anguish and energy, the content of which has probably changed very little since the days of Joachim of Fiore or Meister Eckhart.

In 1948, the Swiss native published *The Mirror of Magic,* the summa of all his knowledge, as indicated by the French edition's subtitle: *On the History of Magic in the Western World.* In his introduction, after acknowledging his debt to James Frazer (definitely a central figure of that era's ethnographical landscape), he does not fail to underscore the singular nature of his position in terms that could also describe the surrealist collective approach to esotericism:

> In addition, my personal library of old books on magic and witchcraft facilitated the investigation and permitted me to select a wealth of illustrations.... As an artist, I was concerned with the aesthetic value of magic and its influence upon man's creative imagination. The relics of ancient peoples indicate that religio-magical beliefs have given a great impulse to artistic activities, a *stimulus* that outlasted paganism and produced belated flowers in the era of Christianity.[44]

(This was written some ten years before *L'Art magique!*)

His works also exercised an influence over the productions of two other surrealists stranded on American shores at the beginning of the 1940s, "two bewitched witches," as Octavio Paz puts it, Remedios Varo and more significantly Leonora Carrington, whom Whitney Chadwick mentioned[45] in the chapter "Women Artists and the Hermetic Tradition" of her book on surrealist women: "Femininity itself, here in hieroglyph, the game and the fire in the bird's eye." Breton wrote in *La Brèche* (n° 7, December 1964) that Remedios Varo had belonged, before the Spanish Civil War, to the "logicofobista" group in Barcelona, which claimed to combine art and metaphysics, a group with whom Wifredo Lam also exhibited. As a Spanish Republican refugee, Varo followed Benjamin Péret to Paris, where she forged Chirico paintings to survive, an exercise that without adulterating it, left traces in her work, just as did her brief liaison with Brauner, "whose art and interest in alchemy would influence her pictorial work," notes Victoria Combalia.[46] Varo found refuge in Mexico with Péret at the end of 1941, where she would remain until her death in 1963. Her friend Octavio Paz has written this about her work:

> She slowly paints fleeting apparitions.
> Appearances are the shadows of archetypes: Varo does not invent; she recalls. Except that these appearances resemble nothing and no one.[47]

About Leonora Carrington, Henri Parisot, who remained her faithful translator, publisher, and friend, wrote in a letter quoted by Branko Aleksic:

> I saw Leonora Carrington for the first time one morning in 1937 in the apartment she shared with Max Ernst on rue Jacob. Brunette, slender, an exquisitely "savage" gaze beneath the arc of a long, dark eyebrow, she brought to mind the Belle Dame sans merci of Keats's poem; the Titania of *A Midsummer Night's Dream*.

Separated by circumstances from Max Ernst,* who had portrayed her in 1935 in the guise of a *Young Chimera in Evening Dress,* the "Bride of the Wind" (Ernst again) was interned in a Spanish psychiatric clinic during the early days of the war, then settled in Mexico in 1942. In her book on Leonora Carrington, Susan L. Aberth notes, "Mexico proved a vibrant influence on . . . Carrington, for whom the power of spells and omens was definitely real."[48] Octavio Paz also noted another reason:

> There are two Mexicos . . . there is a visible Mexico and an invisible Mexico. A past that is buried but still alive; not the indigenous civilization—it met a violent death during the Conquest—but certain mental structures, certain sensibilities and ways of seeing things and the world, and, finally, that which is called the unconscious ideology of a country: myths, obsessions, traditional images of the mother and father, death, sex.[49]

Carrington rapidly became close to Remedios Varo and Benjamin Péret. The two women, who influenced each other, albeit unevenly, shared many common interests, particularly occultism, Celtic mythology, the gnostics, Buddhism, the kabbalah, and magic, as well as cooking. Their reading of that time also left its mark: *The Mirror of the Marvelous* by Pierre Mabille, *The White Goddess* by Robert Graves, and Seligmann's *The Mirror of Magic,* which puts them at the heart of the reflections on these questions, already engaging the attention of many of their peers at this same time. Alejandro Jodorowsky, who spent time with Carrington in Mexico at the beginning of the 1970s, was given a cooking recipe by the Englishwoman, which he describes in his autobiographical account of that time, and which provides an excellent description of her eccentric character:

---

*Max Ernst's coat of arms, as imagined by Marcel Jean, is particularly elaborate: "Quartered on a field of gules and argent with the silhouette of a headless woman in the middle, the first charge is a gold grasshopper, the second is a red ring, the third is a red leaf, and the fourth a gold chimera."

With an unbroken stream of incantation spoken in the voice of a lion, I make my soup on wild rocks while looking at certain stars. The ingredients are simple: half a pink onion, a bit of perfumed wood, some grains of myrrh, a large branch of green mint, three belladonna pills covered with white Swiss chocolate. And a huge compass rose, which I plunge into the soup for one minute before removing it. Just before serving the soup, I add a Chinese "cloud" mushroom, which has snail-like antennae and grows on owl dung.[50]

Delmari Romero Keith wrote this about her:

Huntress of dreams and stars, Leonora has spun the fabric of her reality through the prism of her magical Celto-Irish perception and transmuted it into oneiric metaphors through alchemy. She strides through the labyrinth of myth like a traveler in the night, and travels over an ethereal geography of diaphanous or steep, mountainous landscapes inhabited by lyrical trees on the outskirts of fortified towns.[51]

This describes the matter to a "T" and brings to mind the décor of La Conchita, the "folly" built by Edward James in Xilitla in the Sierra Madre, which Carrington helped decorate, as well as, according to Julotte Roche, "the fresco in which we see a forest, bats, and birds . . . but it is not the forest of here"* that Max Ernst had created in their house in Saint-Martin-d'Ardèche.

Speaking in 1974 of one of Carrington's most famous novels, *The Hearing Trumpet,* which is literally crammed with allusions to every form of esotericism, Mandiargues writes:

---

*Leonora Carrington seems to have tried to effect this transmission in an extremely conscious manner. Didn't she write in her response to the questionnaire accompanying *L'Art magique,* "The true duty of the artist is to know what he is doing and to transmit his knowledge with precision. The artist must always lift up the skirts of Venus or her twin sister Medusa; if he is incapable of that, he should consider changing professions"?

In fact, omitting Michelet as a Frenchman (and the *Trumpet* is far removed from everything French), we note that witchcraft, taken more or less seriously, has been an object of dilection for a great many English, Welsh, and Irish writers since the end of the nineteenth century right into the present. Pell-mell I can cite the names of Yeats, Graves, Machen, Saki, Aleister Crowley, who, from the best to the worst, will make it possible to catch sight of what I am alluding to. It involves, doesn't it, the persistence of the old natural, panic religion, that of the Germanic Wotan, of the horned god and of the Great Mother Goddess (the Great Mother, the Great Goddess), exiled, as Leonora Carrington writes, by God the Father, the Avenger, in other words the God the Jews bequeathed to the Christians. Of the return of the old gods reduced to a temporary clandestine presence, of the war of the gods, or at least of their faithful, Leonora makes a use in *The Hearing Trumpet,* which places her in the top rank of all the fantastic writers ever.[52]

Taking the opposite tack to the religious and scientific orthodoxies of the time, jostling the canons of painting by recourse to a pictorial style reminiscent of the painting from the end of the medieval era, at least in the composition of her canvases, and adopting a sometimes extremely personal writing style, Leonora Carrington, familiar with the Vedanta and with the philosophies of Guénon and Daumal, transmitted her esoteric knowledge in a more or less deliberate manner through both her literary and pictorial work. This is visible, for example, in her *Portrait of Max Ernst* (1939), in which the painter, dressed like the Hermit of Arcanum 9 of the tarot, but with a splendid red fur enhanced with a fish tail, is carrying the alchemical egg (or a crystal ball) like a lantern, at knee height in a white, frozen landscape—wisdom and light—haunted by a white horse, unless it is a mare, which, Pascal Bancourt reminds us, "confers power and sovereignty on the hero." This mare may well be in connection with Macha/Rhiannon/Epona, with Leonora as "la chevalle," as Julotte Roche says in the "investigative narrative" *Max and Leonora* (written in 1997 and published by Le Temps qu'il Fait), or even one of those "wild horses" painted by the Mexican artist Maria Izquierdo, which "can be confused," according to Artaud, "with the evil spirits of the earth" in the context of a "totemism [that] produces a kind of millenary animism."

We can also consider *The Robing of the Bride* by Ernst, also painted in 1939, with its red female figure evolving in a setting in a typically mannerist style in which he depicts himself in the form of a bird entity with a long beak, a kind of representation of the Egyptian god Thoth, the very one the Greeks called Hermes Trismegistus, as a strongly alchemical echo of his former lover's canvas (see plate 16).

In her response to *L'Art magique* questionnaire, the woman who defined "surrealism as the approach we do not yet understand" wrote "truth is the strange, the wonderful," adding a little later in her "prezoological style":

> Let's thus seek out the possibility of having subtle organs that will allow us to spread a beneficial magic or receive it while cultivating the protections against the multiple venoms of the invisible world. It is only in the strange magic ocean that we can find salvation for ourselves and our sick planet.[53]

This same Leonora Carrington was introduced by Elena Poniatowska in a 2008 exhibition in Mexico as follows:

> Leonora, Celtic goddess, Druidess, queen of specters, mistress of the infra-world, knows the formulas of magic potions, and resolves in her paintings the mysteries that sometimes cause us anguish in the dark night.[54]

Paintings like *The Hunt* (a spiritual one, assuredly), *Palatine Predella* (1942), *The House of the Birds*, and *The Twins Are in the Orchard Again* (both 1947) by Carrington, and *The Creation of the Birds*,* *The Useless Science or the Alchemist* (both 1958), or *The*

---

*Recall what Jean Markale said about birds (cited in chapter 1, page 17). Those of the Irish goddess Rhiannon put the living to sleep and awoke the dead.

Ascension of Mount Analogue (1960) by Varo give clear evidence of this desire to transmit an esoteric teaching, with their adepts and athanors, their Celtic figures and the Magna Mater, their allusions to a thought that in its time also attracted René Daumal—that of Gurdjieff, as we saw earlier, whose disciples, the two women, pursuing their quest, encountered at the onset of the 1950s. For her part Remedios Varo was greatly influenced by P. D. Ouspensky, author of *In Search of the Miraculous,* and his theories connected with the fourth dimension,[55] as rightly pointed out by Tere Arcq in the anthology *Cinco Llaves del Mundo Secreto de Remedios Varo.*[56]

Jodorowsky again, in the same autobiographical narrative cited earlier, describes a nocturnal meeting he had with Leonora Carrington, his "surrealist mistress" (without any sexual connotations), and sketches in a few phrases the portrait of a woman who was far from ordinary.

> I saw Leonora seated on a wooden throne whose back was carved with the bust of an angel. Naked except for a Jewish prayer shawl, her gaze fixed unblinking and focused on infinity, she seemed like the figure on the prow of a ship from an ancient civilization. She had left the world of the rational. She continued to recite in English, taking no notice of my presence. I sat on the floor, facing her. There was little left of any individuality in her. She seemed possessed simultaneously by all women who had ever existed. The words poured out of her mouth like an endless river of invisible insects. I remember a few of her verses:
>
>> *I, the eye that sees nine different worlds and tells the tale of each.*
>> *I, Anuba, who saw the guts of pharaoh, embalmer, outcast.*
>> *I, the lion goddess who ate the ancestors and churned them into gold in her belly.*
>> *I, the lunatic and fool meat for worse fools than I.*
>> *I, the bitch of Sirius, landed here from the terrible hyperbole to howl at the moon.*

> *I, the bamboo in the hand of Huang Po.*
> *I, the Queen bee in the entrails of Samson's dead lion.*
> *I, the tears of the archangel that melted it again.*
> *I, the solitary joke made by the snow queen in higher mathematics.*
> *I, the gypsy who brought the first greasy Tarot from Venus.*
> *I, the tree of wisdom whose thirteen branches lead eternally back again.*
> *I, the eleventh commandment: Thou shalt despise no being.*

But an extract from Carrington's *En Bas* (Down Below), a story told "on the return from one of those journeys from which there is little chance of returning" to Jeanne Mégnen, Pierre Mabille's wife, about her stay in Spain, will complete the portrait and clarify my claims better than anything else I could say. It is worth recalling, though, what Jean-Louis Bédouin said about this text, which is amazingly close (and for good reason) to those of Unica Zürn.

> Divinatory, tyrannical, often terrifying, *visions* took possession of the author's mind. The universe was under the thrall of magicians, "masters" that took advantage of their power to create a reign of terror.[57]

And citing Leonora Carrington directly, "on [her] return from this expedition into forbidden territory":

> I knew by dint of divination that the world was congealed, that it was up to me . . . to set it in motion again. . . . I was she who revealed religions and bore on her shoulders the freedom and sins of the earth changed into Knowledge, the union of Man and Woman with God and the Cosmos, all equal between them. . . . The father was the planet Saturn; the son was the Sun and I the Moon, an essential element of the Trinity, with the microscopic knowledge of the earth, its plants and creatures.[58]

Plate 1. *Italian Nun Smoking* by Clovis Trouille
© 2014 Artists Rights Society (ARS), New York/ADAGP, Paris

Plate 2. *They Have an Insatiable Thirst for the Infinite* by Judit Reigl
© 2014 Artists Rights Society (ARS), New York/ADAGP, Paris

Plate 3. *Hide and Seek* by Pavel Tchelitchew

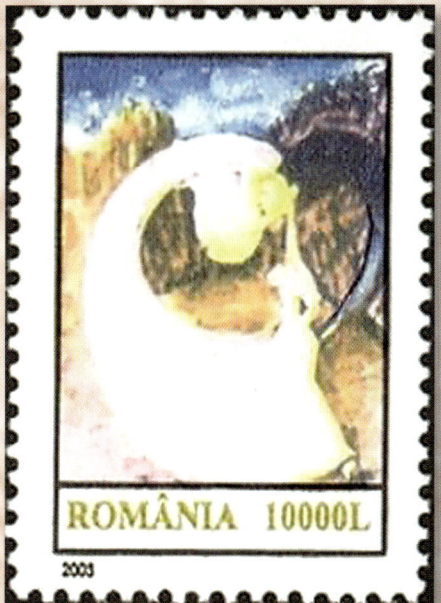

Plate 4. *Heron of Alexandria* by Victor Brauner
© 2014 Artists Rights Society (ARS), New York/ADAGP, Paris

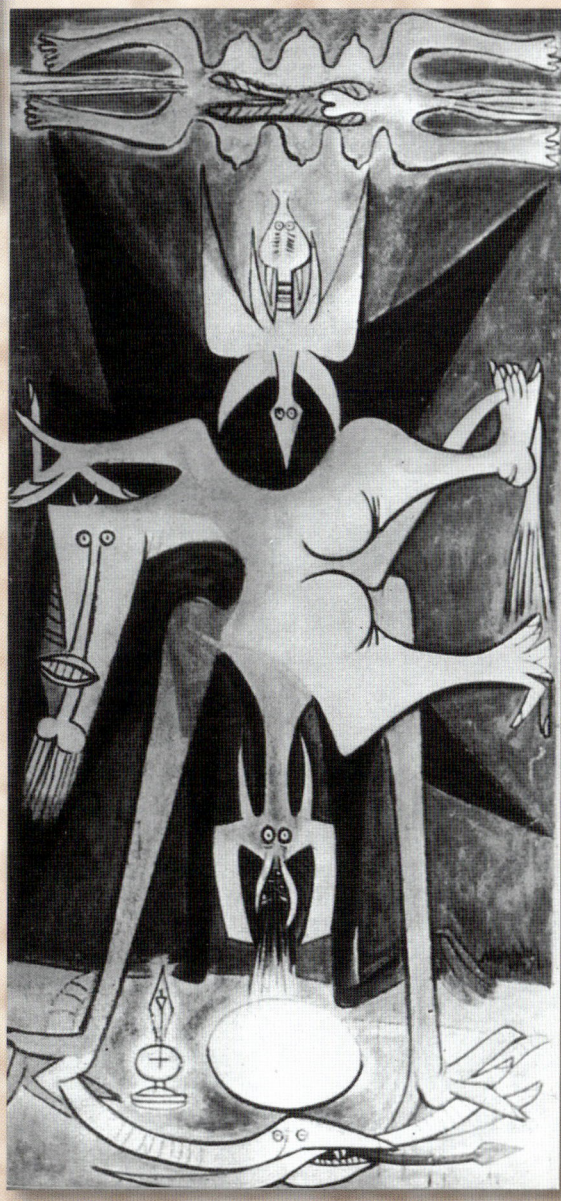

Plate 5. *Clairvoyance* by Wifredo Lam
© 2014 Artists Rights Society (ARS), New York/ADAGP, Paris

Plate 6. *Birth* **by Jackson Pollock**
© 2014 The Pollock-Krasner Foundation/Artists Rights Society (ARS), New York

Plate 7. *Guardians of the Secret* **by Jackson Pollock**
© 2014 The Pollock-Krasner Foundation/Artists Rights Society (ARS), New York

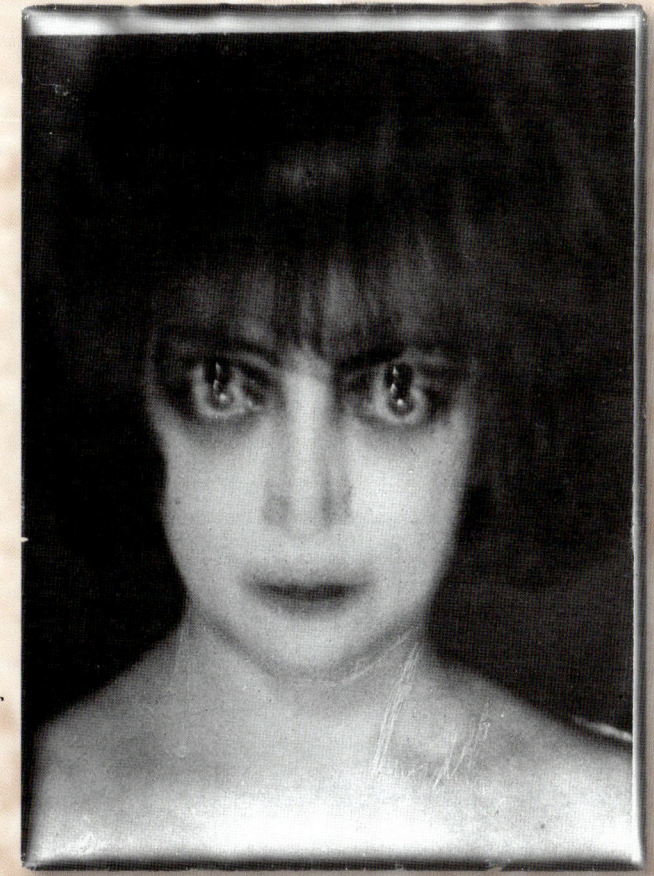

Plate 8. *The Portrait of My Soul* **by Man Ray**
© 2014 Man Ray Trust/Artists Rights Society (ARS), New York/ADAGP, Paris

Plate 9. *The Surrealist* by Victor Brauner

© 2014 Artists Rights Society (ARS), New York/ADAGP, Paris

Plate 10. *The Lovers, Messengers of the Number* by Victor Brauner

© 2014 Artists Rights Society (ARS), New York/ADAGP, Paris

Plate 11. *The Alcove: Interior with Three Women* by Leonor Fini
© 2014 Artists Rights Society (ARS), New York/ADAGP, Paris

Plate 12. *Neither Wings Nor Stones* by Marie Toyen
© 2014 Artists Rights Society (ARS), New York/ADAGP, Paris

Plate 13. *L'Homme du large* by René Magritte
© 2014 C. Herscovici/Artists Rights Society (ARS), New York

Plate 14. *The Green Candle* by Jorge Camacho
© 2014 Artists Rights Society (ARS), New York/ADAGP, Paris

Plate 15. *The Birth of Rabbi Loew* by Leonora Carrington
© 2014 Leonora Carrington/Artists Rights Society (ARS), New York

Plate 16. *The Robing of the Bride* by Max Ernst
© 2014 Artists Rights Society (ARS), New York/ADAGP, Paris

Plate 17. *Palacio Mnemonico* **by Leonora Carrington**
© 2014 Leonora Carrington/Artists Rights Society (ARS), New York

Plate 18. *Vox Angelica* 1942 by Max Ernst

© 2014 Artists Rights Society (ARS), New York/ADAGP, Paris

Plate 19. *Béliar* **by Wifredo Lam**

© 2014 Artists Rights Society (ARS), New York/ADAGP, Paris

Plate 20. *Self-Portrait* by Gustave Moreau

Plate 21. *Wolf Table* by Victor Brauner
© 2014 Artists Rights Society (ARS), New York/ADAGP, Paris

We cannot overlook the fact that Carrington must have known about the Emerald Tablet, mistakenly attributed to Hermes Trismegistus, to make observations like, "The task of the right eye is to peer into the telescope while the left eye peers into the microscope" (as above, so below).[59]

Breton was obviously deeply conversant with esotericism and entirely familiar with Trismegistus, as he had already written in *Les Vases communicants*, as early as 1932, that "every error in the interpretation of man brings about an error in the interpretation of the world."*

---

*In *History of Magic*, Eliphas Levi wrote, "It is in Egypt that Magic attains the grade of completion as a universal science and is formulated as a perfect doctrine. As a summary of all the dogmas which obtained in the ancient world, nothing surpasses and indeed nothing equals those few paragraphs graven on precious stone by Hermes and denominated the Emerald Tablet. . . . The Emerald Tablet contains all Magic in a single page." In fact, the "sentences" carved by Hermes and the precepts proffered by the Emerald Tablet were borrowed from *The Book of the Secret of Creation*, whose Arab author attributed it to a certain "Balinus," who is none other, it seems, than Apollonius of Tyana! On a par with André Breton and Leonora Carrington, Pierre Mabille was perfectly conversant with the teachings of Trismegistus inasmuch as he wrote in 1939—but without quotation marks, which reveals the extent to which he had made this knowledge his own—in the catalog of the Brauner exhibition at Henriette Gallery: "What is below is like what is on high to create the miracle of one sole thing. Here and there, hierarchical planes possess a meaning, a form, a number" (quoted in Pierre Mabille, *Conscience lumineuse, conscience picturale*). This was around the same time that Rolland de Renéville was observing in *L'Expérience Poétique* that "this assertion of the identical structure shared by man and the heavens becomes in some way the password that one poet tosses to another throughout the ages." And what should we say about these remarks made by Jules Monnerot in 1945 in his *La Poésie moderne et le sacré*: "In the most 'surrealist' poetry there figures a kind of picture shot of an inner flow, the objective moving from the *Same* to the *Other*, from the infinitely large to the human scale to the infinitesimally small, from planetary systems to splitting atoms, from wild overestimations to insane underestimations"? Not to mention Gérard Legrand, who ended his *Sur Oedipe* with this phrase: "On condition of removing all expressly or narrowly subjective reading from this metonymy, the Universe is the mirror image of what takes place on the inside." On the other hand, it can be interesting to recall that in the instructions of the Rosicrucian Knight grade, eighteenth degree of the Ancient and Accepted Scottish Rite, we can read, "The analogical relations of man and the universe are defined in the Emerald Tablet of Hermes Trismegistus: as above so below—for all that is and all that will be comes from the One" (cited by Guy Piau in his book *Tradition alchimique et tradition maçonnique*).

And it is under the sign, moreover, of "this same preeminent dialectical concept," completed by Goethe's phrase, "What is inside is also outside," that he places the work of André Masson in *Artistic Genesis and Perspective of Surrealism* before noting:

> It is striking to notice that, despite the fact that neither has influenced the other, both Brauner and Leonora Carrington have been led to interpret this [objective] world from the same spiritual angle, or at least that their work shares this strangely similar spiritual climate.

Brauner occupied a definitely central place in the movement by virtue of his great learning and quick mind, and as Breton says:

> For several years now, he has been safely ensconced in the heart of the "dangerous landscape," deep inside the realm of hallucination. Here he receives the visits of those rare beings who haunt the regions running beneath the surface of human life, holding in their hands the threads of premonitions and flashing correspondences.

It should be clearly noted that the work of this Romanian painter who called himself "emperor of the kingdom of personal myth" (but that's not all) is someone who best illustrates the relationship between surrealism and magic, like his friend and compatriot Jules Perahim. In the catalog for the Victor Brauner: Surrealist Hieroglyphs exhibit in Houston, Texas, Susan Davidson writes:

> His place of birth—the Carpathian Mountains of Romania—was steeped in the mystical and bizarre legends of vampires and werewolves, often explicitly portrayed in his paintings.[60]*

Among all the occult teachings, to which Brauner had already been sensitized during his youth by his family, loomed spiritualism and the

---

*An example is his *Eleonore and the Vampire* (1942).

kabbalah, with its sephirotic tree directly depicted in his paintings from the beginning of the 1930s, during the time of his friendship with Benjamin Fondane (1898–1944). It seems that magic was "revealed" to him by Jean Marquès-Rivière. A controversial figure for good reason, the renegade Mason Jean-Marie Paul Rivière,* better known as Marquès-Rivière, is portrayed as follows by André Combes in his book *La Franc-Maçonnerie sous l'Occupation* (Freemasonry under the Occupation):

> A learned but unbalanced individual, he underwent an exorcism to be purified of all Satanic influence. Coming to Freemasonry in the hopes of obtaining magic powers, he could not help but be disappointed.[61]

Marquès-Rivière quit the Grand Lodge of France in 1931 and was exorcized for that reason by the Jesuit professor Joseph de Toquédec. While collaborating under the pseudonym of Vérax on the weekly *La France catholique,* the news organ of the National Catholic Federation (whose president was his father-in-law, General Édouard de Curières de Castelnau), he wrote *The Spiritual Treason of Freemasonry,* then *The Great Secrets of Freemasonry,* among other books. He also launched the bimonthly magazine *Les Documents nouveaux* (1933–1936) in order to enlighten the right-minded about the Order's misdeeds and condemn its practices. A zealous Collaborator, during the Occupation he organized (with Bernard Faÿ, who had been part of the first team of *Littérature* and a friend of René Crevel) a large anti-Masonic exhibition at the Petit Palais. He was then named deputy director of the Police of Secret Societies and eventually became an outright German agent.

"Like Bernard Faÿ," writes Jean-Louis Coy in *Forces occultes: Le complot judéo-maçonnique au cinéma* (Occult Forces: The Judeo-Masonic Plot on Film), "he put his immense knowledge of Masonic philosophy and its tradition in the service of absolute hate, going so far as to paint, as early as 1936, a vitriolic portrait of Freemasons, based on

---

*He was called Jean Marquès-Rivière, his books are signed Jean Marquès-Rivière, but his full—and real—name was Jean-Marie Paul Rivière.

the physiognomical criteria already used for Jews."[62] In 1943, he created *Occult Force,* the first (and perhaps only) truly anti-Masonic film, for which he was also the author. He wrote the screenplay, along with Paul Riche, alias Jean Mamy, who had participated in the venture of the Alfred Jarry Theater with Antonin Artaud. Hunted after the war, stripped of his citizenship, and condemned to death in absentia, Jean Marquès-Rivière is said to have died in Lyon in 2000. But Marquès-Rivière, whom Brauner met in 1939 or 1940, also wrote *Amulettes, talismans et pantacles dans les traditions orientales et occidentales* (Amulets, Talismans, and Pentacles in Eastern and Western Traditions).[63] Brauner owned a copy that the author signed and dedicated to him, which he gave to Sarane Alexandrian in 1952.[64]

The reading of this book and other books on occultism, combined with the conviction that the loss of his eye was the sign he was being given initiatory access to a magic vision (as Didier Ottinger believes)[65] and the isolation imposed by circumstances led Brauner, during the dark years of his involuntary seclusion in Les Celliers de Rousset (Hautes-Alpes), to produce works of a "magical" nature, reinforcing an already existing tendency (recall his *Heron of Alexandria* of 1939) that was manifested in particular by the "charms" he addressed—perhaps—to the women with whom he was enamored, such as Laurette Séjourné, *Very Beautiful Gold.*

Concerning this period, Jouffroy, in his monograph on the painter, ventured, "Victor Brauner had entered this haunted castle that we are for ourselves. He would only leave thirteen years later."

Which, in passing, offers another explanation for the enduring interest of the surrealists in castles and ghosts, insofar as the author of *Liberté des libertés* (Liberty of Liberties)[66] immediately adds, "Phantom-Personage, he becomes obscurely aware of the phantomatic reality of the inner life!"

Later, Jouffroy states, thereby dating the full flowering of this phase of Brauner's work to 1942:

> This is how Victor Brauner entered magic. This *Empress of Knowledge* can be seen appearing in all her splendor through the

window of *Mythonomie*. A double, half-animal, half-human head with a Cyclopean eye crowned with flames, sits atop a female face whose overly quotidian, inattentive eyes are blindfolded. Clad in the dress of a magician that leaves exposed the Y of the belly and the small planets of her chest, she is holding the Egyptian ankh—a looped *Tau* Cross—in one hand and a snake in the other. She is an empress but also the beloved woman at the same time, lest we forget, and the attraction she exerts is physical as much as it is spiritual. The ghosts around her have vanished. The mountains in the background are deserted. Outer reality is merely some kind of soundtrack, before which the individuals enigmatically continue to guard their silence.

"In 1943," writes Alexandrian—but probably even before his work with his friends on the *Jeu de Marseille*—Brauner began studying "astrological correspondences, planetary spirits, the demons of the kabbalah, the houses of the moon, the astrological alphabets, and the pentacular alphabets used in operative magic," in order to create "talismans of defense and counter-attack"[67]—so much so that Susan Davidson could say without fear of contradiction that he "probably would not have objected to being characterized as a magician."

Going further, Mandiargues writes:

> Brauner, alone, in an old period during which his art was the tragic reflection of his life besieged or invaded by what could easily be called demonic forces, painted a series of image-paintings whose magical power was noted several times.[68]

It is too bad that the author was not more explicit about his opinion! *The Portrait of Novalis, The Lovers, The Image of Increate Reality,* and *Object of Counter-Enchantment,* boxed assemblages under glass created in 1943, are particularly representative of this period of his work, with their abraxas "seals" and kabbalistic or conjuratory signs accompanied by composite figures of stone or clay. Some small figurines, like *Double Vivification,* would not look out of place in a rural wizard's lair.

This was, moreover, the image that came to Sarane Alexandrian's mind in his autobiography, *L'Aventure en soi: Autobiographie,* for describing the studio of the artist with whom he was quite close from 1948 to 1955.

> You would think you were entering the lair of a wizard; sitting everywhere were pentacles, interpreted found objects, pentagrams, books like Paracelsus's Archidoxis Magicae, the huge statue of *Conglomeros,* a monstrous figure with a single head for three bodies, next to a bird skeleton, an adjustable mannequin.

The large canvas *The Palladist,* or *Composition on the Theme of the Palladist* (1943) reveals the same sources of inspiration. "According to Marquès-Rivière," Verena Kuni writes, "the Palladians are small statues that are treated reverently and are thought to protect cities from fire," and "Famous magician priests like Apollonius of Tyana and Hermes Trismegistus allegedly manufactured a variety of these statues for use in conjurations."[69] Taking into account the date this painting was created, this interpretation is possible, but we should also recall, with Alexandrian, that Brauner knew the anti-Masonic book *Palladism: Cult of Satan-Lucifer in the Masonic Triangles* by the renegade Mason Domenico Margiotta,[70] written in the spirit of Leo Taxil and his sidekick "Diana Vaughan," the so-called high priestess of the Luciferian order of the Palladium, from which Brauner could easily have drawn several ideas. Like Tanguy, although in a very different style, Brauner also began to paint (with *The Far-Sighted Mother,* 1943) a figure that "evokes the hieratic and terrifying deities of fertility and the earth revered by the ancient East,"[71] a figure that would find its culmination, but in much warmer tones, twenty-two years later, with the series of the *Feasts of the Mothers.* Meanwhile, as Xavière Gauthier noted, the woman, first and foremost that of Mythonomie, "garbed in a luxurious violet dress is the magician, she who transforms the world and embellishes it. In one hand she holds the Egyptian 'Tau,' symbol of life and death."[72] She is not quite yet the Mother Goddess, but she is already her priestess at least. She simultaneously embodies eroticism and esotericism, as well as the power, inseparable in the artist's eyes in the process of re-enchanting the world.

Says Dominique Bozo, thereby giving strength to Alexandrian's position, who, in a few phrases taken from *L'Aventure en Soi,* adroitly sums up Brauner's overall relationship to esotericism.

> Personal demonology, illustration of fantasies, psychic impulses, investigation of the imaginal realm, illustrated by means of alchemical iconography and that of the tarot. "World of Secret Initiation" (*The Palladist,* 1943). Use and editing of forms originally from the pool of the primitive civilizations of the Americas, Africa, and Europe.
>
> Inasmuch as the dependence of the Ego on the world was commonly accepted, the artist, in order to compensate for it, had to show how the universe depended on the Ego. Victor Brauner therefore identified with a medium emitting signals coming from the microcosm. The mythic images dripped off his paintbrush as if from a cornucopia. I understood the alchemists of the Middle Ages when I saw Victor Brauner, girded by a craftsman's apron, melting beeswax on a stove, glazing a painted surface with it while still warm, marking the lines with an awl, making corrections with a scraper, in order to produce paintings like the relics of a lost civilization: *I am Aganakka, This is the Story of a Poet of Sergimegetusa, Strigoï the Sleepwalker, Lion, Light, Liberty,* and so forth.

Nor does Alexandrian fail to note (in *Création Récréation*) that Brauner goes to the extreme of inventing a technique in order to give form to his intuitions. A technique, that of beeswax painting, he combines in at least four different ways.

> It was not just any works that Brauner decided to create with wax, but only those that expressed a hermetic content, and which required in his opinion the texture of a parchment. The cycle of drawings with candlewax that he created at the same time* also illustrated a mythology derived from the kabbalah; often a beeswax painting had been preceded by a candlewax drawing depicting the same subject.

---

*This was around 1944.

Alain Jouffroy, in his book *Une révolution du regard*, has many similar examples. Describing Brauner as a "mage" where Char speaks of "long effervescences and a maturation of anguish," he writes:

> At the center of modern art, he is the man who is the most aware of the meaning and true psychic range of the symbols inspiration uses so freely. Although cloaked in a variety of doubts and uncertainty, he remains the most faithful to the quest of a new sacred. His attitude toward the world is not only that of an artist but also that of a seer. . . . Thanks to him, the word "master," so tarnished by profane vanity and teaching, could regain its true initiatory meaning.

"This is because the painter has," as Susan Davidson adds, "employed numerology, tarot symbolism, allusions to alchemy and the hexahedral philosopher's stone, and a host of other arcane imagery,* *not simply as superficial references but as integral elements of his pictorial investigations*" (italics added).

Jouffroy showed, in his 1959 book on Brauner, that the painter was not alone in exploring these paths (citing two other names), but it is clear that a long list could be drawn up from among the surrealists or those in their immediate circle of influence.

> This is how, from 1943 to 1944, Victor Brauner, Michaux, and, Breton[73] became aware at the same time of the energy harnessed by magical methods, and used or revivified, for the purposes of a similar banishment of a general misfortune, the signs, rhythms, and formulas that since the dawn of civilization allowed humanity to gain the favor of the unknown forces of nature. For them this magic was not simply a means of defense against anxiety, its purpose was not merely the harmonious integration of man into the universe but it was also simultaneously an ideological instrument against a rationalism that each day grows prouder of its bombs and political police.

---

*As we saw in chapter 4.

In any event, examination of the titles in Victor Brauner's library will confirm, if necessary, his interest in the occult. *The Magic Works of Henry Cornelius Agrippa, with His Occult Secrets* by Pierre d'Aban, Robert Amadou and Robert Kantern's *Literary Anthology of Occultism, Jesus or the Fatal Secret of the Templars, The Book of the Sacred Magic of Abra-Melin the Mage,* and *Martinism* by Robert Ambelain, shared, in fact, the same shelves as *The Dwellings of the Philosophers* by Fulcanelli, *The Magician King and Primitive Society* by Frazer, and Guénon's *Fundamental Symbols of the Sacred Science,* not to mention *The Gnostics of the Revolution* by Louis-Claude de Saint-Martin.

Certainly, as Michel Löwy rightly notes:

> While magic in general and the "science of names," in particular, attracted the attention of the surrealists *with an irresistible force,* (italics added) it was not because they desired—like traditional magicians—to control the forces of nature with ritual acts or secret words. Their—immense—ambition is of an entirely different quality: *to change life.* What interested them in magical practices with language, in the kabbalah, alchemy, and other hermetic arts, is the immense poetic charge that these domains carry. This charge—in the explosive sense of the word—would serve them to dynamite the established cultural order and its sensible positivist conformism. Sparks flying from the different forms of magic could set fire to the powder and thereby help surrealism in its eminently subversive enterprise of poetically re-enchanting the world.[74]

These observations are struck with the imprint of good sense, but it nonetheless remains true that magic, like the other occult sciences, is clearly put into the service of the overall plan, because, to borrow one of the conclusions Robert Amadou made in his postface to Seligmann's *The Mirror of Magic,* "Magic knows and wants man to surpass man" even if, unfortunately, "the paradox is that it forgets and refuses to let him infinitely surpass it. . . ."

10
SURREALISM, FREEMASONRY, AND VOODOO

Ogun Ferraille, the Elect Cohen, and the Great Tradition

Every great work is first and foremost an entombment, and its basic formula is always Goethe's phrase: "Die and become!"

JULIEN GRACQ

As we have seen with the discussion about Victor Brauner in the previous chapter, Freemasonry also deeply interested the surrealists, which is quite logical as it is the putative heir of a number of vanished Western traditions and in Oswald Wirth's somewhat reductive opinion "appears to be nothing but a modern transfiguration of ancient hermetism." Indeed, it was not overlooked in the quest for a knowledge going beyond the limitations of a crazed reason that had led humanity into the cataclysm of two world wars. Guy Piau reminds us that the names of Pythagoras and Hermes Trismegistus as bearers of the tradition figured explicitly in the Cooke Manuscript. This is one of the rare "Old Charges" regarded as the foundational texts of Freemasonry, which go back to the end of the fourteenth and the beginning of the fifteenth centuries, that were not among those destroyed by the Reverends Anderson and Désaguliers, the organizers of so-called speculative Masonry. Piau also supplies a credible explanation for the incontestable connections that can be established between Masonry and alchemy; for example:

> The frequentation of the lodges by alchemists is all the more plausible as it was only the continuation of the presence of alchemists in the builders' lodges where they taught the sacred sciences whose signs appear on those philosophical dwellings—both religious and profane—the most exceptional of which Fulcanelli discovered, analyzed, and interpreted.[1]*

It is worth pointing out the presence (shown by means of the names of Hermes and Pythagoras, which are perhaps merely those of legendary figures), here in the "old charges" (therefore, during the medieval era), of at least traces of an underground hermetic and neo-Platonic tradition. Roger Dachez,† a highly regarded historian of Freemasonry who can hardly be accused of wildly imaginative speculations, indicates in one of his recent books:

---

*With regard to the old texts and manuscripts destroyed by Anderson and Désaguliers, traces of them may survive in the Primitive Scottish Rite conserved by the Supreme Council of Confederated Rites of Edinburgh, if we take Robert Ambelain's word (in *La Franc-Maçonnerie oubliée*).

†With a much more rigorous approach than Guy Piau, Dachez, who admits to turning his back on the Guénonian reading, nevertheless writes, "Once again, the number of symbols and allegories that we would consider essentially Masonic, because it is speculative Freemasonry that has carried them to us, often existed long before the speculative Masons themselves."

Finally, and this is not the least of these texts' value, the Regius and the Cooke manuscripts record a both legendary and mythical traditional history, of the craft, which relates the development of geometry or masonry since the dawn of humanity. It is easy to determine everything the ritual framework of the future grades of speculative Freemasonry borrowed from these references.[2]

We can also see how their origin was implicitly fitted this way into the tradition. Even if the presence of "builders' lodges" in England strictly speaking remains questionable, it seems that Scottish lodges, existing long before the constitution of the Grand Lodge of London and Westminster, in 1717, passed down an esoteric kind of teaching. This has been proven to include the classic art of memory zealously spread by the Dominican Giordano Bruno, perhaps by means of the Giordanisti sect in Germany or the Rosicrucians, as Charles Jameux was first in France to observe.[3] Studied as early as 1966 by Frances A. Yates, this mnemonic process, of which the Schaw Statutes bear undoubtedly the mark, was inherited from ancient Greece. Citing David Stevenson, Jameux notes:

> It was based on a building. The student of the art was instructed to study some large and complex building, memorizing its rooms and layout. . . . In doing this he should establish a specific order in which he visited the individual room and places. When he had memorized a speech, he should then imagine himself to be walking through this building on his set route, and in each of the *loci* or places he had memorized, he should establish *imagines* or images that were to be attached to each argument or point in his speech. . . . When he came to give his speech, the orator would in his own mind walk through the building on his set route, and each image in place would remind him of the point he should come to next in his speech.[4]

This cannot help but remind us of Henri Tort-Nougès's thirty-three room castle (see page 173). It should also bring to mind the fact that

Leonora Carrington titled one of her paintings *Palacio Mnemonico* (see plate 17). In it we "see the shadow of Corrinus,* the Celtic god of animals, in the presence of a luminescent being and a bird holding a fish in its beak, in a cave-filled landscape."[5] The bird, a raven no doubt, is a psychopomp figure (if ever there was one!) for the Celts. As for Corrinus, we should recall the horned god mentioned by Mandiargues.

Returning to Freemasonry, it clearly seems that William Schaw, "Master of the Works" and a Catholic who organized (or perhaps reorganized) the Craft in Scotland at the end of the seventeenth century, was influenced by the "mystical and occult currents of the Renaissance,"[6] as well as by the thought of Giordano Bruno, who considered the art of memory to be "one of the treasures of Egyptian science,"[7] directly invented by Hermes Trismegistus. This Hermes no doubt never existed, but his name was lent to a group of texts that Frédéric Lenoir says are "a synthesis of the thought of Antiquity," the *Corpus Hermeticum*. (Louis Menard's translation of this text figured prominently in Breton's library.) This *Corpus,* which includes the *Poimandres,* goes back to the second or third century CE, and was rescued, it seems, between the sixth and eleventh centuries by the Sabians, then its "only keepers," says Roland Edighoffer. The Sabians may have expanded it a bit, as *The Book of Ostathas,* in which the theory of the microcosm and the macrocosm was first described, according to Sarane Alexandrian, is by a much later gnostic Arab. The Sabians, or more specifically, the Mandeans—sometimes called the Christians of Saint John—lived in Mesopotamia as well as Lebanon and worshipped Hermes Trismegistus and Asclepius, or Agathodaemon, according to Nerval.

Frances A. Yates, as well as Paul Vulliaud, speaks of "mystagogical systems transmitted by traditionalists† or by Plato, Plotinus, Saint Denys the Aeropagite, Trismegistus—all the initiators of the Florentine Theosophists," the so-called Neo-Platonism *of the Renaissance* (italics

---

*I should point out that the alleged Celtic god "Corrinus," appearing in this quote, is quite suspect. I have found no trace of him in Paul Marie Duval's book *Les Dieux de la Gaule,* although this book is highly detailed and covers territory far beyond the frontiers of Gaul, strictly speaking. Perhaps it is Cernunnos, the Gallic god with stag antlers.

†"Traditionalists" refers to kabbalists, in other words.

added), introduced in Florence under Cosmo de Medici[8]* by Marsilio Ficino, a scholar who had also been initiated into the mysteries of the kabbalah by Elias del Medigo (1460–1497). His translations of the texts attributed to Hermes Trismegistus (recently rediscovered in Macedonia), founded on "a vision of the cosmos as a network of magic forces upon which man can work," allowed the emergence of the "figure of the Renaissance mage . . . rooted in the hermetic depths of reborn Neo-Platonism."[9] Yates later adds these lines, which will assume their full importance later.

> And if, as I believe, the Renaissance magus is the immediate ancestor of the seventeenth century scientist, then it proves that "Neo-Platonism" as interpreted by Ficino and Pico[10] was purely and simply the system of thought, occurring between the Middle Ages and the seventeenth century, that paved the way for the emergence of science.[11]

In a 1973 conference on Copernicus, Yates reminds us that the astronomer (1473–1543), considered to be one of the founding fathers of modern science, placed his main work, *De Revolutionibus Orbium Coelestium,* under the auspices of Trismegistus (whom she cites), thereby revealing to what extent the revolution set in motion by the Polish thinker took root in hermetic breeding ground, and to what extent *magia naturalis,* "the pre-modern form of an experimental science still in its infancy," as Antoine Faivre puts it, was based on the philosophia occulta—"a 'magic' notion of the world . . . in accordance with which every thing maintains symbolic, analogical relationships with the other things, so that, as a result, they interact."[12]

The same later holds true for Giordano Bruno, "the missionary for a hermetic reform and philosophy," who saw Copernicus as a man "appointed by the gods to be a dawn heralding the return of the sun of the ancient, true philosophy," the very philosophy contained in the *Corpus Hermeticum.* Yates also goes even a step further

---

*Why did the Reverend Anderson deem it necessary to talk about the Medicis and the history of Italy in the second version of the *Constitutions* which bear his name?

when she recalls how a Venetian follower of Ficino, Fabio Paolini, equated the animated statues described in the *Asclepius* with the clockwork-animated automatons described in Heron of Alexandria's treatise. Yates sees in it "the integration to the animist universe of the Renaissance by means of the magical interpretation of mechanics" of what "would become the supreme symbol of the mechanistic universe installed by the first phase of the Industrial Revolution": the Great Clockmaker, ". . . The supreme engineer, the Great Clockmaker, the Great Architect that Freemasonry, *then coming back to life in England* (italics added), will impose," Charles Porset adds in his *Vampires et lumières* (Vampires and the Enlightenment).[13]

This highlights the influence over the "gentlemen masons" (received since 1590 in the Scottish Lodges!) of the "hermetic-kabbalistic contents" (to borrow Frances A. Yates's phrase, cited by Roger Dachez) of the books of emblems that were all the rage then—"gentlemen masons" with which, it goes without saying, the Templars—the real Templars, I mean—had nothing to do. If we accept Alain Bauer's contention of Newton's decisive importance in the formation of speculative Freemasonry, we cannot help but note that it found its roots through Fludd—another individual well versed in the art of memory—Ashmole, Maïer, and Dee, on the one hand, and Bruno and Copernicus, on the other, in Renaissance neo-Platonism,[14] which itself centered its approach to the world on the writings attributed to Hermes Trismegistus, which went back to the first centuries of the Christian Era, i.e., to the period of intense intellectual and religious ferment that preceded Christianity's triumph, and which primarily echoed gnostic and neo-Platonic philosophies among others.

We should not overlook the traditional knowledge passed on by yet other paths, such as the *Zohar,* which prompted Sarane Alexandrian to wonder if Galilee may not have been kabbalist, after reminding us that it had been claimed "in its Vaiykra section" since the end of antiquity that the world was round and revolved around the sun.

This is by no means subscribing to the "wrong tale that Freemasonry was connected with some kind of occultism";[15] the currents arising out of Renaissance neo-Platonism never actually possessed the organizational structure based on the lodge in the modern sense. But we have to reckon it is not very likely that Masonry emerged fully armed in 1717 out of the thigh of Antony Sayer or even of Jean Théophile Désaguliers. Désaguliers, moreover, who was a native of La Rochelle in France, where a copy of the *Mutus Liber* "was printed and perhaps . . . never released," which, according to Canseliet, "makes it possible to establish that hermeticism, if not operative alchemy, was still cultivated by the intellectual elite in the heroic capital of Aunis* during the course of the eighteenth century." Nor can we pass over in silence the so-called Egyptian Masonry that flourished at this same time at the other end of Europe.

Born fairly mysteriously in Venice at the beginning of the eighteenth century, Egyptian Masonry then appeared in Naples around 1750, where a Masonic Grand Lodge was created around an alchemy enthusiast, Raymond de Sangro, prince of San Vero. This lodge was nourished on the teachings of Michael Sendiwoj, known as "Sendivogius," who would be partially responsible for the origin of the Misraïm Rite (a topic we shall revisit). Objectively, to get back to the heart of our subject, there are some citations, which are a bit troubling to say the least, from the pen of Breton himself (described by Jean Schuster as the "great clockmaker of the surrealist revolution"). Judge for yourself. In the *Second Surrealist Manifesto* we find:

> Let us not lose sight of the fact that the idea of surrealism aims quite simply at the total recovery of our psychic force by a means which is nothing other than the dizzying descent into ourselves, the systematic illumination of hidden places and the progressive darkening of other places.

In 1953, in "On Surrealism in Its Living Works," Breton wrote:

> The definition of surrealism in the First Manifesto merely

---

*[Aunis was a historical province of France, during the Ancient Régime, before the French Revolution. —*Trans.*]

"retouches" a great traditional saying concerning the necessity of "breaking through the drumhead of reasoning reason and looking at the hole," a procedure that will cause symbols that were once mysterious to light up.

José Pierre made a similar observation in 1990 when he wrote:

There is another means of escaping the conflicts of all kinds that crowd our path than attempting to balance night with the day, passion with intelligence, what is above with what is below—on the way to this "point of the spirit" mentioned by Breton as where all the opposites "cease to be perceived as contradictory"; this other means is the "descent into the self" in search of that kind of Ariadne's threat that will allow us to circulate through the thousand twists and turns of the labyrinth in complete tranquility.[16]

Victor Crastre sheds more light on this:

In each of his books from the *Second Manifesto* to *Arcanum 17*, it was always by digging toward the core of esotericism that he [Breton] was able to delve the depths of the so-called unknowable. It even became a method for the "total recuperation of our psychic force" he offers us and this method is the very one used by esoteric or mystical thinkers: the "dizzying descent into ourselves," the "systematic illumination of hidden places and the gradual darkening of others" are the phases of the mystic asceticism.[17]

Guy Girard in *The Shadow and the Request: Surrealist Projections* mentions that Breton "the exploration of the obscure zones of the psyche and the ascent back toward the immediate life of an individual *awakened differently*," which, made possible by the "practice of automatism as a general method of knowledge and liberation," then "provides the impetus for the future of the surrealist utopia."[18]

Descent into the self, illumination of hidden places, light cast on symbols, awakening—we are unquestionably in the presence here of an initiatory kind of language, one that can be compared with these quotes of Paracelsus from *The Seven Books of the Archidoxes of Magic*:

> He who wishes to work on the Great Work should visit his soul, penetrate the deepest part of his being, and carry out a concealed and mysterious labor.

Or

> *Wer da sucht, der findet; wer da sucht in dem inneren Himmel* [We are to search within ourselves, within our conscience, within our inner heaven].[19]

This obviously echoes the advice given the novice Mason who has been asked to descend into himself by following the "perpendicular," the "plumb line"[20]—the same plumb line held in one of the left hands of the Great Transparent presented by Jacques Hérold* at the 1947 exhibition. This analysis is reinforced by this observation by Michel Carrouges: "Surrealism is above all an immense form of rupture. One does not enter it by mean of exams, but by an abrupt alteration of the mind that all at once topples all ways of thinking and feeling."[21]

In *The Mirror of the Marvelous*, which in his own words he wanted to make an "initiation treatise," Pierre Mabille is even more explicit and provides this luminous description in scarcely veiled terms:

> Indeed, those led by their destiny to abandon the ordinary way and overcome the obstacles have been so profoundly changed by the time they enter the marvelous building that they haven't been able to return to the crowd afterward to give them their impressions and tell them what they'd seen. With an altered mental state comes an altered language that makes communication impossible, whether or not it's desired.

---

*Marcel Jean gives Hérold the following coat of arms: "A gule field over a gold terrace with a double rainbow proper, the leading bow rests on the terrace."

We should keep in mind, however, these subtle remarks of Artaud in *Heliogabalus or the Crowned Anarchist*, which remind us that it is incumbent on the initiate himself to do the work: "Besides, one is only ever initiated by workings, rites, outward signs, and hieroglyphic passes that set us on the path of the secret."

This inexpressible transformation is precisely what occurs to the apprentice Mason who receives the light before committing himself to the path, and this is worth comparing with an extract from the autobiography of Sarane Alexandrian, whose father was a Freemason of the Ancient and Accepted Scottish Rite:

> To be a surrealist was to enter a worldwide secret society whose purpose is to establish the reign of "convulsive beauty" on earth, and whose members fraternally loved each other and understood each other intuitively, while sometimes quarreling bitterly in the name of the highest requirements of perfection.

Nor should we ignore this extract by Jacques Abeille about Duits's book on Breton, taken from his article "Un surréel":

> One of the major goals of this book is to convey the idea that meeting Breton was a kind of initiation and it is accidentally, because it is in itself underlying, that the question is raised, for everyone, of the stage every adept has reached or not.

In this respect, Roland Edighoffer's commentary in his short book on the Rosicrucians cannot be overlooked.

> The function of every secret society, as Mircea Eliade has shown, is to participate more intensely in the sacred by virtue of an initiation that is both regeneration and knowledge of a mystery expressed symbolically by the linguistic means of the myth and by the gestural medium of the rite.

Pierre Daix opportunely completes this in *Les Surréalistes: 1917–1932,* noting, "They were equally concerned by establishing restrictive collective rules."[22] Jean Schuster goes even further than Daix. When analyzing the relationship between Breton and Bataille and "the belief they shared . . . in the operational effectiveness of rites," he notes:

> This integration of the ritual as a fundamental element of the *practice*, in the collective activities led separately by the two men, could shed light on the alternation of their conflicts and complicity. Beneath this light, past the quasi profane stage of the recovery of lost powers, we cannot dismiss a will that is sometimes joined and sometimes at odds to reach the sacred, a sacred that has naturally been rid of the dismaying idea of God.[23]

Between 1928 and 1929, Breton and Aragon, "both sons of Masons," according to Jean-Pierre Lasalle,[24] wrote a short theater piece, *The Treasure of the Jesuits*, later published in the special issue of the Belgian "illustrated monthly review on the contemporary spirit," *Variétés*, a play that was brought to the stage for the first—and only—time by Jindrich Honzl in Prague, in 1935, "in that Czechoslovakia created by Freemasons and where all the leaders, from Masaryk to Benes, were Masons."[25] This play, which was undoubtedly inspired by the writings of Léo Taxil* (which were also a source of inspiration for Max Ernst's collages), playfully ridicules Freemasonry, mocking the titles of the dignitaries and the high grades. Some of these are more or less real, for example, "Very Powerful Sovereign Grand Master," "Illustrious Grand Sovereign Inspector General," and "Chevalier Kadosh," while others popped right out of the authors' imaginations, such as "Very Sinister Illustrious Unknown Supreme Authority," and "Grand Klephte," which was obviously inspired by Cagliostro. We also have the example of Robert Desnos "heckling the deiphagous clerics and imbecile Freemasons" in his *Liberty or Love!*

---

*Gabriel Jogand-Pagès, no 1 (1854–1907), who used the pen name Léo Taxil, was an anti-Masonic hoaxer and the author of numerous books denouncing Freemasonry as a Luciferian sect.

When speaking of Max Ernst who, according to Jean Schuster, was "the most surrealist (because he was the most aware) of the surrealist artists," how can I refrain from directing the reader's attention to the presence of the many rules and compasses, but also the more discrete squares, in his 1943 painting *Vox Angelica* (see plate 18), painted in Arizona at the home of a descendent, or so it is said, of Leibniz Werner Spies incidentally, who compared this painting to Matthias Grünewald's Isenheim Altarpiece and its concert of angels![26]

A good while later, Elléouët would see in this painting "quasi Masonic signs, listen: the Altar, the Triangle, the Compass"[27] in the night sky. These are signs also easily found in the works of Duchamp, Picasso—the Picasso of *Les Demoiselles d'Avignon* (1907) in particular—and Chirico. Furthermore, if one examines the *Demoiselles* closely, one cannot help but wonder if their Avignon designation is not somehow connected to the Dominican Dom Pernety, alchemist, hermeticist, and founder (in 1779) of an order of Illuminati, which means—as was often the case in the eighteenth century—mystical Freemasons.

As for Chirico, praised by Mandiargues as "more gifted than any other for pulling from the shadows what could be called the alarming aspect of things," Giovanna Costantini shows that in addition to the signs, numbers, and kabbalistic symbols we find in many of the paintings of his metaphysical period, we can also see the mosaic pavement dear to Freemasons, as well as compasses, squares, and other tools.[28] This metaphysical period is one in which he produced, Carrouges tells us, "a painting that goes beyond the appearances of immediate objectivity to proceed toward a surpassing of these appearances."

Costantini adds, "It is possible Chirico introduced these images in his compositions to echo the concept contained in Robert Fludd's *Mosaic Philosophy,* which expounded the theosophical principles of eternal truth and wisdom based on a mystical geometry and arithmetic."

She additionally points out that the painter often included two towers in the paintings he created between 1911 and 1915, which she claims hold alchemical connotations but primarily compare to the two columns of Masonic temples. They could thereby reflect a symbology in relation with the history of Masonic and Rosicrucian societies, and seem to find their origin in Robert Fludd's engraving *The Temple of Music,* which "illustrated certain architectural precepts proposed by John Dee" relative to the idea that architecture's true beauty proceeds from principles of geometrical and mathematical proportions much more than from the nature of the material used, and represented an imaginary structure accompanied by a philosophical key explaining the "Vitruvian principles of architectural concordance." This University of Michigan–Flint researcher, moreover, underscores the fact that many of Chirico's "metaphysical" works, and she mentions *The Fatal Temple* as an example, include depictions of easily erasable chalk drawings reminiscent of the erasable tracings—that became the tracing boards we use now—originally directly drawn by apprentice Masons on the floor of Lodge or tavern rooms.

During the 1930s, Leiris, showing evidence of a certain sympathy, in his text *The Fall,* wrote:

> *The universe is an organ whose pipes are growing hoarse*
> *in this monstrous church built by the trowels of madness*
> *without even a Freemasonry to unite the faces*
> *by unknown signs . . .*

But he also confided, in *Manhood:*

> My mother sometimes brought me to visit her family's tomb at Père Lachaise cemetery, on which my grandfather's Masonic insignias were displayed under a glass globe. He had been a senior official of the Third Republic, a disciple of Auguste Comte, and a Venerable of the Rose of Perfect Silence Lodge.

Octavio Paz similarly claims a Freemason paternal grandfather in *Solo à deux voix: entretiens avec Julian Rios* (Solo in Two Voices:

Interviews with Julian Rios), and Claude Courtot, musing over Mozart's works in his text *Köchel, 626,* confides:

> I felt a desire to have music heard in the mortuary room where my father lay, Masonic works of Mozart: the *Funeral Ode* and *The Magic Flute.* My father was a Freemason and the first time he took me to the opera it was to see *The Magic Flute.*

Even a self-proclaimed Christian like Joseph Delteil (who was more or less excluded from the group because of it) indicates in *La Deltheillerie* that the subject did not leave him indifferent:

> I sometimes get an urge to take a quick peek at Freemasonry. I am attracted to everything having to do with secret societies and communities. I still have lingering scruples from my childhood though. In my mother's eyes, Freemasonry was something diabolical: Freemason, freethinker, and assassin were synonymous. Nevertheless, here and there, I glance through it. My friend Vassal was totally shocked the other day to learn I owned Lantoine's* *Great History.*

In any event, around Breton, and even among members of the foreign surrealist groups, there were Masons, sometimes high ranking ones. Let's skip past Soupault, a friend of Pierre Brossolette, initiated in 1931 into the Positive Philosophy Lodge of the Grand Orient of France, the former lodge of the symbolist Laurent Tailhade (Soupault only made a quick stay in the Order), and past Ithell Colquhoun, a member of several Masonic lodges—she still paid dues to one in Maida Vale in 1976 to 1977—and at least one chapter of the Order of the Ancient and Accepted Masonry for Men and Women. And let's skip the Chilean Vincente Huidobro, whom Paz called "the seer," a member of the Grand Lodge of France and instigator of the magazine *Mandragora,*

---

*Albert Lantoine (1869–1949) was a very high official (33rd degree) of the Grand Lodge of France.

as well as the Spanish Republican fighter Eugenio F. Granell, exiled to Santo Domingo, where he founded the review *La Poesia Sorprendida,* and who in 1951 was entrusted with the decoration of a temple in San Juan. And let's pass over Jacques Prévert—not a Mason, though—and his group October, who gave their first complete militant popular theater performance on March 10, 1933, on the rue Cadet, in a hall of the Grand Orient of France in front of an audience of Masons; and over Fernand Dumont, too, a member of the surrealist group of Hainaut and of a Masonic lodge in Mons, Belgium; and over Roland Sig, a member of the Parisian group at the beginning of the '50s, and notably a signer of the surrealist tract titled "Masks Off, Hands Off," published in *Le Libertaire,* January 4, 1952. Speaking at his graveside in 1984, Jean Schuster, alluding to his affiliation with Freemasonry, which, he went on to say, "he was overly committed to," noted:

> It seems to me that you Freemasons and we surrealists share the same greed for symbols, a similar belief in their rigor and their richness, and the same vigilance toward the regressive forces that seek to deny them, or make them dull, or recuperate them. Sig was like the embodiment of this common spiritual disposition.[29]

We should also pass over in silence Adrien Dax, who was sufficiently informed about matters touching on Freemasonry to sign a small notice (in the seventh issue of *Médium,* May 1953) concerning the publication at Presses Universitaires de France of a collection of unpublished texts by Fabre d'Olivet, which may have influenced Saint-Yves d'Alveydre, titled *La Vraie maçonnerie et la celeste culture* (The True Masonry and the Celestial Culture). We should also skip over Jean-Louis Bédouin, who attended public lectures at the Grand Lodge of France and frequently resorted to Masonic terminology ("orient," "lost word") in his book *Vingt Ans de surréalisme: 1939–1959* (Twenty Years of Surrealism), as well as over the painter Seigle, who was a member of the Grand Orient for a time, not to mention Charles-Bernard Jameux, who shared the surrealist adventure between 1964 and 1969 before entering the Grand Lodge of France and rising to the position of senior editor for the quarterly review *Initiatory Points of View*. We need to bypass all the above mentioned so we can linger a bit longer on Pierre Mabille, a major figure, "*other* focus," and even "blind spot" of the movement, although always standing a bit back, a charismatic figure who, according to Sarane Alexandrian, made a deeper impression on some surrealists than Breton himself.[30] Jean-Pierre Lassalle would even go so far as to write, "It could even be suggested that in a certain way, Mabille was the link between Guénon and Malcolm de Chazal, whose mysterious family ties to the ancient Rosicrucians were not unknown to Breton."[31] A "man of the great secret," Mabille was initiated into occultism by Pierre Piobb,* which left a deep mark on his work. At the beginning of the '30s he became quite keen on alchemy, "whose schema was inscribed in everything he said," according to Breton, and acquired unusual knowledge about the secret societies of the Renaissance. About this same time, he was received as a Mason in the Parisian Marie Georges Martin Lodge of Le Droit Humain (International Order of Co-Freemasonry) and would end up at the 33rd degree. In 1938, Mabille provided, with *Egregores or the Life of Civilizations,* a work that had a huge impact on the Quebec automatists, particularly Claude Gavreau, who in 1951 declared he "personally endorsed all its conclusions,"[32] an analysis that reveals he probably belonged to the Ancient and Accepted Scottish Rite, as was customary for Le Droit Humain members.

> A special place should be reserved for Freemasonry. Although it claims to be the descendent of the most ancient tradition (a theory that should not be rejected a priori), it came into being at the time

---

*This is the same Pierre V. Piobb (pseudonym of Pierre Vincenti de Piobberta, 1862–1942) whom I discussed in chapter 4 with regard to Nostradamus. He was also the first French translator of Robert Fludd's *Treatises on General Astrology and Geomancy,* which inspired the most theoretical pages of *Arcanum 17.* Breton owned his *Formulaire de Haute Magie,* subtitled *Recettes et formules pour fabriquer soi-même les philtres d'amour, talismans, etc. Clefs absolues des sciences occultes. Esprits. Invocations, Evocations, Tables tournantes,* in the 1907 Darangon edition as well as the 1937 Dangles edition. In 1907, Pierre Piobb published in *L'Année Occultiste et Psychique* (a magazine of which he was the sole editor), the famous talisman of Charles Fourier, about which Adrien Dax spoke in the fourth issue of *La Brèche* in February 1963 and Philippe Audoin in the eight issue in November 1965.

of the Christian dissociation. It took charge of the ritual tools and the symbols abandoned by the Church and which the Jesuits sought to destroy, in agreement, on this point, with the Protestants. The Masons seem increasingly bothered by this cumbersome deposit, whose value they don't know. Their notion of the world and man does not differ from that of the Catholics. The same dualism rages there; however, a greater trust is placed in personal freedom and the possibility of an autonomous, moral evolution there.

Moreover, Mabille borrows his description of the "acceptance of a Master following this ancient and accepted Scottish rite" from "a Masonic Tyler still used for ceremonies." This appears in the chapter "Crossing through Death" in *The Mirror of the Marvelous* as an illustration of the "myth of resurrection." Despite recurring mystical crises during this time, this trained surgeon, who Breton recalled (in "Pont Levis") thought "spirituality is stronger than material forces," joined the surrealist movement in 1934 and became friends with most of its members. About him, José Pierre would even say:

> With Mabille, we are in the presence of something more than the project of an "absolute" man, that is to say the surrealist man insofar as there is nothing he does not know when it comes to what possesses the capability of shedding light not only on humanity's past but on its present and future.

It seems that Mabille was also responsible for fully developing Breton's taste for alchemy and the occult.

> With his work, Pierre Mabille supplies proof that surrealism is definitely on the track of the great tradition and fully participates in the cosmic forces governing human impulses. The quest of the surrealists is therefore far from appearing like a sentimental characteristic; it touches the profound vibrations of the tangible universe; it strives to restore the grandeur of man by restoring to desire all its strength, desire: the secret author of every future.[33]

In the eighth issue of *Minotaure,* Mabille published "Notes on Symbolism," which "with the magazine's perspective in mind," he illustrated with reproductions of Théodore de Bry's superb engravings that embellish Michael Maier's (1618) *Atalanta Fugiens,* plates that are "rigorously adapted to their alchemical context." In 1940, this far-from-ordinary doctor, whose philosophy is sometimes shot through with allusions to a collective unconscious, somewhat reminiscent of Jung's, published *The Mirror of the Marvelous,* which he wished to be "like an initiatory path, a journey through the secret, collective gear works of desire"[34] and universal myths, for which Breton contributed a preface (to the reissue published by Éditions de Minuit in 1962).

Pierre Mabille was also extremely knowledgeable about voodoo. He described one of the ceremonies in a gripping manner in his article "La Manigua," published in Mexico in July–August 1944.[35] This syncretic Caribbean cult was connected with the activities of the escaped slaves known as the Maroons, who fought their guerilla wars into the *mornes* (mountains), and it appeared in Haiti around 1768. It consists of three degrees of initiation: the washing of the head, both baptism and an ordeal by water; the hounsi-canzo, a symbolic ordeal by fire; and the rise to the ancon, the sacred rattle that confers the grade of *houngan* (priest) on a man or *mambo* (priestess) on women. It was also Mabille who afforded Breton (and Wifredo Lam) the rare privilege of witnessing this practice during his stay in Haiti, "not a pseudo-ceremony for tourists, but a ritual performed in secret at night in a remote spot of the island."[36]

Breton became a friend of a houngan who was also a painter, Hector Hyppolite, whom he invited to the international exhibition of 1947, along with his painting *Papa Lauco,* and he dedicated an article to him in *Surrealism and Painting*. In 1949, Mabille portrayed Hyppolite as follows:

> Hyppolite, sorcerer priest of Voodoo, uses his primitive methods—for a long time he used bird feathers for brushes and packing cardboard for canvases—to depict the gods of the Voodoo Olympus.

In "The Smiling Isle of Haiti," a supplement to issue 59 of *La Revue Française* (1950s), poet and playwright Felix Morriseau-Leroy—who was close to the bards of "Negritude" and was the father of the Creole renaissance—wrote these lines, which clearly illustrate the influence wielded by this man:

> Only death has stopped the hand of Hector Hyppolite, who, discovered on the Saint-Marc Road where he was decorating the door to his small home, succeeded in less than four years in selling his paintings to the great experts of modern art and acquiring the reputation of the greatest painter in Haitian history. He claimed to be inspired by the gods of Vodou and spoke of mysterious journeys and loves that were no less mysterious. In front of a crowd made up of common people, artists, and writers, who the sudden death of the painter had plunged in despair, I saw a bourgeois woman from Port-au-Prince lean over the corpse and kiss the forehead of the old houngan from Montrouis.

Breton already knew something on the matter, thanks to articles published on or by William Seabrook,* an unquestionable expert on the subject of voodoo, in issue 6 of Bataille's magazine *Documents* in 1929, then in issue 2–3 of *VVV*. Also informative to Breton was Louis Maximilien's book *Haitian Vodou, Radas-Cauzo Rite* (1945, with

---

*William Seabrook, the traveler and occultist about whom his friend Michel Leiris had written an article in *Documents*, was the author of *The Magic Island*, an extensively developed book on Haitian voodoo that Mabille cites twice in *The Mirror of the Marvelous*, mainly recounting in fairly frightening terms "the ceremony that gave him access to the Voodoo mystery" and discussing the mysterious zombies. In the eighth and final issue of *Documents* (1930), Michel Leiris, following a conversation he had had with Seabrook on the East and occultism, published an article titled "Le 'Caput Mortuum' ou la femme alchimique," inspired by photos of a woman wearing a black leather mask. "Caput Mortuum" "in which life rises from death's grin," in the words of Bédouin, also the "Moor's head"—and Duits reminds us that the kabbalists liked to call themselves "Moors"—is the expression once used by alchemists to describe the phase of the Great Work in which "everything seems rotten but all is regenerated," something that will speak volumes to Masons! Seabrook, who also spent time with Aleister Crowley and George Ivanovich Gurdjieff, also appeared in *Minotaure*.

preface by Mabille). Breton was a spectator of the ceremonies of a form of worship that also interested Michel Leiris: "We spent whole nights with Métraux in the voodoo dens."[37]

Voodoo was also an influence on Max Ernst as well as on the Chinese-Cuban painter Wifredo Lam* (see plate 19) (as Santeria or macumba), as shown by his 1946 work *Ogun Ferraille,* for example, ("the magical Saint James") or *The Wedding* in 1947. Another prime example would be the installation he created in 1947 for the international surrealist exhibition, *Falmer's Hair,* "a voodoo altar with a vever and all the necessary tools, including a luxurious fall of tow-colored hair decorated with upside down crucifixes."[38]

Not to mention Antonin Artaud, who was given a precise, detailed description in 1935 by one of his friends, the Dutchman Hendrik Cramer, the "Captain," who was a former member of the Grand Jeu, on his return from Haiti, as well as Benjamin Péret, who, during his first visit to Brazil (1929–1931), showed interest in the rites and ceremonies of candomblé and macumba. Voodoo would also be an influence later on Hervé Télémaque and his Baron Cimetière. Writing on Lam's painting in 1947, Mabille described it as a "ritual" (as would Alain Jouffroy, who also used the term "sacrificial").

> I remember how enthusiastically he painted his first canvases in which the emotions of black magic were so clearly expressed. I had just come from Haiti, the land of Voodoo, where I had lived for

---

*In his monograph on the painter Wifredo Lam (1902–1982), published in 1972 by editions Georges Fall, Alain Jouffroy states that Lam's "African godmother, Mantonica Wilson," the same—imposing—Mantonica Wilson known as the Santeria priestess Lucumi (who is cited in some of Aimé Césaire's poems, when she is not the dedicatee) "wanted to make him a magician" and had consequently taught him "these signs of the sorcery" from the time he was ten. This may have been why Lam wrote about himself that he "represents the heritage of the convulsion of man and the earth." The coat of arms Marcel Jean created for the painter is "gold clad in sable, with a three pronged dart in carnation. Two points face downward with one on the chief facing dexter." "Gold clad in sable!" We are not far here from the colors of the thirteen *Heads* of 1947 with their many spikes, paintings that were later renamed *Canaïma*.

several years, and easily recognized the deities honored in its ritual ceremonies* in the figures drawn by Lam.[39]

It is true that Lam's *Composition* (1943), subtitled *Nañigo*, makes direct reference, as Lydia Cabrera† notes in her book *La Forêt et les dieux: Religions afro-cubaines et médecines sacrées à Cuba* (Forests and Gods: Afro-Cuban Religions and Sacred Medicines of Cuba),[40] to "adepts of the Abakua Society, a magic and religious secret society founded in Cuba by Carabali slaves—from Calabar in Nigeria—and modeled after ancient African societies."[41] This society had been banned in 1875, which did not mean it vanished. It is perhaps not ridiculous, then, to consider the "divinatory and vaporous" aspect of this painting, as well as that of his *Altar for Elegua* (1944), as a way of "veiling the mystery" around a ceremony, some of whose aspects they revealed without overly betraying its secrets.

Spelled "Elegguà" by Breton in his January 9, 1946, poem "Night in Haiti," the orisha Elegua, a somewhat emblematic figure who reappears constantly in Lam's work, "he who reminds the modern world of primordial terrors and fervor," according to Aimé Cesaire is the guardian of doors and crossroads in Cuba, like the loa Carrefour (Crossroads) in Haiti, "who breathes on the wings of the / Doors." Orishas, who could be somewhat described as Afro-Cuban "saints" from the Yoruba pantheon (from Nigeria), put in an appearance in Lam's paintings frequently. In addition to Elegua, we can also find—identifiable or identified by a title— Yemaya, the orisha of salt water and the sea (*Altar for Yemaya*, 1944), as well as, in Lam's 1943 painting *The Noise*, what is probably Osain, the master of the forest and plants, the keeper of their secrets and virtues.

Péret, speaking of Lam's return to his native land, explains sometime later (in the fourth issue of *Médium*) that the painter is one within whom "merge in order to endure" . . . "the African sorcerer and the Asiatic shaman" and who has "like his ancestors . . . grasped from their

---

*Wifredo Lam himself, however, told Max-Pol Fouchet, who quotes him in the book on this painter published in 1989 by Le Cercle d'Art, "I have never invented my paintings based on a symbolic tradition, but always out of a poetic stimulation."

†Cabrera was an ethnologist who did research on Santéria, and she was often accompanied by Lam and his friend, the author Alejo Carpentier.

source . . 'spirits' seeking their material, compelling them to reveal their secret and only releasing them in sprays of black flame and passionate cries after they have submitted to his desires." There are also photos of some of his works that bear an unsigned commentary that clearly points to the same source of inspiration: "During his stay in the Antilles (Cuba, Haiti), he was keenly moved by the voodoo ceremonies and captivated by the scenes of possession that took place there."

In his autobiography, Sarane Alexandrian recounts Breton's tale of this uncommon experience, mentioning, in passing, Papa Legba, the "Voodoo Saint Peter," keeper of the keys to the invisible world and the first to be summoned in the ritual, as without him nothing is possible:

> He told me every detail, the greeting to Legba-Petro ("Master Carrefour" of the charms and spells), the dance of the possessed around the "poteau-mitan" (which is the "path of the spirits" they descend to enter the sanctuary), while the drummers beat their instruments faster and faster, the scene of the "service" in which the ritually cleansed animal is offered to the loa. He told me that the moment the rooster's throat was slit, the *mambo* (witch possessed by the loa) let out a rooster's crow while the sacrificed bird let out the scream of a woman. Elisa confirmed that she had heard both these cries indicating that the animal and the woman had exchanged roles. We discussed the cause of this illusion falling back on references to psychopathology (auto-suggestion, collective hallucination). Then Breton extended himself on the aftermath of the ceremony, such as the priest's creation of the magic beverage *migan* with the blood of the victim, mixed with sugar and spices.

We should note that the desire to find a plausible explanation for the phenomenon without the desire, yet, "to draw up an ethnographical document," as Mabille points out, consequently establishes a distance that does not exist in Maurice Fourré's *La Nuit du Rose-Hôtel,* in which a number of his characters, says Philippe Audoin, "mention the voodoo pantheon," and in which the author provides, either from *hearsay* or *Nantaise proximity,* a much more colorful, almost Celine-like description:

> In this dark cave, filled with aromatic smoke and in which blood from a sacrificed goat splattered human heads . . . the slow, undulating dance of a human torso from whose arms and legs all life had fled, beneath the flares of sorcery spurting from a head as still as death, in which only two eyes were living, had shaken up my entire being . . . Dance Bamboula! . . . The contagious unrest of the African magicians found themselves transferred at the time of the sacrifice into equatorial America, among the bloody stench of the solar cult.

And yet, odd ulterior motives accompanied Breton's interest, as shown by this passage from *Conversations: The Autobiography of Surrealism*:

> It is worth noting that these phenomena* are considered by Haitian experts in this field as the syncretic product of certain Dahomean and Guinean traditions on the one hand, and on the other, Mesmerian practices [inspired by Franz Anton Mesmer] imported in the eighteenth century to Port-au-Prince by Martinez de Pasqually.

There is also this extract from "Pont Levis":

> We were both inclined to find traces† of mesmerism here,‡ which was rendered plausible—and perfectly fascinating—by the fact that

---

*The phenomena referred to are the possessions.
†In the voodoo cult and, beyond, in other African forms of possession.
‡We should note here the interest often expressed by Breton for "mesmerism," especially in the second Haitian lecture, in which he talks at length about it, suggesting that, "around [Mesmer's] famous wooden tub, convulsive scenes occurred, the description of which does not tangibly differ from that of the crises caused by Haitian loas." Franz Anton Mesmer (1734–1815), also a Freemason and connected with Louis-Claude de Saint-Martin and Jean-Baptiste Willermoz, developed an original therapeutic method based on animal magnetism that enjoyed great success at the end of the eighteenth century and whose "spirit" Breton rediscovered in the works of Freud. In his *Histoire de la philosophie occulte,* Sarane Alexandrian dubs Mesmer "the inventor of psychotherapy." At the end of the eighteenth century and in the first half of the nineteenth century, the Order of Universal Harmony was established, a complete Masonic rite with its high grades, which claimed to follow Mesmer's theories on magnetism. This order had a branch in Port-au-Prince. There could be no better illustration of the extent to which everything, as the surrealists maintained, is connected.

in 1772, accompanied by a Black with "psychic powers," Martinez de Pasqually, in my opinion a most enigmatic and captivating figure, debarked in Santo Domingo. He was to endow the island with a "Sovereign Tribunal," found a lodge in Port-au-Prince, another one in Léogane, and bring his Statute of the Order of the Elect Cohen into its final, definitive form, before dying there in 1774. We expected, by following those tidbits of information we heard, to find clues which might lead us to the exact spot he was buried, still a mystery, and who knows, perhaps even let us lift the phosphorescent veil that kept it hidden.[42]

And there is a note in this text that refers to the "Batavian Martinist" Gérard Van Rijnberk's book *A Thaumaturgist of the Eighteenth Century: Martinez de Pasqually*.[43] Van Rijnberk describes him as a strange individual in any case, who also intrigued Guénon and Papus (so much that he wrote a book on him published by his friend Chamuel* in 1895). In fact, Martinès de Pasqually, said to be a Marrano of Portuguese origin,† and whom Seligmann identified as a "Rosicrucian," influenced by Swedenborg's ideas, had in 1854 founded the Order of the Knight-Masons Elect Cohens of the Universe, a theurgy, a system of white magic used "in order to establish communication with higher deities," as the freethinker Gabriel Naudé defined it in 1625. The author of *The Amorous Devil* (a kind of French precursor of the gothic novel), Jacques Cazotte (esteemed by Eluard and Desnos as well as Leiris and Gengenbach), clearly seems to have been initiated into this "system" (theurgy and Elect Cohen), which was based on incantations and invocations,[44] then raised to the grade of master and granted the right to wear the "long (white) robe of the

---

*The real name of "Chamuel" is Lucien Mauchel, alias Chamuel.
†In his book *Le Secret des Cathares*, Gérard de Sède states that Martinès de Pasqually's real name was Jacques Joachim de Livron de la Tour de la Case. Without indicating the documents on which he bases his contentions, René Trintzius contests that this man was Jewish. "People have been too quick to say he was a Jew. Contrary to what was first believed, he was not at all a kabbalist. His Christianity appears to be as sincere as it was deep." I have left all the different spellings of the name Martinès as they clearly demonstrate the aura of mystery surrounding this individual.

adepts," like those still worn today in some lodges of the "Egyptian" rite. In this regard, we can read in Nerval's *The Illuminati* that the society "of the Martinists,"* of which he became a member, had been introduced into France by Martinez Pasqualis [*sic*] and simply renewed the institution of eleventh-century kabbalistic rites, last echo of the formula of the Gnostics, in which some of the Jewish metaphysics was blended with the obscure philosophies of Alexandrian philosophers, like Iamblichus, for example, who died in 330. This neo-Pythagorian and neo-Platonic disciple of Plotinus was highly esteemed by Nicolas Calas and Odysseus Elytis. Another was Porphyrins, author of *On the Mysteries of Egypt,* who, Ambelain notes, specifically introduced justification for theurgy ("assumption of divine forms, use of divine names" and "descent of deifying energies," as defined by Denis Labouré in his *Masonic Testament*).[45]

It was also to Iamblichus (mentioned by Artaud in *Heliogabalus or the Crowned Anarchist*), Martinès de Pasqually, and Cagliostro that Robert Amadou refers to describe "post-Platonic theurgy" in his *Occident, Orient: parcours d'une tradition,* when he writes:

> "Theurgy": the word appears in the (Pseudo) *Chaldean Oracles,* and it was from there that Iamblichus introduced it into philosophy. The purpose of theurgy is the suprarational union with the divine that Plotinus achieved in pure philosophy: it is a practical method for achieving this aim.

Robert Ambelain (though we know we have to treat his conjectures with caution for his theories were somewhat hazy) ends his book *La Chapelle des damnés* (The Chapel of the Damned) with a note on Martinès, who he claims died in 1779, thereby reinforcing the mystery surrounding this individual. He says here that the members of the group founded by "this mystic philosopher" . . . "claimed they would

---

*Martinezists, in fact. The disciples of Martinès de Pasqually are called "Martinists" but they should be called "Martinésistes"; the "Martinists," strictly speaking, are the disciples of Louis-Claude de Saint-Martin.

purify the terrestrial aura with operations of high magic and struggled against black magic and demonic entities." And he adds, "From this occult masonry was born the current of *Martinism,* with its various orders. The oldest is the one formed in Russia under Catherine II by Tieman von Bérend, of strictly *Martinezist* descent."[46]

Tieman von Bérend was a Réau-Croix and was initiated into the Templar-based Rite of Strict Observance. Alluding to *Saint Petersburg Evenings,* René Trintzius, in his extremely conservative *Jacques Cazotte ou le XVIIIe siècle inconnu* (Jacques Cazotte or the Unknown Eighteenth Century), goes on to say about Martinès, "As Joseph de Maistre saw so clearly, his doctrine was a blend of Platonism, Origenianism, and hermetic philosophy on a Christian base," and casts some light on the master's teaching.

> He wanted adepts to devote their time to the study of the hidden secrets of nature, supernatural sciences, high chemistry, numbers, the esoteric meanings of the oldest religious texts, and divination. Little by little they would make their way to the "Thing," in other words, communication with the Invisible, revelations from the spirits, their apparitions, and certain manifestations that would prepare his disciples to lift a corner of the veil over the Divine.[47]

Roger Dachez and Jean-Marc Pétillot prudently venture in their book *Le Rite Écossais Rectifié* (The Rectified Scottish Rite):

> We still do not know who Martinès's immediate sources were. Certain aspects of the *Treatise on the Reintegration of Beings into Their Primal Property, Virtue, Divine Spiritual Power* are reminiscent of Midrashic literature, which the Jewish ancestry of its author makes easy to grasp, whereas other elements seem to be pulled from the hermetic-kabbalistic substratum on which the Neo-Platonic Renaissance in Italy at the end of the fifteenth century, and more generally what is usually called Christian esotericism, would be grounded.[48]

Returning to Trintzius, his book has the merit of clarifying the context in which the most unbridled irrationality flourished in the shadow of the Enlightenment and the Age of Reason, with illuminism acting as a counterweight to the ambient skepticism.

> Abbé de Villars had already cast a sharp light on hermetic arcana. After him, Dom Pernéty and the Marquis d'Argens would popularize the mysteries of the *Oedipus Aegyptiacus* and the musings of the Florentine Neo-Platonists. Pico Della Mirandola and Marsilio Ficino would be reborn, imbued with what Nerval called "the musky spirit" of the eighteenth century in *The Count de Gabalis* and *Kabbalistic Letters*. No one should write this off (as often happens), as a gratuitous literary parlor game. Because he divulged the entire Rosicrucian doctrine on the spirit world (in a somewhat far-fetched form), the Abbé de Villars was found murdered on the road to Lyon with a dagger planted between his shoulder blades.

In this regard, Seligmann shows in *The Mirror of Magic* that while "this small book was obviously written to amuse Parisians, it is still interesting because it reveals that in Villar's time, there were still Paracelsians supporting the old theories of elemental spirits, kabbalistic signs, talismans, and all the trappings of sixteenth-century magic," Gabalis being, moreover, according to Seligmann, the name Paracelsus gives to the spiritual as opposed to the carnal man.[49]

Completing this picture, François Ribadeau Dumas says:

> Thus standing out behind don Pasqually, mysterious prophet of Reintegration, were, in the eighteenth century, the impulses of the great Rosicrucian magicians of the Renaissance, whose sublime language taught, over and above religion, the divine, dazzling illumination of a theology as the Creator had intended, that of the Edenic truth, the Revelation of happiness through free dialogue with God. The exact same thesis promulgated by Böhme.[50]

Considered by Trintzius as "an attempt to restore the lodges to their mystical, pure, and even Rosicrucian starting point," despite the fact that the Grand Lodge of France had rejected it with its December 12, 1765, decree, Martinès de Pasqually's Cohen Masonry was, with its gnostic connotations (the fallen man-god, prisoner of matter, should reintegrate the boundless substance of the divine, which explains why his position is discussed as the theory of reintegration), in some respects reminiscent of Spinoza's *Theologico-Political Treatise*.[51] Martinès de Pasqually's Order of the Elect Cohen was divided into four classes, with first the three symbolic degrees found in all forms of speculative Masonry, then a second class (the first truly esoteric one), called the Porch, which covered the grades of apprentice, fellow, and master elect cohen. The third class, known as the Temple, included grand master elect cohen, and grand elu de Zorobabel, or knight commander of the Orient. Finally, the fourth class, which was secret, consisted of only one grade, the Réau-Croix. This was practically an order in itself, according to Gérard Van Rijnberk, and, according to Dachez and Pétillot, was "a veritable ordination into a kind of 'primal priesthood.'"

We should note with René Trintzius "that the death of Martinez [*sic*] would greatly disrupt the sect he had founded. Its members broke apart almost immediately. Some joined Freemasonry, others the Swedenborgians."

It is also worth recalling here the names of two figures who played a particularly notable role alongside Martinès de Pasqually in the development of what Serge Caillet (and Andrew Prescott) calls "fringe Freemasonry." These are Jean-Baptiste Willermoz (1730–1824), founder of the Rectified Scottish Rite, and Louis-Claude de Saint-Martin, the "Unknown Philosopher," who would devote part of his remaining years to translating at least four of Jacob Böhme's books. Saint-Martin would also lend his name to Martinism and perhaps his pseudonym to a very high grade of the French Rite, that of Sublime Unknown Philosopher, unless it was borrowed from Baron Tschoudy (1742–1769) and his Order of the Unknown Philosophers, also called the Rite of the Flaming Star. This Louis-Claude de Saint-Martin was introduced by Joseph de Maistre, among his first disciples, as "the most learned, wisest, and most elegant of modern theosophers," as Christian hermeticists were known at the end of the eighteenth century, and his aphoristic thoughts were described by Raymond Christoflour (*Atlantis,* n° 330) as "often as abrupt and obscure as those of the heroes of the tradition he revered, a Paracelsus, an Eckhart, or a Jacob Böhme." This same Louis-Claude de Saint-Martin who, as Jean Van Win noted, wrote in his *On the Spirit of Things:*

> Just as all men are, as for their minds, mere shapeless fragments of the spiritual temple that existed in primitive man, all traditions on earth can similarly consider themselves to be traditions of a fundamental, mother tradition, which from the beginning was entrusted to culpable man and his first offshoots. These fragments nonetheless should always retain traces of the mother tradition; as we can see how the fragments of the first man allow a fair number of meaningful clues to be seen within us, enough to let us recognize our divine origin, and our primal destination.

If we replace "mother tradition" with "primordial tradition," we can easily see where Guénon went to find some of the foundations of his own thought . . .

For his part, Breton cites in his text "Language of the Stones" (in *Perspective Cavalière*) "the unclassifiable 'poem'"—allegorical, initiatory, and fantastic, but mainly in . . . prose—of Claude de Saint-Martin* [*sic*] *The Crocodile or the War of Good and Evil During the Reign of Louis XV* is "an epic-magical poem in 102 cantos," which was nonetheless considered by this theosopher and "enthusiast of hidden things" as a "cheerful book," published in 1799 at the author's expense at the Imprimerie-Librairie du cercle social in Paris, "a philosophical and political club that had emerged from the Masonic milieu," according to Amadou in his preface to the 1962 reprint edition. This club was founded by Nicolas de Bonneville, friend of Thomas Paine and translator of his book on the Druidic origins of Freemasonry.

---

*Breton makes a mistake and calls Saint-Martin "Claude" instead of "Louis-Claude."

The main character of Saint-Martin's text, Eleazar, a "virtuous Israelite" denounced by the Inquisition and forced to leave his native Spain, could easily have borrowed a number of the features of Martinès de Pasqually himself. Robert Amadou grants sufficient importance—both symbolic and artistic—to the poem that he maintains that "by its literary genre, *The Crocodile*, published in 1799, holds in some way the relay between the fantasy tale of the eighteenth century and the Romantic epic of the nineteenth." He does not fail, though, to stress the fact that "the principal design of the book [is to] condemn the errors of modern thought."

Mabille, a "man of the great human fraternities" whose "final message is . . . to extol them," seems to have tried to "convert" Breton to Freemasonry. Breton's poem "Full Margin" (1940), which was dedicated to the surgeon, opens with the following lines, which are fairly transparent to anyone who knows how to read them, although they are a bit casual:

> *I am not for the adepts*
> *I have never lived in the place called* La Grenouillère*
>   *[the frog pond]*
> *My heart's lantern starts smoking and soon sputters*
>   *when approaching the square*†
> *I have only ever been drawn to what does not mind its*
>   *manners.*‡

Jean-Pierre Lasalle suggests this "square," because of the word "carreau," in particular, could be a subtle allusion to the mosaic pavement.[52]

Breton's poem also contains references to Pelagius, a heterodox Celtic monk and possibly a former Druid and as such "crowned with mistletoe, his head erect over all those bent brows." He was, in any

---

*There is also—and more importantly—a pun here: "grenouiller" (the verb), in informal language, means "to indulge in or be involved in shady dealings."
†"Les parvis": the square in front of a church or a Masonic temple.
‡[*Ne pas se tenir à carreau* translated literally would be "does not stick to the square."
—*Trans.*]

event, heir to their monist philosophy, which refused to draw any sharp distinction between good and evil. There was also reference to the Cistercian Joachim de Flore (1130–1202), "led by terrible angels," a mystic theologian who inspired in particular the Dolcinians made famous by Umberto Eco, and destroyed in a Crusade in 1307, the same year the Templars were arrested. In this context, it is worth noting the importance of Joachim de Flore, a disciple of Bernard de Clairvaux, in medieval thought. As the founder of the congregation and order of Flore, recognized by Rome, he wrote three treatises from which stemmed an original philosophical-religious trend that was concerned with humanity's future, Joachinism, which would exert an important influence over thinkers like Campanella, Böhme, Swedenborg, and Hegel![53]

Moreover, the 1947 international exhibition would carry some water to the well in a way that is by no means coincidental. This is evident from the letter Breton sent on January 12, 1947, to those he wanted to take part in it.

> The overall structure of the exhibition will conform to the chief concern of retracing the successive stages of an INITIATION whose gradation will be suggested by the passage from one room to the next.

And in fact, in the review written by Pierre Guerre for *Les Cahiers du Sud,* we can read (in the section) concerning "the large initiatory labyrinth imagined by André Breton":

> Here the mystery is expressed in its poetic, sacred form. Transparent Ariadne's threads stretch above the corridor. Everything is night blue, secret, propitious for ritual and initiation. Within the truly special cloudiness, similar to that of aquariums and some forgotten sanctuaries, open here and there some illuminated cavities. Each is a magic altar modeled on those of Indian or Voodoo worship, dedicated to an individual or an object capable of being endowed with mythic life. The visitor, from one corner to the next, one oratory to another, travels from the dismaying to the extraordinary. He aban-

dons himself, he starts drifting, stumbling, dreaming.... There can be no doubt; the exhibition's purpose has been achieved.

The critic concludes his article, "The spirit breathes there without ever failing in its mission." Philippe Audoin confirms this in his short book on the surrealists, in which he writes, "The staging of this spiritual 'parade' that was the 1947 exhibition was conceived to restrict the visitor to complete the equivalent of an initiatory journey."[54] Sarane Alexandrian described it in his autobiography as an "initiation" or "initiatory labyrinth." In his preface to the exhibition catalog ("Before the Curtain"), Breton, thereby earning the title of initiatory poet that he would be awarded by Jacques Abeille, among others, would even go so far as to say:

> Even if by having the aspirant to knowledge—the visitor in this case—face a cycle of ordeals (reduced practically to a minimum), the only result would be to induce him to let his mind muse over what, throughout the ages, can be strange and disturbing about certain individual and collective modes of behavior, we would already be satisfied that we were on the right track.

Audoin also notes, "The main room [of the exhibition] is clear but it is raining there. Every Mason will know what the expression 'it is raining' means!"*

Whatever the case may be, despite Breton's great esteem for Fred Zeller, the painter and Trotsky's former secretary who was initiated in 1953 and was to be the future grand master of the Grand Orient, the author of the *Manifestoes of Surrealism* remained deaf to the appeals of the luminous delta, perhaps because, as Lassalle indicates:

> The Masons most open to surrealism were the spiritualist and esoteric masons, members of the Grand Lodge which was their

---

*[Raining signifies the presence of the profane in the sacred premises of the temple. —*Trans.*]

holding tank whereas the Grand Orient remained more positivist and anticlerical, if not outright antireligious. This sets up an insoluble contradiction. If one rigorously adhered to virulent anticlericalism, the sole Masons that would appreciate Breton were those of the Grand Orient. But specifically because they represented those values of obtuse scientism and positivism that Breton had ceaselessly combatted, they could only be repulsive for him. Those Masons who would be in league with his major, secret concerns were those who, under the often far too convenient circumlocution of the Great Architect of the Universe, would not be prone to dispensing with God.[55]

Although he was not an initiate, Breton was nevertheless quite conversant with the matter, as shown by Gengenbach's conclusion in *Adieu à Satan*:

> And I cannot overlook the fact that it was not priests who built the cathedrals but master-masons initiated into esotericism. For the most part these cathedrals are not dedicated to the crucified Man-God but to Our Lady. The master-masons knew what they were doing. For them, Our Lady meant much more than the mother of Jesus of Nazareth, who they never wanted to deify out of idolatry. For them she was (on the occult plane) Isis of the Egyptians, who was inseminating and not inseminated, and who engendered the man-god. . . . André Breton meets here all those troubadours and Mason initiates of the cathedrals.

But he only meets them! Conversely, it is quite another matter for a number of the young members of the third surrealist wave. This would only seem natural to them if they thought, like Sarane Alexandrian, that surrealism, an order of modern knighthood comparable to that of the Templars,"

> was an initiatory organization (I am not saying a sect: René Guénon has shown the difference between a "sect," serving a small clique,

and an "initiatory organization," aiming toward universality) in which knowledge is gained by degrees until it reaches the point of rupture, the *conclusive ordeal of the initiation*. One starts as a disciple, then becomes an initiate next (in other words, an individual capable of having disciples), which leads him to withdrawing from the original organization.[56]

With a few subtle differences, Alain Jouffroy confirms this view when he writes:

For Duprey's generation, which is also mine, it was initially important to draw close to Breton—on its own this approach resembled an initiation—but it was equally important to draw away from him, which is not the same as saying it was important to disavow him.[57]

Jacques Abeille echoes this assessment in his article "Un surréel," dedicated to Charles Duits, when he observes:

One of the profound meanings of this book[58] is to say that the frequentation of André Breton consisted in an initiation and it was inadvertently, because it was in itself underlying, that the question was raised, first to every individual, of the degree to which each adept had attained.

Influenced by this climate as well as by the personality of Doctor Henri Hunwald, who was a professor of the School of Anthropology and was fascinated by alchemy and the tradition, a man esteemed by Breton and mentioned by Canseliet in *Médium* n° 4, René Alleau, Elie-Charles Flamand,* Bernard Roger, Guy-René Doumayrou, Roger van Hecke, and Jean Palou[59] became members of the Thebah (the Ark) Lodge n° 347 of the Grand Lodge of France. The members of this Lodge "had taken on the mission of working according to the principles

---

*Flamand, who was born in 1928, also wrote a book titled *La Tour Saint-Jacques,* which he dedicated "to the memory of (his) friends Henri Hunwald, Claude d'Ygé (the adept), Jean Palou, and Gérard Heym, who live in the Light, of which this tower reflects a ray."

of the true esoteric tradition of the Order as well as deeply studying the Masonic symbolism and the practices it engenders." René Guénon was briefly a member of this workshop, which had been founded in 1901 and to which he had been introduced through the efforts of Oswald Wirth, after having frequented the "fringe Masonry"* and attained the grade of chevalier kadosh (thirtieth degree).[60]

René Guénon hardly needs any further introduction. Shot down in a few lines in the *Dictionnaire général du surréalisme et de ses environs,* he believed esotericism was solely linked to "the tradition predating all specific religious forms," according to Sarane Alexandrian. Guénon did much, in his distinctly personal way, to free it from all the faded fin de siècle finery in which it had been rigged out. He was "the great solitary adventurer who rejected faith for knowledge, opposed deliverance to salvation, and freed metaphysics from the ruins of the religion covering it over."[61] He was the man who refused the "bias that attributed to the Greeks and Romans the origin of all civilization,"[62] as well as the man who converted to Islam in 1912, the same year he became a Freemason, and was married in accordance with the Catholic rite, as shown by Jean Van Win. Now if Guénon, who consistently calls on analogy, clearly shares Breton's rejection of the Greeks and Romans, condemning, for example, the "superstition of Greco-Latin classicism" in *The Crisis in the Modern World,* he pushed the tradition back much earlier and even attributes it to a *nonhuman* origin, which is a bit more awkward than a reference to Cthulhu! I should note, in passing, that Guénon "lent credence to a mystical transmission of a primal truth that appeared to human genius in the first ages of the world," as Sylvain Levi, the scholarly expert on India, scolds him in the unfavorable report he wrote on his Ph.D. Guénon does not reject the faith; he simply relegates it to its proper place of exoteric knowledge, indispensable however for grasping the esoteric thought duly reserved for an elite. He was also initially close to (but who wasn't he close to?) the Thomist circle around Jacques Maritain, thanks to whom he was able to publish his attack against the-

---

*The notion of "fringe Masonry," used by Serge Caillet, seems to have been developed by Andrew Prescott, who was responsible for the department of Masonic studies at the University of Sheffield in the United Kingdom.

osophy with the publisher La Nouvelle Librairie nationale, which was connected with the right-wing Action française! He finally, like the surrealists, harshly condemned "modern times" (but not for the same reasons), whose origin he maintained was the destruction of the Order of the Temple,[63] which he considered as not only a link between the East and the West, but also between the spiritual and the temporal. He also condemned the Renaissance and the Reformation, considerd as the starting points for a "regressive mechanism," which made possible the advent of a humanism that reduced everything to the measure of man, to culminate eventually in the current "technicist" civilization in crisis, *the reign of quantity* and uniformity.

> What the modern world has striven after with all its strength, even when it has claimed in its own way to pursue science, is really nothing other than the development of industry and "mechanization"; and in thus seeking to dominate matter and bend it to their service, men have only succeeded in becoming its slaves. Not only have they limited their intellectual—if such a term can still be used in the present state of things—ambitions to inventing and constructing machines, but they have ended by becoming, in fact, machines themselves.[64]

This point of view is worth comparing to the one that Breton expressed in his text "In Self-Defense": "It is not through 'mechanization' that Western populations can be saved . . . that is not how they will escape the moral ill that is killing them." I could go so far as to say that if the illuminated side of the nineteenth century believed in reason and in the advent of a golden age ushered in by scientific progress, Guénon, a few years after, sort of Cassandra announcing the Kali-Yuga, the end of time, represented its dark side, his thought being more or less a synthesis of these ideas. Adopting the opposite course, Guénon believed (in contrast to Eliphas Levi, for example, who retained a bit of his 1848 revolutionary past) that this golden age was behind us. For him, our world lived in the rhythm of a continuous deterioration, punctuated by a few high points that impelled our irresistible slide toward the cataclysm. This makes his ideas close to those of all the currents of the extreme right, who, like him, "relegated democracy among the phenomena of decomposition"![65]

But we should not forget that also at play here, as noted by Jean-Pierre Laurant in *René Guénon: Les enjeux d'une lecture* (René Guénon: The Stakes of a Reading), is that Guénon's "first books were conceived at a time when the disasters of war had caused the certitudes of scientism to waver, separating for a long while human progress and the progress of knowledge."[66] We must also remember that his work, on the whole, despite the suspicions it can legitimately raise, leans toward supplying a "response to the unresolved but perpetually recurring question on the status of the spiritual in contemporary societies and its connection to rationalism." It is worth recalling that Breton and his friends—Artaud,* Leiris, Naville—"fascinated by so-called traditional thought" (as Breton noted in *Entretiens*), were among his very first readers and solicited Guénon's participation in 1925, in *La Révolution surréaliste*. But Guénon, as he wrote in 1932, considered them as "a small group of young men who amused themselves with practical jokes of dubious taste," and he turned them down. Much to Breton's great displeasure (or so it seems), he brought it up again in his interviews with André Parinaud in 1952. "Among the desired collaborations, I see only one missing: it was that of René Guénon."

This was the beginning of a reciprocal misunderstanding aggravated by major divergences of opinion between Guénon and the surrealists on

---

*Here, for example, is what Antonin Artaud wrote to Jean Paulhan on September 16, 1930: "I was extremely disappointed by your letter on the subject of Guénon. I am for Guénon the gullible against all the rest. Guénon the gullible, because he takes the meaningful and human content of all fables and legends literally, appears less infantile to me than the entire modern scientific, biological, and anthropological school that in the footsteps of Edmond Perrier thinks that man first walked on all fours and he became upright by dint of seeking to pick the fruits of trees and he had to sit up to do that. Why wouldn't he have managed to sprout wings by dint of looking at the moon? Me, I believe in the supernatural" (Antonin Artaud, *Oeuvres complètes,* vol. 6). Jean Paulhan, a member of the first editorial team of *Littérature* and incidentally a huge admirer of Louis-Claude de Saint-Martin, always took an interest in Guénon, alternating between phases of irritation and fascination, which drove him to write to Luc Benoist, a faithful supporter of Guénon and director of the collection "Traditions" at Gallimard, "I read him with passion!"

the subjects of psychoanalysis and Marxism, but also love, which the man who would adopt the name Abdel Wahid Yahia (Servant of the One) considered as "a sentimental and therefore a secondary element." Guénon also perceived psychoanalysis in both its Freudian and Jungian forms as a particularly lurid manifestation of "counter-initiation" in its most "Satanic" form, with Jung's form undoubtedly worse because of the place it reserved for symbols. Yet that part of the surrealist spirit aiming at man's exceeding his derisory condition offered convergences, despite everything and perhaps simply due to the spirit of the time, with Guénonian metaphysics.

The members of the Grand Jeu, especially Daumal, who began reading Guénon's works in 1921, also granted, at least initially, major importance to him.[67] Roger Gilbert-Lecomte would even write, "To Monsieur René Guénon, we declare: first of all that his theoretical thought is essentially our own, and the tradition he claims to belong to is surely the only one we recognize." Among the unpublished fragments that would be published after the death of the Reims native under the title *Return to Everything*, Guénon's influence is tangible (as underscored by Alain and Odette Virmaux) in the text "Eternity, Your Name is No," written on a date that is difficult to establish with any precision. According to the Virmauxs, Lecomte mainly demonstrated in this text

> how the power of the Catholic religion, founded on political strength and theological weakness, no longer has anything in common with the true religious spirit as existed in the primitive soul. This religion, which Lecomte by no means was seeking to rehabilitate but simply analyze, gradually deteriorated to the benefit of a mass organization founded on political conservatism and moral order. It has been in a state of constant regression since its primitive stage.

The two authors also cite a study by Michel Random in which this incontestable expert of the Grand Jeu, speaking of Gilbert-Lecomte's world, says:

A neutral world in sum, hence we can see, one where the individual is by his very nature essentially a seer, *because he is instantaneously in the very vision he desires at the moment he conceives it* (italics added).[68]

I cannot help but see this as an example of what Guénon calls "intellectual intuition," the identical nature of knowing and being through which—according to this atypical thinker for whom "knowing is nothing but being"—true metaphysical knowledge is obtained. Shortly before his death, Daumal (as Jean-Marc Vivenza reminds us) made sure to send his last text, *The Holy War*, to "René Guénon, Cairo"—and practically to him alone. Daumal evokes in the first issue of *Le Grand Jeu* "the original spirit of the tradition that we claim as our own with him." This would not prevent Daumal in 1928 from indicating where their proximity ends in the article "Again on the Books of René Guénon":

> René Guénon, I know nothing about your strictly human life; all I know is that you have little concern about convincing the multitudes. But I fear that the happiness of thinking has diverted you from this law—historical in the broadest sense—which impels all that is human in us toward revolt; a revolt we do not regard as a task we are responsible for performing, but as a work that we permit to be completed by means of the human envelopes that we misguidedly call "ours."[69]

Reading Daumal's splendid and unfinished initiatory narrative *Mount Analogue* will make it no less strikingly evident that René Guénon exercised great influence over its author. But judge for yourself! A group of "seekers" led by Father Sogol, "a professor of Alpinism," embark on a quest for a mountain concealed from the sight of all, "the Mountain which connects Heaven and Earth," "located on an island," which is "where our humanity and a higher civilization meet at the place the perpetuation of an instituted truth is carried out." They can only make landfall there after ridding themselves of "their personal affairs, which are so heavy to carry, in their hearts and heads," in other places known as metals, because "the invisible gates of this invisible country" are "opened by those guarding them."

The life led by the community of the "seekers of the mountain," on the shores of Port-des-Singes, seems to owe much to ideas developed by Guénon in various books, particularly *The Crisis of the Modern World*. In fact, this community, which has banned the use of electricity and explosives, lives as people lived before the industrial era. But its chief interest is its social organization because "all authority comes from above, that is from the alpine guides whose delegates direct the administration and municipal police." This wholly mirrors the theocratic society dear to the heart of the author of *East and West,* all the more so as the island dwellers, by virtue of their isolation, have the merit of being "less subject to the nefarious influences of the degenerate cultures that flourish on our continents" (than we are). The authority of these guides is never contested "because it is founded on possession of peradams" ("stones of Adam"), fragments of timeless knowledge—or virtue—that have been recovered through asceticism.

In a way that Guénon would probably not have condemned, the members of the expedition, departing on the conquest of Mount Analogue, that "long, extremely long" adventure, which "shall surely take years," leave behind everything connected to the modern world. Beyond this sacrifice of material things there is a much more significant renunciation that involves shedding the "old man," from which Pierre Sogol (whose name is a transparent reversal of Logos), by seeking his companions' "protection against his pleasure and his dreams, and help to become what he is without imitating anyone," discovers his first "peradam," which is "like a tiny dewdrop." But it certainly seems as if the guides themselves, guardians of the threshold and guarantors of the transmission, are only intermediaries—"still human in some respects"—between us and beings "of a higher type, who hold the keys to everything that is a mystery for us," beings "of a higher type" who I fear have little in common with Breton's Great Transparents!

Daumal puts the following words in the mouth of one of his characters, specifically the one who initiated the expedition. These words exactly sum up his own position with regard to the Guénonian theory concerning the relationship between esotericism and exotericism and the various gurus who left their mark on him:

> Somehow I could not regard this as a simple allegory, this idea of an invisible humanity within visible humanity. Experience has proven, I told myself, that a man can reach truth neither directly nor alone; an intermediary must exist—still human in certain respects yet surpassing humanity in others. Somewhere on our Earth this superior humanity must exist, and it cannot be absolutely inaccessible. And so shouldn't all my efforts be devoted to discovering it? Even if, in spite of my certainty, I were the victim of a monstrous illusion, I would have nothing to lose in making the effort, for in any case, without this hope, all life is meaningless.

Daumal, however, who, contrary to Guénon, mastered Sanskrit perfectly, while recognizing the merit of "never betraying Hindu thought for the benefit of the specific needs of Western philosophy," was not fooled by the quality of some of the esoteric teaching flourishing at that time. Also, as Olivier Pénot Lacassagne reminds us, the author of *A Night of Serious Drinking* could combine enchantment and irony, as shown in his review of an Indian dance and music performance given in Paris in 1931 by Uday Shankar and Timir Baran Bhattâchârya:

> A little authentic, living Hindu thought in flesh and blood, in gestures and spirit was performed publicly in our midst. Nothing disfigured it, no stupid translators, no hypocritical interpreters, not even the slightest shadow of any theosophist, which is a minor miracle.[70]

This criticism is echoed in Artaud's *Heliogabalus or the Crowned Anarchist,* where the author also produces ridicule:

> "The dances of oriental wandering actors and the conjuring tricks of the fakirs recently seen on European stages" are equally unlikely "to restore to us the sense of freedom without images or the mysterious commotion of images resulting from a genuinely sacred gesture."

So much for Helena Blavatsky, whom Guénon violently attacked in his 1921 book *Theosophy: The History of a Pseudo-Religion,* challenging her interpretation of neo-Platonism and rejecting any filiation with this philosophical movement, "a confused mixture of Neoplatonism, Gnosticism, Jewish kabbalah, hermeticism, and occultism, the whole of it being gathered as well as can be expected around two or three ideas, which, like it or not, are of completely modern and purely Western origin" and the secret societies of the seventeenth century. But I should say that his criticism, which he seems to have intended to put in a more general form in *The Occultist Error,* which remained in the planning stages, targeted all of contemporary occultism, which is somewhat paradoxical given his own journey, "which, while representing itself as a restoration of esotericism, only manages to be a vulgar counterfeit because its leaders never possessed any true principles nor any serious initiation," as he writes in *L'Ésoterisme de Dante* (The Esotericism of Dante).

Helena Blavatsky seemed also to be Adrien Dax's chief target when he wrote in his article "Disorienting Orient":

> More often, the faded finery of exoticism ineptly hides actual mental indigence, and this deficiency is aggravated by extreme oversimplification that mainly reveals a relentless mysticism. This mysticism almost always remains envisioned from a Western perspective, which ensures that some antinomies, which the East appears to have dominated, take on, under the pens of overzealous popularizers, a resolutely pessimistic meaning. All forms of renunciation are thereby justified in advance to the benefit of a strange "liberation" about which we truly fear learning more. . . .

It is as if the rather reactionary nature of Guénonian deterministic traditionalism had not really caught his notice any more than it had Breton (despite several temporary clarifications), who like Artaud, Mandiargues, and particularly Queneau, paid close attention to Guénon's work. We can find a trace of Guénon's influence on Artaud in the following passage taken from his text "The Rites of the Kings of Atlantis" (from *Les Tarahumaras*): "Consequently we could say the question of progress does not arise in the presence of any authentic tradition. True traditions do not progress because they are the advanced point of all truth. The sole progress that can be achieved is through conserving the form and force of these traditions." In his February 4, 1937, letter to Jean Paulhan, Artaud speaks, like Guénon, of "a more than human tradition" when describing the symbols appearing on the robes and headbands of the Indians. Queneau was another assiduous reader of Guénon's books and articles from 1921 on and corresponded with him briefly in 1936, according to Michel Lécureur in his *Raymond Queneau, biographie*. In 1937 he began a *Short Treatise on the Democratic Virtues* in a very Guénonian tone, which, left unfinished, would not be published until 1993. He would continue all his life to return to the work of the man who died under the name of Abdel Wahid Yahia, confessing to his son toward its end, "I have read too much René Guénon."

In 1953, in "On Surrealism in Its Living Works," Breton emphasized the convergence of analyses concerning man's place inside "what surrounds him," stating that Guénon's opinion had "always appeared to arise out of elementary good sense." Meanwhile Dax, in the second issue of *Médium* (February 1954)—which clearly shows this involves a matter of concern shared by the group—in these terms the philosophy developed by Guénon in "*Orient, Occident*" [sic] and *The Eastern Metaphysic* in its context:

> If we are to believe René Guénon, whose merit of having placed certain matters beneath the only light suitable for them no one will contest, perfect understanding of the Eastern message requires, above all, a mental availability that is as free of legendary fantasizing as it is of all vague soteriological desires. This is why it is not forbidden to think that the miserable face of the East, ceaselessly offered us with an insistence that is in utter bad taste, is perhaps merely the most faithful reflection of some corrupt spiritualism for which the West, in the final analysis, is solely responsible.

Even André Thirion, in his memoirs, *Révolutionnaires sans Révolutions* (Revolutionaries without Revolutions), eventually admits, "In hindsight, I consider René Guénon as one of the most important authors for understanding the thought and action of the men of the twentieth century . . ." while stating his mistrust of the Grand Jeu, which he condemned as an unoriginal vector "of a new offensive of Oriental philosophies, anarchistic attitudes, the wonders of the fakirs, crystal balls, and hashish. . . ."[71]

Although criticizing the author of *The Multiple States of Being* for his excessive conservatism on the social plane, which made him—for a short time—friends with Leon Daudet and Jacques Bainville of *L'Action française*,* and compelled by his interest in Guénon's work to discreetly pass over in silence the theocratic aspirations it contains, Breton heeded the evolution of his thought so attentively that, as Suzanne Lamy notes in her book *Hermeticism and Poetry in Arcanum 17*, the "supreme point" he mentions on several occasions "can be found at the heart of all esoteric doctrines, in the kabbalah and Taoism, as well as in the intersection of the cross. This is the central point—the point where reintegration occurs at the heart of the human state—it is the point where communication is established with the higher states of being," which reflects Guénon's analysis in *The Symbolism of the Cross*.

> At the center of the cross, therefore, all oppositions are reconciled and resolved; that is the point where the synthesis of all contrary terms is achieved, for in reality they are contrary only from the outward and particular points of view of knowledge in distinctive mode.[72]

> "This reintegration of the being considered as the very center of the human state, that is to say, the restitution of the primordial state" is essential in the effort to reach the supreme goal, which is the identification of the human center with the universal center: "in the first phase the integral human state is realized, in the second the totality of the being."[73]

L'Action française is both a magazine and a political movement.

On the strength of these two quotes, Eddy Batache shows the exact limits of the possible convergences between surrealism and Guénon's thought. If Breton could deem the first phase necessary, there was no way he could recognize himself in the second. This fundamental notion of the supreme point, though, which is at the center of John Dee's sacred geometry, can also be found in the *Zohar*, where, under the name of Kether, meaning "the Indulgent One," the "Star of the Cosmos," or the "Holy Old Man," it is enthroned at the top of the tree of the sephiroth. It is also found in esoteric Islam, where it is called the "divine station," in the Bardic Triads (fragments of ancient Celtic poems) where it is the point of freedom, the equitable combination of all the opposites, one of the three original Unities of Druidism, as well as in "the Far Eastern tradition for which 'The Invariable Center,' site of perfect equilibrium, is 'depicted as the center of *the cosmic wheel*, and is at the same time the point where the 'Activity of the Sky' is directly reflected."[74]

We are sure this point represents for Chazal "the Edenic Golden Number," "the living Golden Point," which is nothing other than "the solar revelation," because he professed this to Adrien Dax in *Médium*. Could this point have a connection with Roger Gilbert-Lecomte's *Punctum stans*, the dead point that Alain and Odette Virmaux tell us corresponds with "a fourth dimension where the opposites are abolished and where speed and motionlessness, empty and full, beginning and end, creation and noncreation reconcile"?[75] This fourth dimension brings to mind Piotr D. Ouspensky, who gave this as a title to one of his books in 1909. Unless it would be "the extreme point of [Daumal's] Mount Analogue," which is "invisible through an excess of light," the place where "at the summit that is sharper than the most slender needle, only that which fills all spaces stands," or "in the most subtle air where everything freezes, all that survives is the crystal of the last stability," or "in the middle of the sky's fire where everything is burning, perpetual incandescence is the sole survivor," or finally, "in the center of everything is the one which sees everything fulfilled in its beginning and its end" (all without a single capital letter!). Could this be, in short "that Point that is not seen but sees . . . tomb of the world . . . but seed of an intense, nonextended Counter-World of visible truth," or "this Point, the only one, identical to the eternal Point," perhaps "the Eye of all eyes," to borrow the term used by the "Phrère Simpliste" Nathaniel* in his 1930 poem "The Backside of the Décor," dedicated—and this is not insignificant—to Joseph Sima? Sima† may have been the sole member of the group, Vera Linhartova tells us, to have attained in his own way—the way of annihilation of the self in the work—the goal this group set for themselves: "the destruction of the individual in order to free the universal forces that the presence of the ego prevents from manifesting." Sima was also the sole member to consistently develop the ideas he had shared with his young friends more profoundly, especially in the second part of his career.[76]

In short, couldn't this supreme point, the concept of which was studied so meticulously by Carrouges, who attempted as best he could to liken it to the idea of God, be Hans Arp's "point of innocence," situated at the crossroads of the undifferentiated?

Artaud adds to this:

> Who cannot see that all these esotericisms are the same and strive to say the same thing in spirit? They indicate one same geometrical, numerical, organic, harmonious, occult idea that reconciles man with nature and life. The signs of these esotericisms are identical. They possess deep analogies between their words, gestures, and screams.[77]

---

*[Phrère Simpliste, meaning "simplistic brother," was one of the terms the core members of the Grand Jeu group used to refer to themselves—an echo of their schooldays in Reims. —*Trans.*]

†Joseph Sima (1891–1971), a Czech painter of the inner vision and of essential oneness, was one of the founding members of the Grand Jeu and thus quite close to Daumal and Gilbert-Lecomte, although much older. Two magnificent portraits he painted of them are housed in the Reims Fine Arts Museum. He also did a portrait of Alexander Salzmann. In 1928, Karel Teige, the primary theoretician of surrealism in Czechoslovakia, including him beneath the banner of this movement that he also sometimes called "introrealism," wrote in the Aventinska Mansarda exhibition catalog, with emphases similar to those that would be stuck later by Nora Mitrani, "Surrealism in Sima's painting and work is the extreme manifestation of romanticism and his intuition." Breton would never officially integrate Sima into the surrealist galaxy, even if, as pointed out by Vera Linhartova in her monograph *Joseph Sima, ses amis, ses contemporains*, there is evidence, "notably after the war," that he made "some gestures of friendship," but "in private."

This same Artaud earned the esteem of Guénon in 1932, who spoke of finding his ideas "interesting" although "a bit confused." Shortly before this time, Artaud had employed a clearly Guénonian tone in "Le Théâtre de la cruauté," "In our current degenerate state, metaphysics must be restored to the mind through the skin," and falls back on it even more strongly in 1934 with this expansion on late Roman antiquity in *Heliogabalus or the Crowned Anarchist:*

> The Orient, far from bringing in its disease and unease, allowed contact to be maintained with the tradition. Principles aren't found, aren't invented; they are kept and communicated; and there are few more difficult operations in the world than to maintain the notion—both clear, and yet absorbed within the body—of a universal principle. All this is to note that from the metaphysical viewpoint, the Orient has always been in a state of reassuring ferment; that it's never thence that things worsen; and that, on the day the magic ass's skin of principles shrinks seriously out there, the face of the world will shrink also, everything will more or less near the end; and that day no longer seems to me far off.

But none of this contradicts in any way the movement's essential presuppositions, insofar as in the secular or even atheist context, in which it evolved, "the divine is merely an abstraction representing the major forces of life spread throughout the entire universe, but somehow concentrated in this point, which is their focal point," as Carrouges cautiously suggests, while emphasizing its "secularizing" and secularized aspect. This does not prevent him from suggesting elsewhere:

> It seems that he [Breton] reutilizes in purely atheist form the kabbalistic notion of the Supreme Point that engenders the whole world . . . . It is the living center of the cosmic totality toward which humanity is wending its way through the dialectical oscillations of its destiny. This is the mythical place surrealism seeks to determine in order to conquer it. What would this place be if not God's and the symbol of divine omnipotence?[78]

Yes, this observation is obviously slanted and has ulterior motives, and it uses sophistry to play on the notions of "God" and the "divine," but its source is undoubtedly a *basic* ambiguity that does not escape the sharp eye of the Catholic militant. When emphasizing that "by choosing Rimbaud [over Marx], Breton had shown that surrealism was not action, but asceticism and spiritual experience," Albert Camus in *The Rebel,* whose suggestions were bitterly criticized by members of the group when first aired, suggests that this "supreme point is the quest for the summit-abyss familiar to mystics." For Camus, "It is a mysticism without God that quenches and illustrates the rebel's thirst for the given," "surrealism's essential enemy [being] rationalism." Camus goes on to say:

> More precisely it is a question of dissolving contradictions in the fires of desire and love, and of demolishing the walls of death. Magic rites, primitive or naïve civilizations, alchemy, the language of fire flowers or sleepless nights, are so many miraculous stages on the road to unity and the philosopher's stone.[79]

This is a road on which the philosopher will not linger. From the side of reason, Victor Crastre opportunely notes:

> André Breton, when he sought to establish the notion of a supreme point where all antinomy between knowable and unknowable would vanish, unknowingly found himself in agreement with the physicist Eddington* when he wrote: "Localization is an artificial concept in a universe in interrelation."[80]

---

*Jean-Louis Bédouin, in his *André Breton* (Paris: Seghers, 1970, reprint edition) also mentions Arthur Stanley Eddington, one of the most important astrophysicists of the twentieth century and the author of a theory attempting to combine those of gravity, relativity, and the quantas, whose "ultimate conclusions . . . little known in France, asserted that the laws established from the observation of phenomena and upon which our theories of physics are based, are only fictions." Bédouin calls him one of "those most eminent scientists, often the most controversial, [who] realize objective knowledge is an illusion."

11
SURREALISM AND GNOSTICISM

Marrano of the hidden religion of the hermeticists...
DAVID LINDENBERG

Logically, the quest for the farthest point in exotic or abolished worlds leads to the absolute.
ALFRED JARRY

Toward the end of the 1940s, the surrealists became infatuated with Malcolm de Chazal's book *Sens-plastique II,* whose "themes and paths lead, for example, to Charles Baudelaire, William Blake, or Jacob Böhme."[1] It so happens that an ancestor of this native of Mauritius, François de Chazal de la Genesté (who moved to the island during the Enlightenment), was a Rosicrucian—whatever that name may mean, as we have seen—and practiced alchemy. According to Alexandrian, "He manufactured alchemical gold at will and... thanks to his gift of second sight, allegedly predicted all the events of the French Revolution" (like Cazotte?). Adding to the mystery, Malcolm de Chazal (who spoke constantly of the "Regeneration of man") revealed in his interview with Adrien Dax (published in the third issue of *Médium,* May 1954) that the location of the tomb of his forefather, which appeared repeatedly to him in *Petrusmok* (1951), remained unknown (like that of Martinès de Pasqually in Haiti). Chazal told Dax, "This is the rule among Rosicrucians: they must ensure all traces of themselves vanish after their death." He then concluded this interview by noting:

> The main thing is that Chazal de la Genesté created alchemical gold, carried out the *Lapis Animalis** and other miraculous feats [see the Backström document where that individual's initiation by Chazal in his Mansion of Crève-Coeur (Heartbreak) on Mauritius is discussed. Backström was one of the Grand Masters of Freemasonry].

Chazal's expatriate ancestor was also a figure of interest to René Guénon, who undoubtedly learned about him in *History and Doctrines of the Rosicrucians* (1932) by Paul Sédir (Yvon Le Loup,† an intimate of Papus). Guénon wrote the following in a letter he sent to Malcolm de Chazal in 1947:

> Since the opportunity has offered itself, I am taking the liberty of asking you a question: I have often heard speak of your family and among other things, I have heard it said that the Marquis de Chazal, who settled in Mauritius toward the end of the eighteenth century, had been a disciple of the Count de Saint-Germain and even a keeper of his secret.

Guénon was certainly well-informed: Chazal's ancestor, although buried according to the author's own words in *Petrusmok* in Pamplemousses Cemetery, an "alchemy sanctuary and Rosicrucian temple," "located next to the church of Bernardin de Saint Pierre," as noted by Christophe Chabbert in *Petrusmok de Malcolm de Chazal:*

**Lapis Animalis is one of the names for potable gold.
†Yvon Le Loup is far better-known as Paul Sédir.

Radioscopie d'un Roman Mythique, was at the very least (a proven fact) the Worshipful Master of a Masonic lodge. Laurent de Beaufils writes:

> Emmanuel Swedenborg, the Count de Saint-Germain, the Rosicrucians, Christian Illuminism, Pansophism, and alchemy all more or less obscurely accompany Malcolm de Chazal's ancestral line.[2]

He adds: "Rosicrucianism, Theosophy, and generally the resources of esotericism have been called to the rescue many times when he had to find reference points on which to harness the message."

The Mauritian whose voice, according to Breton, is an "oracle,"[3] and whose work Alexandrian says hold "digressions originating in Martinism."

In fact, Chazal, who in both the *Dictionnaire général du surréalisme et de ses environs* and in Raymond Abellio's preface to the Creole author's last "philosophical" work, *L'Homme et la Connaissance,* is described as a "gnosis holder," revealed his lifelong "Swedenborgian" influence (although he says he had not been an active follower since he was twenty). However, his family had espoused the church of this illuminated Swedish philosopher, whose works had been translated into French in 1820. Chazal was very "Swedenborgian" in his quest of the meanings hidden in the Bible, which he tried "to decode . . . with the help of numbers and the Apocalypse, which he claimed was its 'condensed container.'"[4] He studied this text relentlessly, as well as the Gospel of John.

This brings us back to Swedenborg, the demi-scientist, demi-mystic—to be more exact, the illumined philosopher, founder of a "cult," and inspirer of a Masonic rite about whom Breton spoke in his first Haitian lecture (and this clearly shows the importance that should be attributed to him).

> It is beyond question that this idea [of the *Correspondences**] was borrowed by Baudelaire from the Swedish mystic Swedenborg,

---

*The *Correspondences* is an analogical system used by Baudelaire in his poems.

whose influence we have seen in the work of Hugo, Balzac, Fourier, and Nerval.

Baudelaire himself, quoted by Rolland de Renéville in *L'Expérience poetique,* had said:

Swedenborg had already taught us that *heaven is a very great man,* that everything—form, movement, number, color, perfume—in the *spiritual* as well as in the *natural* world, is significant, reciprocal, converse, *corresponding.*

But the Mauritius native, who claims he "describes the invisible with angelic images," thinks it worth explaining that "Swedenborg's business is with the other world. I am only making every effort to explain this," which is spelled out more fully in this extract from a letter to the Paris group that was read during their November 18, 1947, meeting at the café on Place Blanche: "(I seek) to grasp the divine through the only antennae of my senses." In a letter to Breton dated 1949, Chazal, who was described by Pastor René Agnel (as quoted in Christopher Chabbert's book) as a "poet, explorer in cosmology and ethnology, expert in esotericism, heterodox theologian, and independent militant," who "will remain until his dying breath an individual tormented by the quest of a truly liberated life, and a truly purified spirituality, like Rimbaud, 'the man with soles of wind,' in pursuit of the transformed life," adds, "France disgusts me. It is lost to true spirituality. *You are not French.* You are German—of the stamp of Novalis and Rilke—with your mind pointed like an arrowhead toward the East—the ever-lit lantern in the clock of divine knowledge."

Several lines later, before concluding his letter, with "And I want you to think of me this way, if I should keep your friendship," he clearly spells out:

He is not a truly great man who accepts an affront to his spirituality. We are merely the priests of the Mystery. We must defend the Temple to the death, like the Jews under Titus.[5]

Spiritual dissolution can only be catastrophic, indeed, for someone who believes, "We are born Carnal, Spiritual is what we should become. Whoever fails to attain Spiritual Regeneration is lost," as Chazal writes in *Le Rocher de Sisyphe*. But Chazal is a native of Mauritius, meaning he is the product of a culture that sits square in the crossroads of the West, Africa, and India, whose Vedas exerted an undeniable fascination on him, as demonstrated by his notion of nature as "God's signature, bearing the seal of the sole principle," as he says in the February 4, 1970, issue of a daily newspaper, *The Advance*. It is therefore correct to infer with Beaufils that Chazal only crossed paths with surrealism "essentially because of this movement's affinities with occultism or the workings of the primitive soul,"[6] even if the Mauritian refused to see the slightest trace of it in his work, although (according to Abellio) it always "drew on the ascension of man and the world in the spirit," and despite, for example, the "Lemurian" inspiration of *Petrusmok,* his story "of a quest whose initiatory dimension is obvious," as Bernard Mouralis notes in Christophe Chabbert's book. *Petrusmok* can even be considered as the story of his own mystical experience, just like its "codicil," *Le Rocher de Sisyphe,* called by Chazal *The Religion of the Stone*.

Further description of the author of *Sens-plastique* is provided by Jean-Louis Curtis, who said after meeting Chazal in 1952 in Mauritius:

> He is permeated by occultism, he believes the island is ancient Lemuria of secret tradition and that the odd profiles of its mountains were sculpted by Lemurian giants.[7]

This was a Lemuria Chazal borrowed from both Jules Hermann, who mentions it in his book *Les Révélations du grand océan,* and the poet Robert Edward Hart. And the Lemurians are the individuals who would once have inhabited the mythical sunken continent of Gondwana that lay somewhere between Africa and India. This is eerily reminiscent of the teachings of Helena Blavatsky, particularly those from *Isis Unveiled* (1877), even if she places this lost continent in the Pacific.

Because of the repeated appearances in Chazal's writing of the transcendence, of the "Grand Unconscious of the Universe" smacking more of pantheism than anything else, of a god in short about whom he told Adrien Dax in May 1954 that although "it had nothing in common with the God of the religions, which to his mind is none other than Satan," it is nonetheless the "Un-conscious and the All-conscious," the idea some members of the group momentarily had of an homage to Chazal in a magazine they planned to publish with Gaston Gallimard's help was scuttled under the pressure of their most violently atheistic comrades. We have to admit that it would not have been easy for them to subscribe, at least all of them, to Chazal's opinions in *Le Rocher de Sisyphe,* for example, when he states loud and clear:

> The author of this book accepts but two forms of truth: revealed truth and analogy. Revealed truth is immediate and supernatural, and is based on faith. The other truth, the analogical truth, is the language of *obvious facts,* the science of *correspondences,* leading to myth, to the truth embodied in Nature, to moral and spiritual pantheism.

Equally incriminating, no doubt, is the idea of the Fall and thus the implicit notion of original sin that haunts the Mauritian's work and which none of Breton's friends could truly accept. This idea peeps out quite clearly in his exchange with Adrien Dax (in *Médium,* 1954). Chazal, in fact, responds to Dax's question, "Since according to you, the Golden Age is repetitive, do you then envision a possible reintegration of man in all the prerogatives he could have known?" by saying:

> We are heading toward that state at this very moment. A new age is in preparation that will come in on the heels of catastrophes and trials. The Golden Age is the specific condition of man partially reintegrated onto Life for a time. Salvation is not the Golden Age, but the Garden of Eden from which we have fallen.

This did not prevent Pierre Mabille from writing what follows at this same time, in an article in *Les Cahiers d'Art* on the English poet and artist William Blake (another disciple of Swedenborg—and close for a time to the ideas of the French Revolution):

> In fact, the adepts of the great Swedish mystic considered man's normal state to be that of a seer, and also that the fact of not seeing corresponded to a deprivation of divine grace; they were thus open to this kind of manifestation.

Thereby through Malcolm de Chazal, "surrealist in pleasure," according to Sarane Alexandrian, we can see the shy manifestation of a particular and often occulted aspect of Breton's philosophy: his interest for the personal quest based on symbols, this philosophical synthesis, as Markale says, of "mystical elements, mythological fables, and cosmological speculations," that ancient gnosis is, much more than a true religion. Perhaps *gnosis* should be in the plural given the number of sects claiming its banner, despite the common "worship" of the gnosis* considered "as knowledge of suprasensible Reality, 'invisibly visible in an eternal mystery.'"[8] However David Lindenberg's statement in "Hypermatérialisme et Gnose" (Hypermaterialism and Gnosis)† that Breton "is no less a 'marrano' of the hidden religion of the hermeticists"[9] is quite on target, and he (Breton) may as well be considered as a "'marrano' of the hidden religion" of the gnostics, at least those who belonged to certain sects for whom Osiris was the

---

*The word *gnosis* is Greek in origin and means knowledge. In Breton's case, it would appear to involve Valentinian gnosis.

†As a reminder, Jacques Matter in his 1828 book *Histoire critique du gnosticisme* defines *gnosis* as "the introduction into Christianity of all the cosmological and theosophical speculations that had formed the bulk of the ancient Eastern religions, and which the Neoplatonists had also adopted in the West." This was cited by Fabrice Bardeau, echoing Jean Doresse, in his introduction to the *Livre sacré des gnostiques d'Égypte* (Paris: Robert Laffont, [coll. "Les Portes de l'étrange"], 1977). As for the term *marrano* used by Lindenberg, it is helpful to recall that the Marranos were the Jews who were forcibly converted on the Iberian peninsula, but also those who did it of their own free will, like the Dunmeh of Salonica and certain Sabbatean groups in Central Europe (see Guy Casaril, *Rabbi Siméon Bar Yochaï*), who continued to secretly practice rituals whose meaning they sometimes no longer understood.

"Master of the Night," or even the demiurge Iadalbaoth. Recall what Seligmann suggested in *The Mirror of Magic:*

> Osiris rules Hell with forty-two assistants who are nothing but the hideous representatives of the sins with them, he judges the souls of the departed. . . . According to the verdict, they receive everlasting life or are punished for their sins. Those whom Osiris brings to reckoning are condemned to hunger and thirst, to lie in the dark and solitary grave from which they may never return to sunlight; or they are tossed to abominable executioners in the shape of crocodiles and hippopotami eager to tear them asunder.

Later, Seligmann adds:

> As Gnosticism originated on Egyptian soil, we may be sure that many elements of the antique Egyptian magic were adopted by the founders of the new doctrine. Magical incantations, powerful words had opened in times the gates of the underworld: formulas had driven away evil powers, which threatened the deceased on his journey to Osiris. Similar words, letters, and phrases were now pronounced by the Gnostic on his ascent to paradise. For the attainment of eternal life, this word-magic was indispensable to him.

Jean Doresse noted that the Hellenic origin of gnostic theology "was beyond debate." We must also keep in mind that "Platonism had already sketched an outline of some of its themes" and that it was deeply influenced by astrology, then accepted throughout the Near East "exactly as we accept the major laws of modern physics," but that it also possessed features in common with hermeticism, the Iranian religions of the time, and above all Judaism.

> Gnosis can be fairly well defined as originating in the powerful penetration of the great Iranian myths in a mystic Judaism, already nourished itself by both Greek influences—philosophical and mystical—and Chaldean influences.

And Jean Doresse's works had an undeniable influence on Breton and the surrealists.[10] Certain Jewish notions, like that of *Tzimtzum* (contraction of God), for example, which can be found both in the *Asclepius* and the Zohar of the twelfth century, then in the fifteenth-century kabbalah of Isaac Louria, would seem to have influenced several currents of gnostic thought, as well as that of some Grand Jeu members, such as Rolland de Renéville. In *L'Experience poetique* he discusses it using the odd name of Zim-Zoum, as a "sacrifice of the deity." He goes on to say:

> Only the voluntary contraction of an infinite consciousness was able to make a place for chance, in other words, the universe. The human being at motion in a world engendered this way by a contraction of the divine consciousness has no other hope of witnessing an end to his damnation except by making his awareness equal to the one that created him, in such a way that he can endeavor through his thought and speech to deny chance and force the universe to vanish into the absolute.

But this influence may have been operated the other way round, as Gershom Scholem, noting that Louria repeats some of Basilides's remarks word for word, insists on the gnostic and neo-Platonic nature of kabbalistic and prekabbalistic writings. But I need to stress that the original path marked out by gnosticism presents, from the surrealist point of view, an interest of an entirely different order, as strongly emphasized by Seligmann in his book on magic: "'The fundamental difference between Gnosticism and Catholicism is their opposing 'concept of *guilt*,'" because while "the Church accepted original sin and professed that the only possible salvation lay in conciliating the offended father," "there were many Gnostic sects who did not admit their own culpability, justifying Adam's deed as being caused by God's injustice."

In his brilliant study on surrealism and atheism, Guy Ducornet quotes these phrases from Breton's interviews edited in *Conversations:*

> The "primacy of matter over mind" even today [1952], I say that such a principle can't claim to be considered as an "article of faith."

It presupposes a dualism that even then I could only accept for the needs of a cause whose main objective—the social transformation of the world—had to be achieved whatever the cost.... Personally, no matter how fiercely I had tried to force myself to stick to it; I could not hew to this line for long.

Ducornet then follows this with a footnote:

Once we start talking about "dualism" we immediately think about all the *gnostic* heresies born during the first centuries of Christianity (or long before that in Upper Egypt) that have left traces in Western culture and psychology from the Middle Ages to Romanticism. Close to both Platonism and Manichaeism, Gnosticism suggests that our world emerged from an ineffable "god" and that matter, which came later, is the principle of evil. It is this dualism we find in the Cathar heresy. . . . André Breton was interested in the discovery of Copt papyrus manuscripts* in Egypt in 1949, which established that gnosis was not necessarily a Christian heresy but perhaps an *autonomous* religion that predated Christianity: "Such a discovery would open up an entirely new vista to the mind, one of unprecedented scope. It is a well-known fact that the esoteric tradition originated with the Gnostics."[11]

Moreover, as Kurt Seligmann says, their myths most often depict the God of Genesis as an evil god.

These people asserted that the creator of the material world was only the imperfect workman of an imperfect world. It was the God of the Old Testament, the Jealous God that had set the Jewish people against Christ.

But we also see, as Jean Doresse reminds us concerning these manuscripts, that "what our Gnostic documents show us is the spiritual

---

*These are the famous manuscripts of Nag Hammadi, sometimes called the Khénoboskion manuscripts (in English, Chenoboskion).

attitude of those who were the most tragically sensitive to the problems of human destiny: Where have I come from? What am I? What is the material world? Where will I go after this life?" which cannot help but arouse echoes, or bring back to mind the notorious idea that "true life is elsewhere," an idea that Unica Zürn illustrated in her own way when saying (about herself), "What she paints is an animal that she has never seen but is certain exists somewhere!"

The gnostic was one of the first to raise the question about why there were several religions and not just one, Sarane Alexandrian explains.

> The Gnostic uses gnosis like a filter to sift through religions and philosophies in order to keep only what he deems best; he forges for himself an intellectual, skillfully crafted religion in the place of a revealed religion whose implausible aspects are justified by collective hallucinations, trances, and visions.[12]

This kind of approach, in passing, would be that of the first Freemasons some centuries later. On the other hand, Jules Monnerot likens "the surrealists to the founders of certain lost cosmologies like Basilides or Valentinus, heresiarchs and leaders of Gnostic schools of the second century" a proximity he explains this way: "The Alexandrian Era and our own are syncretic times. Gnosticism and surrealism are the typical products of this kind of era." Lindenberg explains it like this:

> If life is elsewhere, it is legitimate to think of Valentinus, Thomas, and Carpocrates, who, during the great "Alexandrian" confusion of the Late Empire, were only saying the same thing in their own way. Breton is one of the great "pneumatics" of our time. He seeks to free the mind from its prison.

A "great pneumatic," adds Sarane Alexandrian, is one of those individuals "who can discern true from false by gnosis, and whose *pneuma* (mind or spirit, which is not the same thing as soul or psyche according to the Valentinians) remains continuously incorruptible and immortal, no matter what he or she does."[13] What is strange, to the extent it involves what Doresse calls a "superterrestrial knowledge," is that Breton was extremely conversant with gnostic thought, as shown by this extract from "On Magic Art" (in *Perspective Cavalière*):

> But what I retain most strongly from the thought of Valentinus is the part it gives that sacred terror that takes possession of the artist in the presence of his work created "in the name of God," in other words of an unknown higher principle.

There is also this passage in Breton's 1955 article titled "The Sword in the Clouds," which he wrote about Jean Degottex and his work, which he called akin to "the Zen works of the twelfth century," where he states straightforwardly:

> Indeed, esoteric tradition warns us that standing at the very threshold of this world (*the real world, not the one that is foisted upon us as real*) is the human-headed bull brandishing the Flaming Sword, whose mission it is to separate from the vulgar throng those few fit to enter it (italics added).

I am tempted to describe this as apocalyptic, as a number of apocalypses are gnostic at heart.

Even Simone de Beauvoir, in *Le Deuxième Sexe* (The Second Sex), does not fail to note these singular proximities:

> One finds in Breton the same esoteric naturalism as in the Gnostics who saw in Sophia the principle of redemption as in Dante choosing Beatrice for a guide or Petrarch illuminated by Laura's love.[14]

Jean-Louis Bédouin, meanwhile, rightly reminds us that Breton, when concluding his text "On Surrealism in Its Living Works" (*Médium,* n° 4) and "speaking of the relationship between the mind and the sensorial world ... expressly refers to the doctrine of the Gnostics," as shown by the following extract:

This poetic intuition, finally unleashed by surrealism, seeks not only to assimilate all known forms but also boldly to create new forms—that is to be in a position to embrace all the structures of the world, manifested or not. It alone provides the thread that can put us back on the road of gnosis as knowledge of suprasensible Reality, "invisibly visible in an eternal mystery."

A number of Breton's friends and others who were close to him were in the same position. They shared the same opinions, starting with Toyen, for example, about whom Breton writes in *Surrealism and Painting,* while citing Rorschach, "We are once again treading the ancient gnostic paths of introversion." It seems there was a precursor in 1924 (although the text was not published until 1957) in the person of Roger Gilbert-Lecomte, for whom Breton never hid his admiration. In the third part of his premonitory poem "Mystic Tetanus," the poet quite logically evokes Nicolaitism, that branch of Barbelo-gnosticism whose adepts Clement of Alexandria said "wallow in voluptuous pleasure like billy-goats and plunge their souls into the mud, 'seeking' to exhaust evil by committing it."[15]

> *But to slay the senses I lean*
> *Toward a Nicolaite faith*
> *Heretic and seven time cursed . . .*
> *Instead of a sterile asceticism*
> *I believe that the body destroys itself*
> *Just as well with the poison of vices.*

There is nothing surprising in the fact that this tortured soul, who sought to reach "revelation" through "revolution," would denounce, as Alain and Odette Virmaux say, "the present abject state of the worlds" or the imprisonment of man within his flesh, "that reeking goat hide," from which he invites us to escape through "the initiatory path" and "the law of the Future of the Mind."[16]

This can be crowned with these lines by André Rolland de Renéville, written in 1938:

When the poet approaches Absolute Consciousness in a state of inspiration, either through the destruction of what we call awareness or conversely by its indeterminate expansion, he knows that his mind is only a particle of spiritual fire from which worlds emerge, that he is this fire.

In 1925, Ribemont-Dessaignes (who was friends with the Grand Jeu members) consciously or unconsciously allowed similar concerns to show through. "We could read *Ariadne* based on the later stories of Georges Ribemont-Dessaignes," Jean Roudaut says, "and hear the echo of Gnostic tales in which the imprisoned soul bumps into the bars of his prison."[17] We also have the example of Artaud, who writes in his second "letter on cruelty" to Jean Paulhan:

I employ the word "cruelty" in the sense of an appetite for life, a cosmic rigor and implacable necessity, in the gnostic sense of a living whirlwind that devours the darkness, in the sense of that pain apart from whose ineluctable necessity life could not continue; good is desired, it is the consequence of an act; evil is permanent. When the hidden god creates, he obeys the cruel necessity of creation, which has been imposed on himself by himself, and he cannot *not* create, hence, not admit into the center of the self-willed whirlwind of good a kernel of evil ever more condensed and ever more consumed.

We also know that the idea of the Acéphale, or "headless man," dear to Bataille and illustrated by Masson, finds its origin, as Michel Camus reminds us, in Bataille's discovery in the Cabinet des médailles (coin and antiquity collection) of the National Library, where he had worked since 1924, "of a third- or fourth-century Gnostic intaglio depicting a headless god of Egyptian origin."

It is hard to know, as he never talked about his work, if Yves Tanguy was influenced by gnostic ideas, and surrealist works always resist full analysis for the simple reason they cannot be reduced to rational analysis as they are created outside the categories of reason. But the fact that Carl Jung, who owned Tanguy's 1929 painting *Noyer indifferent,* was inspired to offer a very personal interpretation shows that he found sufficient evidence there.

> The four* together form an unfolded totality symbol, the self in its empirical aspect. The name of one of the Gnostic deities is Barbelo, "God is four." According to an early Christian idea, the unity of the incarnate God rests on the "four," that is to say the pillars of the Evangelists (representing the 3 + 1 structure) just as the Gnostic *monogenes* (*unigenitus,* Only Begotten) stands on the Trapeza (that is to say the trapezium; Trapeza = four-footed table). Christ is the head of the Ecclesia (the Community). As a God, he is the unity of the Trinity, and as the historical Son of Man and anthropos he is the example, the prototype of the individual inner man and at the same time the culmination, goal, and totality of the empirical man. Thus it happens that apparently by chance this picture would figure a hierosgamos taking place in the heavens (sexual cohabitation), followed on earth by the birth of a savior and an epiphany (the expansion of the Self).[18]

"Barbelo the leech," says the Pistis Sophia, the sacred book of the Egyptian Gnostics,[19] or as Alexandrian says, "the First Feminine Power engendered by God." In *The Passive Vampire,* Ghérasim Luca maintains (or cites, for there are quotation marks, but no source) opinions that although associated with Satan have undeniable, shall we say, Valentinian connotations.

> "And the Flesh was made Word. For it has been said that we will be saved by the flesh: we must march naked in life and annihilate Evil by Evil by frenziedly abandoning ourselves to it."

His friend Jacques Hérold, according to Patrick Waldberg, also seems to have borne the stamp of gnostic thought—perhaps unknowingly. Whatever the case may be, Hérold dedicated a drawing

---

*In the painting, four embryonic shapes stand out against a black background.

to Malcolm de Chazal, "the detached loner," on December 15, 1947. Waldberg muses:

> Last summer, while wondering about the meaning of Hérold's work with this article in mind, I thought I had found the key thanks to reading a book that, at first glance, did not seem to have anything at all in common with the subject. It was the second volume of *Les Livres secrets des gnostiques d'Égypte,* which their exegete, Jean Doresse, had recently given me. It appeared clear to me that Hérold, through his behavior in life as in his work, was crafting—unknowingly and by himself—a "gnosis" of gratuitous nature, with no connection whatsoever to salvation. This immediate self-knowledge and grasp of true reality above appearances was a quest he had been stubbornly pursuing since youth. . . . Hérold, this trapper of the moon, is also the man who obeys with the utmost good fortune the deeply moving Gnostic command, deciphered on one of the Nag Hammadi manuscripts: "Be passing."[20]*

Hérold was called "l'or de l'air neuf" (fresh air gold), according to Duchamp, and this "different surrealist," according to Michel Butor, and Pierre Mabille wrote about him in *Les Cahiers d'art* in April 1945,

---

*Historian and archaeologist Jean Doresse, who was able to consult the original documents (i.e., the Chenoboskion manuscripts), notes in his introduction, "Today it is this genesis and religious impetus of gnosis that the library of Chenoboskion suddenly reveals to us with a wealth of detail that far surpasses what historians could have ordinarily hoped or wished for." He goes on to say, "I do not believe the value of a find as rich as that of Chenoboskion in texts that until now were utterly lost (rare were any that even came remotely close to their importance) can be erased or even reduced with respect to the opinion we have of them today. I am even convinced that when these texts are completely and directly known, their religious, historical, and literary value will only grow; that it will be ceaselessly necessary to refer to them and to seek out new revelations from them." He also stresses that among the texts found at Nag Hammadi are manuscripts that fall, strictly speaking, under that category of hermeticism defined as gnosis. Vincent Bounoure also cites this work in his text "Tel Père, tel fils" (in *Les Anneaux de Maldoror et autres chapitres d'un traité des contraires*). As for the "Be Passing" in question, this is from Logion 42 of the Gospel of Thomas, discovered in Nag Hammadi in 1945.

saying, "Once again, free inspiration has put the author in accord with the high science." In 1982, Pierre Demarne noted:

> His quest is the slow transformation of an entirely personal writing, intended to express potent, profound poetic realities, always situated at the boundaries of metaphysical interrogation as often indicated by the titles of his works.[21]

It is in Brauner's "often inaccessible . . . multiple women . . . symbolizing the great mystery of life and death" that Margaret Montagne divines the influence exerted by gnostic thought on the Romanian painter's work. She writes, "They are Sophia and Barbelo, intermediaries between the worlds, who thought by means of the sex act they could restore to humanity a particle of the original light."

She also noted, "In the same way, Brauner used a Gnostic style of drawing with seven planets . . . in *Solivan*" in 1946.

In the third issue of *Médium,* Gérard Legrand goes so far as to develop a hypothesis that seems quite audacious at first glance but that on reflection deserves serious consideration. But judge for yourself! While acknowledging there is little likelihood he could have been familiar with contemporary research on gnosticism, Legrand indicates in his article "Fragment of a Letter to the Count" obvious convergences between the thought of the gnostics and that of Comte de Lautreamont (who Legrand suggests may have inherited it by way of Dante and Milton) and that of the surrealists themselves. He writes:

> In the deserts of Syria and on the banks of the Nile, lived, some twenty centuries ago, men whose thought moved in a way that presents such striking affinities with our own that several of us, completely alien as we may be to the specialist studies required in cases like this, took an interest in them.

Suggesting that Christianity could not have prospered but for them, like "mistletoe on the apple tree," meaning, if I grasp his meaning correctly, Christianity would be some kind of parasite, he adds:

All the Gnostic sects are in agreement with you, Count, in making the "Creator" an essentially evil being, on the principle of initial contradiction that is reminiscent of Böhme's *God versus God*. This demiurge makes necessary a mythic mediator between the Pleroma (Valentinus)—the Universality of post-Platonic ideas—and the Wisdom lost amidst men: what it does not make necessary, in contrary, is a religion.

It is even possible to find traces of gnostic thought in Raymond Queneau's work, according to Sarane Alexandrian in *Le Surréalisme et le rêve* (Surrealism and Dream). Observing that the novels of this "writer imbued with the Pythagorian metaphysics of number" generally have a ternary structure, he suggests the reason for this can be found in gnosis, "which teaches that there are three principles of the Whole: the Darkness, the Pneuma, and the Light." And he provides a truly unsettling example, although with the author of *Zazie in the Metro*, you always have to take his sense of play into account. Alexandrian notes, "Queneau gives a wink to the informed readers when in *Les Temps mêles* [Tangled Times] he gives his prophetic couple the names of Simon and Helen. (Christ's rival, the Gnostic Simon Magus, identified his wife Helen as 'God's first thought.') Simon would tell everyone: 'May the light be with you.'" Alexandrian concludes, "By putting the number 3 into play, Queneau strives to show that he wants 'more light.'" Like Goethe on his deathbed asking for "Mehr Licht!"[22]

In 1948, this novel would be integrated along with *Gueule de Pierre* (Gob of Stone; 1934) into a larger set, *Saint Glinglin*, which would be in seven parts this time; as Alexandrian points out, "7, [is] the number of perfection." It is also, incidentally, the number of the Master among Freemasons.

In March 1984, Alain Calame also noted, with many details, this gnostic saturation and observed that this book's "opacity with which we are confronted perhaps did not exist to the same degree for its first readers . . . informed readers" like "H. C. Puech,* or Georges Bataille

---

*H. C. Puech, who notably worked with Jean Doresse on the Nag Hammadi manuscripts, is a recognized expert on gnosticism.

would have had no trouble identifying an avatar of the god Bes in Baby Toutout, or seeing the Great Mother, Isis, Hecate, Medusa, Typhon, or the 'Acéphale' in Mother Cloche (bell, dome, or cover)."[23] Xavier Bordes, in his preface to *Axion Esti*, vigorously maintains that the poet's "course (another individual heavily influenced by number) is incontestably linked to Gnostic concepts," before going on to say that Elytis, whose thought is closely tied to the East because of his very identity as a Greek, "is a mystic poet developing the incarnation of the Logos as the highest task to which a human being can devote himself." He also reminds us of the recurring gnostic theme of the "micro/macrocosm" appearing in this poet's work: the temple, "working drawing of heavens" that can be reached by the "seven stairs of the Genesis," is, according to the translator, "as much a summary of the macrocosm, 'the unfathomable world' as it is of the microcosm, 'the minimal world.'"

In his book *Mémoire Destituée, Mémoire sans Voisinage*, published after his death in 1976, the painter—and poet—Iaroslav Serpan (founder with Claude Tarnaud and Yves Bonnefoy of the magazine *La Révolution la nuit* in 1946) hurled the following maxim:

> REANIMATE RIGHT HERE
> THE FLAME OF MEMORY
> THE ONE THAT MARKS WITH IRON
> THE NUMBER OF THE BOGOMILS
> (ADAMITES, CATHARS, AND WALDENSIANS
>   INCLUDED)

The same Claude Tarnaud, who lived in the United States for quite some time, criticized in *From (the End of the World)* in terms as surprising as they are scathing this country

> where the official philosophy of the regime aims at protecting the populace against the influence of the Gnostic International whose members from Apollonius of Thyana [*sic*] to the surrealists, by way of the alchemists, German Romantics, Engels, and so forth held the goal

of tearing the individual apart by proposing him in this very world hopes and dreams that are obviously unrealizable and will ever be so / and above all don't see any contradiction therein because although the average American can obtain the complete works of most of the aforementioned Gnostics for a mouthful of enriched bread, he has been vaccinated against their miasms since kindergarten and grade school.[24]

So it is quite logical that the American surrealists of the Chicago group founded and led by Franklin and Penelope Rosemont, in an entirely justified backlash, stated in one text from *The Forecast Is Hot,* the 1977 anthology of their collective tracts and declarations:

> Here as elsewhere, surrealists continue to demand an open-ended and dialectical approach.[25] Our resolute antagonism to the prevailing religious powers has never diminished our sympathetic interests in a wide range of hermetic and gnostic heresies and heterodoxies, or for the mythologies created by the tribal peoples of Polynesia, Melanesia, Africa, and the Americas.[26]

We can see this interest in dualist thought was widely shared throughout the movement, which can seem surprising when we recall the insistence with which they asserted their monist attitude during surrealism's early years. In any case, the surrealists' interest in the gnostics did not dry up with the death of Breton, as shown by José Pierre in his book *La Fontaine close* (published by éditions de l'Instant in 1988), which reveals the hypothetical "secret books" of the Aletheians, an "unknown Gnostic sect" with a very short existence—about thirty years—that was composed solely of women nicknamed the Black Sheep in Alexandria, the Bitches in Antioch, and the Castrators in Rome, but this enthusiast of refined eroticism and practical jokes, despite appearances, clearly appears to be the only person to have noted their existence.[27] It is true that in the scrubland of gnostic sects, it is quite hard to avoid getting lost . . .

The repeated mention of Alexandria, "the privileged site for meetings between intellectuals from different countries and asylum for Jewish refugees of the Diaspora as well as one of the centers of Christianity," according to Jean Markale, and "the most prolific intellectual center, the place where East and West clasped hands," in the words of Kurt Seligmann, cannot help but bring to mind the extraordinary books by Charles Duits, *Nefer* and *Ptah Hotep*.[28] These books are novels of formation (Bildungsroman) in the oriental style in the manner of Beckford and an initiatory Uchronia of a somewhat gnostic nature, crazy texts that Duits himself defined as automatic, "but more in the sense that spiritualists give the term than the surrealist sense." They were engendered by a vision the author experienced in 1968, but fed on "his readings of *The Thousand and One Nights, The Illiad, The Ramayama, The Knights of the Round Table*," and many other things, including the Bible. "Apparently the entity that chose to express itself through me had a medieval notion of writing," he said in the preface to *Nefer*, adding later, "As I share the opinion of the Easterners concerning metempsychosis, I am rather inclined to believe these are the memories from one or more previous lives that make up the substance of *Ptah Hotep* and *Nefer*."[29] In the September 6, 1971, issue of *L'Express*, Matthieu Galey wrote, "Under the appearance of a sword and armor serial, with battles and adventures beyond count, *Ptah Hotep* is a kind of Grail quest in which women play the role of intercessors," an "extravagant monument that could be described as the work of a literary Facteur Cheval." Duits himself described it this way:

> *Ptah Hotep* addresses those people primarily who aspire to free themselves from the hideous illusions inside which humanity is struggling: it is an initiatory text, a radical challenge to the notion that the philosophical and scientific orthodoxy of our time have of reality, and consequently to the arid, sinisterly polar, and pompously false language our orthodoxy uses to express itself.

Duits also borrowed the only surviving words of a gnostic hymn (words he cites on many occasions) for the title of his collection of poems *Fruit sortant de l'Abîme* (Fruit Emerging from the Abyss).[30] In the same letter to Vincent Bounoure that I cited in chapter 7 he develops his various intuitions as follows:

> I found myself quite quickly in the grip of a phenomenon analogous to the one Breton describes in the *First Manifesto*. An unknown hand "was knocking at the window." This hand was brown, exquisitely shaped, and attached by a superb arm to an entity that manifested in the World of Representations under the name Isis, the Supreme Negress, the Sole Woman Who Is Truly Black. It was the muse in the marvelous meaning of the word. She could not be mistaken for a simple rhetorical expression. She revealed herself beneath changing features without losing her identity. Those of the Egyptian goddess, those of Bilquis, the Queen of Sheba, those of Prounicos, the mystic hypostasis of wisdom and lust, those of Sophia, the African with Teeth of Light, who dictated a text to me that was amazing both for its content and its form.[31]

This makes everything quite clear: Isis, the Supreme Negress, who is also Prounicos the Lascivious (some sects also give this name to Barbelo); the Sophia of Down Below, who is also called Pistis, the mother of the celestial powers for the Nicolaites and the Valentinians, the African with Teeth of Light seems like a female reflection of Osiris, the "black god," but also attests, in all her various avatars, to the exceptional importance of the role played by woman for the gnostics. It is curious to note that Jean Markale (in *The Great Goddess, Myths and Sanctuaries*) compares in remarkably similar terms "the Pistis Sophia who will reappear in all the speculations at the beginning of the Christian Era" to the "Wisdom praised in song by Solomon," to "Divine Wisdom, feminine face of an indifferentiated and asexual Creator," and "this Wisdom [that] is not only knowledge [but] also beauty, harmony, fertility, and without [whom] nothing could exist, for the reason life assumes a birth out of the increate by a kind of cosmic scale parturition," which is strikingly reminiscent of the kabbalists' Shechina, mentioned in chapter 8.[32]

Whatever the case may be, this gnostic aspect of the reflection of the

principal organizer of the group personally, as well as that of his friends, whom Sarane Alexandrian would describe as "undeniably representatives of modern gnosis, advocating salvation through dream,"[33] is nicely summed up by David Lindenberg when he says, "Breton's anchorage in *The Time of the Prophets* dear to Paul Bénichou is not a subject of doubt to informed observers," before concluding, "There is therefore a desire for the head of the surrealist group, as for Guénon, to pick up the threads of a forgotten and distorted tradition in order to re-enchant the world."

"For Monnerot,[*] the surrealists are to the Revolution what the Gnostics were for the emerging Christianity," we are told by the extremely erudite Philippe Audoin, author of some fairly profound surveys on these questions.[34] He goes on to say, "We could just as easily orient a parallel toward the late eighteenth-century Illuminists." At the heart of these currents is, for example, Breton's tutelary figure Charles Fourier, who can be considered as the representative of a democratic, egalitarian, and fraternal branch of illuminism (when he began publishing his works after numerous sojourns in Lyon, where Willermoz's influence is generally recognized) that would evolve toward a mystic socialism "in the name of the communion of individuals in a unified world," as Gérard Gengembre[†] writes.[35] Adrien Dax wrote about this same Fourier in 1963 (*La Brèche*, n° 4):

> This is how we can bring up advisedly, concerning Fourier's sources, the influence of Pythagorism and Swedenborg, as well as that of Louis-Claude de Saint-Martin, without thereby coming up with the key to his incontestable creative originality.

---

[*]As for Monnerot, he specifically wrote in *La Poésie moderne et le sacré*, "The surrealists are to the revolutionaries somewhat like the Gnostics were to Christianity, and are to Western culture somewhat like the Gnostics were to Hellenism, Greek philosophy in particular."
[†]It is striking and significant to see in this regard how in 1949 the surrealists Marcel Jean and Arpad Mézei relied on the texts of the symbolist poet and esotericist Stanislas de Guaita to discuss the relationship between Fourier and his disciple Victor Considérant with occultism!

12
SURREALISM AND TRADITION

Occult Sources, Histories of Orders and Churches

Nennen wir die heiligen Dichter auch Seher. (The sacred bards are also called seers.)
ACHIM VON ARNIM

We can see that symbolic powers, occult powers, and poetic powers emerge from the same source, the same depths.
GASTON BACHELARD, PREFACE TO *VICTOR-ÉMILE MICHELET, POÈTE ÉSOTÉRIQUE* BY RICHARD KNOWLES

Pierre Dhainaut notes:

> We label these faculties possessed by the Ancients and cultivated in the Orient as dark, primitive, and inferior. We happily hound and attack those who, despite the scandal it causes, assert they have not vanished, Swedenborg and William Blake and Victor Hugo,

madmen or at best imbeciles. As it happens these abilities are precisely the ones we most need.[1]

This confirms Breton's intuitive grasp of these thinkers, as presented in his first Haitian lecture. In fact, this esoteric philosophy, according to the author of *Nadja,* irrigates all the works of the great nineteenth-century seers and gives them meaning. In this, he shares the ideas developed by August Viatte, author of *Les Sources occultes du romantisme* (The Occult Sources of Romanticism),[2] and Denis Saurat, another author influenced by Gurdjieff and who can sometimes be difficult to follow, in his *Literature and Occult Tradition*. Breton writes:

> Enough flimflam. It is desperately urgent to bring man back to a higher level of awareness of his destiny. The great poets, in touch—though they often had no inkling of this—with the *unknown superiors* (in the extended meaning of the word), some of whose names I merely mention here, have continually proclaimed this for the past hundred years.[3]

Breton then cites their names:

> For my part, this quickly convinces me that those poets whose ascendency we experience today, almost to the exclusion of all others, are those who were most affected by esoteric thought. In France they would be Hugo, Nerval, Baudelaire, Rimbaud, Lautréamont, Jarry, Apollinaire.[4]

He goes on to suggest, "Everything falls out as if high poetry and what is called the 'high science' mark a parallel progression and assist each other."[5]

This echoes an observation Canseliet makes in his preface to René Alleau's *Aspects of Traditional Alchemy* concerning Rimbaud's sonnet "Vowels," despite a fairly vexing and incongruous—but quite understandable on his part—allusion to the divine:

When the young poet was able to follow the colored harmony of the prism, when he almost surely knew nothing about the physical elaboration of the focus, what divine illumination let him select the three main colors of the Great Coction to wit, the *black,* the *white,* and the *red;* the green of the *vitriol,* and the blue of the mercury?

We cannot fail to include Jean Brisset in this prestigious Aeropagus. A place was found for Brisset (derisively elected "prince of thinkers" in 1912) by Breton in his *Anthology of Black Humor,* and Schuster admitted (in *Les Fruits de la passion*) to being tempted to "compare his approach . . . to the incursions of hermetic tradition into the realm of language, through the phonetic kabbalah or the language of the birds," adding that" in other eras, his message would have fit into the Western theosophical—and heretical—current that flows from Joachim de Fiore [*sic*] to Swedenborg by way of Jacob Böhme, whose concern was discovering the truth of man's origins that remains sealed within the sacred scriptures.

Thus, notes Breton in "Before the Curtain":

The great movements of sensibility by which we are still affected, the emotional charter by which we are governed, seem to originate, whether we like it or not, in a tradition entirely different from the one that is taught: that tradition has been kept buried under the most disgraceful, the most vindictive silence.

In his *History of Occult Philosophy,* Alexandrian writes:

All the great occult philosophers were, in one way or another, the successors of the Gnostics, without necessarily making use of their vocabulary and themes. . . . The courses taught by Cornelius Agrippa at the University of Pavia in 1515 revolved entirely around the *Poimander* of Hermes Tresmegistus; Jacob Böhme, Louis-Claude de Saint-Martin, introduced the worship of Sophia into their respective systems; Eliphas Levi picked up anew the idea of the soul's cosmic journey after death from planet to planet toward the divine Absolute; Stanislas de Guaita, although primarily interested in the kabbalah, wrote to Peladan: "'The science' is only one half of wisdom; faith is its other half. But *gnosis* is wisdom itself as it stems from both."[6]

This tops off Breton's remarks, listing the names of the most recent "unknown superiors" he makes the vectors of the tradition: "Martinès, Saint-Martin, Fabre d'Olivet, l'Abbé Constant," and later Saint-Yves d'Alveydre. Jacques Rivière, in his article "The Crisis of the Concept of Literature," published in *NRF* in 1924, tangibly echoes this when he states, "All nineteenth-century literature is a vast incantation toward the miracle," to which Michel Carrouges adds, "Yes, that is definitely the essence of modern literature. No one can make a valid judgment of it if they do not understand that it is primarily the adventure of a magical-mystical movement that competes with religion."[7] Concerning the poetry, literature, and music of his time, the "spiritualist Édouard Schuré" (a "suspect 'thinker'" in Breton's opinion) in the beginning of his essay "Les Grands Initiés" (1889, with ninety-one printings by 1926!) notes:

> An immense draught of unconscious esotericism goes through them. Never before has the aspiration to a spiritual life and the invisible world, repressed by the materialist theories of the scientists and worldly opinion, been more serious or more real. We find this aspiration in the doubts, regrets, black melancholies, and even in the blasphemies of our naturalist novelists and decadent poets. Never has the human soul held a more profound sense of the insufficiency, wretchedness, and insubstantiality of its present life, never before has it so ardently yearned for the invisible beyond, without managing to believe in it. Sometimes even intuition manages to formulate transcendent truths that share no part of the system accepted by reason, contradict the individual's surface opinions and are unintentional flashes of his occult consciousness.[8]*

---

*Kandinsky was quite close to Schuré, who was first a member of Annie Besant's Theosophical Society, then a member of Rudolph Steiner's Anthroposophical Society.

This phenomenon, however, did not only affect metropolitan France, as Nora Mitrani* notes with respect to Portuguese author Fernando Pessoa, who was linked to Crowley but also strongly influenced by Martinism; "Pessoa knew the sources and snares of the occult awareness of things: implicit in his work is the symbol of the Rosicrucians," though not only implicitly as he also wrote three sonnets *about the Grave of Christian Rosenkreutz*.[9] This was also noted by Mabille about a somewhat earlier author dear to his heart, and who Breton, judging on his remarks about Blake in *L'Art magique,* seems to have valued less as an engraver than as a poet and watercolorist. Breton had surely read Marie Louise and Philippe Soupault's translation of *Songs of Innocence and Experience.* Blake also mentions Paracelsus and Böhme and seems heavily influenced by the kabbalah:

> This composite mysticism, whose stable centers are the primacy given clairvoyance and the exaltation of an imaginal realm independent of tangible reality, can be found in the Pre-Raphaelite ambiance and various theosophical movements in England. In France we find

---

*Nora Mitrani (who died of cancer in 1961 at the age of forty) was a young Holocaust survivor who was drawn to Catholicism before becoming a surrealist. She seems to have been the love of Julien Gracq's life, after having been partner to Hans Bellmer. She ended her days at the Goetheanum in Dornach near Basel, in the hope that the spiritualist medicine of Steiner's disciples would provide relief of her suffering. Without going into too much detail about theosophical groups and sects, it will be helpful to say a few words about Rudolf Steiner (1861–1925), whose thought interested several figures in surrealism or the avant-garde, like Mondrian, for example, or his friend Kandinsky, who was also influenced by the thought of Jacob Böhme, and we know that Hans Arp also stayed at Dornach. Aside from Goethe's teaching, whose scientific works he published, and the idea that self knowledge and knowledge of the universe were inseparable, Steiner, author of an essay on the *Chemical Wedding* and of a *Rosicrucian Theosophy,* was first a member of Helena Blavatsky's Theosophical Society, then that of Annie Besant. He founded the Anthroposophical Society, then the Free University (called the Free University of Spiritual Science after 1922) around the Johannesbau, the first Goetheanum, where it seems Masonic ceremonies were held that were organized around a variant of the Rite of Memphis-Misraïm. In contrast to the tenets of Blavatsky's Theosophy, he sought to reconcile—as prompted by his own intellectual course—science and tradition. It appears that his objective was the moral and material betterment—mainly through "anthroposophical therapy"—of humanity.

similar attitudes in Blake's contemporary Claude de Saint-Martin [*sic*], Saint-Yves d'Alveydre, in the more or less occult sects that multiplied during the nineteenth century from which the romantics drew so much of their inspiration.[10]

It so happens that this same Blake, whom Roger Gilbert-Lecomte writes (in the first issue of *Le Grand Jeu*) "has seen the last of the gods in the primordial night, the Mad Creators, who exhale the worlds," and who André Rolland de Renéville (in *L'Experience poetique*) deemed "had achieved a state whose modes escape us, and set the task of lifting us there." Jean-Jacques Mayoux, meanwhile, tells us:

> Like the great Romantics, he was closer to the edge, open to a world of forgotten mysteries and revelations, heir to an obscure, occult tradition the West has scorned right into the present. He, conversely, did not believe in science . . . but constantly relied on this great occultist tradition that links the microscosm man to the cosmos through a system of meaningful relations.[11]

To clarify things yet further, he adds:

> No one has been more instinctively close to the Gnostics, or a quasi Gnostic like Jacob Böhme, and to the vision that identifies the fall with creation and places its responsibility on God or a demiurge that calls himself God, and who by "creating" the world only destroyed the total and perfect integrity of the increate.

This is confirmed by Duits in *The Demonic Consciousness,* which also furnishes a very interesting clarification.[12] "The poet, says Blake, is "on the side of the Devil" (the real Devil of course, "verus Luciferus" according to the Gnostics, who rescues man from the claws of the Archonte)." In passing, Bataille notes in *La Littérature et le mal* (Literature and Evil), "It astounds me that the kinship of Blake and surrealism appears so rarely and so indistinctly."[13]

This is all the more noticeable, if I may say so, as the Englishman has an incontestable libertarian streak that peers out of remarks such as this one, quoted in the fourth issue of *La Brèche:*

> *Prisons are built with stones of Law,*
> *Brothels with bricks of Religion.*

Théophile Gautier, in his *Portraits et souvenirs littéraires* (Literary Portraits and Souvenirs), noted with regard to his friend Gérard de Nerval, whom he claimed was extremely conversant with the writings of Hermes Tresmegistus:

> A preoccupation with the invisible world and cosmogonic myths prompted him to spend some time in the circle of Swedenborg, of Abbe Terrasson (author in 1731 of *Séthos,* which examines the Egyptian Mysteries—N. de A.), and of the author of the *Comte de Gabalis.*[14]

"He had read," Gautier goes on to say, "the *Memorabilia* of Swedenborg and understood the mysterious correspondences of dreams," before putting *Aurélia* in its proper perspective by saying:

> The mysteries of the kabbalah are mixed with Platonic reveries; the pictures of the *Poliphilo's Strife of Love in a Dream* with the visions of *Vita Nuova.* Creuzer with his *Symbology* elbows the Count of Gabalis, and the Cazotte of *The Amorous Devil* is holding the pen there.

Pierre Georges Castex, in his book *The Fantasy Tale in France,* reminds us that even Balzac, as shown by his novel *Séraphita,* was influenced by the ideas of the Swedish thinker and initiated, to boot, into Martinist teachings, while Auguste Viatte, in his book *Victor Hugo and the Illuminati of his Time,* clearly shows what Hugo, for example, owes to the extremely political *Freedom's Testament* by Esquiros and Flora Tristan's friend, Eliphas Levi. Catulle Mendès had introduced Levi to Hugo in 1873, and, as noted by Papus, he had a great influence on artists and writers. Breton insists on this at length in his second Haitian lecture, where he forcefully states, "It was on the very findings of l'Abbé Constant that Hugo built the lyrical work in which he wished to leave us his supreme message," which was *The End of Satan*. In order to give ourselves a critical view of the personality of Eliphas Levi, and those of his peers, it is helpful to remember what Peter Partner wrote in his book *The Murdered Magicians*:

> Popular science was, indeed, the milieu into which a great deal of theosophical and occultist activity was developed during the late nineteenth century. Eliphas Levi (Alphonse Louis Constant) and many similar writers pretended that their theories expressed some kind of "natural supernaturalism" which was a true expression of modern "scientific" thought.... There was also a tendency, strongly evident in Constant's books on magics, to merge all the occultist, mystical theories in a single complex source. Templars and Tarot, Masons and kabbalah, all came together in a single magical mishmash. Esoteric Egyptology, Indian religion, occultist versions of medieval chivalrous epics, tales of the prehistory of Stonehenge and of the supposed traditions of the druids and of Atlantis, doctrines of "Johannine" Gnosticism, all began to flow in and out of one another in a crazy tradition of immemorial "wisdom," which also purported to be a form of science.[15]

Alexandrian sums up Levi as "a great Romantic, in his way." This is undoubtedly all true, and the criticism also applies to the surrealists, but wouldn't there be good reason to explore all roads when the one mapped out for you leads to carnage? "These words that seem to have engaged, expanded, and devastated certain lives are valuable as a sign and a signal. Wavering gleams of the crossroad, they indicate dangerous roads going nowhere," Jules Monnerot notes when speaking "of the men who have been *in communication with forbidden grandeurs*."

Breton, in *Constellations*, states the following:

> They are called Gérard, Xavier, Arthur . . . those who knew that with regard to what would have to be achieved, the well-marked

paths, so proud of their signposts and leaving nothing to be desired when it comes to firm footing, lead strictly nowhere.

Breton echoes this point in *Constellations* (in tandem with Joan Miro), and Pierre Mabille clarifies it yet further in one of his texts on Blake.

> Accordingly, Rimbaud was not asking the poet to raise himself above tangible reality in order to deny it, but in order to see the hidden relationships existing between objects, beings, and the natural powers. Wasn't he attempting to place the poetic process outside the descriptive, sentimental, or intellectual literary domain in that forbidden zone that only adepts of the secret High Science claimed traditionally to respect? Wasn't he counting on the tension of the entire being to attain a marvelous that would be, not a distinct realm, but the incredibly expanded reality of the Illumination?[16]

I think this remark can be legitimately compared with what René Daumal advanced in his "Nerval the Night Blinded":

> *The Egyptian Book of the Dead,* the sacred books of India, the *Zohar,* occultism, folklore, and "primitive mentality" contain an extraordinarily extensive and coherent science of the world of dreams (or astral realm), and I find perfect correspondences in these texts for each of Nerval's visions and experiences.

During this time he confirmed and amplified this theme in his "Clavicules d'un grand jeu poétique" (Little Keys to a Great Poetic Game).

> The poetic works themselves always retain a large number of strictly maniacal repetitions, but elevated to the function of magic procedures, powerful formulas for deliverance and communion; the rhythmic returns of number, rhymes, assonances, and images were originally, in the poet inventing them and who knew their necessity, maniacal expressions promoted by consciousness to the role of

charms. Thanks to the imposition of *numbers,* which are modes of unity, the poem is a totality that has no need to repeat itself in order to be the symbol of the universal and the necessary.[17]

And what is there to say about this programmatic statement by Roger Gilbert-Lecomte from his 1929 text "Ce que devrait être la peinture, ce que sera Sima" (What Painting Should Be, What Sima Will Be), which perfectly echoes while anticipating the preceding?

To write the poems of Nerval or Rimbaud, to paint the paintings of Chirico, Masson, or Sima, it is necessary to have lived the great adventure, stabbed the two-bit tangible perceptible decors, realized that forms metamorphose, that the world dissolves during sleep, that hallucination is not different from perception, and a state of health posited as a norm cannot be opposed to other, so-called pathological states![18]

There is an inexplicable oversight in Breton's list: he omits Saint-Pol Roux, this Magnificent whom he admired immensely and regarded as "the sole authentic precursor of the so-called modern movement." He dedicated his collection of poems *Earthlight* to him, and had had Aragon read him (Saint-Pol Roux). Breton wrote to Saint-Pol Roux:

I have long been outraged by certain literary customs and weary of seeing so many men willing to stoop to anything for honors, and as ever, the noble and selfless attitudes—from Baudelaire to you—completely unknown and prey to what can best ruin them.[19]

This same Saint-Pol Roux whom the members of the group and their intimates referred to in much the same way as Breton, was addressed by Rolland de Renéville in a letter in January 1928 on behalf of the Grand Jeu group, to "place at [his] feet their feelings of veneration and respectful love," as well as later by Yves Elléouët, who, recalling the "ideorealist" poet of Marseille's Breton roots, wrote in 1975:

Very far away, the wind has invested the ruins of the home of the Magnificent One. The play of mirrors on the Iroise Sea. The wreckage of the Manoir of Coecilian sits like an unearthed skull, dirt covered and trepanned, facing into the west of mysteries and the dead.[20]

In the letter quoted above, which was published in the first issue of the magazine from the Reims's natives, *Le Grand Jeu,* with the "Master's" response and an extract from his *Litanies of the Sea,* Rolland de Renéville, representing his friends' concerns, clearly explains the reasons for their admiration:

We have carefully studied the lives and words of those we consider to be Great Initiates. We believe that a certain so-called occult science (which is the only science) remains the basis of the philosophies of Plato and Hegel, the revelations of Buddha and Christ, the poems of Rimbaud and Saint-Pol Roux.

It so happens that Saint-Pol Roux, "surrealist in the symbol," was one of the founders of the group of "artist-magicians"[21]* of the (Catholic and) aesthetic Rose Cross, an offshoot of the Rosicrucian Order of the Temple and the Grail (itself a dissident offshoot of Stanislas de Guaita's Kabbalistic Order of the Rose+Cross). Another founder was Roux's friend Sâr Peladan, known as the "Balzac of occultism," all things

---

*To clarify the label of "artist-magicians" stuck to the names of Peladan and some of his friends, we can cite this extract from Peladan's *De L'Androgyne:* "This colossal undertaking of satisfying spiritual needs achieved by priests and artists since societies first appeared on the earth, represents man's supreme entitlement for immortality." How can we not recall here these remarks by Charles Morice, the "brain" of symbolism, asserting that "every true poet is first and foremost an initiate, reading grimoires awakens in him secrets he had always known virtually?" For more on the subject of the androgyne, we also have Gegenbach, who, in 1953, wrote in *Adieu à Satan,* "I anxiously wondered why I had not succeeded in this fleeting attempt to find my female complement, to rebuild the androgynous block!" Later he said, "In *Arcanum 17,* André Breton analyzed quite well this torment of the man who, conscious of having been stripped of his divine (!) prerogatives, seeks in marvelous love (thanks to which he finds She whom he had lost) the means of restoring the androgynous block in its magnificent unity . . . and to resurrect in its eternal life . . . to escape the intolerable limits of Time and Space."

considered, with his [éthopée] of the Latin Decadence series in particular, "as well as the priest of the idea, the Grail Knight, and the envoy of Montsalvaesche." Concerning Peladan, Paul Arnold, in his *History of the Rose Cross and the Origins of Freemasonry*, tells us, "A certain kinship between his teachings and the doctrine of the Rosicrucian manifestos of 1614–1615 cannot be denied." However, Peter Partner labels him "an esoteric writer obsessed by the theme of bisexuality."[22] Androgyny would be closer to the mark; it was a commonplace of this era's literature, in fact, and can be found, for example, in the work of his friend Catulle Mendès, an author greatly influenced by Swedenborg, whose novel *Zo'har* contains several comic and cynical remarks about spiritualism and astrology.[23]

A great admirer of Barbey d'Aurevilly, "Merodack" Peladan—a dandy of the decadence—exerted an influence over Jacques Vaché and the members (who called each other "Sâr") of what is commonly called the Group of Nantes (this is not simply anecdotal). He was the organizer between 1892 and 1897 of the Salon of the Rose+Cross—a kind of international exhibition of symbolism that took place six times—in which brushing elbows were people like Erik Satie, who composed a "March of the Rose+Cross" for him, Emile Bernard, Fernand Khnopff, Charles Filiger, Georges Rouault, and more or less directly Stéphane Mallarmé, Odilon Redon (the "Prince of mysterious dreams and landscape artist of underground water courses"), and Gustave Moreau, the painter "in Carpocrates and Sade's corner" so highly esteemed by Breton (see plate 20). A short remark by the master in person, spoken at the first exhibition in March 1892, can give a fairly accurate notion of the spirit presiding over these undertakings:

> This day, the Ideal has its temple and its knights, and we Maccabees of the Beautiful have carried to Our Lady, at the foot of our Suzerain Jesus, the homage of the temple and the kowtowing of the Rose-Cross (or Rosicrucians).

Born in Lyon, Joseph Péladan, whose family heritage formed a strange blend of "royalism, dissident Catholicism, as well as occultism and a marked concern for sexuality,"[24] and who had incorporated some of the theories advanced by James Frazer in *The Golden Bough,* was a major figure of the literary, artistic, and occultist milieus of the day. This era, "between the last two decades of the nineteenth century and the first decade of the twentieth," was one "that witnessed a readjustment of the religious, but outside of religion," as noted by Jean Clair in his antisurrealist pamphlet.[25] This happened, in the context of *La Crise de l' humanisme* (The Crisis of Humanism), according to Micheline Tison-Braun, who notes that it only left the "uprooted" a choice between living "in a state of rebellion or anarchist or decadent dissidence,"[26] or to use Pierre Mabille's words, "by an opposite movement seeking to rebuild the lost community by reinforcing—at the expense of all freedom—collective values and disciplines," becoming "the militant of a social mysticism," unless it fell back into the context of an ancestral religion."[27] In this sense, Saint-Pol Roux is fairly representative of this end of the century dominated by a symbolism that was the last flames of romanticism, in which "out of hatred or disgust in the face of materialism and a triumphant determinism, people sought—as in other eras—a path through domains like spiritualism theosophy, demonism."[28] This end of the century was "filled with quarrels we find absurd, but which sought answers for the questions that would truly be raised by the massacres and abominations of World War I."[29] This end of the century "appeared like the inexorable pursuit of curious relations between Science and Alchemy, Magic and Reason, Occultism and Progress" in a process of reconciling the opposites dear to the surrealists and which had come to them by way of Huysmans and Marcel Schwob from the esoteric tradition. This period was a time of paradox in which "Victor Hugo was turning tables, Auguste Comte [created] a religion, Blanqui wrote on the Eternity of the Heavenly Bodies."[30] For this century did not truly come to an end until 1914, and it covered the period of Breton's education, which might explain his incontestable penchant for all forms of hermeticism.

Among the major figures evolving in these milieus at this time, which "was more murky than harried," in which "the "fin de siècle" types communicated at one end with the occultists and at the other with the anarchists,"[31] where, "in the depths, behind those who like to adorn themselves in high grades with redundant names, we can sometimes discern the presence of gurus or intellectual guides, or sometimes retiring but extraordinarily perseverant manipulaters,"[32] Doctor Gérard Encausse, alias Papus, "keystone of Belle Epoque occultism,"[33] stands out clearly. Papus was the instigator or inspirer, noted Pascaline Mourier-Casile of the magazine *Le Voile d'Isis,* whose agenda consisted of "carefully studying the infiltration of occult science into contemporary literature and art." In 1908, Papus also organized with his friends (and this provides a good idea of the general atmosphere reigning at this time) a Spiritualist Masonic Convent in Paris (June 7–10). Among the participants (according to the April 1970 issue of *Planète* dedicated to Guénon) was the former prefect of police, Jean Baylot, who was also a Mason of the National Grand Lodge of France and the kingpin of the Lodge of Research Villard de Honnecourt, "the Great Swedenborgian Lodge, with its high grade compartments, the Velleda Lodge, the Rite of Memphis-Misraïm,* with its progenitor the Humanidad Lodge of Spanish origin, the National Spanish Rite, the ancient and original Masonry, and a swarm of groups and smaller groups of occultist, hermetic, alchemical, neo-Templar, and even spiritualist vocation!"

As a cultural bonus, after the works of the Convent, the event ended with a visit to the Tour Saint-Jacques and the Portal of Notre Dame, with personal commentary by the secretary of the Convent himself—René Guénon.

Mason—but only of the Swedenborgian Rite of Primitive and Original Freemasonry, led by the highly controversial John Yarker (1833–1913) (no French obedience had accepted Papus)—member of the Hermetic Brotherhood of Luxor and theosophist, comrade of Joseph Peladan, Stanislas de Guaita, Victor-Émile Michelet, Villiers de L'Isle Adam, Catulle Mendès, Maurice Barrès, and other "Companions of the Hierophany," seeking to "uncover the occult,"[34] Papus had borrowed his name from Apollonius of Tyana's *Nuctemeron*—Apollonius of Tyana, "the white, that recharges the spirituality of the earth with signs made in the graves," according to Antonin Artaud, a seer who was summoned

---

*Papus was once grand master of the Rite of Memphis-Misraïm.

to appear in Apollinaire's *Rotting Enchanter,* while Artaud dedicated *Heliogabalus or the Crowned Anarchist* to him. In 1889, Papus began to organize the Martinist Order, an initiatory Christian order, with Augustin Chaboseau's valuable aid, perhaps following contact with the Russian "heirs" of Tielman von Berend. Papus's organization was founded on the theories of the kabbalistic adept Jacques (or Jaime) Martinès de Pasqually (whose path we crossed in chapter 10), of his disciples Willermoz and Saint-Martin, and before them, of the (wealthy) cobbler of Görlitz (cited by both Breton and Silbermann), Jacob Böhme (1575–1624), the German mystic whose name we find everywhere.[35] Böhme, who was himself influenced by the "Brothers of the Rose-Cross," tried to show the genesis of a perfect being from imperfect individuals, and with his *Mysterium Magnum,* he developed a concept quite close to the Ein Soph of the kabbalists and provided the basic notion for this entire theoretical current: that of Sophia, divine wisdom, and the female principle that in some respects can be compared with Jung's anima. Let us not overlook, of course, Saint-Yves d'Alveydre (1842–1909), whom Papus considered his "intellectual Master."[36] In other words, it is a good idea to note everyone Breton acknowledged for having the merit of passing on the tradition in his text "Before the Curtain."

Guénon was not prevented from nursing a plan for a book to be titled *The Occultist Error,* although he also belonged for a time to this traditional initiatory society, the Martinist Order, as well as its offshoot, the renovated Order of the Temple, of which he was one of the founders following a spiritualist séance in 1908—which involved automatic writing. The same is true of Gustav Meyrink, a member of the Martinist Blue Lodge in Prague and the author of *The Golem* (whose perfect illustrator would have been that other master Alfred Kubin),[37]* *Walpurgis Night,*

---

*In *L'Art magique,* Breton discusses the painter Alfred Kubin, reader of Nerval and Schopenhauer, who, through personality disorders, pursued the quest of "immediate reality" and chose it as a means of attaining unconscious expression. He was part of the Blaue Reiter (Blue Rider) group, and Kandinsky described his painting as follows: "'An irresistible force precipitates us into the horrible atmosphere of the Void,' that is the soulless content of daily life." An extract from his novel *The Other Side* appeared in the first issue of *La Brèche* (October 1961).

and *The Angel of the Western Window* (whose hero is the esoteric scholar John Dee). Ithell Colquhoun was also a member of this Order.

And it seems the same is true about Picasso, if we can trust the word of Marijo Ariëns-Volker, who in her article "Alchemical, Kabbalistic, and Occult Symbolism in the Work of Pablo Picasso and His Contemporaries" (discussed in chapter 4), brings up several disturbing arguments. According to this researcher, Picasso, at the beginning of his stay in Paris, lived with his friend Ricardo Vines, who frequented the Librairie du Merveilleux, the general headquarters of the "independent group of esoteric studies" created by Papus. Among those closest to the painter at this time, we find André Salmon, who makes reference to Papus, the Martinists, and the Masons in several of his texts.

There were also Juan Gris, "an extremely assiduous Mason,"[38] Max Jacob, who considered kabbalah as his "life philosophy" and will be, before being expelled by Breton for impenitent Catholicism, frequently published in *Littérature,* and Guillaume Apollinaire, who often spoke of Hermes Tresmegistus and whose library held many books by Papus and other Martinists, as well as the official journals of the Order and even a document from the 1908 Spiritualist Congress. According to his grandson, Olivier Widmaier, Picasso was extremely well versed in the kabbalah, read the Zohar, and was a spiritualist adept.[39] In his conversations with Brassai, Picasso admitted he had been a "member of an Order during his cubist period," probably the Martinist Order; some of the collages he made at this time even bear signs that Ariëns-Volker analyzes as allusions to the Martinist grade of unknown superior.[40]*

---

*However, this would not correspond, at least initially, to a Martinist grade, as it should read "S. J." and not "S. I.," that is *souverain juge* (sovereign judge) and not *supérieur inconnu* (unknown superior). Breton (with the support of Gaston Gallimard) briefly contemplated creating a surrealist magazine with this title, *Supérieur Inconnu,* something Sarane Alexandrian would manage to pull off in the 1990s. This same Sarane Alexandrian records in his autobiography that Breton's choice of this title prompted the indignation of "those who suspected this implied the renunciation of surrealism's libertarian and egalitarian ideas," particularly of Jean Ferry, who wrote Breton to advise him, "if he wanted a title with Jesuitical odor," in order to remove any ambiguity he should call it "Secret reverend." It should also be noted that Mandiargues often labeled Breton the "grand superior."

Papus (whose "confused mysticism" would be denounced by Gérard Legrand in *Médium* in November 1953) claimed he had received Martinist initiation from the son of a close friend of Saint-Martin, but he also spent time with the "famous" theoretician of modern occultism, the "priest" (and Mason) Alphonse Louis Constant, alias Eliphas Levi* ("Osiris is a black god," Breton writes in *Arcanum 17*!) and was part of Helena Blavatsky and Colonel Henry Steel Olcott's Theosophical Society. He wanted to make the Martinist Order—which was connected with Christian illuminism—a mystical society, "a school of moral chivalry that would strive to develop the spirituality of its members by the study of the invisible world and its laws, through the exercise of devotion and intellectual assistance, and by the creation in each spirit of a faith that would be more solid by being based on observation and science." He adopted as his goal the teaching of the great lines of the Western tradition and "to struggle against the nefarious effect of low materialism and atheism." A co-ed order, it consisted of three grades, the highest of which was that of unknown superior—sometimes rebaptized solitary initiate or sovereign judge. The movement had its own official organ, the monthly *L'Initiation,* which appeared until 1912 and was relaunched in 1953 by Papus's son, Philippe Encausse. It still exists today. It is also helpful to note that Martinism is not so different from Freemasonry, in particular through the Rite of Memphis-Misraïm and, especially, the Rectified Scottish Rite, the blue lodge offshoot of the Order of the Knights Beneficent of the Holy City, which was founded by Willermoz, a disciple of Martinès de Pasqually and friend of Louis-Claude de Saint-Martin, and author of *L'Homme de désir;* it was the same down to the detail that the name of the great architect of the universe is Yeshua.

In order to make things a little clearer, it would help to provide a little information about these rites, in other words, about these Masonic practices. For example, article 1 of the General Rules of the Independent Grand Priory of France, its regulatory authority, stipulates that "the Rectified Scottish Rite fits into a modern Freemasonry that

---

*In his second Haitian lecture, Breton analyzed at length the influence exerted by Eliphas Levi (whose rigor is specifically contested by Colin Wilson for reason of "exacerbated" romanticism) on the work of Victor Hugo.

seeks to preserve the purest tradition," a tradition in which the neotestamentary contribution is clear-cut. The Rite of Memphis-Misraïm was the result of the 1881 union, under Garibaldi's leadership, of the Rite of Misraïm—plural for the word *Egyptian*—which (as we saw in chapter 10) was connected with the prince of San Vero, then, after 1788, with Cagliostro's teaching, and the Rite of Memphis, created in 1815 on the initiative of the former members of the Egyptian mission that had accompanied Bonaparte. These Bonaparte associates, as noted by Robert Ambelain, were often

> masons of the old initiation rites: *Philalethes, African Brothers, Hermetic Rite, Primitive Rite,* not to omit for all the *Grand Orient of France*. Having discovered a surviving Gnostic-hermetic tradition in Cairo, then the same Druse Freemasonry later encountered by Gérard de Nerval in Lebanon . . . the Brothers of the Egyptian Mission subsequently decided to abandon the Masonic line of descent from the *Grand Lodge of London* and start over again with a new Rite* that owed nothing to England, but undoubtedly did owe much to their Eastern discoveries.[41]

Today, Yves Fred Boisset, current senior editor of *L'Initiation*, notes that Martinism is a traditional initiatory society whose members, "Utopians of a world of love and peace," "know how to expand their field of vision to all esoteric teachings, which they study and analyze in a spirit of great tolerance." Furthermore, "they strive for the greatest

---

*The Primitive Rite was organized in Prague in 1759 by the Viscount Chefdebien d'Aigrefeuille. Baron Tschoudy's Hermetic Rite, organized in seven grades, the last two of which were *Perfect Initiate of Egypt* and *Knight of the Sun,* was, as its name indicates, founded on hermeticism and alchemy. The Order of the Philalethes, founded in 1779 by Savalette de Langes, contained alchemical and theurgical practices. For more on the "Druze Masonry" that Nerval encountered in Lebanon, see the section "Druses et maronites" in his *Voyage en Orient,* vol. 2, which says, "The Druze have been successively compared to the Pythagorians, the Essenes, and the Gnostics, and it seems that the Templars, the Rosicrucians, and modern Freemasons have borrowed many ideas from them." A very odd—and quite instructive—Druze catechism appears in the appendix of volume 3.

human fraternity and for progress, because they are traditionalists (in the Guenonian sense of the word) not conservatives or backward looking. They are always tuned in to others and remain available if their fellows are suffering." He adds, "Desire is the watchword of Martinism; the Martinist is a man of desire," and remarks on their "desire to grasp the inner workings of spirituality," a desire that is understood as "the ardor that pushes a soul forward toward the knowledge of spiritual things,"* in short, "desire for God." Robert Amadou tells us, "Mallarmé, the poet, was a man of desire, take that to mean spirit-man." And it was the surrealist Pierre Demarne, in a 1951 text, who wrote:

> To Lead the Total Man into this fundamental SURREAL in which touching the archetype is the timeless trance of our veritable revealed First Motor: DESIRE.[42]

"Key to man, key to the world, desire is the key to freedom in the pure sense of the word as we understand it," adds Jean-Louis Bédouin. But is it always the same thing? In any case we can conclude with Breton that it is the "sole motive for the world"! Doesn't "thought," as Malcolm de Chazal indicates, "travel at the speed of desire"?

Another unforgettable figure from this fin de siècle period was Stanislas de Guaita, whom Bachelard introduced in his preface to Richard Knowles' book on Victor-Emile Michelet as follows:

> In the very first pages of *Les Compagnons de la Hiérophanie,* Michelet gives us a quick sketch of what was, with Guaita, the neo-classicism of occultism, the passion to assert alchemical knowledge at a time of such furious advances in science. Stanislas de Guaita, who when graduating from the Lycée of Nancy, was still only the poet of *The Dark Muse,* soon found work in Sainte-Claire Deville's laboratory: "Like the majority of modern alchemists," Michelet tells us, "chemistry with its series of variable findings would inevitably lead him to alchemy, the immemorially doctrinal science."

---

*According to Simone Rihouët-Coroze.

The symbolist author of *The Dark Muse* (1883) and particularly of *Rosa Mystica* (1885), who Jean-Marc Debenedetti reminds us "exercised a nonnegligible influence on the poets of his generation by revealing the symbolism of esotericism to them," Guaita "restored" in 1888 the Kabbalistic Order of the Rose+Cross, for which Papus would be a dignitary, then the leader. This was a Rosicrucian order, which served for a time as a Martinist inner circle and was also intended—in reaction to the "orientalism" of the Theosophical Society—to give new life to the Western esoteric tradition, but undoubtedly not the same tradition Artaud had in mind. The decidedly omnipresent figure of Papus was also consecrated a gnostic bishop, under the name of Tau Vincent,* by Jules Doinel (Valentine II), the "restorer"—after a spiritualist experiment at the home of Lady Caithness—and briefly head (in 1889) of the Gnostic Church of the Cathar Rite. In 1911, a treaty was concluded between the Martinist Order and Jean Bricaud's Gnostic Catholic Church, a dissident offshoot of the Gnostic Church that would become the Universal Gnostic Church, of which another omnipresent figure in these milieus, René Guenon, before breaking with everyone, would be one of the primary heads, under the name of Tau Paligenius† (Re-Né),‡ bishop of Alexandria.

---

*"Metempsychosis," writes Paul Vulliaud, "is in the common tongue what palingenesis is in esoteric language," the passage "from death to the whole life."

†The Greek letter "tau" is traditionally placed before the name chosen by the gnostic bishops. See Alfred Jarry's play *César-Antéchrist*, prologue Act, Scene III: "I am the Tau, protector of the ancient mages." Moreover, as Jules Boucher writes in his *Symbolique Maçonnique*, "The Tau is an even more expressive symbol than the cross because it connects the hylic world, the material world to the invisible. Just as an invisible pillar rests within the long square, the branch of the cross that corresponds to the transcendental world does not appear to our physical eyes. This is how the very objectivity and reality of spirituality appear in a clearly marked manner to those who are not under the total grip of matter. The Latin cross indicates mind-aided evolution—the human head—whereas the Tau indicates a purely spiritual elevation." The "tau" is also a symbol of Osiris. The mendicant order of the Antonins, keeper during the Middle Ages of vast scientific and esoteric knowledge, was endowed by its grand master, Guillaume le Roux, in 1160 with an escutcheon bearing an azure "tau" on a gold field, as noted by Guy Tarade in his book *Les Derniers Gardiens du Graal*. Gold signifies wealth and azure wisdom.

‡"Re-Né" is the translation into French of "Paligenius." It means "Born-Again." But René (as in René Guénon) is also a first name, in France.

A perfect representative of what Guénon criticized as "pseudo-initiation" and someone he condemned for his confused syncretism was the highly controversial Jean (or "Joanny") Bricaud (1881–1934), a former seminarian turned Martinist and the head of an essentially Lyonnais branch of the Order in 1918 after the death of Charles Détré. Bricaud was called "Téder," and was Papus's dubious successor; he was therefore grand master as well of the Rite of Memphis-Misraïm and was consecrated a bishop in 1913 by Louis-Marie-François Giraud. Bricaud became the patriarch Tau John II of the Universal Gnostic Church, where he ordained numerous bishops. One of these was the high-ranking Mason Robert Ambelain (who in time would also become a grand master of this Rite), who under the name of Tau John III, in 1953, created the Apostolic Gnostic Church before taking on the succession of the Universal Gnostic Church in 1960. A Masonic "godchild" of Constant Chevillon, Ambelain* initiated in 1943 into the clandestine Alexandria of Egypt Lodge (Rite of Memphis-Misraïm) another brother who aroused Breton's interest and who would ultimately join the Grand Lodge of France, Robert Amadou (1924–2006), an expert on Martinès de Pasqually and Saint-Martin.

---

*Ambelain (1907–1977) is described this way in his book *La Vie secrète de Saint Paul*: "Robert Ambelain, Grand Master and honorary Grand Master of several French and foreign Masonic obediences, as well as of two traditional initiatory organizations." He held all the degrees of the Ancient and Accepted Scottish Rite, the Rectified Scottish Rite, the Rite of Memphis-Misraïm (no less than ninety-five!) and the Swedish Rite, and he was also a member of the Union Compagnonnique des devoirs unis. Author of numerous articles and lectures, Ambelain published more than forty books between 1936 and 1985 devoted to occultism, gnosis, kabbalah, secret societies, and so on, some of which are controversial, to say the least. He took part in the preliminary survey for *L'Art magique*, as did Eugène Canseliet, René Alleau, Raymond Abellio, and Denis Saurat. In addition, it may be interesting to read Joanny Bricaud's book *Joris-Karl Huysmans et le Satanisme*. This book shines a most interesting light on the quarrels that stirred up the little world of occultism of that era. It is particularly revealing about the Boullan affair, named for the fiendish Lyonnais clergyman with whom Gengenbach identified in his *Adieu à Satan*. Bricaud's small tome also contains "Une Séance de Spiritisme chez J.-K. Huysmans," published in 1908 by an intimate of Gustave Boucher, the author of *Là-Bas*, who demonstrates the persistent appeal—from Hugo's séances on Guernsey to the surrealist period of hypnotic sleeps—of spiritualism in literary milieus.

Lassalle says:

> Amadou's publication of *The Journal of Saint-Martin* was an event that inspired discussions inside the surrealist group. I recall that I was singing its praises, while Mimi Parent* was expressing her misgivings, saying she was troubled by God's omnipresence in his work.

Jean-Pierre Lassalle's observation† was confirmed by Nora Mitrani, in the fifth issue of *Médium* in March 1953, in these terms:

> From Claude de Saint-Martin, whose original manuscripts Robert Amadou has recently discovered in a London attic, we only retain a certain rising line that human desire should pursue; breaking down myths and words in accordance with their natural progression to the higher principles they reflect.

It is telling that both Ambelain and Amadou dedicated some of their books to Breton in warm and highly personal terms, and it is perhaps this recurring interest in Martinism by the author of *Nadja* and some of his friends that allowed Marijo Ariëns-Volker to make her assertions. She relied, in part, on some of the allusions made by Raymond Queneau, who cheerfully ridicules in *Odile* (his second autobiographical novel) "the little booklets published by his friends that

---

*Parent was the companion of Jean Benoît.

†Lassalle, a member of the group between 1959 and 1966, wrote an interesting personal dedication (envoi) to the painter Brauner, when he sent him his collection of poems *Le Grand Patagon*: "To Victor Brauner, this attempt at *Gnostic poetry* (italics added), respectful homage from Jean-Pierre Lasalle" (in *Victor Brauner dans les collections du MNAM-CCI*).

More broadly, David Nadeau writes about Lasalle's poetry as we can read it in his *Rituels de Gueules:* "Blazons, mythologies, initiatory brotherhoods, the sources of his inspiration are secret and erudite." Moreover, a quote by Saint-Martin (in François Ribadeau Dumas) casts a helpful light on this thinker, Saint-Martin himself: "It is clearly the ignorance and hypocrisy of priests that is one of the primary causes for the ills that have afflicted Europe for several centuries until the present day. I do not include the alleged transmission of the Church of Rome, which, in my opinion, transmits nothing as Church."

(he) first took for theosophical publications." Ariëns-Volker writes, "It seems that in this circle something called 'papusism' [in reference to Papus] was one of the disciplines appearing at the heart of surrealism. Papusism appeared, but also, pell-mell, chiromancy, criminology, and, even Stalinism." But this "papusism" does not seem to meet with Queneau's approval, as shown by the scathing humor of the following remark concerning the evening gatherings on the rue Fontaine:

> After dinner, the experiments began—for they brazenly claimed to be part of the experimental sciences, mentioning the names of Claude Bernard, Charcot, and Dr. Encausse, better known by his Latin name.*

Robert Amadou, also a contributor to *L'Art magique,* I recall, collaborated on the activities of the International Metaphysical Institute and even became the head editor of *La Revue métapsychique.* It was on these grounds and at his request that Breton sent him a letter, published in this same magazine and included in the anthology *Perspective Cavalière,* concerning an article by Jean Bruno, "André Breton et la magie quotidienne," about which he said he had "nothing to object" or add, a letter that specifically concerned the illustration which could accompany this study. At the end of his text, devoted to Chirico's *The Child's Brain,* Breton, who accorded a particular importance to this painting (which he owned), found that a phrase by Robert Amadou best expressed his feelings—a phrase that is well worth citing: "Magic is a practice providing a means of acting upon an element of the universe by using the analogical correspondences that this element shares with every other element of the universe." Breton, at the end of his letter, assured his correspondent of his "lively esteem." Amadou, who would later write, "The heart of my quest is God," was ordained priest on January 25, 1945, and was consecrated as a gnostic bishop on January 28 of that same year, before being ordained Réau-Croix—the highest grade—in

---

*During the evening gatherings at rue Fontaine, the surrealists also talked a lot about politics and particularly Stalinism. They were not only interested in esotericism but also in politics!

the Order of the Elect Cohen and admitted in the Kabbalistic Order of the Rose+Cross by Robert Ambelain, alias Aurifer, who had conferred the Martinist initiation on him, under the name of Ignifer, in 1942. This great initiate left the International Metaphysical Institute in 1955 and founded *La Tour Saint-Jacques,* a magazine dedicated to occultism in the broad sense. In 1978, he published a book of interviews on alchemy with Eugène Canseliet, *Le Feu du soleil.* He also seems to have played a role in the 1994 merger of the two rival branches of the Rosicrucian Apostolic Church, which then became the Rosicrucian Gnostic Apostolic Church, where Paul Sanda was consecrated as a bishop under the name of Tau Sendivogius.*

A phrase by François Ribadeau Dumas in 1970 clearly establishes the ties connecting all these men and the roles they played in the transmission of a clearly esoteric philosophy.

> Marc Haven,[†] Stanislas de Guaita, Fulcanelli, Sédir, Papus, René Guénon, Oswald Wirth, brilliant leaders whose successors are

---

*Michael Sendiwoj, known as "Sendivogius" (1566–1646), was an alchemist of Polish origin and a disciple of the Scotsman Alexander Seton, known as the "Cosmopolite," who, Seligmann says, succeeded in transmuting metal in front of two scientists, the German Wolfgang Dienheim and the Swiss Zwinger. Sendivogius was a councilor at the Prague court of "the alchemist emperor," Rudolph II of the Hapsburgs, where he was highly esteemed. He is the author of *The Cosmopolite or the New Chemical Light,* a copy of which was found in Newton's famous "trunk," and *Treatise on Mercury, Sulfur, and Salt.* According to Seligmann, Sendivogius only used the projection powder bequeathed him by Seton, who had received it from a very mysterious "shipwrecked Dutchman." Angelo Ripellino, author of *Praga Magica,* seems to consider him nothing more than a vulgar "puffer."

†Marc Haven, also known as Doctor Emmanuel Lalande, and Paul Sédir, alias Yvon Le Loup, who were both quite close to Papus, numbered among the primary dignitaries of the Martinist Order. Paul Sédir (an anagram of *désir*) seems to have borrowed his pseudonym from the eponymous character of Louis-Claude de Saint-Martin's *Crocodile,* that is to say from the invaluable right-hand man to the "worthy" Eleazar. Paul Naudon is one of the main historians of Freemasonry, although some of his theories are challenged today by his successors. Meanwhile, concerning Oswald Wirth, whom I cited in chapter 4, Alain Bauer observes about him in his book *Le Crépuscule des Frères,* "Like Newton, but in accordance with a reversed timetable, he was a magnetic healer or an hermeticist by day, a committed humanist by night—and Freemason all the time."

today's occultists: Robert Amadou, Doctor Philippe Encausse, the son of Papus, Robert Ambelain, Jules Boucher, historian Paul Naudon, Canseliet, and others, whose works of great erudition provide the greatest contribution to the occult sciences and ceremonial practices.[43]

These histories of orders and churches that come into being, vanish, then reappear are complex, to say the least, but as Yves Fred Boisset writes:

> The true initiates know that over and beyond their differences generated by time and space, the Truth is one, like light is one despite its multiple diffractions, and the verb is one despite the multiplicity of languages.

In issue 55 of the *French Review* (October 1981) we find these remarks by André Pieyre de Mandiargues, collected by Joyce O. Laurie:

> But Breton's interest was increasingly drawn* toward a certain thought—secret, rebellious, nonconformist—and then he certainly read and studied Swedenborg,† and then what was called French Illuminism at the end of the eighteenth century, Martinism.

---

*This occurred after 1947 and Breton's writing of "Devant le Rideau."
†On the subject of Swedenborg, Paul Valéry wrote, "I entered (his writings) without suspecting I was penetrating an enchanted forest, where each step caused the rise of sudden flights of ideas, where crossroads and echoes multiplied, where each glance glimpsed perspectives completely overgrown in enigmas, where the intellectual veneer becomes excited and goes astray, losing, rediscovering, and losing the trail again. But this is hardly a waste of time, I love hunting for its own sake, and there are few hunts as absorbing and diverse as the hunt for the Swedenborg mystery"; cited by François Ribadeau Dumas in *Les Magiciens de Dieu: Les Grands Initiés des XVIIIe et XIXe siècles* (Paris: Robert Laffont ["Les énigmes de l'univers"], 1970). When we know the exchanges shared by Breton and Valéry, it is possible to think that Breton's interest in the Swedish philosopher occurred earlier than the date proposed by Mandiargues, even if he regrets, in *L'Art magique,* that Baudelaire "had believed he should claim to follow Swedenborg—and even Lavater—to the express exclusion of Charles Fourier."

It all adds up, especially as the Breton auction revealed the presence in his library of a veritable Bibliotheca Philosophica Hermetica, as Marijo Ariëns-Volker puts it, with Saint-Yves d'Alveydre's five main works, but also *The Literary Anthology of Occultism, Raymond Lulle and Alchemy,* and *Louis-Claude de Saint-Martin and Martinism* by Robert Amadou, as well as *In the Shadow of the Cathedrals, Martinism,* and *Adam the Red God,* with its subtitle *Judeo-Christian Esotericism, Gnosis and the Ophits,* and *Luciferians and Rose+Cross* by Robert Ambelain.

Bertrand Schefer writes:

> There is a principle in hermeticism that by itself sums up one of the fundamental attitudes of Western culture: during a time of intellectual crises and historic mutations, a *tradition* inescapably re-emerges in an attempt to resolve the contradictions of the present. Trapped between a past reduced to an archival record and a present that is no more contemporary, the world in crisis runs athwart the very movement that creates it. According to the paradox expounded by Husserl, the tradition, which is by essence ignorance of the origins, contains within itself the articulation of a new life. The present, rethinking the conditions of its birth within tradition and rediscovering a new spiritual temporality, emerges from its self-sustaining narrow-mindedness and can be reborn. This is how the wisdom tradition passed down by hermetic literature (since the beginning of the Christian era to the most recent theosophies) accompanies the moments of doubt and experimentation of a knowledge in quest of new foundations that is constantly striving to extend its own boundaries.[44]

The period covering the ascent of nationalist power—that of the European nations in particular—then the hot and cold wars that followed, is without a doubt one of these times of crisis that led to the collapse of the old world and make the contours of the future vague, to say the least.

13
Surrealism and Myth

Continue to advance in the only valid way possible: through the flames.
ANDRÉ BRETON AND ANDRÉ MASSON

The marvelous befalls only those who sacrifice to its cult.
JACQUELINE CHÉNIEUX-GENDRON

The poet is the one who destroys and builds myths, who destroys them in order to construct different ones, which are always more real.
VITEZSLAV NEZVAL, *THE PASSERBY OF PRAGUE*

It has been too easily forgotten today that the era preceding the birth of surrealism was placed throughout Europe under the sign of an extraordinary violence: class violence, state violence, the intellectual and political terrorism of the war mongers that could not help but rub off on society and corrupt it. The totalitarian regimes that would soon establish themselves were already embryonic, but this was where their seeds lay and not in a movement like surrealism, which was created, we should remember, by *survivors* desperately seeking to re-enchant the world. Criticism formulated by revisionists like Jean Clair mistake the effect for the cause and their purpose is undoubtedly ideological! According to Bataille, in *The Tears of Eros,* "The wars of our century mechanized war; war has become senile. The world eventually surrendered to reason."

Paul Virilio forcefully points this out in his conversations with Enrico Baj:

> We cannot understand what happened after cubism to the time of abstract art and the Viennese action painters, if we do not make the connection with the horrors of war, wars made even more horrible by technology, gas, and new kinds of bombs. This gave rise to a permanent torture of the body and the latent terrorism of the avant-gardes, with the Dadaists, Surrealists, and Situationists. . . .[1]

We should add here the accompanying atmosphere of "intellectual" catastrophe, the twilight of thought noted by Jean-Marie Domenach in his *Barrès par lui-même* ([Maurice] Barrès in His Own Words), which recreates "that formidable torrent of nationalist and 'anti-Kraut' nationalism in which the French intelligentsia faltered for a moment, losing its respect for truth and bordering on racist justification." To get a more concrete idea of the context, it is good to keep in mind these words by Max Ernst, quoted in the catalog for his Beaubourg retrospective in 1991:

> We other young men returned from the war in a daze and our indignation needed an outlet. It naturally found one in violent attacks against the basic fundamentals of the civilization that had brought on the war, attacks against language, syntax, logic, literature, painting and so forth.

Even Gengenbach observed in *Judas or the Surrealist Vampire:*

> All these young men who escaped from the nightmare and were marked by the war they had waged without joy, returned full of disgust and animated by a radical nihilism against all manifestations

of civilization, and against the law and morality of a Society that had so casually sent them off to death. They wanted to free and deliver man forever from the systems straitjacketed by reason, logic, and religious mysticism that had led to this vile butchery. They spit on a sordid reality and set off in search of an unreal, unknown world that was more true than the other and inhabited by strange creatures in never-before seen landscapes. . . . Poetry restored to its original state would become a magic that would transform humanity, and change life and the world. The poet would again become a seer, medium, and prophet, and rediscover the enchanted spring and the treasures of a paradise from which he had been banished by twenty centuries of Christian oppression. The surrealists sought to have done with the ideas of family, country, religion, and with the current aesthetics and moralities. They ripped away their pseudo-civilized masks in order to achieve metempsychosis.

As if picking up the relay, Carrouges adds, "The question of death posed by the war had not yet stopped being raised in all its violence."

Claude Gavreau, the Quebec automatist, called this "the instrumental cause, as some contemporary Thomist might say." But he made his position even clearer in his *Seventeen Letters to a Ghost,* an unpublished work cited by André G. Bourassa:

> This is what I think, worldwide crises are the normal effect of the disintegration of the Christian myth. Surrealism is the result of the realization—first completely empirical then more and more thought out—of this state of disintegration of the myth.[2]

Surrealism was born of the disgust felt when facing "the indecency of a culture collapsing in on itself," as Annie Le Brun said, and from the rejection of rationalism and the political, religious, and social values that had led to the butchery of 1914–1918.[3]* "Very present in our

---

*Artaud writes, "And I think that for four hundred years European consciousness has been living on an immense factual error. This fact is the rationalist concept of the world whose application within our everyday life in the world provides what I will call

minds were the human sacrifices these gods had asked for and would ask for again," Breton wrote in *Conversations*. This is why surrealism, devoted to the conquest of the inner world "before being the exaltation of a higher reality," sought since the outset to be "critical of the facts and reason's movement in these facts," and to reject "a world in which the most lugubrious of all games is played, that of man playing hide and seek with himself."[4] This is the basis for its attempt of a "complete liberation of poetry and through it, of life,"[5] specifically, as Desnos said in 1940, for a "revolt against mediocrity," far from all the artistic or literary concerns to which people today are trying to herd it back. But it was equally foreign to a quest for "a path to salvation," as Carrouges sought to imply.

This was a recurring idea, moreover. Schuster and Hantaï would write in *Médium* (1955):

> Since the beginning it has seemed to the surrealists that if balance was restored, that is if the irruption into daily life of so-called paranormal phenomena (which go from simple dreams to prophetic signs, from "visions," to clairvoyance) ceased being controlled and finally systematically devalued by the rationalist force that organizes the human mind as poorly as it does social relations, the very key to the interpretation and transformation of the world would fall into their hands.[6]

This is why, as Jules Monnerot points out, "Everything that might serve as a rallying sign against this *hated* world can count on a warm welcome." In order to implement its plans, the movement aimed quite wide, as Tzara notes in his "Essay on the Situation of Poetry," published in the fourth issue of *Le Surréalisme au service de la révolution*, basing itself on:

(continued from p. 399) *separate consciousness.*" For her part, Nora Mitrani writes, "The major party responsible (I would be tempted to say the major guilty party) of this dizzying hunt, called modern rationalism, is Descartes." But it goes without saying, as Charles Jameux points out, that this shameful reason has only remote connections with the "ardent reason" of Gaston Bachelard or Ferdinand Alquié.

> the love of ghosts, witchcraft, occultism, magic, vice, dream, madness, passions, true or invented folklore, mythology (or even mystifications), social or other kinds of utopias, real or imaginary journeys, bric-a-brac, marvels, the adventures and mores of primitive peoples and generally everything that did not fit into the rigid frameworks in which beauty had been placed to identify itself with the mind.

Aware that the radical moral evolution to which it aspired could only occur within the much larger context of profound social transformation, the movement sought support from revolutionary thought. This is the significance of the transition from *La Révolution surréaliste* to *Le Surréalisme au service de la révolution*. After the betrayal of Bolshevik ideals by Stalin and those like him, after the murder of Trotsky and the break-up of the Fourth International, after the new carnage of the Second World War, realizing, as Bédouin noted, all this would only lead to failure "so long as revolutionaries confine themselves to certain specific aspects of social life without attacking the spiritual structure of society directly," it was somewhat paradoxically that the movement sought political asylum among the anarchists.

But following the crushing end of the Spanish Revolution, anarchism was increasingly viewed as "the political formulation of despair" and the crucible of inaccessible utopias.[7]

> Because despair is in no way a stagnant milieu in which the imaginations of the weak are forever bathing. Despair does not wait. Despair is torrential. Despair forces doors. Despair causes cities to split at the seams. Despair is the storm beneath which are ripening unheard of worlds of deliverance.[8]*

---

*Indeed: "Only despair precipitates consciousness to the bottom of the inner gulf through which it must inevitably cross in order to ascend in a leap toward the high zones of illumination," said Michel Carrouges. Couldn't surrealism be the *moral* formulation—without nihilism—of a despair opportunely redeemed by love, or rather "unhope," to borrow Annie Le Brun's expression? "Despair feeding, as it always does, on phantasmagoria, is imperturbably leading men of letters to the rejection, en masse, of moral and social laws and to practical and theoretical wickedness," Lautréamont wrote in *Poésies 1*.

Anarchism and its utopias also possessed the merit of not being overly criminal, should we keep in mind (as Philippe Audoin wrote) that "no mistake, utopia is the blessed isle, nature beneath the tumultuous wind of charms, in a word, the possible."[9] Breton, in his desire to bring to fruition "the mission, assigned to man, to violently break with the ways of thinking and feeling that had led him to no longer tolerate his existence,"[10] as a "revolutionary [then] forged for himself a highly uncommon tradition: the family of the great heresiarchs."[11] We can also wonder if the desire to occult surrealism expressed in the *Second Surrealist Manifesto* was not inversely proportional to the rising perils that would lead to another war and if the consolidation of the esoteric path after 1945 did not correspond in some way to the creation of a climate of permanent insecurity connected with the entrance into the atomic age.

> *There would be only the war*
> *Nothing like it for giving new life*
> *To the hermetic life*

Breton wrote this in his poem "Postcard," dedicated to Benjamin Péret and published in the Belgian magazine *L'Invention collective* in April 1940. As Maurice Mourier underscores:

> Whatever the case may be, incapable of hunting for this other world in the spiritual space that overlays this expression in a religious context, or build his aerie in any transcendental ecological niche, he was condemned to this squaring: inventing the world beyond right here, painting its innate transcendence with an utterly pure immanence. This is undoubtedly the secret of surrealism.[12]

"Initiated" Breton was, though, according to Gracq, and it remains up to us "to question (his) dark and crystalline messages."[13] Around 1931 or 1932 he wrote, "The *end*, in my opinion, can only be knowledge of man's eternal destination, of man in the general, that the Revolution alone can carry to this destination,"[14] knowing that "revolutions are achieved in spectacular fashion in men's imaginations. Then they carve an often dark path toward reality."[15] "Revolution Revelation...."

Again we need to know just what revolution! Would it be that "total reintegration of man who, at the end of the alchemical process, would be accompanied by a veritable transformation of understanding," about which Claude Tarnaud speaks in *From (the End of the World)*? Or should it be understood, as indicated by Rémy Laville with regard to Pierre Mabille and the surrealist movement, that "to be a revolutionary is to indicate the path of a new world out of chaos, to make the new sensible forms tangible and intelligible,"[16] as can be glimpsed in Mabille's article "Del Nuevo Mundo," without going so far as "to prepare for the coming of the future Gods,"[17] as then feverishly urged by Duits and Matta, according to the former's account. What if we were to take up Roger Gilbert-Lecomte's suggestion in his text "La Lézarde" (The Crack) to

> give to the rational, scientific culture of today's man its base, foundation, roots, and old soul of bygone days, its bushy soul with its dialectical monism, destroyer of all antinomies (matter-mind, dream-reality, and so on), its sense of symbols and analogies, of the universal myths and rites that join man to the earth and earth to the heavens?[18]

And wouldn't it be time to go back to the idea thrown out by Breton in 1935, in his preface to *Political Position of Surrealism,* that surrealism is the "mode for creating a collective myth," knowing that, as Mircea Eliade had shown, myth (thus like poetry) was inseparable from the sacred? And wouldn't it be time, by borrowing the suggestion made by René Etiemble at the beginning of 1942, for nothing less than this "practical preparation for an intervention into the mythical life that initially takes on the widest scale—a cleansing face...," which is mentioned in *Situation of Surrealism Between the Two Wars* and appears even more clearly in the following citation?

> But ever since the reasonable and rational approach of consciousness got the upper hand over the impassioned approach of the

unconscious, that is since the last myths became congealed within a deliberate mystification, the secret of knowledge and action—of acting without alienating the acquisition of knowledge—appears to have become lost. The time has come to put forth a new myth capable of carrying humanity to a higher stage of its ultimate destination. This is surrealism's specific enterprise. It is its great rendezvous with History.

And, considering, in the terms later used by Paul-Émile Bourdas* and the Quebec automatists, that "a new civilization must arise that refuses to be based exclusively on the instruments of reason, logic, and intention," and hoping "it would make way for magic and the freedom of automatism,"[19] couldn't it also imply "choosing, or adopting and imposing a myth fostering the society we deem desirable," as Breton writes in *Prolegomena to a Third Surrealist Manifesto or Not?*

Couldn't it also involve offering a reply to the anxieties bedeviling Breton, which Alexandrian records in his autobiography?

> The West is going to perish ignominiously, Breton maintained, and the entire world with it, if poets and artists do not urgently teach the means of transcending it through the imagination. Surrealism's desire was to enable everyone to rediscover the freshness of inspiration, the luxury of belief, the sense of the sacred, the lyrical accord between the Ego and nature characteristic of the primitive peoples of Oceania.

---

*During and after World War II, Paul-Émile Bourdas led a surrealism-inspired group, the Sagittarians, that claimed to go further, with some significant local specificities, and which ultimately became the group of the surrational automatists. It is interesting to note that the texts of the automatists, particularly their 1948 manifesto, *Refus global,* were published by Mithra-Myth editions! Another group, closer to the "line" defined by Breton, formed under the leadership of Alfred Pellan before submitting in the 1950s to the influence of revolutionary surrealism and Edouard Jaguer's Phases movement. Members of these local avatars of surrealism included Léon Bellefleur, Jean Benoît, Mimi Parent, Claude Gavreau, Roland Giguère, Fernand Leduc, and Jean-Paul Riopelle.

And what if we had, as Pastoureau suggests, "recourse to myth as a kind of collective psychoanalysis?"[20] Or "mythanalysis," as suggested by Malcolm de Chazal in the development of the following rumination:

> We need a new Freudianism that would be religious.
> Surrealism knows this.
> The World of the Spirit feels it.
> Surrealism discovered automatic writing—written confession of the ego. But an abyss separates it from psychoanalysis, and there is yet another abyss between psychoanalysis and religion.
> Bind. We have to bind. By the myth, we should reach the religious poet of the subconscious, the Visionary, the prophet of the spirit. But what spirit? And the response looms forth: "The Universal Mind that is both inside the world and inside the human being,"

Chazal asks in *Le Rocher de Sisyphe*. How? By bouncing back, moreover, as if by the effect of an imperceptible return to the sources, to the fundamentals, that is to the German romantics, who are, according to Annie Le Brun, "impassioned about making the notion of myth one of the cornerstones of their consideration, up to dreaming of a new mythology as of another foundation" even if that myth is called on to become a "mythology of reason."[21]

Jean-Marc Debenedetti adds:

> In short, lets consider the distress of a humanity deprived of any exalting myth! Because myth gives meaning to the world, and thereby man finds a place and a design in a universe that is animated by the dictates of his desire. Myth is just as necessary to the human being—first and foremost a *desiring* being—on the spiritual plane as the air he breathes and the water which is his major constituent element, or the dream that he fashions out of his absolute need for freedom.[22]

Gérard Legrand,* who by education was the most "philosophical" mind of the post–World War II surrealist generation, echoes this with

---

*Legrand is the surrealist who thinks that surrealism is "philosophy in discovery of itself."

more exactitude in his article "Sur Oedipe" (On Oedipus), published in issue 3 of *Médium*, in May 1954, and as a book published by Le Terrain Vague:

> The *mythos** is, in fact, the efflorescence of that zone of language where desire, no longer being an object of knowledge, expresses itself in a quasi-conceptual manner. This efflorescence pursues its course in tandem with the crystallization of speech. It is neither pre-logical nor "another kind of logic," it is next to logic, but *only* in the same way that the artifices of calligraphy can govern or strive toward a text's presentation.[23]

This important clarification can only remind us of the surrealists' constant desire to undo the straitjacket of a reason that was only good for engendering monsters.

Indeed Artaud had already, as he said in his "Third Letter on Language," addressed to Jean Paulhan in December 1932, sought a means of getting around this problem and again restoring myth to the heart of a society and era that saw "its old values collapsing," assigning, in the direct line of his personal concerns, this mission to the theater: "If the present time has turned away and lost all interest in the theater it is because the theater has ceased to represent it. It no longer has any hope that it may provide myths on which it can rely."[24] At the end of this same document, he summarizes his hopes this way:

> The creation of myths is the true purpose of the theater, translating life beneath its immense, universal aspect, and extracting from this life images in which we would like to rediscover ourselves.... Let it free us within a Myth having sacrificed our little human individuality, like Figures from the Past, with forces rediscovered in the Past.[25]

Mythos is a term that Legrand prefers to *myth*—hence the italics.

In "La Théâtre de la cruauté" he continues with:

> [These] themes [which] will be cosmic and universal, interpreted in accordance with the most ancient texts, taken from old Mexican, Hindu, Jewish, Iranian, cosmogonies, among others, [that have] been updated [of course] in order to introduce into man, on an equal footing with life, the reality of imagination and dreams.[26]

Similar universalist presuppositions were presumably at work in the development of Breton's thought. With respect to Henri Rousseau, "Le Douanier" (the customs officer), he explains to Masson in *The Creole Dialogue* (1941):

> Thus, beyond all the obstacles created by civilization, a mysterious, *second* communication, would still be possible between people based on what originally united them and what separated them.[27]

And he received in answer:

> You touch on something that moves me to the core. You always defended the idea of a Mediumistic quality necessary to the poet and the artist. One could, in fact, express the idea that Henri Rousseau was the receiver of dreams, age-old desires; his nostalgia for an innocent life in the Garden is compelling.

How could we not see an allusion here to the collective unconscious as the foundation of mythologies? Or of the new myth in becoming, this "myth in formation *behind the veil of events*" (italics added), traces of which can be found in the programmatic declaration of the first issue of *VVV*. This is also the angle that I personally believe is the correct one for analyzing the interests of the French surrealists, as well as those of the Americans, who, in particular, care for popular culture (far removed from any intention of transforming the movement into some kind of manifestation of popular art, for which advertising would be one of the current avatars). This interest in popular culture includes the films of

Louis Feuillade, such as *Les Vampires,* "for love and sensuality," with Irma Vep-Musidora in her form-fitting costume, and *Fantômas,* "that modern epic," for instance, "for revolt and freedom," in the words of Robert Desnos. *Fantômas* had already been a source of fascination for Picasso and Apollinaire, and André Salmon wrote in 1931 that "his shadow (had fallen) over Montmartre." This dark figure is most often clad in a black cape and mask—perhaps the same mask Chirico put on the poet in his *Portrait of Apollinaire*—and the ritual attributes of the Martinists, for whom they symbolize renunciation of the profane world. Consider even Jules Verne, whom Nicolas Saucy squarely views as the man who provided surrealism with its prime matter. A Verne whose Professor Otto Lidenbrock, with features close to those given him by Edouard Riou, haunts the paintings of the parasurrealist Paul Delvaux, while the *Sphinx of the Ice Fields,* unless it is his brother, the Sphinx of the Sands, offers his enigmas in Desnos's *Liberty or Love!* whose hero, the corsair Sanglot, seems to be akin to Captain Nemo (and Long John Silver).

But it is true that Desnos was particularly *receptive* in this domain *also,* and he saw in Jules Verne "a romantic writer" who was "influenced by Hoffmann [and who] was able to give fantastic literature a new form." He added that Verne "is clearly of the same lineage who, through Perrault and Madame d'Aulnoy, Andersen, and so many others, conducts us from the kingdom of Peau d'âne [Donkey Skin] to the kingdom of science." He thus sums up in a perfectly surrealist spirit, from Verne's "Le château des Carpathes" (The Castle of the Carpathians), "a love story . . . enveloped in the fog of dream":

> The old castle in which the plot unfurls must have been the lair at some time of a ghost or vampire. The forest surrounding it must still hold in its caves more than seven dwarves along with a Tom Thumb. . . . In any case, it does protect a sleeping beauty . . . but you will see.[28]

Yet this text dates from September 1940!

In her *André Breton, Explorateur de la Mère-Moire,* Pascaline Mourier-Casile skillfully demonstrated the subtle connections *Arcanum 17* maintained with Jules Verne's *Les Indes Noires* (*The Underground*

City), and she even suggests that "while Breton rarely cites Jules Verne . . . it is because he made this imaginary universe his own once and for all, and traversed it as if it were his own land." According to her, the influence of the Nantes native made itself felt, either directly or through the intervention of reminiscences, from the time of *The Magnetic Fields!* There is really nothing surprising about this, as she notes quite rightly "that the author of *Extraordinary Voyages* was in no way foreign to the initiatory tradition, if only through the intermediary of Freemasonry."

In 1955, it was the turn of Maurice Fourré, whose own wondrous qualities cannot be denied and who was in some respect Verne's neighbor. He put the following words in the mouth of the narrator of *La Marraine du sel,* this Clair Harondel who seems to owe Verne so much:

> I opened Jules Verne's book, *Five Weeks in a Balloon.* Oblivious to everything around me in my refound intoxication from a book of my childhood, I followed like an enthusiastic young boy the poet of new mechanisms and traveling, the strange visionary haunted by the immensities of cosmic poetry.

Julien Gracq confided to Jean Carrière in 1986 that "Jules Verne was his reading passion during his entire childhood," after having explained to Jean-Louis Tissier in 1978 that the work of the Nantes native was for him "a kind of Book of Wonders." He acknowledged again in 2000, despite his advanced age and his proclaimed retirement from active "literary life," that Verne was sufficiently important to grant Jean-Paul Dekiss a full and rich interview of some sixty pages for the tenth issue of the *Revue Jules Verne*. A Vernian red thread clearly crosses through his entire opus, as eloquently shown by this short extract from the *Narrative,* a posthumous text undoubtedly dating from the end of 1941 or the beginning of 1942, regarding an episode of the France Campaign in 1940:

> For the first time, Lieutenant G. overheard in conversation, without any particular explanation, the name of *Admiral North,* under whose command it appeared the regiment was now passing. . . .

Through the unusual name, he saw rising the figure of an admiral of the ice fields, a Hyperborean navigator, a masked silhouette with an extraordinary resolution and fanaticism who has just leapt to the bridge and claimed authority in the city of pirates like Captain Hatteras on a vessel in distress.... "On the orders of Admiral North ..." This was an entirely different matter, unimaginable—it was unheard of—it went far beyond Jules Verne.[29]

Le Visage effleuré de peine (Pain's Grazed Visage) by Gisèle Prassinos[30] (filled incidentally with allusions to the codes of the gothic novel) may also resonate with a few echoes of Verne's *Master Zacharias*, whose hero claims to have "discovered the secrets of the mysterious union of the body and the soul," this aspect also truly present in the work of the author of *From the Earth to the Moon*.

Claude Tarnaud chooses to evoke Nemo, in *From (the End of the World)*, under his true name of an anticolonialist breaking with everything and a figure of absolute defiance:

> This is why the high figure of Prince Dakkar never ceased to surprise me. Descendent of a long line of wanderers, he used technical innovation deliberately to invent his freedom, the right to recognize *all* without having to justify himself to anyone. As the emerged lands no longer offered a safe haven, he used *science* to create a land that clung to *nothing*. This is why he is exemplary. In addition to the abysses, he chose many other depths to draw from in accordance with the inseparable criteria of gestural poetry.

Robert Benayoun, in the review *Médium* (November 1953), had already written a forthright article in this same spirit titled "Is Science Fiction?" In it he explains:

> In expectation of a return to the Faustian theme, begetter of Melmothes, and a new breakdown of the apparent reality, our authors would more likely be Edgar Rice Burroughs, dispenser of all Golden Ages, Sir H. Rider Haggard, father of eternal loves, and

Clark Ashton Smith, sophisticated gleaner of worlds (as well as a colleague and friend of H. P. Lovecraft).

Getting back to the main topic, can we accept the opinions of Jacques Meuris that myth is "a poetic narrative used to develop ideas,"[31] and of Amina Osman that it "is a foundation of social and cultural life," revealing "the irruption of the sacred into the world," which then becomes "quite similar to dream"?[32] Then there is Pierre Brunel, who believes it is "a dynamic system of symbols, archetypes, and patterns with great emotional resonance,"[33] that is additionally capable of mobilizing energies, for Breton, and knowing, with Jules Monnerot, that "the authentic meaning of myth is felt like the innermost initiation, the privileged personal experience of dream." So it is not impossible that we find ourselves in the presence here of an attempt to create something comparable to what in its time (under the leadership of James Anderson and Jean-Théophile Désaguliers and the high patronage of Newton and the Royal Society) was speculative Freemasonry, which can be analyzed as the regenerative myth of eighteenth-century thought. In the words of Eric Hobsbawm, it is the "key example of an invented, innovative tradition."[34] Especially, when we consider, like Legrand, that "myth is not *recommencement*" but is the timeless figure (of the beginning, "among other things").[35] In passing, as we are talking about "invention," it may be worth pointing out that the person who finds a treasure is also called an "inventor." Discovery assumes concealment, that the thing rediscovered had been hidden. What better way to suggest that this "invention of tradition, the invention of Freemasonry," in Roger Dachez's words, may at least indicate the partial resurgence of a "knowledge" that had been wending its way underground? This would be a real acknowledgment of the power of words!

This is also clearly evident in the theory advanced by Charles Imbert (although it can be hard to accept all of this author's intuitions) in his work *Les Sources souterraines de la franc-maçonnerie: Mithra et le tarot* (The Subterranean Sources of Freemasonry: Mithra and the Tarot), which explains why it is plausible that what we are dealing with in the form of modern Masonry (after the year 1717) is actually a much older secret society that had carried "philosophies" through the ages that had not been subject to "the blessing of the intolerant totalitarian thought of the Church."[36] He posits an entire tradition whose veritable "coming out" was staged by the Grand Lodge of London and Westminster, illuminated by ideas that would become those of the Enlightenment. Let's include, though, the exception of this naturally complementary nuance that "the invention of Freemasonry" appeared as the "invention of a tradition," resolutely *facing the future,* "where customary recourse to the occult can only be interpreted as a *return to a tradition anchored in the more or less mythical past,* perceived as a Golden Age, whose gentle nature needs to be restored." Here again it should not be overlooked that the surrealists' activities and thoughts aimed at recasting human understanding, "gleaning" what interested them from the tradition without subscribing to the idea of a lost Eden that reeks of the Fall, a Fall in which they specifically refused to believe and whose presuppositions they refuted. What the movement "has already achieved in poetry, art, and morality," Jean-Louis Bédouin wrote in 1961, "must be taken up anew and recast so that it can be incorporated into a new kind of Great Work: the creation of a mythology that is living because it is freely and deeply experienced," with the cautionary note that "the place must be prepared free of all confusion," so that "the adventure in which surrealism is engaged has nothing in common with any attempt of religious restoration. It does not aim at a mystical renaissance," even if "an enrichment of surrealist thought" can be viewed there—and this advice should not be ignored!

As early as 1940, with the publication of his book *The Mirror of the Marvelous,* which Jacqueline Chénieux-Gendron describes as a "subtle reflection on initiation and the magic mentality," Pierre Mabille, whose importance can never be stressed enough, supplied

> proof that surrealism is clearly on the path of the great tradition and is taking part in the cosmic forces governing human movements. The quest of the surrealists is therefore far from appearing as a sentimental singularity; it is affected by the profound vibrations of the tangible universe; it is attempting the restoration of human

grandeur by giving desire back all its strength—desire, the secret author of all becoming, (and that) its contribution to the historical revolution that must be carried out goes through the crafting of a collective myth.[37]

Let me remind you in passing that the Martinists called themselves "men of desire."

"An image of the world that is valid for each man, taken individually as well as in his connections with the human community," resumes Jean-Louis Bédouin, "that is the myth we are looking for!" But it should be made clear that this is a myth inserted within a very specific framework, one that Jacques Bernard Brunius defined in these terms in his article "Danger of Death" in *VVV,* in which we note that this author does not shy away at all from the use of the word *mystic:*

> For the great intellectuals of today, it involves nothing less than the replacement of a myth of oppression by a myth of liberation, a myth that allows man to escape God without selling his soul to the devil, a myth that does not leave the man freed of God alone with himself, a collective mysticism in which the individual is not hoodwinked by the group or a leader, a myth in which neither capital nor captain will be synonymous with virility, a myth of moral and material emancipation in which order and disorder will only be one and the same activity.

The contents of this new myth, whose source is to be found in the works of Lautreamont, Rimbaud, and Jarry, among others, and of which the 1947 exhibition would "offer a completely exterior glimpse,"[38] was crafted under the gaze of the Great Transparents, to whom Ithell Colquhoun devoted a poem in 1944, who are seen again in Octavio Paz,[39] and in Matta's "glaziers, high chamberlain[s] of Hermes's return to our time."[40] These contents, which are summed up in the seven commandments that allude to the seven stages of purification of the hermeticists, are borrowed from *The Legendary Life of Max Ernst* by Henri Béhar, who attributed to Breton the desire to copy the contours of this new myth on the way in which, "in tune with creators endowed with great powers of anticipation like Rimbaud, Nietzsche, Sade, Lautreamont, and so forth, contemporary artists [such as Max Ernst] prefigure the world to come: to free objects from their gangue; to discover through wandering; to recreate desire; to display convulsive beauty; to deprive oneself to attain revelation; never to doubt; to love because love is always in the lead."[41] We have to admit this is a bit more alluring than Bataille's curt response expressed in various occasions.... While he professed his desire for the advent of a "great surrealism," in the second issue of the magazine *Troisième Convoi* (January 1946), he was satisfied with stating in the second issue of the same magazine (November 1946) that "the absence of myth is the sole inevitable myth: which fills the depths like wind the void."[42]

For Armand Hoog (1913–1999), a literature professor at Princeton and a friend of Breton, as well as a fellow prisoner of war with Julien Gracq in Silesia, who had earlier noted several contradictions of surrealism in his article "The Fall of the Black House," the stakes are as he explained in the first issue of *Archibras* in 1967:

> Carry the transfiguration of life yet farther, rescue history emerging from the wreckage of the war, truly and for the first time construct a surrealist *transcendence*. Times call for nothing less.[43]

But we must keep in mind what Roger Caillois said as early as 1938: "if there is any value to myth as such, it is by no means aesthetic in nature."

Even for Albert Camus, who drew up the balance sheet a bit prematurely:

> If surrealism did not change the world, it furnished it with a few strange myths, which partly justified Nietzsche's announcement of the return of the Greeks, partly only because he was referring to unenlightened Greece, the Greece of mysteries and dark gods. Finally, just as Nietzsche's experience culminated in the acceptance of the light of day, surrealist experience culminates in the exaltation of the darkness of night, the agonized and obstinate cult of the tempest.[44]

While he obviously did not have Jean Terrosian's *Mythe decisif** in mind (it was created long after), could he refer to one of the "exalting and marvelous myths that will compel the entire world to the assault of the unknown," which is a theme in the 1943 text *La Parole est à Péret?* In any case we are dealing with a return to the source of romanticism, which may be black and certainly has its sources on the Atlantic shores!

In 1957, again (in *L'Art magique*) Breton reasserted the deadline's imminence and set out the line to follow: "to maintain and . . . to renew, while preparing the hatching of new myths, which can *already be spotted for their moral value,* the 'old fanaticism' of the legendary, the sumptuous and the irrepressible." This unfinished quest is always on the agenda among those claiming to follow the surrealist spirit. As proof I offer these lines by Bertrand Schmitt, published in 2003 (*S.U.R.R.,* n° 4):

> Standing today as aghast, furious witnesses of this revolting farce that is our allegedly modern world, we still have the mysteries of the myth from which we expect the light under which we shall labor building the arks of a new civilization.

And we should still keep in mind, as Pascal Bancourt says in *Les Mystères de la ville d'Ys: L'héritage spirituel des légendes celtiques* (The Mysteries of the City of Ys: The Spiritual Heritage of the Celtic Legends), that it cannot "be fully grasped until it has been realized within the individual personally as the result of assiduous contemplation."[45] But is this quest really unfinished? Couldn't Jacques Abeille be right when he writes:

> We could well ask ourselves if surrealism is not already the myth it gives itself as expectation and provocation. A foundational movement whose history, *to be truthful,* could only be legendary—suspended by the adherence, belief, and magical participation of the narrator?[46]

---

*[This is a pun on the myth of Sisyphus (the subject of another book by Camus) and the decisive myth. Formatted like a tarot card, it depicts a slingshot and a boulder. — *Trans.*]

This brings us back to Hobsbawm!

In any event, the crafting of the myth (to come?) fits fully onto the tradition, as shown, for example, by the costume ("whose beauty is like the encounter of the eternal tragic and the tragedy of our time")[47] created and worn by Jean Benoît in 1959 for the extraordinary magical performance of *The Execution of the Last Will and Testament of the Marquis de Sade*. Alain Jouffroy tells us:

> According to Jean Benoît, who conceived and executed the costume, the entire array symbolizes "the symbolic transfer of the tomb of D.A.F. de Sade," and its color was "specially conceived to take on its full intensity from the warm light of the setting sun." All the arrows adorning it were vertical, oblique, or curved: not a single one was horizontal. Each detail had its symbolic key. All together they invited a resurrection of the mythic life. Everything in it displayed an absolute fidelity to a traditional language of signs. One only has to visit the exhibition of masks at the Musée Guimet to get a true sense of the inventive summa of rites and meanings that Jean Benoît realized with this costume.[48]

This was confirmed by Jean-Louis Bédouin, an expert on primitive masks, among other things, in *Vingt Ans de surréalisme: 1939–1959*, when he talks of this "costume-mask . . . reminiscent of those from the Pacific or British Columbia,"[49] and by José Pierre, who observes:

> The need to be entirely one with what he created would find its particular outlet in painted costumes accompanied by essential accessories. Thanks to this solution, an exceptional one in the West, he rediscovered the ritual meaning that accompanies the artistic art among so-called primitive peoples.[50]

An approach like this is quite remote, of course, in appearance from the tabula rasa of commencements, but it irresistibly calls to mind Artaud's 1932 remarks about "symbolic gestures and the magical beauty of costumes taken from certain ritual models" in "La Théâtre de la cruauté."⁵¹ It sparked some condescending criticisms, as well, like those of Jules-François Dupuis:

> From a fortress open to every wind blowing in from the old world, it [surrealism] began—after the fashion of the Romantics reinventing an idyllic Middle Ages, complete with valiant knights, in the very shadow of the stock exchanges, banks, and factories—to set against the misery of the spectacle the power of a myth, purified of any religious overtones that would draw its strength from a reconsecration of human relationships modeled on the reconsecration of art.

Which would not be so bad! And the prosecutor cruelly goes on to say:

> Thus the surrealists take up the defense of myth, at a time when myth no longer exists, against the spectacle, which is everywhere. They are Don Quixotes tilting against housing projects; no one in that time of change so much resembles the Cervantes character as these latter-day knights wandering between the devil of total freedom and the death of culture.⁵²

The observation may not be entirely unfounded but should be brought back to its proper proportions. We should remind ourselves that even aged and despite the losses in their ranks, the heroes of the Round Table continue in these times of want to boldly stride through the Western imaginal realm today behind the black-and-red flags of Pré-Saint-Gervais,* and "strictly speaking, surrealism may well be the epic of our time."⁵³

Hardly suspect for recuperation of the movement or illicit inflection of his guiding ideas—and moreover, his observations were never contested—Julien Gracq, in his *André Breton, quelques aspects de l'écrivain,* had already brought up the issue by suggesting:

---

*[Pré-Saint-Gervais was a radical, working-class suburb of Paris. —*Trans.*]

Surrealism (it is merely a symptom) has presided as a preliminary draft of a religious form over a phenomenon of spontaneous social segregation and embryonic reorganization on the *human scale,* which deserves our attention—which may one day thrive inside a social body that discourages with the despondency of its immensity and uniformity, a "human being"—always the same—who has not grown. This group, quite mindful of its closed nature, or in any case restricted, tended to provide its members with everything (except bread): a doctrine—a mysticism—summary rites—a "soul" bond that was not extended to such a large number of initiates that the *human warmth* we thirst for so greatly cannot circulate from stem to stern.

In 1942, like Carrouges, Raoul Ubac spoke of "atheist mysticism," adding:

To be specific, it would involve diverting the mystical experience from its essential object: the quest for God, and to keep its methodology of knowledge as well as its "states" like a key that allows the human being to be realized in his totality. Under these aspects the mystic experience coincides with the poetic experience.[54]

In his 1945 article in *Confluences,* Jules Monnerot would go even further:

It will be incumbent upon the true historians to say how surrealism tipped over from dream into myth. Let's keep in mind here that it seems fairly futile to maintain that this has nothing in common with religious phenomena. To the contrary, certain signs could lead us to believe that it heralds a transformation of the spirit of a kind similar only to what can be found in the history of religions. I am well aware that this methodological comparison will inspire the same aversion among both surrealists and Christians: this does not make it any less a matter of prejudice. Nothing characterizes better their religious streak than the surrealists' anti-Catholicism.

How not to recall here what Xavier Bordes says about Elytis carrying out in *Axion Esti,* "under the aegis of the surrealism of Saint John [*sic*], the Eagle of Pathmos," the synthesis "of the values of the Greek religious tradition—Christian—and the values of the pre-Christian Greek world," carried, among others, by "the disciples of Hermes with the pointed caps and the caduces of sooty smoke?"

Victor Crastre notes in 1963 that "Breton thinks and expresses himself mystically each time he surrenders to the natural slope of his thought," even adding, "If Breton always exhibited a vibrant fondness for the Middle Ages, it was because mysticism shone with a particular brilliance in these times. . . . Knowledge could then be attained by nonrational means."[55]

As we are discussing the Middle Ages, I should say a word about the attachment (strange to say the least) that Breton's daily companion for twenty years, Jean Schuster, displayed toward Bernard de Clairvaux. He was regularly mentioned in Schuster's last books, one of those "three priests to spare from a massacre" (with Bartolomé de Las Casas and Dom Perignon) that he cites in *T'as vu ça d'ta f'nêtre!* Perhaps it is because of the very preromantic tones of these words by the Cistercian: "You will find more in forests than in books: trees and rocks can teach you things no professor can tell you."

This affection was one he shared with René Guénon, author of *Saint Bernard* (published in 1929 by Éditions Publiroc), in which he speaks of the "reincarnated Templar" who, guided by spirits, sought to renew the Templar Order as a "Knight of the Virgin," before admiringly enumerating the qualities "of the great saint called the Last of the Church Fathers, and in whom some saw, not without reason, the prototype of Sir Galahad, the ideal and pure knight. . . ."

In Schuster's *Le Ramasse-Miettes* (Crumb Collector), we can read, "I always had a desire to write a *true* book that would be a long, breathless reflection on the juncture between a man and his work. When I was twenty, it was Max Ernst and then, much later, it was Stendhal, Benjamin Constant, and above all Bernard de Clairvaux," who was a maker of popes and a key figure of the Christian West. The man who founded the abbey that bears his name near Troyes wrote the statutes of the Order of the Temple, obtained the condemnation of Abelard's theology (to whom Artaud devoted two texts in 1925 and 1927), opposed the progression of Catharism, preached the Second Crusade, and with his sermons wielded a real influence over medieval mysticism. It is true that Bernard de Clairvaux, author of *Praise for the New Knighthood* (that of the Temple in particular), whose goal was to attain full spiritual realization, provides the perfect example of a contemplative individual immersed unwillingly in political and profane life. It is similar to the Celtic monks like Corentin in the legend of the city of Ys, who, for example, attempted—in this instance by delegation in the good city of Quimper—to exercise temporal power in the place of the sovereign. It was also like Saint Bernard, who was also Dante's guide—the kadosh of this Fede Santa—which Guénon tells us in his *L'Ésotéricism de Dante* "displays certain analogies with what was later the Rosicrucian Fraternity, although this fraternity is in no way more or less a direct offshoot."[56] Dante, together with is friends Cino da Postoia, Guido Cavalcanti, and Cecco d'Ascoli, was a member of the group Lieges of Love, who were influenced by the thought of the kabbalists, and he was acknowledged by Breton as a remote precursor of surrealism. Saint Bernard, to return to him, is Dante's guide into paradise in that "sacred poem" *The Divine Comedy* (Paradiso XXVI), placed beneath the sign of three women (perhaps as well "the three great Black Women / raising their arms while facing the East" in the opening verses of *Axion Esti*). Mary the Sacred Feminine, Santa Luci the Light, and Beatrice the incarnation of Sophia d'En Haut,* "the divine Wisdom or universal intelligence," in the words of Franco Peregrino, were decidedly part of this initiatic text, written in a coded language, a "mysteriosophy,"[57] but in the common tongue, which, Mandiargues claims in *The Moon Dial*, exercised a certain influence on Lautreamont, who would have known the version illustrated by Gustave Doré. Praising, by means of a citation from Geoffroy of Auxerre, "the inner beauty of that man," Schuster also explains (in "The Discreet Charm of God") that "God's massive presence† *pushes* man *back* within himself where, as Bernard said, the spirit of wisdom bases interiority on unity." Schuster later added:

---

*From heaven
†Schuster refers here to God's presence in the setting of the worship place.

> The cause of Bernard de Clairvaux, in my opinion, is more the cause of the mind being stretched to its uttermost limits toward its inner unity and the "divine" radiance that presumes, than the secular combat to which his words and actions were reduced. This God, who traveled into the imaginal realm of men, was only a vast reflection of their desire to be. I believe Bernard nearly succeeded in creating the true man. After him, everything became spoiled and ruined. The slope descends for five centuries, and from the neighboring Touraine we learn that the soul is forever separate from the body. From this point, God is no longer the metaphor for the yearning spirit, but the customs officer at its borders.[58]

Régis Debray, therefore, is right when he echoes Schuster in his response to Jean Clair's detestable pamphlet (mentioned in the introduction):

> Yes, the hunt was spiritual, and the requisitioning ethical, between duty and destiny. To ask of imagination what others ask of prayer, an increase on a general level, reminds us that we can only destroy what we replace: fire on the divine, make way for the surreal. To make poetry a lifestyle, a rule of life, and the equivalent of a solemn vow catapults us far beyond the aesthetic domain. Beneath the somewhat laughable exteriors of black magic and the mystery sect, with its rites of initiation, hot irons on the chest, and the expulsion of the relapsed heretic into outer darkness, far beyond the crystal balls and gothic novels, it is definitely a *religiosity* that is cropping up here. And not only because it involved, for the lay Druid, binding together dissimilar individuals and turning a heap into a coherent whole; nor because one cannot combine with impunity a certain world weariness and disdain for the grandeurs of the established order with the idea of a higher consciousness reserved for the emotional and the oneiric. But because the hope in a reconciliation between heaven and earth, the ardent expectation of the "supreme point" is truly Gnostic. A classic example of the finger in the unbeliever's eye. Despite their declared scorn for all religions, and to the

tune of the thousand times repeated cry of "back to your kennels, yelpers of God," the atheist surrealists have decidedly replayed the straw and beam game of the religions of salvation. Like all those who expect from the literary act the same kind of redeeming grace and the same somewhat esoteric election that the faithful expect of the sacramental action. We are no longer in the domain of literary games, nor even in one of philosophical choices, but purely and simply in the sacred from the time a life choice has been elected, by means of a vocation, that places the entire individual under a tension that could potentially be fatal.[59]

At an earlier time (March 1957), Frédérick Tristan, who made sure to clarify that "he was not part of the clan of young surrealists" but rather "close to the magazine *La Tour Saint-Jacques* and René Alleau" (himself a member of the surrealist group), pointed out in his article "Gradiva Rediva," published in the first issue of *Structure,* that "current surrealist research [was] of a purely metaphysical origin, like it or not."[60] Didn't Roger Gilbert-Lecomte (surrealist in drug use) say, "The Grand Jeu is a game of chance, in other words a gratuitous one, or better yet a game of 'grace': the grace of God and the grace of gestures"?

In Debray's long extract (which was impossible for me to abbreviate) there is an allusion to the 1948 tract "Back to Your Kennels, Yelpers of God," signed by fifty-two members of the group, a text intended to counteract the attempt to recuperate surrealism by Christians for apologetic purposes. For example, a certain Dom Claude Jean-Nesmy, a Benedictine, shamelessly spouted, "André Breton's program shows evidence of aspirations that are completely parallel to our own," and a Claude Mauriac talked about "Saint André Breton," [!] or "Breton as a moralist and mystic" in the magazine *La Nef.*[61] The tract concludes with this strong language:

> Whether the politicians among them (the Christians) tactically renounce the anathema is not enough for us to renounce what they call blasphemies, invectives which are clearly devoid in our eyes of

any objective when it comes to the divine but continue to express our irreducible aversion toward anyone who gets down on their knees."[62]

Jean Clair tells us that 1948 was the year when "the Church no longer held any real power and to the contrary had just revealed the blood tribute it had been forced to pay to Nazism."[63] Alas, the good apostle forgot that the church, Artaud's "Apostolic and Roman madam," had seriously compromised itself with the Vichy government and found itself proportionately discredited, whereas Constant Chevillon, for example, Jean Bricaud's successor at the head of the Lyonnaise branch of the Martinist Order but also grand master of the Rite of Memphis-Misraïm, had perished thanks to the bullets of French Fascist militiamen! He did not deem it helpful, either, to clarify that this blood tribute had been paid in large part by the Jews, on whose behalf Pope Pius XII refused to intercede, although perfectly informed as to what was happening to the east.

Guy Ducornet in his book *Surrealism and Atheism* had the idea in 2006 of asking 175 surrealists from all countries to "countersign" this manifesto ("Back to Your Kennels, Yelpers of God") in order to "revalidate" it. Paul Sanda's name appears there, in between those of Fabio de Sanctis and Maria Santana. . . . Not to mention Sanda's small pamphlet *God Is Love (etc.),* published by L'Âne qui butine in Mouscron, Belgium, in which there is a passage from which I cannot resist quoting:

> Since the time I began this book it has become common knowledge how the Church has recently undertaken the task of studying itself more thoroughly, particularly its personal concerns, and this thanks to the work of those remarkable scholars with such lofty and profound minds: the pedophile priests, and thanks to the fantastical nature of those highly qualified brothels known as theological schools, and the charitable movements overseeing pornographic, pastoral, and missionary activities, whose purpose is to bugger the blacks as deeply as possible, and all the dirty wogs living in the underdeveloped countries where no one can any longer pursue any

real sexual tourism in peace. . . . It would take too long to list, even as simple allusions, the abundant theological literature whose subject is the Church's personal study of itself.

Ah Great! One worthy document (which gives an *orgasmic* hit to the present exposition), I cannot omit: the *Encyclical Mystici Corporis* by Pipe [*sic*] Pius VII (not sure of the year), a document that offers a vast, clear doctrine on the divine institution through which Jesus continues his work of buggered buggerer in the world. So here are the words of the Vatican's big ballsack: "The doctrine of Christ's mystical body, which is the Church, was originally received from the Redeemer's own lips." In the name of god . . . god damn, good god. . . . Come on, your Holy ballsiness!

One small detail: it was Bataille who pointed out that when the fathers of the church used the word *god* without a capital "G," it was to designate the devil.

Paul Sanda, then, to make his point perfectly clear, states:

This little book is definitely a pamphlet against the Roman Catholic Church and not against Belief. Sacrilege is necessary to advance in the initiatory order; the right to blaspheme is fundamental for free spiritual adhesion.

These remarks, only the most benign of which I've quoted here, are in a line of direct descent from those that conclude the 1948 tract cited above, and even those of Benjamin Péret, who writes in *Le Déshonneur des poètes* (The Dishonor of Poets) that it is up to them "to utter the ever sacrilegious words and permanent blasphemies,"[64] and Jehan Mayoux, who were both notorious, virulent anticlerics. Furthermore, as Alquié notes, "Humanism being first asserted theoretically, the revolt against God is no longer a desperate revolt against being, but a revolt against the illusions that, according to Breton, specifically prevent the human being from succeeding to be!" Schuster writes, "It is common knowledge that at the beginnings of surrealism there was a quest for a *metareason* and the necessity for drawing from the most varied and best hidden sources of thought in order to release a new logic founded on the wreckage of rationalism."⁶⁵ Paul Sanda also emphasizes, "One thing we expect from this inner exploration is first and foremost the integral restoration of proper freedom."* Sanda then merely advanced a step further than Breton, even if it is a giant step but on the same path.† This does not deserve the loss of a tool like the House of the Surrealists in Cordes-sur-Ciel at a time when their voices desperately need to be heard, a time when "the transformations, ruptures, and mutations that lead traditional cultures to the world we know are taking away from us—irremediably or not—the orphic notion of a world heeding a secret harmony from which a few vibrations could be gathered by an inspired poetry, and do not leave in a better state what originates in the marvelous!"⁶⁶

Philippe Audoin heads in the same direction with these remarks, which now seem well ahead of their time and in the current state of things reveal the caducity of the objections raised by Paul Sanda's mockers:

> Jules Monnerot was completely justified in comparing surrealism to Alexandrian gnosis some time ago. Moreover, Breton had publically accepted this strange kinship. Wouldn't it be enough, after all, that a plan of collective liberation animating a group of men who are exemplary or striving to be, for him to feel on familiar territory? *The most aberrational Gnostic sect, even if it takes sides against life, even if it ruins or contaminates life, only does so with a higher, freer life in mind, one that in the final analysis is accessible in this world.*

---

*This is a phrase that can be compared to something I quoted in the foreword from Breton's *Second Surrealist Manifesto*: "Remember that the idea of surrealism tends simply to the total recuperation of our psychic strength by a means that is nothing less than a vertiginous descent within us, the systematic illumination of hidden places and the gradual darkening of others, a perpetual promenade in the heart of the forbidden zone."

†Additionally, as Nadja said, "There are no lost steps!" And didn't Breton emphasize in "Perspective Cavalière" (*La Brèche,* n° 5, October 1963), "Surrealism is a dynamic whose vector today is not to be found in *La Révolution surréaliste* but in *La Brèche!*" And in 2013?

> *Furthermore, beyond the tawdry Judeo-Christian fineries and angelologies, the God of the Gnostics appears on more than one occasion as* immanent *(italics added).*[67]

Audoin's remarks should be compared with this phrase of Louis-Claude de Saint-Martin: "What's more, gnosis, a formless radiance, pays no heed to religion, vital burst of the form." Finally, Breton, again, states in the *First Surrealist Manifesto:*

> Under the pretense of civilization and progress, we have managed to banish from the mind everything that may rightly or wrongly be termed superstition or fancy; forbidden is any kind of search for truth that is not in conformance with accepted practices.

Later, still faithful to himself, Breton writes:

> It is deplorably shortsighted and timid to admit that the world can be changed once and for all, and then to deny oneself beyond that, as if it were profanatory, any incursion upon the immense lands that still remain to be explored.

It might be the case, however, if the implicit future makes it possible to avoid the iceberg visible on the horizon that Claude Tarnaud had already identified in 1968:

> Once rid of their barbaric, Semitic-Babylonian, and crassly individualistic nostalgias, hermeticism and alchemy may be extrapolated to the socio-economic-scientific plane.

Breton's words take on their full meaning when compared with a recent remark by Alain Joubert (a former player—though a minor one—in the surrealist adventure).

> This "position of the mind" that is surrealism evolves over time and, having neither a precise shape nor privileged aesthetic, it cor-

responds with an approach to life that cannot be reduced to many others.[68]

This is undoubtedly not false, even if its irreducible character remains quite mysterious, given the artistic vagaries and ambiguities surrounding it, which allows Joubert to cast anathemas that contradict his own remarks, when he may have been better advised to contemplate this remark by Alain Jouffroy: "Surrealism never confused itself with a dogma, nor would it ever have presented itself as such to those who understand it or who fit into its perspective,"[69] or even this passage from the first issue of *La Révolution surréaliste:* "Surrealism does not present itself as the exposition of a doctrine. Some ideas that currently serve it as departure points can in no way be permitted to prejudice its later development!"

"The true initiates," says Yves Fred Boisset, "free and conscientious seekers, strive to remain faithful to a tradition, which, over the course of the ages, has demonstrated its fidelity to spiritual ideals and its attachment to a social deontology that neither religions nor politics have been capable of respecting, as every page of History can show."

14
KEEPING A LEVEL HEAD?

As if the volcano had frozen the poets in terror
   GÉRARD LEGRAND, *LE RETOUR DU PRINTEMPS*

To / Public Writers / And to / Poets poets / To / Expansion / To / Mania / To / Confidence / To / Vanity / To / Candor / To the prophets / As to the virtuosos / Let us tirelessly remind ourselves / That / THE EXPERIENCE CONTINUES
   PAUL NOUGÉ, *HISTOIRE DE NE PAS RIRE*

We must, if I dare say so, keep a level head. Heirs of the occultist tradition of romanticism and symbolism, there were many individuals in all the groups in France and elsewhere who claimed to be surrealists, and Breton was the first, who, in the attempt to re-enchant the world, examined the various components of esotericism, shared its goals, and borrowed certain objectives from it. This is an incontestable fact. But how is it possible to imagine that they could have subscribed, for example, to the gnostics' rejection of the physical world and their disdain of sexuality and thus human love? How is it possible to imagine that they could have adopted as their own the very Guénonian notion that "the tradition has a nonhuman origin that guarantees its doctrine's infallibility," as Jean During puts it? How could they have have accepted for even an instant the idea that alchemy holds "the conviction that an intelligent, conscious energy is involved in the origin of life; the belief in a possible form of the physical immortality of the human being; a representation of the world subject to an inescapable law," as Françoise Leclecq-Bolle de Bal maintains? It is impossible to assume they were so weak as to subscribe, although they momentarily followed the same path, to Amadou's position.

> Among other things, my research thus has a bearing on astrology, alchemy, magic, and occultism in general. Does this surprise you? You doubt that these may be paths for finding God? His paths, which are sciences, go hand in hand with a personal approach that culminates in theosophy. Etymologically, theosophy is defined as the Wisdom of God, the presence of God, outside Himself in the world.[1]

Nor is it possible to imagine even for an instant that surrealists shared Carrouges's notion that "the essential role of religion and hermeticism was to repair the consequences of this fall and reintroduce man into a definitive *wonderland*." All the more so since this fall is to be understood as the cause for man's misery on Earth. How could they entertain even momentarily a notion like that of *reintegration*, for example, or, as Carrouges discreetly puts it, the *recuperation of lost powers* (and not "psychic powers," as Breton specifically puts it), which, presupposing the fall, redemption, and the existence of a redemptive God, is obviously foreign to all their mental categories, especially, as good Hegelians, if any idea concerning some kind of fall occurred to them, it would be rather that of God himself? At best, far from acknowledging "in any way the fact of a primordial fall," as Carrouges implies Breton did, they asked themselves what occultists like Martinès de Pasqually could have meant by it. In other words, if we think the dominant thought of the eighteenth century was expressed in two basic currents—a "materialist" trend embodied by the philosophers and encyclopediasts; the other spiritualist, represented by the illuminati of all kinds—then the first current led to modern rationalism and the world that was ruined in the catastrophe of the First World War, thus making explorations of the spiritualist path legitimate, but with God recused, the operation became aleatory, to say the least! And everyone seems to be in accord on this point.

Looking in from the outside in 1956, Robert Amadou (in his postface to *The Mirror of Magic*) points out:

> Mysticism and pseudo-mysticisn, demonic possession and pseudo possession, theology and cosmology: if both God and the Devil are denied and if all transcendent morality is not only rejected but violently attacked and contravened, these opposites are meaningless. Surrealism's decidedly materialistic position makes *exclusive* its insistence on the reality of the psyche whose gulfs it sounds with a rare audacity and a perfect mastery (italics added).

From the inside, in his preface to the reissue of *L'Art magique* in 1991, Gérard Legrand writes:

> Deep down, the *act of faith* an orthodoxy demands (even a heretical one) was absolutely impossible for Breton, and I believe I can vouch for it: whatever the certainties and uncertainties of each surrealist, not one would have held a different opinion in this regard.[2]

Yet curiosity seems to have played a large role in their approach, as shown by this remark from Breton's interview by José M. Valverdo for the *Correo Literario* of Madrid in 1950:

> I haven't given up the idea of further exploring the question of whether surrealism truly meets up with "traditional" thought—let's say that of Swedenborg or Fabre d'Olivet—to the point of eventually merging with it; or if it only intersects it at various points.

Nonetheless we should accept the pertinence of this observation by Jacques Van Lennep: "Of course the majority of surrealists rejected

God, but they kept what we called the being's progressive concentration."[3] This is how Jean-Claude Silbermann, echoing the question Breton raises in *Nadja* ("is it true that the *beyond,* the entire beyond, is present in this life?"), can say in a somewhat convoluted way in an interview with Jean Schuster (in May 1990):

> Immanance, spoken of so highly in surrealism, is a joke. I think there is transcendence, but one without God. . . . If we have any kind of intellectual *mission,* it would be to *steal* from the monotheistic religions' *thieves* anything divine there might be.

Schuster concurred with these remarks,[4] which simply echoed those made by Philippe Audoin at the Cerisy Symposium in 1966.

> Transcendence, if there is any transcendence, is an inner transcendence, and what has been invested in entities that have been more or less imposed by tradition, culture, and society, must be recovered and restored to the subject.[5]

In 1924, in *Deuil pour Deuil (Mourning for Mourning),* Robert Desnos put it this way:

> I do not believe in God, but I have a sense of the infinite. No one has a more religious spirit than I. I ceaselessly collide with insoluble questions. The questions I definitely would like to accept are insoluble. The others can only be posed by individuals with no imagination and cannot interest me.[6]

Nonetheless it is equally true that some persistent ambiguities pose a problem, ambiguities illustrated by the following phrase by Philippe Soupault's hero Julien, from *En Joue! (Take aim!)* written in 1925. In his 1979 foreword to *Take aim!* he admitted that this character owed much to himself, of course, and to Desnos as well as to Jacques Rigaut, Pierre Drieu La Rochelle, and René Crevel.

Atheists are the ones who make me believe in God's existence. They are the true believers, not those crowding around an altar. To deny it is necessary to believe.[7]

From this perspective the Carrouges affair is also emblematic. It exploded after the release of the book *André Breton and the Basic Fundamentals of Surrealism*, at a time when it became clear that Breton, the author of *Les États généraux*, retained all his trust and friendship in Michel Carrouges, who was associated with the work of the group but who, as noted by Alquié, had claimed in *La Mystique du surhomme* (a serious study published some three years earlier by Gallimard and not some tiny, marginal publisher) "to insert the surrealist project in the context of a great Promethean project, through which man would strive to annex the entire religious territory." Carrouges wrote the following, perfectly crystalline words:

> The idea of an impersonal and immanent god is unthinkable. This is not a dialectical contradiction; it is pure nonsense. The word "God" as a noun can only designate the divine powers insofar as they relate to themselves primarily as autonomous, free, conscious, and self-acting entities. To call God just anything, such as the whole of everything, but stripped of the supreme independence conferred by self-awareness and will, in other words self-determining freedom, has no meaning whatsoever. It is simply giving a false name to something that could at most be the divine, in other words the deity as adjective, a characterization related to this world with which it identifies. We can then speak only on the divine as a general quality of the universe, or perhaps the most eminent part of the universe. *In any case we have broken the circle of God's omnipotence and replaced the conscious sovereignty of his free will by the wheel of fortune and the blind empire of Fatum*," [which] "buries man in animality"[8] (italics added).

This is the kind of stuff that would perturb any atheist materialist but would draw the attention of a Chazal, for example, who, in the twenty-third part of the second book of *Petrusmok* implicitly admits the influence that *La Mystique du surhomme* may have exerted on him. Not to mention the allusions in Carrouges's 1950 book to the "original and future glory of man," to a "wonderland" (poor Alice!) openly compared to the lost Eden and thereby giving off a strong whiff of sacristy, to a "humanity that [occupying] the supreme point would be radiantly sovereign, instead of being subject to the whip blows of antagonisms, as it would have ceased at this level . . . would find itself freed of all hurt and servitude, because it would be carried above their conflicts like a vessel that rules the waves!" In all likelihood Breton knowingly accepted Carrouges's presence in the group—especially as he had frequented it since 1945 and had been in contact with Breton since before the war. The question therefore arises, it seems, "to know whether Carrouges used his surrealist training for the profit of the 'Church,'" to use the terms of Duchamp—who refused to take a stand on the matter—in a letter published in the fourth issue of *Médium*. The disrupters of the lecture "Is Surrealism Dead?" given in 1951 by the Catholic writer, were effective in "forcing Breton to take a position,"[9] as Gérard de Cortanze put it. There was thus clearly confrontation between two lines in a recurring crisis in the life of the movement, that of the partisans—including Breton—of a certain esoteric approach and that of the upholders of a strictly hard-line atheism, a crisis whose beginnings, according to Pastoureau, went back to the disagreements about what standing to give the "occult" that arose when preparing the 1947 exhibition, which explains the tone of his letter to Fardoulis-Lagrange cited in the introduction.

And it was Breton, the alleged inflexible chief (he was, in fact, says Alquié, surrealism's "intellectual and reflective conscience," basically a good definition of Régis Debray's "fratriarch"), who, to preserve the unity of the movement, yielded, although this did not prevent some people from leaving the group. In any case, this affair clearly shows the limits of what the group could accept but also shows how much its main organizer could tolerate personally.

It should be clearly acknowledged that the surrealists who ventured on the paths of esotericism did so in the purpose of sweeping away "the modes of thought of a bygone era,"[10] to counterbalance or even eliminate the influence of institutional churches because "while they preach revolt against the human condition and proclaim hopes of a transfiguration of life by poetic magic," as Carrouges says, they do so with other words, for the purpose of also combatting the positivist reason that has been conceived and presented to the world as a guarantee of the advent of a radiant future by contributing to "the hieroglyphic interpretation of the world," in the words of Jean-Louis Bédouin, and by exploring new paths to the imaginal realm and the marvelous.

We must keep in mind, as Philippe Noble quite rightly notes in his foreword to Hester Albach's book *Léona: The Heroine of Surrealism*, that "the intention" of this movement "was never to resolve enigmas but to propose new ones." We should also recall with Raoul Ubac:

> It would be futile to believe that the artist invents symbols; on the other hand, he can rediscover them, finding them within himself so as to give them, plastically speaking at least, a new life. The modern artist therefore finds himself confronted by a problem that his freedom alone cannot resolve. But fortunately for him, symbols live a latent life; plastically they are not codified and every era finds them anew, or rather rediscovers those for which it feels a profound need, by giving them a new form.[11]

This opinion mirrors that of Breton when he speaks of "the eternal vigor of symbols, which impose on human behavior a constant harmonic reference to that irrational and fabulous element concerning origins and endings,"[12] but also Carrouges's emphasis in *Le Sismographe surréaliste* that "symbolism refuses to be bivouacked, it is universal or it does not exist."[13] We can only concur with these observations, although it is necessary to temper their apparent focus on the arts by recalling that Ubac stated elsewhere in the same book (*Tracés sur la plage*), "Surrealism was also an ethic, a global vision of the world that needs to be called back into question. It had to take action on every plane." Breton would put the final touch on his Belgian friend's analysis with this quote taken from Raymond Abellio's study *The Modern Spirit and Tradition*:

The evocative power possessed by symbolism stems from this implicit structuration, which props up its connections and confers upon them an integrational power independent of the "literal nature" of the symbol, a power that proclaims each symbol is itself integrable and only a focal point of meaning provisionally isolated within a much larger focal point that awaits naming.[14]

In view of which, the surrealists adopted a specific attitude to symbols and the values they support, which was clearly noted by Marcel Lecomte in 1946. In his article "The Lost Secrets," previously discussed in chapter 8, he partially echoes Guénon's claim that symbolism is "the preeminent metaphysical language" and says about Dali, Ernst, or Breton:

> Far from still wishing to remain in a state of attentive humility or submission in their quest of these secret values, these men, in their conviction that the primary virtues and meanings of these traditional values had been forgotten since the disappearance of the ancient societies in which they had been mysteriously formed and which no longer reappeared, for example in medieval, renaissance, and modern art, except as incantation and suggestion sometimes indeed singularly potent and radiant. And these men, so to speak, sought to recreate them by themselves. They no longer wished their sovereign protection. They wished their help in grasping a memory.

This could apply to many more figures in the surrealist circles of influence! The "invention of a tradition," which was made necessary after the alleged "war to end all wars" that had definitively ruined the ideology of "progress," and was made essential after the escalation of horror that was World War II and the atomic threat (a technological version of the sword of Damocles), thus clearly seems to have traveled through a certain rediscovery of the tradition, but not at the price, however, of a return to God. From the alchemist's motto, *ora et labora* (pray and work), Breton's friends could, if need be, accept the second term but certainly never the first. "The surrealists," Bédouin lucidly notes, "for all their passions for the cursed sciences, especially the one whose origin [in the West] is attributed to Hermes, nonetheless were only more rigorous in their decision to move cautiously through this domain." This was specifically to the degree that "there is no poetic physics, strictly speaking [and that] poetry, differing in this way from alchemy, is not *operative!*" Not to mention theurgy . . .

What this means concretely, as Pascaline Mourier-Casile notes when writing about only Breton, is that what the kabbalistic tradition provided him with "was a fascinating reserve of the imaginal realm, which could be drawn from to reactivate and give new life to the great human myths," and that the majority of surrealists simply took possession of traditional symbols and images for use as their prime matter, without the spirituality that goes with them, a little in the same way as the two initiators of the movement were inspired by the scientific methods of Freud and Janet for writing *The Magnetic Fields.* Not to the point, however, of falling into the excess embodied by the ominously colorful figures of Jacques Bergier and Louis Pauwels, authors of the famous *Morning of the Magicians.* This book was demolished by Robert Benayoun in his article "The Twilight of the Hucksters" (*La Brèche,* n° 1, October 1961), in which he denounces "the authors' superficial almost exotic curiosity," the "almost incredible sloppiness of the whole work" and for good measure, "its reactionary method," [*sic*] which was only capable of interesting "all the cartomancers, all the suburban spiritualists, subprefecture theosophists, and Icelandic swamis of the hemisphere."

Alongside his attempt to detour the basic fundamentals of surrealism, Michel Carrouges was obliged to acknowledge, "The distinguishing feature of surrealism is to approach such ideas* as closely as possible without ever giving them unrestricted right of the city, so to speak, and remaining continuously ambiguous." Nadia Choucha even states:

> The surrealists adopted occult theories, not so much as a challenge to the facts of science and logic, but as a challenge to the values attached to these facts.[15]

---

*He refers to those ideas linked with occultism.

This observation is directly echoed by Guy Girard when he stresses:

In the battle against capitalist abjectness and the miserable situation provided for the mind's resources, it involved the interrogation of ancient social harmonies and the secrets of their magic art* (and why not?), convincing revolutionary circles that the creative power of language was not lost. A power which came from the deepest valleys of New Guinea gave life to the Golem of Prague as it did the mechanics of passions in Fourier's work, determined oneiric freedoms and offered to whoever sought to seize them, its tools of dreams on the anvil of days.[16]

Antoine Faivre, speaking of Jacob Böhme, then writes:

Finally, theosophy believes the human being possesses the ability, generally in sleep, but always potential, to establish contact with the divine world and with entities from a higher order of reality—to "plug" into them, in some way. This ability is based on the existence of a specific organ inside us, a kind of *intellectus,* which is the "*creative* (or '*magical*') *imagination.*" This mainly allows the subject to have the experience of a "central" vision or intuition, in order to explore all levels of reality, and to experience a "second birth."[17]

If we follow Faivre's example here, we could be tempted, once the unacceptable reference to the divine is removed, to ask ourselves it there wasn't a "secular theosophy" aspect in surrealism, if I may put it this way†—and perhaps this is the same as the "atheist metaphysics" of

---

*This "magic art" is that of primitive civilizations.
†In *Major Trends in Jewish Mysticism,* Gershom Scholem writes, "Theosophy signifies a mystical doctrine or school of thought which purports to perceive and to describe the mysterious workings of the Divinity, perhaps also believing it is possible to become absorbed in its contemplation." If we accept, with Breton, that the spiritual element only takes form with the individual psyche, that is if we replace transcendence with immanence, we could venture so far as to speak of a "secular theosophy," if this oxymoron is not entirely devoid of meaning.

Silbermann[18]—that is capable of explaining the many incursions into esoteric domains explored in this book, in quest of the occult philosophy described by Eliphas Levi in *Transcendental Magic*.

> Behind the veil of all the hieratic and mystical allegories of ancient doctrines, behind the darkness and strange ordeals of all initiations, under the seal of all sacred writings, in the ruins of Nineveh or Thebes, on the crumbling stones of old temples and on the blackened visage of the Assyrian or Egyptian sphinx, in the monstrous or marvelous paintings, which interpret to the faithful of India the inspired pages of the Vedas, in the cryptic emblems of our old books on alchemy, in the ceremonies practiced at reception by all secret societies, there are found indications of a doctrine that is everywhere the same and everywhere carefully concealed. Occult philosophy seems to have been the nurse or godmother of all the religions, the secret lever of all intellectual forces, and the absolute queen of society in those ages—when it was reserved exclusively for the education of priests and of kings.

Born in the seventeenth century of the reinterpretation and reorganization of what had been handed down or recovered from the various ancient traditions—the neo-Pythagorian, neo-Platonic, hermetic, gnostic, early Christian, kabbalistic, and even, more recently, alchemical traditions—Freemasonry invented itself as a tradition to promote the values of tolerance, progress, and freedom of conscience. In the same way, it clearly seems that surrealism, starting from the same "material," augmented in particular by the contribution of the German romantics,* Hegel, Marx to a certain degree, and a somewhat interpreted Freud, but

---

*The remark about the role of romanticism is based on André Rolland de Renéville, about whom Alain and Odette Virmaux write in the *Dictionnaire général du surréalisme et de ses environs*, "His true importance has yet to be precisely measured." In *L'Expérience Poétique,* Rolland de Renéville himself writes, "Surrealism, today, despite its doctrinal weaknesses, appears in the final analysis as an attempt to resolve antinomic realities, most particularly the distinction that opposes the center of the consciousness to the dark edges of the mind. The effort it has put upon this inner darkness places

fiercely rejecting the idea of God, if not that of transcendence entirely, had the ambition to invent itself in turn as a tradition for the twentieth century and beyond, based on the three luminous pillars of freedom, love, and poetry, grasped as the ultimate school of knowledge, not to mention the hidden pillar of revolution! In any case, if I can borrow an image, we can compare those who took or are taking part in this adventure to a group of men and women walking very close to the edge of the crater of a volcano* ("Mouth of the heavens, yet mouth of Hell," wrote Breton in *Mad Love*), such as Etna, the gate to Tartarus, for example, unless it is the caldera of Absalon, "the very materialization of the crucible in which poetic images are forged until they are strong enough to shake worlds."[19]

Or as Georges Ribemont-Dessaignes asks in a poem titled (striking coincidence) *Absolute Absalon*, "What are we seeking among the abysses and peaks?"

After all, didn't Pierre Mabille suggest in *The Mirror of the Marvelous* that "the inside of craters" forms part of "piercings toward the marvelous," and didn't René Char write to Breton in *La Lettre hors commerce* in 1947, "I will never be so far gone, so lost in my independence or its illusion, to no longer have the heart to love those tough, disobedient minds who descend into the depths of the crater paying no attention to the calls from its edges!" Some, like Pliny or Empedocles of the past, have fallen; they followed the path of classic initiations into Masonry, in obediences, or rites more or less attached

---

(continued from p. 438) surrealism in the romantic tradition. On consideration of its conclusions, the spiritual domains that have gone unrecognized by man up to the present would be revealed to him by the poet, and this conquest would seem to know no other limits than those of a mind whose frontiers are pushed back by every attempt to approach them."

*Gui Rosey in *Le Miroir du solitaire* (vol. I of *Tirer au Clair la nuit: Oeuvres Vives*), writes, "Wandering to the edge of the precipice in my solitude / I love its attractive turmoil that transports me / Like a cursed wine drawn from a lost vine stock." And André Breton, in *L'air de l'eau*, writes, "The Marquis de Sade has gone back inside the erupting volcano, from which he had come." Alquié notes, meanwhile, "Colored by occultism, if not by religion, surrealism remains *on the edge of belief* and refuses the precise formulation offered by a faith" (italics added).

to the tradition, as did Sanda, Jameux, Colquhoun, Mabille, or Palou; received the teachings of master alchemists, as did Camacho and Flamand, or even of gurus of the Gurdjieff (or Salzmann) variety, as did Daumal. But didn't Jean Lacoste ask (in issue 1012 of *La Quinzaine littéraire*) if it would not be more appropriate to see "Empedocles' death in Etna, with the 'bronze sandal' linked to worship of Hecate," as "the symbol of a descent into hell, the precondition for any rebirth," not neglecting to mention that "fire purifies, regenerates, and confers immortality."

Some have gotten burned, although remaining at a "distance from the hearth," as André Breton wrote. Others have experienced "savage initiations," rediscovering by their own means in a more or less complete or consistent way, a little like Nerval, or like an Oswald Wirth declaring at the end of the nineteenth century, "One is not initiated, one initiates oneself," the paths of this tradition whose contours, despite all, remain fairly vague, seems be passed down through the ages and know periods of revival at times when the crises of civilizations come to a head. But didn't Édouard Jaguer say, "Let us not forget that surrealism is nothing other than the crisis of the mind turned into a movement."[20] Others, finally, were more or less satisfied enjoying the spectacle or inhaling some more or less sulfurous fumes before going on their way.

The point here is not to formulate any kind of judgment about the contents of this tradition—or about the values it carries or could carry—without seeing anything else there, in fact, than a relationship with the world different from the one that has prevailed in the ossified form given it by Latinity and Christianity, but simply to emphasize that, obviously, many resorted to it, most of whom employed it for a new reading of the world in the rather secularized context of the technological age. "Splendid heir," writes Guy Dupré in his article "Le grand indésirable," "of what in the tradition was most childish but also least teachable, keeper of the sole spiritual power we are in any mood to acknowledge, he [Breton] urges all to *journey* by means that remain each individual's responsibility to discover that have to be prompted to each individual by his own demon."[21]

I believe in this domain* as in any other, in the pure surrealist joy of the man who, forewarned that all others before him have failed, refuses to admit defeat, sets off from whatever point he chooses, along any other path save a reasonable one, and arrives wherever he can.[22]

Keeping in mind however that "the transformation of the world will be tied to the image man has of this world; it will reestablish the primordial contacts of man and the universe, whose rupture is one cause for the stupor of our existence."[23]

For Breton's friends as well as their predecessors, Monnerot notes, "It involves no less than entering alive a 'world' conceived as a counter to daily life, within the magic circle of the challenge that finitude casts at itself." The Caribbean philosopher adds:

Men who nurture such devastating pipe dreams are, when seen from a sufficient distance, the choice site for a drama that cedes nothing in grandeur—just think about it—to those ancient myths that have gripped human nostalgia most tenaciously!

So, adjacent to surrealism's active nature, stamped by a constant political commitment, there is clearly a "contemplative" aspect symbolized by the transversal quest of the marvelous. Esotericism, in a variety of forms and taking what Annie Le Brun calls "the substantial part of unconscious makeshift efforts" into account, has thus left its mark on surrealism, that "doctrine containing its own corrections,"[24] an imprint that, without being truly determinative, is still, in the final analysis, much more than decorative or simply anecdotal. As Silbermann notes:

The tradition travels invisibly but entirely through the air—and mainly in the air of language. It is in the original rumor, babble, respiration, breath, the silence between words, between the lines; in

---

*Here Breton refers to the domain of "scientific reverie, so unseemly, in the final analysis, in all regards."

that aura of words through which forms, even before they are given names, are made flesh within us and among us, the world's shared intuition and covenant: tradition.

But it is also because its "understanding of what it means to be human led surrealism to rediscover the spirit of metaphysics on many points, and to oppose the trend of an era that exhibited no concern about the essential absence."* As a means of simultaneously emphasizing the ambiguous nature of this vestige and the fairly persistent, universal nature of the presence of esotericism among the different groups claiming to be surrealist as well as the permanence of its own spirit, I would like to cite this particularly eloquent piece written in 1981 by Philip Lamantia. He was one of the youngest members—and American to boot—of the circle that gathered around Breton in New York during World War II, as well as one of the first to join the Chicago group formed in 1966 by Franklin and Penelope Rosemont.

> The stone I tossed into the air of chance shall come to you one great day and exfoliate the original scarab, the carbuncle of delights, the pomegranate inviolate, the sonorous handkerchief of the Comte de Saint-Germain, all the reinvented perfumes of ancient Egypt, the map of the earth in the Age of Libra when the air shall distribute our foods, the sempiternal spectrum of sundown at Segovia (the stork carrying the golden egg from the Templar's tower), Chief Seattle's lost medicine pouch, our simultaneous presence in all the capitals of Europe while traveling Asia and listening to the million-throated choir of tropical birds, your lost candlewax empire, a madrone forest to live inside of, which we can wrap up in a set of "secret bags" and open on our wanderlust, the turbulent cry beneath the oceans, the extinct birdcalls to a magical vessel Christian Rosenkreutz dropped on his way out of Damcar, beads of coral dissolving the last motors, the redolent eyes of firstborn seers, the key to the bank of sanity, the ship of honey at the height of storms through which we sail to new

---

*This understanding is Breton's, but also that of the movement he represents.

islands rising from the sunken continents and the bridge between sleep and waking we will traverse in constant possession of "the great secret" become transparent as a tear drop—*with no other work but the genius of present life.*[25]

It is all there—or almost. As summed up in Breton's *Constellations,* "Each of us passes and repasses, tirelessly tracking his chimera, calabash head at the end of his pilgrim staff."

In this world where quantity—given the status of a value—rules unchallenged to the devastation of all; this world that is sinking entirely unawares into an utterly sinister "iron age," this world where the "hatred of poetry" triumphs and the "golden key is still beneath the mattress of 'ardent reason,'" this world in which "the sudden darkening of the landscape is connected with the obvious return of the packs to their consecrated kennels," this world to which only the "minds fossilized by utilitarianism and rationalism"* can remain insensitive, in this world the surrealist idea scintillates more than ever like one of Hérold's crystals, Brauner's philosopher's stone, or Breton's star, with all its brilliance highlighted by dream, love, knowledge, revolution, and the true life to be built . . .

In this quest for meaning through the forests of Celtia, over the broken branches left by Galahad and Perceval, or of the East with the companions of Hugues de Payns, to each one his own grail,† in the light of the marvelous . . . without however scattering "cursed bread to the birds."

---

*These quotes are by Jean Schuster and Simon Hantaï, Annie Le Brun, and Michel Carrouges respectively.
†In his text on Breton in *Alternating Currents,* Octavio Paz also rightly recalls, "Surrealism was his chivalrous order and all his activity a *Grail Quest.*"

Notes

INTRODUCTION. TOLERANCE AND ACCEPTANCE OF DIFFERENCE

1. Carrouges, *La Mystique du surhomme*.
2. Batache, *Surréalisme et tradition*.
3. Biro and Passeron, *Dictionnaire général du surréalisme et de ses environs*.
4. Aelberts and Auquier, *Poètes singuliers du surréalisme et autres lieux*.
5. Durozoi, *History of the Surrealist Movement*.
6. Daix, *Les Surréalistes: 1917–1932*.
7. Virmaux and Virmaux, *Roger Gilbert-Lecomte et le Grand Jeu*.
8. Blanc, *Troisième Convoi*.
9. Schuster, *Les Fruits de la passion*.

CHAPTER ONE. UNDER THE SIGN OF THE GOOSE: SURREALISM AND LIBERATION OF THE MIND

1. Guy Ducornet, *Le Punching Ball et la vache à lait*.
2. Schuster, *Lettre à André Liberati contre les acolytes de Dieu et les judas de l'athéisme*.
3. Jean, "Un banquet de têtes."
4. Alexandrian, *L'Aventure en soi: Autobiographie*.
5. Jouffroy, "Lettre rouge."
6. Leiris, *Le ruban autour du cou d'Olympia*.
7. Desnos, *La Liberté ou l'amour!*
8. Ribemont-Dessaignes, "Cahiers Nouveaux," *Ariane*.
9. Mabille, *Égrégores ou la vie des civilisations*; Mabille, *Thérèse de Lisieux*.
10. Jean, "Un banquet de têtes."
11. Buñuel, *My Last Sigh*.
12. Turrent and Colina, "Conversations avec Luis Buñuel"; Paz, *The Bow and the Lyre*.
13. Canonne, *Le Surréalisme en Belgique, 1924–2000*.

14. Ibid.
15. Schmitt and Massoni, *Jan Svankmajer, un surréaliste du cinéma d'animation*. This publication accompanied an exhibit of Svankmajer's works at the Museum of Modern and Contemporary Art in Strasbourg, France.
16. Schuster, *Archives 57–69: Batailles pour le Surréalisme*.
17. Silbermann, "Pas même un tison, sa brûlure."
18. Girard, *L'Ombre et la demande: projections surréalistes*.
19. Audricourt, *Lettres à la cantonade*. Philippe Audoin's text is titled "Contribution à l'histoire des religions occidentales."
20. Charpentier, *Les Jacques et le mystère de Compostelle*.
21. Markale, *L'Épopée celtique en Bretagne*.
22. Crastre, *Le Drame du surréalisme*.
23. Le Brun, *Qui vive: Considérations actuelles sur l'inactualité du surréalisme*.
24. Carrouges, *La Mystique du surhomme*.
25. Breton, *Le Surréalisme et la peinture*.
26. Mandiargues, *Le Point où j'en suis*.
27. Schuster, *Lettre à André Liberati*.
28. Duits, *La Conscience démonique*.
29. Ducornet, *Ça va chauffer! Situation du Surréalisme aux U.S.A. (1966–2001)*.
30. Nadeau, *Histoire de Surréalisme*.
31. Gracq, "André Breton ou l'âme d'un movement"; Decottignies, "La vie poétique d'Ernest de Gengenbach."
32. Gengenbach, *Satan à Paris*.
33. Pierre, *Recherches sur la sexualité: Archives du surréalisme*; Pierre, *Investigating Sexuality*.
34. Alexandrian, *Les Libérateurs de l'amour*.
35. Péan, *La Diabolique de Caluire*.
36. Quoted by Maurice Nadeau in his *History of Surrealism*.
37. Beaufils, *Malcolm de Chazal*.
38. Gengenbach, *L'expérience démoniaque*.
39. Gengenbach, *Surréalisme et christianisme*.
40. Conversation on March 16, 2010, with Charles Bernard Jameux, a member of the group from 1964 to 1969. Most of the remarks attributed to Jameux were gleaned from this discussion.
41. Chazal, *Le Rocher de Sisyphe*.
42. Leiris and Schuster, *Entre augures*.
43. Malraux, *La Tête d'obsidienne*.
44. Alleau, "En Pleine santé."
45. Legrand, "Rationalisme et raisons de vivre."
46. Vendryès, *Vie et probabilité*.
47. The quotation comes from an article, "Théorie de la Dérive," by Guy-Ernest Debord in the ninth issue of the Belgian surrealist magazine, *Les Lèvres Nues* edited by Marcel Mariën and Paul Nougé.

CHAPTER TWO. SURREALISM AND THE SACRED

1. Breton, *Nadja*.
2. Mourier, "Breton/Berkeley: De l'idéalisme absolu comme tentation et comme terreur."
3. Breton, *Le Surréalisme et la peinture*.
4. Laville, *Pierre Mabille: un compagnon du surréalisme*.
5. Breton, *Les Pas perdus*; Alquié, *Philosophie du Surréalisme*.
6. Holten and Pierre, *D'Orgeix*.
7. Gilbert-Lecomte, *Le Grand Jeu*, n° 1, *La Force des renoncements*.
8. Artaud, *Héliogabale ou l'anarchiste couronné*.
9. Breton, *Les Pas perdus*.
10. Aragon, "Une vague de rêves."
11. Lotringer, *Fous d'Artaud*.
12. Casaril, *Rabbi Siméon Bar Yochaï*.
13. Barrault, "L'Homme-théâtre."
14. Legrand, "Rationalisme et raisons de vivre."
15. Ibid.
16. Béresniak, *La Rose et le compas: Rose-Croix et franc-maçonnerie*.
17. Paz, "Henri Michaux."
18. Schuster, *Docsur*, n° 6, summer 1988.
19. Macaire, "Le sommeil de la raison: approches de l'inconscient dans l'expérience de l'Acéphale, 1936–1939."
20. *Acéphale*, n° 5.
21. Artaud, "Lettres sur la cruauté," *Le Théâtre et son double*; Royer, "Connaissance et reconnaissance."
22. Queneau, *Odile*.
23. Albach, *Léona, héroïne du surréalisme*.
24. Imbert, *Les Sources souterraines de la franc-maçonnerie: Mithra et le tarot*.
25. Lebel, "Tanguy, joueur/inventeur."
26. Audoin, *Les Surréalistes*.
27. Saint-Martin, *L'Homme de désir*.
28. Daumal, "Le Paradoxe de la communication."
29. The Zohar was probably written (as shown by Gershom Scholem) between 1280 and 1286 by Moses Ben Shem-Tov and Joseph Gikatila. Artaud's "Le Théâtre de la cruauté (Second Manifeste)" is an article in the book *Le Théâtre et son double*.
30. Daumal, "Le Paradoxe de la communication."
31. Janet, *L'Automatisme psychologique*.
32. Jameux, *Le Vaisseau de feu*.
33. Jameux, *Souvenirs de la maison des vivants*.
34. Dupré, "Visage nu, poitrine à découvert"; Another article, "Unique Annie," was published in 1982, also in *La Quinzaine littéraire*, and was reprinted in Dupré's book *Dis-moi qui tu hantes*.

35. In *Littérature,* n° 11–12, 1923, for example.
36. "The thirtieth issue of *Mélusine, cahiers de recherche sur le surréalisme,* is about Serbo-Croatian surrealism, nadrealizam.
37. Breton, *L'Art magique.*
38. Breton, *Second Manifeste du surréalisme.*
39. Crastre, *Le Drame du Surréalisme.*
40. Bédouin, "Surrealism and Occultism" (*Cahiers d'Hermès,* n° 2, 1949).
41. Pierre, "Coup de semonce."
42. *NRF,* November 1928, on Péret. The name of the author is Gabriel Bounoure. There are two Bounoures, Gabriel, a criticist writing in the NRF, in particular, and Vincent, a member of the surrealist group. This article is a critical note on the collection of poems by Benjamin Péret entitled *Le Grand Jeu.* It is also the title of the article.
43. Gabriel Bounoure, *Marelle sur les parvis.*
44. During, "Nothing on Initiation," which appeared in the issue of *Planète Plus* devoted to René Guénon in April 1970. I cite this magazine with the greatest circumspection, aware that "to associate with *Planète* is to enlist for the great workings of every type of reaction, it is to encourage an attempted generalized lobotomy" (Tract, *Sauve qui doit,* 1961). Jean During, obviously, is quoted, but also the surrealist tract *Sauve qui doit,* hostile to *Planète* and its dubious contents. The quotation is taken from this tract and aims at showing how reluctant the surrealists were toward *Planète.*
45. Breton, *Lettres à Aube.*
46. Breton, *Entretiens,* in *Oeuvres complètes,* vol. 3.
47. Virmaux and Virmaux, *Roger Gilbert-Lecomte et le Grand Jeu.*
48. Monnerot, *La Poésie moderne et le sacré.*
49. Jean Schuster mentioned Denis de Rougemont in a footnote.
50. *La Brèche,* n° 7, December 1964, but also Legrand, *Pour connaître la pensée des présocratiques.*
51. From Caillois's memoirs, *Le Fleuve Alphée* (Gallimard, 1978).
52. "The Star Eaters" was Bataille's contribution to the book *André Masson,* which was published in 1940, on the initiative of Robert Desnos and Armand Salacrou but not reprinted until André Dimanche did so in 1993.
53. Battistini, *Trois Présocratiques.* The first edition appeared under the more meaningful title of *Trois Contemporains.*
54. Kingsley, *Ancient Philosophy, Mystery, and Magic.*
55. Queneau, *Pierrot mon ami.*
56. Bédouin, *André Breton.*
57. Bourassa, André G., quoted in *Surréalisme et Littérature Québecoise.*
58. Chazal, quoted in *L'Ile Maurice protohistorique.*
59. Paz, "André Breton, or the Quest for the Beginning."
60. Artaud, "La Montagne des signes."
61. Artaud, quoted in "La Rite des rois de l'Atlantide."

62. Chazal, *L'Île Maurice protohistorique, folklorique et légendaire*. Chazal's book was cited by Amina Osman in his article "Le Mage de l'île Maurice" on Sur Malcolm de Chazal (collective work put together under the auspices of the Charles Baudelaire Center of Mauritius).
63. Ibid.
64. Gilbert-Lecomte, "L'Horrible Révélation . . . la seule," in *Les Poètes du Grand Jeu*; Gilbert-Lecomte, "Les Atlantes." This is just another poem by Gilbert-Lecomte published in *Oeuvres complètes,* vol. 2 (Gallimard, 1977). *Les Poètes du Grand Jeu* is listed in the bibliography under Zéno Bianu, who compiled and introduced the anthology of poems entitled *Les Poètes du Grand Jeu*.
65. Artaud, *Oeuvres*.
66. Girard and Massoni, "37° North, 73° East."
67. *The King of the World* was mentioned in the correspondence between Martinès de Pasqually, Jean-Baptiste Willermoz, and Louis-Claude de Saint-Martin! *La Mission de l'Inde en Europe, Mission de l'Europe en Asie: La Question du Mahatma et sa Solution* (full title), Saint-Yves d'Alveydre (Dorbon, 1910, reprinted Belisane, 1995); Guénon, *The King of the World* (Paris: Ch Bosse, 1927).
68. Daumal, *Mount Analogue*.
69. Gilbert-Lecomte, *Le Grand Jeu,* n° 3.
70. Suzuki, *Essays in Zen Buddhism*.
71. Duits, "Je suis né à Paris . . ."
72. Arcq, *Cinco Llaves del Mundo Secreto de Remedios Varo*.
73. As noted by Jean-Pierre Lassalle in the December 2006 issue of *Cahiers d'Occitanie,* n° 39.
74. Jouffroy, *Manifeste de la Poésie Vécue*.
75. Linhartova, quoted in *Dada et surréalisme au Japon*.
76. del Renzio, "Incendiary Innocence."
77. This was recorded in the biographical supplement to Colquhoun's exhibition catalog, *Surrealism: Paintings, Drawings, Collages, 1936–1976,* at Newlyn Orion Galleries, February–March 1976.
78. Republished in 1987 by Phebus under the title *Rue des Maléfices*.
79. Flamand, *Les Méandres du sens*.
80. Kober, "Dans le verger de la salamandre (Elie-Charles Flamand)."
81. Sabatier, *La Poésie du XXe siècle*.
82. Published on the web at http://melusine.univ-paris3.fr (accessed July 2, 2013). Eléonora Antzenberger's article about Whitney Chadwick's book *Les Femmes dans le mouvement surréaliste* was first published on this site.
83. "Etoile double" is a collective text probably written by Jean Schuster and José Pierre, signed by all the surrealists who had published articles in *Le Libertaire* and collected by José Pierre in *Surréalisme et Anarchie*.
84. Cited in Adamowicz, *Ceci n'est pas un tableau, les écrits surréalistes sur l'art*. This text also appears in three works by Paul Nougé: *Histoire de ne pas Rire,*

and "Les Images défendues": "Our open eye passes over many things that in the physical sense of the word remain invisible!"
85. Bonnefoy, *Breton à l'avant de soi.*
86. Clair, *Du Surréalisme considéré dans ses rapports avec le totalitarisme et les tables tournantes.*
87. Abbou, *Jean Clair ou la misère intellectuelle française.*
88. Eisner, *Haunted Screen.*
89. Jouffroy, *Une revolution du regard.*

CHAPTER THREE. SURREALISM AND THE LABYRINTH OF THE MIND

1. Duprey, *La Fin et la manière.*
2. Carassou, *René Crevel*. Also see Aragon, "Une vague de rêves," cit. René Crevel: "Au revenant s'oppose le devenant."
3. Carassou, *René Crevel.*
4. Ibid.
5. Duits, *André Breton a-t-il dit passe.* The Anglicist Denis Saurat, who died in 1958 and was the author of several books whose contents are questionable to say the least, is cited in Breton's books *Alouette du parloir* and *Le Surréalisme et la peinture.* He also took part in the questionnaire for Breton's *L'Art magique.*
6. Swedenborg, *Concerning the earths in our solar system.*
7. Carrouges, "Le Hasard objectif." This paper was written for the Symposium on Surrealism at Cerisy, France, July 10–18, 1966 (read by Michel Zéraffa). Interviews were supervised and published by Alquié in *Entretiens sur le surréalisme.* In the notes of his *Le Ramasse-Miettes/Lettre différée à Philippe Soupault,* Schuster also mentions "the influence of Myers and Flournoy" in the genesis and development of surrealism, which he "deemed underestimated," whereas Marguerite Bonnet categorically refutes Myers's influence.
8. Breton, "Sur Robert Desnos," in *Perspective Cavalière* (Paris, Gallimard, 1970).
9. Duprey, *Derrière son double/Spectreuses.*
10. Alexandrian, "Techniques du surréalisme."
11. Guyon, in a footnote to his article on Nerval, "Comme une suite à un ajour d'*Arcane 17*," which gives another definition, about one of the favorite poets of the surrealists, by another surrealist of the "split personality."
12. Zürn, *L'Homme-Jasmin*. These quotes are from "Meeting with Unica," Ruth Henry's preface to the 1977 German edition, *Der Mann im Jasmin.*
13. Rodanski, *Requiem for Me.*
14. Ibid.
15. Gracq, *Au château d'Argol*; Duprey, *Derrière son Double.*
16. Fourré, *Tête-de-Nègre.*
17. Leclercq-Bolle De Bal, *La Métamorphose, mystère Initiatique.*
18. Mansour, "Napoléon," in *Histoires nocives.*
19. Mansour, "Jules César," in *Histoires nocives.*

20. Leclercq-Bolle De Bal, *La Métamorphose, mystère Initiatique*.
21. Jameux, *Le Vaisseau de feu*.
22. Courtot, "Ouverture Italienne" in *Bonjour Monsieur Courtot*.
23. Duits, "Les Fantômes."
24. Caillois, *Le Fleuve Alphée*.
25. Among other works, Yves Elléouët (1932–1975) published two novels with Gallimard "in which the noise of dead kings plays out," *Le Livre des rois de Bretagne* in 1974 and *Falc'hun,* with a preface by Michel Leiris, in 1976. See also the catalogue for the exhibition Yves Elléouët, held at the Quimper Fine Arts Museum, Quimper, France, from June 19 to September 14, 2009, then at the castle of Tours from November 6, 2009, to January 10, 2010.
26. Audoin, *Bourges, cité première*.
27. Sudre, *Introduction à la métapsychique humaine*.
28. Murnau, *Nosferatu*.
29. Also recall Breton's splendid text "Braise au trépied de Keridwen," which serves as the preface to Markale's book *Les Bardes Gallois*.
30. Jameux, *Murnau*.
31. Pierre, quoted in "Le gouvernement de la foudre."
32. Ibid.
33. Reeve, *Old English Baron*.
34. Bouvier and Leutrat, *Nosferatu*.
35. Desnos, *Mines de rien*.
36. See also Ernst, *Première conversation mémorable avec la chimère;* and Aleksic, *Amour, nature et plaisir en picto-poésie*. Cornelius Agrippa, discussed here, was influenced by hermetic thought and neo-Platonism.
37. Luca, *Le Vampire passif*.
38. Leiris, *Images de marque*.
39. Leiris, *La Possession et ses aspects théâtraux chez les Éthiopiens de Gondar*. This is an expanded version of his article "The Bull of Seyfu Tchenger" in the second issue of *Minotaure,* also mentioned in Leiris's *L'Âge d'Homme*.
40. Le Brun, *De l'éperdu*.
41. Caillois, *Le Mythe et l'homme*.
42. Alexandrian, "Techniques du surréalisme."
43. *View 2,* October 1940.
44. Schwartz, "Automatism and Shamanism."
45. Emmerling, *Jackson Pollock*.
46. Houellebcq, *H. P. Lovecraft: Contre le monde, contre la vie*.
47. Jaguer, *Le Surréalisme face à la littérature*.
48. Malestroit, *Julien Gracq: Quarante ans d'amitié; 1967–2007*.

CHAPTER FOUR. SURREALISM AND DIVINATION

1. Eigeldinger, "Notes on the Poetics of Clairvoyances" in *Revue des sciences humaines,* n° 193, January–March 1984.

2. Breton, *La Clé des Champs.*
3. Nezval, *Rue-Gît-le-Coeur.*
4. Caillois, *Les Impostures de la poésie.*
5. Limbour, *Le Bridge de Madame Lyane.*
6. Sudre, *Introduction à la métapsychique humaine.*
7. Alexandrian, *L'Homme des lointains.*
8. As indicated by Rike Felka in her preface, "Franco-German Floating Leaf," for the French edition of Unica Zürn's *MistAKE and Other French Writings,* by the woman who was Hans Bellmer's companion in poverty.
9. Leiris, *Aurora.*
10. *Voix plurielles* 06–01, electronic review of the Association of French Professors of Canadian Universities and Colleges. brock.scholarsportal.info/journals/voix plurielles/article/view/169.
11. Aleksic, "Amour, nature et plaisir en picto-poésie."
12. Desnos, *Trois Livres de prophéties.*
13. Brisset, *Prophéties accomplies.*
14. Piobb, *Le Secret de Nostradamus.*
15. These quotations are from texts for the Raymond Queneau symposium organized by Limoges University in March 1984, published by Clancier-Guénaud in 1985.
16. Breton, quoted in Daix, *Les Surréalistes: 1917–1932.*
17. Grillot de Givry, *Le Musée des sorciers, mages et alchimistes.* The preface is by René Alleau, and the book was translated by J. Courtenay Locke as *Witchcraft, Magic, and Alchemy.*
18. Perks, "Fatum and Fortuna: André Masson, Surrealism, and the Divinatory Arts." This was published in *Papers of Surrealism,* an online journal published by the AHRB, Research Center for Studies of Surrealism and its Legacies, with the support of Essex and Manchester Universities and the Tate Gallery. www.Surrealismcentre.ac.uk/papersofsurrealism.
19. Seligmann, *Mirror of Magic.*
20. Ariëns-Volker, "Alchemical, Kabbalistic, and Occult Symbolism."
21. *Arts,* n° 7, March 1952.
22. Chirico, *Hebdomeros.*
23. Audoin, *Bourges, cité première.*
24. Fini, *Rogomelec.*
25. Roger, "Le jour de l'Étoile."
26. Breton, *Entretiens.*
27. Abeille, *Le Veilleur du jour.*
28. Abeille, *Les Jardins statuaires.*
29. Vanci-Perahim, "Quand les couloirs du sommeil traversent la Roumanie, de la rehabilitation du rêve à l'oniromancie obsessionnelle (1929–1947)."

CHAPTER FIVE. SURREALISM AND ASTROLOGY

1. Bachelard, *L'Eau et les rêves*.
2. Breton, "Sur l'astrologie."
3. Breton, *Les Vases communicants*.
4. Legrand, *André Breton en son temps*.
5. Breton, "Sur l'astrologie."
6. Le Gros, *André Breton et la Bretagne*. Paul Choisnard, who was cited by Alexandrian and mentioned by Le Gros, was a former student of the École Polytechnique.
7. Sebbag, *L'Imprononçable Jour de ma Naissance André Breton*.
8. Nezval, *Rue Git-le-Coeur*.
9. Rodanski, *Requiem for Me*.
10. Duits, "Je suis né à Paris . . ." See also the article "Charles Duits et l'immense oui," by Christian Le Mellec as well as "Un surréel" by Jacques Abeille.
11. Mandiargues, *Un Saturne gai: Entretien avec Yvonne Caroutch*.
12. Biro and Passeron, *Dictionnaire général du surréalisme et de ses environs*.
13. Mezei, "Le Surréalisme en Hongrie aujourd'hui."
14. Doumayrou, *Géographie sidérale*. See also Doumayrou, *Cinq Paradigmes de la géométrie sacrée et leur signature monumentale*.
15. Breton, "Les États généraux."
16. Delteil, *La Deltheillerie*.
17. Dhainaut, *Jean Malrieu*.
18. Pierre, *Le belvédère Mandiargues*.

CHAPTER SIX. SURREALISM AND DARK ROMANTICISM: "IN THE CLOSED PALACE"

1. Le Brun, quoted in "Les premiers romans noir ou l'ébauche d'une science revolutionnaire."
2. Lévy, Preface to *Vathek*.
3. Audoin, *Maurice Fourré, rêveur définitif/Le Caméléon mystique*.
4. Audoin, "Le noir des sources."
5. Bataille, *Les Larmes d'Éros*.
6. Penrose, *Erzébet Bathory: la Comtesse sanglante*.
7. Dauxois, *L'Empereur des alchimistes: Rodolphe II de Habsbourg*.
8. Kobry, "L'effet Arcimboldo."
9. Serbanne, "Panorama."
10. Mabin, "Origines de la création et création des origins." This is an article about the author of *Falc'hun* in the catalog for the 2009 exhibition of his works in Quimper and Tours.
11. Fini, *Rogomelec*; Godard, *Léonor Fini ou les métamorphoses d'une oeuvre*.
12. Lacomblez, *Conversation avec Claude Arlan*.
13. Schmitt and Massoni, *Jan Svankmajer: un surréaliste du cinema d'animation*.

14. Praz, *La Chair, la mort et le diable*.
15. Péret, "Actualité du roman noir."
16. Vadé, *Pour un tombeau de Merlin: du barde celte à la période modern*.
17. Dupré, "Visage nu, poitrine à découvert."
18. Le Brun, *Les Châteaux de la subversion*; Le Brun, *Soudain: un bloc d'abîme* (English translation by Camille Naish, as *Sade: A Sudden Abyss*); Le Brun, *On n'enchaîne pas les volcans*.
19. Ibid.
20. Doumayrou, *Château, comme poindre*.
21. Benayoun, *Petite Pièces pouvant server à approcher (même à comprendre) sinon à expliquer dans son ensemble le surréalisme*. For more on the Désert de Retz, see Cendres and Radiguet, *Le Désert de Retz, paysage choisi*.
22. Galfetti, *Maisons excentriques*.
23. Nocé, "Le réveil du bois dormant."
24. Duprey, *La Fin et la manière*.
25. See Bauer and Morbach, "Les Racines d'un ordre initiatique et le rôle de l'Écosse dans l'apparition de la franc-maçonnerie."
26. Mabille, *Le Miroir du merveilleux*. English translation by Jody Gladding, *The Mirror of the Marvelous*.

CHAPTER SEVEN. THE UNAPPEASABLE SHADOW OF ARTHUR'S COMPANIONS: SURREALISM AND CELTICISM

1. Breton, *Le Surréalisme et la peinture*.
2. Elléouët, "James Joyce."
3. Audoin, "Préface."
4. Julien Gracq, "Foreword." Vincent Bounoure, in *Les Anneaux de Maldoror et autres chapitres d'un traité des contraires,* speaks with respect to surrealism of a "strange knighthood dedicated to a more than perilous quest," but these texts probably date from the beginning of the 1970s.
5. Hubert, *Les Celtes*; Anitchkoff, *Joachim de Flore et les Milieux Courtois*.
6. Albach, *Léona: héroïne du surréalisme*. Foreword by Philippe Noble.
7. Baron, "Le Village marin."
8. Artaud, *Oeuvres*.
9. We should also keep in mind Breton's very beautiful text "Braise au trépied de Keridwen," which serves as the preface to Jean Markale's book *Les Bardes Gallois*.
10. Roy, "Un profil d'André Breton," in *André Breton en perspective cavalière*.
11. Breton, *Lettre à Robert Tatin,* cited by Gérard Bodinier in "La Domaine international du surréalisme."
12. Markale, "Mystères et enchantements des littératures celtiques," *Médium* n° 4, 1955.

13. Lengyel, *L'Art gaulois dans les médailles.*
14. Duits, "Je suis né à Paris . . ."
15. Flahutez, *Nouveau monde et nouveau mythe: Mutation du surréalisme de l'exil américain à l'Écart absolu (1941–1965).* See also Markale, *L'Épopée celtique en Bretagne.*
16. Markale, "Rome et l'épopée celtique," introduction to the main work bearing the same title in *Les Cahiers du Sud,* n° 355, April–May 1960.
17. Published in Breton, *Le Surréalisme et la peinture.*
18. Cabanel, *Croisant le verbe* (including Jorge Camacho's wonderful drawings).
19. Mayoux, *Sous des vastes portiques: études de littérature et d'art anglais.*
20. Mandiargues, *Le Musée noir.*
21. Breton, "Genèse et perspective," a short text incorporated in *Le Surréalisme et la peinture.*
22. Morgane-Tanguy, *D'Armorique en Amérique: Yves Tanguy, druide surréaliste.*
23. Mingam, *Yves Tanguy, surréaliste: "La Conviction du jamais vu"; essai psychanalytique.*
24. Vieuille, *Kay Sage ou le surréalisme américain.*
25. Quoted in Ford, *Yves Tanguy et l'automatisme.*
26. Ibid.
27. Anne Desclos (1907–1998) wrote *Histoire d'O* (Story of O) using the pen name Pauline Réage. She also wrote under the name Dominique Aury.
28. This 1942 painting is described in the catalog *Wifredo Lam, Voyages entre Caraïbes et avant-gardes.*
29. Markale, *Le Grande Déesse: mythes et sanctuaires.* Translated into English by Jody Gladding, *The Great Goddess.*
30. Markale, "Rome et l'épopée celtique."
31. *Le Courrier de l'Unesco,* in "Les Celtes."
32. Le Gros, *André Breton et la Bretagne.*
33. Gracq, *La Forme d'un Ville.*
34. Rodanski, *Requiem for Me.* "Who am I? Always the same ghost, which amounts to saying the other."
35. Fourré, *La Marraine du sel.*
36. Fourré, *La Nuit de Rose-Hôtel.*
37. Mabin, *Yves Elléouët.*
38. Elléouët, *Falc'hun, Livre des rois de Bretagne* (for the second quote), and *Tête cruelle* for the last. Markale's quote about *Falc'hun* comes from the second and last issue of *Surréalisme,* published by Savelli, under the initiative of Vincent Bounoure and friends.
39. Dugué, "Dans un pays de lointaine mémoire."
40. Elléouët, *Tête cruelle.*
41. Graves, *White Goddess.*
42. Breton, *Constellations.*
43. Hobsbawm and Ranger, *The Invention of Tradition,* cited by Andrew

Prescott in his lecture, "Druidic Myth and Freemasonry." The serious drawback to such an approach (that is to say from the point of view of tradition) is that it entirely leaves out surrealism's political dimension.
44. Rémy, *Au treizième coup de minuit: Anthologie du surréalisme en Angleterre.*
45. Keith, "Leonora Carrington." The author bases his article on a text by Salomon Grimberg, *Leonora Carrington, Encultura Reciente. The Book of Kells,* a masterpiece of Irish art, is a medieval illuminated manuscript created by the monks of the religious community founded in that town by Saint Colomban.
46. Le Brun, *Qui vive: Considérations inactuelles sur l'actualité du surréalisme.*
47. This extract is from *Le Mouvement PHASES de 1952 à l'Horizon 2001,* the catalog for the exhibition at the Noroît Center in Arras, France, January 22–April 30, 2000. Created by Édouard Jaguer, former member of La Main à plume, La Révolution La Nuit, Revolutionary Surrealism, and COBRA, the Phases group (and the magazine of the same name) quickly established him, writes Jean-Michel Goutier in this same catalog, as "an energy converter, whose essential task consists of capturing the echoes of scattered forces and spreading them in such a way that their necessary native anarchy melts into a current of ideas," which were on the margins of surrealism strictly speaking, but around very similar ideas.
48. Published in 2003 by L'Escampette with a preface by Pierre Peuchmaurd.
49. Audoin, *Les Surréalistes.*
50. Dupuis, *Histoire désinvolte du surréalisme.* Here, Jules-François Dupuis, concierge at 7 rue du Faubourg Montmartre, and the last man to see Lautreamont alive, lends his name to Raoul Vaneigem, the situationist accomplice of Guy Debord.
51. Flahutez, *Nouveau monde et nouveau mythe: Mutation du surréalisme de l'exil américain à l'Écart absolu (1941–1965).*
52. Elléouët, *Falc'hun.*
53. Audoin, "Baron Zéro."
54. Van Langhenhoven, "Saynètes oecuméniques."
55. Breton, *La Lampe dans l'horloge;* Breton, *La Clé des Champs.*
56. Elléouët, *Falc'hun* for the first quote, *Tête cruelle* for the second.
57. Breton, *Le Surréalisme et la peinture.*
58. Elléouët, *Falc'hun.*
59. Mr. Maurice is the "director" in Fourré's *Tête-de-Nègre.*
60. Leiris, *L'Âge d'homme.*
61. Breton, "Le Pont suspendu," which is an account, moreover, of an event where "another, unknown dimension" manifested itself.
62. Schmied, in "André Breton et le surréalisme international."
63. As described by Goutier in *Lettres à Aube.*
64. Dunne, *Experiment with Time.*
65. Carrouges, "Le Hasard objectif."
66. Desnos, "Journal of an Apparition."

CHAPTER EIGHT. SURREALISM AND ALCHEMY: "YOU WITH LEAD IN THE HEAD, MELT IT DOWN TO MAKE SURREALIST GOLD"

1. Bounan, "Préface pour un anniversaire."
2. Alleau, *Alchimie*. In the third issue of *Médium* (May 1954), Alleau published a text titled "Psychoanalyse et Alchimie." See also Bachelard, *La Psychanalyse du feu*, published in English as *The Psychoanalysis of Fire*.
3. Alleau's March 9, 1953, lecture was cited by Doumayrou in "Surréalisme, esotérisme." With respect to these lectures, Breton writes (*Médium* n° 1, November 1952), "Impeccable presentation, highly qualified speaker. The discussion he engaged at the end of each session with what was inevitably the most mixed kind of audience is a model for *high class*." When *L'Art magique* came out, Breton sent a copy to Alleau with the following dedication: "To René Alleau who knows he will find nothing but ashes here, understanding what distance I was from the hearth when I was burned." (See Benayoun and Polac, *Passage Breton*.)
4. Ressoun-Demigneux, "Artificiala and Naturalia."
5. Amadou, *Occident, Orient: parcours d'une tradition*.
6. Piau, *Tradition alchimique et tradition maçonnique*.
7. Bounoure, "Preface à un traité des matrices." Grillot de Givry writes, incidentally, "You are the very substance of the great work."
8. Albach, *Léona, héroine du surréalisme*.
9. Van Lennep, *Art et alchimie*.
10. Breton, *Second Manifeste du surréalisme*.
11. Breton, *Lettres aux voyantes*.
12. Leiris, "Éléments pour une biographie."
13. Leiris, *Aurore*.
14. Audoin, "La Fontaine de Fortune."
15. Apollinaire, *Le Flâneur des deux rives*.
16. Larguier, *Le Faiseur d'or, Nicolas Flamel*.
17. Clébert, "Jacques Hérold et le surréalisme."
18. Duprey, *Derrière son Double*.
19. Choucha, *Surrealism and the Occult*.
20. Ibid.
21. Poisson, *Théories et symboles des alchimistes*.
22. Lebel, *Marcel Duchamp: Von der Erscheinung Konzeption*.
23. Roob, *Alchimie et mystique: le monde hermétique*.
24. Trouche, "Une morphologie totémique de l'invisible," in the collective work *Wifredo Lam: Voyages entre Caraïbes et avant-gardes*.
25. Interview with Brumagne, broadcast on Radio Télévision Belge Francophone in Belgium, May 22, 2009.
26. Lecomte, *Le Sens des tarots*.

27. Srp, *Toyen, une femme surréaliste*. Catalog for the exhibition organized at the Saint Etienne Museum of Modern Art, June 28–September 30, 2002.
28. Biès, *René Daumal*.
29. Artaud, *Le Théâtre et son double*.
30. Murphy, *L'Alchimie des Philosophes*.
31. Canseliet, "Hermétiques Rudiments d'Héraldiques."
32. Alleau, "Au periscope du temps."
33. Letter of José Lezama Lima to Jorge Camacho, August 1971. In Carlos Franqui, *Jorge Camacho* (Ediciones Poligrafa, 1979). "In Lezama Lima," writes Paz, "the vision of the myths is mythical and he himself, as poet, is a myth of myths" (*Solo a deux voix*).
34. In 2001, Camacho and Roger, along with Eduardo Fernández Sánchez, published *La Cathédrale de Séville et le Bestiaire hermétique du portail de Saint-Christophe et de l'Immaculée Conception,* about which Marie-Dominique Massoni says, "With Jorge Camacho and Bernard Roger as light bearers, alchemy and Freemasonry become the morning and evening star, and poetry, the polar star, arrives like the language of Nature" (*S.U.R.R.*, n° 5). Roger, at the "transparent crossroads where the meeting of the interior world and the interior of the world takes place" (as he wrote concerning Camacho's Le Ton Haut exhibition in 1969), whose article "le Jour de l'etoile" is quoted by Doumayrou in his *Géographie sidérale,* is also the author of the extremely rare *Paris et l'Alchimie* and *À la découverte de l'alchimie: L'art d'Hermès à travers les contes, l'histoire, et les rituels maçonniques*.
35. Camacho, "Jorge Camacho, oeuvres 1964–1996." In this regard, on the subject of Camacho, Jacqueline Storme, a Lille gallery owner and a member of the Atelier de la Monnaie, a parasurrealist group under the leadership of Roger Frézin (of Edouard Jaguer's Phases movement) and Pierre Olivier (a group which presented an exhibition of Camacho, Matta, and Silbermann at the beginning of the '70s), told me the following anecdote, which is worth repeating. There was a bread oven on Storme and Olivier's vacation property in Picardy that greatly fascinated Camacho when he discovered it, and he expressed an interest in renting the property. It was Hervé Telemarque, a friend to all three, who dissuaded Storme and Olivier from accepting this proposition, by explaining to them that with his operative alchemy experiments, their guest would "blow up the whole place."
36. With respect to this exhibition at the Mathias Fels Gallery, Guy-René Doumayrou writes, in his article "Surréalisme, ésotérisme," "Then something never before seen occurred, the paintings signed Jorge Camacho instead of ceremoniously borrowing suggestive images from the suggestive vocabulary of the tradition, founded on concrete experience a poetic language whose allusions could only be deciphered by the initiates."
37. Canseliet, *L'Alchimie expliquée sur ses textes classiques*.
38. See Roger, *À la découverte de l'alchimie*.

39. See Camacho and Gruger, *Héraldique alchimique nouvelle*.
40. Silbermann, "Le Saumon, la cerise et le gardien du trait."
41. Colquhoun, "Waterstone of the Wise," cited by Richard Shillitoe in *Ithell Colquhoun, Magician Born of Nature*.
42. Tristan, "Hérold, 'l'or de l'air.'" The quote from Hérold is taken from Jean-Paul Clébert's article "Jacques Hérold et le surréalisme." It is worth noting in passing that Frédérick Tristan, under the pseudonym of Danielle Sarréra, which he cooked up (with Gaston Criel) "during a party at La Pergola on the Boulevard Saint Germain" (as noted in the foreword to *L'Obsédante*, June 1991), figures among Aelberts and Auquier's *Poètes singuliers du surréalisme et autres lieux*.
43. Cited in Pierre's *Le belvédère Mandiargues*.
44. Van Lennep, *Art et alchimie*.
45. Audoin, "Baron Zéro."
46. Simonelli, "À la recherche de Fol-Yver" [In Search of Fol-Yver].
47. Fourré, *Tête-de-Nègre*.
48. Fourré, *Le Caméléon mystique*.
49. Schmitt and Massoni, *Svankmajer E & J Bouche à Bouche*.
50. Canseliet, preface to *Mute Book*.
51. Bounoure, Pierre, and Courtot, "Lettre sur l'exposition Le Principe de plaisir."
52. Penrose, *Erzébet Bathory: la Comtesse sanglante*.
53. Dauxois, *L'Empereur des alchimistes: Rodolphe II de Hapsbourg*.
54. Ibid.
55. Landemont, *Les Grandes Figures de l'ésotérisme*.
56. Penrose, quoted in *Erzébet Bathory: la Comtesse sanglante*.
57. Ibid.
58. Koyré, "Paracelse."
59. Masson, *Le Rebelle du surréalisme: Écrits*.
60. Van Lennep, quoted in *Art et alchimie*.
61. Roob, *Alchimie and mystique: le monde hermétique*.
62. Sède, *La Rose-Croix*.
63. See the preface to Emmanuel Swedenborg's *Delights of Wisdom*.
64. We should recall that Fulcanelli's *Le Mystère des cathédrales* is dedicated "To the Brothers of Héliopolis," just like Canseliet's *Trois Anciens Traités d'alchimie*. Canseliet always followed his signature with an "F.C.H.," for "Frère Chevalier d'Hermopolis" (Brother Knight of Hermopolis). In his book *Tradition alchimique et tradition maçonnique*, Guy Piau indicates moreover, "The fraternity of Hermopolis is a community whose existence is proven fact. Its members, acknowledged if not well-known alchemists, philosophers, and spagyrists, gathered together during Fulcanelli and Canseliet's time in the back room of a book store specializing in hermetic works."
65. See Frances A. Yates, *Fragments Autobiographiques*.

66. Edighoffer, *Les Rose-Croix*.
67. Sède, *La Rose-Croix*.
68. Hutin, *Les Disciples anglais de Jacob Boehme*.
69. Guyon, "Comme suite à un ajour d'*Arcane 17*."
70. Breton, "Genèse et perspective," in *Surrealism and painting*.
71. Surany, *Alchimie du visible à l'invisible*.
72. Crastre, *Le Drame du surréalisme*.
73. Bounoure, *Moments de surréalisme*.
74. Allendy, "Paracelse, le médecin maudit."

CHAPTER NINE. SURREALISM AND MAGIC

1. Legrand, *André Breton et son temps*.
2. Paz, "Baudelaire as Art Critic."
3. Biro and Passeron, *Dictionnaire général du surréalisme et de ses environs*.
4. Mézei, "Liberté du langage," cited in Choucha, *Surrealism and the Occult*.
5. Paz, "André Breton or the Quest for the Beginning."
6. Löwy, "Langage et magie."
7. Cited by Michel Löwy in Scholem, *Le Nom et les symboles de Dieu dans la mystique juive*.
8. Cited by Michel Löwy in Scholem, "Le Golem de Prague et le Golem de Rehovot."
9. Casaril, *Rabbi Siméon Bar Yochaï*.
10. Jan Potocki, *Manuscript Found in Saragossa*. Taking into account the general issues and questions of this work, it is interesting to note the opinions aired by Axel Preiss in his article on this Polish writer in volume 3 of the *Dictionnaire des littérateurs de langue française:* "This quest (for the Other or the Elsewhere) also makes it possible to see in the *Manuscript* the stages of an initiation, perhaps a Masonic one, in any case one inspired by a certain form of theosophy or illuminism that was in vogue toward the end of the eighteenth century.... This kind of reading is, in fact, possible when we know the extent to which the Potocki family was involved with these doctrines."
11. Löwy, "Langage et magie."
12. *Sefer Yetzirah* (Book of Formation or Book of Creation) is another key text of the kabbalah, which also has similarities to gnosis. This book was translated into French in 1552 by Guillaume Postel and retranslated at the end of the nineteenth century by Papus.
13. Scholem, *On the Kabbalah and Its Symbolism*.
14. Jouffroy, *Une révolution du regard*.
15. Pierre, *Le belvédère Mandiargues*.
16. Seligmann, *History of Magic and the Occult*. The French edition of this book (*Le Miroir de la magie: Histoire de la magie dans le monde occidental*) includes a postface by Robert Amadou ending in these words: "For

our amusement and our edification, Kurt Seligmann invites us as he once invited the amateurs of painted canvases where he led a similar quest, to accompany him on his 'heraldic wanderings.'"

17. Flahutez, *Nouveau monde et nouveau mythe: Mutation du surréalisme de l'exil américain à l'Écart absolu (1941–1965)*.
18. Le Brun, *Qui vive: Considérations actuelles sur l'inactualité du surréalisme*.
19. Rabourdin, "André Breton et Julien Gracq à Nantes: l'anneau de Béatrix."
20. Yates, "Hermetic Tradition in Renaissance Science."
21. Breton, *Signe Ascendant*.
22. "Surréalistes français et yougoslaves" is a file probably organized by Branko Aleksic and published in the April 23, 1990, issue of *La Revue parlée*. Milan Dedinac is listed as "one of the Belgrade Thirteen."
23. Alexandrian, *L'Aventure en soi: Autobiographie*.
24. François de Nomé and Didier Barra were seventeenth-century French painters using the name Monsu Désidério.
25. *L'Art magique* by Breton and Legrand.
26. Choucha, *Surrealism and the Occult*.
27. Legrand, "Rationalisme et raisons de vivre." The tone of this text and the references to Frazer remind us of Gérard Legrand's full role in the production of *L'Art magique*.
28. Béhar, *André Breton, le grand indésirable*. In a September 20, 1956, letter to Yves Elléouët, Breton also wrote concerning *L'Art magique*, "That detestable book you know, still awaits completion, and once I begin to apply myself to it again, the great torments and nightly menaces begin recurring. There are even demons that push impudence so far as to give themselves names; the one of the night before last thought a good idea to keep repeating that he called himself 'Jappard'"(*Lettres à Aube*). The element of comparison he gives his correspondent is also highly interesting as it brings us back to the fin-de-siècle occultism we have already discussed so much: "Everything that could give you an idea close to the atmosphere it creates for me can be found, I think in Huysmans' *En Rade*."
29. Kyrou, *Le Surréalisme au cinéma*.
30. Kral, "L'art du saut dans le vide."
31. Péret, *Au Soleil Noir*.
32. Seibel, "The Fête in vacuity or the Conjunction of Opposites in the paintings of Léonor Fini."
33. Mandiargues, "Story of Psyche."
34. Chénieux-Gendron, "Masks and Metamorphoses."
35. Mandiargues, *Tout disparaîtra*.
36. Brauner's sketchpads are conserved in the National Museum of Modern Art in Paris. The drawing cited appears in *Victor Brauner: Surrealist Hieroglyphs*, the catalog for the 2002 exhibition of the Menil Collection in Houston.

37. Flahutez, *Nouveau monde et nouveau mythe: Mutation du surréalisme de l'exil américain à l'Écart absolu (1941–1965)*.
38. Seligmann, "Dialogue with a Tsimshian."
39. Dedieu, preface to Fini's *Fêtes secrètes: Dessins*.
40. Mandiargues, "L'École du songe."
41. Onfray, *Métaphysique des ruines*.
42. Dedieu, preface to Fini's *Fêtes secrètes: Dessins*.
43. Hames, *The Cinema of Jan Svankmajer: A Dark Alchemy*.
44. Seligmann, *Le Miroir de la magie*.
45. Chadwick, *Women Artists and the Surrealist Movement*.
46. Combalia, "Remedios Varo and Benjamin Péret."
47. Paz, "Remedios Varo's Appearances and Disappearances."
48. Aberth, *Leonora Carrington: Surrealism, Alchemy, and Art*. Cited by Keith in "Leonora Carrington, une somnambule dans la lumière."
49. Paz, *Solo à deux voix: entretiens avec Julian Rios*.
50. Jodorowsky, *Spiritual Journey of Alejandro Jodorowsky*.
51. Keith, *Leonora Carrington, Bride of the Wind*.
52. Mandiargues, "Le Cornet acoustique."
53. Quoted by Le Brun in "Je n'ai plus 'une seul dent."
54. Poniatowska, *Leonora Carrington en la ciudad de Mexico, février 2008*; quoted by Keith in *Leonora Carrington, Bride of the Wind*.
55. Ouspensky, *Fragments d'un enseignement inconnu*.
56. Arcq, *Cinco Llaves del Mundo Secreto de Remedios Varo*.
57. Carrington, *En Bas, précédé d'une lettre à Henri Parisot*.
58. Breton, quoted in *Anthologie de l'humour noir*.
59. In his presentation (André Breton, *Oeuvres completes*, vol. 2) of Breton's *Fata Morgana* (included in *Oeuvres completes*, vol. 2), Étienne-Alain Hubert draws attention to this passage of the poem, in which Breton uses "the enigmatic expression 'Ibis mummy'" and reminds us that the sacred ibis of the Egyptians, one of whose mummies Breton may have seen at the Borély Museum in Marseille, is the symbol of Thoth, who was incorporated into the Hermes Trismegistus of the occultist tradition.
60. Davidson, "Introduction: 'Vivifying Presence'" in *Victor Brauner: Surrealist Hieroglyphs*.
61. Combes, *La Franc-Maçonnerie sous l'Occupation*.
62. Coy, *Forces occultes: Le complot judéo-maçonnique au cinéma*.
63. Marquès-Rivière, *Amulettes, talismans et pantacles dans les traditions orientales et occidentales*.
64. Alexandrian, "L'Être secret de Victor Brauner."
65. Ottinger, *La Collection d'art moderne et contemporain*. In "The Painter's Eye," Mabille came up with a very plausible theory, which he presented as follows: "Our friend's concern for attaining a higher degree of energy through the sacrifice of a serious mutilation was entirely fulfilled. The man

I knew before the accident was self-effacing, shy, pessimistic, and demoralized by his last sojourn in Romania. Today he is free, asserting his ideas clearly and authoritatively, he works with new vigor and achieves his goals more fully."

66. Jouffroy, *Liberté des libertés,* illustrated by Miro.
67. Alexandrian, "L'Être secret de Victor Brauner."
68. Mandiargues, "Certains visionnaires."
69. Kuni, *Victor Brauner dans les collections du MNAM-CCI.* I should also give the following explanation, suggested by Doumayrou in *Géographie sidérale:* "In archaic Greece, the power of this goddess [Pallas-Minerva] was depicted by the *palladia,* real or supposed (supposed) aerolites, black things, heavy and magnetic, mysteriously fallen from the spheres of the imponderable", which "emerging from some rift of the celestial vault ... carry a particle of sidereal fire, the Word."
70. Margiotta, *Le Palladisme, culte de Satan-Lucifer dans les triangles maçonniques.* Published in Grenoble in 1895.
71. Ottinger, *La Collection d'art moderne et contemporain.*
72. Gauthier, *Surréalisme et Sexualité.*
73. Respectively, Michaux with *Exorcismes* and, of course, Breton with *Arcanum 17.*
74. Löwy, "Langage et magie."

CHAPTER TEN. SURREALISM, FREEMASONRY, AND VOODOO: *OGUN FERRAILLE,* THE ELECT COHEN, AND THE GREAT TRADITION

1. Piau, *Tradition alchimique et tradition maçonnique.*
2. Dachez, *L'Invention de la franc-maçonnerie: Des opératifs aux spéculatifs.*
3. Jameux, "Les Sources antiques de la transmission initiatique en franc-maçonnerie: art classique de la mémoire." Jameux mainly cites Stevenson, *The Origins of Freemasonry,* a major book, and Yates, *The Art of Memory.*
4. Ibid.
5. Keith, "Leonora Carrington, une somnambule dans la lumière."
6. Dachez, *L'Invention de la franc-maçonnerie: Des opératifs aux spéculatifs.*
7. Ibid.
8. Vulliaud, *La Pensée ésotérique de Léonard de Vinci.*
9. Canseliet, "Introduction." According to Canseliet, however, a certain Martinus Ortholanus, known as Hortulanus, "the gardener philosopher of maritime gardens," about whom "we know nothing specific," allegedly wrote a "luminous commentary to the Emerald Tablet of Hermes Trismegistus in the fourteenth century," in 1323 to be precise.
10. De la Mirandola.
11. Yates, "La Tradition hermétique dans la science de la Renaissance."
12. Faivre, "L'Obsession de la Renaissance."

13. Porset, *Vampires et lumières*.
14. Bauer, *Isaac Newton's Freemasonry*, with a preface by Michel Barat and a postface by Roger Dachez.
15. Barat, preface in *Isaac Newton's Freemasonry*.
16. Pierre, *Le belvédère Mandiargues*.
17. Crastre, *Le Drame du surréalisme*.
18. Girard, *L'Ombre et la demande: projections surréalistes*.
19. Paracelsus, *The Seven Books of the Archidoxes of Magic*.
20. Breton, *Le Puits enchanté*. "Behold in the glint of the plumbline she who is privy to the secret of moles." Couldn't we in the same way imagine another level than the immediate in the reading of these verses of Maurice Fourré in *La Nuit du Rose-Hôtel*: "And / the sun / of the Equator / in front of / the steps of the man in full flight 'defeated man' / slays / the Shadow / beneath / the implacable plumbline / of the / Vertical"?
21. Carrouges, *André Breton et les données fondamentales du surréalisme*.
22. Daix, *Les Surréalistes: 1917–1932*.
23. Schuster, *Les Fruits de la passion*.
24. Lassalle, "André Breton et la franc-maçonnerie." While it is certain that the Prefect Andrieux, Aragon's natural father, was definitely a Mason up to 1885, the membership of Breton's father in this philosophical school has not been proven, as Lassalle rightly notes. No trace of his membership could be found in the archives of the Grand Orient de France.
25. Ibid.
26. Bischoff, *Max Ernst*.
27. Elléouët, *Falc'hun*.
28. Costantini, Wall and Pylon.
29. Schuster, *Les Fruits de la passion*.
30. Alexandrian, *Le Surréalisme et le rêve*. It is Jacqueline Chénieux-Gendron, though, who uses the expressions "other focus" and "blind spot" in her article "Pierre Mabille, 'Point aveugle' du surréalisme."
31. Lassalle, "André Breton et la franc-maçonnerie."
32. Claude Gavreau, as quoted in Bourassa, *Surréalisme et Littérature Québecoise*. English translation by Mark Czarneci.
33. Laville, *Pierre Mabille: un compagnon du surréalisme*.
34. Ibid. Also Jacqueline Chénieux-Gendron and Rémy Laville, in their preface to Pierre Mabille's posthumously published book, *Conscience lumineuse, conscience picturale*, note that the title of *The Mirror of the Marvelous* is echoed by that of the book published a few years later by Kurt Seligmann, *The Mirror of Magic*. They go on to say, "The coincidence of the titles is not by chance as their abundant private correspondence can confirm."
35. According to Laville, in *Pierre Mabille: un compagnon du surrealisme*, in 1947 Mabille wrote a text, "Surréalisme et vaudou," for the Haitian magazine *Conjonction*, a text that unfortunately appears to be lost.

36. Leiris and Schuster, *Entre augures*.
37. Alexandrian, *L'Aventure en soi: Autobiographie*.
38. In the words of Jacques Leenhardt, quoted in *Wifredo Lam: Voyages entre Caraïbes et avant-gardes*.
39. Mabille, "La Peinture rituelle de Wifredo Lam."
40. Cabrera, *La Forêt et les dieux: Religions afro-cubaines et médecines sacrées à Cuba*.
41. In *Wifredo Lam, Voyages entre Caraïbes et avant-gardes*.
42. Breton, "Pont Levis."
43. Van Rijnberk, *A Thaumaturgist of the Eighteenth Century: Martinez de Pasqually*.
44. Ziegler, *Histoire secrète de Paris*. Cazotte is also the author of *Continuation of the Thousand and One Nights*, whose oriental inspiration, although clearly in the spirit of the age, brings Beckford, the author of *Vathek*, to mind.
45. Labouré, *Testament maçonnique*.
46. Ambelain, *La Chapelle des damnés*.
47. Trintzius, *Jacques Cazotte ou le XVIIIe siècle inconnu*.
48. Dachez and Pétillot, *La Rite Écossais Rectifié*.
49. Anonymous, *Le Comte de Gabalis*.
50. Dumas, *Les Magiciens de Dieu: Les Grands Initiés des XVIIIe et XIXe siècles*. The allusion to the "prophet of reintegration" can be explained by the title of the book Martinès de Pasqually left us: *Traité sur la réintégration des êtres dans leurs premières propriétés, vertus et puissances spirituelles et divines*.
51. See Frère, *L'Occultisme*.
52. Lassalle, "André Breton et la franc-maçonnerie."
53. Homs, "Joachim de Flore." In his book *T'as vu ça d'ta f'nêtre*, Schuster writes, "It is certainly not by chance if André Breton, in search of psychic unity perhaps like no other in his time, was passionately interested in Bernard's disciple, Joachim de Flore."
54. Audoin, *Les Surréalistes*.
55. Lassalle, "André Breton et la franc-maçonnerie."
56. Alexandrian, *Georges Henein*.
57. Jouffroy, "Lettre rouge."
58. Duits, *André Breton a-t-il dit passe*.
59. Lassalle, "André Breton et la franc-maçonnerie." A collaborator on *La Brèche*, Jean Palou (1917–1967) wrote a remarkable book, *La Franc-Maçonnerie*, which is continuously reprinted. His book ends with the following sentence: "Freemasonry in our poor contemporary world in which Science no longer seems to have much Consciousness, remains the place, the mountaintop, the court of the sun, the white isle, the isle of Splendor, the Forest of Brocéliande, the Temple of the Grail, and the furthest edge of Thule where the—salvational—light still shines," a sentence that definitely

deserves emphasis. He is like David Nadeau, who indicates that "among the surrealist writers affiliated with the Thebah Lodge, several discreetly claimed to be members of an initiatory tradition represented by various smith gods of pre-Hellenic Antiquity," the "theurgists of fire," of whom René Alleau speaks in *Aspects de l'alchimie traditionnelle*. The relations of Brother Henri Hunwald, then one of the most active members of this workshop, with the surrealist movement "unfortunately remain scarcely documented." Henri Hunwald was cited in 1949 by Mezei and Jean in *Genèse de la pensée moderne dans la littérature française*.

60. Flamand, *Les Méandres du sens*.
61. Breton, "René Guénon jugé par le surréalisme," *N.N.R.F.*, July 1953, in Batache, *Surréalisme et Tradition*. The Nouvelle Revue Française was renamed N.N.R.F. (Nouvelle Nouvelle Revue Française) after World War II for a few years.
62. Guénon, *Introduction générale à l'étude des doctrines hindoues*.
63. In "Le Pont Neuf," about the place Dauphine, Breton notes, "The execution of the Templars was carried out on this spot on 13 March, 1313, and was largely responsible, according to some, for the revolutionary destiny of the city." A revolutionary destiny that Guénon would scarcely have found pleasant!
64. Guénon, *La Crise du monde moderne*.
65. Van Win, *Contre Guénon*.
66. Laurant, *René Guénon: Les enjeux d'une lecture*.
67. Ottinger, "Le Grand Jeu et le surréalisme français."
68. This appeared in issue 7 of *L'Originel*, January 1978–). Michel Camus, "Le Gardien du Seuil."
69. Daumal, *Chaque fois que l'aube paraît: Essais et notes*.
70. Lacassagne, *Vies et morts d'Antonin Artaud*.
71. Thirion, *Révolutionnaires sans Révolutions*.
72. Guénon, *Le Symbolisme de la Croix*.
73. Ibid.
74. Ibid. Cited in Batache, *Surréalisme et Tradition*.
75. Virmaux and Virmaux. *Roger Gilbert-Lecomte et le Grand Jeu*.
76. Daumal, *Le Contre-Ciel/Les Dernières Paroles du poète*.
77. Artaud, "L'Homme contre le destin."
78. Footnote by Carrouges in *Book of Zohar*.
79. Camus, *The Rebel*.
80. Crastre, *Le Drame du surréalisme*.

CHAPTER ELEVEN. SURREALISM AND GNOSTICISM

1. Beaufils, *Malcolm de Chazal*.
2. Ibid.
3. Breton, *La Lampe dans l'horloge*.

4. *Médium.*
5. Chazal, in "Almanach surréaliste du demi-siècle."
6. Beaufils, *Malcolm de Chazal.*
7. Curtis, "Rencontre avec Malcolm de Chazal."
8. Breton, quoted in *Du Surréalisme en ses oeuvres vives.*
9. Lindenberg, "Hypermatérialisme et Gnose."
10. Bardeau, *Le Livre sacré des gnostiques d'Égypte.*
11. Breton, quoted in *Flagrant délit.*
12. Alexandrian, *Histoire de la philosophie occulte.*
13. Ibid.
14. Beauvoir, *Le Deuxième Sexe.*
15. Lacarrière, *Les Gnostiques.* English translation by Nina Rootes.
16. Virmaux and Virmaux, *Roger Gilbert-Lecomte et le Grand Jeu.*
17. Roudaut, in his preface to the reprint edition of Ribemont-Dessaigne's *Ariane.*
18. Jung, *Flying Saucers.*
19. The Pistis Sophia.
20. Waldberg, "Jacques Hérold ou l'enfance de l'art." Waldberg mentions a book by Jean Doresse here that was published in two volumes by Plon in 1957 and 1963, whose full title is *Les Livres secrets des gnostiques d'Égypte: Introduction aux écrits gnostiques coptes découvert à Khénoboskion* (reprinted by Le Rocher as *Les Livres secrets de l'Égypte: Les Gnostiques* in their Champollion collection, 1992).
21. Demarne, *Art Artistes 2: Ecrits 1977–1988.*
22. Alexandrian, *Le Surréalisme et le rêve.*
23. Calame, *Le Chiendent: Des Mythes à la Structure.*
24. Tarnaud, *De (Le Bout du monde),* written sometime between December 1967 and April 1974.
25. *The Marvelous against Religion.* In Ducornet *Ça va chauffer! Situation du Surréalisme aux U.S.A. (1966–2001).*
26. Ducornet, *Ça va chauffer! Situation du Surréalisme aux U.S.A. (1966–2001).*
27. Pierre Drachline, the director of the collection "Griffons" of les éditions de l'Instant, confirmed for me during a brief conversation we had on May 1, 2008, that José Pierre found amusement in inventing the adventure of the Aletheians from whole cloth. The names of the three "founders," Zoe (life), Alithea (truth), and Sigé (silence or the abyss), refer to the names of two aeons for the first two and the female part of the Pro-Pator, the before-father, for the latter, in the Valentinian cosmogony.
28. Duits, *Ptah Hotep;* Duits, *Néfer.*
29. Duits, preface to *Néfer,* in *Vision et hallucination: L'expérience du Peyotl en littérature.*
30. Duits, *Fruit sortant de l'Abîme.*
31. Duits, "Lettre à Vincent Bounoure," in *Vision et hallucination: L'expérience du Peyotl en littérature.*

32. Markale, *The Great Goddess, Myths and Sanctuaries.*
33. Alexandrian, *Histoire de la philosophie occulte.*
34. See, for example, Audoin, "Le Talisman de Charles Fourier."
35. Gengembre, "Illuminisme et littérature."

CHAPTER TWELVE. SURREALISM AND TRADITION: OCCULT SOURCES, HISTORIES OF ORDERS AND CHURCHES

1. Dhainaut, "Charles Duits, un grand indésirable." Dhainaut also reminds us that Duits made the poet Hugo a bodhisattva in his *Victor Hugo, le grand échevelé de l'air.*
2. Viatte, *Les Sources occultes du romantisme.*
3. Breton, *La Lampe dans l'horloge.*
4. The same sentence can be found in "Devant le Rideau." In the first Haitian lecture, Breton also mentioned Aloysius Bertrand and Petrus Borel, whom he often cites elsewhere.
5. Breton, "Le Surréalisme et la tradition."
6. Alexandrian, *Histoire de la philosophie occulte.*
7. Carrouges, *La Mystique du surhomme.*
8. Schuré, *Les Grands Initiés.*
9. Mitrani, "Poésie, Liberté d'Être." For more on Pessoa and Martinism, see Maros, "Fernando Pessoa et la tradition martiniste."
10. Mabille, "William Blake." Mabille grants Blake such importance, "pure of any greed [and who] was accepted into the contemplation of the whole of Reality without having to pay the price of steep punishments for the light," that he cites him three times in *The Mirror of the Marvelous,* the final text quoted in Mabille's *Mirror of the Marvelous* is by Blake, an extract from the *First Prophetic Books* and serves as the book's conclusion.
11. Mayoux, "La Damnation de William Beckford" in *Sous de vastes portiques.*
12. Duits, *La Conscience démonique.*
13. Bataille, *La Littérature et le mal.*
14. Gautier, *Portraits et souvenirs littéraires.*
15. Partner, *The Murdered Magicians.*
16. Mabille, "William Blake."
17. Daumal, "Nerval le Nyctalope"; Daumal, "Clavicules d'un grand jeu poétique." It may be helpful to note that the term *clavicule,* meaning "little key," is often used in the titles of hermetic books, for example, *Clavicule de la philosophie hermétique* by T. F. Géron (1753), not to mention the *Clavicule de Salomon.*
18. Gilbert-Lecomte, "Ce que devrait être la peinture, ce que sera Sima."
19. Briant, *Saint-Pol Roux.* It is interesting to quickly note that Peladan called his peers inside the Order of the Aesthetic Rosicrucians "Magnificents," a label that others would obviously remember later (see Da Silva, *Le Salon de la Rose-Croix*).

20. Elléouët, *Falc'hun.*
21. Partner, *The Murdered Magicians.*
22. Ibid.
23. Mendès, *Zo'har.*
24. Da Silva, *Le Salon de la Rose-Croix.*
25. Clair, *Du Surréalisme considéré dans ses rapports avec le totalitarisme et les tables tournantes.*
26. Tison-Braun, *La Crise de l'humanisme.*
27. Mabille, *Initiation à la connaissance de l'homme* (1949). Cited by Rémy Laville in *Pierre Mabille: Un compagnon du surréalisme.* Laville also stresses the fact that the genesis of this work owes much to "the reading of Cardan, Lulle, Gerber, and Paracelsus."
28. Devaux, "Joris-Karl Huysmans, un créateur de mondes étonnants." It is also desirable to recall that Peladan's avowed purpose was to "detoxify France of its materialism."
29. Juin, preface to *Un Coeur en peine.* As illustration of Juin's observation, how could I refrain from alluding to Laurent Tailhade, "fin-de-siècle" poet, anarchist, and Freemason, from whom Breton borrowed the title "La Claire Tour" for one of his articles—on revolt—which was included in *La Clé des Champs?* With respect to the symbolists we should perhaps recall (along with Jean-Marc Debenedetti) what Breton said about them in his *Entretiens:* "It was thanks to them that a corpus of essential values was persevered and kept untarnished. . . . Mostly I retained my veneration (the word is not excessive) for these great witnesses of a bygone era, even as the shadows were deepening around them—shadows they had loved and that suited them so well. These men had resisted any compromise, and looked upon the pitiful place the critics had reserved for them without bitterness."
30. Bauer, *Isaac Newton's Freemasonry.*
31. Juin, preface to *Un Coeur en peine.*
32. Sède, *Le Secret des Cathares.*
33. Estoile, *"Qui Suis-je?" Papus.*
34. Cited by Alexandrian in his *André Breton par lui-même,* with the following commentary by Breton: "Surrealism must go yet farther: we must disoccul. the occult and occult everything else." See Michelet, *Les Compagnons de la Hiérophanie.* In his preface to *Victor-Émile Michelet, Poète Ésotérique* by Richard Knowles, Gaston Bachelard noted about this symbolist—and the atmosphere of that era—"And this is how the poet was drawn to alchemy books his entire life. His proselytism never took a break. He himself cites a letter in which Mallarmé, this obscure poet with clear dreams, writes: 'Occultism is the commentary of pure signs, to which all literature, the immediate burst of the spirit, obeys.'" Later, the philosopher goes on to say, still on Michelet: "The poet wants to update traditional alchemy poetically."

35. We should note here that the three main protagonists of the Grand Jeu, René Daumal, Roger Gilbert-Lecomte, and André Rolland de Renéville, were perfectly conversant with the works of Martinez de Pasqually, Louis-Claude de Saint-Martin, and Jean-Baptiste Willermoz. Colin Wilson writes in *The Occult,* "Romanticism, the new spirit created by Goethe, Schilling, Hoffmann, Wordsworth, Shelley, Berlioz, was the artistic expression of the mysticism of Claude de Saint-Martin." Later he adds, "The romantics were driven by the spirit of magic, which is the very spirit of the evolution of the human race." This concurs with Rudolph Steiner's opinion, as presented by Simone Rihouët-Corroze in her "Analyse du '*Crocodile,*'" the introduction to the reprint of this book *Le Crocodile* by Louis-Claude de Saint-Martin, first printed in 1799, then reprinted in 1962 and 1979 with a preface by Robert Amadou and an "Analyse" by Simone Rihouët-Coroze of the "Unknown Philosopher" (Saint-Martin); anthroposophist Rudolf Steiner, who had only read the German translation of *Des erreurs et de la vérité ou les hommes rappelés aux principes de la science* (1775), "assigned a major place" to this thinker, "going so far as to say that without Saint-Martin's influence, the great German romantics and Goethe himself would not have been what they were." For more on Breton and *Le Crocodile,* see the footnote by Étienne-Alain Hubert on Breton's text "Langue des pierres" in *Perspective Cavalière.*
36. Artaud also quoted Saint-Yves d'Alveydre in his lecture on surrealism and revolution. Gérard Legrand also cites him in his *Sur Oedipe.*
37. Breton, *L'Art magique.*
38. Lassalle, "André Breton et la franc-maçonnerie."
39. Widmaier, *Picasso: portraits de famille.*
40. Brassai, *Conversations avec Picasso.* Translated into English by Jane Marie Todd.
41. Ambelain, *Franc-Maçonnerie d'autrefois: Cérémonies et rituels de Memphis et de Misraïm.*
42. Demarne, "Inde, mère enfin liberée de l'énergie spirituelle."
43. Ribadeau Dumas, *Les Magiciens de Dieu: Les Grands Initiés de XVIIIe et XIXe siècles.*
44. Schefer, foreword to *Hermétisme et Renaissance.*

CHAPTER THIRTEEN. SURREALISM AND MYTH

1. Virilio, *Discours sur l'horreur de l'art.* Interviews with Enrico Baj.
2. Bourassa, *Surréalisme et Littérature Québecoise.*
3. Artaud, "L'Homme contre le destin."
4. Artaud, "Surréalisme et révolution."
5. Césaire, "Alain et l'esthétique."
6. Schuster and Hantaï, "Une démolition au platane."
7. Henein, quoting from a catalog for the El Telmisany exhibition.
8. Ibid.

9. Audoin; *L'Archibras,* n° 6, December 1968.
10. Breton, "Un grand poète noir."
11. Paz, "André Breton: la Brume et l'Éclair."
12. Mourier, "Breton/Berkeley: De l'idéalisme absolu comme tentation et comme terreur."
13. Gracq, *André Breton: quelques aspects de l'écrivain.*
14. Breton, *Les Vases communicants.*
15. Schuster, *Les Fruits de la passion.*
16. Laville, *Pierre Mabille: un compagnon du surréalisme.*
17. Mabille, "Del Nuevo Mundo." Published in Mexico in *Cuadernos Americanos.*
18. Gilbert-Lecomte, "La Lézarde." Cited by Michel Random in *Le Grand Jeu,* vol. 1.
19. Bourassa, *Surréalisme et Littérature Québecoise.*
20. Henri Pastoureau, "Le Surréalisme de l'après-guerre, 1946–1950," in Henri Jones *Le Surréalisme ignoré.* It should be noted that this highly contestable book is of little worth except for the thirty pages of eyewitness testimony contributed by Pastoureau.
21. Le Brun, *Si rien avait une forme, ce serait cela.*
22. Debenedetti, "Mythe et poésie."
23. Legrand, *Sur Oedipe.*
24. Pastoureau, "Le Surréalisme de l'après-guerre, 1946–1950."
25. Artaud, "Lettres sur la langage."
26. Artaud, "Le Théâtre de la cruauté (Second Manifeste)."
27. Breton, *Martinique Charmeuse de serpents.*
28. Desnos, "Le château des Carpathes," in Desnos, *Mines de rien.*
29. Gracq, *Manuscrits de guerre.*
30. Prassinos, *Le Visage effleuré de peine.*
31. Meuris, *Magritte et les mystères de la pensée.*
32. Osman, "Le Mage de l'île Maurice."
33. Brunel, *Dictionnaire des mythes littéraires.*
34. Hobsbawm and Ranger, *The Invention of Tradition.* Cited by Prescott in his lecture "Druidic Myths and Freemasonry." The serious drawback of this book's approach to surrealism is that it entirely leaves out surrealism's political dimension.
35. Legrand, *Sur Oedipe.*
36. Imbert, *Les Sources souterraines de la franc-maçonnerie: Mithra et le tarot.*
37. Laville, *Pierre Mabille: un compagnon du surréalisme.*
38. Breton, "Devant le Rideau."
39. Paz, *Deux Transparents: Marcel Duchamp et Claude Lévi-Strauss.*
40. Tristan, on Jacques Hérold's Grand Transparent, in his "Hérold, l'Or de l'air."
41. Béhar, *André Breton, le grand indésirable.*

42. Bataille, in *Troisième Convoi*, n° 2, January 1946.
43. Hoog, "The Fall of the Black House."
44. Camus, *The Rebel*.
45. Bancourt, *Les Mystères de la ville d'Ys: L'héritage spirituel des légendes celtiques*.
46. Abeille, "Un surréel."
47. Schuster, *Archives 57/68: Batailles pour le surréalisme*.
48. Jouffroy, *Une révolution du regard*.
49. Bédouin, *Vingt Ans de surréalisme: 1939–1959*.
50. Lambert, quoted in *General History of Painting*. See the section on surrealism.
51. In this regard, in "Connaissance et reconnaissance," his article on Artaud, Royer writes, "The actor should play in 'cipher,' letting it be understood that his gestures and words are 'dictated by higher intelligences.' Costumes will be chosen for their revelatory values: their intention is ritual. Light should perform a physical action, to be 'a fusillade of fire arrows,' produce heat, cold, anger, fear. . . . Mannequins, enormous masks, 'invented beings made from wood and cloth,' objects with distinctive proportions will be the essential element of the stage décor."
52. Dupuis, *Histoire désinvolte du surréalisme*.
53. Audoin, "La Fontaine de Fortune." Philippe Audoin, to whom Marcel Jean's text "Les Quinzaines Héraldiques" is dedicated, is the bearer of the coat of arms: "Silver field with gules dove essorant," used to title the evocation by Silbermann of his three acknowledged masters—including Breton, who is easily identifiable in the second place—in *Le jour me nuit*.
54. Ubac, *Tracés sur la plage*.
55. Crastre, *Le Drame du surréalisme*.
56. Guénon, *L'Ésotérisme de Dante*.
57. "Mysteriosophy" is related to "the initiatory science of the mysteries" (in *Il Linguaggio Segreto di Dante e dei Fedeli d'Amore*).
58. Schuster, *Le Ramasse-Miettes/Lettre différée à Philippe Soupault;* Schuster, *T'as vu ça d'ta f'nêtre*.
59. Debray, *L'Honneur des funambules, réponse à Jean Clair sur le surréalisme*.
60. Tristan, *L'Obsédante*.
61. In his *André Breton*, Mauriac also wrote, though, "Surrealism is following in the opposite direction—and often unconsciously—the path that civilization traveled to ultimately rediscover the magic of the first ages."
62. Schuster, "Back to Your Kennels, Yelpers of God." The tract was written by Schuster and signed by many members of the group, including Acker.
63. Clair, *Du Surréalisme consideré dans ses rapports avec le totalitarisme*.
64. Péret, *Le Déshonneur des poètes*.
65. Schuster, *Docsur n° 6*.
66. Vadé, *Pour un tombeau de Merlin: du barde celte à la période moderne*.

67. Audoin, *Breton*.
68. Joubert, "Antipodistes complémentaires."
69. Jouffroy, "Lettre rouge."

CHAPTER FOURTEEN. KEEPING A LEVEL HEAD?

1. Amadou, *Occident, Orient: parcours d'une tradition*.
2. Legrand, "Libre Promenade."
3. Van Lennep, *Art et alchimie*.
4. Schuster, "Conversation de Schuster avec Silbermann."
5. Audoin, in "Discussion générale."
6. Desnos, *Deuil pour deuil*.
7. Soupault, *En joue!*
8. Carrouges, *La Mystique du surhomme*.
9. Cortanze, *Le Surréalisme*.
10. Breton, "Braise au trépied de Keridwen."
11. Ubac, *Tracés sur la plage*.
12. Patri, Interview with Aimé.
13. Carrouges in *Polarité du symbole, études carmélitaines*.
14. Carrouges, quoted in *La Mystique du surhomme*.
15. Choucha, *Surrealism and the Occult*.
16. Girard, *L'Ombre et la demande: projections surréalistes*.
17. Faivre, "Une Théologie de l'image."
18. Silbermann, "Le Saumon, la cerise et la gardien du trait."
19. Breton, "Un grand poète noir."
20. Jaguer, "Le Surréalisme par-dessus L'Ancien et le Nouveau Monde."
21. Dupré. *Dis-moi qui tu hantes?*
22. Breton, *First Manifesto of Surrealism*.
23. Bédouin, *Vingt Ans de surréalisme*.
24. Legrand, quoted in "PMF = 1788?"
25. Lamantia, *Becoming Visible*.

Bibliography

Abbou, Malek. *Jean Clair ou la misère intellectuelle française.* Paris: Des amis de Benjamin Péret, 2002.
Abeille, Jacques. *Les Jardins statuaires.* Paris: Joëlle Losfeld, 2004.
———. "Un surréal." In *Vision et Hallucination: L'experiénce du Peyotl en littérature,* by Charles Duits. Paris: Albin Michel, 1994.
———. *Le Veilleur du jour.* Paris: Flammarion ("L'Âge d'or") 1986.
Aberth, Susan L. *Leonora Carrington: Surrealism, Alchemy, and Art.* Hampshire, UK: Lund Humphries, 2004.
Acker, Adolphe, Sarane Alexandrian, Maurice Baskine, et al. *À La niche les Glapisseurs de Dieu.* Paris: Éditions Surrealistes, 1948.
Adamowicz, Eliza. *Ceci n'est pas un tableau, les écrits surréalistes sur l'art.* Paris: L'Age d'homme (coll. "Bibliothèque Mélusine"), 2004.
Aelberts, Alain-Valéry, and Jean-Jacques Auquier. *Poètes singuliers du surrealism et autres lieux.* Paris: Union Générale d'Édition, 1971.
Albach, Hester. *Léona, héroine du surréalisme.* Arles, France: Actes Sud, 2009.
Alexandrian, Sarane. *André Breton par lui-même.* Paris: Éditions du Seuil, 1971.
———. *L'Aventure en soi: Autobiographie.* Paris: Mercure de France, 1990.
———. *Création, Récréation.* Paris: Donoël/Gonthier (coll. "Bibliothèque meditations"), 1976.
———. "L'Être secret de Victor Brauner." *Superieur inconnu,* n° 4, July–December 2006.
———. *Georges Henein.* Paris: Seghers (coll. "Poètes d'aujourd'hui"), 1981.
———. *Histoire de la philosophie occulte.* Paris: Seghers, 1983.
———. *L'Homme des lointains.* Paris: Flammarion, 1960.
———. *Les Libérateurs de l'amour.* Paris: Le Seuil, 1977.
———. *Le Surréalisme et le rêve.* Paris: Gallimard, 1974.
———. "Techniques du surrealisme." In *Création, Récréation,* by Sarane Alexandrian. Paris: Donoël/Gonthier (coll. "Bibliothèque meditations"), 1976.
Aleksic, Branko. "Amour, nature et plaisir en picto-poésie." In *Première*

Conversation mémorable avec la chimère, by Max Ernst. Thaon, France: Amiot-Lenganey, 1991.

———. "Surréalistes français et yougoslaves." *La Revue parlée,* April 23, 1990.

Alleau, René. *Alchimie.* Paris: Allia, 2008.

———. *Aspects de l'alchimie traditionelle.* Paris: Éditions de Minuit, 1953.

———. "Psychanalyse et Alchimie." *Médium,* n° 3, May 1954.

Allendy, René. "Paracelse, le médecin maudit." In *La Rose-Croix,* by Gérard de Sède, Paris: J'ai Lu (coll. "L'Aventure mysterieuse"), 1978.

Alquié, Ferdinand. *Entretiens sur le surréalisme.* Paris: Éditions Mouton, 1968.

———. *Philosophie du Surréalisme.* Paris: Flammarion (coll. "Champs"), 1977.

———. *The Philosophy of Surrealism.* Translated by Bernard Waldrop. Ann Arbor: University of Michigan Press, 1960.

Amadou, Robert. *Occident, Orient: parcours d'une tradition.* Paris: Caniscript, 2010.

———. *Occultisme: Esquisse d'un monde vivant.* Paris: Juillard, 1950.

Ambelain, Robert. *La Chapelle des damnés.* Paris: Robert Laffont, 1983.

———. *Franc-Maçonnerie d'autrefois: Cérémonies et rituels de Memphis et de Misraïm.* Paris: Robert Laffont (coll. "Les aventures de l'esprit"), 1988.

———. *La Vie secrete de Saint Paul.* Paris: Robert Laffont (coll. "Les enigmes de l'univers"), 1972.

Anitchkoff, Eugène. *Joachim de Flore et les Milieux Courtois.* Geneva: Droz, 1931.

Anonymous. *Le Comte de Gabalis.* Richmond, Va.: Macoy and Masonic Supply Co., 1922.

Apollinaire, Guillaume. *Le Flâneur des deux rives.* Paris: Éditions de la Sirène, 1918.

Aragon, Louis. "Entrance of the Succubi." *La Révolution surréaliste,* n° 6, March, 1926.

———. *Paris Peasant.* New York: Prentice-Hall, 1970.

———. *Le Paysan de Paris.* Paris: Gallimard, 1972.

———. "Une vague de rêves." In *Commerce,* Autumn 1924. Paris: Seghers, 1990.

Arcq, Tere. *Cinco Llaves del Mundo Secreto de Remedios Varo.* Mexico City: Artes de Mexico, 2008.

Ariëns-Volker, Marijo. "Alchemical, Kabbalistic, and Occult Symbolism in the Work of Pablo Picasso and His Contemporaries." In *Masonic and Esoteric Heritage,* papers of the First International Conference of the OVN, the foundation for the promotion of university research on the history of Freemasonry in Holland, 2005.

Artaud, Antonin. *Héliogabale ou l'anarchiste couronné.* Paris: Gallimard (coll. "L'imaginaire"), 1979.

———. *Heliogabalus or the Crowned Anarchist.* London: Solar Books, 2006.

———. "L'Homme contre le destin." *Messages révolutionnaires.* Paris: Gallimard, 1971.

———. Lecture on surrealism and revolution.

———. "Lettres sur la cruauté." In *Le Théâtre et son double*. Paris: Gallimard (coll. "Idées"), 1964.

———. "Lettres sur le langage." In *Le Théâtre et son double*. Paris: Gallimard (coll. "Idées"), 1964.

———. *Messages révolutionnaires*. Paris: Gallimard, 1971.

———. "La Montagne des signes." *Voyage au Pays des Tarahumaras*. Paris: Éditions de la revue "Fontaine," 1945.

———. *Oeuvres*. Paris: Quarto, 2004.

———. "La Rite des rois de l'Atlantide." In *Les Tarahumaras*. Paris: Gallimard, 1971.

———. "Surréalisme et revolution." In *Messages révolutionnaires*. Paris: Gallimard, 1971.

———. *Les Tarahumaras*. Paris: Gallimard, 1971.

———. *The Theater and Its Double*. New York: Grove Press, 1960.

———. "Le Théâtre de la cruauté (Second Manifeste)." In *Le Théâtre et son double*. Paris: Gallimard (coll. "Idées"), 1964.

———. *Le Théâtre et son double*. Paris: Gallimard (coll. "Idées"), 1964.

———. "Witchcraft and the Cinema." In *Collected Works* vol. 3. Translated by Alastair Hamilton. London: Calder and Boyars, 1972.

Audoin, Philippe. "Baron." *L'Archibras,* n° 7, 1967.

———. *Bourges, cité première*. Paris: Julliard, 1972.

———. *Breton*. Paris: Gallimard (coll. "Pour une bibliothèque ideale"), 1970.

———. "Discussion générale." Finale, *Entretiens sur le surréalisme,* under the supervision of Fernand Alquié. Proceedings of the Symposium of Cerisy, July 10–18, 1966. Paris: Mouton and Co., 1968.

———. *Entretiens sur le surréalisme*. Paris: Mouton and Co., 1968.

———. "La Fontaine de Fortune." In *1968, année surréaliste: Cuba, Prague, Paris,* by Jérôme Duwa. Paris: IMEC éditeur (coll. "Pièces d'archives"), 2008.

———. *Maurice Fourré, rêveur définitif/Le Caméléon mystique*. Paris: Le Soleil Noir, 1978.

———. "Le noir des sources." *La Brèche,* n° 6, June 1964.

———. "Preface." In *Les Minutes de sable memorial/César-Antechrist,* by Alfred Jarry. Paris: Gallimard, 1977.

———. *Les Surréalistes*. Paris: Le Seuil (coll. "Écrivains de toujours"), 1973.

———. "Le Talisman de Charles Fourier." *La Brèche,* n° 8, November 1965.

Audricourt, Pierre Schumann. *Lettres à la cantonade*. Paris: Le Terrain Vague–Eric Losfeld (coll. "Le desordre"), 1971.

Aury, Dominique (Anne Desclos). *Histoire d'O*. Paris: Jean Jacques Pauvert, 1954.

Bachelard, Gaston. *L'Eau et les rêves*. Paris: José Corti, 1942.

———. Preface to *Victor-Émile Michelet, Poète Ésoterique,* by Richard Knowles. Paris: Vrin, 1954.

———. *La Psychanalyse du feu.* Paris: Gallimard, 1949.
———. *The Psychoanalysis of Fire.* Boston: Beacon, 1964.
———. *Water and Dreams.* Dallas, Tex.: Dallas Institute, 1999.
Bancourt, Pascal. *Les Mystères de la ville d'Ys: L'héritage spirituelle des légendes celtiques.* Monaco: Le Rocher, 2003.
Barat, Michel. Preface in *Isaac Newton's Freemasonry,* by Alain Bauer. Rochester, Vt.: Inner Traditions, 2007.
Bardeau, Fabrice. *Livre sacré des gnostiques d'Egypte.* Paris: Robert Laffont (coll. "Les Portes de l'étrange"), 1977.
Baron, Jacques. "Le Village marin." *L'Enfant perdu du surréalisme, La Nouvelle Revue nantaise,* n° 5, 2009.
Barrault, Jean-Louis. "L'Homme-théâtre." Paris: Gallimard, 1957.
Batache, Eddy. *Surréalisme et tradition.* Paris: Éditions Traditionnelles, 1978.
Bataille, Georges. *L'Éxperience Intérieure.* Paris: Gallimard, 1978.
———. *Les Larmes d'Éros.* Paris: Jean-Jacques Pauvert, 1961.
———. *La Littérature et le mal.* Paris: Gallimard (coll. "Idées"), 1957.
———. "The Star Eaters." In *André Masson.* Rouen: Imprimerie Wolf, 1940.
———. *The Tears of Eros.* San Francisco: City Lights, 2001.
Battistini, Yves. *Trois Présocratiques.* Paris: Gallimard, 1968.
Bauer, Alain. *Le Crépuscule des Frères.* Paris: La Table Ronde, 2005.
———. *Isaac Newton's Freemasonry.* Rochester, Vt.: Inner Traditions, 2007.
Bauer, Alain, and Phillipe Morbach. "Les Racines d'un ordre initiatique et le role de l'Écosse dans l'apparition de la franc-maçonnerie." *Points de vue initiatiques,* n° 10, December 1995, January–February 1996.
Baulot, Isaac. *L'Alchimie et son Livre muet.* Paris: J. J. Pauvert, 1967.
Beaufils, Laurent de. *Malcolm de Chazal.* Paris: Éditions de la Différence, 1995.
Beauvoir, Simone de. *La Deuxième Sexe.* Paris: Gallimard, 1949.
Beckford, William. *Vathek.* Paris: Garnier-Flammarion, 1981.
Bédouin, Jean-Louis. *André Breton.* Paris: Seghers, 1970.
———. *Sauve qui doit.* Paris: Planète, 1961.
———. *Vingt Ans de surréalisme: 1939–1959.* Paris: Denoël, 1961.
Béhar, Henri. *André Breton: le grand indésirable.* Paris: Calmann-Lévy, 1990.
Benayoun, Robert. *Petite Pièces pouvant server à approacher (même à comprendre) sinon à expliquer dans son ensemble le surréalisme.* Paris: L'Écart Absolu, 2001.
Benayoun, Robert, and Michel Polac. *Passage Breton.* Documentary film, 1975.
Beresniak, Daniel. *La Rose et le Compas: Rose-Croix et franc-maçonnerie.* Escalquens, France: Trajectoire, 2004.
Bériou, Jean Yves. *Le Château périlleux* [Castle Perilous]. Paris: L'Escampette, 2003.
Bianu, Zéno. *Les Poètes du Grand Jeu.* Paris: Gallimard (coll. "Poésies"), 2003.
Biès, Jean. *René Daumal.* Paris: Seghers (coll. "Poètes d'aujourd'hui"), 1973.
Biro, Adam, and René Passeron. *Dictionnaire général du surréalisme et de ses environs.* Paris: P.U.F., 1982.

Bischoff, Ulrich. *Max Ernst.* Cologne, Germany: Benedikt Taschen Verlag, 1948.
Bodinier, Gerald. "La Domaine international du surréalisme." Special issue, *Le Puits et l'Ermite,* n° 29–30, 31, 1978.
Boll, Marcel. *L'Occultisme devant la science.* Paris: P.U.F. ("Que sais-je?"), 1944.
Bonnefoy, Yves. *Breton à l'avant de soi.* Paris: Éditions Léo Scheer, 2001.
Boucher, Jules. *Symbolique Maçonnique.* Paris: Dervy, 1990.
Bounan, "Préface pour un anniversaire," in Alleau, *Alchimie.* Paris: Allia, 2008.
Bounoure, Gabriel. *Marelle sur les parvis.* Saint-Clément-de-Rivière, France: Fata Morgana (coll. "Hermès"), 1995.
Bounoure, Vincent. *Les Anneaux de Maldoror et autres chapitres d'un traité des contraires.* Paris: L'Écart Absolu, 1999.
———. *Moments du surréalisme.* Paris: L'Harmatton, 1999.
———. "Preface à un traité des matrices." In *Moments du surréalisme.* Paris: L'Harmatton, 1999.
Bounoure, Vincent, José Pierre, and Claude Courtot. "Lettre sur l'exposition Le Principe de plaisir." *1968, année surréaliste: Cuba, Prague, Paris,* edited by Jérôme Duwa. Paris: IMEC éditeur (coll. "Pièces d'archives"), 2008.
Bourassa, André G. *Surréalisme et Littérature Québecoise.* Montréal: Éditions l'Étincelle, 1977.
Bouvier, Michel, and Jean-Louis Leutrat. *Nosferatu.* Paris: Gallimard, 1981.
Brassaï. *Conversations avec Picasso.* Paris: Gallimard, 1964.
———. *Conversations with Picasso.* Chicago: University of Chicago Press, 1999.
Breton, André. *L'air de l'eau.* Paris: Éditions Cahiers d'Art, 1934.
———. *Alouette du parloir.* Paris: Grasset, 1954.
———. *Anthologie de l'humour noir.* Paris: Livre de poche, 1986.
———. *Anthology of Black Humor.* San Francisco, City Lights, 2001.
———. *Arcanum 17.* Los Angeles, Calif.: Green Integer, 2004.
———. *L'Art magique.* Paris: Éditions Phébus et Adam Biro, 2003.
———. "Braise au trépied de Keridwen." Preface to *Les Bardes Gallois,* by Jean Markale. Paris: Falaize, 1956.
———. *Break of Day.* Lincoln: University of Nebraska Press, 2008.
———. *La Clé des Champs.* Paris: Les Éditions du Sagittaire, 1953.
———. *Communicating Vessels.* Lincoln: University of Nebraska Press, 1997.
———. *Constellations of Miro.* San Francisco: City Lights, 2000.
———. "Devant le Rideau." *La Clé des Champs.* Paris: Les Éditions du Sagittaire, 1953.
———. *Earthlight.* Los Angeles, Calif.: Green Integer, 2003.
———. *Entretiens.* In *Oeuvres complètes,* vol. 3. Paris: Gallimard (coll. "Bibliothèque de la Pléiade"), 1988–2008.
———. *Les États généraux.* In *Oeuvres complètes.* Paris: Gallimard (coll. "Bibliothèque de la Pléiade"), 1988–2008.
———. *Flagrant délit.* Paris: J. J. Pauvert, 1964.

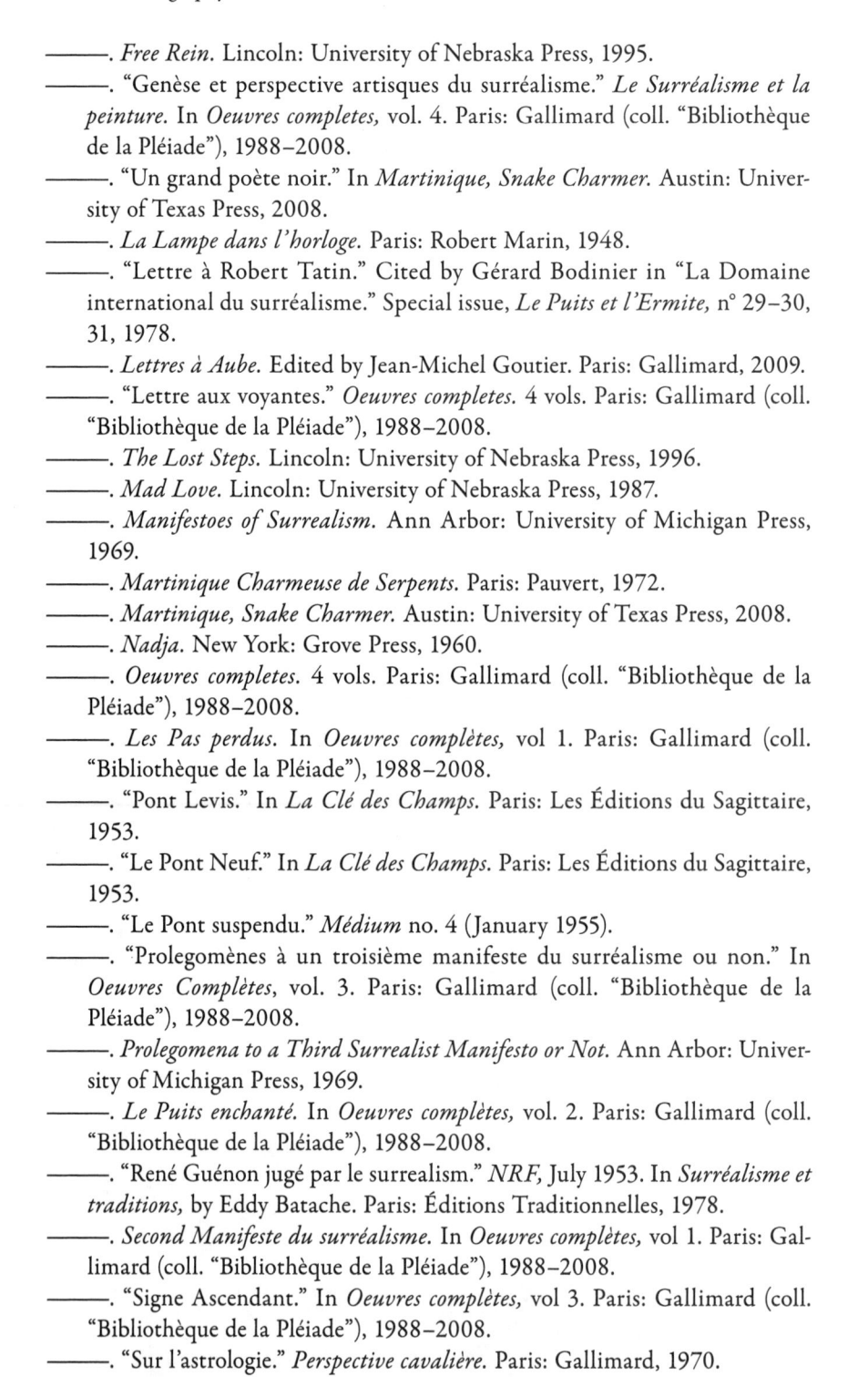

———. *Free Rein*. Lincoln: University of Nebraska Press, 1995.

———. "Genèse et perspective artisques du surréalisme." *Le Surréalisme et la peinture*. In *Oeuvres completes*, vol. 4. Paris: Gallimard (coll. "Bibliothèque de la Pléiade"), 1988–2008.

———. "Un grand poète noir." In *Martinique, Snake Charmer*. Austin: University of Texas Press, 2008.

———. *La Lampe dans l'horloge*. Paris: Robert Marin, 1948.

———. "Lettre à Robert Tatin." Cited by Gérard Bodinier in "La Domaine international du surréalisme." Special issue, *Le Puits et l'Ermite*, n° 29–30, 31, 1978.

———. *Lettres à Aube*. Edited by Jean-Michel Goutier. Paris: Gallimard, 2009.

———. "Lettre aux voyantes." *Oeuvres completes*. 4 vols. Paris: Gallimard (coll. "Bibliothèque de la Pléiade"), 1988–2008.

———. *The Lost Steps*. Lincoln: University of Nebraska Press, 1996.

———. *Mad Love*. Lincoln: University of Nebraska Press, 1987.

———. *Manifestoes of Surrealism*. Ann Arbor: University of Michigan Press, 1969.

———. *Martinique Charmeuse de Serpents*. Paris: Pauvert, 1972.

———. *Martinique, Snake Charmer*. Austin: University of Texas Press, 2008.

———. *Nadja*. New York: Grove Press, 1960.

———. *Oeuvres completes*. 4 vols. Paris: Gallimard (coll. "Bibliothèque de la Pléiade"), 1988–2008.

———. *Les Pas perdus*. In *Oeuvres complètes*, vol 1. Paris: Gallimard (coll. "Bibliothèque de la Pléiade"), 1988–2008.

———. "Pont Levis." In *La Clé des Champs*. Paris: Les Éditions du Sagittaire, 1953.

———. "Le Pont Neuf." In *La Clé des Champs*. Paris: Les Éditions du Sagittaire, 1953.

———. "Le Pont suspendu." *Médium* no. 4 (January 1955).

———. "Prolegomènes à un troisième manifeste du surréalisme ou non." In *Oeuvres Complètes*, vol. 3. Paris: Gallimard (coll. "Bibliothèque de la Pléiade"), 1988–2008.

———. *Prolegomena to a Third Surrealist Manifesto or Not*. Ann Arbor: University of Michigan Press, 1969.

———. *Le Puits enchanté*. In *Oeuvres complètes*, vol. 2. Paris: Gallimard (coll. "Bibliothèque de la Pléiade"), 1988–2008.

———. "René Guénon jugé par le surrealism." *NRF,* July 1953. In *Surréalisme et traditions,* by Eddy Batache. Paris: Éditions Traditionnelles, 1978.

———. *Second Manifeste du surréalisme*. In *Oeuvres complètes,* vol 1. Paris: Gallimard (coll. "Bibliothèque de la Pléiade"), 1988–2008.

———. "Signe Ascendant." In *Oeuvres complètes,* vol 3. Paris: Gallimard (coll. "Bibliothèque de la Pléiade"), 1988–2008.

———. "Sur l'astrologie." *Perspective cavalière*. Paris: Gallimard, 1970.

———. *Surrealism and Painting*. New York: Harper, 1973.

———. *Surrealism and Painting*. Boston: MFA Publications, 2002.

———. *Le Surréalisme et la peinture*. In *Oeuvres completes,* vol. 4. Paris: Gallimard (coll. "Bibliothèque de la Pléiade"), 1988–2008.

———. "Le Surréalisme et la tradition." *Perspective cavalière.* Paris: Gallimard, 1970.

———. *Les Vases communicants.* In *Oeuvres completes,* vol. 2. Paris: Gallimard (coll. "Bibliothèque de la Pléiade"), 1988–2008.

Breton, André, and Jean-Michel Goutier. *Lettres à Aube.* Paris: Gallimard, 2010.

Briant, Théophile. *Saint-Pol Roux.* Paris: Seghers (coll. "Poètes d'aujourd'hui"), 1952.

Bricaud, Johnny. *Joris-Karl Huysmans et le Satanisme.* Paris: À Rebours, 2009.

Brisset, Jean-Pierre. *Prophéties accomplises.* Paris: Leroux, 1906.

Brunel, Pierre. *Dictionnaire des mythes littéraires.* Monaco: Éditions du Rocher, 1988.

Buñuel, Louis. *Lettres à Aube.* Paris: Gallimard, 2009.

———. *My Last Sigh.* New York: Knopf, 1983.

Cabanel, Guy. *Croisant le verbe.* Paris: L'Éther Vague, 1995.

Cabrera, Lydia. *La Forêt et les dieux: Religions afro-cubaines et médecines sacrées à Cuba.* Paris: Jean-Michel Place, 2005.

Caillois, Roger. *La Fleuve Alphée.* Paris: Gallimard (coll. "L'imaginaire"), 1978.

———. *Les Impostures de la poésie.* Paris: Gallimard (coll. "Metamorphoses"), 1945.

———. *Le Mythe et l'homme.* Paris: Gallimard (coll. "Idées"), 1972.

Calame, Alain. *Le Chiendent: Des Mythes a la Structure.* Limoges Symposium, 1984.

Camacho, Jorge, "Jorge Camacho, oeuvres 1964–1996." Interview with Gérard Durozoi in catalog produced for the exhibition Jorge Camacho, les détours de soi, at Idem+Arts in Maubeuge, France.

Camacho, Jorge, and Alain Gruger. *Héraldique alchimique nouvelle.* Paris: Le Soleil Noir, 1978.

Camus, Albert. *The Rebel.* New York: Vintage, 1960.

Camus, Michel. "Le Gardien du Seuil" (Sur René Daumal). *L'Originel,* n° 7, January 1978.

Canonne, Xavier. *Le Surréalisme en Belgique, 1924–2000.* Fonds Mercator-Ville-de-Mons; Mons, Belgium: 2006; Arles, France: Actes Sud, 2007.

Canseliet, Eugène. *L'Alchimie expliquée sur ses textes classiques.* Paris: Pauvert, 1972.

———. "Hermétiques Rudiments d'Héraldiques." *Atlantis,* n° 291 n° 2, January–February 1975.

———. "Introduction." In *L'Alchimie et son Livre muet,* by Isaac Baulot. Paris: J. J. Pauvert, 1967.

———. "Preface." In *The Mute Book.* Paris: J. J. Pauvert, then Gutenberg Reprints in 1996.

———. *Trois Anciens Traités d'alchimie.* Paris: Jean-Jacques Pauvert, 1975.
Carassou, Michel. *René Crevel.* Paris: Fayard, 1989.
Carrington, Leonora. *Down Below.* Chicago: Black Swan Press, 1983.
———. *En Bas.* Paris: Le Terrain Vague–Eric Losfeld (coll. "Le désordre"), 1973.
———. *Lettre à Henri Parisot.* Paris: Le Terrain Vague–Eric Losfeld (coll. "Le désordre"), 1973.
Carrouges, Michel. *André Breton and the Basic Concepts of Surrealism.* Tuscaloosa: University of Alabama Press, 1974.
———. *André Breton et les données fondamentales du surréalisme.* Paris: Gallimard, 1950.
———. "Le Hasard objectif." Paper presented at symposium on surrealism, Cerisy, France, July 10–18, 1966.
———. *La Mystique du surhomme.* Paris: Gallimard (coll. "Bibliothèque des idées"), 1948.
———. *Polarité du symbole: études carmélitaines.* Bruges, Belgium: Desclée De Brouwer, 1960.
Casaril, Guy. *Rabbi Siméon Bar Yochaï et la Cabbala.* Paris: Le Seuil (coll. "Points"), 2004.
Cendres, Julien, and Chloé Radiguet. *Le Désert de Retz, paysage choisi.* Paris: Éclat, 2009.
Césaire, Suzanne. "Alain et l'esthétique." In *Le Grand Camouflage.* Paris: Seuil, 2009.
———. "Surréalisme et revolution." In *Le Grand Camouflage.* Paris: Seuil, 2009.
Chabbert, Christophe. *Petrusmok de Malcolm de Chazal: Radioscopie d'un Roman Mythique.* Paris: L'Harmattan, 2001.
Chadwick, Whitney. *Women Artists and the Surrealist Movement.* New York: Bulfinch, 1985.
Charpentier, Louis. *Les Jacques et le mystère de Compostelle.* Paris: Robert Laffont (coll. "Les énigmes de l'univers"), 1971.
Chazal, Malcolm de. "Almanach surréaliste du demi-siècle." Special issue of *La Nef,* March 1950; reprint edition (as book), Paris: Plasma, 1978.
———. *L'Île Maurice protohistorique, folklorique et légendaire.* Paris: Mauritius Printing, 1973.
———. *Le Rocher de Sisyphe.* Paris: L'Ether Vague, 1996.
Chénieux-Gendron, Jacqueline. "Masks and Metamorphoses." In the catalog for the exhibition Yves Elléouët.
———. "Pierre Mabille, 'Point aveugle' du surréalisme." *Révue des sciences humaines,* n° 193, January–March 1984.
Chénieux-Gendron, Jacqueline, and Rémy Laville. Preface to *Conscience lumineuse, conscience picturale,* by Pierre Mabille. Paris: José Corti, 1989.
Chirico, Giorgio de. *Hebdomeros.* New York: PAJ, 1988.
Choucha, Nadia. *Surrealism and the Occult.* Rochester, Vt.: Inner Traditions, 1992.

Clair, Jean [Gérard Regnier]. *Du Surréalisme considéré dans ses rapports avec le totalitarisme et les tables tournantes.* Paris: Mille et Une Niuits, 2003.

Clébert, Jean-Paul. "Jacques Hérold et le surréalisme." *La Revue des sciences humaines,* 1984.

Colquhoun, Ithell. *The Goose of Hermogenes.* London: Peter Owen, 2003.

———. *Sword of Wisdom.* New York: Neville Spearman, 1975.

———. "The Waterstone of the Wise." In *New Roads, 1943,* edited by Alex Comfort and John Bayliss. Billericay, Essex, England: Gray Walls Press, 1944.

Combalia, Victoria. "Remedios Varo and Benjamin Péret." In *Benjamin Péret et les Amériques,* by Gérard Roche. Paris: Association des amis de Benjamin Péret, 2010.

Combes, André. *La Franc-Maçonnerie sous l'Occupation.* Monaco: Rocher, 2001.

Cortanze, Gérard de. *Le Surréalisme.* Paris: MA Éditions (coll. "Le Monde de"), 1985.

Costantini, Giovanna. "Wall and Tower: Freemasonry in the Art of Giorgio de Chirico." Lecture, Masonic and Esoteric Heritage Conference, Royal Library, the Hague, the Netherlands, October 20–21, 2005."

"Coup de semonce." *Tracts surréalistes et déclarations collectives,* vol. 2. Paris: Eric Losfeld, 1982.

Le Courrier de l'Unesco. "Les Celtes," December 1975.

Courtot, Claude. *Bonjour, Monsieur Courtot.* Paris: Ellebore, 1984.

Coy, Jean-Louis. *Forces occultes: Le complot judéo-maçonnique au cinéma.* Paris: Véga, 2008.

Crastre, Victor. *Le Drame du surréalisme.* Paris: Les Éditions du Temps (coll. "Les documents du temps"), 1963.

Curtis, Jean-Louis. "Rencontre avec Malcolm de Chazal." In *Le Surréalisme et ses insoumis, La Nouvelle Revue de Paris,* n° 14. Monaco: Le Rocher, 1988.

Dachez, Roger. *L'Invention de la franc-maçonnerie: Des opératifs aux spéculatifs.* Paris: Véga, 2008.

Dachez, Roger, and Jean-Marc Pétillot. *Le Rite Écossais Rectifié.* Paris: P.U.F. ("Que sais-je?"), 2010.

Daix, Pierre. *Les Surréalistes: 1917–1932.* Paris: Hachette Littératures ("Pluriel"), 1993.

Dali, Salvador, and Louis Pauwels. *The Passions According to Dali.* St. Petersburg, Fla.: Salvador Dali Museum, 1985.

Da Silva, Jean. *Le Salon de la Rose-Croix.* Paris: Éditions Syros-Alternatives, 1991.

Daumal, René. *Chaque fois que l'aube paraît: Essais et notes,* vol. 1. Paris: Gallimard, 1953.

———. "Clavicules d'un grand jeu poétique." In *Le Contre-Ciel,* by René Daumal. Paris: Gallimard (coll. "Poésies"), 1990.

———. *Le Contre-Ciel/Les Dernières Paroles du poète.* Paris: Gallimard (coll. "Poésies"), 1990.

———. *Mont Analogue.* Paris: Gallimard (coll. "L'imaginaire"), 1981.

———. *Mount Analogue.* San Francisco: City Lights, 1968.

———. "Nerval le Nyctalope." In *Le Grand Jeu,* n° 3, from *Le Grand Jeu: Collection complète.*

Dauxois, Jacqueline. *L'Empereur des alchimistes: Rodolphe II de Habsbourg.* Paris: JC Lattès, 1996.

Debenedetti, Jean-Marc. "Mythe et poésie." In *Poésie 1/Vagabondages.* Special issue, 19, *Le Poète et le Mythe,* n° 19, September 1999.

Debray, Régis. *L'Honneur des funambules: réponse à Jean Clair sur le surréalisme.* Paris: L'Échoppe, 2003.

Decottignies, Jean. "La vie poétique d'Ernest de Gengenbach." *La Revue des sciences humaines,* n° 193, January–March 1984.

Decron, Benoît. "Mythologie et la fête des mères." *Cahiers de l'Abbaye Sainte-Croix,* n° 84, 1997.

Del Renzio, Toni. "Incendiary Innocence." In *Au trezième coup de minuit: Anthologie du surréalisme en Angleterre,* by Michel Rémy. Paris: Éditions Dilecta, 2008.

Delteil, Joseph. *La Deltheillerie.* Paris: Grasset, 1968.

Demarne, Pierre. *Art Artistes 2: Ecrits 1977–1988.* Cordes-sur-Ciel: Rafael de Surtis, 1998.

———. "Inde, mère enfin libérée de l'énergie spirituelle." In *Le Surréalisme et ses insoumis.*

Desnos, Robert. "Le château des Carpathes." *Aujourd'hui,* September 14, 1940.

———. "The Journal of an Apparition." *La Révolution surréaliste,* n° 9–10, October 1927.

———. *La Liberté ou l'amour!* Paris: Gallimard (coll. "L'imaginaire"), 1982.

———. *Liberty or Love!* London: Atlas Press, 1924.

———. *Mines de rien.* Bazas, France: Éditions Le Temps Qu'il Fait, 1985.

———. *Trois Livres de prophéties.* In *Oeuvres.* Paris: Gallimard (Coll. "Quarto"), 2003.

Devaux, Yves. "Joris-Karl Huysmans: un créateur de mondes étonnants." *Arts et métiers du livre,* n° 258, February–March 2007.

Dhainaut, Pierre. "Charles Duits, un grand indésirable." *Vision et hallucination: L'expérience du Peyotl en littérature,* by Charles Duits. Paris: Albin Michel, 1994.

———. *Jean Malrieu.* Paris: Éditions des Vanneaux (coll. "Présence de la poésie"), 2007.

Dictionnaire des littératures de langue française. 2 vols. Paris: Bordas, 1987.

Dunne, John William. *An Experiment with Time.* London: Faber and Faber, 1927.

Doresse, Jean. *Les Livres secrets des gnostiques de l'Égypte: Introduction aux écrits gnostiques coptes découverts à Khénoboskion.* 2 vols. Paris: Plon, 1957, 1963.

Doumayrou, Guy-René. "Château, comme poindre." In *Surréalisme,* n° 1. Paris: Éditions Savelli, 1977

——. *Cinq Paradigmes de la géométrie sacrée et leur signature monumentale.* Paris: Arma Artis, 2003.

——. *Géographie sidérale.* Paris: Éditions 10/18, 1976.

——. "Surréalisme, esotérisme." *Docsur,* n° 8, April 1989.

Ducornet, Guy. *Ça va chauffer! Situation du Surréalisme aux U.S.A. (1966–2001).* Mons, Belgium: Éditions Talus d'Approche, 2001.

——. *Le Punching Ball et la vache à lait.* Angers, France: Deleatur-Actual, 1992.

Dugué, Michel. "Dans un pays de lointaine mémoire." *Littérature de Bretagne, Europe,* n° 625, May 1981.

Duits, Charles. *André Breton a-t-il dit passe.* Paris: Denoël, 1969.

——. *La Conscience démonique.* Paris: Denoël, 1974.

——. "Les Fantômes." In *La Conscience démonique.* Paris: Denoël, 1974.

——. *Fruit sortant de l'Abîme.* L'Isle sur la Sorgue, France: Le Bois d'Orion, 1993.

——. "Je suis né à Paris . . ." *Vision et hallucination: L'expérience du Peyotl en littérature, about Charles Duits.* Paris: Albin Michel, 1994.

——. "Lettre à Vincent Bounoure." *Vision et hallucination: L'expérience du Peyotl en littérature, about Charles Duits.* Paris: Albin Michel, 1994.

——. *Nefer.* Paris: Henri Veyrier, 1978.

——. *Ptah Hotep.* 2 vols. Paris: Denoël, 1971.

——. *Victor Hugo: le grand échevelé de l'air.* Paris: Belfond (Coll. "Mandala"), 1975.

——. *Vision et hallucination: L'expérience du Peyotl en littérature.* Paris: Albin Michel, 1994.

Ribadeau Dumas, François. *Les Magiciens de Dieu: Les Grands Initiés des XVIIIe et XIXe siècles.* Paris: Robert Laffont (coll. "Les énigmes de l'univers"), 1970.

Dupré, Guy. *Dis-moi qui tu hantes.* Monaco: Éditions du Rocher, 2003.

——. "Visage nu, poitrine à découvert." *La Quinzaine littéraire,* n° 581, July 1–15, 1991.

Duprey, Jean-Pierre. *Derrière son Double.* Paris: Le Soleil Noir, 1964.

——. *La Fin et la manière.* Paris: Le Soleil Noir, 1965.

Dupuis, Jules-François (Raoul Vaneigen). *A Cavalier History of Surrealism.* Oakland, Calif.: AK Press, 2001.

——. *Histoire désinvolte du surréalisme.* Paris: Éditions Paul Vermont, 1977.

During, J. "Notes on Initiation." *Planète Plus,* April 1970.

Durozoi, Gérard. *Histoire du surréalisme.* Paris: Hazan, 1997.

——. *History of the Surrealist Movement.* Translated by Alison Anderson. Chicago: University of Chicago Press, 2004.

Duval, Paul Marie. *Les Dieux de la Gaule.* Paris: Petite Bibliothèque Payot, 1976.

Duwa, Jérôme. *1968 année surréaliste: Cuba, Prague, Paris.* Paris: IMEC éditeur (coll. "Pièces d'archives"), 2008.

Edighoffer, Roland. *Les Rose-Croix.* Paris: P.U.F. ("Que sais-je?"), 1982.

Eisner, Lotte. *The Haunted Screen*. Berkeley: University of California, 1965.
Elléouët, Yves. *Falc'hun*. Paris: Gallimard, 1976.
———. "James Joyce." In *Tête cruelle*. Paris: Calligrammes, 1982.
———. *Le Livre des rois de Bretagne*. Paris: Gallimard, 1974.
———. *Tête cruelle*. Paris: Calligrammes, 1982.
Emmerling, Leonhard. *Jackson Pollock*. Berlin: Taschen, 2004.
Ernst, Max. *Première Conversation mémorable avec la chimère*. Thaon, France: Amiot-Lenganey, 1991.
Estoile, Arnaud de l'. *"Qui Suis-je?" Papus*. Paris: Pardès, 2006.
Faivre, Antoine. "L'Obsession de la Renaissance." *20 Clés pour comprendre l'ésoterisme*, January 6, 2009.
———. "Une Théologie de l'image." *20 Clés pour comprendre l'ésoterisme*, January 6, 2009.
Fauré, Michel. *Histoire du surréalisme sous l'Occupation*. Paris: La Table Ronde, 1982.
Felka, Rike. "Franco-German Floating Leaf." Preface for *MistAKE and Other French Writings,* by Unica Zürn. Paris: Ypsilon, 2008.
Fini, Leonor. *Fêtes secrétes: Dessins*. Paris: Éditions du Regard, 1978.
———. *Rogomelec*. Paris: Stock, 1979.
Flahutez, Fabrice. *Nouveau monde et nouveau mythe: Mutation du surréalisme de l'exil américain à l'Écart absolu (1941–1965)*. Dijon, France: Presses du Réel, 2007.
Flamand, Elie-Charles. *Les Méandres du sens*. Paris: Dervy, 2004.
———. *La Tour Saint-Jacques*. Paris: La Table d'Émeraude, 1991.
Ford, Gordon Onslow. *Yves Tanguy et l'automatisme*. Baye, France: Éditions La Digitale, 2002.
Fourré, Maurice. *Le Caméléon mystique*. Paris: Caligrammes, 1981.
———. *La Marraine du sel*. Paris: Gallimard, 1955.
———. *La Nuit du Rose-Hôtel*. Paris: Gallimard, 1950.
———. *Tête-de-Nègre*. Paris: Gallimard, 1960.
Frère, Jean-Claude. *L'Occultisme*. Paris: Grasset, 1974.
Fulcanelli. *Les Demeures philosophales*. Paris: Pauvert, 1965.
———. *The Dwellings of the Philosophers*. Boulder, Colo.: Archive Press and Communications, 1999.
———. *Le Mystère des cathédrales et l'interprétation ésotérique des symboles hermétiques du Grand Oeuvre*. Paris: Pauvert, 1974.
———. *The Mystery of the Cathedrals: Esoteric Intrepretation of the Hermetic Symbols of the Great Work*. Albuquerque, N.Mex.: Brotherhood of Light, 1984.
Galfetti, Gustau Gili. *Maisons excentriques*. Paris: Le Seuil, 1999.
Garin, Eugénio. *Hermétisme et Renaissance*. Paris: Allia, 2001.
Gautier, Théophile. *Portraits et souvenirs littéraires*. Paris: Michel Lévy Frères, 1875.
Gengembre, Gérard. "Illuminisme et littérature." *Dictionnaire des littératures de langue française*. 3 vols. Paris: Bordas, 1987.

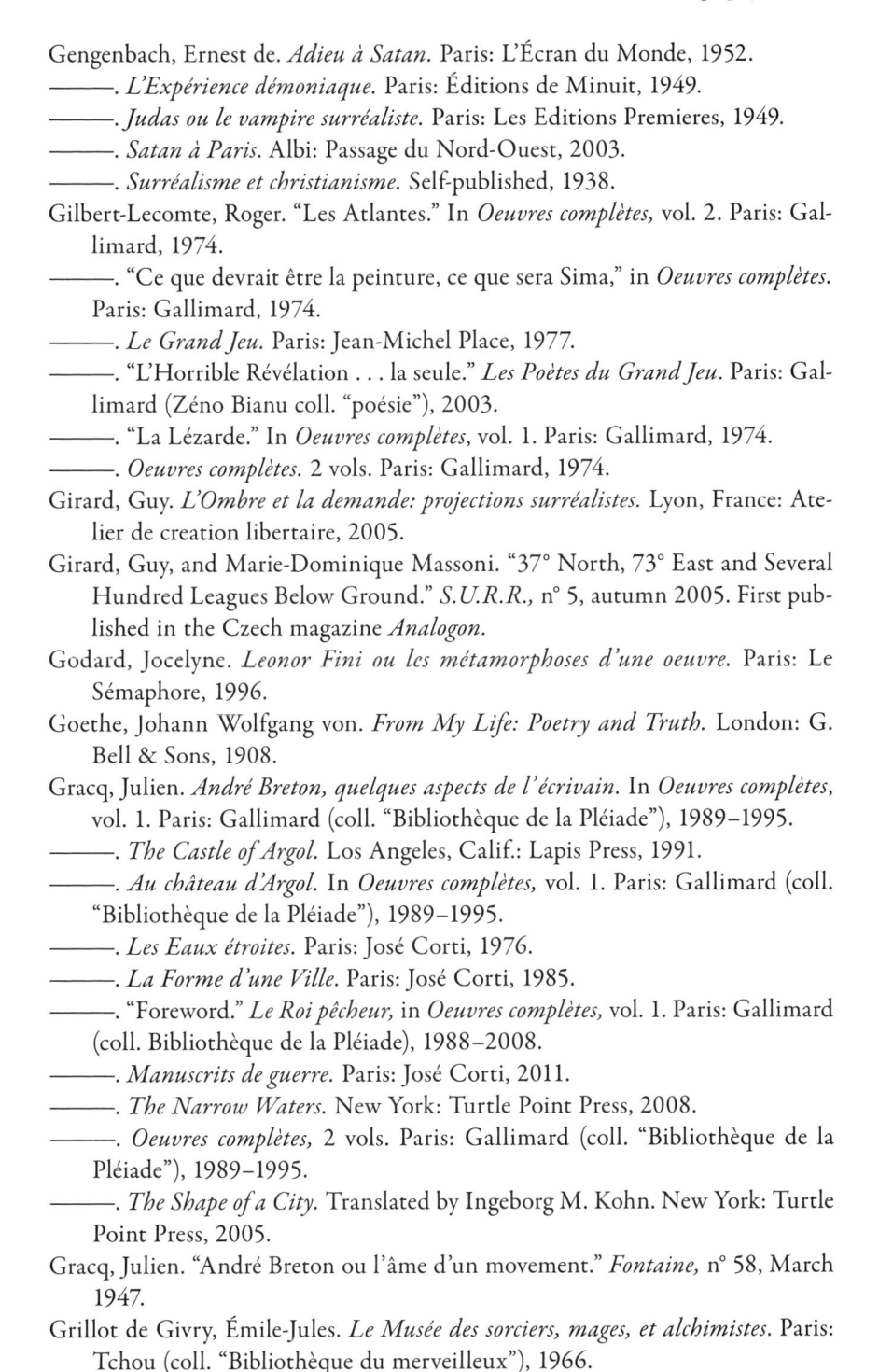

Gengenbach, Ernest de. *Adieu à Satan*. Paris: L'Écran du Monde, 1952.
———. *L'Expérience démoniaque*. Paris: Éditions de Minuit, 1949.
———. *Judas ou le vampire surréaliste*. Paris: Les Editions Premieres, 1949.
———. *Satan à Paris*. Albi: Passage du Nord-Ouest, 2003.
———. *Surréalisme et christianisme*. Self-published, 1938.
Gilbert-Lecomte, Roger. "Les Atlantes." In *Oeuvres complètes,* vol. 2. Paris: Gallimard, 1974.
———. "Ce que devrait être la peinture, ce que sera Sima," in *Oeuvres complètes*. Paris: Gallimard, 1974.
———. *Le Grand Jeu*. Paris: Jean-Michel Place, 1977.
———. "L'Horrible Révélation . . . la seule." *Les Poètes du Grand Jeu*. Paris: Gallimard (Zéno Bianu coll. "poésie"), 2003.
———. "La Lézarde." In *Oeuvres complètes*, vol. 1. Paris: Gallimard, 1974.
———. *Oeuvres complètes*. 2 vols. Paris: Gallimard, 1974.
Girard, Guy. *L'Ombre et la demande: projections surréalistes*. Lyon, France: Atelier de creation libertaire, 2005.
Girard, Guy, and Marie-Dominique Massoni. "37° North, 73° East and Several Hundred Leagues Below Ground." *S.U.R.R.,* n° 5, autumn 2005. First published in the Czech magazine *Analogon*.
Godard, Jocelyne. *Leonor Fini ou les métamorphoses d'une oeuvre*. Paris: Le Sémaphore, 1996.
Goethe, Johann Wolfgang von. *From My Life: Poetry and Truth*. London: G. Bell & Sons, 1908.
Gracq, Julien. *André Breton, quelques aspects de l'écrivain*. In *Oeuvres complètes*, vol. 1. Paris: Gallimard (coll. "Bibliothèque de la Pléiade"), 1989–1995.
———. *The Castle of Argol*. Los Angeles, Calif.: Lapis Press, 1991.
———. *Au château d'Argol*. In *Oeuvres complètes,* vol. 1. Paris: Gallimard (coll. "Bibliothèque de la Pléiade"), 1989–1995.
———. *Les Eaux étroites*. Paris: José Corti, 1976.
———. *La Forme d'une Ville*. Paris: José Corti, 1985.
———. "Foreword." *Le Roi pêcheur,* in *Oeuvres complètes,* vol. 1. Paris: Gallimard (coll. Bibliothèque de la Pléiade), 1988–2008.
———. *Manuscrits de guerre*. Paris: José Corti, 2011.
———. *The Narrow Waters*. New York: Turtle Point Press, 2008.
———. *Oeuvres complètes,* 2 vols. Paris: Gallimard (coll. "Bibliothèque de la Pléiade"), 1989–1995.
———. *The Shape of a City*. Translated by Ingeborg M. Kohn. New York: Turtle Point Press, 2005.
Gracq, Julien. "André Breton ou l'âme d'un movement." *Fontaine,* n° 58, March 1947.
Grillot de Givry, Émile-Jules. *Le Musée des sorciers, mages, et alchimistes*. Paris: Tchou (coll. "Bibliothèque du merveilleux"), 1966.
———. *Witchcraft, Magic, and Alchemy*. New York: Houghton Mifflin, 1931.

Grimberg, Solomon. *Leonora Carrington: Encultura Reciente.* Mexico City: Impronta, 1999.
Guénon, René. *La Crise du monde moderne.* Paris: Gallimard, 1946.
———. *The Crisis of the Modern World.* Hillsdale, N.Y.: Sophia Perennis, 2004.
———. *L'Erreur Spritiste.* Paris: Traditionnelles, 1984.
———. *L'Ésotérisme de Dante.* Paris: Bosse, 1925.
———. *Introduction générale à l'étude des doctrines hindoues.* Paris: Guy Trédaniel, 1997.
———. *The Symbolism of the Cross.* London: Luzac, 1975.
———. *Le Symbolisme de la Croix.* Paris: Guy Trédaniel, 1996.
Guyon, Robert. "Comme suite à un ajour d'*Arcane 17*." *La Brèche,* n° 6, June 1964.
Hames, Peter. *The Cinema of Jan Svankmajer: Dark Alchemy.* London: Wallflower Press, 2007.
Hammond, Paul. *Constellations of Miró, Breton.* San Francisco: City Lights, 2001.
Henein, Georges. Catalog for the El Telmisany exhibition, Cairo, 1941. In *Georges Henein,* by Sarane Alexandrian. Paris: Seghers (coll. "Poètes d'aujourd'hui"), 1981.
Hobsbawm, Eric, and Terence Ranger. *The Invention of Tradition.* Cambridge: Cambridge University Press, 1983.
Holten, Ragnar von, and José Pierre. *D'Orgeix.* Paris: Musée de Poche, 1975.
Homs, Henry. "Joachim de Flore." In *Le Rite français du premier grade au Ve Ordre.* Edited by Edmond Mazet. Paris: Éditions Télètes, 2003.
Hoog, Armand. "The Fall of the Black House, contradictions of the Surrealism." *ESPRIT,* July 1945.
Houellebecq, Michel. *H. P. Lovecraft: Contre le monde, contre la vie.* Monaco: Le Rocher, 1981.
Hubert, Henri. *Les Celtes.* 2 vols. Paris: Albin Michel, 1932, 1933.
Hutin, Serge. *Les Disciples anglais de Jacob Boehme.* Paris: Denoël, 1960.
Huysman, Joris-Karl. *En Rade.* Paris: Plon, 1928.
Imbert, Charles. *Les Sources souterraines de la franc-maçonnerie: Mithra et le tarot.* Paris: Véga, 2009.
Ivsic, Radovan. *Cascades.* Paris: Gallimard, 2006.
Jaguer, Édouard. *Le Surréalisme face à la littérature.* Bazas, France: Actual/Le Temps Qu'il Fait, 1989.
———. "Le Surréalisme par-dessus L'Ancien et le Nouveau Monde." In *André Breton et le surréalisme international.* Special issue, *Opus* 123–24 (April–May, 1991).
Jameux, Charles. *Murnau.* Paris: Éditions Universitaires, 1965.
———. "Les Sources antiques de la transmission initiatique en franc-maçonnerie: art classique de la mémoire." *Points de vue Initiatiques,* n° 100, December 1995–January 1996.
———. *Souvenirs de la maison des vivants.* Paris: AG Éditions, 2008.

———. *Le Vaisseau de feu*. Self-published, 1980.
Janet, Pierre. *L'Automatisme psychologique*. Paris: Alcan, 1889.
Jarry, Alfred. *Les Minutes de sable mémorial/César-Antechrist*. Paris: Gallimard, 1977.
Jean, Marcel. "Un banquet de têtes." In *Jacques Prévert: Collages*. Paris: Maeght Éditeur, 1995.
Jodorowsky, Alejandro. *The Spiritual Journey of Alejandro Jodorowsky*. Rochester, Vt.: Inner Traditions, 2008.
Jones, Henri. *Le Surréalisme ignoré*. Montréal, Que.: Centre éducative et cultural, Inc., 1969.
Joubert, Alain. "Antipodistes complémentaires." *La Quinzaine littéraire*, n° 987, March 1–15, 2009.
Jouffroy, Alain. "Lettre rouge." In *La Fin et la manière*, by Jean-Pierre Duprey. Paris: Le Soleil Noir, 1965.
———. *Liberté des libertés*. Paris: Le Soleil Noir, 1971.
———. *Manifeste de la Poésie Vécue*. Paris: Gallimard (coll. "L'infini"), 1995.
———. *Une révolution du regard*. Paris: Gallimard, 1964.
Juin, Hubert. Preface. In *Un Coeur en peine*, by Joseph Peladan. Paris: Union Générale d'Edition 1984.
Jung, Carl Gustav. *Flying Saucers: A Modern Myth*. Princeton, N.J.: Princeton University Press, 1969.
Keith, Delmari Romero. *Leonora Carrington, Bride of the Wind*. Latin American House in Paris, May 30–July 18, 2008.
———. "Leonora Carrington, A Sleepwalker in the Light." In *Leonora Carrington, Bride of the Wind*, the catalog for the exhibition held at the Latin American House in Paris, May 30–July 18, 2008.
———. *Leonora Carrington, la mariée du vent*. Paris: Gallimard, 2008.
———. "Leonora Carrington, une somnambule dans la lumière." In *Leonora Carrington, la mariée du vent*. Paris: Gallimard, 2008.
Kingsley, Peter. *Ancient Philosophy, Mystery, and Magic: Empedocles and Pythagorean Tradition*. New York: Oxford University Press, 1995.
Knowles, Richard. *Victor-Émile Michelet, Poète Ésoterique*. Paris: Vrin, 1954.
Kober, Marc. "Dans le verger de la salamandre (Elie-Charles Flamand)." *La Soeur de l'ange*, n° 3, éditions A Contrario. Study Center for New Literary Spaces (CENEL)—Paris University XIII.
Kobry, Yves. "L'effet Arcimboldo." In "Arcimboldo (1526–1593)." Special issue of the *Beaux-Arts* review, 2007.
Koyré, Alexander. *Mystiques, spirituels, alchimistes du XVIe siècle allemand*. Paris: Gallimard (coll. "Idées"), 1971.
———. "Paracelse." In *Mystiques, spirituels, alchimistes du XVIe siècle allemand*. Paris: Gallimard (coll. "Idées"), 1971.
Kral, Petr. "L'art du saut dans le vide." In "André Breton et le surréalisme international." Special issue, *Opus* 123–24 (April–May 1991).

Kuni, Verena. *Victor Brauner dans les collections du MNAM-CCI.* Paris: Éditions du Centre Pompidou, 1996.
Kyrou, Ado. *Le Surréalisme au cinéma.* Paris: Le Terrain Vague, 1963.
Labouri, Denis. *Testament maçonnique.* Paris: Rafael de Surtis, 2008.
Lacarrière, Jacques. *The Gnostics.* San Francisco: City Lights, 1989.
———. Les Gnostiques. Paris: Gallimard (coll. "Idées"), 1973.
Lacassagne, Olivier Pénot. Vie et mort d'Antonin Artaud. Saint-Cyr-Sur-Loire, France: Christian Pirot, 2007.
Lamantia, Philip. *Becoming Visible.* San Francisco: City Lights, 1981.
Lambert, Jean-Clarence, *André Masson.* Rouen: Imprimerie Wolf, 1940.
———. ed. *General History of Painting.* Paris: Rencontre Éditions, 1967.
Landemont, Sébastien. *Les Grandes Figures de l' ésotérisme.* Paris: de Vecchi, 2005.
Larguier, Léo. *Le Faiseur d'or, Nicolas Flamel.* Paris: Arléa, 2010.
Lasalle, Jean-Pierre. "André Breton et la franc-maçonnerie." *Histoires littéraires,* n° 1, 2000.
———. *Le Grand Patagon.* Paris: Saligardes, 1963.
Laurant, Jean-Pierre. *René Guénon: Les enjeux d'une lecture.* Paris: Dervy, 2006.
Laville, Rémy. *Pierre Mabille: un compagnon du surréalisme.* Paris: Publications de la faculté des lettres de Clermont II, 1983.
Lebel, Jean-Jacques. "Tanguy, joueur/inventeur." In *Yves Tanguy, l'univers surréaliste.* Catalog for the exhibit at the Quimper Fine Arts Museum, Quimper, France, June 29–September 30, 2007.
Lebel, Robert. *Marcel Duchamp: Von der Erscheinung Konzeption.* Cologne, Germany: DuMont Schauberg, 1962.
Le Brun, Annie. *Les Châteaux de la subversion.* Paris: J. J. Pauvert aux Éditions Garnier, 1982.
———. "L'Inconscient." *A Distance.* Paris: Carrere, 1984.
———. "Je n'ai plus une seul dent." In *Leonora Carrington, la mariée du vent,* under the supervision of Delmari Romero Keith. Paris: Gallimard, 2008.
———. *De l'éperdu.* Paris: Stock, 2000.
———. *On n'enchaîne pas les volcans.* Paris: Gallimard, 2006.
———. "Les premiers romans noir ou l'ébauche d'une science revolutionnaire." *La Brèche,* n° 8, November 1965.
———. *Qui vive: Considérations inactuelles sur l'inactualité du surréalisme.* Paris: Ramsay/J. J. Pauvert, 1991.
———. *Sade: A Sudden Abyss.* San Francisco: City Lights, 2001.
———. *Si rien avait une forme, ce serait cela.* Paris: Gallimard, 2010.
———. *Soudain un bloc d'abîme, Sade.* Translated by Camille Naish. Paris: J. J. Pauvert, 1985.
Leclercq-Bolle De Bal, Françoise. *La Métamorphose: mystère Initiatique.* Paris: Maison de vie éditeur, 2009.
Lecomte, Marcel. *Le Sens des tarots.* Brussels: Ensaad, 1948.

Lécureur, Michel. *Raymond Queneau, biographie.* Paris: Les Belles Lettres, 2002.
Legrand, Gérard. *André Breton en son temps.* Paris: Le Soleil Noir, 1976.
———. "Libre Promenade." In *L'art magique,* by André Breton. Paris: Éditions Phébus et Adam Biro, 2003.
———. *Pour connaître la pensée des présocratiques.* Paris: Bordas, 1970.
———. "Rationalisme et raisons de vivre." *Le Libertaire,* November 30, 1951.
———. *Sur Oedipe.* Paris: Le Terrain Vague–Eric Losfeld (coll. "Le désordre"), 1972.
Le Gros, Marc. *André Breton et la Bretagne.* Paris: Blanc Silex Éditions, 2000.
Leiris, Michel. *L'Âge d'homme.* Paris: Gallimard, 1939.
———. *Aurora.* London: Atlas Press, 1993.
———. *Aurora.* Paris: Gallimard, 1939.
———. "Éléments pour une biographie." In *André Masson.* Rouen: Imprimerie Wolf, 1940.
———. *Haut Mal.* Paris: Gallimard, 1969.
———. *Images de marque.* Bazas, France: Éditions le Temps qu'il fait, 2002.
———. *La Possession et ses aspects théâtraux chez les Éthiopiens de Gondar.* Paris: Plon, 1958.
———. *Le ruban autour du cou d'Olympia.* Paris: Gallimard (coll. "L'imaginaire"), 2006.
Leiris, Michel, and Jean Schuster. *Entre augures.* Paris: Le Terrain Vague (coll. "Le désordre"), 1990.
Le Mellec, Christian. "Charles Duits et l'immense oui." In *Vision et hallucination: L'expérience du Peyotl en littérature.* Paris: Albin Michel, 1994.
Lengyel, Lancelot. *L'Art gaulois dans les médailles.* Paris: Éditions Corvina, 1954.
Le Scouezec, Gwenc'hlan. *Guide de la Bretagne mystérieuse.* Paris: Tchou Princesse, 1979.
Levi, Eliphas. *History of Magic.* Freeport, Maine: Weiser, 1999.
———. *Transcendental Magic.* London: Rider & Co., 1964.
Ligou, Daniel. *Dictionary of Freemasonry.* Paris: P.U.F., 1987.
Limbour, Georges. *Le Bridge de Madame Lyane.* Paris: Gallimard, 1948.
Lindenberg, David. "Hypermatérialisme et Gnose." In *Surréalisme et Philosophie,* by Christian Descamps. Paris: Éditions du Centre Georges Pompidou, 1992.
Linhartova, Vera. *Dada et surréalisme au Japon.* Paris: Publications Orientalistes de France, 1987.
Lotringer, Sylvère. *Fous d'Artaud.* Paris: Sens & Tonka, 2003.
Löwy, Michel. "Langage et magie." *S.U.R.R.,* n° 4: *Transmutation du langage,* Spring 2003.
Luca, Ghérasim. *Le Vampire passif.* Paris: José Corti, 2001.
———. *The Passive Vampire.* Prague: Twisted Spoon Press, 2008.
Mabille, Pierre. *Conscience lumineuse, conscience picturale.* Paris: José Corti, 1989.

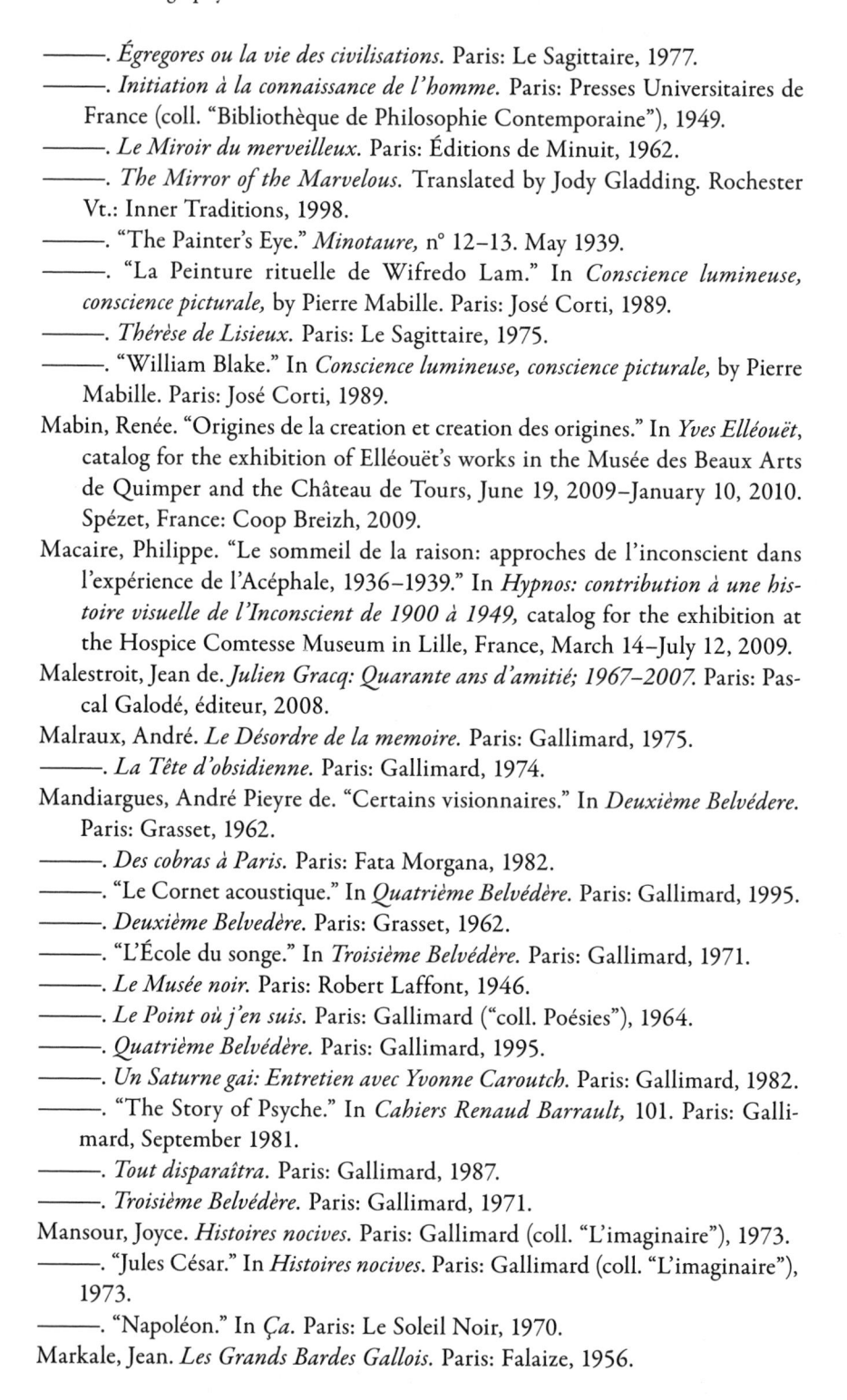

———. *Égregores ou la vie des civilisations.* Paris: Le Sagittaire, 1977.

———. *Initiation à la connaissance de l'homme.* Paris: Presses Universitaires de France (coll. "Bibliothèque de Philosophie Contemporaine"), 1949.

———. *Le Miroir du merveilleux.* Paris: Éditions de Minuit, 1962.

———. *The Mirror of the Marvelous.* Translated by Jody Gladding. Rochester Vt.: Inner Traditions, 1998.

———. "The Painter's Eye." *Minotaure,* n° 12–13. May 1939.

———. "La Peinture rituelle de Wifredo Lam." In *Conscience lumineuse, conscience picturale,* by Pierre Mabille. Paris: José Corti, 1989.

———. *Thérèse de Lisieux.* Paris: Le Sagittaire, 1975.

———. "William Blake." In *Conscience lumineuse, conscience picturale,* by Pierre Mabille. Paris: José Corti, 1989.

Mabin, Renée. "Origines de la creation et creation des origines." In *Yves Elléouët,* catalog for the exhibition of Elléouët's works in the Musée des Beaux Arts de Quimper and the Château de Tours, June 19, 2009–January 10, 2010. Spézet, France: Coop Breizh, 2009.

Macaire, Philippe. "Le sommeil de la raison: approches de l'inconscient dans l'expérience de l'Acéphale, 1936–1939." In *Hypnos: contribution à une histoire visuelle de l'Inconscient de 1900 à 1949,* catalog for the exhibition at the Hospice Comtesse Museum in Lille, France, March 14–July 12, 2009.

Malestroit, Jean de. *Julien Gracq: Quarante ans d'amitié; 1967–2007.* Paris: Pascal Galodé, éditeur, 2008.

Malraux, André. *Le Désordre de la memoire.* Paris: Gallimard, 1975.

———. *La Tête d'obsidienne.* Paris: Gallimard, 1974.

Mandiargues, André Pieyre de. "Certains visionnaires." In *Deuxième Belvédere.* Paris: Grasset, 1962.

———. *Des cobras à Paris.* Paris: Fata Morgana, 1982.

———. "Le Cornet acoustique." In *Quatrième Belvédère.* Paris: Gallimard, 1995.

———. *Deuxième Belvédère.* Paris: Grasset, 1962.

———. "L'École du songe." In *Troisième Belvédère.* Paris: Gallimard, 1971.

———. *Le Musée noir.* Paris: Robert Laffont, 1946.

———. *Le Point où j'en suis.* Paris: Gallimard ("coll. Poésies"), 1964.

———. *Quatrième Belvédère.* Paris: Gallimard, 1995.

———. *Un Saturne gai: Entretien avec Yvonne Caroutch.* Paris: Gallimard, 1982.

———. "The Story of Psyche." In *Cahiers Renaud Barrault,* 101. Paris: Gallimard, September 1981.

———. *Tout disparaîtra.* Paris: Gallimard, 1987.

———. *Troisième Belvédère.* Paris: Gallimard, 1971.

Mansour, Joyce. *Histoires nocives.* Paris: Gallimard (coll. "L'imaginaire"), 1973.

———. "Jules César." In *Histoires nocives.* Paris: Gallimard (coll. "L'imaginaire"), 1973.

———. "Napoléon." In *Ça.* Paris: Le Soleil Noir, 1970.

Markale, Jean. *Les Grands Bardes Gallois.* Paris: Falaize, 1956.

———. *L'Épopée celtique en Bretagne*. Paris: Payot, 1971.

———. *Le Grande Déesse: mythes et sanctuaires*. Paris: Albin Michel (coll. "Spiritualités"), 1997.

———. *The Great Goddess*. Translated by Jody Gladding. Rochester, Vt.: Inner Traditions, 1998.

———. "Mystères et enchantements des littératures celtiques." *Médium,* n° 4, 1955.

———. "Rome et l'épopée celtique." *Les Cahiers du Sud,* n° 355, April, May 1960.

———. *Les Saints Fondateurs de Bretagne et des pays celtes*. Paris: Pygmalion, 2002.

Maros, Jorge de. "Fernando Pessoa et la tradition martiniste." In *L'Ésotérisme chrétien et les valeurs de notre temps*. Papers of the symposium on Louis-Claude de Saint-Martin, Sintra, Portugal, May 29 and 30, 2004. Paris: Éditions Rafael de Surtis, 2009.

Marques-Rivière, Jean. *Amulettes, talismans et pantacles dans les traditions orientales et occidentales*. Paris: Payot, 1938.

Masson, André. *Le Rebelle du surréalisme: Écrits*. Paris: Éditions Hermann (coll. "Savoir sur l'art"), 1994.

Mauriac, Claude. *André Breton*. Paris: Flores, 1949.

Mayoux, Jean-Jacques. "La Damnation de William Beckford." *Sous de Vastes Portiques*. N.p.: English Miscellany, 1961.

———. *Sous des vastes portiques: études de littérature et d'art anglais*. Paris: Maurice Nadeau/Papyrus, 1981.

Mendès, Catulle. *Zo'har*. Paris: Charpentier, 1886.

Meuris, Jacques. *Magritte et les mystères de la pensée*. Brussels: Éditions de La Lettre Volée, 1992.

Mezei, Arpad. "Liberté du langage." *Le Surréalisme*. Paris: Maeght Editeur, 1947.

———. "Le Surréalisme en Hongrie aujourd'hui." In "André Breton et le surréalisme International." Special issue, *Opus* 123–24 (April–May 1991).

Mezei, Arpad, and Marcel Jean. *Genèse de la pensée moderne dans la littérature française*. Lausanne, Switzerland: Éditions de l'Âge d'Homme (coll. "Bibliothèque Mélusine"), 2001.

Michelet, Victor-Émile. *Les Compagnons de la Hiérophanie*. Paris: Dorbon-Ainé, 1938.

Migam, Josick. *Yves Tanguy, surréaliste: "La Conviction du jamais-vu"; essai psychanalytique*. Paris: Penta/L'Harmattan, 2007.

Mitrani, Nora. "Poésie, Liberté d'Être." In *Rose au Coeur Violet*, by Nora Mitrani. Paris: Le Terrain Vague (coll. "Le Désordre"), 1988.

———. *Rose au Coeur Violet*. Paris: Le Terrain Vague (coll. "Le Désordre"), 1988.

Monnerot, Jules. *La Poésie moderne et le sacré*. Paris: Gallimard, 1945.

Morgane-Tanguy, Geneviève. *D'Armorique en Amérique: Yves Tanguy, druide surréaliste*. Paris: Fernand Lanore, 1995.

Mourier, Maurice. "Breton/Berkeley: De l'idéalisme absolu comme tentation et comme terreur." In *Surréalisme et philosophie*. Edited by Christian Descamps. Paris: Éditions du Centre Pompidou, 1992.

Mourier-Casile, Pascaline. *André Breton, Explorateur de la Mère-Moire*. Paris: P.U.F. (Coll. "Ecrivains"), 1986.

Murphy, Juliette. In the catalog for the *Alchemy of the Philosophers* exhibition, 2009, published by the Gala and Salvador Dali Foundation.

Murnau, F. W., director. *Nosferatu, a Symphony of Horror*. Prana Film, 1922.

Nadeau, Maurice. *Histoire du Surréalisme*. Paris: Seuil (coll. "Points"), 1970.

———. *History of Surrealism*. New York: Macmillan, 1965.

Nerval, Gérard de. *Voyage en Orient*. Paris: Nouvelle Librarie française, 1981.

Nezval, Vitezslav. *Rue Git-le-Coeur*. Avignon, France: Éditions de l'Aube, 1988.

Nocé, Vincent. "Le réveil du bois dormant," *Libération*, January 23–24, 2010.

Nougé, Paul. *Histoire de ne pas Rire*. Paris: L'Age d'Homme (coll. "Cistre-Lettres différentes"), 1980.

———. "Les Images défendues" (Prohibited Images). *Le Surréalisme au service de la révolution*, n° 5, 1933.

Onfray, Michel. *Métaphysique des ruines*. Paris: Mollat-LGF, 2010.

Osman, Amina. *Le Mage de l'île Maurice*. Paris: L'Ether Vague, 1996.

Ottinger, Didier. "Le Grand Jeu et le surréalisme français." In *Grand Jeu et surréalisme, Reims, Paris, Prague*. Exposition, December 16, 2003–March 28, 2004.

———. *La Collection d'art moderne et contemporain*. Museum of the Holy Cross Abbey, Les Sables d'Olonne, 1990.

Ouspensky, P. D. *Fragments d'un enseignement inconnu*. Paris: Stock, 1949.

———. *In Search of the Miraculous*. London: Routledge, 1950.

———. *A New Model of the Universe*. Mineola: N.Y., 1997.

Paine, Thomas. *The Origins of Freemasonry*. New York: G. P. Putnam's Sons, 1896.

Palou, Jean. *La Franc-Maçonnerie*. Paris: Payot, 1964.

Paracelsus, *The Seven Books of the Archidoxes of Magic*. Preface by Marc Haven. London: The Theosophical Publishing Society, 1907.

Partner, Peter. *The Knights Templar and Their Myth*. Rochester, Vt.: Destiny Books, 1990.

Passeron, René. *Histoire de la Peinture surréaliste*. Paris: Le Livre de pouche, 1968.

Pastoureau, Henri. "Le Surréalisme de l'après-guerre, 1946–1950." In *Le Surréalisme ignoré*, by Henri Jones. Montreal, Que.: Centre éducatif et culturel, Inc., 1969.

Paz, Octavio. *Alternating Current*. New York: Viking, 1967.

———. "André Breton or the Quest for the Beginning." In *Alternating Current*. New York: Viking, 1967.

———. "Baudelaire as Art Critic: Presence and Present." In *On Poets and Others*. New York: Arcade, 1990.

———. *The Bow and the Lyre*. Austin: University of Texas Press, 1987.

———. *Deux Transparents: Marcel Duchamp et Claude Lévi-Strauss*. Paris: Gallimard, 1970.

———. "Henri Michaux." In *Alternating Current*. New York: Viking, 1967.

———. *On Poets and Others*. New York: Arcade, 1990.

———. "Remedios Varo's Appearances and Disappearances." In *Alternating Current*. New York: Viking, 1967.

———. *Solo a deux voix: entretiens avec Julian Rios*. Paris: Ramsay/De Cortanze, 1992.

Péan, Pierre. *La Diabolique de Caluire*. Paris: Fayard, 1999.

Peladan, Joseph. *Un Coeur en peine*. Paris: Broché, 1908.

———. *De L'Androgyne*. Paris: Éditions Allia, 2010.

Penrose, Valentine. *The Bloody Countess*. New York: Solar Books, 2006.

———. *Erzébet Bathory: la Comtesse sanglante*. Paris: Mercure de France, 1962.

Peregrino, Pierre F. *La Lettre G,* n° 4, Spring 2006.

Péret, Benjamin. "Actualité du roman noir." *Arts,* n° 361, May–June 1952.

———. *Le Déshonneur des poètes*. Paris: Actual/José Corti, 1986.

———. *The Heart of the Comet* in *Death to the Pigs*. London: Atlas Press, 1988.

———. *Oeuvres Complete*. 7 vols. Paris: Eric Losfeld, 1978–1988; José Corti, 1988–1997.

———. *Au Soleil Noir*. Paris: Éditions Sokolova, 1953.

Perks, Simone. "Fatum and Fortuna: André Masson, Surrealism, and the Divinatory Arts." *Papers of Surrealism,* n° 3, Spring 2005. www.Surrealismcentre.ac.uk/papersofsurrealism (accessed May 17, 2013).

Piau, Guy. *Tradition alchimique et tradition maçonnique*. Paris: Éditions DETRAD aVs, 2005.

———. *Le belvédère Mandiargues*. Paris: Artcurial et Éditions Adam Biro, 1990.

———. "Coup de semonce." In *Tracts surréalistes et déclarations collectives,* by José Pierre. 2 vols. Paris: Eric Losfeld, 1982.

———. "Le gouvernement de la foudre." Introduction to *Wolfgang Paalen*. New York: Jupiter Books, 1982.

———. *Investigating Sexuality*. New York: Verso, 1994.

———. *Recherches sur la sexualité: Archives du surréalisme*. Paris: Gallimard, 1990.

———. *Surréalisme et anarchie*. Paris: Plasma, 1983.

———. *Tracts surréalistes et déclarations collectives*. 2 vols. Paris: Eric Losfeld, 1982.

Piobb, Pierre. *Le Secret de Nostradamus*. Escalquens, France: Dangles, 1945.

Pistis Sophia. Paris: Robert Laffont (coll. "Les Portes de l'Étrange"), 1972.

Poisson, Albert. *Théories et symboles des alchimistes*. Paris: Éditions Traditionnelles, 1891.

Poniatowska, Elena. *Leonora Carrington en la ciudad de Mexico* (Exhibit), February 2008.

Porset, Charles. *Vampires et lumières*. Paris: À l'Orient, 2007.
Potocki, Jan. *The Manuscript Found in Saragossa*. London: Penguin, 1995.
Prassinos, Gisèle. *Le Visage effleuré de peine*. Paris: Grasset, 1964.
Praz, Mario. *La Chair: la mort et le diable*. Paris: Gallimard (coll. "Tel"), 1999.
Prescott, Andrew. "Druidic Myth and Freemasonry." Lecture, presented at the Centre for Research into Freemasonry, Sheffield University, 2000.
Prevost, Pierre. *La Spiritualité et ses Parodies Modernes*. Paris: Dervy (coll. "Pierre Vivante"), 2007.
Queneau, Raymond. *Odile*. Paris: Gallimard, 1937.
———. *Pierrot mon ami*. Paris: Gallimard, 1942.
Rabourdin, Dominique. "André Breton et Julien Gracq à Nantes: l'anneau de Béatrix." In *Le Rêve d'une ville, Nantes et le surréalisme*, edited by Henri-Claude Cousseau. Paris: Coedition of the Réunion des musées nationaux et du Musée des Beaux-Arts de Nantes, 1994.
Random, Michel. *Le Grand Jeu*, vol 1. Paris: Denoöl, 1970.
Ratcliffe, Eric. *Ithell Colquhoun: Pioneer Surrealist Artist, Occultist, Writer, and Poet*. London: Mandrake, 2007.
Reeve, Clara. *The Old English Baron*. London: Mawman, Poultry, 1778.
Rémy, Michel. *Au trezième coup de minuit: Anthologie du surréalisme en Angleterre*. Paris: Éditions Dilecta, 2008.
Ressoun-Demigneux, Karim. "Artificiala and Naturalia." In "Arcimboldo (1526–1593)." Special issue of the *Beaux-Arts* review, 2007.
Ribemont-Dessaigne, Georges. *Ariadne*. Paris: Jean-Michel Place, 1977.
Rihouët-Corroze, Simonne. "Analyse du 'Crocodile.'" Paris: Triades-Édition, 1962.
Ripellino, Angelo. *Praga Magica*. Paris: Plon (coll. "Terre humaine"), 1993.
Roche, Gérard. *Benjamin Péret et les Amériques*. Paris: Association des amis de Benjamin Péret, 2010.
Rodanski, Stanislas. *Requiem for Me*. Paris: Éditions des Cendres, 2009.
———. *La Victoire à l'ombre des ailes*. Paris: Le Soleil Noir, 1975.
Roger, Bernard. *À la découverte de l'alchimie: L'art d'Hermès à travers les contes, l'histoire, et les rituels maçonniques*. Paris: Dangles, 2003.
———. "Le jour de l'étoile." *L'Archibras*, n° 7, March 1969.
———. *Paris et l'Alchimie*. Paris: Éditions William Alta-Umbra Solis, 1981.
Roger, Bernard, Jorge Camacho, and Eduardo Fernández Sánchez. *La Cathédrale de Séville et le Bestiaire hermétique du portail de Saint-Christophe et de l'Immaculée Conception*. Pol-François Lambert Foundation.
Rolland de Renéville, André. *L'Expérience Poétique*. Genève, Switzerland: A la Baconnière, 1948.
Roob, Alexander. *Alchimie et mystique: le monde hermétique*. Cologne, Germany: Taschen, 2001.
Rosey, Gui. *Tirer au Clair la nuit: Oeuvres Vives*. Vol. I, *Le Miroir du solitaire*. Paris: José Corti, 1963.

Roudaut, Jean. *Preface for Ariadne.* Paris: Jean-Michel Place, 1977.
Roy, Claude. *André Breton en perspective cavalière.* Paris: Gallimard, 1976.
Royer, Jean-Michel. "Connaissance et reconnaissance." *Cahiers Renaud-Barrault,* n° 69. Paris: Gallimard, first trimester, 1957.
Sabatier, Robert. *La Poésie du XXe siècle.* Paris: Albin Michel, 1988.
Saint-Martin, Louis Claude de. *Des erreurs et de la vérité ou les hommes rappelés aux principes de la science.* Edinburgh: Unknown publisher, 1775. Reprinted, University of Michigan, 2009.
———. *L'Homme de désir.* Monaco: Le Rocher, 1985.
Schefer, Bernard. Foreword to *Hermétisme et Renaissance,* by Eugénio Garin. Paris: Allia, 2001.
Schmitt, Bernard, and Marie-Dominique Massoni. *Jan Svankmajer: un surréaliste du cinema d'animation.* Paris: Éditions Ciné-Fils, 1999.
———. *Svankmajer E & J Bouche à Bouche.* Annecy, France: Éditions de l'Oeil, 2002.
Scholem, Gershom. "Le Golem de Prague et le Golem de Rehovot." In *Le Messianisme juif: Essai sur la spiritualité du judaïsme.* Paris: Calmann-Lévy, 1974.
———. *Major Trends in Jewish Mysticism.* New York: Schocken Books, 1946.
———. *Le Nom et les symboles de Dieu dans la mystique juive.* Paris: Le Cert, 1983.
———. *On the Kabbalah and Its Symbolism.* New York: Schocken Books, 1965.
Schuré, Édouard. *Les Grands Initiés.* Paris: Perrin (coll. "Librairie académique"), 1960.
Schuster, Jean. *Archives 57–69: Batailles pour le Surréalisme.* Paris: Eric Losfeld, 1969.
———. "Conversation de Schuster avec Silbermann." In "André Breton et le Surréalisme International." Special issue, *Opus* 123–24 (April–May 1991).
———. *Docsur,* n° 6, summer 1988.
———. *Les Fruits de la passion.* Paris: Éditions de l'Instant, 1988.
———. *Lettre à André Liberati contre les acolytes de Dieu et les judas de l'athéisme.* Bazas, France: Éditions Le Temps qu'il fait, 1986.
———. *Le Ramasse-Miettes/a Lettre différée à Philippe Soupault.* Bordeaux, France: Pleine Page/Opales, 1991.
———. *T'as vu ça d'ta f'nêtre.* Levallois-Perret, France: Manya, 1990.
———. "À La niche les Glapisseurs de Dieu" by Adolphe Acker, Sarane Alexandrian, Maurice Baskine, et al. Paris: Éditions Surrealistes, 1948.
Schuster, Jean, and Simon Hantaï. "Une démolition au platane." *Médium* (1955): 58.
Schwartz, Stephen. "Automatisme et Shamanisme." *Bulletin de liaison surréaliste,* December 7, 1973.
Seabrook, William. *The Magic Island.* New York: Harcourt Brace, 1929.
Sebbag, Georges. *L'Imprononçable Jour de ma Naissance André Breton.* Paris: Éditions Jean-Michel Place, 1988.

Sède, Gérard de. *La Rose-Croix.* Paris: J'ai Lu (coll. "L'Aventure mysterieuse"), 1978.

———. *Le Secret des Cathares.* Paris: J'ai Lu (coll. "L'Aventure mysterieuse"), 1974.

Seibel, Castor. "The Fête in the Conjunction of Opposites in the Painting of Leonor Fini." *Connaissance des Arts,* n° 274, December 1974.

Seligmann, Kurt. "Dialogue with a Tsimshian." *Minotaure.* May 1939.

———. *The History of Magic and the Occult.* New York: Pantheon Books, 1948.

———. *Le Miroir de la magie: Histoire de la magie dans le monde occidental.* Paris: Fasquelle, 1956.

———. *The Mirror of Magic.* New York: Pantheon Books, 1948.

Sendivogius. *The New Chemical Light Drawn from the Fountain of Nature and of Manual Experience to Which Is Added a Treatise on Sulphur.* Whitefish, Mont.: Kessinger Publishing, 2010.

———. *Treatise on Mercury, Sulphur, and Salt.* London: A. Clark, 1674.

Serbanne, Claude. "Panorama. Surréalistes étrangers." *Les Cahiers du Sud,* n° 280, 1946.

Shillitoe, Richard. *Ithell Colquhoun, Magician Born of Nature.* Lulu.com, 2010. www.ithellcolquhoun.co.uk (accessed May 17, 2013).

Silbermann, Jean-Claude. *Le Jour me nuit.* Paris: HC and D'Arts, 1999.

———. *Pas meme un tison, sa brûlure.* Paris: L'écart Absolu, 1999.

———. "Le Saumon, la cerise et la gardien du trait." *Le Jour me nuit.* Paris: HC and D'Arts, 1999.

Simonelli, Jacques. "À la recherche de Fol-Yver" (In Search of Fol-Yver). *Fleur de lune,* n° 19, April 2008, edited by the Association of Friends of Maurice Fourré.

Soupault, Philippe. *En joue!* Paris: Lachenal et Ritter, 1984.

Srp, Karel. *Toyen, une femme surréaliste.* Saint Etienne, France: Éditions Artha, 2002.

Stevenson, David. *The Origins of Freemasonry.* Cambridge: Cambridge University Press, 1990.

Sudre, René. *Introduction à la métapsychique humaine.* Paris: Payot, 1926.

Surany, Marguerite. *Alchimie du visible à invisible.* Presses de l'Échiquier, 1967.

Suzuki, D. T. *Essays in Zen Buddhism.* New York: Grove Press, 1961.

———. *The Mute Book.* J. J. Pauvert, then by Gutenberg Reprints, 1996.

Swedenborg, Emanuel. *Concerning the earths in our solar system, which are called planets: and concerning the earths in the starry heavens together with an account of their inhabitants, and also of the spirits and angels there: from what hath been seen and heard.* London: Swedenborg Society, 1962.

———. *Delights of Wisdom Pertaining to Conjugal Love.* London: Swedenborg Society, 1962.

Tarade, Guy. *Les Derniers Gardiens du Graal.* Paris: Dervy, 1993.

Tarnaud, Claude De. *Le Bout du monde.* Paris: L'Écart absolu, 2003.

Thirion, André. *Révolutionnaires sans Révolutions.* Paris: Robert Laffont, 1972.
Tison-Braun, Micheline. *La Crise de l'Humanisme.* Paris: Nizet, 1967.
Trintzius, René. *Jacques Cazotte ou le XVIIIe siècle inconnu.* Paris: Éditions Athéna, 1944.
Tristan, Frédérick. "Hérold, 'l'Or de l'air.'" *Libération,* March 19, 1987.
———. *L'Obsédante.* Paris: Le Cherche-Midi, 1992.
Turrent, Thomas Pérez, and José de la Colina. "Conversations avec Luis Buñuel: Il est dangereux de se pencher au-dedans." In *Cahiers du cinema.* Paris: Seuil, 1993.
Ubac, Raoul. *Tracés sur la plage.* Paris: Maeght, 2005.
Vadé, Yves. *Pour un tombeau de Merlin: du barde celte à la période moderne.* Paris: José Corti (coll. "Les essais"), 2008.
Valli, Luigi. *Il Linguaggio Segreto di Dante e dei Fedeli d'Amore.* Rome: Optima, 1928.
Van Langhenhoven, Jehan. "Saynètes oecuméniques." In *Chroniques d'un mal au pas lent: Réponse aux serruriers.* Paris: Rafael de Surtis, 2009.
Van Lennep, Jacques. *Art et alchimie.* Paris: Meddens, 1966.
Van Rijnberk, Gérard. *A Thaumaturgist of the Eighteenth Century: Martinez de Pasqually.* Paris: Librarie Felix Alcan, 1935.
Van Win, Jean. *Contre Guénon: Les enjeux d'une lecture.* Paris: Éditions de la Hutte, Collection Essais, 2010.
Vanci-Perahim, Marina. "Quand les couloirs du sommeil traversent la Roumanie, de la rehabilitation du rêve à l'oniromancie obsessionnelle (1929–1947)." In *Hypnos: contribution à une histoire visuelle de l'Inconscient de 1900 à 1949,* catalog for the exhibition at the Hospice Comtesse Museum in Lille, France, March 14–July 12, 2009.
Vendryès, Pierre. *Vie et probabilité.* Paris: Albin Michel, 1942.
Viatte, Auguste. *Les Sources occultes du romantisme.* Paris: Champion, 1927. Reprint, Paris: Slatkine, 2009.
Victor Brauner: Surrealist Hieroglyphs. Catalog for exhibition at the Menil Collection, Houston, Texas, October 2001–January 2002.
Vieuille, Chantal. *Kay Sage ou le surréalisme américain.* Paris: Éditions Complicités, 1995.
Virilio, Paul. *Discours sur l'horreur de l'art.* Paris: Atelier de creation libertaire, 2003.
Virmaux, Alain, and Odette Virmaux. *Les Grandes figures du surréalisme.* Paris: Bordas, 1964.
———. *Roger Gilbert-Lecomte et le Grand Jeu.* Paris: Belfond, 1981.
Vulliaud, Paul. *La Pensée ésotérique de Léonard de Vinci.* Paris: Dervy Poche, 2009.
Waldberg, Patrick. "Jacques Hérold ou l'enfance de l'art." In "André Breton et le surréalisme international." London: Thames and Hudson, 1965.
Widmaier, Olivier. *Picasso, portraits de famille.* Paris: Ramsay, 2002.

Wifredo Lam: Voyages entre Caraïbes et avant-gardes. Catalog of the artist's exhibition at the Nantes Fine Arts Museum, Nantes, France, April 29–August 29, 2010.
Wilson, Colin. *The Occult*. London: Watkins, 2006.
Yates, Frances A. *The Art of Memory*. Chicago: University of Chicago Press, 2001.
———. *Fragments Autobiographiques*. Paris: Allia, 2009.
———. "Hermetic Tradition in the Science of the Renaissance." In *Science et traditions hermétiques*. Paris: Allia, 2009.
Ziegler, Gilette. *Histoire secrete de Paris*. Paris: Bibliothèque Marabout, 1967.
Zürn, Unica. *L'Homme-Jasmin*. Paris: Gallimard (coll. "L'imaginaire"), 1971.
———. *The Man of Jasmine*. London: Atlas Press, 1994.
———. *Oracles et spactacles*. Paris: Éditions George Visat, 1967.
———. *Surréalisme et sexualité*. Paris: Gallimard, 1971.

SELECTED PERIODICALS

Acéphale (1936–1939) reprint edition, Paris: Jean-Michel Place, 1995.
"Almanach surréaliste du demi-siècle." Special issue of *La Nef* (March 1950). Reprint edition, Paris: Plasma, 1978
Analogon (1967–2013)
"André Breton et le surréalisme international." Special issue, *Opus* 123–24, April–May 1991
Archibras (1967–1969)
Bief (1958–1960)
La Brèche (1961–1965)
Bulletin de liaison Surréaliste (1970–1976) reprint edition, Paris: Savelli, 1977
Documents (1929–1930)
Le Grand Jeu (1928–1930) reprint edition, Paris: Jean-Michel Place, 1977
Littérature (1919–1924).
Médium (first and second series, 1950–1955)
Minotaure (1933–1939)
Néon (1948–1949)
Opus 19–20, Surréalisme international, October, 1970
La Révolution surréaliste (1924–1929)
S.U.R.R. (1996–2005)
Surréalisme (1977)
Le Surréalisme au service de la révolution (1932)
Le Surréalisme même (1956–1959)
Troisième Convoi (1945–1951)
VVV (1942–1944)
View (1940–1947)

INDEX

Page numbers followed by an "n" indicate notes.

Abeille, Jacques, 138–39, 309, 333, 415
Abellio, Raymond, 434–35
Adieu à Satan (Gengenbach), 28–29, 39, 277–78, 332, 381n
African religions, 109–11
Agarttha, 68–69
Agrippa de Nettesheim, Cornelius, 108–9
Albach, Hester, 219–20, 434
alchemy, 216–56
    beliefs of, 429
    Breton and, 219–22, 225, 233–34
    Camacho and, 235–36
    Chazal and, 348–49
    Freemasonry and, 301
    Mandiargues and, 241–43
    Paris as center of, 224–25
    poetry and, 231
    as sacred science, 219
    stages of the "great work," 219–20
    surrealism and, xii
    theater and, 231–32
Alcove: Interior with Three Women, The (Fini), 204, Plate 11
Alexandria, 367–68
Alexandrian, Sarane
    astrology and, 122–23, 145
    autobiography, 9, 234n, 295–96, 309, 321

on Gnosticism, 358
God and Goddess, 194
History of Occult Philosophy, 76n, 261, 373–74
on hypnotic trance, 90
on surrealism, 309, 332–33
Alleau, René
    Aspects of Traditional Alchemy, 217, 372–73
    Breton's friendship with, 233–34
    lectures at Hall of Geography, xii
    on shadows, 31
    surrealists encounter with, 217–18
Allendy, René, 256, 256n
Alquié, Ferdinand, 33, 100–101
Amadou, Robert
    about, 393–94
    on alchemy, 218
    on astrology, 143–44
    path of, 429
    on post-Platonic theurgy, 324
    on surrealism, 430
Ambelain, Robert, 235n, 324–25, 388, 391, 391n
Amun, 16–17
anarchism, 401–2
androgyne, 63, 92n, 227, 239, 240, 381n
anticlericalism, 17–18, 20–21, 34

499

Antzenberger, Éleonore, 78
Apollinaire's coat of arms, 176n
Aragon, Louis, 88–89, 90–91, 107
Arcane 17, 212, 219, 225, 226, 229–30, 240
Arcimboldo, Giuseppe, 161–62
Ariëns-Volker, Marijo, 392–93
Artaud, Antonin
   address to the Pope, 29–30
   astrology and, 147, 157
   on Atlantis, 67–68
   on the cinema, 99
   on the cross, 20
   described, 158–59
   on Druids, 182
   on esotericisms, 345–46
   Guénon and, 336n, 341–42
   Heliogabalus or the Crowned Anarchist, 37, 58, 134, 147, 187, 228, 255, 309, 324, 340–41, 346
   "letter on cruelty," 45, 361
   on magic, 271–72
   "Mountain of Signs, The," 65
   on the Orient, 346
   premonitions, 212–13
   on separate consciousness, 399–400n
   surrealism and, xii
   "Surrealism and Revolution" lecture, 38–39
   on theater and alchemy, 231–32
   voodoo and, 319
artists-magicians, 381, 381n
Aspects of Traditional Alchemy (Alleau), 217, 372–73
astrology, 142–55
atheism, 18, 418, 433
Atlantis, 67–68
Audoin, Philippe
   astrology and, 133
   "Baron Zéro," 208, 243–44
   on Breton, 185–86
   on castles, 170
   on Gnosticism, 425–26

   on God, 15–16
   "La Fontaine de Fortune," 223–24
   on sacred geography, 195
   on surrealists, 48–49
automatic writing, 85, 87, 88, 118
automatons, 109, 272, 305

Barbault, André, 144
"Baron Zéro" (Audoin), 208, 243–44
Baskine, Maurice, 234
Bastien, Sophie, 124
Batache, Eddy, 3
Bataille, Georges, 42, 43, 59, 70, 281, 310, 361
Beaufils, Laurent, 26
Beckford, William, 159–60
Bédouin, Jean-Louis
   on Alleau, 217–18
   on Breton, 61–62, 181
   on Carrington's *En Bas* (Down Below), 290
   "Eros and the Death Instinct," 63–64, 193
   on Péret, 87
beeswax painting, 297
"Before the Curtain" (Breton), 373
Béhar, Henri, 212
Béliar (Lam), Plate 19
Bellmer's doll, 264
Benayoun, Robert, 114–15, 167–68, 410–11
Bérend, Tieman von Bérend, 324–25
Bidermanas, Israël, 168–69
Birth of Rabbi Loew, The (Carrington), 262, Plate 15
Birth (Pollock), 113, Plate 6
black masses, 25
Blake, William, 94, 116, 353–54, 375–76
Blavatsky, Helena, 341, 352
Böhme, Jacob, 49–50, 376, 385, 437
Bonnefoy, Yves, 81, 276

Bounoure, Vincent, 50, 101, 256, 363n
Bourdas, Paul-Emile, 64–65, 404
Brauner, Victor
　baptizing his home, 234n
　Biosensitive Ultrapainting, 263
　doubles and, 93
　esotericism of, 297
　eye enucleation of, 211
　Heron of Alexandria, 108, Plate 4
　Jouffroy on, 211, 294–95, 298
　Lovers, Messengers of the Number, 137–38, Plate 10
　magic and, 292–99
　Murmur of the Wall, 140
　spiritualism of, 89–90
　Strigoï the Sleepwalker, 89–90
　succubi and, 278
　Surrealist, The, 137, Plate 9
　visionary drawing by, 120
　Wolf Table, Plate 21
Breton, André
　alchemy and, 219–22, 225, 233–34
　Arcane 17, 212, 219, 225, 226, 229–30, 240
　astrology and, 144–46
　on castles, 157–58
　on clairvoyance, 118–19, 120
　Constellations, 378–79, 443
　Conversations, 356–57, 400
　"Before the Curtain," 373
　distain for the pope, 18–19
　First Surrealist Manifesto, 46, 73, 90, 119, 157, 170, 306–7, 369, 426
　Freemasonry and, 332
　"Fronton-Virage," 233
　"Full Margin" (poem), 329–30
　Gengenbach, Ernest de and, 25
　on Gnosticism, 358–60
　on gothic novels, 165–66
　on high poetry and high science, 372
　initiatory labyrinth of, 330–31
　last café meeting, xi

　Les Vases communicants, 33, 103, 157, 291
　"Limits not Frontiers of Surrealism," 170
　Literature and Occult Tradition, 372
　Mad Love, 63, 171, 209, 215, 219, 225
　magic and, 267–70
　"Poetry Is at This Price," 2
　on point of mind, 54–55
　as "pope," 27–28, 180–81
　premonitions, 212, 213–14, 215
　role in the surrealist movement, 5, 433
　science and, 30–31, 33–34
　Second Surrealist Manifesto, 46, 222, 225–26, 306, 307, 401, 402, 425n
　sense of the sacred, 56–57
　on spiritualism, 85, 88
　on the "supreme point," 343, 344–45
　"On Surrealism in Its Living Works," 240, 259, 306–7, 342, 359–60
　tarot and, 133–34
　Toyen's portrait of, 230–31
　on vampiric lamia, 99–100
　voodoo and, 318–19, 321, 322–23
　"What Tanguy Veils and Reveals," 191, 193
Bricaud, Jean ("Joanny"), 391
bridge, crossing, 103–4
Brisset, Jean-Pierre, 125–26, 373
Brothers of the Rose Cross, 250
Brumagne, Françoise, 229, 230
Brunius, Jacques Bernard, 413
Buñuel, Louis, 13

Caillois, Roger, 98, 126–27, 249
Camacho, Jorge
　Green Candle, The, 236, Plate 14
　interest in alchemy, 235–36
　Silbermann on, 239
Campana-Rochefort, Marie-Noëlle, 128

Camus, Albert, 347, 414–15
Canseliet, Eugène, xi, 218–19, 222–23, 238
Carrington, Leonora
  about, 284–91
  Birth of Rabbi Loew, The, 262, Plate 15
  En Bas (Down Below), 290
  Hearing Trumpet, The, 162, 203–4, 286–87
  Palacio Mnemonico, 302–3, Plate 17
  Portrait of Max Ernst, 287–88
Carrouges, Michel
  on castles, 157–58
  on ghosts/hauntings, 94, 156
  on God, 432
  on mediums, 214
  Mysticism of the Superman, The, 3, 18
  on religion, 429
  on spiritualism, 86–87, 88
  on the Supreme Point, 346
  on surrealism, 308, 436
Casaril, Guy, 261
castles, 153, 156, 157–60, 164–65, 170–72, 173, 188, 189
Cathars, 154, 155
Cazotte, Jacques, 323–24
Celtism, 175–215
  Christianity and, 187
  culture of, 188–89
  Druidic revival, 201–2
  dualist thought and, 178–79
  Gallic art, 175–76, 186–87
  myths of, 181–85, 197–200
  quest for the Grail, 196, 210
  sacred geography, 195
  Western path of, 177–78
Char, René, 72–73, 119, 232, 439
Chateaubriand, François-René de, 196–97
Chazal, Malcolm de
  alchemy and, 348–49
  described, 351–53
  as gnosis holder, 350
  Le Rocher de Sisyphe, 65–66, 67, 353, 405
  mythanalysis, 405
Chénieux-Gendron, Jacqueline, 276
Chirico, Giorgio de
  artistry of, 311–12
  Breton and, 132, 212
  Child's Brain, The, 393
  on forebodings, 215
  ghosts and, 106–7
Choucha, Nadia, 227–28, 267–68, 436–37
Christ, 11, 29, 362
Christian illuminism, 387
cinema/films, 13–14, 97–99, 407–8
Clair, Jean, 3, 11, 81–82
Clairvaux, Bernard de, 419–21
clairvoyance, 116–20
Clairvoyance (Lam), 111–12, Plate 5
collective unconscious, 218, 316, 407
Colquhoun, Ithell
  book on Ireland, 188
  influences on, 200–201
  occultism of, 74–76
  Philosopher's Stone, 239
  tarot of, 139
  "Waterstone of the Wise, The," 240–41
  writings and paintings, 202–3, 239–40
Constellations (Breton), 378–79, 443
Conversations (Breton), 356–57, 400
Cooke manuscripts, 301–2
Copernicus, 304
Corpus Hermeticum, 303
Corrinus, Celtic god, 302–3
costumes, 416–17
"Coup de semonce" [Warning Shot], 17
Courtot, Claude, 95, 313
Crastre, Victor, 255, 307, 347
Crevel, René, 11–12, 30, 85
cross, the, 20–21

Dachez, Roger, 301–2, 325
Daix, Pierre, 4, 309–11
Dali, Salvador, 13, 124, 138, 232–33
Dante, 189, 190, 359, 420
Darget, Louis, 99
Daumal, René, 10, 88, 231, 338, 339–40, 379–80
Dax, Adrien, 69–70, 71, 72, 108, 178–79, 314, 341, 342, 370
death omens, 209–10
Debenedetti, Jean-Marc, 405
Debray, Régis, 421–22
Decottignies, Jean, 21–22
Dedieu, Claude, 282
Dedieu, Jean-Claude, 280–81
Dedinac, Milan, 266
Dee, John, 251, 312, 344
Dekiss, Jean-Paul, 409–10
Delteil, Joseph, 313
Demarne, Pierre, 389
Désert de Retz, 167–70, 169–70
Desiderio, Monsu, 281
Desnos, Robert
    on Christ, 11
    on cinema, 97
    expulsion from surrealist movement, 78–79
    on the infinite, 431
    Jules Vernes and, 408
    premonitions, 213
    prophecies of, 124–25
    spiritualism of, 88–89, 90
Dhainaut, Pierre, 153–54, 371–72
divination, 116–41
    automatic writing, 85, 87, 88, 118
    clairvoyance, 116–20
    fortune-tellers, 123–24
    mediumship, 85, 86–87, 90, 91–92n, 121–22
    number symbology, 127–28
    objective chance, 124
    prophets and prophecies, 124–27
    See also tarot

Doresse, Jean, 260–61, 355–56, 357–58, 363n
double, the, 21, 91n, 92–93, 94, 95–96, 101
Doumayrou, Guy René, 152–53
Druids, 177–78, 180, 182, 186, 191, 201–2
Duchamp, Marcel, 140, 227–28
Ducornet, Guy, 20, 356–57, 423
Duits, Charles
    astrology and, 148–49
    on Breton, 71–72
    on God and Goddess, 194
    intuitions, 368–69
    on magic, 273–74
    Nefer, 368
    poets and the Church, 20
    Ptah Hotep, 50–51, 87, 368
    science and, 32–33
    spiritualism of, 87–88, 100
    Vision et hallucination, 118
    visions of, 98
Dumas, François Ribadeau, 326
Dumont, Claude, 19
Dunne, John William, 214
Duprey, Jean-Pierre
    on castles, 171–72
    prediction post of, 150
    rampart against madness, 174
    spiritualism of, 84, 89, 92–93
    suicide of, 92n
Dupuis, Jules-François, 267, 417

Eddington, Arthur Stanley, 347n
Edighoffer, Roland, 251–53, 309
egregore, 47–48
Eigeldinger, Marc, 117–18
Elléouët, Yves
    Ankou portrayed by, 207
    Celtism of, 200
    Falc'hun, 98–99, 171, 187–88, 198–99
    on heraldry, 106

"Not Wilted on My Lapel," 196
Portrait of a Castle, 162
on Saint-Pol Roux, 380–81
as surrealist, 176–77
Emerald Tablet, 252, 291
Emmerling, Leonhard, 113–14
En Bas (Down Below) (Carrington), 290
Encausse, Gérard (Papus), 384–85, 387, 390, 393
Ernst, Max
Carrington and, 284–85
"For the Eighty Years of Max Ernst," 108
Little Girl Dreams of Taking the Veil, A, 13
portrait of, 287–88
Robing of the Bride, The, 288, Plate 16
Vox Angelica, 311, Plate 18
on war, 298
"Eros and the Death Instinct" (Bédouin), 63–64, 193
esotericism, 76–77n, 374, 433–34, 441
esoteric tradition, 40–41
Étiemble, René, 80–81

Fabre d'Olivet, Antonine, 157
Faivre, Antoine, 304, 437
Falc'hun (Elléouët), 98–99, 171, 187–88, 198–99
fall, the, 429
Ferry, Jean, 233
Fêtes secrétes: Dessins (Fini), 280–81
fetishes, 274
Ficino, Marsilio, 265, 303–4
films/cinema, 13–14, 97–99, 407–8
Fini, Leonor
Alcove: Interior with Three Women, The, 204, Plate 11
Fêtes secrétes: Dessins, 280–81
magic and, 275–76
First Surrealist Manifesto, 46, 73, 90, 119, 157, 170, 306–7, 369, 426

Flamand, Elie-Charles, 76–77, 107–8, 234
Flamel, Nicolas, 222–24, 225–26
Flore, Joachim de, 330
Flournoy, Théodore, 101n, 214
Fludd, Robert
Mosaic Philosophy, 311
Temple of Music, The, 312
"For the Eighty Years of Max Ernst," 108
fortune-tellers, 123–24
Fourier, Charles, 370
Fourré, Maurice, 198, 243–44, 321–22, 409
Freemasonry
alchemy connections, 301
interest in surrealism, 331–32
myth and, 411–13
occultism and, 305–6
practices of, 387–88
secret common with surrealism, xii
as secret society, 411–12
speculative, 305
surrealists' interest in, 300–301, 306–11
texts ("Old Charges") of, 301–2
frescoes of Santa Maria Novella, 99–100
"Fronton-Virage" (Breton), 233
Fulcanelli, xii, 234, 235n
"Full Margin" (Breton), 329–30

Galfetti, Gustau Gili, 169
Gallic art, 175–76, 186–87
Gauthier, Xavière, 120
Gautier, Théophile, 377
Gavreau, Claude, 315, 399
Gazzotti, Elzevia, 267
Gengenbach, Ernest de
about, 20–29
Adieu à Satan, 28–29, 39, 277–78, 332, 381n
Judas ou le vampire surréaliste, 57, 158, 398–99

Satan à Paris, 20, 22–23, 24
geography, sacred, 152–53, 195
Gérard, Francis, 101–2
German romanticism, 248
ghosts, 84–85, 94, 99, 100–101, 103, 106–7, 109
Gilbert-Lecomte, Roger
  on astrology, 146
  on clairvoyance, 119–20
  experimental metaphysics, 57
  on painting and poetry, 380
  on science, 31–32, 403
  as seer, 337–38
  as surrealist, 88, 89
Girard, Guy, 15, 55–56, 68, 307, 437
Gnosticism, 348–70
  Alexandrian on, 358
  Audoin on, 425–26
  beliefs of, 248, 428
  Catholicism versus, 356
  Christianity and, 364–65
  doctrine of, 359–60
  dualism and, 357
  in novels and poetry, 365–66
  origins of, 355
God, 2, 10, 11, 247, 429, 431, 432
Golden Fleece, xii–xiii, 217
Goldfayn, Georges, 154
Golem, the, 262–65
goose, 16–17
gothic novels, 156–57, 158–59, 164–66
Gracq, Julien, 11, 28, 105, 157, 184–85, 409–10, 417–18
Grail myth, 210
Grand Orient, 331, 332
Greek philosophers, 59–61
Green Candle, The (Camacho), 236, Plate 14
Guaita, Stanislas de, 389–90
Guardians of the Secret (Pollock), 113–14, Plate 7
Guénon, René
  attack on Blavatsky, 341
  Chazal and, 349
  Crisis of the Modern World, The, 339
  influence of, 341–42, 344
  on spiritualism, 90
  as surrealist and mason, 334–39
  Symbolism of the Cross, The, 343
Gurdjieff, 50–53

Haven, Marc, 394n
Hearing Trumpet, The (Carrington), 162, 203–4, 286–87
Hédéra (poem), 140–41
Heliogabalus or the Crowned Anarchist (Artaud), 37, 58, 134, 147, 187, 228, 255, 309, 324, 340–41, 346
Henein, Georges, 61
heraldry, 106, 152, 235, 279, 280
Hermes, xii, 265, 291, 301, 303, 304, 305
Hérold, Jacques, 150, 241, 308, 362–64
Heron of Alexandria (Brauner), 108, Plate 4
Hide and Seek (Tchelitchew), 84, Plate 3
high science, 372, 379
History of Occult Philosophy (Alexandrian), 373–74
homunculus, 239
Hoog, Armand, 414
House of the Surrealists, 1
Hugo, Victor, 117, 377–78
Huidobro, Vincente, 313–14
Hunwald, Henri, 333
hypnotic sleeps, 85, 87, 107
Hyppolite, Hector, 317–18

Imbert, Charles, 411–12
immanence, 431
"In Carpocrates and Sade's corner," 382, Plate 20
initiation, 41–42, 43–46, 317
interest in astrology
  Mandiargues, André Pieyre de, 149–50

Italian Nun Smoking (Trouille), 23, Plate 1
Ivsic, Radovan, 274–75

Jameux, Charles
   on castles, 173
   on Christianity, 12
   Freemasonry affiliation, 314
   on Gengenbach, 29
   on Gurdjieff, 52–53
   hallucination of, 208–9
   on memory/mnemonic process, 302
   on mirrors, 94–95
   on *Nosferatu*, 105, 106
   on the surrealist movement, 5
   visions of, 102
Jean, Marcel, 12, 150–51
Jeu de Marseille (card deck), 86, 166–67
Jodorowsky, Alejandro, 285–86, 289–90
Jouffroy, Alain
   on Bellmer's doll, 264
   on Brauner, 211, 294–95, 298
   on Breton, 333
   on costumes, 416
   on surrealism, 5–6, 9, 427
Judas ou le vampire surréaliste (Gengenbach), 57, 158, 398–99
Jung, Carl, 218, 361–62

kabbalah, 235n, 240, 260, 261–62, 278, 293, 436
Keith, Delmari Romero, 286
King Arthur, 180
Konaï, Teodor bar, 115
Koyré, Alexandre, 247–48
Kubin, Alfred, 385
Kyrou, Ado, 159n

Lacomblez, Jacques, 154–55, 163
"La Fontaine de Fortune" (Audoin), 223–24

Lam, Wilfredo
   about, 319–21
   Béliar, Plate 19
   Clairvoyance, 111–12, Plate 5
   heraldry and, 229
   Light of the Forest, 193
   voodoo and, 319–21, Plate 19
Lamantia, Philip, 442–43
Lambert, Jean-Clarence, 133
language, 259–60, 262, 265
Lassalle, Jean-Pierre, 392
Le Brun, Annie, 165, 166, 205, 265, 399, 405
Lecomte, Marcel, 64, 230, 435
Legrand, Gérard
   astrology and, 144
   on faith, 430
   gnosticism and, 364
   on language and poetry, 39–40
   on magic, 266, 269
   on myth, 405–6
   on narrow-minded rationalism, 31
   "Return of Spring, The," 67–68
Le Gros, Marc, 145–46
Leiris, Michel, 30, 66, 111, 123–24, 142, 210, 223, 249, 312
Lemuria, 352
Le Rocher de Sisyphe (Chazal), 65–66, 67, 353, 405
Les Demoiselles d'Avignon (Picasso), 132, 229, 311
"Les Jeux à Deux," (Zürn), 204–5
Les Vases communicants (Breton), 33, 103, 157, 291
L'Étoile scellée (the Sealed Star), xii, 233–34
Levaillant, Francoise, 248
Levi, Eliphas, 221, 269, 378, 438
L'Expérience Poétique, 127–28, 258, 260, 351, 356, 376
L'Homme du large (Magritte), 229, 230, Plate 13
Limbour, Georges, 121–22

"Limits not Frontiers of Surrealism"
  (Breton), 170
Linhartova, Vera, 118
Literature and Occult Tradition
  (Breton), 372
Little Girl Dreams of Taking the Veil, A
  (Ernst), 13
Ljubomir, Popovic Alekse (Ljuba),
  242–43
Lovecraft, Howard Phillips, 114–15
Lovers, Messengers of the Number
  (Brauner), 137–38, Plate 10
Löw, Rabbi Juda Ben Betsalel, 262,
  Plate 15
Löwy, Michel, 299
Luca, Ghérasim
  clairvoyance, 213
  on doubles, 93
  magic and, 276–77
  observations from 1941, 10
  Passive Vampire, The, 109, 213,
    276–77, 362
  on the world of "tomorrow," 109
Lucifer's fall, 248

Mabille, Pierre
  on Christianity, 12
  on clairvoyance, 116–17
  as Freemason, 315–17
  on Hector Hyppolite, 317
  knowledge about voodoo, 317
  Mirror of the Marvelous, The, 131,
    173–74, 308, 316, 412–13
  on Seligmann, 279–80
  on Wilfredo Lam, 319–20
  on William Blake, 353–54
Madam Raffa, 121–22
Mad Love (Breton), 63, 171, 209, 215,
  219, 225
magic, 257–99
  art and, 267–68
  curses, 270
  defined, 257–59, 268

  dogma in, 269
  fetishes, 274
  Golem, the, 262–65
  language and, 259–60, 265
  as natural, 247
  occult philosophy and, 8–9
  poetry as, 257–58, 299
  science and, 273
  soul and, 267
Magnetic Fields, The, 101, 409, 436
Magnus, Albertus, 235n
Magritte, René (*L'Homme du large*),
  229, 230, Plate 13
Maistre, Joseph de, 325
Malrieu, Jean, 153–54
Mandiargues, André Pieyre de
  on Breton, 395
  on Carrington's novel, 286–87
  on castles, 172
  Hédéra (poem), 140–41
  iconoclastic theory of, 63
  interest in alchemy, 241–43
  interest in astrology, 149–50
  L'Anglais décrit dans le château fermé,
    159
  magic and, 276, 281
  on premonitions, 96
  ring of, 155
  on Unica Zürn, 95–96
mannerisms, 164, 243, 275, 281, 282
Man of Jasmine, The (Zürn), 91–92,
  95–96, 128, 273, 278–79
Man Ray
  drawings signed with a 11112, 127
  The Portrait of My Soul, 121, Plate 8
  portrait of Sade, 166
Manuscript Found in Saragossa
  (Potocki), 262
Mariën, Marcel, 14
Maritain, Jacques, 27
Markale, Jean, 139, 369
Marquès-Rivière, 293–94
Martinist Order/Martinism, 74, 86,

324–25, 385, 386, 387, 388–89, 390, 423
marvelous, the, 1, 85, 174, 177
Masson, André, 42–43, 45, 46, 59, 113, 248
materialism, 48, 49–50
Mauriac, Claude, 422–23
Mayoux, Jean-Jacques, 376
mediums, 85, 86–87, 90, 91–92n, 121–22, 214
memory, art of, 302, 303
Mesmer, Franz Anton, 322n
Mézei, Arpad, 151–52, 259
Miller, Henry, 181
Mirror of Magic, The (Seligmann), 146–47, 174, 218, 270, 283, 285, 299, 326, 354–55, 430
Mirror of the Marvelous, The (Mabille), 131, 173–74, 308, 316, 412–13
mirrors, 94–97
Misraïm Rite, 306
"MistAKE" (Zürn), 123
Mitrani, Nora, 158, 375
Mona Lisa, 228
Monnerot, Jules
  on God, 22
  on myth, 418
  on poetry and magic, 257–58
  on the sacred, 34
  surrealism and, 6, 55, 358, 370n, 441
Montagne, Margaret, 263, 364
Mont-Saint-Michel (monastery), 24–25
Moreau, Gustave, *Self-Portrait*, 382, Plate 20
Morganwg, Iolo, 201–2
Morice, Charles, 381n
Morriseau-Leroy, Felix, 317
Mosaic Philosophy (Fludd), 311
"Mountain of Signs, The" (Artaud), 65
Murdered Magicians, The, 378
Murmur of the Wall (Brauner), 140
Murnau, F. W., 103

Myers, Frederic, 86, 101n, 214
Mysticism of the Superman, The (Carrouges), 3, 18
myth, 397–427
  collective, 403
  creation of, 403, 406–7, 416–17
  described, 405–6, 411
  dreams and, 418–19
  Freemasonry and, 411–13
  mysticism and, 418–19
  new, xii, 241, 413–15
  the sacred and, 403
  value of, 414–15

Naglowska, Maria de, 25
names, science of, 260
Nefer (Duits), 368
Neither Wings Nor Stones; Wings and Stones (Toyen), 230, Plate 12
Nerval, Gérard de, 227, 377
Newton, Isaac, 252
Nezval, Vitezslav, 148, 235n
Nocé, Vincent, 169
No Performance (Toyen), 140
Nosferatu (film), 103, 104, 105
Nostradamus, Michel de, 126
Nougé, Paul, 19–20, 78–80
numbers, 127–28

objective chance, xi, 1, 34
occultism, 74–75, 108, 143, 258
Onfray, Michel, 281
"On Surrealism in Its Living Works," 240, 259, 306–7, 342, 359–60
Order of the Elect Cohen, 323, 327
Osiris, 229–30, 354–55
Ouspensky, P. D., 140, 289

Paalen, Wolgang, 104
Païni, Lotus de, 267
Palacio Mnemonico, Plate 17
Palacio Mnemonico (Carrington), 302–3, Plate 17

Papus. *See* Encausse, Gérard (Papus)
Paracelsus, 247–50, 308
Partner, Peter, 378
Pasqually, Martinès de, 323, 324–25, 327
Passions According to Dali, The, 232–33
Passive Vampire, The (Luca), 109, 213, 276–77, 362
Paz, Octavio, 65, 258–60, 284, 285, 312–13
Péladan, Joseph (Sâr), 381–83
Pelagius, 329–30
Penrose, Valentine, 161, 246
Perahim, Jules, 139–40
Péret, Benjamin
  on castles, 171
  on God and religion, 12
  on gothic novels, 165
  magic and, 272
  on the sacred, 58
  study of African religions, 109–11
  voodoo's influence on, 319
Perks, Simone, 131
Pessoa, Fernando, 375
Pétillot, Jean-Marc, 325
Petitclerc, Gilles, 206
phantasmagoria, 97–98
Philidor, Paul, 97–98
philosopher's stone, 221–22
Philosopher's Stone (Colquhoun), 239
photographs, paranormal, 99, 107
Piau, Guy, 300–301
Picasso, Pablo
  Les Demoiselles d'Avignon, 132, 229, 311
  occult interests, 132
Pierre, José, 16, 174, 264, 307, 316, 416
Piobb, Pierre V., 315n
Plotinus, 143, 144
Poe, Edgar Allen, 160
poetic science, 33

poetry
  alchemy and, 231
  Gnosticism and, 365–66
  great poets, 372
  as magic, 257–58
  the sacred and, 56–57
Pollock, Jackson
  Birth, 113, Plate 6
  Guardians of the Secret, 113–14, Plate 7
pope, 18–19, 29–30
Portrait of Max Ernst (Carrington), 287–88
Portrait of My Soul, The (Man Ray), 121, Plate 8
possession phenomena, 109, 112
Potocki, Jan, 261–62
Prague, as "high holy," 246
Praz, Mario, 164
premonitions, 210–15
Prévert, Jacques, 12–13, 16, 314
prophets and prophecy, 124–27
psychoanalysis, 85, 337
Ptah Hotep (Duits), 50–51, 87, 368
Pythagoras, 301

Queneau, Raymond, 365–66

Rabinowitz, Celia, 7–8
Randolph, Pascal Beverly, 25
Random, Michel, 337–39
Réage, Pauline, 193
Reigl, Judit, 128, Plate 2
religion
  African, 109–11
  sacred, the, 42–43
  surrealism versus, 7–19
"Return of Spring, The" (Legrand), 67–68
revelations, 10, 65, 360
Ribemont-Dessaignes, Georges, 11, 361
Ristic, Marko, 53, 54, 108

Robing of the Bride, The (Ernst), 288, Plate 16
Rodanski, Stanislas, 92, 95, 148, 197
Roger, Bernard, xi–xiv, 237
Rolland de Renéville, André
  on Absolute Consciousness, 360–61
  L'Expérience Poétique, 127–28, 258, 260, 351, 356, 376
  on occult science, 381
  role of romanticism and, 438n
Rosenkreutz, Christian, 250
Rosicrucians, 68, 249n, 250, 251–53, 254, 349, 382, 390
Roussel, Raymond, 111, 233

Sabians, 303
sacred, the, 35–83
  approaches to, 55–56
  esoteric tradition, 40–41
  Greek philosophers and, 59–61
  initiation and rituals, 41–42, 43–46
  love as, 58
  metaphysics and, 35–38
  myth and, 403, 411
  poetry and, 56–57
  religion and, 42–43
Sade, Marquis de, 157n, 416
Saint-Jacques-de-la-Boucherie Church, 224, 225
Saint James, 226–27
Saint-Martin, Louis-Claude de, 327–28, 329, 392n, 426
Saint-Pol Roux, 380–81, 383
Sanda, Paul, 1–2, 394, 423–24, 425, 427
Satan à Paris (Gengenbach), 20, 22–23, 24
Satanism in the style of Clovis Trouille, 23, Plate 1
Savinio, Alberti, 249
Schaw, William, 303
Schefer, Bertrand, 396
Schuré, Édouard, 374

Schuster, Jean
  attacks on God, 14
  Bernard de Clairvaux and, 419–21
  on Breton, 57–58
  Freemasonry affiliation, 314
  on ghosts, 103
  letter to a "Group of militants," 79
  Letter to André Liberati, 8, 19
  on metareason, 424–25
  on paranormal phenomena, 400
  on rituals, 310
  on surrealism, 1, 6, 8, 37
  on transcendence, 431
  science, 30–34, 273, 403
Scutenaire, Louis, 10, 263–64
Seabrook, William, 318, 318n
Seal of Solomon, 254–55
Sébillot, Paul, 209
Second Surrealist Manifesto, 46, 222, 225–26, 306, 307, 401, 402, 425n
secret societies, 44, 45–49, 309, 313
Sède, Gérard de, 249n, 256
Seibel, Castor, 275
Self-Portrait (Moreau), Plate 20
Seligmann, Kurt
  about, 282–84
  character of, 279–80
  on gnostic myths, 357
  on the Golem, 264
  Mirror of Magic, The, 146–47, 174, 218, 270, 283, 285, 299, 326, 354–55, 430
  translating texts, 248–49
Sena, ancient, 182–83
Sendiwoj, Michael, 394n
Serpan, Iaroslav, 266
Shakespeare, 189–90
shamanism, 112–13
Silbermann, Jean-Claude, 14–15, 238–39, 431, 441–42
Sima, Joseph, 118, 188–89, 345, 345n
Simonelli, Jacques, 244–45
Sogol, Father, 338

Soupault, Philippe, 18, 101, 182, 235n, 313, 375, 431–32
spiritualism
  risks of, 88, 90–91, 101–2
  surrealists and, 85–87, 103–5
Stankov "Castle," 164
Steiner, Rudolf, 114, 267, 375n
Stoker, Bram, 103, 161
Story of O, 193
Strand, Penmarch, 197–98
Strange Visitor (Toyen), 277
Strigoï the Sleepwalker (Brauner), 89–90
succubi, 277–78
Sudre, René, 101, 122
Summers, Montague, 8–9
supreme point, 55, 343, 344–45, 346, 347
surrealism
  beliefs of, 435–36
  birth of, 397–401
  described, 3–6, 9, 34
  dissolution in 1969, xi, 4
  misinterpretations on, 7–9
  quest of, 1, 412–13
  as a tradition, 438–41
  "traditional" thought and, 428–30
  weakness of, 8–9
Surrealist, The (Brauner), 137, Plate 9
Svankmajer, Jan, 162, 163–64, 274
Svankmajerova, Eva, 30, 245
Swedenborg, Emmanuel, 86, 250n, 265–66, 350–51
symbolism, 435

Taliesin, 183–84
Talking Heads Dinner in Paris (Prévert), 16
Tanguy, Yves, 190–92, 194, 361–62
Tarnaud, Claude, 366–67, 410, 426
tarot, 128–40
  Fool, 132–33
  Hanged Man, 139–40
  Hermit, 139
  Juggler, 131–32
  Star, 135–37
  Tower, 133–34
Tatin, Robert, 183n
Tchelitchew, Pavel (*Hide and Seek*), 84, Plate 3
Teige, Karel, 4–5
Templars, 249n, 305
Temple of Music, The (Fludd), 312
theater, 231–32, 406–7
theurgy, 324
They Have an Insatiable Thirst for the Infinite (Reigl), 128, Plate 2
Thirion, André, 343
Tibetan Buddhism, 73
Toland, John, 201
Tort-Nougès, Henri, 302
Tour Saint-Jacques, 225
tower of Babel, 133, 169
Toyen
  Château of Silling and, 160
  described, 142–43
  drawings of, 230–31
  magic and, 272
  mannerism and, 282
  Neither Wings Nor Stones; Wings and Stones, 230, Plate 12
  No Performance, 140
  Strange Visitor, 277
tradition
  esoteric, 40–41
  invention of, 435
  surrealism, 438–42
transcendence, 9, 36, 38, 186, 431
Transcendental Magic (Levi), 438
Treasure of the Jesuits (play), 212, 310
Trintzius, René, 323n, 325, 326–27
Trismegistus, Hermes, xii, 265, 291, 301, 303, 304, 305
Tristan and Iseult, 197–98
Tristan Tzara, 154
Trithemius, Johannes, 247
Troménies (processions), 176n

Tronche, Anne, 229
Trouille, Clovis, 23, Plate 1

Ubac, Raoul, 434
unconscious, the, 91n

Valentinus, Basil, 241
Van de Wrouwer, Roger, 14
Van Lennep, Jacques, 221, 229, 230, 243, 430–31
Van Win, Jean, 328
Varo, Remedios, 284, 285, 289
Vendryès, Pierre, 34
Verne, Jules, 408–10
Villars, Abbé de, 326
voodoo, 317–23, Plate 19
Vox Angelica (Ernst), 311, Plate 18

Waite, Arthur Edward, 131

"Waterstone of the Wise, The" (Colquhoun), 240–41
"What Tanguy Veils and Reveals" (Breton), 191, 193
Willermoz, Jean-Baptiste, 327
Wolf Table (Brauner), Plate 21

Yarker, John, 384
Yates, Frances A., 303–5
Yochaï, Rabbi Bar, 261

Zeller, Fred, 331–32
Zen buddhism, 70–71, 72
Zohar, 305, 344
Zürn's, Unica
  "Les Jeux à Deux,," 204–5
  Man of Jasmine, The, 91–92, 95–96, 128, 273, 278–79
  "MistAKE," 123

BOOKS OF RELATED INTEREST

Surrealism and the Occult
Shamanism, Magic, Alchemy, and the Birth of an Artistic Movement
by Nadia Choucha

The Mystery Traditions
Secret Symbols and Sacred Art
by James Wasserman

Secret Societies and the Hermetic Code
The Rosicrucian, Masonic, and Esoteric Transmission in the Arts
by Ernesto Frers

Psychomagic
The Transformative Power of Shamanic Psychotherapy
by Alejandro Jodorowsky

The Spiritual Journey of Alejandro Jodorowsky
The Creator of El Topo
by Alejandro Jodorowsky

Aleister Crowley: The Beast in Berlin
Art, Sex, and Magick in the Weimar Republic
by Tobias Churton

Lords of the Left-Hand Path
Forbidden Practices and Spiritual Heresies
by Stephen E. Flowers, Ph.D.

Introduction to Magic
Rituals and Practical Techniques for the Magus
by Julius Evola and the UR Group

INNER TRADITIONS • BEAR & COMPANY
P.O. Box 388
Rochester, VT 05767
1-800-246-8648
www.InnerTraditions.com

Or contact your local bookseller